Anonymous

Message of the Pres. of the U. S.

Anonymous

Message of the Pres. of the U. S.

ISBN/EAN: 9783337810429

Printed in Europe, USA, Canada, Australia, Japan

Cover: Foto ©ninafisch / pixelio.de

More available books at **www.hansebooks.com**

NITED STA

CUMENTS

OF STA

WASHINGTON:
GOVERNMENT PRINTING OFFICE.
1861.

MESSAGE.

Fellow-citizens of the Senate and House of Representatives:

In the midst of unprecedented political troubles, we have cause of great gratitude to God for unusual good health, and most abundant harvests.

You will not be surprised to learn that, in the peculiar exigencies of the times, our intercourse with foreign nations has been attended with profound solicitude, chiefly turning upon our own domestic affairs.

A disloyal portion of the American people have, during the whole year, been engaged in an attempt to divide and destroy the Union. A nation which endures factious domestic division, is exposed to disrespect abroad; and one party, if not both, is sure, sooner or later, to invoke foreign intervention.

Nations thus tempted to interfere, are not always able to resist the counsels of seeming expediency and ungenerous ambition, although measures adopted under such influences seldom fail to be unfortunate and injurious to those adopting them.

The disloyal citizens of the United States who have offered the ruin of our country, in return for the aid and comfort which they have invoked abroad, have received less patronage and encouragement than they probably expected. If it were just to suppose, as the insurgents have seemed to assume, that foreign nations, in this case, discarding all moral, social, and treaty obligations, would act solely, and selfishly, for the most speedy restoration of commerce, including, especially, the acquisition of cotton, those nations appear, as yet, not to have seen their way to their object more directly, or clearly, through the destruction, than through the preservation, of the Union. If we could dare to believe that foreign nations are actuated by no higher principle than this, I am quite sure a sound argument could be made to show them that they can reach their aim more readily, and easily, by aiding to crush this rebellion, than by giving encouragement to it

The principal lever relied on by the insurgents for exciting foreign nations to hostility against us, as already intimated, is the embarrassment of commerce. Those nations, however, not improbably, saw from the first, that it was the Union which made, as well our foreign, as our domestic commerce. They can scarcely have failed to perceive that the effort for disunion produces the existing difficulty; and that one strong nation promises more durable peace, and a more extensive, valuable and reliable commerce, than can the same nation broken into hostile fragments.

It is not my purpose to review our discussions with foreign states; because whatever might be their wishes, or dispositions, the integrity of our country, and the stability of our government, mainly depend, not upon them, but on the loyalty, virtue, patriotism, and intelligence of the American people. The correspondence itself, with the usual reservations, is herewith submitted.

I venture to hope it will appear that we have practiced prudence, and liberality towards foreign powers, averting causes of irritation; and, with firmness, maintaining our own rights and honor.

Since, however, it is apparent that here, as in every other state, foreign dangers necessarily attend domestic difficulties, I recommend that adequate and ample measures be adopted for maintaining the public defences on every side. While, under this general recommendation, provision for defending our sea-coast line readily occurs to the mind, I also, in the same connexion, ask the attention of Congress to our great lakes and rivers. It is believed that some fortifications and depots of arms and munitions, with harbor and navigation improvements, all at well selected points upon these, would be of great importance to the national defence and preservation. I ask attention to the views of the Secretary of War, expressed in his report, upon the same general subject.

I deem it of importance that the loyal regions of East Tennessee and western North Carolina should be connected with Kentucky, and other faithful parts of the Union, by railroad. I therefore recommend, as a military measure, that Congress provide for the construction of such road, as speedily as possible. Kentucky, no doubt, will co-operate, and, through her legislature, make the most judicious selection of a line. The northern terminus must connect with some existing railroad; and whether the route shall be from Lexington, or Nicholasville, to the Cumberland Gap; or from Lebanon to the Tennessee line, in the direction of Knoxville; or on some still different line, can easily be determined. Kentucky and the general government co-operating, the work can be completed in a very short time; and when done, it will be not only of vast present usefulness, but also a valuable permanent improvement, worth its cost in all the future.

Some treaties, designed chiefly for the interests of commerce, and having no grave political importance, have been negotiated, and will be submitted to the Senate for their consideration.

Although we have failed to induce some of the commercial powers to adopt a desirable melioration of the rigor of maritime war, we have removed all obstructions from the way of this humane reform, except such as are merely of temporary and accidental occurrence.

I invite your attention to the correspondence between her Britannic Majesty's minister accredited to this government, and the Secretary of State, relative to the detention of the British ship Perthshire in June last, by the United States steamer Massachusetts, for a supposed breach of the blockade. As this detention was occasioned by an obvious misapprehension of the facts, and as justice requires that we should commit no belligerent act not founded in strict right, as sanctioned by public law, I recommend that an appropriation be made to satisfy the reasonable demand of the owners of the vessel for her detention.

I repeat the recommendation of my predecessor, in his annual message to Congress in December last, in regard to the disposition of the surplus which will probably remain after satisfying the claims of American citizens against China, pursuant to the awards of the commissioners under the act of the 3d of March, 1859. If, however, it should not be deemed advisable to carry that recommendation into effect, I would suggest that authority be given for investing the principal, over the proceeds of the surplus referred to, in good securities, with a view to the satisfaction of such other just claims of our citizens against China as are not unlikely to arise hereafter in the course of our extensive trade with that Empire.

By the act of the 5th of August last, Congress authorized the President to instruct the commanders of suitable vessels to defend themselves against, and to capture pirates. This authority has been exercised in a single instance only. For the more effectual protection of our extensive and valuable commerce, in the eastern seas especially, it seems to me that it would also be advisable to authorize the commanders of sailing vessels to re-capture any prizes which pirates may make of United States vessels and their cargoes, and the consular courts, now established by law in eastern countries, to adjudicate the cases, in the event that this should not be objected to by the local authorities.

If any good reason exists why we should persevere longer in withholding our recognition of the independence and sovereignty of Hayti and Liberia, I am unable to discern it. Unwilling, however, to inaugurate a novel policy in regard to them without the approbation of Congress, I submit for your consideration the expediency of an appropriation for maintaining a chargé d'affaires near each of those new states. It does not admit of doubt that important commercial advantages might be secured by favorable treaties with them.

The operations of the treasury during the period which has elapsed since your adjournment have been conducted with signal success. The patriotism of the people has placed at the disposal of the government the large means demanded by the public exigencies. Much of the national loan has been taken by citizens of the industrial classes, whose confidence in their country's faith, and zeal for their country's deliverance from present peril, have induced them to contribute to the support of the government the whole of their. limited acquisitions. This fact imposes peculiar obligations to economy in disbursement and energy in action.

The revenue from all sources, including loans, for the financial year ending on the 30th June, 1861, was eighty-six million eight hundred and thirty-five thousand nine hundred dollars and twenty-seven cents, and the expenditures for the same period, including payments on account of the public debt, were eighty-four million five hundred and seventy-eight thousand eight hundred and thirty-four dollars and forty-seven cents; leaving a balance in the treasury, on the 1st July, of two million two hundred and fifty-seven thousand sixty-five dollars and eighty cents. For the first quarter of the financial year, ending on the 30th September, 1861, the receipts from all sources, including the balance of 1st of July, were one hundred and two million five hundred and thirty-two thousand five hundred and nine dollars and twenty-seven cents, and the expenses ninety-eight million two hundred and thirty-nine thousand seven hundred and thirty-three dollars and nine cents; leaving a balance, on the 1st of October, 1861, of four million two hundred and ninety-two thousand seven hundred and seventy-six dollars and eighteen cents.

Estimates for the remaining three quarters of the year, and for the financial year 1863, together with his views of ways and means for meeting the demands contemplated by them, will be submitted to Congress by the Secretary of the Treasury. It is gratifying to know that the expenditures made necessary by the rebellion are not beyond the resources of the loyal people, and to believe that the same patriotism which has thus far sustained the government will continue to sustain it till Peace and Union shall again bless the land.

I respectfully refer to the report of the Secretary of War for information respecting the numerical strength of the army, and for recommendations having in view an increase of its efficiency and the well being of the various branches of the service intrusted to his care. It is gratifying to know that the patriotism of the people has proved equal to the occasion, and that the number of troops tendered greatly exceeds the force which Congress authorized me to call into the field.

I refer with pleasure to those portions of his report which make allusion to the creditable degree of discipline already attained by our troops, and to the excellent sanitary condition of the entire army.

The recommendation of the Secretary for an organization of the militia upon a uniform basis, is a subject of vital importance to the future safety of the country, and is commended to the serious attention of Congress.

The large addition to the regular army, in connexion with the defection that has so considerably diminished the number of its officers, gives peculiar importance to his recommendation for increasing the corps of cadets to the greatest capacity of the Military Academy.

By mere omission, I presume, Congress has failed to provide chaplains for hospitals occupied by volunteers. This subject was brought to my notice, and I was induced to draw up the form of a letter, one copy of which, properly addressed, has been delivered to each of the persons, and at the dates respectively named and stated, in a schedule, containing also the form of the letter, marked A, and herewith transmitted.

These gentlemen, I understand, entered upon the duties designated, at the times respectively stated in the schedule, and have labored faithfully therein ever since. I therefore recommend that they be compensated at the same rate as chaplains in the army. I further suggest that general provision be made for chaplains to serve at hospitals, as well as with regiments.

The report of the Secretary of the Navy presents in detail the operations of that branch of the service, the activity and energy which have characterized its administration, and the results of measures to increase its efficiency and power. Such have been the additions, by construction and purchase, that it may almost be said a navy has been created and brought into service since our difficulties commenced.

Besides blockading our extensive coast, squadrons larger than ever before assembled under our flag have been put afloat and performed deeds which have increased our naval renown.

I would invite special attention to the recommendation of the Secretary for a more perfect organization of the navy by introducing additional grades in the service.

The present organization is defective and unsatisfactory, and the suggestions submitted by the department will, it is believed, if adopted, obviate the difficulties alluded to, promote harmony, and increase the efficiency of the navy.

There are three vacancies on the bench of the Supreme Court— two by the decease of Justices Daniel and McLean, and one by the resignation of Justice Campbell. I have so far forborne making nominations to fill these vacancies for reasons which I will now state. Two of the outgoing judges resided within the States now overrun by revolt; so that if successors were appointed in the same localities, they could not now serve upon their circuits; and many of the most competent men there, probably would not take the personal hazard of accepting to serve, even here, upon the supreme bench. I have been unwilling to throw all the appointments northward, thus disabling myself from doing justice to the south on the return of peace; although I may remark that to transfer to the north one which has heretofore been in the south, would not, with reference to territory and population, be unjust.

During the long and brilliant judicial career of Judge McLean his circuit grew into an empire—altogether too large for any one judge to give the courts therein more than a nominal attendance—rising in population from one million four hundred and seventy thousand and eighteen, in 1830, to six million one hundred and fifty-one thousand four hundred and five, in 1860.

Besides this, the country generally has outgrown our present judicial system. If uniformity was at all intended, the system requires that all the States shall be accommodated with circuit courts, attended by supreme judges, while, in fact, Wisconsin, Minnesota, Iowa, Kansas, Florida, Texas, California, and Oregon, have never had any such courts. Nor can this well be remedied without a change of the system; because the adding of judges to the Supreme Court, enough for the accommodation of all parts of the country, with circuit courts, would create a court altogether too numerous for a judicial body of any sort. And the evil, if it be one, will increase as new States come into the Union. Circuit courts are useful, or they are not useful. If useful, no State should be denied them ; if not useful, no State should have them. Let them be provided for all, or abolished as to all.

Three modifications occur to me, either of which, I think, would be an improvement upon our present system. Let the Supreme Court be of convenient number in every event. Then, first, let the whole country be divided into circuits of convenient size, the supreme judges to serve in a number of them corresponding to their own number, and independent circuit judges be provided for all the rest. Or, secondly, let the supreme judges be relieved from circuit duties, and circuit judges provided for all the circuits. Or, thirdly, dispense with circuit courts altogether, leaving the judicial functions wholly to the district courts and an independent Supreme Court.

I respectfully recommend to the consideration of Congress the present condition of the statute laws, with the hope that Congress will be able to find an easy remedy for many of the inconveniences and evils which constantly embarrass those engaged in the practical administration of them. Since the organization of the government, Congress has enacted some five thousand acts and joint resolutions, which fill more than six thousand closely printed pages, and are scattered through many volumes. Many of these acts have been drawn in haste and without sufficient caution, so that their provisions are often obscure in themselves, or in conflict with each other, or at least so doubtful as to render it very difficult for even the best informed persons to ascertain precisely what the statute law really is.

It seems to me very important that the statute laws should be made as plain and intelligible as possible, and be reduced to as small a compass as may consist with the fullness and precision of the will of the legislature and the perspicuity of its language. This, well done, would, I think, greatly facilitate the labors of those whose duty it is to assist in the administration of the laws, and would be a lasting benefit to the people, by placing before them, in a more accessible and intelligible form, the laws which so deeply concern their interests and their duties.

I am informed by some whose opinions I respect, that all the acts of Congress now in force, and of a permanent and general nature, might be revised and re-written, so as to be embraced in one volume (or at most, two volumes) of ordinary and convenient size. And I respectfully recommend to Congress to consider of the subject, and, if my suggestion be approved, to devise such plan as to their wisdom shall seem most proper for the attainment of the end proposed.

One of the unavoidable consequences of the present insurrection is the entire suppression, in many places, of all the ordinary means of administering civil justice by the officers, and in the forms of existing law. This is the case, in whole or in part, in all the insurgent States; and as our armies advance upon and take possession of parts of those States, the practical evil becomes more apparent. There are no courts nor officers to whom the citizens of other States, may apply for the enforcement of their lawful claims against citizens of the insurgent States; and there is a vast amount of debt constituting such claims. Some have estimated it as high as two hundred million dollars, due, in large part, from insurgents, in open rebellion, to loyal citizens who are, even now, making great sacrifices in the discharge of their patriotic duty to support the government.

Under these circumstances, I have been urgently solicited to establish, by military power, courts to administer summary justice in such cases. I have thus far declined to do it, not because I had any doubt that the end proposed—the collection of the debts—was just and right in itself, but because I have been unwilling to go beyond the pressure of necessity in the unusual exercise of power. But the powers of Congress I suppose are equal to the anomalous occasion, and therefore I refer the whole matter to Congress, with the hope that a plan may be devised for the administration of justice in all such parts of the insurgent States and Territories as may be under the control of this government, whether by a voluntary return to allegiance and order, or by the power of our arms. This, however, not to be a permanent institution, but a temporary substitute, and to cease as soon as the ordinary courts can be re-established in peace.

It is important that some more convenient means should be provided, if possible, for the adjustment of claims against the government, especially in view of their increased number by reason of the war. It is as much the duty of government to render prompt justice against itself, in favor of citizens, as it is to administer the same, between private individuals. The investigation and adjudication of claims, in their nature belong to the judicial department; besides it is apparent that the attention of Congress, will be more than usually engaged, for some time to come, with great national questions. It was intended, by the organization of the court of claims, mainly to remove this branch of business from the halls of Congress; but while the court has proved to be an effective, and valuable means of investigation, it in great degree fails to effect the object of its creation, for want of power to make its judgments final.

Fully aware of the delicacy, not to say the danger, of the subject, I commend to your careful consideration whether this power of making judgments final, may not properly be given to the court, reserving the right of appeal on questions of law to the Supreme Court, with such other provisions as experience may have shown to be necessary.

I ask attention to the report of the Postmaster General, the following being a summary statement of the condition of the department:

The revenue from all sources during the fiscal year ending June 30, 1861, including the annual permanent appropriation of seven hundred thousand dollars for the transportation of "free mail matter," was nine million forty-nine thousand two hundred and ninety-six dollars and forty cents, being about two per cent. less than the revenue for 1860.

The expenditures were thirteen million six hundred and six thousand seven hundred and fifty-nine dollars and eleven cents, showing a decrease of more than eight per cent. as compared with those of the previous year, and leaving an excess of expenditure over the revenue for the last fiscal year of four million five hundred and fifty-seven thousand four hundred and sixty-two dollars and seventy-one cents.

The gross revenue for the year ending June 30, 1863, is estimated at an increase of four per cent. on that of 1861, making eight million six hundred and eighty-three thousand dollars, to which should be added the earnings of the department in carrying free matter, viz: seven hundred thousand dollars, making nine million three hundred and eighty-three thousand dollars.

The total expenditures for 1863 are estimated at twelve million five hundred and twenty-eight thousand dollars, leaving an estimated deficiency of three million one hundred and forty-five thousand dollars to be supplied from the treasury, in addition to the permanent appropriation.

The present insurrection shows, I think, that the extension of this District across the Potomac river, at the time of establishing the capital here, was eminently wise, and consequently that the relinquishment of that portion of it which lies within the State of Virginia was unwise and dangerous. I submit for your consideration the expediency of regaining that part of the District, and the restoration of the original boundaries thereof, through negotiations with the State of Virginia.

The report of the Secretary of the Interior, with the accompanying documents, exhibits the condition of the several branches of the public business pertaining to that department. The depressing influences of the insurrection have been especially felt in the operations of the Patent and General Land Offices. The cash receipts from the sales of public lands during the past year have exceeded the expenses of our land system only about two hundred thousand dollars. The sales have been entirely suspended in the southern States, while the interruptions to the business of the country, and the diversion of large numbers of men from labor to military service, have obstructed settlements in the new States and Territories of the northwest.

The receipts of the Patent Office have declined in nine months about one hundred thousand dollars, rendering a large reduction of the force employed necessary to make it self-sustaining.

The demands upon the Pension Office will be largely increased by the insurrection. Numerous applications for pensions, based upon the casualties of the existing war, have already been made. There is reason to believe that many who are now upon the pension rolls and in receipt of the bounty of the government, are in the ranks of the insurgent army, or giving them aid and comfort. The Secretary of the Interior has directed a suspension of the payment of the pensions of such persons upon proof of their disloyalty. I recommend that Congress authorize that officer to cause the names of such persons to be stricken from the pension rolls.

The relations of the government with the Indian tribes have been greatly disturbed by the insurrection, especially in the southern superintendency and in that of New Mexico. The Indian country south of Kansas is in the possession of insurgents from Texas and Arkansas. The agents of the United States appointed since the 4th of March for this superintendency have been unable to reach their posts, while the most of those who were in office before that time have espoused the insurrectionary cause, and assume to exercise the powers of agents by virtue of commissions from the insurrectionists. It has been stated in the public press that a portion of those Indians have been organized as a military force, and are attached to the army of the insurgents. Although the government has no official information upon this subject, letters have been written to the Commissioner of Indian Affairs by several prominent chiefs, giving assurance of their loyalty to the United States, and expressing a wish for the presence of federal troops to protect them. It is believed that upon the repossession of the country by the federal forces the Indians will readily cease all hostile demonstrations, and resume their former relations to the government.

Agriculture, confessedly the largest interest of the nation, has, not a department, nor a bureau, but a clerkship only, assigned to it in the government. While it is fortunate that this great interest is so independent in its nature as to not have demanded and extorted more from the government, I respectfully ask Congress to consider whether something more cannot be given voluntarily with general advantage.

Annual reports exhibiting the condition of our agriculture, commerce and manufactures would present a fund of information of great practical value to the country. While I make no suggestion as to details, I venture the opinion that an agricultural and statistical bureau might profitably be organized.

· The execution of the laws for the suppression of the African slave trade has been confided to the Department of the Interior. It is a subject of gratulation that the efforts which have been made for the suppression of this inhuman traffic have been recently attended with unusual success. Five vessels being fitted out for the slave trade have been seized and condemned. Two mates of vessels engaged in the trade, and one person in equipping a vessel as a slaver, have been convicted and subjected to the penalty of fine and imprisonment, and one captain, taken with a cargo of Africans on board his vessel, has been convicted of the highest grade of offence under our laws, the punishment of which is death.

The Territories of Colorado, Dakotah and Nevada, created by the last Congress, have been organized, and civil administration has been inaugurated therein under auspices especially gratifying, when it is considered that the leaven of treason was found existing in some of these new countries when the federal officers arrived there.

The abundant natural resources of these Territories, with the security and protection afforded by organized government, will doubtless invite to them a large immigration when peace shall restore the business of the country to its accustomed channels. I submit the resolutions of the legislature of Colorado, which evidence the patriotic spirit of the people of the Territory. So far the authority of the United States has been upheld in all the Territories, as it is hoped it will be in the future. I commend their interests and defence to the enlightened and generous care of Congress.

I recommend to the favorable consideration of Congress the interests of the District of Columbia. The insurrection has been the cause of much suffering and sacrifice to its inhabitants, and as they have no representative in Congress, that body should not overlook their just claims upon the government.

At your late session a joint resolution was adopted authorizing the President to take measures for facilitating a proper representation of the industrial interests of the United States at the exhibition of the industry of all nations to be holden at London in the year 1862. I regret to say I have been unable to give personal attention to this subject—a subject at once so interesting in itself, and so extensively and intimately connected with the material prosperity of the world. Through the Secretaries of State and of the Interior a plan, or system, has been devised, and partly matured, and which will be laid before you.

Under and by virtue of the act of Congress entitled "An act to confiscate property used for insurrectionary purposes," approved August 6, 1861, the legal claims of certain persons to the labor and service of certain other persons have become forfeited ; and numbers of the latter, thus liberated, are already dependent on the United States, and must be provided for in some way. Besides this, it is not impossible that some of the States will pass similar enactments for their own benefit respectively, and by operation of which, persons of the same class will be thrown upon them for disposal. In such case I recommend that Congress provide for accepting such persons from such States, according to some mode of valuation, in lieu, *pro tanto*, of direct taxes, or upon some other plan to be agreed on with such States respectively ; that such persons, on such acceptance by the general government, be at once deemed free ; and that, in any event, steps be taken for colonizing both classes, (or the one first mentioned, if the other shall not be brought into existence,) at some place, or places, in a climate congenial to them.   It might be well to consider, too, whether the free colored people already in the United States could not, so far as individuals may desire, be included in such colonization.

To carry out the plan of colonization may involve the acquiring of territory, and also the appropriation of money beyond that to be expended in the territorial acquisition.   Having practiced the acquisition of territory for nearly sixty years, the question of constitutional power to do so is no longer an open one with us.   The power was questioned at first by Mr. Jefferson, who, however, in the purchase of Louisiana, yielded his scruples on the plea of great expediency. If it be said that the only legitimate object of acquiring territory is to furnish homes for white men, this measure effects that object ; for the emigration of colored men leaves additional room for white men remaining or coming here.   Mr. Jefferson, however, placed the importance of procuring Louisiana more on political and commercial grounds than on providing room for population.

On this whole proposition, including the appropriation of money with the acquisition of territory, does not the expediency amount to absolute necessity—that, without which the government itself cannot be perpetuated?

The war continues.   In considering the policy to be adopted for suppressing the insurrection, I have been anxious and careful that the inevitable conflict for this purpose shall not degenerate into a violent and remorseless revolutionary struggle.   I have, therefore, in every case, thought it proper to keep the integrity of the Union prominent as the primary object of the contest on our part, leaving all questions which are not of vital military importance to the more deliberate action of the legislature.

In the exercise of my best discretion I have adhered to the blockade of the ports held by the insurgents, instead of putting in force, by proclamation, the law of Congress enacted at the late session for closing those ports.

So, also, obeying the dictates of prudence, as well as the obligations of law, instead of transcending, I have adhered to the act of

Congress to confiscate property used for insurrectionary purposes. If à new law upon the same subject shall be proposed, its propriety will be duly considered. The Union must be preserved; and hence, all indispensable means must be employed. We should not be in haste to determine that radical, and extreme measures, which may reach the loyal as well as the disloyal, are indispensable.

The inaugural address at the beginning of the Administration, and the message to Congress at the late special session, were both mainly devoted to the domestic controversy out of which the insurrection and consequent war have sprung. Nothing now occurs to add or subtract, to or from, the principles, or general purposes, stated and expressed, in those documents.

The last ray of hope for preserving the Union peaceably, expired at the assault upon Fort Sumter; and a general review of what has occurred since may not be unprofitable. What was painfully uncertain then, is much better defined and more distinct now; and the progress of events is plainly in the right direction. The insurgents confidently claimed a strong support from north of Mason and Dixon's line; and the friends of the Union were not free from apprehension on the point. This, however, was soon settled definitely, and on the right side. South of the line, noble little Delaware led off right from the first. Maryland was made to *seem* against the Union. Our soldiers were assaulted, bridges were burned, and railroads torn up, within her limits; and we were many days, at one time, without the ability to bring a single regiment over her soil to the capital. Now, her bridges and railroads are repaired and open to the government; she already gives seven regiments to the cause of the Union and none to the enemy; and her people, at a regular election, have sustained the Union, by a larger majority, and a larger aggregate vote than they ever before gave to any candidate, or any question. Kentucky, too, for some time in doubt, is now decidedly, and, I think, unchangeably, ranged on the side of the Union. Missouri is comparatively quiet; and I believe cannot again be overrun by the insurrectionists. These three States of Maryland, Kentucky, and Missouri, neither of which would promise a single soldier at first, have now an aggregate of not less than forty thousand in the field, for the Union; while, of their citizens, certainly not more than a third of that number, and they of doubtful whereabouts, and doubtful existence, are in arms against it. After a somewhat bloody struggle of months, winter closes on the Union people of western Virginia, leaving them masters of their own country.

An insurgent force of about fifteen hundred, for months dominating the narrow peninsular region, constituting the counties of Accomac and Northampton, and known as eastern shore of Virginia, together with some contiguous parts of Maryland, have laid down their arms; and the people there have renewed their allegiance to, and accepted the protection of, the old flag. This leaves no armed insurrectionist north of the Potomac, or east of the Chesapeake.

Also we have obtained a footing at each of the isolated points, on the southern coast, of Hatteras, Port Royal, Tybee Island, near Savannah, and Ship island; and we likewise have some general accounts of popular movements, in behalf of the Union, in North Carolina and Tennessee.

These things demonstrate that the cause of the Union is advancing steadily and certainly southward.

Since your last adjournment, Lieutenant General Scott has retired from the head of the army. During his long life, the nation has not been unmindful of his merit; yet, on calling to mind how faithfully, ably, and brilliantly he has served the country, from a time far back in our history, when few of the now living had been born, and thenceforward continually, I cannot but think we are still his debtors. I submit, therefore, for your consideration, what further mark of recognition is due to him, and to ourselves, as a grateful people.

With the retirement of General Scott came the executive duty of appointing, in his stead, a general-in-chief of the army. It is a fortunate circumstance that neither in council nor country was there, so far as I know, any difference of opinion as to the proper person to be selected. The retiring chief repeatedly expressed his judgment in favor of General McClellan for the position; and in this the nation seemed to give a unanimous concurrence. The designation of General McClellan is, therefore, in considerable degree, the selection of the country, as well as of the Executive; and hence there is better reason to hope there will be given him, the confidence, and cordial support thus, by fair implication, promised, and without which, he cannot, with so full efficiency, serve the country.

It has been said that one bad general is better than two good ones; and the saying is true, if taken to mean no more than that an army

Ex. Doc. 1——2

is better directed by a single mind, though inferior, than by two superior ones, at variance, and cross-purposes with each other.

And the same is true, in all joint operations wherein those engaged, *can* have none but a common end in view, and *can* differ only as to the choice of means. In a storm at sea, no one on board *can* wish the ship to sink; and yet, not unfrequently, all go down together, because too many will direct, and no single mind can be allowed to control.

It continues to develop that the insurrection is largely, if not exclusively, a war upon the first principle of popular government—the rights of the people. Conclusive evidence of this is found in the most grave and maturely considered public documents, as well as in the general tone of the insurgents. In those documents we find the abridgment of the existing right of suffrage, and the denial to the people of all right to participate in the selection of public officers, except the legislative, boldly advocated, with labored arguments to prove that large control of the people in government, is the source of all political evil. Monarchy itself is sometimes hinted at as a possible refuge from the power of the people.

In my present position, I could scarcely be justified were I to omit raising a warning voice against this approach of returning despotism.

It is not needed, nor fitting here, that a general argument should be made in favor of popular institutions; but there is one point, with its connexions, not so hackneyed as most others, to which I ask a brief attention. It is the effort to place *capital* on an equal footing with, if not above *labor*, in the structure of government. It is assumed that labor is available only in connexion with capital; that nobody labors unless somebody else, owning capital, somehow by the use of it, induces him to labor. This assumed, it is next considered whether it is best that capital shall *hire* laborers, and thus induce them to work by their own consent, or *buy* them, and drive them to it without their consent. Having proceded so far, it is naturally concluded that all laborers are either *hired* laborers, or what we call slaves. And further, it is assumed that whoever is once a hired laborer, is fixed in that condition for life.

Now, there is no such relation between capital and labor as assumed; nor is there any such thing as a free man being fixed for life in the condition of a hired laborer. Both these assumptions are false, and all inferences from them are groundless.

Labor is prior to, and independent of, capital. Capital is only the fruit of labor, and could never have existed if labor had not first existed. Labor is the superior of capital, and deserves much the higher consideration. Capital has its rights, which are as worthy of protection as any other rights. Nor is it denied that there is, and probably always will be, a relation between labor and capital, producing mutual benefits. The error is in assuming that the whole labor of community exists within that relation. A few men own capital, and that few avoid labor themselves, and, with their capital, hire or buy another few to labor for them. A large majority belong to neither class—neither work for others, nor have others working for them. In most of the southern States, a majority of the whole people of all colors, are neither slaves nor masters; while in the northern, a large majority are neither hirers nor hired. Men with their families—wives, sons, and daughters—work for themselves, on their farms, in their houses, and in their shops, taking the whole product to themselves, and asking no favors of capital on the one hand, nor of hired laborers or slaves on the other. It is not forgotten that a considerable number of persons mingle their own labor with capital—that is, they labor with their own hands, and also buy or hire others to labor for them; but this is only a mixed, and not a distinct class. No principle stated is disturbed by the existence of this mixed class.

Again: as has already been said, there is not, of necessity, any such thing as the free hired laborer being fixed to that condition for life. Many independent men everywhere in these States, a few years back in their lives, were hired laborers. The prudent, penniless beginner in the world, labors for wages awhile, saves a surplus with which to buy tools or land for himself; then labors on his own account another while, and at length hires another new beginner to help him. This is the just, and generous, and prosperous system, which opens the way to all—gives hope to all, and consequent energy, and progress, and improvement of condition to all. No men living are more worthy to be trusted than those who toil up from poverty—none less inclined to take, or touch, aught which they have not honestly earned. Let them beware of surrendering a political power which they already possess, and which, if surrendered, will surely be used to close the door of advancement against such as they, and to fix new disabilities and burdens upon them, till all of liberty shall be lost.

From the first taking of our National Census to the last, are seventy years; and we find our population, at the end of the period, eight times as great as it was at the beginning. The increase of those other things, which men deem desirable, has been even greater. We thus have, at one view, what the popular principle, applied to government, through the machinery of the States and the Union, has produced in a given time; and also what, if firmly maintained, it promises for the future. There are already among us those who, if the Union be preserved, will live to see it contain two hundred and fifty millions. The struggle *of* to-day is not altogether *for* to-day— it is for a vast future also. With a reliance on Providence, all the more firm and earnest, let us proceed in the great task which events have devolved upon us.

ABRAHAM LINCOLN.

WASHINGTON, *December* 3, 1861.

LIST OF PAPERS

RELATING TO

FOREIGN AFFAIRS,

ACCOMPANYING

THE PRESIDENT'S MESSAGE TO CONGRESS, AT THE OPENING OF ITS SESSION IN DECEMBER, 1861.

CIRCULARS.

INSTRUCTIONS AND DESPATCHES.

PRUSSIA.

BELGIUM.

MEXICO.

GREAT BRITAIN.

GREAT BRITAIN—Continued.

GREAT BRITAIN—Continued.

CASE OF THE "PERTHSHIRE."

AUSTRIA.

FRANCE.

FRANCE—Continued.

SPAIN.

ROME.

RUSSIA.

DENMARK.

ITALY.

SWITZERLAND.

SWITZERLAND—Continued.

NETHERLANDS.

TURKEY.

SWEDEN.

PORTUGAL.

PERU.

GUATEMALA.

NICARAGUA.

EGYPT.

CORRESPONDENCE.

Mr. Black (Secretary of State) to all the ministers of the United States.

CIRCULAR.

DEPARTMENT OF STATE,
Washington, February 28, 1861.

SIR : You are, of course, aware that the election of last November resulted in the choice of Mr. Abraham Lincoln; that he was the candidate of the republican or anti-slavery party; that the preceding discussion had been confined almost entirely to topics connected, directly or indirectly, with the subject of negro slavery; that every northern State cast its whole electoral vote (except three in New Jersey) for Mr. Lincoln, while in the whole south the popular sentiment against him was almost absolutely universal. Some of the southern States, immediately after the election, took measures for separating themselves from the Union, and others soon followed their example. Conventions have been called in South Carolina, Georgia, Florida, Alabama, Mississippi, Louisiana, and Texas, and those conventions, in all except the last-named State, have passed ordinances declaring their secession from the federal government. A congress, composed of representatives from the six first-named States, has been assembled for some time at Montgomery, Alabama. By this body a provisional constitution has been framed for what it styles the "Confederated States of America."

It is not improbable that persons claiming to represent the States which have thus attempted to throw off their federal obligations will seek a recognition of their independence by the Emperor of Russia. In the event of such an effort being made, you are expected by the President to use such means as may in your judgment be proper and necessary to prevent its success.

The reasons set forth in the President's message at the opening of the present session of Congress, in support of his opinion that the States have no constitutional power to secede from the Union, are still unanswered, and are believed to be unanswerable. The grounds upon which they have attempted to justify the revolutionary act of severing the bonds which connect them with their sister States are regarded as wholly insufficient. This government has not relinquished its constitutional jurisdiction within the territory of those States, and does not desire to do so.

It must be very evident that it is the right of this government to ask of all foreign powers that the latter shall take no steps which may tend to encourage the revolutionary movement of the seceding States, or increase the danger of disaffection in those which still remain loyal. The President feels assured that the government of the Emperor will not do anything in these affairs inconsistent with the friendship which this government has always heretofore experienced from him and his ancestors. If the independence of the "Confederated States" should be acknowledged by the great powers of Europe it would tend to disturb the friendly relations, diplomatic and commercial, now existing between those powers and the United

States. All these are consequences which the court of the Emperor will not fail to see are adverse to the interests of Russia as well as to those of this country.

Your particular knowledge of our political institutions will enable you to explain satisfactorily the causes of our present domestic troubles, and the grounds of the hope still entertained that entire harmony will soon be restored.

I am, sir, respectfully, your obedient servant,

J. S. BLACK.

John Appleton, Esq., &c., &c., &c.

The same, *mutatis mutandis*, to W. Preston, Esq., Madrid; E. G. Fair, Esq., Brussels; Theo. S. Fay, Esq., Berne; Jos. A. Wright, Esq., Berlin; J. G. Jones, Esq., Vienna; J. Williams, Esq., Constantinople; Geo. M. Dallas, Esq., London; Chas. J. Faulkner, Esq., Paris; Henry C. Murphy, Esq., Hague.

Mr. Seward (Secretary of State) to all the ministers of the United States.

CIRCULAR.

Department of State,
Washington, March 9, 1861.

Sir: My predecessor, in his despatch, number 10, addressed to you on the 28th of February last, instructed you to use all proper and necessary measures to prevent the success of efforts which may be made by persons claiming to represent those States of this Union in whose name a provisional government has been announced to procure a recognition of their independence by the government of Spain.

I am now instructed by the President of the United States to inform you that, having assumed the administration of the government in pursuance of an unquestioned election and of the directions of the Constitution, he renews the injunction which I have mentioned, and relies upon the exercise of the greatest possible diligence and fidelity on your part to counteract and prevent the designs of those who would invoke foreign intervention to embarrass or overthrow the republic.

When you reflect on the novelty of such designs, their unpatriotic and revolutionary character, and the long train of evils which must follow directly or consequentially from even their partial or temporary success, the President feels assured that you will justly appreciate and cordially approve the caution which prompts this communication.

I transmit herewith a copy of the address pronounced by the President on taking the constitutional oath of office. It sets forth clearly the errors of the misguided partisans who are seeking to dismember the Union, the grounds on which the conduct of those partisans is disallowed, and also the general policy which the government will pursue with a view to the preservation of domestic peace and order, and the maintenance and preservation of the federal Union.

You will lose no time in submitting this address to the Spanish minister for foreign affairs, and in assuring him that the President of the United States entertains a full confidence in the speedy restoration of the harmony and unity of the government by a firm, yet just and liberal bearing, cooperating with the deliberate and loyal action of the American people.

You will truthfully urge upon the Spanish government the consideration that the present disturbances have had their origin only in popular passions, excited under novel circumstances of very transient character, and that while not one person of well-balanced mind has attempted to show that dismemberment of the Union would be permanently conducive to the safety and welfare of even his own State or section, much less of all the States and sections of our country, the people themselves still retain and cherish a profound confidence in our happy Constitution, together with a veneration and affection for it such as no other form of government ever received at the hands of those for whom it was established.

We feel free to assume that it is the general conviction of men, not only here but in all other countries, that this federal Union affords a better system than any other that could be contrived to assure the safety, the peace, the prosperity, the welfare, and the happiness of all the States of which it is composed. The position of these States, and their mining, agricultural, manufacturing, commercial, political, and social relations and influences, seem to make it permanently the interest of all other nations that our present political system shall be unchanged and undisturbed. Any advantage that any foreign nation might derive from a connexion that it might form with any dissatisfied or discontented portion, State, or section, even if not altogether illusory, would be ephemeral, and would be overbalanced by the evils it would suffer from a disseverance of the whole Union, whose manifest policy it must be hereafter, as it has always been heretofore, to maintain peace, liberal commerce, and cordial amity with all other nations, and to favor the establishment of well-ordered government over the whole American continent.

Nor do we think we exaggerate our national importance when we claim that any political disaster that should befall us, and introduce discord or anarchy among the States that have so long constituted one great pacific, prosperous nation, under a form of government which has approved itself to the respect and confidence of mankind, might tend by its influence to disturb and unsettle the existing systems of government in other parts of the world, and arrest that progress of improvement and civilization which marks the era in which we live.

The United States have had too many assurances and manifestations of the friendship and good will of her Catholic Majesty to entertain any doubt that these considerations, and such others as your own large experience of the working of our federal system will suggest, will have their just influence with her, and will prevent her Majesty's government from yielding to solicitations to intervene in any unfriendly way in the domestic concerns of our country. The President regrets that the events going on here may be productive of some possible inconvenience to the people and subjects of Spain; but he is determined that those inconveniences shall be made as light and as transient as possible, and, so far as it may rest with him, that all strangers who may suffer any injury from them shall be amply indemnified. The President expects that you will be prompt in transmitting to this department any information you may receive on the subject of the attempts which have suggested this communication.

I am, sir, respectfully, your obedient servant,

WILLIAM H. SEWARD.

W. PRESTON, Esq., *Madrid.*

The same, *mutatis mutandis,* to E. G. FAIR, Esq., Brussels; THEO. S. FAY, Esq., Berne; JOS. A. WRIGHT, ESQ., Berlin; J. G. JONES, Esq., Vienna; J. WILLIAMS, Esq., Constantinople; GEO. M. DALLAS, Esq., London; CHAS. J. FAULKNER, Esq., Paris; JOHN APPLETON, ESQ., St. Petersburg; HENRY C. MURPHY, Esq., Hague.

Ex. Doc. 1——3

Mr. Seward to ministers of the United States in Great Britain, France, Russia, Prussia, Austria, Belgium, Italy, and Denmark.

CIRCULAR.

DEPARTMENT OF STATE,
Washington, April 24, 1861.

SIR: The advocates of benevolence and the believers in human progress, encouraged by the slow though marked meliorations of the barbarities of war which have obtained in modern times, have been, as you are well aware, recently engaged with much assiduity in endeavoring to effect some modifications of the law of nations in regard to the rights of neutrals in maritime war. In the spirit of these movements the President of the United States, in the year 1854, submitted to the several maritime nations two propositions, to which he solicited their assent as permanent principles of international law, which were as follows:

1. Free ships make free goods; that is to say, that the effects or goods belonging to subjects or citizens of a power or State at war are free from capture or confiscation when found on board of neutral vessels, with the exception of articles contraband of war.

2. That the property of neutrals on board an enemy's vessel is not subject to confiscation unless the same be contraband of war.

Several of the governments to which these propositions were submitted expressed their willingness to accept them, while some others, which were in a state of war, intimated a desire to defer acting thereon until the return of peace should present what they thought would be a more auspicious season for such interesting negotiations.

On the 16th of April, 1856, a congress was in session at Paris. It consisted of several maritime powers, represented by their plenipotentiaries, namely, Great Britain, Austria, France, Russia, Prussia, Sardinia, and Turkey. That congress having taken up the general subject to which allusion has already been made in this letter, on the day before mentioned, came to an agreement, which they adopted in the form of a declaration, to the effect following, namely:

1. Privateering is and remains abolished.

2. The neutral flag covers enemy's goods, with the exception of contraband of war.

3. Neutral goods, with the exception of contraband of war, are not liable to capture under enemy's flag.

4. Blockades, in order to be binding, must be effective; that is to say, maintained by forces sufficient really to prevent access to the coast of the enemy.

The agreement pledged the parties constituting the congress to bring the declaration thus made to the knowledge of the States which had not been represented in that body, and to invite them to accede to it. The congress, however, at the same time insisted, in the first place, that the declaration should be binding only on the powers who were or should become parties to it as one whole and indivisible compact; and, secondly, that the parties who had agreed, and those who should afterwards accede to it, should, after the adoption of the same, enter into no arrangement on the application of maritime law in time of war without stipulating for a strict observance of the four points resolved by the declaration.

The declaration which I have thus substantially recited of course prevented all the powers which became parties to it from accepting the two propositions which had been before submitted to the maritime nations by the President of the United States.

The declaration was, in due time, submitted by the governments represented in the congress at Paris to the government of the United States.

The President, about the 14th of July, 1856, made known to the States concerned his unwillingness to accede to the declaration. In making that announcement on behalf of this government, my predecessor, Mr. Marcy, called the attention of those States to the following points, namely:

1st. That the second and third propositions contained in the Paris declaration are substantially the same with the two propositions which had before been submitted to the maritime States by the President.

2d. That the Paris declaration, with the conditions annexed, was inadmissible by the United States in three respects, namely: 1st. That the government of the United States could not give its assent to the first proposition contained in the declaration, namely, that "Privateering is and remains abolished," although it was willing to accept it with an amendment which should exempt the private property of individuals, though belonging to belligerent States, from seizure or confiscation by national vessels in maritime war. 2d. That for this reason the stipulation annexed to the declaration, viz: that the propositions must be taken altogether or rejected altogether, without modification, could not be allowed. 3d. That the fourth condition annexed to the declaration, which provided that the parties acceding to it should enter into no negotiation for any modifications of the law of maritime war with nations which should not contain the four points contained in the Paris declaration, seemed inconsistent with a proper regard to the national sovereignty of the United States.

On the 29th of July, 1856, Mr. Mason, then minister of the United States at Paris, was instructed by the President to propose to the government of France to enter into an arrangement for its adherence, with the United States, to the four principles of the declaration of the congress of Paris, provided the first of them should be amended as specified in Mr. Marcy's note to the Count de Sartiges on the 28th of July, 1856. Mr. Mason accordingly brought the subject to the notice of the imperial government of France, which was disposed to entertain the matter favorably, but which failed to communicate its decision on the subject to him. Similar instructions regarding the matter were addressed by this department to Mr. Dallas, our minister at London, on the 31st day of January, 1857; but the proposition above referred to had not been directly presented to the British government by him when the administration of this government by Franklin Pierce, during whose term these proceedings occurred, came to an end, on the 3d of March, 1857, and was succeeded by that of James Buchanan, who directed the negotiations to be arrested for the purpose of enabling him to examine the questions involved, and they have ever since remained in that state of suspension.

The President of the United States has now taken the subject into consideration, and he is prepared to communicate his views upon it, with a disposition to bring the negotiation to a speedy and satisfactory conclusion.

For that purpose you are hereby instructed to seek an early opportunity to call the attention of her Majesty's government to the subject, and to ascertain whether it is disposed to enter into negotiations for the accession of the government of the United States to the declaration of the Paris congress, with the conditions annexed by that body to the same; and if you shall find .that government so disposed, you will then enter into a convention to that effect, substantially in the form of a project for that purpose herewith transmitted to you; the convention to take effect from the time when the due ratifications of the same shall have been exchanged. It is presumed that you will need no special explanation of the sentiments of the President on this subject for the purpose of conducting the necessary conferences with the government to which you are accredited. Its assent is expected on the ground that the proposition is accepted at its suggestion, and in the form it has

preferred. For your own information it will be sufficient to say that the
President adheres to the opinion expressed by my predecessor, Mr. Marcy,
that it would be eminently desirable for the good of all nations that the
property and effects of private individuals, not contraband, should be exempt
from seizure and confiscation by national vessels in maritime war. If the
time and circumstances were propitious to a prosecution of the negotiation
with that object in view, he would direct that it should be assiduously pursued. But the right season seems to have passed, at least for the present.
Europe seems once more on the verge of quite general wars. On the other
hand, a portion of the American people have raised the standard of insurrection, and proclaimed a provisional government, and, through their organs,
have taken the bad resolution to invite privateers to prey upon the peaceful
commerce of the United States.

Prudence and humanity combine in persuading the President, under the
circumstances, that it is wise to secure the lesser good offered by the Paris
congress, without waiting indefinitely in hope to obtain the greater one
offered to the maritime nations by the President of the United States.

I am, sir, respectfully, your obedient servant.

WILLIAM H. SEWARD.

CHARLES FRANCIS ADAMS, Esq., &c., &c., &c.

The same, *mutatis mutandis*, to the ministers of the United States in France,
Russia, Prussia, Austria, Belgium, Italy, and Denmark.

---

*Convention upon the subject of the rights of belligerents and neutrals in time of
war, between the United States of America and her Majesty the Queen of
Great Britain and Ireland.*

The United States of America and her Majesty the Queen of Great Britain
and Ireland, being equally animated by a desire to define with more precision the rights of belligerent and neutrals in time of war, have, for that
purpose, conferred full powers, the President of the United States upon
Charles F. Adams, accredited as their envoy extraordinary and minister
plenipotentiary to her said Majesty, and her Majesty the Queen of Great
Britian and Ireland, upon

And the said plenipotentiaries, after having exchanged their full powers,
have concluded the following articles :

ARTICLE I.

1. Privateering is and remains abolished. 2. The neutral flag covers
enemy's goods, with the exception of contraband of war. 3. Neutral goods,
with the exception of contraband of war, are not liable to capture under
enemy's flag. 4. Blockades in order to be binding, must be effective; that
is to say, maintained by a force sufficient really to prevent access to the
coast of the enemy.

ARTICLE II.

The present convention shall be ratified by the President of the United
States of America, by and with the advice and consent of the Senate, and
by her Majesty the Queen of Great Britain and Ireland, and the ratifications
shall be exchanged at Washington, within the space of six months from the
signature, or sooner if possible. In faith whereof, the respective plenipotentiaries have signed the present convention in duplicate, and have thereto
affixed their seals.

Done at London, the   day of   , in the year of our Lord, one
thousand eight hundred and sixty-one (1861.)

PRUSSIA.

Mr. Seward to Mr. Judd.

[Extract.]

No. 1.]   DEPARTMENT OF STATE,
                                Washington, March 22, 1861.

SIR: Contrary to what usually happens in giving instructions to a minister
going abroad, I am directed by the President to ask you to fix your attention in the first instance, and to keep it constantly fixed, on the actual condition of affairs at home. I allude, of course, to the unlawful and unconstitutional attempt which is being made to detach several of the States
from the federal Union, and to organize them as an independent republic
under the name of the "Confederate States of America."

You are well aware of what you will find Europeans unable to understand, namely, that owing to the very peculiar structure of our federal government, and the equally singular character and habits of the American
people, this government not only wisely but necessarily hesitates to resort
to coercion and compulsion to secure a return of the disaffected portion of
the people to their customary allegiance. The Union was formed upon
popular consent and must always practically stand on the same basis. The
temporary causes of alienation must pass away; there must needs be disasters
and disappointments resulting from the exercise of unlawful authority by
the revolutionists, while happily it is certain that there is a general and
profound sentiment of loyalty pervading the public mind throughout the
United States. While it is the intention of the President to maintain the
sovereignty and rightful authority of the Union everywhere with firmness as
well as discretion, he at the same time relies with great confidence on the
salutary working of the agencies I have mentioned, to restore the harmony
and Union of the States. But to this end it is of the greatest importance
that the disaffected States shall not succeed in obtaining favor or recognition
from foreign nations.

It is understood that the so-called Confederate States of America have
sent, or are about to send, agents to solicit such recognition in Europe,
although there is no special reason for supposing Prussia to be one of the
nations to which application will be made. An almost electric political connexion, however, exists between the several capitals of western Europe,
and therefore your most efficient and unfailing efforts must be put forth
directly, and even indirectly, to prevent the success of that ill-starred
design.

This matter was deemed so important by the late administration that my
predecessor, on the 28th of February last, made it a subject of a circular
despatch, of which an original part was transmitted by him to Mr. Wright,
who preceded you in your mission.

The present administration entertain the same general view of the subject which in that despatch was taken by Mr. Buchanan. Accordingly, on
the 9th day of March instant, I sent to our representatives abroad a new
circular letter in which I reiterated and amplified the instructions which

had thus been given to them by Mr. Black. Although that circular will be found in the archives of your legation, yet for your greater convenience I append a copy of it to this communication.

This department has little more to add to that paper when it is read, as it ought to be, in connexion with the President's inaugural address, on which it rests for its basis.

It may, however, be well to call your attention to the fact that in that communication, as in this, I have forborne altogether from discussing the groundless complaints and pretexts which have been put forth by the organs of disunion to justify the rash and perilous revolution which they are attempting to inaugurate. I have practiced this reticence not because the point is unimportant, but because the dispute is purely a domestic one, and the President would not willingly have the archives of our legations bear testimony to so un-American a proceeding as an acknowledgment, even by indirection, that this government ever consented to join issue upon a purely family matter of this kind with a portion of our own citizens before a foreign tribunal. Nevertheless, should you find that any weight is given to those complaints and pretexts in the court to which you are accredited, your perfect knowledge of all the transactions involved, will, I am sure, enable you to meet them conclusively and satisfactorily without precise instructions on that point.

You will not take up any subject of controversy or debate that may arise between the governments of Prussia and the United States, without first communicating the matter to this department, and you will practice the same forbearance on any subject of controversy which your predecessor may have left for your attention. These instructions are given you because it is our first and most earnest desire and expectation that you will avoid all possible forms of offence or irritation, and will, on the other hand, endeavor to establish the most friendly and cordial relations with the government of the King of Prussia. With this view you will assure his Majesty that the President and people of the United States entertain sentiments of the highest respect and sincere good will for his Majesty and the people of Prussia.

*   *   *   *   *   *   *   *   *   *

I am, sir, your obedient servant,

WILLIAM H. SEWARD.

NORMAN B. JUDD, Esq , &c., &c., &c.

Mr. Wright to Mr. Seward.

[Extract.]

No. 173.]   UNITED STATES LEGATION,
                                          Berlin, May 8, 1861.

SIR: I have, since my return, had a long interview with Baron Von Schleinitz, the minister for foreign affairs, who, whilst he expressed the earnest sympathy of his government with the American people in their present troubles, not only because of the effect of such disturbances upon the commerce of Europe, but also on account of the intimate relations between the two countries, owing to the presence of a large German population in the United States, gave me the most positive assurance that his government, from the principle of unrelenting opposition to all revolutionary movements, would be one of the last to recognize any *de facto* government of the disaffected States of the American Union.

The news of to-day has exerted the most unhappy influence upon the Americans here, and the universal sentiment is a profound desire and a hope for the restoration of peace in the United States. *   *   *
*   *   *   *   *   *   *

I have the honor to be, most respectfully, your very obedient servant,
JOSEPH A. WRIGHT.
His Excellency Hon. WILLIAM H. SEWARD,
Secretary of State, Washington, D. C.

Mr. Wright to Mr. Seward.

[Extract.]

No. 174.]   UNITED STATES LEGATION,
                                             Berlin, May 15, 1861.
SIR:
*   *   *   *   *   *

The proclamation of the President was received by the previous mail, and the subject has received due consideration.

On receipt of your circular dated the 20th of April, I immediately called upon Baron de Schleinitz, minister of foreign affairs, who had received the proclamation of the President, and he at once promptly informed me that, in his opinion, no apprehension need be entertained as to Prussian subjects engaging under the authority of the so-called Confederate States in fitting out privateers, or in any manner interfering with our commerce. Prussia has but few ports. Hers is not a sea-faring people, and the sympathies of the government and of the people are with the United States. Whatever danger may be apprehended on this subject must come from Bremen, Hamburg, and other ports situated in Oldenburg, Hanover, &c. Due vigilance will be used to prevent any such unlawful interference, and if any such be detected the proper authorities will be promptly advised thereof, and every effort will be made to suppress it. Not knowing whether your circular has been sent to the consuls, I have forwarded copies to several already.
*   *   *   *   *   *   *   *

I have the honor to be, very respectfully, your obedient servant,
JOSEPH A. WRIGHT.
His Excellency Hon. WILLIAM H. SEWARD,
Secretary of State, Washington, D. C.

Mr. Wright to Mr. Seward.

[Extract.]

No. 175.]   UNITED STATES LEGATION,
                                             Berlin, May 26, 1861.
SIR:
*   *   *   *   *   *

Enclosed is a copy of a recent communication to the minister of foreign affairs. Prussia will take efficient steps to sustain the government of the

United States in the protection of property and commerce, and will do all she can, consistently with her obligations to other governments, to sustain the vigorous action of our government in maintaining law and order.

The minister of foreign affairs, Baron Von Schleinitz, informed me on yesterday that it was the intention of the government to issue a proclamation touching these questions.

The government and people are, in spirit and feeling, with us. I am in the receipt of hundreds of letters and personal calls seeking positions in the American army, and asking for means of conveyance to our shores. So numerous, indeed, are the applications, that I have been compelled to place on the doors of the legation a notice to the purport that "This is the legation of the United States, and not a recruiting office." The fidelity and firmness exhibited with such unanimity by our own people in sustaining the administration in their efforts to put down the outrages of the so-called "Confederate States," whilst it astonishes the people of the old world, is at the same time rapidly creating a sentiment of confidence in our ability to maintain unimpaired the institutions of our fathers.

Let the cost be what it may, we must vindicate the memory of our fathers from the slanders announced by those in high places in the so-called "Confederate States," wherein they have proclaimed ours is only a confederation of States, and not a national union.

*   *   *   *   *   *

I have the honor to be, most respectfully, your obedient servant,

JOSEPH A. WRIGHT.

His Excellency Hon. WILLIAM H. SEWARD,
    Secretary of State, Washington, D. C.

Mr. Wright to Mr. Seward.

[Extracts.]

No. 176.]   UNITED STATES LEGATION,
Berlin, June 8, 1861.

SIR: Although the Prussian government has not issued a proclamation upon the subject referred to in my last despatch, I still continue to receive from the minister of foreign affairs the strongest assurances of the sympathies and friendship of this government.   *   *   *   *

*   *   *   *   *   *

Your circular of the 6th of May has been received, but the subject had been duly considered previously thereto. No opportunity will be neglected to counteract any efforts that may be made by individuals or associations in negotiations hostile to the United States.

*   *   *   *   *   *

I have the honor to be, most respectfully, your obedient servant,

JOSEPH A. WRIGHT.

Hon. WILLIAM H. SEWARD,
    Secretary of State, Washington, D C.

Mr. Wright to Mr. Seward.

[Extract.]

No. 178.]   UNITED STATES LEGATION,
                                                         Berlin, June 25, 1861.

SIR:

*   *   *   *   *   *

I have received this moment a copy of the *National Zeitung*, containing the despatch of Baron Schleinitz to Baron Gerolt; and also an order from the minister of commerce, addressed to Prussian subjects engaged in trade and commerce. This is not what I had expected. I was anticipating a proclamation from the King more full and distinct. This will doubtless have the desired effect, as it will be published in all the German journals, and coming from Prussia will be duly respected by the German States and Free Cities. Their sympathy and spirit is with the United States government.

Mr. Judd is expected on the 27th instant.

I have the honor to be, very respectfully, your obedient servant,
                                                         JOSEPH A. WRIGHT.

Hon. WILLIAM H. SEWARD,
      Secretary of State, Washington City.

Baron Schleinitz to Baron Gerolt.

[Translation.]

                                                         BERLIN, *June 13, 1861.*

The various herewith enclosed statements, by which your excellency has given me a knowledge of the occurrences through which the internal tranquillity of the Union is disturbed, have called forth my serious consideration. The hope which, until now, we so willingly entertained, that the inchoate conflict between the government of the United States and sundry of the southern States of the Union would be brought to an amicable settlement, is now, unhappily, in view of existing conditions, borne back to a far distance.

The indubitable fact of the state of the intestine warfare in which the Union is placed is a source of deep regret to the King's government. The relations of close friendship which connect Prussia and the government of the United States exist from the foundation of the Union. They have endured nearly a hundred years; never at any time disturbed by change of circumstances, nor in any wise impaired.

By a series of treaties, by means of which the improvement of the interests of manufacture and commerce on either side has been eminently developed, the intimate relations between the two States have attained a prosperous durability. At no time, between these two powers, has any collision of antagonistic interests found a foothold. The soaring flight which the internal prosperity of the Union has taken, extending its range from year to year by means of the bond of unity of the States thus knit together, the commanding attitude which North America has attained, abroad, has been looked upon by Prussia not merely with no dissatisfaction but has rather been greeted by her with honest sympathy.

The more earnestly, then, do we regret that the continuance of so prosperous a condition of things should appear to be placed in question by the inchoate disturbance of that internal unity, the unshaken existence of which had, until this time, formed the surest foundation of the Union. It behooves not the royal government either to discuss the causes of existing controversies or to pass judgment upon those debatable questions which belong entirely to the domestic relations of the Union. Our whole endeavor in this matter must be addressed to sustaining the United States in their heretofore existing relations with us, even under the difficult circumstances of the present time.

Nevertheless, by the serious turn which the conflict that has broken ont has already taken, and by the consequent self-reliant mode of proceeding of the government of the United States in relation to blockades, and the treatment of neutral navigation, essential and important interests on this side are also affected, and the royal government has taken into earnest consideration the protection thereof on grounds of international law and in conformity with treaty stipulations.

Your excellency has full knowledge of the negotiations which, through a series of years, were carried on between Prussia and the United States, upon the principles which ought to be brought into application in naval warfare in relation to the rights of neutral shipping. It is to the credit of the North American Cabinet that, in the year 1854, it availed itself of the plan of a treaty, proposed with us, to be first to take the initiative for putting the rights above mentioned in liberal and practical shape upon a broader foundation of well settled principles. We then willingly acceded to the North American proposition, and although the negotiations conducted by your excellency were closed without attaining the desired result, because a stand was then taken against that abolition of privateering which was suggested by us, it has, meantime, nevertheless, so fallen out that the general united desire to establish the recognition of the rights of neutral shipping during maritime warfare upon more extended and unassailable foundations has attracted, in praiseworthy degree, the attention of the great powers of Europe. The declaration upon maritime rights by the Paris convention, on the 16th April, 1856, stands in evidence of this. The collective States of Europe, with the exception of Spain only, gave their adhesion thereto. But the United States of North America, in regard to the first principle concerning the abolition of privateering, to our regret, thought proper to qualify their assent to the Paris declaration, if we do not misapprehend the liberal and well-intentioned views by which that cabinet was guided in the matter. These were made known in the proposition of President Pierce upon the subject, according to which the principle that private property on the seas should be altogether inviolable, should be included among the provisions of the law of nations. It is to be regretted that the President did not succeed in giving effect to his proposition. The estimation with which we regarded his course is sufficiently known to your excellency.

By reason of the consequently prevailing doubts about the treatment to which neutral shipping may be subjected during the condition of things there connected with an incipient state of war, I must request your excellency will please to make this interesting question the subject of a friendly and unreserved conference with the Secretary of State of that country.

It would certainly be most desirable to us that the government of the United States might embrace this occasion to announce their adhesion to the Paris declaration. Should this not be attained, then, for the present, we would urge that an exposition might be made, to be obligatory during the now commencing intestine war, in regard to the application generally of the second and third principles of the Paris declaration to neutral shipping. The provision of the second principle, that the neutral flag covers the enemy's cargo, (with exception of contraband of war,) is already assured to Prussian shipping by our treaty with the United States of May 1, 1828, again adopting article twelve of the treaty of September 10, 1785.

We lay much stress upon this toward bringing round a determination to make application of this principle at the present time to neutral shipping generally and universally. We doubt this the less because, according to a despatch from the then President, addressed by the Secretary of State, L. Cass, under date of June 27, 1859, to the minister of the United States in Paris, and also communicated to us, without further referring to the Paris declaration, it is expressly mentioned that the principle that the neutral flag covers the enemy's cargo (contraband of war excepted) would be reduced to application in respect to the shipping of the United States always, and in its full extent.

The import of the third principle, by which neutral private property under an enemy's flag (except contraband of war) is inviolable, becomes, in respect of its immediate recognition by the United States, a stringent necessity to the neutral powers.

Let there be a doubt of the application of this principle, and the business enterprises of neutral States are exposed to inevitable shocks, and collisions of every conceivable kind are to be dreaded. To provide for the avoidance of these in due season, *we* must at least anxiously desire.

It would minister greatly to my satisfaction if your excellency, as soon as may be, could officially inform me that the overtures and propositions which you are commissioned to make to the administration have found a favorable reception.

SCHLEINITZ.

His Excellency BARON VON GEROLT, &c., &c., &c., *Washington.*

[Translation.]

On the same subject the minister of commerce issued the notification annexed to the mercantile classes in the Baltic ports:

It is my duty to make known to you that during the continuance of the conflict which has broken out among the North American States the mercantile classes must abstain from all enterprises which are forbidden by the general principles of international law, and especially by the ordinance of the 12th of June, 1856, which has relation to the declaration of the 12th of April, 1856, upon the principles of maritime law. Moreover, I will not omit to make it especially noticeable by you that the royal government will not permit to its shipping or its subjects, which may mix up in these conflicts by taking letters of marque, sharing in privateering enterprises, carrying merchandise contraband of war, or forwarding despatches, to have the benefit of its protection against any losses which may befall them through such transactions.

The equipment of privateers in the ports of this country is forbidden by the laws of the land, as is known to the mercantile community.

Mr. Seward to Baron Gerolt.

DEPARTMENT OF STATE,
Washington, July 16, 1861.

The undersigned, Secretary of State of the United States, has the honor of acknowledging the receipt of a copy of a letter of instruction, under the date of the 13th of June, from Baron Schleinitz, the minister of foreign affairs of his Majesty the King of Prussia, to Baron Gerolt, his Majesty's envoy extraordinary and minister plenipotentiary to the United States, which Baron Gerolt has submitted for perusal to the undersigned.

Baron Gerolt, in pursuance of this instruction, has referred to doubts said to prevail in Europe about the treatment to which neutral, shipping may be subjected during the continuance of the internal disturbance now existing in the United States, and has requested from the undersigned an explanation of the views of this government thereupon.

Baron Schleinitz, in this communication, has remarked that it would certainly be most desirable for Prussia that this government should embrace this occasion to announce its adhesion to the celebrated declaration of Paris. But that if this could not be attained, then, for the present, the government of Prussia would urge that an exposition might be made to be obligatory during the present intestine disturbances in the United States, in regard to the application generally of the second and third principles of the Paris declaration to neutral shipping.

The second principle of the Paris declaration is, that the neutral flag covers the enemy's goods, not contraband of war.

The third principle is, that the goods, not contraband of war, of a neutral found on board an enemy's vessel are exempt from confiscation.

The undersigned has the pleasure of informing Baron Gerolt, by authority of the President of the United States, that the government cheerfully declares its assent to these principles in the present case, and to continue until the insurrection which now unhappily exists in the United States shall have come to an end, and they will be fully observed by this government in its relations with Prussia.

But the undersigned would be doing injustice to this government if he should omit to add, by way of explanation, that so long ago as the 24th of April last he transmitted ample instructions and powers to Mr. Judd, the then newly appointed Minister of the United States to Berlin, authorizing him to enter into a treaty (subject to the consent of the Senate of the United States) with the kingdom of Prussia for the adhesion of this government to the declaration of the congress at Paris. Similar instructions and powers were given to all the ministers appointed to conduct diplomatic intercourse with all existing maritime powers. This government in these instructions declared its continued desire and preference for the amendment of the Paris declaration proposed by this government in 1856, to the effect that the private or individual property of non-combatants, whether belonging to belligerent States or not, should be exempted from confiscation in maritime war. But recurring to the previous failure to secure the adoption of that amendment, this government instructed its ministers, if they should find it necessary, to waive it for the present, and to negotiate our adhesion to the declaration pure and simple.

The delay of Mr. Judd in his departure for Berlin is probably the cause why this proposition was not made by him to the Prussian government previous to the date of the instruction given by Baron Schleinitz to Baron Gerolt, which formed the occasion of the present note.

This government having thus practically anticipated the wishes of the Prussian government, the undersigned has, of course, been the more at liberty to accede to those wishes in the more limited extent in which they are expressed by Baron Schleinitz.

The undersigned at the same time holds himself none the less bound to proceed with a view to a more ample and more formal establishment of the benign principles of maritime war in regard to neutral commerce as indicated in the instructions given to Mr. Judd.

Of course the undersigned will be understood as not qualifying or modifying by this communication the right of the United States to close any of the national ports which have already fallen or which may fall into the hands of the insurgents, either directly or in the lenient and equitable form of the blockade which is now in full force.

The undersigned cannot close this communication without expressing to Baron Gerolt the great satisfaction with which this government has learned, through the communication now acknowledged, that his Majesty the King of Prussia faithfully adheres to the existing treaties between the two countries, and fulfils, without question or reservation, all their obligations. This announcement is accompanied by assurances of good feeling and good will that will not fail, under the peculiar circumstances of the times, to make a deep and lasting impression on the government and the people of the United States, and to perpetuate the friendship that for near a century has existed between the two countries to the great advantage and lasting honor of both.

Baron Gerolt may be assured that the government and the people of the United States have deliberately and carefully surveyed the unhappy disturbance of their social condition which has caused so much anxiety to all friendly commercial nations, and have adopted the necessary means for its speedy and complete removal, so that they expect to be able to prosecute their accustomed career of enterprise, and, while fulfilling all the national obligations, to co-operate with enlightened nations engaged, like Prussia, in enlarging and increasing the sway of commerce, and in promoting and advancing the high interests of civilization and humanity.

The undersigned offers to Baron Gerolt renewed assurances of his high consideration.

WILLIAM H. SEWARD.

Baron Fr. Gerolt, &c., &c., &c.,
Washington.

Baron Gerolt to Mr. Seward.

[Translation.]

Legation of Prussia,
Washington, July 17, 1861.

The undersigned, envoy extraordinary and minister plenipotentiary of his Majesty the King of Prussia, has had the honor to receive the note of the honorable Mr. Seward, Secretary of the United States, in reply to the instructions which Baron de Schleinitz, minister of foreign affairs at Berlin, transmitted to the undersigned to be communicated to the honorable Secretary of State of the United States.

The undersigned cannot but felicitate himself on the declaration made in this note in favor of the treatment of neutrals pending the duration of intestine disturbances in the United States, as well as on the sentiments of friendship and good understanding expressed in the note of the honorable W. H. Seward towards the government of his Majesty, to which the undersigned will hasten to communicate these demonstrations of the government of the United States.

The undersigned seizes this occasion to renew to the honorable W. H. Seward the protestations of his most distinguished consideration.

FR. VON GEROLT.

Hon. WILLIAM H. SEWARD,
Secretary of State of the United States, Washington.

Mr. Judd to Mr. Seward.

[Extracts.]

LEGATION OF THE UNITED STATES,
Berlin, July 2, 1861.

SIR: I arrived in Berlin on Thursday, the twenty-seventh ultimo, and was cordially welcomed by my predecessor, Mr. Wright, whose attentions and civilities, together with the information imparted to me in connexion with the mission, have tended very much to make my entry into Berlin and induction into office agreeable and pleasant.

Mr. Wright's position here and his influence, as the representative of our government, with the authorities, has been alike creditable and honorable to himself and useful to the citizens of the United States.

His firm straightforward Americanism has won the respect of, and exerted a decided influence upon, the ruling powers of this kingdom.

On the 28th of June Mr. Wright applied to his excellency Baron Schleinitz, minister of foreign affairs, for an interview, for the purpose of presenting his open letter of recall, and affording me the opportunity of presenting the copy of my letter of credence, and requesting my presentation to his Majesty the King.

The baron named the next day, at three o'clock p. m.; and, in accordance with the appointment, Mr. Wright and myself called upon the minister and presented our respective letters. In reply to my request for an audience, the baron stated that the King was at Potsdam; that he would notify him of our wishes, and advise of his Majesty's pleasure upon the subject.

*   *   *   *

On Monday, the first of July, a note from the minister advised me that the King would receive me in private audience at his palace in Berlin at half past four p. m. of that day.

Mr. Wright and myself attended, in pursuance of the summons, and were presented to his Majesty by Baron Schleinitz.

Mr. Wright presented his letter of recall, and addressed his Majesty some remarks appropriate to the occasion, of which his despatch of to-day will contain an account.

I then presented my letter of credence, and stated to his Majesty that I was instructed by the President to convey to him the President's wishes for his health and happiness, and for the prosperity of his kingdom. That our government desired that the friendly relations so long existing between the two governments might continue and increase with the growing prosperity of the two nations. That for myself, personally, I hoped that my residence near his Majesty's government might be useful to the citizens of my country, and acceptable to his Majesty. That I should endeavor in my official action to promote and increase the harmony, good will, and friendly feelings that had so long existed between the two nations, and that I presented my own best wishes for the health and happiness of his Majesty.

The King, in reply, expressed his warm feelings towards Mr. Wright, and stated that he regretted the troubles in our country; that he hoped soon to see them ended, and the integrity and majesty of our government and law maintained, and order triumph.

He thanked Mr. Wright for his allusion to the past friendly relations, and the manner in which he had promoted the same, and assured us that he was happy to hear through me the assurance of the continuance of the same.

The day following my presentation was occupied by me in establishing my relations with the ministers of state and the several diplomatic function-aries residing at this court.

I have the honor to be your obedient servant,

N. B. JUDD.

Hon. WILLIAM H. SEWARD,
  Secretary of State, Washington, D. C.

Mr. Judd to Mr. Seward.

[Extract.]

No. 4.]   LEGATION OF THE UNITED STATES,
                                             Berlin, July 24, 1861.

SIR: On the 9th of July instant, in pursuance of the special instructions contained in despatch No. 4, from the Department of State to this legation, under date of April 24, 1861, to seek an early opportunity to ascertain whether the government of Prussia is disposed to enter into negotiations for the accession of the government of the United States to the articles of the declaration of the congress assembled at Paris, April 16, 1856, on the question of privateering and maritime war, I had an interview with Baron Von Schleinitz, minister of foreign affairs of his Majesty the King of Prussia. In communicating to the baron my instructions on that subject, and inform-ing him of the disposition of the government of the United States to bring the negotiation on the basis of the Paris declaration to a speedy and satis-factory conclusion, I, at the same time, expressed to him how eminently desirable for the good of all nations the President deems it that the property and effects, not contraband of war, of private individuals, although citizens of belligerent States, should be exempt from seizure and confiscation by national vessels in time of maritime war. The baron, in response, assured me that his Majesty's government desired to adopt the most liberal policy on that subject.

I then alluded to his instructions to Baron Von Gerolt, the Prussian minis-ter in Washington, as published in the official journal, the "Staats Arzeiger," and inquired if it was desired to transfer the negotiations to Washington. He replied in the negative, adding that the purpose and intent of the document chiefly was to give utterance to, and make manifest the good will of, his Majesty's government towards that of the United States, and to furnish a full and free communication and exchange of views between the two governments.

In reply to his inquiry, whether the President of the United States, through me, was prepared to submit propositions for a convention, I informed him that I had special powers to negotiate a treaty based upon the Paris declaration, and that a memorandum for that purpose had been prepared by the Department of State for my guidance.· To my inquiry, whether the production of the evidence of my special authority was desired at this time, he replied negatively, but asked to be informed whether the treaty was intended to be a joint one with all the parties to the Paris conference, or a separate convention with each one of the parties. I responded that my instructions directed me to negotiate with the Prussian government only. He then requested that the propositions of the government of the United States be submitted in writing, promising, in that event, an early consideration of the same. Accordingly, on the 11th day of July instant, I addressed a communication to Baron Von Schleinitz, minister of foreign affairs, together with a copy of the memorandum for a convention upon the subject of belligerents and neutrals in time of war between the United States of America and his Majesty the King of Prussia, as furnished me by the Department of State, in connexion with its despatch No. 4, under date of April 24, 1861. A copy of my communication accompanies this despatch, marked Exhibit No. 1. No reply has yet been received from Baron Von Schleinitz to that communication.

*   *   *   *   *   *   *   *   *

I have the honor to be, respectfully, your obedient servant,

N. B. JUDD.

Hon. W. H. SEWARD,
    Secretary of State, Washington, D. C.

Exhibit No. 1.

LEGATION OF THE UNITED STATES,
Berlin, July 11, 1861.

MONSIEUR LE BARON: The undersigned, envoy extraordinary and minister plenipotentiary, has the honor herewith to present the memoranda referred to in our conversation of yesterday, it being simply a statement of the articles of the declaration adopted by the congress assembled at Paris, April 16, 1856.

While the President has instructed the undersigned to present and assent to a convention in terms substantially that of the congress at Paris, the President, nevertheless, desires the undersigned to submit to the government of his Majesty the King of Prussia how just and eminently desirable for the good of all nations he considers it that the property and effects of private individuals, not contraband of war, should be exempt from seizure and confiscation by national vessels in time of maritime war, although belonging to the citizens and subjects of the belligerent States; and in view of this fact, the undersigned begs leave to state to your excellency that he feels authorized and prepared to so modify the propositions he has the honor herewith to submit as to embrace the principle above stated, if it should meet the views and be deemed desirable by the government of his Majesty the King of Prussia.

The undersigned avails himself of this opportunity to assure your excellency of his high and distinguished consideration.

N. B. JUDD.

His Excellency Baron Von SCHLEINITZ,
Minister of Foreign Affairs, &c., &c., &c.

Mr. Seward to Mr. Judd.

No. 7.]
DEPARTMENT OF STATE,
Washington, July 26, 1861.

SIR: Mr. Wright's despatch, No. 177, dated June 22, was duly received.

Baron Gerolt has handed to me a copy of the instruction from his government, to which Mr. Wright refers. I have acknowledged the tenor of that paper as not unacceptable, but I agree with Mr. Wright in thinking it desirable that the strongest possible expressions be obtained from Prussia for their moral effect.

Our army on the Potomac encountered a reverse on the 21st, which, for the moment, produced a shock; but the evil effects of the disaster have already passed away, while a more vigorous and determined resolution exists now than ever to strengthen and preserve the Union.

We have put all the candidates recommended to us by Baron Schleinitz into military employment.

I am, sir, your obedient servant,

WILLIAM H. SEWARD.

NORMAN B. JUDD, Esq., &c., &c., &c., *Berlin.*

Mr. Seward to Mr. Judd.

[Extract.]

No. 12.]
DEPARTMENT OF STATE,
Washington, August 12, 1861.

SIR: Your despatch of July 24, No. 3, has been received. Your conduct in relation to the subject of negotiations for a convention with the government of Prussia on the subject of the rights of neutrals in maritime war, as referred to in that paper, is approved. * * * * *
* * * * * * * * *

I am, sir, your obedient servant,

WILLIAM H. SEWARD.

NORMAN B. JUDD, Esq., &c., &c., &c.

Ex. Doc. 1——4

Mr. Judd to Mr. Seward.

[Extract.]

No. 6.]   LEGATION OF THE UNITED STATES,
                                                Berlin, August 27, 1861.

SIR: *   *   *   *   *   *   *   *   *

Since my written communication to Baron Von Schleinitz on the subject of the maritime treaty, a copy of which was sent to the State Department in my despatch No. 4, I have not heard from this government directly upon the subject; but Baron Von Mohrenheim, of the Russian legation, informs me that, in conversation with Baron Von Schleinitz, the latter expressed the opinion that the object sought by the United States could be attained by a simple adhesion on its part to the articles of the Paris treaty, and that there was no necessity for a formal and separate treaty. I also learned from Baron Von Mohrenheim that the Russian government inclined to the same opinion. My conversations with the members of the diplomatic corps here have convinced me that they are not only thoroughly advised of the views and action of their own governments in this matter, but that every step taken by any government interested is promptly communicated, so that each representative is fully advised of the condition of the question with all the governments, and that there is concerted action, with England at the head.

*   *   *   *   *   *   *   *   *

I have the honor to be, very respectfully, your obedient servant,
                                                        N. B. JUDD.
Hon. W. H. SEWARD,
    Secretary of State.

Mr. Judd to Mr. Seward.

[Extract.]

No. 10.]   LEGATION OF THE UNITED STATES,
                                                Berlin, October 10, 1861.

SIR: I have the honor to acknowledge the receipt of your despatch (No. 14) bearing date September 21, 1861. Since my communication to the foreign office here in relation to the maritime treaty, a copy of which accompanied despatch No. 4, from this legation, I have no word or note from the Prussian government on the subject.

*   *   *   *   *   *   *   *   *

I have the honor to be, respectfully, your obedient servant,
                                                        N. B. JUDD.
Hon. W. H. SEWARD,
    Secretary of State, Washington, D. C.

Mr. Seward to Mr. Judd.

No. 16.]   DEPARTMENT OF STATE,
                                          Washington, October 21, 1861.

SIR: Your despatch of September 24 (No. 8) has been received. It treats
of many matters interesting, though not of chief importance. Your proceedings in regard to them are approved. Disunion, by surprise and
impetuous passion, took the first successes, and profited by them to make
public opinion in Europe. Union comes forward more slowly, but with
greater and more enduring vigor. This nation, like every other, in the
present as in all other cases, stands by its own strength. Other powers will
respect it so long as it exhibits its ability to defend and save itself. More,
perhaps, ought not to be wished; certainly it could not be reasonably expected.

    I am, &c.,

                                          WILLIAM H. SEWARD.

N. B JUDD, Esq.,
    &c., &c., &c., Berlin.

BELGIUM.

Mr. Seward to Mr. Sanford.

No. 2.]
Department of State,
Washington, March 26, 1861.

Sir: Having spent the winter in Washington, you need not be informed of the attempts of a misguided party of citizens in several of the southern States, not unattended with violence and spoliation, to dismember the federal republic, and of their scheme to organize several of the States in a new revolutionary government, under the name of the Confederate States of America. Formidable as this conspiracy seemed at the beginning, it is now confidently believed that the policy of the present administration in regard to it will be supported by the people—a policy of conciliationr forbearance, and firmness—and that the conspiracy will thus fail for want of ultimate adoption by the States themselves which are expected to constitute the new confederacy. Aware of this danger, the movers in that desperate and destructive enterprise are now understood to be making every effort to gain external advantage by appeals to prejudice or supposed interest in foreign nations for a recognition of the independence of the proposed new confederacy.

Under these circumstances the most important duty of the diplomatic representatives of the United States in Europe will be to counteract by all proper means the efforts of the agents of that projected confederacy at their respective courts. It was your extensive acquaintance on the continent, taken in connexion with your activity and energy here, which induced the President to confer upon you the appointment of minister resident in Belgium.

The general considerations to be urged against such a recognition will be found in the inaugural address of the President, delivered on the 4th of March instant, and in a circular letter despatched by me on the 9th instant to our ministers, an original part of which will be found in the archives of your legation. For your present convenience I enclose a copy of this circular letter.

The President, confident of the ultimate ascendancy of law, order, and the Union, through the deliberate action of the people in constitutional forms, does not expect you to engage in any discussion which the agents of the disunionists may attempt to initiate on the merits of their proposed revolution. He will not consent, directly or indirectly, to the interpellation of any foreign power in a controversy which is merely a domestic one.

There is some reason to suppose that the agents of the disunionists will attempt to win favor for their scheme of recognition by affecting to sympathize with the manufacturing interests of the European nations in their discontent with the tariff laws of the United States, and by promising to receive the fabrics of such nations on more favorable terms. You will be able to reply to such seductions as these that the new tariff laws thus complained of are revenue laws deemed by the legislature of the United States necessary under new and peculiar circumstances; that all experience shows that such laws are not and cannot be permanent; that if, as is now pretended, they shall prove to be onerous to foreign commerce, they will, of course, prove also to be unfruitful of revenue, and that in that case they will necessarily be promptly modified. The inconvenience, if any shall result from them, will therefore be temporary and practically harmless. Nor will any statesman of a foreign country need to be informed that the consumption of the fabrics which it is proposed shall be favored by the so-called seceding States chiefly takes place, not within those States, but in a very large degree in the States which remain undisturbed by this unhappy attempt at revolution.

It hardly needs be added that the recognition which the insurgents States desire tends through either peace or war to the establishment of a new government. That new government, like the government of the United States, must levy imports on foreign merchandise, while it must also resort to an export duty on cotton, its great staple, for its support; and these two measures combined would constitute a policy largely prohibitive, instead of the liberal and genial one which is now promised by the disunion party.

You will not fail to represent to the government of the King of the Belgians that all the interests of European manufactures and commerce are identified with the promotion of peace and the undisturbed activity of the American people. An act of recognition in favor of a now discontented party would necessarily tend to encourage that party to attempt to establish their separation from the Union by civil war, the consequences of which would be disastrous to all the existing systems of industrial activity in Europe, and when once they had begun, those consequences would be likely to continue indefinitely; whereas no nation in Europe can hope that their own interests would be as safe and prosperous under any change of government here as they are now and have so long been under our present system.

It is quite manifest already that differences and embarrassing questions may soon arise concerning the conduct of commerce, and that the commercial States of Europe may be subjected to strong seductions to violate our revenue laws and regulations. You will say generally on this subject that the government of the United States will expect the same respect to those laws and regulations which has hitherto been shown and which our treaties of amity and commerce entitle us to demand, and that it will not hold itself bound to favor or exempt from consequences any parties, of whatever nation, who may violate them. It does not at all distrust its ability to maintain them or the good disposition of its allies to observe them.

I shall not enlarge on these subjects, insomuch as the phase of the whole affair changes almost daily. The President willingly expects to rely on your astuteness in discovering points of attack and your practical skill and experience in protecting the interests of the United States. He will expect you, however, to communicate to this department very fully and frequently, and you will receive prompt instructions in every new emergency.

I am, sir, your obedient servant,

WILLIAM H. SEWARD.

HENRY S. SANFORD, Esq., &c., &c., &c.

Mr. Sanford to Mr. Seward.

[Extract.]

No. 1.]   LEGATION OF THE UNITED STATES,
                                    Brussels, May 10, 1861.

SIR: *   *   *   *   *   *   *   *   *
I was received by the King, to present my letter of credence, on the 8th, in "solemn audience," and made on the occasion an address, of which I enclose a copy, (A.)

The King replied that he highly appreciated the sentiments of friendly feeling, of which I bore to him the expression, from the President, and the flattering terms, as he expressed it, in which they were couched. He desired me to tender to the President his thanks for them, and to say that he reciprocated fully the desire for the continuance of the friendly and cordial relations which, during the more than thirty years that had elapsed since the formation of his government, had marked our intercourse, and he hoped for the continued prosperity of the United States. After some remarks complimentary to myself and my former residence in Europe, he entered into general conversation, in which he showed great interest in and knowledge of the United States, manifesting a warm desire to have the means of direct intercourse increased between the two countries. The genius of his people, he said, was rather for industrial pursuits at home, and in which they had been very successful; but they had failed upon the seas; and he thought if the enterprise and practical knowledge of our people could be brought to bear in favor of steam communication between Belgium and the United States, a large trade could be diverted through this channel, Antwerp being a natural entrepôt for Central Europe.

His Majesty spoke but generally of the insurrection in the southern States; said he hoped that some peaceful issue would be found, and that the spirit of conciliation would prevail, and then referred to the growing markets they had for their manufactures in the United States. My audience, which was lengthened by a long conversation on general subjects, was most satisfactory, in the very kind and cordial spirit manifested by his Majesty.
*   *   *   *   *   *   *   *   *   *
I have the honor to be, with great respect, your obedient servant,
                                                    H. S. SANFORD.
Hon. WILLIAM H. SEWARD,
          Secretary of State.

Mr. Sanford to Mr. Seward.

[Extracts.]

No. 5.]   LEGATION OF THE UNITED STATES,
                                    Brussels, May 26, 1861.

SIR: I had a conversation to-day with M. de Vrière on the subject of the efforts of the commissioners of the so-called "Confederate States" to obtain recognition of the European powers.

He informed me that no application had been made to him in this view, nor would it now be entertained if made. The revolution would receive no sanction by any act of Belgium. A small State, he continued, whose prosperity depended on the full exercise of the industrial pursuits of its people, they did not mingle in foreign politics, their policy being not to imperil their interests by stepping beyond the limits of strict neutrality in their intercourse with other States. They should, therefore, remain "neutral," as he expressed it, in respect to this question. They had not even yet recognized the Italian government, he added. We desired, I told him, not to be subjected to any interference in the settlement of our domestic affairs, whether in the form of recognition of political existence or of belligerent rights of those who were in open rebellion to the government and laws of the United States. It was an issue between order and anarchy which we were fully able to cope with, and all Europe was interested that its settlement be in the most prompt and effective manner, as least liable to cause permanent derangement to commerce.

In reply to my inquiry, he said he had received no official information of the blockade of our southern ports, proclaimed by the President, although he had late advices from the Belgian minister at Washington. He had only knowledge of it, he said, as printed in the papers. In answer to his inquiry, I said I thought it would not injuriously affect the supply of cotton, as the crop of the past year had mostly gone forward; and, moreover, that while the blockade would be rigorously enforced with regard to supplies, or vessels bearing the "confederate" flag, I presumed, although I had no instructions on the subject, that the vessels now loading, or under engagements to load in those ports, would be allowed reasonable time to leave; that there was every desire to make this condition of things, which was but temporary, as little embarrassing as possible to foreign commerce. The minister expressed great satisfaction at this, and said that the possibility of failure of the cotton supply, growing out of these troubles in our southern States, was causing great anxiety.

M. de Vrière then spoke of the new tariff with a great deal of feeling; said that it was highly prejudicial to their interests, instancing in point that forty furnaces for the manufacture of window glass had been stopped in consequence, and expressed his surprise that, in this age of progress, when Europe was abandoning the exploded system, as he expressed himself, of differential duties, the United States should pursue such a course. Their own experience as a manufacturing people had convinced them of the bad policy of such a system for the interests of the manufacturers themselves. I replied that I presumed the general interruptions of trade consequent upon apprehended war in the United States was, quite as much as the new tariff, a cause for suspension of the traffic he referred to. The tariff had been augmented by the last Congress to produce more revenue; if it failed to produce such result, it would probably be changed; it was a matter dependent on the will of Congress, and he was aware we had had several changes in the past few years, none of which had apparently given satisfaction to the manufacturing States of Europe which desired to supply our markets; still, it was our main source of revenue, and the system of raising means for the expenses of the government by a duty on importations would probably long continue.

*   *   *   *   *   *   *   *   *

I took my leave of M. de Vrière with the repeated assurance that no countenance would be given, in any form, to the rebellion in our southern States.

I have the honor to be, with great respect, your most obedient servant,

H. S. SANFORD.

Hon. WILLIAM H. SEWARD,
   Secretary of State.

Mr. Sanford to Mr. Seward.

[Extract.]

No. 9.]   LEGATION OF THE UNITED STATES,
                                    Brussels, June 22, 1861.

SIR: As M. de Vrière is out of town, I directed the attention of Monsieur Saluremont, the secretary general, who is charged with the affairs of the department in the absence of the minister, in an interview with him to-day, as to the propriety of a proclamation warning Belgians from taking service under those in rebellion to the federal government, furnishing them "aid and comfort," and, especially, closing the ports of Belgium to their "*privateers*"—declared by the President to be pirates—or permitting them to be fitted out in her ports. I said that while the assurances I had received from M. de Vrière, soon after my arrival, of the attitude of his government had been satisfactory, I hoped it would now give public expression to them, both as due to a friendly power and as a warning to their own citizens of the perils of such enterprises.

Mons. Saluremont replied that the matter had been under consideration; that the position which England and France had taken had not seemed to be satisfactory to the government of the United States, and they had delayed, in consequence, taking any formal steps; but not, he begged me to be assured, from any want of friendly spirit or desire to do all the occasion called for at their hands.

I replied that he was correct in his views of our sentiments as to the course which England and France had seen fit to pursue. We could not look upon the recognition of belligerent rights to those who, under our laws, were rebels, and before we had attempted to employ forcible means of coercion, as evincing the friendly spirit we had a right to expect; that these people would be treated none the less as rebels on the land as pirates on the seas—they or those of whatever nationality who joined them; and we counted, on the part of Belgium, upon no such qualification of our citizens in rebellion, whom we were engaged in submitting to the action of our laws.

He said their legislation provided generally for the cases I had instanced, but that attention would be immediately given to the subject, and he thought we need not have any reason to be dissatisfied with the action they would take in the premises.

He then told me that our new tariff law was a subject of great complaint in Belgium, and great distress in some branches of industry which it had destroyed, referring specially to glass and some kinds of woollen goods.

I again explained our system of revenue, which all manufacturing States this side the Atlantic insist upon believing to be disadvantageous to their interests.

  *   *   *   *   *   *

I have the honor to be, with great respect, your most obedient servant,
                                            H. S. SANFORD.

Hon. WILLIAM H. SEWARD,
 Secretary of State, &c., &c., &c.

Mr. Sanford to Mr. Seward.

[Extract.]

No. 10.]   LEGATION OF THE UNITED STATES,
                                                         Brussels, July 2, 1861.

SIR: Referring to a conversation detailed in my despatch No. 9, I have
the honor to enclose a notice published in the official journal (the *Moniteur*)
of the 25th ultimo, in which, basing its action upon the stipulations of the
declaration of the congress of Paris of April 16, 1856, it is announced that
instructions have been addressed to the judicial, maritime, and military
authorities to inform them that privateers of no nation or flag, alone or with
their prizes, will be permitted, save in cases of extreme danger by stress of
weather, to enter the ports of Belgium; enjoining upon them to recognize
no commission or letter of marque as having validity; and warning all
subject to the Belgian laws that in taking part or service in any privateers
they incur risk of being treated as pirates abroad, and of being prosecuted
with the utmost rigor of the laws at home. In thanking the acting minister
for this prompt response to my request, I observed that while this was sufficient, in so far as it went, for the occasion that called it forth—as we had,
and expected to have, no privateers upon the sea at this time—still, so long
as we were not a party to the declaration of Paris, the employment of privateers by the United States was undoubtedly as much a belligerent right as the
employment of militia on land; and in the event of a foreign war we should
expect, on the part of friendly powers, no such impediment to its exercise
by any injurious distinction between it and the other arms of the public
service.

      *   *   *   *   *   *

I have the honor to be, with great respect, your most obedient servant,
                                                         H. S. SANFORD.

·

[Translation.]

Belgium has given its adhesion to the principles laid down in the declaration of the congress of Paris of April 16, 1856. This adhesion was published, together with said declaration, in the Belgian *Moniteur* of June
8, 1856.

The commercial public is notified that instructions on this subject have
been given to the judicial, maritime, and military authorities, warning them
that privateers, under whatever flag or commission, or letters of marque, are
not to be allowed to enter our ports except in case of imminent perils of the
sea. The aforesaid authorities are charged, consequently, to keep a strict
watch upon all such privateers and their prizes, and to compel them to put
to sea again as soon as practicable.

The same authorities have been charged not to recognize the validity of
any commission or letter of marque whatsoever.

All persons subject to the laws of Belgium, who shall fit out or take any
part in any privateering expedition, will therefore expose themselves to the
danger, on the one hand, of being treated as pirates abroad, and, on the
other, to prosecution before Belgian tribunals with all the rigor of the laws.

Mr. Seward to Mr. Sanford.

No. 4.]   DEPARTMENT OF STATE,
                                                    Washington, May 6, 1861.

SIR: Herewith I transmit a copy of a despatch of the 24th ultimo, which has been addressed to the several ministers of the United States accredited to the maritime powers whose plenipotentiaries composed the congress of Paris of the 16th April, 1856, calling their attention to the importance of endeavoring to negotiate with those powers conventions upon the subject of the rights of belligerents and neutrals in time of war. The government of Belgium was not represented in the Paris congress; but the negotiation of a similar convention with that government is considered desirable, and you will therefore be governed by the instruction of which I enclose a transcript, and endeavor to effect that object. With this view I herewith send you a full power and a draft of the proposed convention.

I am, sir, your obedient servant,

WILLIAM H. SEWARD.

HENRY S. SANFORD, Esq., &c., &c., *Brussels.*

Mr. Seward to Mr. Sanford.

No. 9.]   · DEPARTMENT OF STATE,
                                                    Washington, June 21, 1861.

SIR: Your despatches (No. 5, dated May 26, and No. 6, of the same date) have been received. We are especially pleased with Mr. De Vrière's just and friendly sentiments in regard to our affairs.

You are aware that the declaration of Paris enjoins each of the parties that have signed it not to negotiate any other changes of the law of nations concerning the rights of neutrals in maritime war. We have supposed that this would operate to prevent Great Britain, and probably France, from receiving our accession to the declaration, if we should insist on the amendment proposed by Mr. Marcy, namely, the exemption of private property of non-belligerents from confiscation. But we should now, as the instructions heretofore given you have already informed you, vastly prefer to have that amendment accepted. Nevertheless, if this cannot be done, let the convention be made for adherence to the declaration pure and simple.

The feverish excitement which prevailed when you left the country is passing away. Public confidence in the ability of the government to repress the insurrection and preserve the Union is practically restored, and the beneficial result that two months ago seemed problematical is now regarded as only a question of time.

I am, sir, your obedient servant,

WILLIAM H. SEWARD.

H. S. SANFORD, Esq., &c., &c., *Brussels.*

Mr. Seward to Mr. Sanford.

No. 11.]   DEPARTMENT OF STATE,
                                           Washington, June 22, 1861.

SIR: Your despatch of the 5th June, (No. 8,) accompanied by a copy of your letter to Mr. De Vrière, on the subject of our proposed adherence to the declaration of the congress of Paris, has been received. We see no reason to doubt the propriety of that communication.

    I am, sir, your obedient servant,

                               WILLIAM H. SEWARD.

HENRY S. SANFORD, Esq., *&c., &c., &c*, *Brussels.*

Mr. Sanford to Mr. Seward.

[Extract.]

No. 11.]   UNITED STATES LEGATION,
                                           Brussels, July 3, 1861.

SIR: I have not been unmindful of your instructions (No. 2) respecting a convention for the abrogation of passports for our citizens travelling or sojourning in Belgium.

As already intimated in my first despatch, passports are already almost virtually abolished here, the *visa* being no longer necessary. The usual course of this government in respect to this subject is, upon notification by a government that Belgians are not required to be provided with passports to enter upon or travel within its territories, to exempt equally citizens or subjects of such nations in Belgium.

This course has been pursued with Sweden and Holland, and will be soon followed with France and England.

In view of the disturbances in our southern States, and the consequent impossibility of assuring entire reciprocity of exemption from passports throughout our territory, I have not deemed it advisable at this time to make any proposition on this subject.

I am assured by Mr. De Vrière that, on formal notification that Belgians will not be required to present passports in the United States, the proper authorities here will direct the exemption of citizens of the United States travelling here from the requirement of passports.

They would need, however, in case of domicile here, some document to prove their identity. In this connexion, it may not be out of place to refer to a conversation I had some time since on this subject of the abolition of passports, with the officer in charge of that branch of the public service in France.

He said that they had already exempted British subjects coming to France from the action of the passport regulations, and had lately made similar exemptions with regard to Sweden, and were about to make the same exemptions with respect to Belgium, and would with most other nations on a footing of reciprocity. This was, however, a purely administrative act, liable to be recalled whenever considered for the interest of the state. They would in no case make a treaty which should bind them to the perpetual abolition of passports *vis-a-vis* to my nation.

In the present aspect of affairs in the United States, they deemed it important to have a control over the movements of their citizens to the United States and *vice versa* of ours in French territory; and deemed the present an inopportune time to make any change in the passport system with respect to the United States.

When matters returned to their normal condition, there would be no objection, he said, to suspend their passport regulations for citizens of the United States, and a simple administrative order was all that was necessary on their part, and could be made at any time when deemed expedient.

* * * * * * * * *

* * * * * * * * *

* * * * * * * * *

I have the honor to be, with great respect, your most humble servant,

H. S. SANFORD.

Hon. WILLIAM H. SEWARD,
Secretary of State.

Mr. Seward to Mr. Sanford.

No. 12.]   DEPARTMENT OF STATE,
                                                 Washington, July 8, 1861.

SIR: Your despatch of June 22 (No. 9) was duly received. It is, in the main, not unsatisfactory, so far as the subject of our domestic affairs is concerned.

In regard to the rights of friendly or neutral powers in maritime war, the subject has become somewhat complicated, and it would be a tedious labor to make a distinct explanation to each of our ministers abroad. I send you instead, *confidentially*, a copy of my last despatch on this subject to Mr. Dayton. It may serve as a guide to your own conduct in relation to the subject.

I am, sir, respectfully, your obedient servant,

WILLIAM H. SEWARD.

HENRY S. SANFORD, Esq., *Brussels.*

Mr. Sanford to Mr. Seward.

No. 15.]   LEGATION OF THE UNITED STATES,
                                                 Brussels, July 18, 1861.

SIR: I have the honor to acknowledge the receipt of your despatches Nos. 9, 10, and 11, under dates of the 20th and 22d respectively.

I have as yet received no reply from M. De Vrière to my note to him of the 5th ultimo, on the subject of our adhesion to the declaration of the congress of Paris. I referred to it a few days since on the occasion of a visit to the foreign office, and was told that my proposition had been communicated to the French government, and that communication had been made by it to this government of the main points of the note addressed by M. Thouvenel to M. Mercier in the month of May upon this subject of neutral rights. I inferred from this that they were awaiting the result of the communications made to you by the French and English governments through their ministers at Washington.

I will take an early opportunity to bring the subject again to the attention of the minister.

I have the honor to be, with great respect, your most obedient servant,

H. S. SANFORD.

Hon. WILLIAM H. SEWARD,
  Secretary of State, &c., &c., &c.

Mr. Seward to Mr. Sanford.

No. 20.]   DEPARTMENT OF STATE,
                                                 Washington, July 30, 1861.

SIR: The accompanying transcript of an instruction to our minister to Great Britain, dated the 21st instant, and numbered 42, will place you in possession of the views of this government concerning the principle of the law which authorizes the President to close the ports that have been seized by the insurgents.

I am, sir, your obedient servant,

WILLIAM H. SEWARD.

HENRY S. SANFORD, Esq., &c., &c., &c., *Brussels.*

Mr. Sanford to Mr. Seward.

No. 16.]   LEGATION OF THE UNITED STATES,
                                                 Brussels, July 30, 1861.

SIR: I called yesterday at the department of foreign affairs to press again upon the attention of Baron De Vrière the proposition of adhesion to the declaration of Paris, made to him near two months since, and he being out of town, I saw the secretary general, who, as before said, replaces the minister in his absence.

In reply to my question whether the government had come to any decision, he said that they were not yet sufficiently informed of the condition of this subject at other courts to give me any positive answer; that while he would not say that they would give a negative one, the policy and acts of Belgium being, as I was aware, doubtless most liberal, yet they did not feel, as a smaller power, justified in taking any step of this nature in advance of their neighbors.

I inquired whether there was any other objection to this proposed convention than he had indicated, in order to learn whether the addition of the Marcy proposition was considered an impediment. He said he was not prepared to give any other; that their position with regard to neighboring powers, to whom Belgium owed, in one sense, her nationality, was a delicate one, and they did not feel authorized to take any initiative in negotiations of this character; they left that to those powers who must necessarily have a controlling influence in general politics.

It is thus evident that this government will do nothing till after the great powers have decided upon a course of action in this matter.

I have the honor to be, with great respect, your most obedient servant,

H. S. SANFORD.

Hon. WILLIAM H. SEWARD,
    Secretary of State, &c., &c., &c.

P. S.—I open my despatch to acknowledge the receipt of your despatches Nos. 12, 13, and 14, with their respective enclosures, which will have immediate action.

H. S. S.

Mr. Seward to Mr. Sanford.

No. 22.]
DEPARTMENT OF STATE,
    Washington, August 5, 1861.

SIR: Your despatch No. 15, dated July 18, has been received.

There is no especial urgency on our part for consideration by the Belgium government of our proposition to accede to the declaration of the congress of Paris before the similar propositions submitted to the British and French governments shall have been acted upon by them, although we hold ourselves ready to carry our overtures into effect when the Belgium government shall desire.

I am, sir, respectfully, your obedient servant,
    WILLIAM H. SEWARD.

HENRY S. SANFORD, Esq., &c., &c., &c., *Brussels.*

Mr. Seward to Mr. Sanford.

No. 23.]
DEPARTMENT OF STATE,
    Washington, August 12, 1861.

SIR: Your despatch dated July 3 (No. 11) has been received.

I am quite content, under existing circumstances, with the disposition you propose in that paper to make of the subject of passports, and I acquiesce very cheerfully in the views which you take of the importance of vigilance in regard to the movements of disaffected citizens of our own country travelling in Europe.

I am, sir, respectfully, your obedient servant,
    WILLIAM H. SEWARD.

HENRY S. SANFORD, Esq., &c., &c., &c., *Brussels.*

Mr. Seward to Mr. Sanford.

No. 24.]
DEPARTMENT OF STATE,
    Washington, August 21, 1861.

SIR: Your despatch of July 30 (No. 16) has been received.

I am not disappointed, nor do I think we ought to be dissatisfied, with Mr. De Vrière's reply to your inquiry on the subject of maritime relations.

You are so frequently at Paris and London, that I may refer you to the legations at one of those places for the latest phase of our negotiation on the same subject with the government of Great Britain. That government having taken the lead in determining European relations to us, and other powers having silently acquiesced, we shall hardly expect them to anticipate her own final decision upon the case, as it is presented to all alike.

I am, sir, respectfully, your obedient servant,

WILLIAM H. SEWARD.

HENRY S. SANFORD, Esq., &c., &c., &c., *Brussels.*

MEXICO.

Mr. Seward to Mr. Corwin.

No. 2.]
DEPARTMENT OF STATE,
Washington, April 6, 1861.

SIR: The actual condition of affairs in Mexico is so imperfectly understood here that the President finds it very difficult to give you particular and practical directions for the regulation of your conduct during your mission.

Our latest information was, in substance, that the provisional government of President Juarez, so long confined to the sea-coasts of the country, had finally overthrown its adversaries and established itself at the capital; that the opposing armies had been demoralized and dispersed, and that there was no longer any armed resistance in the States; that an election for president had been held, in conformity with the constitution of 1857, and that the now provisional president had probably secured a majority of the votes, although the result was as yet not certainly known. The pleasure which these events have inspired is unhappily diminished by rumors that the government is without sufficient authority or hold on the public confidence to maintain order; that robberies are of frequent occurrence on the high roads, and even that a member of our late legation in the country has been murdered on his way from the city of Mexico to Vera Cruz.

You will apply yourself at once, with energy and diligence, to investigate the truth of this last-mentioned occurrence, which, if found to have been accurately reported, will not only be regarded as a high offence against the dignity and honor of the United States, but will prove a severe shock to the sensibilities of the American people.

The President is unable to conceive that any satisfactory explanation of a transaction so injurious to the character of Mexico can be made. He will, however, wait for your report concerning it, though with the deepest anxiety, before taking action upon the subject.

I find the archives here full of complaints against the Mexican government for violations of contracts and spoliations and cruelties practiced against American citizens. These complaints have been lodged in this department, from time to time, during the long reign of civil war in which the factions of Mexico have kept that country involved, with a view to having them made the basis of demands for indemnity and satisfaction whenever government should regain in that country sufficient solidity to assume a character for responsibility. It is not the President's intention to send forward such claims at the present moment. He willingly defers the performance of a duty which at any time would seem ungracious, until the incoming administration in Mexico shall have had time, if possible, to cement its authority and reduce the yet disturbed elements of society to order and harmony. You will, however, be expected, in some manner which will be marked with firmness as well as liberality, to keep the government there in mind that such of these claims as shall be found just will, in due time, be presented and urged upon its consideration.

While now, as heretofore, it is a duty of this government to reason with

Ex. Doc. 1——5

that of Mexico, and deprecate a continuance of the chronic reign of disorder there, a crisis has unhappily arrived, in which the performance of this duty is embarrassed by the occurrence of civil commotions in our own country, by which Mexico, in consequence of her proximity, is not unlikely to be affected. The spirit of discontent seems, at last, to have crossed the border, and to be engaged in an attempt to overthrow the authority of this government in some parts of the country which adjoin the Mexican republic. It is much to be feared that new embarrassments of the relations of the two countries will happen when authority so long prostrated on the Mexican side finds the power of the United States temporarily suspended on this side of the frontier. Whatever evils shall thus occur, it is much to be feared will be aggravated by the intervention of the Indians, who have been heretofore with difficulty restrained from violence, even while the federal authority has been adequately maintained.

Both of the governments must address themselves to this new and annoying condition of things, with common dispositions to mitigate its evils and abridge its duration as much as possible.

The President does not expect that you will allude to the origin or causes of our domestic difficulties in your intercourse with the government of Mexico, although that government will rightfully as well as reasonably ask what are his expectations of their course and their end. On the contrary, the President will not suffer the representatives of the United States to engage in any discussion of the merits of those difficulties in the presence of foreign powers, much less to invoke even their censure against those of our fellow-citizens who have arrayed themselves in opposition to its authority.

But you are instructed to assure the government of Mexico that these difficulties, having arisen out of no deep and permanent popular discontent, either in regard to our system of government itself, or to the exercise of its authority, and being attended by social evils which are as ruinous as they are unnecessary, while no organic change that is contemplated could possibly bring to any portion of the American people any advantages of security, peace, prosperity, or happiness equal to those which the federal Union so effectually guaranties, the President confidently believes and expects that the people of the United States, in the exercise of the wisdom that hitherto has never failed them, will speedily and in a constitutional way adopt all necessary remedies for the restoration of the public peace and the preservation of the federal Union.

The success of this government in conducting affairs to that consummation may depend in some small degree on the action of the government and people of Mexico in this new emergency. The President could not fail to see that Mexico, instead of being benefited by the prostration or the obstruction of federal authority in this country, would be exposed by it to new and fearful dangers. On the other hand, a condition of anarchy in Mexico must necessarily operate as a seduction to those who are conspiring against the integrity of the Union to seek strength and aggrandizement for themselves by conquests in Mexico and other parts of Spanish America. Thus, even the dullest observer is at last able to see what was long ago distinctly seen by those who are endowed with any considerable perspicacity, that peace, order, and constitutional authority in each and all of the several republics of this continent are not exclusively an interest of any one or more of them, but a common and indispensable interest of them all.

This sentiment will serve as a key to open to you, in every case, the purposes, wishes, and expectations of the President in regard to your mission which, I hardly need to say, he considers at this juncture perhaps the most interesting and important one within the whole circle of our international relations.

The President of the United States does not know, and he will not consent to know, with prejudice or undue favor any political party, religious class, or sectional interest in Mexico. He regrets that anything should have occurred to disturb the peaceful and friendly relations of Mexico with some of the foreign States lately represented at her capital. He hopes most sincerely that those relations may be everywhere renewed and reinvigorated, and that the independence and sovereignty of Mexico and the government which her people seem at last to have accepted, after so many conflicts, may be now universally acknowledged and respected.

Taking into view the actual condition and circumstances of Mexico, as well as those of the United States, the President is fully satisfied that the safety, welfare, and happiness of the latter would be more effectually promoted if the former should retain its complete integrity and independence, than they could be by any dismemberment of Mexico, with a transfer or diminution of its sovereignty, even though thereby a portion or the whole of the country or its sovereignty should be transferred to the United States themselves. The President is moreover well aware that the ability of the government and people of Mexico to preserve and maintain the integrity and the sovereignty of the republic might be very much impaired, under existing circumstances, by hostile or unfriendly action on the part of the government or of the people of the United States. If he needed any other incentive to practice justice and equality towards Mexico, it would be found in the reflection that the very contention and strife in our own country which at this moment excite so much domestic disquietude and so much surprise throughout a large part of the world, could probably never have happened if Mexico had always been able to maintain with firmness real and unquestioned sovereignty and independence. But if Mexico has heretofore been more unfortunate in these respects than many other modern nations, there are still circumstances in her case which justify a hope that her sad experience may be now coming to an end. Mexico really has, or ought to have, no enemies. The world is deeply interested in the development of her agricultural, and especially her mineral and commercial, resources, while it holds in high respect the simple virtues and heroism of her people, and, above all, their inextinguishable love of civil liberty.

The President, therefore, will use all proper influence to favor the restoration of order and authority in Mexico, and, so far as it may be in his power, he will prevent incursions and every other form of aggression by citizens of the United States against Mexico. But he enjoins you to employ your best efforts in convincing the government of Mexico and even the people, if, with its approval, you can reach them, that the surest guaranty of their safety against such aggressions is to be found in a permanent restoration of the authority of that government. If, on the other hand, it shall appear in the sequel that the Mexican people are only now resting a brief season to recover their wasted energies sufficiently to lacerate themselves with new domestic conflicts, then it is to be feared that not only the government of the United States but many other governments will find it impossible to prevent a resort to that magnificent country of a class of persons, unhappily too numerous everywhere, who are accustomed to suppose that visionary schemes of public interest, aggrandizement, or reform will justify even lawless invasion and aggression.

In connexion with this point it is proper that you should be informed that the Mexican government has, through its representative here, recently complained of an apprehended attempt at invasion of the State of Sonora by citizens of California, acting, as is alleged, with the knowledge and consent of some of the public authorities in that State. You will assure the Mexican government that, due care being first taken to verify the facts thus presented, effective means shall be adopted to put our neutrality laws into activity.

The same representative has also expressed to the President an apprehension that the removal of the federal troops from the Texan border may be followed by outbreaks and violence there. There is, perhaps, too much ground for this apprehension. Moreover, it is impossible to forsee the course of the attempts which are taking place in that region to subvert the proper authority of this government. The President, however, meantime directs you to assure the Mexican government that due attention shall be bestowed on the condition of the frontier, with a view to the preservation and safety of the peaceable inhabitants residing there. He hopes and trusts that equal attention will be given to this important subject by the authorities of Mexico.

These matters, grave and urgent as they are, must not altogether withdraw our attention from others to which I have already incidentally alluded, but which require more explicit discussion.

For a few years past, the condition of Mexico has been so unsettled as to raise the question on both sides of the Atlantic whether the time has not come when some foreign power ought, in the general interest of society, to intervene to establish a protectorate or some other form of government in that country and guaranty its continuance there. Such schemes may even now be held under consideration by some European nations, and there is also some reason to believe that designs have been conceived in some parts of the United States to effect either a partial dismemberment or a complete overthrow of the Mexican government, with a view to extend over it the authority of the newly projected confederacy, which a discontented part of our people are attempting to establish in the southern-part of our own country You may possibly meet agents of this projected confederacy, busy in preparing some further revolution in Mexico. You will not fail to assure the government of Mexico that the President neither has, nor can ever have, any sympathy with such designs, in whatever quarter they may arise or whatever character they may take on.

In view of the prevailing temper and political habits and opinions of the Mexican people, the President can scarcely believe that the disaffected citizens of our own country, who are now attempting a dismemberment of   ⸝
the American Union, will hope to induce Mexico to aid them by recognizing the assumed independence which they have proclaimed, because it seems manifest to him that such an organization of a distinct government over that part of the present Union which adjoins Mexico would, if possible, be fraught with evils to that country more intolerable than any which the success of those desperate measures could inflict even upon the United States. At the same time it is manifest that the existing political organization in this country affords the surest guaranty Mexico can have that her integrity, union, and independence will be respected by the whole people of the American Union.

The President, however, expects that you will be watchful of such designs as I have thus described, however improbable they may seem, and that you will use the most effective measures in your power to counteract any recognition of the projected Confederate States by the Mexican government, if it shall be solicited.

Your large acquaintance with the character of the Mexican people, their interests and their policy, will suggest many proper arguments against such a measure, if any are needful beyond the intimations I have already given.

In conclusion, the President, as you are well aware, is of opinion that, alienated from the United States as the Spanish American republics have been for some time past—largely, perhaps, by reason of errors and prejudices peculiar to themselves, and yet not altogether without fault on our own part—that those States and the United States nevertheless, in some respects, hold a common attitude and relation towards all other nations; that it is the interest of them all to be friends as they are neighbors, and to mutually maintain and support each other so far as may be consistent with the individual sovereignty which each of them rightly enjoys, equally against all disintegrating agencies within and all foreign influences or power without their borders.

The President never for a moment doubts that the republican system is to pass safely through all ordeals and prove a permanent success in our own country, and so to be commended to adoption by all other nations. But he thinks also that that system everywhere has to make its way painfully through difficulties and embarrassments, which result from the action of antagonistical elements which are a legacy of former times and very different institutions. The President is hopeful of the ultimate triumph of this system over all obstacles, as well in regard to Mexico as in regard to every other American State; but he feels that those States are nevertheless justly entitled to a greater forbearance and more generous sympathies from the government and people of the United States than they are likely to receive in any other quarter.

The President trusts that your mission, manifesting these sentiments, will reassure the government of Mexico of his best disposition to favor their commerce and their internal improvements. He hopes, indeed, that your mission, assuming a spirit more elevated than one of merely commerce and conventional amity, a spirit disinterested and unambitious, earnestly American in the continental sense of the word, and fraternal in no affected or mere diplomatic meaning of the term, while it shall secure the confidence and good will of the government of Mexico, will mark the inauguration of a new condition of things directly conducive to the prosperity and happiness of both nations, and ultimately auspicious to all other republican States throughout the world.

I am, sir, your obedient servant,

WILLIAM H. SEWARD.

Thomas Corwin, Esq., &c., &c., &c.

Mr. Corwin to Mr. Seward.

[Extract.]

No. 1.]   Legation of the United States,
          City of Mexico, May 29, 1861.

Sir: *   *   *   *   *   *   *   *

I deem it of the very first importance that our consuls at every port on the Gulf of Mexico should be at their respective posts, with careful and specific instructions as to their treatment of vessels sailing under the flag of the Confederate States, or having papers from ports within those States, made out by officers under their authority.

Should the relations now existing, or which may hereafter exist, between the United States and the seceding States be such as to require of me any specific act in relation to such state of things, I beg to be advised of it by the department as early as possible.

The present government of Mexico is well affected towards us in our present difficulties, but, for obvious reasons, will be unwilling to enter into any engagement which might produce war with the south, unless protected by promise of aid from the United States.

   * * * * * * * *

   I am, &c.,

                 THOMAS CORWIN.

  Hon. W. H. Seward, &c., &c., &c.

Mr. Corwin to Mr. Seward.

[Extracts.]

No. 2.   LEGATION OF THE UNITED STATES,
                   Mexico, June 29, 1861.

SIR: * * * * * * * *

The present time is most propitious for securing the advantages and preventing the evils which I have suggested. The government here feels the strongest sympathy with the United States.

   * * * * * * * *

It has been my constant endeavor since my arrival here to possess the Mexican mind of the true causes of our difficulties, and thus enable them to estimate the danger to this republic which will result from any unfavorable termination of them. I am quite sure that whilst this government will endeavor to preserve peaceful relations with all the European powers on fair terms, it regards the United States as its true and only reliable friend in any struggle which may involve the national existence. That this should be so is somewhat remarkable, when we regard the deep prejudices engendered in the general Mexican mind by the loss of Texas, which they attribute to our citizens, and the compulsory cession of territory which was a consequence of our war with them.

   * * * * * * * *

   I am, &c.,

                 THOMAS CORWIN.

  Hon. W. H. Seward,
    Secretary of State, U. S., &c., &c., &c.

GREAT BRITAIN.

No. 2.]

DEPARTMENT OF STATE,
Washington, April 10, 1861.

SIR: Although Great Britain and the United States possess adjacent dominions of large extent, and although they divide, not very unequally, a considerable portion of the commerce of the world, yet there are at present only two questions in debate between them. One of these concerns the line of boundary running through Puget's Sound, and involves the title to the island of San Juan. The other relates to a proposition for extinguishing the interest of the Hudson's Bay and Puget's Sound agricultural companies in the Territory of Washington. The discussion of these questions has hitherto been carried on here, and there is no necessity for removing it to London. It is expected to proceed amicably and result in satisfactory conclusions. It would seem, therefore, on first thought, that you would find nothing more to do in England than to observe and report current events, and to cultivate friendly sentiments there towards the United States. Nevertheless, the peculiar condition of our country in the present juncture renders these duties a task of considerable delicacy.

You will readily understand me as alluding to the attempts which are being made by a misguided portion of our fellow citizens to detach some of the States and to combine them in a new organization under the name of the Confederate States of America. The agitators in this bad enterprise, justly estimating the influence of the European powers upon even American affairs, do not mistake in supposing that it would derive signal advantage from a recognition by any of those powers, and especially Great Britain. Your task, therefore, apparently so simple and easy, involves the responsibility of preventing the commission of an act by the government of that country which would be fraught with disaster, perhaps ruin, to our own.

It is by no means easy to give you instructions. They must be based on a survey of the condition of the country, and include a statement of the policy of the government. The insurrectionary movement, though rapid in its progress, is slow in revealing its permanent character. Only outlines of a policy can be drawn which must largely depend on uncertain events.

The presidential election took place on the 6th of November last. The canvass had been conducted in all the southern or slave States in such a manner as to prevent a perfectly candid hearing there of the issue involved, and so all the parties existing there were surprised and disappointed in the marked result. That disappointment was quickly seized for desperate purposes by a class of persons until that time powerless, who had long cherished a design to dismember the Union and build up a new confederacy around the Gulf of Mexico. Ambitious leaders hurried the people forward, in a factious course, observing conventional forms but violating altogether the deliberative spirit of their constitutions. When the new federal administration came in on the 4th of March last, it found itself confronted by an insurrectionary combination of seven States, practicing an insidious strategy to seduce eight other States into its councils.

One needs to be as conversant with our federative system as perhaps only American publicists can be to understand how effectually, in the first instance, such a revolutionary movement must demoralize the general government. We are not only a nation, but we are States also. All public officers, as well as all citizens, owe not only allegiance to the Union but allegiance also to the States in which they reside. In the more discontented States the local magistrates and other officers cast off at once their federal allegiance, and conventions were held which assumed to absolve their citizens from the same obligation. Even federal judges, marshals, clerks, and revenue officers resigned their trusts. Intimidation deterred loyal persons from accepting the offices thus rendered vacant. So the most important faculties of the federal government in those States abruptly ceased. The resigning federal agents, if the expression may be used, *attorned* to the revolutionary authorities and delivered up to them public funds and other property and possessions of large value. The federal government had, through a long series of years, been engaged in building strong fortifications, a navy yard, arsenals, mints, treasuries, and other public edifices, not in any case for use against those States, but chiefly for their protection and convenience. These had been unsuspectingly left either altogether or imperfectly garrisoned or guarded, and they fell, with little resistance, into the hands of the revolutionary party. A general officer of the army gave up to them a large quantity of military stores and other property, disbanded the troops under his command, and sent them out of the territory of the disaffected States.

It may be stated, perhaps without giving just offence, that the most popular motive in these discontents was an apprehension of designs on the part of the incoming federal administration hostile to the institution of domestic slavery in the States where it is tolerated by the local constitutions and laws. That institution and the class which especially cherishes it are not confined to the States which have revolted, but they exist in the eight other so-called slave States; and these, for that reason, sympathize profoundly with the revolutionary movement. Sympathies and apprehensions of this kind have, for an indefinite period, entered into the bases of political parties throughout the whole country, and thus considerable masses of persons, whose ultimate loyalty could not be doubted, were found, even in the free States, either justifying, excusing, or palliating the movement towards disunion in the seceding States. The party which was dominant in the federal government during the period of the last administration embraced, practically, and held in unreserved communion, all disunionists and sympathizers. It held the executive administration. The Secretaries of the Treasury, War, and the Interior were disunionists. The same party held a large majority of the Senate, and nearly equally divided the House of Representatives. Disaffection lurked, if it did not openly avow itself, in every department and in every bureau, in every regiment and in every ship-of-war; in the post office and in the custom-house, and in every legation and consulate from London to Calcutta. Of four thousand four hundred and seventy officers in the public service, civil and military, two thousand one hundred and fifty-four were representatives of States where the revolutionary movement was openly advocated and urged, even if not actually organized. Our system being so completely federative and representative, no provision had ever been made, perhaps none ever could have been made, to anticipate this strange and unprecedented disturbance. The people were shocked by successive and astounding developments of what the statute book distinctly pronounced to be sedition and treason, but the magistracy was demoralized and the laws were powerless. By degrees, however, a better sentiment revealed itself. The executive administration hesitatingly, in part, reformed itself. The capital was garrisoned; the new President came in unresisted, and soon constituted a new and purely loyal administration. They found the disunionists perseveringly engaged in raising armies and laying sieges around national fortifications situate within the territory of the disaffected States. The federal marine seemed to have been scattered everywhere except where its presence was necessary, and such of the military forces as were not in the remote States and Territories were held back from activity by vague and mysterious armistices which had been informally contracted by the late President, or under his authority, with a view to postpone conflict until impracticable concessions to disunion should be made by Congress, or at least until the waning term of his administration should reach its appointed end. Commissioners who had been sent by the new confederacy were already at the capital demanding recognition of its sovereignty and a partition of the national property and domain. The treasury, depleted by robbery and peculation, was exhausted, and the public credit was prostrate.

It would be very unjust to the American people to suppose that this singular and unhappy condition of things indicated any extreme favor or toleration of the purpose of a permanent dissolution of the Union. On the contrary, disunion at the very first took on a specious form, and it afterwards made its way by ingenious and seductive devices. It inculcated that the Union is a purely voluntary connexion, founded on the revocable assent of the several States ; that secession, in the case of great popular discontent, would induce consultation and reconciliation, and so that revolution, instead of being war, is peace, and disunion, instead of being dissolution, is union. Though the ordinances of secession in the seceding States were carried through impetuously, without deliberation, and even by questionable majorities, yet it was plausibly urged that the citizens who had remained loyal to the Union might wisely acquiesce, so as ultimately to moderate and control the movement, and in any event that if war should ensue, it would become a war of sections, and not a social war, of all others, and especially in those States, the form of war most seriously to be deprecated. It being assumed that peaceful separation is in harmony with the Constitution, it was urged as a consequence that coercion would, therefore, be unlawful and tyrannical ; and this principle was even pushed so far as to make the defensive retaining by the federal government of its position within the limits of the seceding States, or where it might seem to overawe or intimidate them, an act of such forbidden coercion. Thus it happened that for a long time, and in very extensive districts even, fidelity to the Union manifested itself by demanding a surrender of its powers and possessions, and compromises with or immunity towards those who were engaged in overthrowing it by armed force. Disunion under these circumstances rapidly matured. On the other hand, the country was bewildered. For the moment even loyal citizens fell naturally into the error of inquiring how the fearful state of things had come about, and who was responsible for it, thus inviting a continuance of the controversy out of which it had arisen, rather than rallying to the duty of arresting it. Disunion, sustained only by passion, made haste to attain its end. Union, on the contrary, required time, because it could only appeal to reason, and reason could not be heard until excitement should in some degree subside. Military spirit is an element always ready for revolution. It has a fuller development in the disaffected than in the loyal States. Thousands of men have already banded themselves as soldiers in the cause of disunion, while the defenders of the Union, before resorting to arms, everywhere wait to make sure that it cannot be otherwise preserved. Even this cautious and pacific, yet patriotic disposition has been misunderstood and perverted by faction to encourage disunion.

I believe that I have thus presented the disunion movement dispassionately and without misrepresenting its proportions or its character.

You will hardly be asked by responsible statesmen abroad why has not the new administration already suppressed the revolution. Thirty-five days are a short period in which to repress, chiefly by moral means, a movement which is so active while disclosing itself throughout an empire.

You will not be expected to promulgate this history, or to communicate it to the British government, but you are entitled to the President's views; which I have thus set forth in order to enable you to understand the policy which he proposes to pursue, and to conform your own action to it.

The President neither looks for nor apprehends any actual and permanent dismemberment of the American Union, especially by a line of latitude. The improvement of our many channels of intercourse, and the perfection of our scheme of internal exchanges, and the incorporation of both of them into a great system of foreign commerce, concurring with the gradual abatement of the force of the only existing cause of alienation, have carried us already beyond the danger of disunion in that form. The so-called Confederate States, therefore, in the opinion of the President, are attempting what will prove a physical impossibility. Necessarily they build the structure of their new government upon the same principle by which they seek to destroy the Union, namely, the right of each individual member of the confederacy to withdraw from it at pleasure and in peace. A government thus constituted could neither attain the consolidation necessary for stability, nor guaranty any engagements it might make with creditors or other nations. The movement, therefore, in the opinion of the President, tends directly to anarchy in the seceding States, as similar movements in similar circumstances have already resulted in Spanish America, and especially in Mexico. He believes, nevertheless, that the citizens of those States, as well as the citizens of the other States, are too intelligent, considerate, and wise to follow the leaders to that disastrous end. For these reasons he would not be disposed to reject a cardinal dogma of theirs, namely, that the federal government could not reduce the seceding States to obedience by conquest, even although he were disposed to question that proposition. But, in fact, the President willingly accepts it as true. Only an imperial or despotic government could subjugate thoroughly disaffected and insurrectionary members of the State. This federal republican system of ours is of all forms of government the very one which is most unfitted for such a labor. Happily, however, this is only an imaginary defect. The system has within itself adequate, peaceful, conservative, and recuperative forces. Firmness on the part of the government in maintaining and preserving the public institutions and property, and in executing the laws where authority can be exercised without waging war, combined with such measures of justice, moderation, and forbearance as will disarm reasoning opposition, will be sufficient to secure the public safety until returning reflection, concurring with the fearful experience of social evils, the inevitable fruits of faction, shall bring the recusant members cheerfully back into the family, which, after all, must prove their best and happiest, as it undeniably is their most natural home. The Constitution of the United States provides for that return by authorizing Congress, on application to be made by a certain majority of the States, to assemble a national convention, in which the organic law can, if it be needful, be revised so as to remove all real obstacles to a reunion, so suitable to the habits of the people, and so eminently conducive to the common safety and welfare.

Keeping that remedy steadily in view, the President, on the one hand, will not suffer the federal authority to fall into abeyance, nor will he, on the other, aggravate existing evils by attempts at coercion which must assume the form of direct war against any of the revolutionary States. If, while he is pursuing this course, commended as it is by prudence as well as patriotism, the scourge of civil war for the first time in our history must fall upon our country during the term of his administration, that calamity will then have come through the agency, not of the government, but of those who shall have chosen to be its armed, open, and irreconcilable enemies; and he will not suffer himself to doubt that when the value of the imperilled Union shall be brought in that fearful manner home to the business and the bosoms of the American people, they will, with an unanimity that shall vindicate their wisdom and their virtue, rise up and save it.

It does not, however, at all surprise the President that the confidence in the stability of the Union, which has been heretofore so universally entertained, has been violently shocked both at home and abroad. Surprise and fear invariably go together. The period of four months which intervened between the election which designated the head of the new administration and its advent, as has already been shown, assumed the character of an interregnum, in which not only were the powers of the government paralyzed, but even its resources seemed to disappear and be forgotten.

Nevertheless, all the world know what are the resources of the United States, and that they are practically unencumbered as well as inexhaustible. It would be easy, if it would not seem invidious, to show that whatever may be the full development of the disunion movement, those resources will not be seriously diminished, and that the revenues and credit of the Union, unsurpassed in any other country, are adequate to every emergency that can occur in our own. Nor will the political commotions which await us sensibly disturb the confidence of the people in the stability of the government. It has been necessary for us to learn, perhaps the instruction has not come too soon, that vicissitudes are incident to our system and our country, as they are to all others. The panic which that instruction naturally produced is nearly past. What has hitherto been most needful for the reinvigoration of authority is already occurring. The aiders, abettors, and sympathizers with disunion, partly by their own choice and partly through the exercise of the public will, are falling out from the civil departments of the government as well as from the army and the navy. The national legislature will no longer be a distracted council. Our representatives in foreign courts and ports will henceforth speak only the language of loyalty to their country, and of confidence in its institutions and its destiny.

It is much to be deplored that our representatives are to meet abroad agents of disunion, seeking foreign aid to effect what, unaided, is already seen to be desperate. You need not be informed that their success in Great Britain would probably render their success easy elsewhere. The President does not doubt that you fully appreciate the responsibility of your mission. An honored ancestor of yours was the first to represent your whole country, after its independence was established, at the same court to which you now are accredited. The President feels assured that it will happen through no want of loyalty or of diligence on your part if you are to be the last to discharge that trust. You will have this great advantage, that from the hour when that country, so dear to us all, first challenged the notice of nations, until now, it has continually grown in their sympathy and reverence.

Before considering the arguments you are to use, it is important to indicate those which you are not to employ in executing that mission:

First. The President has noticed, as the whole American people have, with much emotion, the expressions of good will and friendship toward the United States, and of concern for their present embarrassments, which have been made on apt occasions by her Majesty and her ministers. You will make due acknowledgment for these manifestations, but at the same time you will not rely on any more sympathies or national kindness. You will make no admissions of weakness in our Constitution, or of apprehension on the part of the government. You will rather prove, as you easily can, by comparing the history of our country with that of other states, that its Constitution and government are really the strongest and surest which have ever been erected for the safety of any people. You will in no case listen to any suggestions of compromise by this government, under foreign auspices, with its discontented citizens. If, as the President does not at all apprehend, you shall unhappily find her Majesty's government tolerating the application of the so-called seceding States, or wavering about it, you will not leave them to suppose for a moment that they can grant that application and remain the friends of the United States. You may even assure them promptly in that case that if they determine to recognize, they may at the same time prepare to enter into alliance with the enemies of this republic. You alone will represent your country at London, and you will represent the whole of it there. When you are asked to divide that duty with others, diplomatic relations between the government of Great Britain and this government will be suspended, and will remain so until it shall be seen which of the two is most strongly entrenched in the confidence of their respective nations and of mankind.

You will not be allowed, however, even if you were disposed, as the President is sure you will not be, to rest your opposition to the application of the Confederate States on the ground of any favor this administration, or the party which chiefly called it into existence, proposes to show to Great Britain, or claims that Great Britain ought to show to them. You will not consent to draw into debate before the British government any opposing moral principles which may be supposed to lie at the foundation of the controversy between those States and the federal Union

You will indulge in no expressions of harshness or disrespect, or even impatience, concerning the seceding States, their agents, or their people. But you will, on the contrary, all the while remember that those States are now, as they always heretofore have been, and, notwithstanding their temporary self-delusion, they must always continue to be, equal and honored members of this federal Union, and that their citizens throughout all political misunderstandings and alienations still are and always must be our kindred and countrymen. In short, all your arguments must belong to one of three classes, namely : First. Arguments drawn from the principles of public law and natural justice, which regulate the intercourse of equal States. Secondly. Arguments which concern equally the honor, welfare, and happiness of the discontented States, and the honor, welfare, and happiness of the whole Union. Thirdly. Arguments which are equally conservative of the rights and interests, and even sentiments of the United States, and just in their bearing upon the rights, interests, and sentiments of Great Britain and all other nations.

We freely admit that a nation may, and even ought, to recognize a new State which has absolutely and beyond question effected its independence, and permanently established its sovereignty; and that a recognition in such a case affords no just cause of offence to the government of the country from which the new State has so detached itself. On the other hand, we insist that a nation that recognizes a revolutionary State, with a view to aid its effecting its sovereignty and independence, commits a great wrong against the nation whose integrity is thus invaded, and makes itself responsible for a just and ample redress.

I will not stop to inquire whether it may not sometimes happen that an imperial government or even a federative one may not so oppress or aggrieve its subjects in a province or in a State as to justify intervention on the plea of humanity. Her Majesty's government, however, will not make a pretence that the present is such a case. The United States have existed under their present form of government seventy and more years, and during all that time not one human life has been taken in forfeiture for resistance to their authority. It must be the verdict of history that no government so just, so equal, and so humane, has ever elsewhere existed. Even the present disunion movement is confessedly without any better cause than an apprehension of dangers which, from the very nature of the government, are impossible; and speculations of aggressions, which those who know the physical and social arrangements of this continent must see. at once are fallacious and chimerical.

The disunionists will, I am sure, take no such ground. They will appeal, not to the justice, or to the magnanimity, but to the cupidity and caprice of Great Britain.

It cannot need many words to show that even in that form their appeal ought to be promptly dismissed. I am aware that the revenue law lately passed by Congress is vehemently denounced in Great Britain. It might be enough to say on that subject that as the United States and Great Britain are equals in dignity, and not unequal in astuteness in the science and practice of political economy, the former have good right to regard only their own convenience, and consult their own judgment in framing their revenue laws. But there are some points in this connexion which you may make without compromising the self-respect of this government.

In the circumstances of the present case, it is clear that a recognition of the so-called Confederate nations must be deemed equivalent to a deliberate resolution by her Majesty's government that this American Union, which has so long constituted a sovereign nation, shall be now permanently dissolved, and cease to exist forever. The excuse for this resolution, fraught, if effectual, with fearful and enduring consequences, is a change in its revenue laws—a change which, because of its very nature, as well as by reason of the ever-changing course of public sentiment, must necessarily be temporary and ephemeral. British censors tell us that the new tariff is unwise for ourselves. If so, it will speedily be repealed. They say it is illiberal and injurious to Great Britain. It cannot be so upon her principles without being also injurious to ourselves, and in that case it will be promptly repealed. Besides, there certainly are other and more friendly remedies for foreign legislation that is injurious without premeditated purpose of injury, which a magnanimous government will try before it deliberately seeks the destruction of the offended nation.

The application of the so-called Confederate States, in the aspect now under consideration, assumes that they are offering, or will offer, more liberal commercial facilities than the United States can or will be disposed to concede. Would it not be wise for Great Britain to wait until those liberal facilities shall be definitely fixed and offered by the Confederate States, and then to wait further and see whether the United States may not accord facilities not less desirable?

The union of these States seventy years ago established perfectly free trade between the several States, and this, in effect, is free trade throughout the largest inhabitable part of North America. During all that time, with occasional and very brief intervals, not affecting the result, we have been constantly increasing in commercial liberality towards foreign nations. We have made that advance necessarily, because, with increasing liberality, we have at the same time, owing to controlling causes, continually augmented our revenues and increased our own productions. The sagacity of the British government cannot allow it to doubt that our natural course hereafter in this respect must continue to be the same as heretofore.

The same sagacity may be trusted to decide, first, whether the so-called Confederate States, on the emergency of a military revolution, and having no other sources of revenue than duties on imports and exports levied within the few ports they can command without a naval force, are likely to be able to persevere in practicing the commercial liberality they proffer as an equivalent for recognition. Manifestly, moreover, the negotiation which they propose to open with Great Britain implies that peace is to be preserved while the new commerce goes on. The sagacity of her Majesty's government may be trusted to consider whether that new government is likely to be inaugurated without war, and whether the commerce of Great Britain with this country would be likely to be improved by flagrant war between the southern and northern States.

Again, even a very limited examination of commercial statistics will be sufficient to show that while the staples of the disaffected States do, indeed, as they claim, constitute a very important portion of the exports of the United States to European countries, a very large portion of the products and fabrics of other regions consumed in those States are derived, and must continue to be derived, not from Europe, but from the northern States, while the chief consumption of European productions and fabrics imported into the United States takes place in these same States. Great Britain may, if her government think best, by modifying her navigation laws, try to change these great features of American commerce; but it will require something more than acts of the British Parliament and of the proposed revolutionary Congress to modify a commerce that takes its composite character from all the various soils and climates of a continent, as well as from the diversified institutions, customs and dispositions of the many communities which inhabit it.

Once more: All the speculations which assume that the revenue law recently passed by Congress will diminish the consumption of foreign fabrics and productions in the United States are entirely erroneous. The American people are active, industrious, inventive, and energetic, but they are not penurious or sordid. They are engaged with wonderful effect in developing the mineral, forest, agricultural and pastoral resources of a vast and, practically, new continent. Their wealth, individual as well as public, increases every day in a general sense, irrespective of the revenue laws of the United States, and every day also the habit of liberal—not to say profuse—expenditure grows upon them. There are changes in the nature and character of imported productions which they consume, but practically no decline in the quantity and value of imports.

It remains to bring out distinctly a consideration to which I have already adverted. Great Britain has within the last forty-five years changed character and purpose. She has become a power for production, rather than a power for destruction. She is committed, as it seems to us, to a policy of industry, not of ambition; a policy of peace, not of war. One has only to compare her present domestic condition with that of any former period to see that this new career on which she has entered is as wise as it is humane and beneficent. Her success in this career requires peace throughout the civilized world, and nowhere so much as on this continent. Recognition by her of the so-called Confederate States would be intervention and war in this country. Permanent dismemberment of the American Union in consequence of that intervention would be perpetual war—civil war. The new confederacy which in that case Great Britain would have aided into existence must, like any other new state, seek to expand itself northward, westward, and southward. What part of this continent or of the adjacent islands would be expected to remain in peace?

The President would regard it as inconsistent with his habitually high consideration for the government and people of Great Britain to allow me to dwell longer on the merely commercial aspects of the question under discussion. Indeed he will not for a moment believe that, upon consideration of merely financial gain, that government could be induced to lend its aid to a revolution designed to overthrow the institutions of this country, and involving ultimately the destruction of the liberties of the American people.

To recognize the independence of a new state, and so favor, possibly determine, its admission into the family of nations, is the highest possible exercise of sovereign power, because it affects in any case the welfare of two nations, and often the peace of the world. In the European system this power is now seldom attempted to be exercised without invoking a consultation or congress of nations. That system has not been extended to this continent. But there is even a greater necessity for prudence in such cases in regard to American States than in regard to the nations of Europe. A revolutionary change of dynasty, or even a disorganization and recombination of one or many States, therefore, do not long or deeply affect the general interests of society, because the ways of trade and habits of society remain the same. But a radical change effected in the political combinations existing on the continent, followed, as it probably would be, by moral convulsions of incalculable magnitude, would threaten the stability of society throughout the world.

Humanity has indeed little to hope for if it shall, in this age of high improvement, be decided without a trial that the principle of international law which regards nations as moral persons, bound so to act as to do to each other the least injury and the most good, is merely an abstraction too refined to be reduced into practice by the enlightened nations of Western Europe. Seen in the light of this principle, the several nations of the earth constitute one great federal republic. When one of them casts its suffrages for the admission of a new member into that republic, it ought to act under a profound sense of moral obligation, and be governed by considerations as pure, disinterested, and elevated as the general interest of society and the advancement of human nature.

The British empire itself is an aggregation of divers communities which cover a large portion of the earth and embrace one-fifth of its entire population. Some, at least, of these communities are held to their places in that system by bonds as fragile as the obligations of our own federal Union. The strain will some time come which is to try the strength of these bonds, though it will be of a different kind from that which is trying the cords of our confederation. Would it be wise for her Majesty's government, on this occasion, to set a dangerous precedent, or provoke retaliation? If Scotland and Ireland are at last reduced to quiet contentment, has Great Britain no dependency, island, or province left exposed along the whole circle of her empire, from Gibraltar through the West Indies and Canada till it begins again on the southern extremity of Africa?

The President will not dwell on the pleasing recollection that Great Britain, not yet a year ago, manifested by marked attention to the United States her desire for a cordial reunion which, all ancient prejudices and passions being buried, should be a pledge of mutual interest and sympathy forever thereafter. The United States are not indifferent to the circumstances of common descent, language, customs, sentiments, and religion, which recommend a closer sympathy between themselves and Great Britain than either might expect in its intercourse with any other nation. The United States are one of many nations which have sprung from Great Britain herself. Other such nations are rising up in various parts of the globe. It has been thought by many who have studied the philosophy of modern history profoundly, that the success of the nations thus deriving their descent from Great Britain might, through many ages, reflect back upon that kingdom the proper glories of its own great career. The government and people of Great Britain may mistake their commercial interests, but they cannot become either unnatural or indifferent to the impulses of an undying ambition to be distinguished as the leaders of the nations in the ways of civilization and humanity.

I am, sir, respectfully, your obedient servant,

WILLIAM H. SEWARD.

Mr. Dallas to Mr. Seward.

[Extracts.]

No. 325.]   LEGATION OF THE UNITED STATES,
London, March 22, 1861.

SIR: I have recently had the honor to receive your despatches, numbered 304 and 305.

Having noticed that the despatch No. 304, bearing date the 28th of February, respecting the newly-formed confederacy of seceded States, was in harmony as well with the views enunciated in the inaugural address on the 4th instant as with those of the presidential message of December last, I lost no time in seeking an interview with her Majesty's principal secretary of state for foreign affairs, and in stating the opposition which I am in that despatch instructed to make to any recognition by the Queen of England of the independence of those who have thus attempted to throw off their federal obligations.

The necessary opportunity was accorded to me on the day after the receipt of the despatch, yesterday. Lord John Russell then listened to the communication as one he expected; though on its purport the British cabinet, if they had interchanged opinions at all, had reached no definite conclusion as to their proper course of action.

I took the liberty to inquire whether any one professing to represent the southern republic had approached this government on the subject, and his lordship, with prompt frankness, assured me that he felt no hesitation in answering in the negative, adding that he had been shown a private letter from which he inferred that accredited ministers or commissioners, authorized to negotiate for the recognition, would shortly be sent by the provisional authorities of Montgomery.

I have the honor to be, sir, your most obedient servant,

G. M. DALLAS.

The Hon. the SECRETARY OF STATE, *Washington.*

Mr. Dallas to Mr. Seward.

[Extract.]

No. 329.]   LEGATION OF THE UNITED STATES,
                                  London, April 5, 1861.

SIR: I have the honor to acknowledge the receipt of your despatches, numbered 306 and 307, and a circular, dated the 9th of March, 1861, respecting the probable efforts of persons claiming to represent a southern provisional government to obtain the recognition of their independence by Great Britain.

Respecting this last-mentioned subject, I addressed yesterday, as soon as your instruction was received, a note to her Majesty's principal secretary of state for foreign affairs requesting an early interview, deeming it not impossible that I might be enabled to send you something by this steamer. My note, however, is yet unanswered, owing, I presume, to the absence of Lord John Russell from town. The commissioners from the new confederacy have not yet arrived, and may not arrive until late in this month. You were apprised by my despatch of the 22d ultimo (No. 325) that, on the receipt from the department of your predecessors, No. 304, I had lost no time in placing the matter properly before this government. Your own views will be communicated in greater fullness when the opportunity is allowed me.

        *   *   *   *   *   *   *   *

I have the honor to be, sir, your obedient servant,
                                      G. M. DALLAS.

The Hon. WILLIAM H. SEWARD, *Secretary of State*

Mr. Dallas to Mr. Seward.

No. 330.]   LEGATION OF THE UNITED STATES,
                                    London, April 9, 1861.

SIR: Referring to my despatch of the 5th instant, (No. 329,) I have now the honor to state that Lord John Russell accorded me an interview at the foreign office yesterday, and enabled me to submit fully to his consideration the representations of your circular, with the inaugural address of the President.

We conversed for some time on the question of recognizing the alleged southern confederacy, of which no representative has yet appeared, and may not appear until the end of the month.

His lordship assured me with great earnestness that there was not the slightest disposition in the British government to grasp at any advantage which might be supposed to arise from the unpleasant domestic differences in the United States, but, on the contrary, that they would be highly gratified if those differences were adjusted and the Union restored to its former unbroken position.

I pressed upon him, in concluding, if that were the case—and I was quite convinced that it was—how important it must be that this country and France should abstain, at least for a considerable time, from doing what, by encouraging groundless hopes, would widen a breach still thought capable of being closed.

He seemed to think the matter not ripe for decision one way or the other,

Ex. Doc. 1——6

and remarked that what he had said was all that at present it was in his power to say. The coming of my successor, Mr. Adams, looked for from week to week, would doubtless be regarded as the appropriate and natural occasion for finally discussing and determining the question. In the intermediate time whatever of vigilance and activity may be necessary shall, of course, and as a high duty, be exerted.

English opinion tends rather, I apprehend, to the theory that a peaceful separation may work beneficially for both groups of States and not injuriously affect the rest of the world. They cannot be expected to appreciate the weakness, discredit, complications, and dangers which we instinctively and justly ascribe to disunion.

I beg to add that a phase of this subject will be introduced in the House of Commons to-night by Lord Alfred Churchill, and that on the 15th instant a motion favoring the recognition will be pressed by Mr. W. H. Gregory, member for Galway.

I have the honor to be, sir, your most obedient servant,

G. M. DALLAS.

Hon. WILLIAM H. SEWARD,
    Secretary of State.

PARLIAMENTARY NOTICES.

HOUSE OF LORDS, *Tuesday, April 9.*

Blackpool and Lytham railroad bill.

ORDERS OF THE DAY.

Middleton's estate.—Standing order No. 141 to be considered, in order to its being dispensed with, on the petition for a private bill.
Lunacy regulation bill.—Committee.
Queensland government bill.—Committee.

HOUSE OF COMMONS, *Tuesday, April 9.*

NOTICES OF MOTIONS.

Lord STANLEY.—To ask the under secretary of state for war what steps have been or are being taken to abolish purchase in the army above the rank of major, as recommended by the commission of 1856.

Lord ALFRED CHURCHILL.—To ask the secretary of state for foreign affairs whether it is the intention of her Majesty's government to recognize the Confederate States of America without a guarantee that the flag of that confederation shall not be made subservient to the slave trade, and whether it is the intention of her Majesty's government to invite a conference of the European powers on the subject, so as to prevent the African slave trade being reopened or carried on under the flag of the said confederation.

Mr. Seward to Mr. Adams.

No. 4.]   DEPARTMENT OF STATE,
                                Washington, April 27, 1861.

SIR: A despatch has just been received from Mr. Dallas, dated the 9th of April instant, the record of which (No. 330) you doubtless will find in the archives of the legation when you shall have arrived at London.

In that paper Mr. Dallas states that he had had a conversation with Lord John Russell, the minister of foreign affairs of her Britannic Majesty's government, on the subject of a protest against any recognition of the so-called Confederate States of America, the protest having been presented to him by Mr. Dallas, in obedience to a circular letter of instructions sent to him from this department, under the date of the 9th ultimo.

Mr. Dallas represents that his lordship assured him, with great earnestness, that there was not the slightest disposition in the British government to grasp at any advantage which might be supposed to arise from the unpleasant domestic differences in the United States; but, on the contrary, that they would be highly gratified if those differences were adjusted, and the Union restored to its former unbroken position.

This, by itself, would be very gratifying to the President. Mr. Dallas, however, adds that he endeavored to impress upon his lordship how important it must be that Great Britain and France should abstain, at least for a considerable time, from doing what, by encouraging groundless hopes, would widen a breach still thought capable of being closed ; but that his lordship seemed to think the matter not ripe for decision one way or the other, and remarked that what he had already said was all that at present it was in his power to say.

When you shall have read the instructions at large which have been sent to you, you will hardly need to be told that these last remarks of his lordship are by no means satisfactory to this government. Her Britannic Majesty's government is at liberty to choose whether it will retain the friendship of this government by refusing all aid and comfort to its enemies, now in flagrant rebellion against it, as we think the treaties existing between the two countries require, or whether the government of her Majesty will take the precarious benefits of a different course.

You will lose no time in making known to her Britannic Majesty's government that the President regards the answer of his lordship as possibly indicating a policy that this government would be obliged to deem injurious to its rights and derogating from its dignity.

I am, sir, respectfully, your obedient servant,

WILLIAM H. SEWARD.

C. F. ADAMS, Esq.,
&c., &c., &c.

Mr. Dallas to Mr. Seward.

No. 333.] LEGATION OF THE UNITED STATES,
London, May 2, 1861.

SIR: In my No. 329 I mentioned having received your Nos. 306 and 307, and "a circular of the 9th of March, 1861." As I have got no despatch from you, numbered 308, it is probable that this "circular" was considered at the department as representing that number in the series. I have now to acknowledge your several despatches, numbered, respectively, 309, 310, 311, and 312, whose contents have had my careful and prompt attention.

You have doubtless noticed that the motion of Mr. Gregory, in the House of Commons, on the recognition of the southern confederation—which motion I mentioned at the conclusion of my No. 330—underwent postponement from the 16th to the 30th ultimo, and has again been deferred a fortnight, for the reasons stated in the extract from the "Times" newspaper of the 30th April, hereto annexed.

The solicitude felt by Lord John Russell as to the effect of certain measures represented as likely to be adopted by the President induced him to request me to call at his private residence yesterday. I did so. He told me that the three representatives of the southern confederacy were here; that he had not seen them, but was not unwilling to do so, *unofficially;* that there existed an understanding between this government and that of France which would lead both to take the same course as to recognition, whatever that course might be; and he then referred to the rumor of a meditated blockade of southern ports and their discontinuance as ports of entry—topics on which I had heard nothing, and could therefore say nothing. But as I informed him that Mr. Adams had apprised me of his intention to be on his way hither, in the steamship "Niagara," which left Boston on the 1st May, and that he would probably arrive in less than two weeks, by the 12th or 15th instant, his lordship acquiesced in the expediency of disregarding mere rumor, and waiting the full knowledge to be brought by my successor.

The motion, therefore, of Mr. Gregory may be further postponed, at his lordship's suggestion.

I have the honor to be, sir, your most obedient servant,

G. M. DALLAS.

Hon. WILLIAM H. SEWARD,
    Secretary of State.

[From the London Times, April 30, 1861.]

AMERICA.—In reply to a question from Mr. W. E. Foster, Mr. Gregory stated that in deference to the expressed opinion of the foreign secretary, who had informed him that a discussion at the present moment upon the expediency of a prompt recognition of the southern confederation of America would be embarrassing to the public service, and in deference, also, to the wishes of several honorable friends of his, he should postpone for a fortnight the motion which stood in his name for to-morrow night. The noble lord at the head of the foreign office believed that the motion might then be brought forward without inconvenience.

[From the London Times, May 3, 1861.]

AMERICA.—SOUTHERN LETTERS OF MARQUE.—Mr. J. Ewart asked the secretary of state for foreign affairs whether, seeing the possibility of privateering being permitted and encouraged by the southern confederation of the States of America, her Majesty's government had placed a sufficient naval force, or intended to increase it, in the Gulf of Mexico, with a view to protect British shipping and British property on board of American ships ; and if privateers, sailing under the flag of an unrecognized power, would be dealt with as pirates.

Lord J. Russell said : In answer to the first part of the question of the honorable gentleman, I beg to say that her Majesty's government has directed that a naval force, for the protection of British shipping, should be sent to the coast of America. As to the latter part of the question, I will state to the house that the government has, from day to day, received the most lamentable accounts of the progress of the war in the States of America. Her Majesty's government heard the other day that the Confederated States have issued letters of marque ; and to-day we have heard that it is intended there shall be a blockade of all the ports of the southern States. As to the general provisions of the law of nations on these questions, some of the points are so new as well as so important that they have been referred to the law officers of the crown for their opinion in order to guide the government in its instructions both to the English minister in America and the commander of the naval squadron. Her Majesty's government has felt that it was its duty to use every possible means to avoid taking any part in the lamentable contest now raging in the American States. (Hear, hear.) And nothing but the imperative duty of protecting British interests, in case they should be attacked, justifies the government in at all interfering. We have not been involved in any way in that contest by any act or giving any advice in the matter, and, for God's sake, let us if possible keep out of it! (Cheers.)

Mr. Adams to Mr. Seward.

[Extracts.]

No. 1.]   LEGATION OF THE UNITED STATES,
                                        London, May 17, 1861.

SIR: I have the satisfaction to announce my safe arrival at this place on Monday evening, the 13th of this month. The steamer reached Liverpool at eleven in the morning, where I was received with the utmost kindness, and strongly solicited to remain at least one day. A large deputation of the American Chamber of Commerce waited upon me and delivered an address, to which I made a brief reply. Both have been printed in the newspapers, and I transmit a copy of the Times containing them. I could not fail to observe, in the course of these proceedings, the great anxiety and the fluctuating sentiment that prevail in regard to the probable issue of affairs in America. I could also perceive that my arrival had been expected with far more solicitude than I had anticipated. It was not disguised from me that a supposed community of interest in the cotton culture was weighing heavily in that city in favor of the disaffected; and that much misapprehension prevailed as to the relative position of parties in the United States, which it was of some consequence to dispel. To this end it had been the wish that I could have found it convenient to make a longer stay in the place.

Under other circumstances I might have so far deferred to these representations as to delay my departure for twenty-four hours. But, on the other hand, some incidental allusions to the state of things in London convinced me of the importance of losing no time on my way. Accordingly I took the next train in the afternoon, and was in a condition to proceed at once to business on the morning of Tuesday, the 14th. In the interval between my departure from Boston on the 1st and my arrival on the 14th, I discovered that some events had taken place deserving of attention. The agents of the so-called Confederate States had arrived, and, as it is supposed, through their instigation certain inquiries and motions had been initiated in Parliament for the purpose of developing the views of the ministry in regard to American affairs. I allude more particularly to the questions proposed by Mr. Gregory, of Galway, and to the motion of Mr. Horsfall, the member for Liverpool, touching the effect of the blockade proclaimed by the President against the southern ports. The answer given by Lord John Russell, in the proceedings of the 6th of May, will, of course, have attracted your attention long before these lines meet your eye. I need not say that it excited general surprise, especially among those most friendly to the government of the United States. There seemed to be not a little precipitation in at once raising the disaffected States up to the level of a belligerent power, before it had developed a single one of the real elements which constitute military efficiency outside of its geographical limits. The case of the Greeks was by no means a parallel case, for the declaration had not been made until such time had intervened as was necessary to prove, by the very words quoted by Lord John Russell from the instructions of the British government, that the power was sufficient "to cover the sea with its cruisers." Whereas in the present instance there was no evidence to show as yet the existence of a single privateer afloat. The inference seemed almost inevitable that there existed a disposition at least not to chill the hopes of those who are now drawing the very breath of life only from the expectation of sympathy in Great Britain. Yet I am not quite prepared to say that there is just ground for the idea. On the contrary, I am led to believe, from the incidental discussion afterwards held in both houses, as well as from other information, that the language of Lord John Russell was viewed as not altogether sufficiently guarded, and that the ministry as a whole are not prepared to countenance any such conclusion.

There are still other reasons which occasion in me great surprise at the action of his lordship. I need not say that I was received by my predecessor, Mr. Dallas, with the greatest kindness and cordiality. I immediately learned from him that he had declined himself to enter into any discussions on the subject, because he knew that I was already on my way out, and that I should probably come fully possessed of the views of my government, and ready to communicate them freely to the authorities here. To this end he had already concerted with Lord John Russell the earliest possible measures for my presentation and for a conference with him. In regard to the ceremony, there were circumstances attending it which, in the precise posture of affairs, give it some significance. * * On Tuesday morning Mr. Dallas called on me to accompany him on his visit to Lord John Russell, at his house, at eleven o'clock. Great was our disappointment, however, to find that he had been suddenly called away, at an early hour, to visit his brother, the Duke of Bedford, at Woburn Abbey, who was very ill, and who actually died at two o'clock in the afternoon of that day. This, of course, has put an end to all further communication with him for the present. I very much regretted this circumstance, as I should have been glad to converse with him prior to the final action upon the proclamation which was adopted by the Privy Council, and which was issued in the Gazette on the very same day. A copy of that proclamation is to be found in the Times of the 15th of May, the same paper which I have already desired to transmit for another purpose. I submit it to your consideration without comment.

Feeling doubtful how the informal arrangement of Lord John Russell might have been affected by his sudden departure, I at once addressed to him the customary announcement of my arrival, and a request for an audience of her Majesty at an early day. This brought me immediate replies from the minister and from his secretary, Mr. Hammond, confirming the appointment of Thursday (yesterday) as the time for my presentation, while the latter gentleman notified me that in the absence of Lord John Russell Lord Palmerston would be in waiting at the palace at three o'clock to present me. At the same time Mr. Dallas received a similar notification, appointing the same hour and place for his audience of leave. This arrangement was fully carried out yesterday according to the programme. Mr. Dallas was introduced first, and took his leave, after which I presented my credentials, with a few words expressive of the desire of my government to maintain the friendly relations existing between the two countries; and thus I became the recognized minister.

Thus an end is put to all the speculations which have been set afloat in some quarters for interested purposes touching the probable position of the minister of the United States at this court. I might add, that so far I have every reason to be fully satisfied with the reception which I have met with from everybody. Fortunately the news which came from the United States by the same steamer which brought me was calculated to dispel many of the illusions that had been industriously elaborated during the period of isolation of the city of Washington, and to confirm the faith of those who had permitted themselves to doubt whether all government in the United States was of any more cohesiveness than a rope of sand. Yet I cannot say that the public opinion is yet exactly what we would wish it. Much depends upon the course of things in the United States, and the firmness and energy made visible in the direction of affairs.

The morning papers contain a report of the debate in the House of Lords on the Queen's proclamation, to which I beg to call your particular attention. I cannot say that the tone of it is generally such as I could wish. There is undoubtedly a considerable influence at work here both in and out of the ministry which must be met and counteracted at as early a moment as practicable. Mr. Gregory yesterday gave notice of a postponement of the consideration of his motion until the 7th of June. The reason assigned is the situation of Lord John Russell. * * The same cause, however, which postpones this debate also delays my opportunities of conference with the minister. My wish has been to confer with him rather than with any of the subordinates, for reasons which will readily occur to you. Next week come the Whitsuntide holidays, and the adjournment of Parliament for ten days, during which little can be done with effect. I propose, nevertheless, at once to apply for a conference at as early a period as possible.

I have just received a visit from a Mr. Arrowsmith, who came on behalf of Mr. Cunard's Steamship Company, to know whether the government would desire any number of their steam vessels to further their operations of blockade. I said, in reply, that I had no instructions on that point, and could give no information, but that I was now writing and would communicate the proposal. Mr. Arrowsmith says that fifteen or twenty vessels could be furnished at a moment's notice, which, by preparations of cotton pressed between decks, could be made to sustain guns, and thus be efficient instruments in closing the southern ports.

I have the honor to be your obedient servant,

CHARLES FRANCIS ADAMS.

Hon. WILLIAM H. SEWARD,
    Secretary of State, Washington, D. C.

P. S.—I have this moment received your despatches No. 3 and No. 4. They are of such importance that I immediately addressed a note to the foreign office requesting an early interview.

Mr. Seward to Mr. Adams.

[Extracts.]

No. 10.]   DEPARTMENT OF STATE,
                                          Washington, May 21, 1861.

SIR: This government considers that our relations in Europe have reached a crisis, in which it is necessary for it to take a decided stand, on which not only its immediate measures, but its ultimate and permanent policy can be determined and defined. At the same time it neither means to menace Great Britain nor to wound the susceptibilities of that or any other European nation. That policy is developed in this paper.

The paper itself is not to be read or shown to the British secretary of state, nor are any of its positions to be prematurely, unnecessarily, or indiscreetly made known. But its spirit will be your guide. You will keep back nothing when the time arrives for its being said with dignity, propriety, and effect, and you will all the while be careful to say nothing that will be incongruous or inconsistent with the views which it contains.

Mr. Dallas, in a brief despatch of May 2, (No. 333,) tells us that Lord John Russell recently requested an interview with him on account of the solicitude which his lordship felt concerning the effect of certain measures represented as likely to be adopted by the President. In that conversation the British secretary told Mr. Dallas that the three representatives of the southern confederacy were then in London, that Lord John Russell had not yet seen them, but that he was not unwilling to see them unofficially. He further informed Mr. Dallas that an understanding exists between the British and French governments which would lead both to take one and the same course as to recognition. His lordship then referred to the rumor of a meditated blockade by us of southern ports, and a discontinuance of them as ports of entry. Mr. Dallas answered that he knew nothing on those topics, and therefore could say nothing. He added that you were expected to arrive in two weeks. Upon this statement Lord John Russell acquiesced in the expediency of waiting for the full knowledge you were expected to bring.

Mr. Dallas transmitted to us some newspaper reports of ministerial explanations made in Parliament.

You will base no proceedings on parliamentary debates further than to seek explanations, when necessary, and communicate them to this department.

The President regrets that Mr. Dallas did not protest against the proposed unofficial intercourse between the British government and the missionaries of the insurgents. It is due, however, to Mr. Dallas to say that our instructions had been given only to you and not to him, and that his loyalty and fidelity, too rare in these times, are appreciated.

Intercourse of any kind with the so-called commissioners is liable to be construed as a recognition of the authority which appointed them. Such intercourse would be none the less hurtful to us for being called unofficial, and it might be even more injurious, because we should have no means of knowing what points might be resolved by it. Moreover, unofficial intercourse is useless and meaningless if it is not expected to ripen into official intercourse and direct recognition. It is left doubtful here whether the proposed unofficial intercourse has yet actually begun. Your own antecedent instructions are deemed explicit enough, and it is hoped that you have not misunderstood them. You will, in any event, desist from all intercourse whatever, unofficial as well as official, with the British government, so long as it shall continue intercourse of either kind with the domestic enemies of this country. When intercourse shall have been arrested for this cause, you will communicate with this department and receive further directions.

Lord John Russell has informed us of an understanding between the British and French governments that they will act together in regard to our affairs. This communication, however, loses something of its value from the circumstance that the communication was withheld until after knowledge of the fact had been acquired by us from other sources. We know also another fact that has not yet been officially communicated to us, namely: That other European states are apprized by France and England of their agreement, and are expected to concur with or follow them in whatever measures they adopt on the subject of recognition. The United States have been impartial and just in all their conduct towards the several nations of Europe. They will not complain, however, of the combination now announced by the two leading powers, although they think they had a right to expect a more independent, if not a more friendly course, from each of them. You will take no notice of that or any other alliance. Whenever the European governments shall see fit to communicate directly with us, we shall be, as heretofore, frank and explicit in our reply.

As to the blockade, you will say that by our own laws and the laws of nature, and the laws of nations, this government has a clear right to suppress insurrection. An exclusion of commerce from national ports which have been seized by insurgents, in the equitable form of blockade, is a proper means to that end. You will not insist that our blockade is to be respected, if it be not maintained by a competent force; but passing by that question as not now a practical or at least an urgent one, you will add that the blockade is now, and it will continue to be, so maintained, and therefore we expect it to be respected by Great Britain. You will add that we have already revoked the exequatur of a Russian consul who had enlisted in the military service of the insurgents, and we shall dismiss or demand the recall of every foreign agent, consular or diplomatic, who shall either disobey the federal laws or disown the federal authority.

As to the recognition of the so-called Southern Confederacy, it is not to be made a subject of technical definition. It is, of course, direct recognition to publish an acknowledgment of the sovereignty and independence of a new power. It is direct recognition to receive its embassadors, ministers, agents or commissioners, officially. A concession of belligerent rights is liable to be construed as a recognition of them. No one of these proceedings will pass unquestioned by the United States in this case.

Hitherto, recognition has been moved only on the assumption that the so-called Confederate States are *de facto* a self-sustaining power. Now, after long forbearance, designed to sooth discontent and avert the need of civil war, the land and naval forces of the United States have been put in motion to repress insurrection. The true character of the pretended new State is at once revealed. It is seen to be a power existing in pronunciamento only. It has never won a field. It has obtained no forts that were not virtually betrayed into its hands or seized in breach of trust. It commands not a single port on the coast nor any highway out from its pretended capital by land. Under these circumstances, Great Britain is called upon to intervene and give it body and independence by resisting our measures of suppression. British recognition would be British intervention, to create within our territory a hostile State by overthrowing this republic itself.

*   *   *   *   *   *   *   *   *

As to the treatment of privateers in the insurgent service, you will say that this is a question exclusively our own. We treat them as pirates. They are our own citizens, or persons employed by our citizens, preying on the commerce of our country. If Great Britain shall choose to recognize them as lawful belligerents, and give them shelter from our pursuit and punishment, the laws of nations afford an adequate and proper remedy.

Happily, however, her Britannic Majesty's government can avoid all these difficulties. It invited us in 1856 to accede to the declaration of the congress of Paris, of which body Great Britain was herself a member, abolishing privateering everywhere in all cases and forever. You already have our authority to propose to her our accession to that declaration. If she refuse it, it can only be because she is willing to become the patron of privateering when aimed at our devastation.

These positions are not elaborately defended now, because to vindicate them would imply a possibility of our waiving them. We are not insensible of the grave importance of this occasion. We see how, upon the result of the debate in which we are engaged, a war may ensue between the United States and one, two, or even more European nations. War in any case is as exceptional from the habits as it is revolting from the sentiments of the American people. But if it come it will be fully seen that it results from the action of Great Britain, not our own; that Great Britain will have decided to fraternize with our domestic enemy either without waiting to hear from you our remonstrances and our warnings, or after having heard them. War in defence of national life is not immoral, and war in defence of independence is an inevitable part of the discipline of nations.

The dispute will be between the European and the American branches of the British race. All who belong to that race will especially deprecate it, as they ought. It may well be believed that men of every race and kindred will deplore it. A war not unlike it between the same parties occurred at the close of the last century. Europe atoned by forty years of suffering for the error that Great Britain committed in provoking that contest. If that nation shall now repeat the same great error, the social convulsions which will follow may not be so long, but they will be more general. When they shall have ceased, it will, we think, be seen, whatever may have been the fortunes of other nations, that it is not the United States that will have come out of them with its precious Constitution altered, or its honestly obtained dominions in any degree abridged. Great Britain has but to wait a few months, and all her present inconveniences will cease with all our own troubles. If she take a different course she will calculate for herself the ultimate, as well as the immediate consequences, and will consider what position she will hold when she shall have forever lost the sympathies and affections of the only nation on whose sympathies and affections she has a natural claim. In making that calculation she will do well to remember that in the controversy she proposes to open we shall be actuated by neither pride, nor passion, nor cupidity, nor ambition; but we shall stand simply on the principle of self-preservation, and that our cause will involve the independence of nations and the rights of human nature.

I am, sir, respectfully, your obedient servant,

WILLIAM H. SEWARD.

CHARLES FRANCIS ADAMS, Esq., &c., &c., &c.

Mr. Adams to Mr. Seward.

[Extracts.]

No. 2.]   LEGATION OF THE UNITED STATES,
                           London, May 21, 1861.

SIR: At the close of my last despatch I stated my purpose to ask an early interview with Lord John Russell. A note to that effect was immediately sent to the foreign office. An answer was received on Saturday morning, saying that his lordship would be happy to see me, if I would take the trouble to go out to Pembroke Lodge, at Richmond, where he is retired for the present, on Monday at twelve or one o'clock, or, if I preferred it, he would see me at one o'clock on that same day, (May 18.) Although it was approaching eleven o'clock when I got the answer, and the distance exceeds nine miles from the city, I replied by accepting the earlier appointment, and was probably myself at the Lodge before he received my note.

Be this as it may, I found his lordship ready to receive me, so that I proceeded at once to business. After expressing the general feeling which I believed prevailing in the United States of good will towards Great Britain, and the confident expectations I had entertained, down to the period of my arrival, that these sentiments were fully reciprocated to my government on the part of the government here, I signified my sense of disappointment in not finding this quite so unequivocally manifested as I had hoped. There were now fewer topics of direct difference between the two countries than had probably existed at any preceding time, and even these had been withdrawn from discussion at this place to be treated on the other side of the water. I therefore came out here with little to do beyond the duty of preserving the relations actually existing from the risk of being unfavorably affected by the unfortunate domestic disturbances prevailing in my own country. It was not without pain that I was compelled to admit that from the day of my arrival I had felt in the proceedings of both houses of Parliament, in the language of her Majesty's ministers, and in the tone of opinion prevailing in private circles, more of uncertainty about this than I had before thought possible. This sentiment alone would have impelled me to solicit an early interview; but I was now come under a much stronger motive. I had just received a despatch from my government, based upon a letter from Mr. Dallas, of much earlier date than any of the matters to which I had alluded. In that letter he had reported a conversation with his lordship, the close of which had been deemed so unsatisfactory that I had been directed at once to seek for a further elucidation of his meaning. It was the desire of my government to learn whether it was the intention of her Majesty's ministers to adopt a policy which would have the effect to widen, if not to make irreparable, a breach which we believed yet to be entirely manageable by ourselves.

At this point his lordship replied by saying that there was no such intention. The clearest evidence of that was to be found in the assurance given by him to Mr. Dallas in the earlier part of the conversation referred to. With regard to the other portion, against which I understood him to intimate he had already heard from Lord Lyons that the President had taken exception, he could only say that he hardly saw his way to bind the government to any specific course, when circumstances beyond their agency rendered it difficult to tell what might happen. Should the insurgent States ultimately succeed in establishing themselves in an independent position, of the probability of which he desired to express no opinion, he presumed, from the general course of the United States heretofore, that they did not mean to require of other countries to pledge themselves to go further than they had been in the habit of going themselves. He therefore, by what he had said to Mr. Dallas, simply meant to say that they were not disposed in any way to interfere.

To this I replied by begging leave to remark that, so far as my government was concerned, any desire to interfere had never been imputed to Great Britain; but in her peculiar position it was deserving of grave consideration whether great caution was not to be used in adopting any course that might, even in the most indirect way, have an effect to encourage the hopes of the disaffected in America. It had now come to this, that without support from here, the people of the United States considered the termination of this difficulty as almost entirely a question of time. Any course adopted here that would materially change that calculation would inevitably raise the most unpleasant feelings among them. For independently of the absolute influence of Great Britain, admitted to be great, the effect of any supposed inclination on her part could not fail to be extensive among the other nations of Europe. It was my belief that the insurgent States could scarcely hope for sympathy on this side of the Atlantic, if deprived of any prospect of it here. Hence anything that looked like a manifestation of it would be regarded among us as inevitably tending to develope an ultimate separation in America; and, whether intended or not, the impression made would scarcely be effaced by time. It was in this view that I must be permitted to express the great regret I had felt on learning the decision to issue the Queen's proclamation, which at once raised the insurgents to the level of a belligerent State, and still more the language used in regard to it by her Majesty's ministers in both houses of Parliament before and since. Whatever might be the design, there could be no shadow of doubt that the effect of these events had been to encourage the friends of the disaffected here. The tone of the press and of private opinion indicated it strongly. I then alluded more especially to the brief report of the lord chancellor's speech on Thursday last, in which he had characterized the rebellious portion of my country as a belligerent State, and the war that was going on as *justum bellum.*

To this his lordship replied that he thought more stress was laid upon these events than they deserved. The fact was that a necessity seemed to exist to define the course of the government in regard to the participation of the subjects of Great Britain in the impending conflict. To that end the legal questions involved had been referred to those officers most conversant with them, and their advice had been taken in shaping the result. Their conclusion had been that, as a question merely of *fact,* a war existed. A considerable number of the States, at least seven, occupying a wide extent of country, were in open resistance, whilst one or more of the others were associating themselves in the same struggle, and as yet there were no indications of any other result than a contest of arms more or less severe. In many preceding cases, much less formidable demonstrations had been recognized. Under such circumstances it seemed scarcely possible to avoid speaking of this in the technical sense as *justum bellum,* that is, a war of two sides, without in any way implying an opinion of its justice, as well as to withhold an endeavor, so far as possible, to bring the management of it within the rules of modern civilized warfare. This was all that was contemplated by the Queen's proclamation. It was designed to show the purport of existing laws, and to explain to British subjects their liabilities in case they should engage in the war. And however strongly the people of the United States might feel against their enemies, it was hardly to be supposed that in practice they would now vary from their uniformly humane policy heretofore in endeavoring to assuage and mitigate the horrors of war.

To all which I answered that under other circumstances I should be very ready to give my cheerful assent to this view of his lordship's. But I must be permitted frankly to remark that the action taken seemed, at least to my mind, a little more rapid than was absolutely called for by the occasion. It might be recollected that the new administration had scarcely had sixty days to develop its policy ; that the extent to which all departments of the government had been demoralized in the preceding administration was surely understood here, at least in part; that the very organization upon which any future action was to be predicated was to be renovated and purified before a hope could be entertained of energetic and effective labor. The consequence had been that it was but just emerging from its difficulties, and beginning to develop the power of the country to cope with this rebellion, when the British government took the initiative, and decided practically that it is a struggle of two sides. And furthermore, it pronounced the insurgents to be a belligerent State before they had ever shown their capacity to maintain any kind of warfare whatever, except within one of their own harbors, and under every possible advantage. It considered them a marine power before they had ever exhibited a single privateer on the ocean. I said that I was not aware that a single armed vessel had yet been issued from any port under the control of these people. Surely this was not the case in the instance which had been relied upon in his speech by his lordship as authority for the present action. There the Greeks, however small as a people, had long been actively and effectually waging war, before the interposition of Great Britain, and, to use the language of the government, as quoted by himself, had "covered the sea with cruisers." It did seem to me therefore as if a little more time might have been taken to form a more complete estimate of the relative force of the contending parties, and of the probabilities of any long drawn issue. And I did not doubt that the view taken by me would be that substantially taken both by the government and the people of the United States. They would inevitably infer the existence of an intention more or less marked to extend the struggle. For this reason it was that I made my present application to know whether such a design was or was not entertained. For in the alternative of an affirmative answer it was as well for us to know it, as I was bound to acknowledge in all frankness that in that contingency I had nothing further left to do in Great Britain. I said this with regret, as my own feelings had been and were of the most friendly nature.

His lordship replied by an assurance that he participated in those feelings; neither did he see the action that had been thus far taken at all in the light in which I saw it. He believed that the United States, in their own previous history, had furnished examples of action taken quite as early as that now complained of. He instanced two cases. The first I do not now remember, for it seemed to me not important at the time; the other was the insurrection in Hungary under Kossuth, at which period, he believed, they had gone so far as actually to send an agent to that country with a view to recognition, and that to the great dissatisfaction and against the remonstrances of Austria.

I replied only to the second case, by remarking that the incidents attending that affair were not fresh in my mind, neither was I sure that I ever knew the whole action of the government; but it was my impression that the object of the mission was only confined to the acquisition of the facts necessary to form an opinion, and that, after they were obtained, no public step of any kind had been taken. Neither could I myself recollect an instance in which ample time had not been given by the United States for the development of events sufficiently decisive to justify any action that might have followed; for I begged it to be understood that the government did not mean at all to deny that there were cases in which recognition of a revolutionary government might be both expedient and proper. The rule was clear, that whenever it became apparent that any organized form of society had advanced so far as to prove its power to defend and protect itself against the assaults of enemies, and at the same time to manifest a capacity to maintain binding relations with foreign nations, then a measure of recognition could not be justly objected to on any side. The case was very different when such an interference should take place, prior to the establishment of the proof required, as to bring about a result which would not probably have happened but for that external agency.

And here I stop for a moment to make two remarks upon this part of the conversation. The first of these is, that I have an impression that the agent to go to Hungary, alluded to by his lordship, was Mr. Mann, the same gentleman who is now figuring in the commission of the confederates at this place. If in this I am right, we can be at no loss for his lordship's sources of information. The other remark is, that the Hungarian precedent was unquestionably one in which a very strong sympathy with the insurgent party actually existed in the United States. Are we therefore to infer a similar impulse to actuate the precipitate measure now taken here?

I did not say this to his lordship, though I might have done so; but I proceeded to observe that I had come to England prepared to present the views of my government on the general question, and that I should have done so in full but for the interposition of this more immediate despatch. At the present moment I should touch only upon one point in connexion with the acknowledgment of the insurgents even as a belligerent State. It seemed necessary to call the attention of his lordship to the fact which must be obvious to him, that as yet they had not laid any foundation for government solid enough to deserve a moment's confidence. They had undertaken to withdraw certain States from the government by an arbitrary act which they called secession, not known to the Constitution, the validity of which had at no time been acknowledged by the people of the United States, and which was now emphatically denied; but not content with this, they had gone on to substitute another system among themselves, avowedly based upon the recognition of this right of States to withdraw or secede at pleasure. With such a treaty, I would ask, where could be vested the obligation of treaties with foreign powers, of the payment of any debts contracted, or, indeed, of any act performed in good faith by the common authority for the time being established. For my own part, I fully believed that such a system could not deserve to be denominated, in any sense, a government; and therefore I could not but think any act performed here, having a tendency to invest it in the eye of the world with the notion of form and substance, could be attended only with the most complete disappointment to all the parties connected with it.

His lordship here interposed by saying that there was not, in his opinion, any occasion at present for going into this class of arguments, as the government did not contemplate taking any step that way. Should any such time arrive in the future, he should be very ready to listen to every argument that might be presented against it on the part of the United States. At this moment he thought we had better confine ourselves to the matter immediately in hand.

I then remarked that there was another subject upon which I had received a despatch, though I should not, after so long a conference, venture to do more than open the matter to-day. This was a proposal to negotiate in regard to the rights of neutrals in time of war. The necessary powers had been transmitted to me, together with a form of a convention, which I would do myself the honor to submit to his consideration if there was any disposition to pursue the matter further. His lordship then briefly reviewed the past action of the two countries since the meeting of the congress at Paris, and expressed the willingness of Great Britain to negotiate; but he seemed to desire to leave the subject in the hands of Lord Lyons, to whom he intimated that he had already transmitted authority to assent to any modification of the only point in issue which the government of the United States might prefer. On that matter he believed there would be no difficulty whatever. Under these circumstances, I shall not press the subject further at this place until I receive new directions to that effect from the department.

His lordship then observed that there were two points upon which he should be glad himself to be enlightened, although he did not know whether I was prepared to furnish the information. They both related to the President's proclamation of a blockade. The first question was upon the nature of the blockade. The coast was very extensive, stretching along the Atlantic and the Gulf of Mexico a great way. Was it the design of the United States to institute an effective blockade in its whole extent, or to make only a declaration to that effect as to the whole, and to confine the actual blockade to particular points? Considering the uniform doctrine of the government refusing to recognize the validity of mere paper blockades, he could hardly suppose they designed the latter.

To this I replied that I knew nothing directly of the President's intentions on this subject; but that inasmuch as the government had always protested against mere paper blockades, I could not suppose that it was now disposed to change its doctrine. On the contrary, I had every reason for affirming that it was the intention to make an effective blockade; and this was more practicable than at first sight might appear from the fact that there were few harbors along the coast, however great its extent, and these were not very easy of access. I thought, therefore, that even though the blockade might not be perfect, it would be sufficiently so to come within the legitimate construction of the term.

His lordship then alluded to the other point, which was, that the proclamation assigned no precise date for the commencement of the blockade, which he believed was necessary; but he presumed that that defect might be remedied at any time. To which I added that I did not doubt any such omission of form would be supplied as soon as it was pointed out.

His lordship then made some remarks upon the adoption of the tariff; to which I replied that, in my belief, that law was mainly passed as a revenue measure, with incidental protection; that it was not in any way aimed in a hostile spirit to foreign nations; and that the people of the United States would always buy from Great Britain as much as they could pay for, and generally a good deal more. This last remark raised a smile; and thus ended his lordship's series of inquiries.

Having thus disposed of these secondary questions, I returned once more to the charge, and asked him what answer I should return to the inquiry which I had been directed to make. In order to avoid any ambiguity, I took out of my pocket your despatch No. 4, and read to him the paragraph recapitulating the substance of Mr. Dallas's report of his interview, and the very last paragraph. I said that it was important to me that I should not make any mistake in reporting this part of the conversation; therefore I should beg him to furnish me with the precise language. He said that he did not himself know what he was to say. If it was expected of him to give any pledge of an absolute nature that his government would not at any future time, no matter what the circumstances might be, recognize an existing State in America, it was more than he could promise. If I wished an exact reply, my better way would be to address him the inquiry in writing. I said that I was well aware of that, but I had hoped that I might be saved the necessity of doing so. On reflection, he proposed to avoid that by offering to transmit to Lord Lyons directions to give such a reply to the President as, in his own opinion, might be satisfactory. To this arrangement I gave my assent, though not without some doubt whether I was doing right. In truth, if I were persuaded that her Majesty's government were really animated by a desire to favor the rebellion, I should demand a categorical answer; but thus far I see rather division of opinion, consequent upon the pressure of the commercial classes. Hence I preferred to give the short time demanded, as well as to place in the hands of the President himself the power to decide upon the sufficiency of the reply.

*   *   *   *   *   *

*   *   *   *   *   *

It may be as well to state that, both in matter and manner, the conference, which has been reported as fully and as accurately as my memory would permit, was conducted in the most friendly spirit.

   *   *   *   *   *   *

 *   *   *   *   *   *

I have the honor to be, sir, your obedient servant,

CHARLES FRANCIS ADAMS.

Hon. WILLIAM H. SEWARD,
   Secretary of State, Washington, D. C.

Mr. Adams to Mr. Seward.

[Extracts.]

No. 4.]   LEGATION OF THE UNITED STATES,
London, May 31, 1861.

SIR :

  *   *   *   *   *   *

  *   *   *   *   *   *

I have likewise to acknowledge the reception of a printed circular addressed to my predecessor, Mr. Dallas, and dated the 27th of April, 1861, transmitting the proclamation of the President declaring the blockade of the ports of Virginia and North Carolina. In this connexion it may be as well to call your attention to the manner in which these measures are viewed here, so far as it may be gathered from what is casually dropped by members of Parliament as well as what is published in the newspapers. A leading article in the Times newspaper of this morning is especially deserving of attention. It would seem from this that a scheme to overturn the old and recognized British law of blockade, through the means of a joint declaration of the European powers, somewhat after the fashion of the armed neutrality of the last century, is among the things now floating in the minds of people here. Great Britain, so long known and feared as the tyrant of the ocean, is now to transform herself into a champion of neutral rights and the freedom of navigation, even into the ports of all the world, with or without regard to the interests of the nations to whom they may belong.

   *   *   *   *   *   *

I beg to call your attention to the language used by Lord John Russell and by Mr. Gladstone in the debate in the House of Commons last evening, in relation to a passing remark of Sir John Ramsden upon American affairs on the preceding Monday. They indicate what I believe to be true, that the feeling toward the United States is improving in the higher circles here. It was never otherwise than favorable among the people at large. I was myself present and heard Sir John Ramsden on Monday night. His remark was partially cheered by the opposition, who were ready to receive anything favorably from a new convert ; but I have reason to believe that it met with decided condemnation from a large majority of the members. The proof of this was established last night in the manner in which the castigation of Mr. Gladstone, which I also witnessed, was listened to and approved. Sir John seems to have gained no laurels in this conflict. The ministry sustained themselves in the division last night, which is, I presume, the decisive test for the year. I believe this may be regarded as a favorable result to the

United States. I shall reserve some general observations on the subject for a separate despatch in the early part of next week.

I have the honor to be, sir, your obedient servant.

CHARLES FRANCIS ADAMS.

Hon. WILLIAM H. SEWARD,
Secretary of State.

Mr. Seward to Mr. Adams.

No. 14.]

DEPARTMENT OF STATE,
Washington, June 3, 1861.

SIR : Your despatch of May 17 (No. 1) has been received.

Your speech at Liverpool was equally prudent and happy. Your promptness in passing through the town to the seat of government, although to be regretted in some respects, is, in view of the circumstances, approved.

Every instruction you have received from this department is full of evidence of the fact that the principal danger in the present insurrection which the President has apprehended was that of foreign intervention, aid, or sympathy ; and especially of such intervention, aid, or sympathy on the part of the government of Great Britain.

The justice of this apprehension has been vindicated by the following facts, namely :

1. A guarded reserve on the part of the British secretary of state, when Mr. Dallas presented to him our protest against the recognition of the insurgents, which seemed to imply that, in some conditions, not explained to us, such a recognition might be made.

2. The contracting of an engagement by the government of Great Britain with that of France, without consulting us, to the effect that both governments should adopt one and the same course of procedure in regard to the insurrection.

3. Lord John Russell's announcement to Mr. Dallas that he was not unwilling to receive the so-called commissioners of the insurgents unofficially

4. The issue of the Queen's proclamation, remarkable, first, for the circumstances under which it was made, namely, on the very day of your arrival in London, which had been anticipated so far as to provide for your reception by the British secretary, but without affording you the interview promised before any decisive action should be adopted; secondly, the tenor of the proclamation itself, which seems to recognize, in a vague manner, indeed, but does seem to recognize, the insurgents as *belligerent* national *power.*

That proclamation, unmodified and unexplained, would leave us no alternative but to regard the government of Great Britain as questioning our free exercise of all the rights of self-defence guaranteed to us by our Constitution and the laws of nature and of nations to suppress the insurrection.

I should have proceeded at once to direct you to communicate to the British government the definitive views of the President on the grave subject, if there were not especial reasons for some little delay.

These reasons are, first, Mr. Thouvenel has informed our representative at Paris that the two governments of Great Britain and France were preparing, and would, without delay, address communications to this government concerning the attitude to be assumed by them in regard to the insurrection. Their communications are hourly expected.

Second. You have already asked, and, it is presumed, will have obtained, an interview with the British secretary, and will have been able to present the general views of this government, and to learn definitely the purposes of Great Britain in the matter, after it shall have learned how unsatisfactory the action of the British government hitherto has been to the government of the United States.

The President is solicitous to show his high appreciation of every demonstration of consideration for the United States which the British government feels itself at liberty to make. He instructs me, therefore, to say that the prompt and cordial manner in which you were received, under peculiar circumstances arising out of domestic afflictions which had befallen her Majesty and the secretary of state for foreign affairs, is very gratifying to this government.

A year ago the differences which had partially estranged the British and the American people from each other seemed to have been removed forever. It is painful to reflect that that ancient alienation has risen up again under circumstances which portend great social evils, if not disaster, to both countries.

Referring you to previous instructions, and reserving further directions until we shall have your own report of the attitude of the British government as defined by itself for our consideration,

I am, sir, respectfully, your obedient servant,

WILLIAM H. SEWARD.

CHARLES FRANCIS ADAMS, Esq., &c., &c., &c.

Mr. Adams to Mr. Seward.

[Extract.]

No. 5.]   LEGATION OF THE UNITED STATES,
                                                  London, June 7, 1861.

SIR: I have the honor to acknowledge the receipt of your several despatches, No. 7, of the 11th of May, with copies of the correspondence relating to the slave trade and to San Domingo ; No. 8, of the 20th, enclosing the commission of Neil McLachlan, esq., as consul at Leith ; and No. 9, of the 21st, enclosing the commission of Edward Leavenworth, esq., as consul at Sydney, New South Wales. These commissions have been duly transmitted to her Majesty's secretary for foreign affairs, with the customary request for recognition. The earlier papers have been carefully read, and will be made the subject of consideration at the next conference, which I purpose to ask of his lordship at an early day.

I think I can report with confidence a considerable amelioration of sentiment here towards the government of the United States. This may be partly ascribed to the impression made by the news received of vigorous and effective measures in America, and partly to a sense that the preceding action of her Majesty's ministers has been construed to mean more than they intended by it. It cannot be denied that it had opened a most grave question touching the use that might be made of all the ports of Great Britain as a shelter for captures by privateers purporting to be authorized by the rebellious States. After a careful examination of the subject, I had come to the conclusion that, without some further positive action, the preceding practice in this country would authorize the retention of such captures until condemned as prizes in some admiralty court set up by the insurgents at home and the sale of them afterwards. The effect of this, in giving them encouragement, can scarcely be estimated. It would at once enlist in their behalf most of the daring and desperate adventurers of every nation, whose sole object is plunder, and would initiate a struggle between a community of planters, who have nothing to lose on the ocean, and a commercial nation which whitens every sea with the sails of a peaceful navigation. That so serious a consequence as this was ever intended to flow from the precipitate act of the government here I did not believe. Hence it was with great satisfaction that I learned, on Monday, that the question would be proposed on that day by Mr. Forster in the House of Commons, which you will have seen before this in the record of the proceedings of that body, and that it would be fully answered by Lord John Russell on behalf of her Majesty's ministers. This answer, as since made, may be regarded as satisfactory, so far as it closes the door to one bad effect of the proclamation; but it does not remove the main difficulty of putting the legitimate and the spurious authority in the same category. Although in practice the operation is favorable to the former, in theory the admission of equality is equally vicious. The only consolation is to be found in the evident desire betrayed by the government here to avoid in any way a collision with the United States or any direct encouragement of the insurgents.

This is the day assigned for the consideration of the motion of Mr. Gregory, the member for Galway. I understand that he means to enter largely into the question of recognition of the confederates, and that he will probably be answered as fully. It is stated to me that the ministry are willing to have the discussion go on. For obvious reasons I do not think it advisable to attend the debate myself; but I shall take measures to obtain the best information of the actual state of feeling in the House from personal observation, and to transmit my own conclusions in the next despatch. Unfortunately it will be necessary to close the present one before evening, in order to be in time for the steamer.

* * * * * * * * *

I have the honor to be, sir, your obedient servant,

CHARLES FRANCIS ADAMS.

Hon. WILLIAM H. SEWARD,
  Secretary of State, Washington, D. C.

Mr. Seward to Mr. Adams.

No. 16.]
DEPARTMENT OF STATE,
Washington, June 8, 1861.

SIR: I enclose a copy of a note of this date addressed to Lord Lyons, which will dispel any uncertainty which the British government may entertain in regard to our recognition of a rule of international law which they may deem important.

I am, sir, respectfully, your obedient servant,

WILLIAM H. SEWARD.

CHARLES FRANCIS ADAMS, Esq., &c., &c., &c.

Mr. Seward to Lord Lyons.

DEPARTMENT OF STATE,
Washington, June 8, 1861.

MY LORD: I have the honor to acknowledge the receipt of your note of the 5th instant, with the accompanying papers, relative to a claim in the case of the cargo of the bark Winifred, a part of which is represented to belong to British subjects.

In reply, I regret that at this juncture I do not feel at liberty to interfere in the case, as it is understood that the usual proceedings in the prize court at New York have been set on foot against the vessel and her cargo.

If, however, that court shall be satisfied of the ownership by British subjects of the part of the cargo claimed, it cannot be doubted that restitution will be decreed, as this government recognizes the right of the property of a friendly nation in the vessels of an insurgent to be exempted from condemnation.

The papers which accompanied your note are herewith returned.

I have the honor to be, with the highest consideration, your lordship's most obedient servant,

WILLIAM H. SEWARD.

The Right Honorable Lord Lyons, &c., &c., &c.

Mr. Seward to Mr. Adams.

No. 15.]   DEPARTMENT OF STATE,
                                        Washington, June 8, 1861.

SIR: I have the pleasure of acknowledging the receipt of your despatch of May 21, (No. 2,) which contains a report of the conversation which you had held with Lord John Russell on the 18th day of that month.

This government insists, as all the world might have known that it must and would, under all circumstances, insist, on the integrity of the Union, as the chief element of national life. Since, after trials of every form of forbearance and conciliation, it has been rendered certain and apparent that this paramount and vital object can be saved only by our acceptance of civil war as an indispensable condition, that condition, with all its hazards and deplorable evils, has not been declined. The acceptance, however, is attended with a strong desire and fixed purpose that the war shall be as short and accompanied by as little suffering as possible. Foreign intervention, aid, or sympathy in favor of the insurgents, especially on the part of Great Britain, manifestly could only protract and aggravate the war. Accordingly, Mr. Dallas, under instructions from the President, in an interview conceded to him by the British secretary of state for foreign affairs, presented our protest against any such intervention.

Lord John Russell answered with earnestness that there was not in the British government the least desire to grasp at any advantages which might be supposed to arise from the unpleasant domestic differences in the United States, but, on the contrary, that they would be highly gratified if those differences were adjusted, and the Union restored to its former unbroken position.

Mr. Dallas then, as he reported to us, endeavored to impress upon his lordship how important it must be that Great Britain and France should abstain, at least for a considerable time, from doing what, by encouraging groundless hopes, (of the insurgents,) would widen a breach still thought capable of being closed; but his lordship seemed to think that the matter was not ripe for decision, one way or another, and remarked that what he had already said was all that at present it was in his power to say.

Upon this report you were instructed to inform her Britannic Majesty's government that the President regarded the reply made by his lordship to Mr. Dallas's suggestion as possibly indicating a policy which this government would be obliged to deem injurious to its rights, and derogating from its dignity. This government thought the reply of the secretary unjustifiably abrupt and reserved. That abruptness and reserve unexplained, left us under a seeming necessity of inferring that the British government might be contemplating a policy of encouragement to the insurgents which would widen the breach here which we believed it possible to heal if such encouragement should not be extended. A vital interest obliged the United States to seek explanation, or to act on the inference it thus felt itself obliged to adopt.

Your despatch of the 21st of May, (No. 2,) which has just been received, shows how you have acquitted yourself of the duty imposed upon you. After stating our complaint to his lordship, you very properly asked an elucidation of his meaning in the reply to which exception had been taken by us, and very rightly, as we think, asked whether it was the intention of her Majesty's ministers to adopt a policy which would have the effect to widen, if not to make irreparable, a breach which we believe yet to be entirely manageable by ourselves. His lordship disclaimed any such intention. A friendly argument, however, then arose between the secretary and yourself concerning what should be the form of the answer to us which his lordship could properly give, and which would, at the same time, be satisfactory to this government. The question was finally solved in the most generous manner by the proposition of his lordship that he would instruct Lord Lyons to give such a reply to the President as might, in his own opinion, be satisfactory, which proposition you accepted.

I hasten to say, by direction of the President, that your course in this proceeding is fully approved. This government has no disposition to lift questions of even national pride or sensibility up to the level of diplomatic controversy, because it earnestly and ardently desires to maintain peace, harmony, and cordial friendship with Great Britain. Lord John Russell's proposition, by authorizing the President to put the most favorable construction possible upon the response which was deemed exceptionable, removes the whole difficulty without waiting for the intervention of Lord Lyons. You will announce this conclusion to Lord John Russell, and inform him that the settlement of the affair in so friendly a spirit affords this government sincere satisfaction.

Your conversation with the British secretary incidentally brought into debate the Queen's late proclamation, (which seems to us designed to raise the insurgents to the level of a belligerent state;) the language employed by her Majesty's ministers in both houses of Parliament, the tone of the public press, and of private opinion, and especially a speech of the lord chancellor, in which he had characterized the insurgents as a belligerent State, and the civil war which they are waging against the United States as *justum bellum.*

The opinions which you expressed on these matters, and their obvious tendency to encourage the insurrection and to protract and aggravate the civil war, are just, and meet our approbation. At the same time, it is the purpose of this government, if possible, consistently with the national welfare and honor, to have no serious controversy with Great Britain at all; and if this shall ultimately prove impossible, then to have both the defensive position and the clear right on our side. With this view, this government, as you were made aware by my despatch No. 10, has determined to pass over without official complaint the publications of the British press, manifestations of adverse individual opinion in social life, and the speeches of British statesmen, and even those of her Majesty's ministers in Parliament, so long as they are not authoritatively adopted by her Majesty's government. We honor and respect the freedom of debate, and the freedom of

the press. We indulge no apprehensions of danger to our rights and interests from any discussion to which they may be subjected, in either form, in
any place. Sure as we are that the transaction now going on in our country
involves the progress of civilization and humanity, and equally sure that
our attitude in it is right, and no less sure that our press and our statesmen
are equal in ability and influence to any in Europe, we shall have no cause to
grieve if Great Britain shall leave to us the defence of the independence of
nations and the rights of human nature.

My despatch No. 14 presented four distinct grounds on which this government apprehended a policy on the part of her Majesty's government to
intervene in favor of the insurgents, or to lend them aid and sympathy. The
first ground was the reserve practiced by the British secretary for foreign
affairs in his conversation with Mr. Dallas, referred to in the earlier part of
this despatch. I have already stated that the explanations made and offered
by Lord John Russell have altogether removed this ground from debate.

The second was the contracting of an engagement by the government of
Great Britain with that of France, without consulting us, to the effect that
both governments would adopt one and the same course of proceeding in
regard to the subject of intervention in our domestic affairs. You were informed in my despatch No. 10 that, as this proceeding did not necessarily
imply hostile feelings towards the United States, we should not formally
complain of it, but should rest content with a resolution to hold intercourse
only with each of those States severally, giving due notice to both that the
circumstance that a concert between the two powers in any proposition each
might offer to us would not modify in the least degree the action of the
United States upon it.

The third ground was Lord John Russell's announcement to Mr. Dallas
that he was not unwilling to receive the so-called commissioners of the insurgents unofficially. On this point you already have instructions, to which
nothing need now be added.

The fourth ground is the Queen's proclamation, exceptionable first for the
circumstances under which it was issued, and secondly, for the matter of that
important state paper.   ·

My despatch No. 14 apprised you of our reason for expecting a direct
communication on this subject from her Majesty's government. I reserve
instructions on this fourth ground, as I did in that despatch, expecting to
discuss it fully when the promised direct communication shall bring it authoritatively before this government in the form chosen by the British government itself.

My silence on the subject of the defence of that proclamation made by
Lord John Russell in his conversation with you being grounded on that
motive for delay, it is hardly necessary to say that we are not to be regarded
as conceding any positions which his lordship assumed, and which you so
ably contested on the occasion referred to in your despatch. Your argument
on that point is approved by the President.

The British government having committed the subject of the proposed
modifications of international law on the subject of the right of neutrals in
maritime war to Lord Lyons before you were prepared by our instructions
to present the subject to that government, no objection is now seen to the
discussion of that matter here. No communication on any subject herein
discussed has yet been received from Lord Lyons. Despatches which you
must have received before this time will have enabled you to give entire
satisfaction to his lordship concerning the blockade. We claim to have a
right to close the ports which have been seized by insurrectionists, for the
purpose of suppressing the attempted revolution, and no one could justly

complain if we had done so decisively and peremptorily. In resorting to the milder and very lenient form of the blockade, we have been governed by a desire to avoid imposing hardships unnecessarily onerous upon foreign as well as domestic commerce. The President's proclamation was a notice of the intention to blockade, and it was provided that ample warning should be given to vessels approaching and vessels seeking to leave the blockaded ports before capture should be allowed. The blockade from the time it takes effect is everywhere rendered actual and effective.

Your remarks on the subject of the late tariff law were judicious. The subject of revenue policy in the altered condition of affairs is not unlikely to receive the attention of Congress.

We are gratified by the information you have given us of the friendly spirit which has thus far marked the deportment and conversation of the British government in your official intercourse with it.

I am, sir, respectfully, your obedient servant,

WILLIAM H. SEWARD.

CHARLES FRANCIS ADAMS, Esq., &c., &c., &c.

Mr. Adams to Mr. Seward.

LONDON, *June* 8, 1861.

DEAR SIR: I send herewith a copy of the London Times of this morning, containing an account of the termination of Mr. Gregory's movement.

Subsequent events only can now do anything to improve the prospect of the confederates at this court. Yours, &c.,

C. F. ADAMS.

Hon. W. H. SEWARD, *Washington, D. C.*

Mr. Adams to Mr. Seward.

[Extracts.]

No. 8.]

LEGATION OF THE UNITED STATES,
London, June 14, 1861.

SIR: I have to acknowledge the reception of your despatches No. 10, dated the 21st of May, and No. 11, dated on the 24th, with a copy of a letter from Mr. O. Vandenburgh, and also a printed circular from the department of the 20th of May, relating to purchases made here of articles contraband of war.

The intelligence of the feeling expressed in America upon the reception of the Queen's proclamation was fully expected by me, so that it excited no surprise, and much of the course of your argument in your despatch will be found to have been already adopted in my conference with Lord John Russell, an account of which is before this time in your hands.

*   *   *   *   *   *   *   *   *

However this may be, my duty was plain. I applied for an interview with Lord John Russell, and he appointed one for ten o'clock on Wednesday, the 12th, at his own house. After some slight preliminary talk, I observed to him that I had been instructed to press upon her Majesty's government the expediency of early action on the subject of privateering; that in the present state of excitement in the United States consequent upon the measures which it had felt it necessary to adopt, I did not know of anything which would be so likely to allay it as an agreement on this point. His lordship then said that he did not know whether I knew it, but the fact was that Mr. Dayton had made a proposition to France for negotiation on the basis of the articles as agreed upon in Paris. France had communicated the fact through her minister, the Compte de Flahault; and he intimated' that there had been a cabinet conversation on the subject, without arriving at a decision. I then referred to what had passed at our former interview. I mentioned my proposal to negotiate, and the inclination shown by his lordship to leave the subject with Lord Lyons, with authority to arrange the only point in dispute as the government at Washington might desire. There I had left the matter. His lordship replied that he did not mean to be quite so understood. His intention was to say, that having agreed upon the three articles, he should be ready to consent to the total omission of the fourth article, if that would be agreeable at Washington. I said that I had not so understood him, and from my present recollection, I am confident that my report of his language was not incorrect.

*   *   *   *   *   *   *   *   *

I next approached the most delicate portion of my task. I descanted upon the irritation produced in America by the Queen's proclamation, upon the construction almost universally given to it, as designed to aid the insurgents by raising them to the rank of a belligerent State, and upon the very decided tone taken by the President in my despatches in case any such design was really entertained. I added that from my own observation of what had since occurred here, I had not been able to convince myself of the existence of such a design. But it was not to be disguised that the fact of the continued stay of the pseudo commissioners in this city, and still more the knowledge that they had been admitted to more or less interviews with his lordship, was calculated to excite uneasiness. Indeed, it had already given great dissatisfaction to my government. I added, as moderately as I could, that in all frankness any further protraction of this relation could scarcely fail to be viewed by us as hostile in spirit, and to require some corresponding action accordingly.

His lordship then reviewed the course of Great Britain. He explained the mode in which they had consulted with France, prior to any action at all, as to the reception of the deputation from the so-called Confederate States. It had been the custom both in France and here to receive such persons unofficially for a long time back. Poles, Hungarians, Italians, &c., &c., had been allowed interviews, to hear what they had to say. But this did not imply recognition in their case any more than in ours. He added that he had seen the gentlemen once some time ago, and once more some time since; he had no expectation of seeing them any more.

*   *   *   *   *   *   *   *   *

I shall continue my relations here until I discover some action apparently in conflict with it, or receive specific orders from the department dictating an opposite course.

I ventured to repeat my regret that the proclamation had been so hastily issued, and adverted to the fact that it seemed contrary to the agreement said to have been proposed by Mr. Dallas and concurred in by his lordship, to postpone all action until I should arrive, possessed with all the views of the new administration. But still, though I felt that much mischief had ensued in the creation of prejudices in the United States, not now easy to be eradicated, I was not myself disposed in any part of my conduct to aggravate the evil. My views had been much modified by opportunities of more extended conversation with persons of weight in Great Britain, by the improved tone of the press, by subsequent explanations in Parliament, by the prohibition of all attempts to introduce prizes into British ports, and, lastly, by the unequivocal expression of sentiment in the case of Mr. Gregory when the time came for him to press his motion of recognition. I trusted that nothing new might occur to change the current again, for nothing was so unfortunate as the effect of a recurrence of reciprocal irritations, however trifling, between countries, in breaking up the good understanding which it was always desirable to preserve.

His lordship agreed to this, but remarked that he could not but think the complaint of the proclamation, though natural enough perhaps at this moment, was really ill founded. He went over the ground once more which he occupied in the former interview—the necessity of doing something to relieve the officers of their ships from the responsibility of treating these persons as pirates if they met them on the seas. For his part, he could not believe the United States would persevere in the idea of hanging them, for it was not in consonance with their well-known character. But what would be their own situation if they should be found practicing upon a harsher system than the Americans themselves.

Here was a very large territory—a number of States—and people counted by millions, who were in a state of actual war. The fact was undeniable and the embarrassment unavoidable. Under such circumstances the law officers of the crown advised the policy which had been adopted. It was designed only as a preventive to immediate evils. The United States should not have thought hard of it. They meant to be entirely neutral.

I replied that we asked no more than that. We desired no assistance. Our objection to this act was that it was practically not an act of neutrality. It had depressed the spirits of the friends of the government. It had raised the courage of the insurgents. We construed it as adverse, because we could not see the necessity of such immediate haste. These people were not a navigating people. They had not a ship on the ocean. They had made no prizes, so far as I knew, excepting such as they had caught by surprises. Even now, I could not learn that they had fitted out anything more than a few old steamboats, utterly unable to make any cruise on the ocean, and scarcely strong enough to bear a cannon of any calibre. But it was useless to go over this any more. The thing was now done. All that we could hope was that the later explanations would counteract the worst effects that we had reason to apprehend from it ; and, at any rate, there was one compensation, the act had released the government of the United States from responsibility for any misdeeds of the rebels towards Great Britain. If any of their people should capture or maltreat a British vessel on the ocean, the reclamation must be made only upon those who had authorized the wrong. The United States would not be liable.

I added that I could not close the interview without one word upon a subject on which I had no instructions. I saw by the newspapers an account of a considerable movement of troops to Canada. In our situation this would naturally excite attention at home, and I was therefore desirous to learn whether they were ordered with any reference to possible difficulties with us. His lordship said that the country had been denuded of troops for some time back, and it was regarded only as a proper measure of precaution, in the present disordered condition of things in the United States, to restore a part of them. He said he did not know but what we might do something. He intimated a little feeling of uneasiness at the mission of Mr. Ashmun, without any notice given to them of his purposes ; and he likewise said something about a threat uttered by yourself to Lord Lyons to seize a British vessel on Lake Ontario without ceremony. To this I replied, that inasmuch as I had understood Mr. Ashmun's mission had been made known to the governor of Canada, it did not seem to me that it could be of much concealed significance ; and that as to the other matter, if there was any reality in the threat, it surely was an odd way of proceeding to furnish at once the warning in time to provide against its execution.

*   *   *   *   *   *   *   *   *

I did not touch at all on the subject of the blockade, as referred to in your despatch No. 10, for the reason that I do not now understand the government as disposed in any way to question its validity or to obstruct it. On the contrary, his lordship, incidentally referring to it in this interview, said that instructions had been sent out to the naval officers in command to respect it, and never themselves to seek to enter any of the ports blockaded, unless from some urgent necessity to protect British persons or property.

I have the honor to be, sir, your obedient servant,

CHARLES FRANCIS ADAMS.

Mr. Seward to Mr. Adams.

No. 21.]   DEPARTMENT OF STATE,
Washington, June 19, 1861.

SIR: On the 15th day of June instant, Lord Lyons, the British minister, and Mr. Mercier, the French minister, residing here, had an appointed interview with me. Each of those representatives proposed to read to me an instruction which he had received from his government, and to deliver me a copy if I should desire it. I answered, that in the present state of the correspondence between their respective governments and that of the United States, I deemed it my duty to know the characters and effects of the instructions, respectively, before I could consent that they should be officially communicated to this department. The ministers therefore, confidentially, and very frankly, submitted the papers to me for preliminary inspection. After having examined them so far as to understand their purport, I declined to hear them read, or to receive official notice of them.

I proceed now to give you our reasons for this course, that you may, if you find it necessary or expedient, communicate them to the government of Great Britain.

When we received official information that an understanding was existing between the British and French governments that they would take one and the same course concerning the insurrection which has occurred in this country, involving the question of recognizing the independence of a revolutionary organization, we instructed you to inform the British government that we had expected from both of those powers a different course of proceeding. We added, however, that insomuch as the proposed concert of action between them did not necessarily imply any unfriendliness of purpose or of disposition, we should not complain of it, but that we should insist in this case, as in all others, on dealing with each of those powers alone, and that their agreement to act together would not at all affect the course which we should pursue. Adhering to this decision, we have not made the concert of the two powers a ground of objection to the reading of the instruction with which Lord Lyons was charged.

That paper purports to contain a decision at which the British government has arrived, to the effect that this country is divided into two belligerent parties, of which this government represents one, and that Great Britain assumes the attitude of a neutral between them.

This government could not, consistently with a just regard for the sovereignty of the United States, permit itself to debate these novel and extraordinary positions with the government of her Britannic Majesty; much less can we consent that that government shall announce to us a decision derogating from that sovereignty, at which it has arrived without previously conferring with us upon the question. The United States are still solely and exclusively sovereign within the territories they have lawfully acquired and long possessed, as they have always been. They are at peace with all the world, as, with unimportant exceptions, they have always been. They are living under the obligations of the law of nations, and of treaties with Great Britain, just the same now as heretofore; they are, of course, the friend of Great Britain, and they insist that Great Britain shall remain their friend now just as she has hitherto been. Great Britain, by virtue of these relations, is a stranger to parties and sections in this country, whether they are loyal to the United States or not, and Great Britain can neither rightfully qualify the sovereignty of the United States, nor concede, nor recognize any rights, or interests, or power of any party, State, or section, in contravention to the unbroken sovereignty of the federal Union. What is now seen in this country is the occurrence, by no means peculiar, but frequent in all countries, more frequent even in Great Britain than here, of an armed insurrection engaged in attempting to overthrow the regularly-constituted and established government. There is, of course, the employment of force by the government to suppress the insurrection, as every other government necessarily employs force in such cases. But these incidents by no means constitute a state of war impairing the sovereignty of the government, creating belligerent sections, and entitling foreign States to intervene or to act as neutrals between them, or in any other way to cast off their lawful obligations to the nation thus for the moment disturbed. Any other principle than this would be to resolve government everywhere into a thing of accident and caprice, and ultimately all human society into a state of perpetual war.

We do not go into any argument of fact or of law in support of the positions we have thus assumed. They are simply the suggestions of the instinct of self-defence, the primary law of human action, not more the law of individual than of national life.

This government is sensible of the importance of the step it takes in declining to receive the communication in question. It hopes and believes, however, that it need not disturb the good relations which have hitherto subsisted between the two countries which, more than any other nations, have need to live together in harmony and friendship.

We believe that Great Britain has acted inadvertently, and under the influence of apprehensions of danger to her commerce, which either are exaggerated or call for fidelity on her part to her habitual relations to the United States, instead of a hasty attempt to change those relations.

Certainly this government has exerted itself to the utmost to prevent Great Britain from falling into the error of supposing that the United States could consent to any abatement of their sovereignty in the present emergency. It is, we take leave to think, the common misfortune of the two countries that Great Britain was not content to wait before despatching the instruction in question, until you had been received by her Majesty's government, and had submitted the entirely just, friendly, and liberal overtures with which you were charged.

Although the paper implies, without affirming, that the insurgents of this

country possess some belligerent rights, it does not name, specify, or indicate one such right. It confines itself to stating what the British government require or expect the United States to do. Virtually, it asks us to
concede to Great Britain the principles laid down in the declaration of the
congress held at Paris in 1856. It asks indeed a little less, certainly nothing
more or different from this, The British government ask this of us to-day,
the 15th of June, in ignorance of the fact that we had, so early as the 25th
of April, instructed you to tender, without reservation, to Great Britain our
accession, pure and simple, to that declaration. We have all the while, since
that instruction was sent forth, been ready, as we now are ready, to accede
to the declaration, where and whenever Great Britain may be ready and
willing to receive it. The argument contained in the instruction seems,
therefore, to have been as unnecessary and irrelevant as it is unacceptable.
Lord Lyons thinks that his instructions do not authorize him to enter into
convention with us here. You will inform the government of Great Britain
of the fact, and, if they prefer, you will enter into the convention at London.

Of course it is understood that the concessions herein made do not affect
or impair the right of the United States to suppress the insurrection as well
by maritime as by land operations, and for this purpose to exclude all commerce from such of the ports as may have fallen into the hands of the insurgents, either by closing the ports directly or by the more lenient means of a
blockade, which we have already adopted.

It is thus seen that, in the present case, there is only an embarrassment
resulting from the similar designs of the two governments to reach one common object by different courses without knowledge of each others dispositions in that respect. There is nothing more. We propose, as a nation at
peace, to give to Great Britain as a friend what she as a neutral demands of
us, a nation at war. We rejoice that it happens so. We are anxious to
avoid all causes of misunderstanding with Great Britain; to draw closer, instead of breaking, the existing bonds of amity and friendship. There is
nothing good or great which both nations may not expect to attain or effect
if they may remain friends. It would be a hazardous day for both the
branches of the British race when they should determine to try how much
harm each could do the other.

We do not forget that, although thus happily avoiding misunderstanding
on the present occasion, Great Britain may in some way hereafter do us
wrong or injury by adhering to the speculative views of the rights and duties
of the two governments which she has proposed to express. But we believe
her to be sincere in the good wishes for our welfare, which she has so constantly avowed, and we will not, therefore, suffer ourselves to anticipate occasions for difference which, now that both nations fully understand each
other, may be averted or avoided.

One point remains. The British government while declining, out of regard to our natural sensibility, to propose mediation for the settlement of
the differences which now unhappily divide the American people, have nevertheless expressed, in a very proper manner, their willingness to undertake the
kindly duty of mediation, if we should desire it. The President expects you
to say on this point to the British government, that we appreciate this generous and friendly demonstration; but that we cannot solicit or accept mediation from any, even the most friendly quarter. The conditions of society here,
the character of our government, the exigencies of the country, forbid that
any dispute arising among us should ever be referred to foreign arbitration.
We are a republican and American people. The Constitution of our government furnishes all needful means for the correction or removal of any possible political evil. Adhering strictly as we do to its directions, we shall

surmount all our present complications, and preserve the government complete, perfect, and sound, for the benefit of future generations. But the integrity of any nation is lost, and its fate becomes doubtful, whenever strange hands, and instruments unknown to the Constitution, are employed to perform the proper functions of the people, established by the organic laws of the State.

Hoping to have no occasion hereafter to speak for the hearing of friendly nations upon the topics which I have now discussed, I add a single remark by way of satisfying the British government that it will do wisely by leaving us to manage and settle this domestic controversy in our own way.

The fountains of discontent in any society are many, and some lie much deeper than others. Thus far this unhappy controversy has disturbed only those which are nearest the surface. There are others which lie still deeper that may yet remain, as we hope, long undisturbed. If they should be reached, no one can tell how or when they could be closed. It was foreign intervention that opened and that alone could open similar fountains in the memorable French revolution.

I am, sir, respectfully, your obedient servant,

WILLIAM H. SEWARD.

Charles F. Adams, &c., &c., &c.

Mr. Adams to Mr. Seward.

[Extracts]

No. 9.]
Legation of the United States,
London, June 21, 1861.

Sir: *   *   *   *   *   *   *   *
            *   *   *   *   *   *   *   *

I have not deemed it necessary to ask a special interview to communicate to Lord John Russell the sense entertained by the President of the manner of my reception here, as directed in yours of the 3d of June. Presuming it to be altogether likely that another despatch, prepared after the reception of my No. 2, is now near at hand, I have preferred to wait and see if that may not give me other matter to submit at the same time.

The intelligence received from the United States of the effect produced by the reception of the Queen's proclamation has not been without its influence upon opinion here. Whilst people of all classes unite in declaring that such a measure was unavoidable, they are equally earnest in disavowing any inferences of want of good will which may have been drawn from it. They affect to consider our complaints as very unreasonable, and are profuse in their professions of sympathy with the government in its present struggle. This is, certainly, a very great change from the tone prevailing when I first arrived. It is partly to be ascribed to the accounts of the progress of the war, but still more to the publications in the London *Times* of the letters of its special correspondent. There is no longer any floating doubt of the capacity of the government to sustain itself, or any belief that the insurgents will make their own terms of accommodation. The idea still remains quite general that there will never be any actual conflict, and it is connected in many cases with an apprehension that the reunion may be cemented upon the basis of hostile measures against Great Britain. Indeed, such has been the motive hinted at by more than one person of influence as guiding the policy of the President himself. Whenever such a suggestion has been

made to me, I have been careful to discountenance it altogether, and to affirm that the struggle was carried on in good faith, and from motives not subject to be affected by mere considerations of policy, or by temporary emotions. More especially have I endeavored to disavow any "arrière pensée" which has the effect to confirm the suspicion of our sincerity, I regret to say, by far too much disseminated.   *   *   *   *   *
*   *   *   *   *   *   *   *
I am now earnestly assured on all sides that the sympathy with the government of the United States is general; that the indignation felt in America is not founded in reason; that the British desire only to be perfectly neutral, giving no aid nor comfort to the insurgents. I believe that this sentiment is now growing to be universal. It inspires her Majesty's ministers, and is not without its effect on the opposition. Neither party would be so bold as to declare its sympathy with a cause based upon the extension of slavery, for that would at once draw upon itself the indignation of the great body of the people. But the development of a positive spirit in the opposite direction will depend far more upon the degree in which the arm of the government enforces obedience than upon any absolute affinity in sentiments. Our brethren in this country, after all, are much disposed to fall in with the opinion of Voltaire, that "Dieu est toujours sur le coté des gros canons." General Scott and an effective blockading squadron will be the true agents to keep the peace abroad, as well as to conquer one at home. In the meanwhile the self-styled commissioners of the insurgents have transferred their labors to Paris, where, I am told, they give out what they could not venture publicly to say here, that this government will recognize them as a State. The prediction may be verified, it is true; but it is not now likely to happen, under any other condition than the preceding assent of the United States.
I have the honor to be your obedient servant,
CHARLES FRANCIS ADAMS.
Hon. William H. Seward,
Secretary of State.

Mr. Adams to Mr. Seward.

[Extracts.]

No. 10.]   Legation of the United States,
London, June 28, 1861.
Sir: *   *   *   *   *   *   *
My interview with his lordship was intended only to express to him the views entertained by the President, as communicated to me in your despatches No. 14 and No. 15 of the reports made by me of our first conference. His lordship said that he had just received despatches as late as the 15th, communicating the same information, and that Lord Lyons had learned, through another member of the diplomatic corps, that no further expression of opinion on the subject in question would be necessary. This led to the most frank and pleasant conversation which I have yet had with his lordship, in which we reviewed the various points of difficulty that had arisen in a manner too desultory to admit of reporting, excepting in the general result.   *   *
*   *   *   *   *   *   *   *   *   *   *   *   *
I added that I believed the popular feeling in the United States would subside the moment that all the later action on this side was known. There

was but a single drawback remaining, which was what I could not but regard as the inopportune despatch of the Great Eastern with the troops for Canada. He said that this was a mere precaution against times of trouble.

*   *   *   *   *   *   *   *

His lordship then said something about difficulties in New Granada, and the intelligence that the insurgents had undertaken to close several of their ports. But the law officers here told him that this could not be done as against foreign nations, excepting by the regular form of blockade. He did not know what we thought about it, but he had observed that some such plan was said to be likely to be adopted, at the coming meeting of Congress, in regard to the ports of those whom we considered as insurgents. I replied that such was one of the several projects reported at the last session of Congress, to which I was a member, but I had heard some serious constitutional objections raised against it. My own opinion was that the blockade would be persevered in, which would obviate all difficulty.

On the whole, I think I can say that the relations of the two countries are gradually returning to a more friendly condition. My own reception has been all that I could desire. I attach value to this, however, only as it indicates the establishment of a policy that will keep us at peace during the continuance of the present convulsion.

I have the honor to be, sir, your obedient servant,

CHARLES FRANCIS ADAMS.

Hon. WILLIAM H. SEWARD,
    Secretary of State, Washington, D. C.

Mr. Seward to Mr. Adams.

No. 32.]

DEPARTMENT OF STATE,
Washington, July 1, 1861.

SIR: Your despatch No. 8 (dated June 14) has been received.

My despatch, No. 21, of 19th ultimo, has anticipated the matter you have discussed in the paper before me. It remains only to say that while we would prefer to add Mr. Marcy's amendment, exempting private property of non-belligerents from confiscation in maritime war, and desire you to stipulate to that effect if you can, yet we are, nevertheless, ready and willing to accede to the declaration of the congress of Paris, if the amendment cannot be obtained. In other words, we stand on the instructions contained in my aforesaid despatch.

We, as you are well aware, have every desire for a good understanding with the British government. It causes us no concern that the government sends a naval force into the Gulf and a military force into Canada. We can have no designs hostile to Great Britain so long as she does not, officially or unofficially, recognize the insurgents or render them aid or sympathy. We regard the measures of precaution on her part, to which I have alluded, as consequences of the misunderstanding of our rights and her own real relation towards us that she seemed precipitately to adopt, before she heard the communication with which you were charged on our behalf. These consequences may be inconvenient to herself, but are not all occasion of irritation to the United States. Under present circumstances, the more effectually Great Britain guards her possessions and her commerce in this quarter the better we shall be satisfied. If she should change her course and do us any injury, which we have not the least idea now that she purposes to do, we should not be deterred from vindicating our rights and our unbroken sovereignty against all the armies and navies that she could send here.

Before the Queen's proclamation was issued, and at the moment when privateers were invited and a naval force announced as being organized by the insurrectionists, it was reported to this government that the iron steamer Peerless, lying at Toronto, had been sold to insurgents to be used as a privateer to prey upon our commerce, and that she was, nevertheless, to pass under British papers and the British flag down the St. Lawrence to be delivered over to a pirate commander in the open sea. It was said that the governor general declined to interfere. I asked Lord Lyons to request the governor general of Canada to look into the facts, and prevent the departure of the vessel if he should find the report to be true. Lord Lyons answered that he had no authority to do so. I then said that I should direct our naval forces to seize and detain the vessel if they should have good reason to believe the facts reported to be true, and to refer the parties interested to this government. I did this at once, and his lordship protested. Afterwards, as we understand, the governor general did interfere, and the Peerless was prevented from sailing until the danger of her being converted into a pirate was prevented. Here the matter ended. Certainly the British government could not expect us to permit the St. Lawrence to become a harbor for buccaneers. Had the vessel been seized or detained we should at once have avowed the act and tendered any satisfaction to the British government if it should appear that the character of the vessel had been misunderstood.

Mr. Ashmun went to Canada to watch and prevent just such transactions as the sale or fitting out of the Peerless for a pirate would have been. It was not supposed that his visit there would be thought objectionable, or could give any uneasiness to the British government. Lord Lyons here viewed the subject in a different light and complained of it. I instantly recalled Mr. Ashmun.

These are the two grievances presented to you by Lord John Russell. I trust that the British government will be satisfied that in both cases we were only taking care that the peace of the two countries should not be disturbed through the unlawful action of covetous and ill-disposed persons on the border which separates them.

I conclude with the remark that the British government can never expect to induce the United States to acquiesce in her assumed position of this government as divided in any degree into two powers for war more than for peace. At the same time, if her Majesty's government shall continue to practice absolute forbearance from any interference in our domestic affairs, we shall not be captious enough to inquire what name it gives to that forbearance, or in what character it presents itself before the British nation in doing so. We hold ourselves entitled to regard the forbearance as an act of a friendly power, acting unconsciously of a domestic disturbance among us, of which friendly States can take no cognizance. On this point our views are not likely to undergo any change. In maintaining this position we are sure we do nothing derogating from the dignity of the British government, while we inflexibly maintain and preserve the just rights and the honor of the United States.

I am, sir, respectfully, your obedient servant,

WILLIAM H. SEWARD.

Charles Francis Adams, Esq., &c., &c., &c.

Mr. Adams to Mr. Seward.

[Extract.]

No. 14.] 　　　　　　　　　　　　　LEGATION OF THE UNITED STATES,
　　　　　　　　　　　　　　　　　　　　　London, July 12, 1861.

SIR: Your despatches, from No. 2 to No. 25, inclusive, were received at this office early in the present week.

I have read the first of these papers, containing further instructions to me, and dated on the 21st of June, with close attention. My prevailing feeling has been one of profound surprise at the course of this government throughout the present difficulty. First. It prepares, in the form of an instruction to Lord Lyons, a paper to be presented to you, among other things "virtually asking you to concede the principles laid down in the declaration of the congress held in Paris in 1856." Secondly. When in obedience to my instructions I propose to offer a project to Lord John Russell, actually designed to do the very thing desired, I am told the directions have already been sent out to Lord Lyons to arrange the matter on the basis proposed by the American government of the three articles, omitting the fourth altogether. Thirdly. Lord Lyons expresses the opinion to you that his instructions do not authorize him to enter into a convention with you in the United States. Fourthly. When, concurrently with these events, Mr. Dayton proposes to negotiate on the same basis with France, I am informed that this proposal has been communicated to the ministry here, and that no definite conclusion had been arrived at. I must say that a more remarkable series of misunderstandings has seldom come within my observation.

I now propose to bring this matter to a distinct issue. To this end I have addressed a letter to Lord John Russell, to know whether, under the renewed instructions of the present despatch, he is disposed to open the negotiation here. The advantage of this will be that I shall get an answer in writing, which will admit of no misconception. A copy of that answer will be forwarded so soon as it is received.

　*　　　*　　　*　　　*　　　*　　　*　　　*　　　*　　　*

I have the honor to be, sir, your obedient servant,
　　　　　　　　　　　　　　　　　　　CHARLES FRANCIS ADAMS.
Hon. WILLIAM H. SEWARD, &c., &c., &c.

Mr. Adams to Mr. Seward.

No. 17.] 　　　　　　　　　　　　　LEGATION OF THE UNITED STATES,
　　　　　　　　　　　　　　　　　　　　　London, July 19, 1861.

SIR : Your despatch, No. 32, dated the 1st of July, relating to the communications between the two governments respecting the declaration of the convention at Paris, in 1856, reached me soon after I had addressed a formal letter to Lord John Russell, designed to bring the matter to a definite point. In my No. 14, dated on the 12th, I stated the fact that I had sent such a letter, and I promised that I would forward his lordship's answer so soon as it should be received. I now transmit copies of my letter and of the answer.

It is not a little singular that his lordship's memory of what passed at our first interview on this subject should differ so widely from mine. It would seem, by his account, that he had been the first to mention the instructions to Lord Lyons to propose a negotiation on the subject of the declaration of Paris, and that I had thereupon expressed the opinion that it would be well to leave it in your hands, in which opinion he fully concurred.

Ex. Doc. 1——8

On my side, I am quite certain that the discussion which actually took place between us involved a wholly different class of topics of a very critical nature, and never touched upon the declaration of Paris, until it had exhausted itself on the others. It was by that time late, and I then opened the new subject by remarking that there would be no time to do more than to allude to it at this conference. I first mentioned the fact that I had instructions to propose a negotiation upon the disputed point of the Paris declarations, and the necessary powers to perfect an agreement, if her Majesty's government were disposed to enter into it. It was this proposal that elicited the explanations of his lordship as to what had been already done, and the expression of an opinion that the instructions sent to Lord Lyons were of such a kind as to make some agreement on your side so very likely as to render any treatment of the same matter here unadvisable; and . it was then that I concurred in his opinion.

As things now stand, perhaps this difference of recollection in the present instance may not be material. But there might be cases in which it would be of so much moment that I think hereafter I shall prefer, upon essential points, to conduct the affairs of this legation a little more in writing than I have heretofore thought necessary.

At the hour appointed in his note, I waited upon his lordship for the first time, at his official residence in Downing street. After comparing our respective remembrance of the facts in dispute, I went on to repeat what I maintained I had at first proposed, to wit: that I was ready to negotiate if her Majesty's government were so disposed. To that end I had brought my powers, and also the project of a convention, copies of both of which papers I offered to leave with him. He remarked that at this stage it was not necessary to look at the powers. The other one he took and examined. The first remark which he made was that it was essentially the declaration of Paris. He had never known until now that the government of the United States were disposed to accede to it. He was sure that I had never mentioned it. To this I assented, but observed that the reason why I had not done so was that my government had directed me to make a preliminary inquiry, and that was to know whether her Majesty's ministers were disposed to enter into any negotiation at all. It was because of my understanding his lordship to say that he preferred to leave the matter with Lord Lyons, that I had considered negotiation here to be declined. I had also heard, through his lordship, of a proposition since made by Mr. Dayton on this subject to the French government, and which had been communicated to him, that led me to suppose the matter might be taking its shape at Paris. His lordship observed that Mr. Dayton's proposal was nothing more than a repetition of that made by Mr. Marcy, which they were not willing to accede to. I then said that Mr. Marcy's amendment was undoubtedly the first wish of my government. I also had instructions to press it, if there was the smallest probability of success; but I understood that this matter had been definitively settled. His lordship signified his assent to this remark, and added that I might consider the proposition as inadmissible. He would therefore take the copy of the project of a convention which I had offered him, for the purpose of submitting it to the consideration of his colleagues in the cabinet, and let me know when he should be ready to meet again.

In the course of conversation, I took the occasion to remark upon that passage of his lordship's note to me which related to the manner in which other states had signified their adherence to the declaration. I called his attention to the fact that, whatever might be the course elsewhere, the peculiar structure of our government required some distinct form of agreement or convention to be made with foreign States upon which the Senate could exercise their legitimate authority of confirmation or rejection. He seemed at once to understand the force of this observation, and to assent to the necessity. Yet I foresaw at the time the difficulty in which it would place the British government in its relations with the other parties to the convention at Paris. The reply of his lordship, this moment come to hand, a copy of which is herewith submitted, explains it fully, and leaves the matter in the same state of suspense that it was in before.

Under these circumstances, and presuming it to be the wish of the President that no time be lost, I shall write to Mr. Dayton, at Paris, to know whether he considers himself authorized to proceed to conclude a similar arrangement with the French government; if so, I shall try to go on without waiting for further instructions; if not, I shall hold myself ready to act here so soon as this difficulty shall have been removed elsewhere.

I have the honor to be, sir, your obedient servant,

CHARLES FRANCIS ADAMS.

Hon. WM. H. SEWARD,
   Secretary of State, Washington, D. C.

Mr. Adams to Lord John Russell.

LEGATION OF THE UNITED STATES,
London, July 11, 1861.

MY LORD: From the tenor of the last despatches received from the Department of State at Washington, I am led to suppose that there has been some misunderstanding in regard to the intentions of her Majesty's government respecting a proposal to negotiate upon the basis of the declaration of the congress held at Paris in 1856. In the first conversation which I had the honor to hold with your lordship, so long ago as the 18th of May last, in answer to an offer then made by myself, under instructions from my government, I certainly understood your lordship to say that the subject had already been committed to the care of Lord Lyons, at Washington, with authority to accept the proposition of the government of the United States, adopting three articles of the declaration at Paris, and to drop the fourth altogether. For this reason you preferred not to enter into the question on this side of the water. I am now informed that Lord Lyons thinks his instructions do not authorize him to enter into convention with the authorities at Washington, and am instructed to apprise her Majesty's government of the fact.

Under these circumstances, I am directed once more to renew the proposition here, and to say that, if agreeable to your lordship, I am prepared to present to your consideration a project of a convention at any moment which it may be convenient to you to appoint.

Seizing the occasion to renew the assurance of my highest consideration, I have the honor to be your lordship's most obedient servant,

CHARLES FRANCIS ADAMS.

The Right Honorable Lord JOHN RUSSELL,
   &c., &c., &c.

Lord John Russell to Mr. Adams.

FOREIGN OFFICE, *July* 13, 1861.

SIR: I have just had the honor to receive your letter dated the 11th instant. In the first conversation I had the honor to hold with you, on the 18th of

May, I informed you that instructions had been sent to Lord Lyons to propose to the government of the United States to adopt the second, third, and fourth articles of the declaration of Paris, dropping the first altogether.

You informed me that you had instructions on the same subject; but I understood you to express an opinion, in which I fully concurred, that it would be well to leave the question in the hands of the Secretary of State at Washington.

Lord Lyons had instructions to make an agreement with the government of the United States, but he had no express authority to sign a convention.

The States who have adhered to the declaration of Paris have generally, if not invariably, done so by despatches or notes, and not by conventions.

As, however, you have been instructed to present to her Majesty's government, for consideration, a project of a convention, I shall be happy to see you at the foreign office at three o'clock to-day, for the purpose of receiving that project.

I request you to receive the assurance of my highest consideration, and have the honor to be, sir, your most obedient servant,

J. RUSSELL.

CHARLES FRANCIS ADAMS, Esq., &c., &c., &c.

Lord John Russell to Mr. Adams.

FOREIGN OFFICE, July 18, 1861.

SIR: Upon considering your propositions of Saturday last I have two remarks to make.

First. The course hitherto followed has been a simple notification of adherence to the declaration of Paris by those states which were not originally parties to it.

Secondly. The declaration of Paris was one embracing various powers, with a view to general concurrence upon questions of maritime law, and not an insulated engagement between two powers only.

Her Majesty's government are willing to waive entirely any objection on the first of these heads, and to accept the form which the government of the United States prefers.

With regard to the second, her Majesty's government are of opinion that they should be assured that the United States are ready to enter into a similar engagement with France, and with other maritime powers who are parties to the declaration of Paris, and do not purpose to make singly and separately a convention with Great Britain only.

But as much time might be required for separate communications between the government of the United States and all the maritime powers who were parties to or have acceded to the declaration of Paris, her Majesty's government would deem themselves authorized to advise the Queen to conclude a convention on this subject with the President of the United States so soon as they shall have been informed that a similar convention has been agreed upon, and is ready for signature, between the President of the United States and the Emperor of the French, so that the two conventions might be signed simultaneously and on the same day.

I have the honor to be, with the highest consideration, sir, your most obedient, humble servant,

J. RUSSELL.

CHARLES FRANCIS ADAMS, Esq., &c., &c., &c.

Mr. Seward to Mr. Adams.

No. 42.]   DEPARTMENT OF STATE,
                                              Washington, July 21, 1861.

SIR: Your despatch of June 28, No. 10, has been received.

I have already, in a previous communication, informed you that this government has not been disturbed by the action of the British authorities in sending three regiments into Canada, nor by the announcement of the coming of British armed vessels into American waters. These movements are certainly not very formidable in their proportions; and we willingly accept the explanation that they proceed from merely prudential motives.

Doubtless it had been better if they had not been made. But what government can say that it never acts precipitately, or even capriciously. On our part the possibility of foreign intervention, sooner or later, in this domestic disturbance is never absent from the thoughts of this government. We are, therefore, not likely to exaggerate indications of an emergency for which we hold ourselves bound to be in a measure always prepared.

Another subject which, according to your report, was discussed in your late interview with Lord John Russell demands more extended remarks. I refer to the portion of your despatch which is in these words: " His lordship then said something about difficulties in New Grenada, and the intelligence that the insurgents there had passed a law to close their ports. But the law officers here told him that this could not be done as against foreign nations, except by the regular form of a blockade. He did not know what we thought about it; but he had observed that some such plan was said to be likely to be adopted at the coming meeting of Congress in regard to the ports of those whom we considered as insurgents."

Much as I deprecate a reference in official communications of this kind to explanations made by ministers in Parliament, not always fully or accurately reported, and always liable to be perverted when applied to cases not considered when the explanations are given, I nevertheless find it necessary, by way of elucidating the subject, to bring into this connexion the substance of a debate which is said to have taken place in the House of Commons on the 27th of June last, and which is as follows:

Mr. H. Berkly asked the secretary of state for foreign affairs whether her Majesty's government recognized a notification given by Señor Martin, minister plenipotentiary to this court from the Grenadian confederation, better known as the Republic of New Grenada, which announces a blockade of the ports of Rio Hacha, Santa Marta, Savanilla, Carthagena, and Zaporte, and which government did her Majesty's government recognize in the so-called Grenadian confederation.

Lord John Russell said the question is one of considerable importance. The government of New Grenada has announced, not a blockade, but that certain ports of New Grenada are to be closed. The opinion of her Majesty's government, after taking legal advice, is, that it is perfectly competent for the government of a country in a state of tranquillity to say which ports shall be open to trade and which shall be closed; but in the event of insurrection or civil war in that country, it is not competent for its government to close the ports that are *de facto* in the hands of the insurgents, as that would be an invasion of international law with regard to blockade. Admiral Milne, acting on instructions from her Majesty's government, has ordered the commanders of her Majesty's ships not to recognize the closing of their ports.

Since your conversation with Lord John Russell, and also since the debate which I have extracted occurred, the Congress of the United States has by law asserted the right of this government to close the ports in this country which have been seized by the insurgents.

I send you herewith a copy of the enactment. The connecting by Lord John Russell of that measure when it was in prospect with what had taken place in regard to a law of New Granada, gives to the remarks which he made to you a significance that requires no especial illustration. If the government of the United States should close their insurrectionary ports under the new statute, and Great Britain should, in pursuance of the intimation made, disregard the act, no one can suppose for a moment that the United States would acquiesce. When a conflict on such a question shall arrive between the United States and Great Britain, it is not easily to be seen what maritime nation could keep aloof from it. It must be confessed, therefore, that a new incident has occurred increasing the danger that what has hitherto been, and, as we think, ought to be, a merely domestic controversy of our own, may be enlarged into a general war among the great maritime nations. Hence the necessity for endeavoring to bring about a more perfect understanding between the United States and Great Britain for the regulation of their mutual relations than has yet been attained.

In attempting that important object I may be allowed to begin by affirming that the President deprecates, as much as any citizen of either country or any friend of humanity throughout the world can deprecate, the evil of foreign wars, to be superinduced, as he thinks unnecessarily, upon the painful civil conflict in which we are engaged for the purpose of defending and maintaining our national authority over our own disloyal citizens.

I may add, also, for myself, that however otherwise I may at any time have been understood, it has been an earnest and profound solicitude to avert foreign war; that alone has prompted the emphatic and sometimes, perhaps, impassioned remonstrances I have hitherto made against any form or measure of recognition of the insurgents by the government of Great Britain. I write in the same spirit now; and I invoke on the part of the British government, as I propose to exercise on my own, the calmness which all counsellors ought to practise in debates which involve the peace and happiness of mankind.

The United States and Great Britain have assumed incompatible, and thus far irreconcilable, positions on the subject of the existing insurrection.

The United States claim and insist that the integrity of the republic is unbroken, and that their government is supreme so far as foreign nations are concerned, as well for war as for peace, over all the States, all sections, and all citizens, the loyal not more than the disloyal, the patriots and the insurgents alike. Consequently they insist that the British government shall in no way intervene in the insurrection, or hold commercial or other intercourse with the insurgents in derogation of the federal authority.

The British government, without having first deliberately heard the claims of the United States, announced, through a proclamation of the Queen, that it took notice of the insurrection as a civil war so flagrant as to divide this country into two belligerent parties, of which the federal government constitutes one and the disloyal citizens the other; and consequently it inferred a right of Great Britain to stand in an attitude of neutrality between them.

It is not my purpose at this time to vindicate the position of the United States, nor is it my purpose to attempt to show to the government of Great Britain that its position is indefensible.

The question at issue concerns the United States primarily, and Great Britain only secondarily and incidentally. It is, as I have before said, a question of the integrity, which is nothing less than the life of the republic itself.

The position which the government has taken has been dictated, therefore, by the law of self-preservation. No nation animated by loyal sentiments and inspired by a generous ambition can even suffer itself to debate with parties within or without a policy of self-preservation. In assuming this position and the policy resulting from it, we have done, as I think, just what Great Britain herself must, and therefore would do if a domestic insurrection should attempt to detach Ireland, or Scotland, or England from the United Kingdom, while she would hear no argument nor enter into any debate upon the subject. Neither adverse opinions of theoretical writers, nor precedents drawn from the practice of other nations, or, even if they could be, from her own, would modify her course, which would be all the more vigorously followed if internal resistance should fortify itself with alliances throughout the world. This is exactly the case now with the United States.

So, for obvious reasons, I refrain from argument to prove to the government of Great Britain the assumed error of the position it has avowed.

First. Argument from a party that maintains itself to be absolutely right, and resolved in no case to change its convictions, becomes merely controversial. Secondly. Such argument would be only an indirect way of defending our own position, which is unchangeable. Thirdly. The position of Great Britain has been taken upon the assumption of a certain degree of probability of success by the insurgents in arms; and it must be sooner or later abandoned, as that probability shall diminish and ultimately cease, while in any case that circumstance does not affect our position or the policy which we have adopted. It must, therefore, be left to Great Britain to do what we have done, namely, survey the entire field, with the consequences of her course deemed by us to be erroneous, and determine as those consequences develope themselves how long that course shall be pursued.

While, however, thus waiving controversy on the main point, I am tempted by a sincere conviction that Great Britain really must desire, as we do, that the peace of the world may not be unnecessarily broken, to consider the attitude of the two powers, with a view to mutual forbearance, until reconciliation of conflicting systems shall have become in every event impossible.

The British government will, I think, admit that so soon as its unexpected, and, as we regard it, injurious position assumed in the Queen's proclamation became known to us, we took some pains to avert premature or unnecessary collision, if it could be done without sacrificing any part of the sovereignty which we had determined in every event to defend. We promptly renewed the proposition which, fortunately for both parties, we had tendered before that proclamation was issued, to concede as one whole undivided sovereignty to Great Britain, as a friend, all the guarantees for her commerce that she might claim as a neutral from this government as one of her two imagined belligerents. It seemed to us that these two great and kindred nations might decline to be dogmatic, and act practically with a view to immediate peace and ultimate good understanding.

So, on the other hand, it is my duty to admit, as I most frankly do, that the directions given by the British government that our blockade shall be respected, and that favor or shelter shall be denied to insurgent privateers, together with the disallowance of the application of the insurgent commissioners, have given us good reason to expect that our complete sovereignty, though theoretically questioned in the Queen's proclamation, would be practically respected. Lord Lyons, as you are aware, proposed to read to me a despatch which he had received from his government, affirming the position assumed in the Queen's proclamation, and deducing from that position claims as a neutral to guarantees of safety to British commerce less than those we had, as I have already stated, offered to her as a friend. I declined, as you have been advised, to hear the communication, but nevertheless renewed through you, as I consistently could, the offer of the greater guarantees before tendered.

The case then seemed to me to stand thus: The two nations had, indeed, failed to find a common ground or principle on which they could stand together; but they had succeeded in reaching a perfect understanding of the nature and extent of their disagreement, and in finding a line of mutual, practical forbearance. It was under this aspect of the positions of the two governments that the President thought himself authorized to inform Congress on its coming together on the 4th of July instant, in extra session that the sovereignty of the United States was practically respected by all nations.

Nothing has occurred to change this condition of affairs, unless it be the attitude which Lord John Russell has indicated for the British government in regard to an apprehended closing of the insurrectionary ports, and the passage of the law of Congress which authorizes that measure in the discretion of the President.

It is my purpose not to anticipate or even indicate the decision which will be made, but simply to suggest to you what you may properly and advantageously say while the subject is under consideration. First. You will, of course, prevent misconception of the measure by stating that the law only authorizes the President to close the ports in his discretion, according as he shall regard exigencies now existing or hereafter to arise.

Secondly. The passage of the law, taken in connexion with attendant circumstances, does not necessarily indicate a legislative conviction that the ports ought to be closed, but only shows the purpose of Congress that the closing of the ports, if it is now or shall become necessary, shall not fail for want of power explicitly conferred by law. When, on the 13th of April last, disloyal citizens defiantly inaugurated an armed insurrection by the bombardment of Fort Sumter, the President's constitutional obligation to suppress the insurrection became imperative.

But the case was new, and had not been adequately provided for by express law. The President called military and naval forces into activity, instituted a blockade, and incurred great expense, for all which no direct legal provisions existed. He convened Congress at the earliest possible day to confirm these measures, if they should see fit.

Congress, when it came together, confronted these facts. It has employed itself less in directing how and in what way the Union shall be maintained, than in confirming what the President had already done, and in putting into his hands more ample means and greater power than he has exercised or asked.

The law in question was passed in this generous and patriotic spirit. Whether it shall be put into execution to-day or to-morrow, or at what time, will depend on the condition of things at home and abroad, and a careful weighing of the advantages of so stringent a measure against those which are derived from the existing blockade.

Thirdly. You may assure the British government that no change of policy now pursued, injuriously affecting foreign commerce, will be made from motives of aggression against nations which practically respect the sovereignty of the United States, or without due consideration of all the circumstances, foreign as well as domestic, bearing upon the question. The same spirit of forbearance towards foreign nations, arising from a desire to confine the calamities of the unhappy contest as much as possible, and to bring it to a close by the complete restoration of the authority of the government as speedily as possible, that have hitherto regulated the action of the government will continue to control its counsels.

On the other hand, you will not leave it at all doubtful that the President fully adheres to the position that this government so early adopted, and which I have so continually throughout this controversy maintained; consequently he fully agrees with Congress in the principle of the law which authorizes him to close the ports which have been seized by the insurgents, and he will put into execution and maintain it with all the means at his command, at the hazard of whatever consequences, whenever it shall appear that the safety of the nation requires it.

I cannot leave the subject without endeavoring once more, as I have so often done before, to induce the British government to realize the conviction which I have more than once expressed in this correspondence, that the policy of the government is one that is based on interests of the greatest importance, and sentiments of the highest virtue, and therefore is in no case likely to be changed, whatever may be the varying fortunes of the war at home or the action of foreign nations on this subject, while the policy of foreign States rests on ephemeral interests of commerce or of ambition merely. The policy of these United States is not a creature of the government but an inspiration of the people, while the policies of foreign States are at the choice mainly of the governments presiding over them. If, through error, on whatever side this civil contention shall transcend the national bounds and involve foreign States, the energies of all commercial nations, including our own, will necessarily be turned to war, and a general carnival of the adventurous and the reckless of all countries, at the cost of the existing commerce of the world, must ensue. Beyond that painful scene upon the seas there lie, but dimly concealed from our vision, scenes of devastation and desolation which will leave no roots remaining out of which trade between the United States and Great Britain, as it has hitherto flourished, can ever again spring up.

I am, sir, respectfully, your obedient servant,

WILLIAM H. SEWARD.

Mr. Adams to Mr. Seward.

[Extracts.]

No. 20.]   LEGATION OF THE UNITED STATES,
                                                London, July 26, 1861.

SIR: At the close of my despatch, No. 17, on the subject of my last conference with Lord John Russell, I mentioned my intention to write to Mr. Dayton, at Paris, to know whether he felt authorized to proceed in a simultaneous negotiation on the subject of the declaration of the congress at Paris. I have now to report that I executed my purpose on the 19th instant.

On the evening of the 24th I received a note from Mr. Dayton announcing his arrival in town and his wish to confer with me upon this matter.

Yesterday morning I had the pleasure of a full and free conversation with him, in the course of which we carefully compared our respective instructions and the action taken under them.

I am very glad he has taken the trouble to come over to see me, for I confess that I was a little embarrassed by not knowing the precise nature of his proposal to the French government at the time when I heard of it from Lord John Russell. Had I been informed of it I should perhaps have shaped my own course a little differently. So I doubt not that he would have been pleased to know more exactly my own proceedings as well as the more specific character of my instructions. An hour's interview has had the effect to correct our impressions better than could have been accomplished by an elaborate correspondence.

I can now perfectly understand as well as enter into the reasons which prompted his proposal of the declaration of Paris, connected as it was with the modification first suggested by Mr. Marcy. There can be no doubt that the attempt to secure such an extension of the application of the principle contained in the first point of that declaration was worth making, on the part of the new administration, particularly at a place where there was no reason to presume any disinclination to adopt it. Neither did the reply of Mr. Thouvenel entirely preclude the hope of ultimate success, so far as the disposition of France may be presumed.

The obstacles, if any there are, must be inferred to have been thought to exist elsewhere. And an advance could be expected only when the efforts to remove them had been applied with effect in the proper quarter. It was, therefore, both natural and proper for Mr. Dayton, after having made his offer, and received such an answer, to wait patiently until it should become apparent that such efforts had been made, and made without success.

There can be no doubt that the opposition to this modification centres here. Independently of the formal announcement of Lord John Russell to me that the proposition was declined, I have, from other sources of information, some reason to believe that it springs from the tenacity of a class of influential persons, by their age and general affinities, averse to all sudden variations from established ideas. Such people are not to be carried away by novel reasoning, however forcible. We have cause to feel the presence of a similar power at home, though in a vastly reduced degree.

All modifications of the public law, however beneficent, naturally meet with honest resistance in these quarters for a time. It is to be feared that this may have the effect of defeating, at this moment, the application of the noble doctrines of the declaration of Paris, in the full expansion of which they are susceptible. But to my mind the failure to reach that extreme point will not justify the United States in declining to accept the good which is actually within their grasp. The declaration of the leading powers of civilized Europe, made at Paris in 1856, engrafted upon the law of nations for the first time great principles for which the government of the United States had always contended against some of those powers, and down to that time had contended in vain.

That great act was the virtual triumph of their policy all over the globe. It was the sacrifice, on the part of Great Britain, of notions she had ever before held to with the most unrelenting rigidity. It would therefore seem as if any reluctance to acknowledge this practical amount of benefit, obtained on the mere ground that something remained to require, was calculated only to wither the laurels gained by our victory.

It would almost seem like a retrograde tendency to the barbarism of former ages. Surely it is not in the spirit of the reformed government in America to give countenance to any such impression. Whatever may have been the character of the policy in later years, the advent of another and a better power should be marked by a recurrence to the best doctrines ever proclaimed in the national history. And if it so happen that they are not now adopted by others to the exact extent that we would prefer, the obvious course of wisdom would seem to be to accept the good which can be obtained, and patiently to await another opportunity when a continuance of exertions in the same direction may enable us to secure everything that is left to be desired.

I think that Mr. Dayton has waited only to be convinced that his proposed modification cannot be secured before he acts upon the authority given him to accede to the declaration of Paris, pure and simple.

On my part, I have apprised him of the answer made to me by Lord John Russell at our last conference. But he wishes some evidence upon which he can rely a little more securely than a report of conversation. And considering the remarkable discrepancy in the recollection of the conferences with his lordship which has thus far taken place, I am not surprised. In order to meet this difficulty he has addressed to me a letter of inquiry, which I propose to answer. At the same time I design to address a letter to his lordship recapitulating the portion of his conversation that is in question, and informing him that, *on the assumption that I understood him right,* Mr. Dayton consents to proceed. This will, of course, render it necessary for him to explain himself, if the fact should be otherwise.

Mr. Dayton will, of course, communicate directly with the department as to the later measures which he may think proper to take.

You will have been already informed by the newspapers of the changes which the ministry has undergone in consequence of the necessity imposed upon Lord Herbert by his failing health to retire from his post. As a consequence, Lord John Russell has been called to the House of Lords, though retaining his official station, and some shifting of other places has occurred. The only new appointment is that of Sir Robert Peel.

*   *   *   *   *   *   *   *   *   *
*   *   *   *   *   *   *   *   *   *
*   *   *   *   *   *   *   *   *   *
*   *   *   *   *   *   *   *   *   *

But I have not time at the close of this communication to enter into any speculations so intimately connected with a general view of the state of affairs in the other countries of Europe as well as in the United States. I shall therefore reserve what views I may have to submit on this subject to a future opportunity.

I have the honor to be, sir, your obedient servant,

CHARLES FRANCIS ADAMS.

Hon. William H. Seward,
    Secretary of State, Washington, D. C.

Mr. Seward to Mr. Adams.

[Confidential.]

No 46.] Department of State,
    Washington, July 26, 1861.

Sir: My despatch, No. 42, dated July 21, was delayed beyond the proper mail day by circumstances entirely beyond my control. I trust, however, that it will still be in time.

Our army of the Potomac on Sunday last met a reverse equally severe and unexpected. For a day or two the panic which had produced the result was followed by a panic that seemed to threaten to demoralize the country. But that evil has ceased already. The result is already seen in a vigorous reconstruction upon a scale of greater magnitude and increased enthusiasm.

It is not likely that anything will now be done here, hastily or inconsiderately, affecting our foreign relations.

I am, sir, respectfully, your obedient servant,

WILLIAM H. SEWARD.

Charles Francis Adams, Esq., &c., &c., &c.

Mr. Seward to Mr. Adams.

[Confidential.]

No. 49.]
DEPARTMENT OF STATE,
Washington, July 29, 1861.

SIR: Your despatch of July 12, 1861, No 14, has been received.

Your proposition of making a distinct appeal to the British government on the subject of the issue between it and this government, upon the questions so long discussed, is approved. We shall look with much interest for the answer of that government.

You will hear of a reverse of our arms in Virginia. The exaggerations of the result have been as great as the public impatience, perhaps, which brought it about. But the affair will not produce any serious injury. The strength of the insurrection is not broken, but it is not formidable. The vigor of the government will be increased, and the ultimate result will be a triumph of the Constitution. Do not be misled by panic reports of danger apprehended for the capital.

Some important points in your despatch will be treated of in another paper.

I am, sir, respectfully, your obedient servant,

WILLIAM H. SEWARD.

CHARLES FRANCIS ADAMS, Esq., &c., &c., &c.

Mr. Adams to Mr. Seward.

No. 22.]
LEGATION OF THE UNITED STATES,
London, August 2, 1861.

SIR: I have the honor to transmit the copy of a note addressed by me, on the 29th of July last, to Lord John Russell, and likewise a copy of his lordship's reply. I must frankly admit that I do not understand the meaning of the last paragraph.

I have transmitted a copy of his lordship's note to Mr. Dayton. I doubt not that it will be deemed by him so far satisfactory as to induce him to take the necessary measures for a simultaneous negotiation as soon as the customary arrangements with the French government can be made

I have the honor to be, sir, your obedient servant,

CHARLES FRANCIS ADAMS.

Hon. WM. H. SEWARD,
Secretary of State, Washington, D. C.

LEGATION OF THE UNITED STATES,
London, July 29, 1861.

MY LORD: I have the honor now to inform your lordship that, in consonance with the intention expressed in my note of the 19th instant, I have written to Mr. Dayton, at Paris, touching the extent of his powers to negotiate upon the same basis proposed by me to you, with the government of France, to which he is accredited. I have also to say that since the date of my writing I have had the pleasure to converse personally with him as well as to receive a letter from him in answer to my inquiry.

Mr. Dayton informs me that, some time since, he made a proposal to the French government to adopt the declaration of the congress of Paris in 1856, with an addition to the first clause, in substance the same with that heretofore proposed by his predecessor, Mr. Mason, under instructions given by Mr. Marcy, then the Secretary of State of the United States. To that proposal he received an answer from the French minister of foreign affairs, declining to consider the proposition, not for any objection entertained against it, but because it was a variation from the terms of the original agreement requiring a prior reference of it to the other parties to that convention. This answer does not, in his opinion, make the ultimate acceptance of his addition impossible, and he does not feel as if he ought to abandon the support of what he considers as so beneficent an amendment to the original plan until he has reason to despair of success. He has therefore requested to know of me whether I have reason to believe perseverance in this direction to be fruitless.

For my part I entirely concur in the view entertained by Mr. Dayton of the value of this amendment. I also know so well the interest that my government takes in its adoption as to be sure that it would refuse to justify a further procedure on our part which was not based upon a reasonable certainty that success is not attainable, at least at the present moment. I have, therefore, ventured to state to Mr. Dayton my belief that I have that certainty. I have therefore mentioned to him, what I have likewise communicated to the proper department of the government of the United States, the fact that in the last conference I had the honor to hold with your lordship, allusion having been made to the amendment of Mr. Dayton, I said that that amendment was undoubtedly the first wish of my government, and that I had instructions to press it if there was the smallest probability of success, but that I supposed this matter to have been already definitively acted upon. To which I understood your lordship to signify your assent, and to add that I might consider the proposition as inadmissible. If I have made no mistake in reporting the substance of what passed between us, Mr. Dayton tells me he is satisfied, and expresses his readiness to proceed on the basis proposed by me to your lordship with the French government. But in order to remove all probability of misconception between him and myself, I have taken the liberty of recalling your lordship's attention to the matter before it may be too late. Should there have been any essential error of fact on the main point, I trust your lordship will do me the favor to set me right.

Should it happen, on the contrary, that I am correct, I believe it will not be necessary to interpose any delay in the negotiation for further reference to the government of the United States. Mr. Dayton will take the necessary steps to apprise the government of the Emperor of the French of his intention to accede to the declaration of Paris, pure and simple, and the negotiations may be carried on simultaneously in both countries as soon as the necessary arrangements can be perfected on the respective sides.

However my government may regret that it has not been able to expand the application of the principles of the declaration of Paris to the extent which it deems desirable, it is too well convinced of the great value of the recognition actually given to those principles by the great powers of Europe in that act, longer to hesitate in giving in its cordial adhesion. But it ardently cherishes the hope that time and the favoring progress of correct opinion may before long bring about opportunities for additional developments of the system they initiate, through the co-operation of all maritime nations of the earth, and most especially of one so enlightened and philanthropic as Great Britain.

Renewing the assurances of my highest consideration, I have the honor to be your lordship's most obedient servant,

CHARLES FRANCIS ADAMS.

The Right Hon. Lord JOHN RUSSELL, &c., &c., &c.

FOREIGN OFFICE, *July* 31, 1861.

SIR: I have had the honor to receive your letter of the 29th instant, in which you inform me that Mr. Dayton, some time since, made a proposal to the French government to adopt the declaration of the congress of Paris in 1856, with an addition to the first clause, in substance the same with that heretofore proposed by his predecessor, Mr. Mason, under instructions given by Mr. Marcy, then the Secretary of State of the United States. After giving an account of the reception given to that proposition by the French government, and the value attached to it by Mr. Dayton and yourself, you proceed to state that in a conversation with me you told me that the addition proposed was the first wish of your government, and that you had instructions to press it if there was the smallest probability of success, but that you supposed this matter to have been already definitively acted upon. You represent me as signifying my assent, and adding that I considered the proposition as inadmissible.

So far as I am concerned, this statement is perfectly correct.

You go on to inform me that in the case of your statement being correct, Mr. Dayton will take the necessary steps to apprise the French government of his intention to accede to the declaration of Paris, "pure and simple, and that the negotiations may be carried on simultaneously in both countries as soon as the necessary arrangements can be perfected on the respective sides."

You will doubtless recollect that in my letter of the 18th instant, I stated that "her Majesty's government are of opinion that they should be assured that the United States are ready to enter into a similar engagement with France, and with the other maritime powers who are parties to the declaration of Paris, and do not propose to make simply and separately a convention with Great Britain only."

But as I agreed in the same letter to waive this assurance, and as I conclude, in point of fact, the United States are willing to sign similar conventions with all the states parties to the declaration of Paris, I shall be ready to carry on the negotiations as soon as the necessary arrangements can be perfected in London and Paris, so that the conventions may be signed simultaneously at those two capitals.

I need scarcely add that on the part of Great Britain the engagement will be prospective, and will not invalidate anything already done.

I have the honor to be, with the highest consideration, sir, your most obedient, humble servant,

J. RUSSELL.

CHARLES FRANCIS ADAMS, Esq., &c., &c., &c.

Mr. Seward to Mr. Adams.

No. 55.]   DEPARTMENT OF STATE,
Washington, August 6, 1861.

SIR: Your despatch, No. 17, of the date of July 19th, has been received.

I entirely approve of the letter which you addressed to Lord John Russell, of the 11th, a copy of which accompanied that despatch, and I wait now with impatience, yet not without some solicitude, for the action of the British government upon our propositions which we so early sent forward in good faith, and which by such strange accidents have been so long in reaching the cabinet of Great Britain.

I need hardly tell you that the same mail which conveyed our propositions concerning maritime rights for the consideration of the British government, carried also propositions literally the same for the consideration of the French government, and that of every other maritime power in Europe.

All those powers are understood to be awaiting the action of the government of Great Britain.

I am, sir, respectfully, your obedient servant,

WILLIAM H. SEWARD.

CHARLES FRANCIS ADAMS, Esq., &c., &c., &c.

Mr. Seward to Mr. Adams.

No. 58.]   DEPARTMENT OF STATE,
                                           Washington, August 12, 1861.

SIR: Your despatch of July 24th (No. 20) has been received. I am glad that you have had a full and satisfactory conversation with Mr. Dayton. It seems probable that we shall now be able to arrive at an understanding with the governments of Great Britain and France on the subject of international law relating to maritime war.

The shock produced by the reverse of our arms at Bull Run has passed away. The army is reorganized; the elections show that reaction against disunion has begun in the revolutionary States, and we may confidently look for a restoration of the national authority throughout the Union.

If our foreign relations were once promptly re-established on their former basis, the disunion sentiment would languish and perish within a year.

I am, sir, respectfully, your obedient servant,

WILLIAM H. SEWARD.

CHARLES FRANCIS ADAMS, Esq., &c., &c., &c.

Mr. Adams to Mr. Seward.

[Extract.]

No. 29.]   LEGATION OF THE UNITED STATES,
                                           London, August 16, 1861.

SIR: I have read with great attention the contents of your despatch, No. 42, dated the 21st July, and shall avail myself of the argument upon the next occasion of an interview with Lord Russell. But I have not thought it necessary to solicit one, for the reason that the government here does not appear to contemplate any change of position, so long as the blockade shall be kept up.

In the last conference which I had with his lordship, I took occasion towards the close of it to intimate to him that he must not infer, from my not having entered into discussion of the merits of the question, that I gave any assent to the position taken by him about the right of a government to close its own ports, when held by forcible possession of persons resisting its authority. On the contrary, I desired to reserve for my government the treatment of it as an open question whenever it should take any practical shape.

In the meantime I had every reason to believe that it was the design of the President to persevere in the blockade, and to that end that the necessary forces were in constant process of accumulation. This course, being understood to be one against which his lordship had signified an intention not to raise any objection, I did not think it worth while now to go further.

At the time of this interview no mention had been made of the precise form of the legislation contemplated by Congress. We received more precise intelligence on this side of the water a few days before the prorogation of Parliament. On the very last day for transacting business the subject was brought up in the House of Commons on a question addressed to Lord Palmerston by Mr. Wyld. His lordship's answer has doubtless attracted your attention long ere this. He considered the law as merely giving a discretionary power. But if carried into practice he construed it as putting an end to the blockade. So that, whether under blockade or under a levy of duties, foreign nations would have a rule to go by. His reply was, however, rather specious than solid, for it did not touch the difficulty presented by the fourth section, nor that involved in a possible levy of a double set of duties, one by the government on ship-board, and another by the insurgents on land. I am inclined to believe that serious objection would be made here in either of these contingencies. For this reason I do not deem it expedient to stir the matter until the necessity for it shall become positive. Believing the government to be on the whole favorably disposed towards us, and also that it is of great importance to avoid all complications of the present struggle which would practically benefit the insurgents, I shall delay to open any sources of controversy which I think may be avoided until especially instructed to do otherwise.

* * * * * * * * *

I have the honor to be, sir, your obedient servant,

CHARLES FRANCIS ADAMS.

Hon. WILLIAM H. SEWARD,
    Secretary of State, Washington, D. C.

Mr. Seward to Mr. Adams.

No. 61.]   DEPARTMENT OF STATE,
                                   Washington, August 17, 1861.

SIR: Your despatch of August 2 (No. 22) has been received. It is accompanied by a correspondence which has just taken place between yourself and Lord John Russell, with a view, on your part, to remove possible obstructions against the entrance upon negotiations, with which you have so long been charged, for an accession on our part to the declaration of the congress of Paris on the subject of the rights of neutrals in maritime war. It was also understood by you that a further result of the correspondence would be to facilitate, indirectly, the opening of similar negotiations for a like object, by Mr. Dayton, with the government of France.

Your letter to Lord John Russell is judicious, and is approved. Lord John Russell's answer is satisfactory, with the exception of a single passage, upon which it is my duty to instruct you to ask the British secretary for foreign affairs for an explanation.

That passage is as follows:

"I need scarcely add that on the part of Great Britain the engagement will be prospective, and will not invalidate anything already done."

A brief statement of the objects of the proposed negotiation will bring the necessity for an explanation of this passage into a stong light. We have heretofore proposed to other maritime states certain meliorations of the laws of maritime war affecting the rights of neutrals. These meliorations are: 1st. That the neutral flag shall protect enemy's goods not contraband of war. 2d. That the goods of neutrals, not contraband, though found under an enemy's flag, shall not be confiscated. 3d. That blockades, to be respected, must be effective.

The congress at Paris adopted these three principles, adding a fourth, namely, that privateering shall be abolished. The powers which constituted that congress invited the adhesion of the United States to that declaration. The United States answered that they would accede on condition that the other powers would accept a fifth proposition, namely, that the goods of private persons, non-combatants, should be exempt from confiscation in maritime war.

When this answer was given by the United States, the British government declined to accept the proposed amendment, or fifth proposition, thus offered by the United States, and the negotiation was then suspended. We have now proposed to resume the negotiation, offering our adhesion to the declaration of Paris, as before, with the amendment which would exempt private property from confiscation in maritime war.

The British government now, as before, declares this amendment or fifth proposition inadmissible It results that, if the United States can at all become a party to the declaration of the congress of Paris by the necessary consent of the parties already committed to it, this can be done only by their accepting that declaration without any amendment whatever, in other words, "pure and simple." Under these circumstances you have proposed in your letter to Lord John Russell to negotiate our adhesion to the declaration in that form. It is at this stage of the affair that Lord John Russell interposes, by way of caution, the remark, that "on the part of Great Britain the engagement will be prospective, and will not invalidate anything already done."

I need dwell on this remark only one moment to show that, although expressed in a very simple form and in a quite casual manner, it contains what amounts to a preliminary condition, which must be conceded by the United States to Great Britain, and either be inserted in the convention, and so modify our adhesion to the declaration of Paris, or else must be in some confidential manner implied and reserved, with the same effect.

Upon principle this government could not consent to enter into formal negotiations, the result of which, as expressed in a convention, should be modified or restricted by a tacit or implied reservation. Even if such a proceeding was compatible with our convictions of propriety or of expediency, there would yet remain an insuperable obstacle in the way of such a measure.

The President can only initiate a treaty. The treaty negotiated can come into life only through an express and deliberate act of ratification by the Senate of the United States, which ratification sanctions, in any case, only what is set down in the treaty itself. I am not, by any means, to be understood in these remarks as implying a belief that Lord John Russell desires, expects, or contemplates the practice of any reservation on the part of the United States or of Great Britain. The fact of his having given you the caution upon which I am remarking, would be sufficient, if evidence were necessary, to exclude any apprehension of that sort. It results from these remarks that the convention into which we are to enter must contain a provision to the effect that "the engagements" to be made therein are "on the part of Great Britain prospective, and will not invalidate anything already done."

I must, therefore, now discuss the propriety of inserting such a stipulation in the convention which you have been authorized to consummate. The proposed stipulation is divisible into two parts, namely: First. That the engagements of Great Britain are "prospective" [only.]

I do not see any great objection to such an amendment. But why should it be important. ' A contract is always prospective, and prospective only, if it contains no express stipulation that it shall be retrospective in its operation. So much, therefore, of the stipulation asked is unnecessary, while, if conceded, it might possibly give occasion to misapprehension as to its effect. You will, therefore, decline to make such a condition without first receiving a satisfactory explanation of its meaning and its importance.

The second part of the proposed condition is, that the "engagement will not invalidate anything already done." I am not sure that I should think this proposed condition exceptionable, if its effect were clearly understood. It is necessary, however, to go outside of his lordship's letter to find out what is meant by the words "anything already done." If "anything" pertinent to the subject "has been already done" which ought not to be invalidated, it is clear that it must have been done either by the joint action of the United States and Great Britain, or by the United States only, or by Great Britain acting alone. There has been no joint action of the United States and Great Britain upon the subject. The United States have done nothing affecting it; certainly nothing which they apprehend would be invalidated by the simple form of convention which they propose. I am left to conclude, therefore that the "thing" which "has been done already," and which Great Britain desires shall not be invalidated by the convention, must be something which she herself has done. At the same time we are left to conjecture what that thing is which is thus to be carefully saved. It would be hazardous on our part to assume to know, while I have no doubt that the British government, with its accustomed frankness, and in view of the desirableness of a perfect understanding of the matter, will at once specify what the thing which has been done by her, and which is not to be invalidated, really is. You will, therefore, respectfully ask the right honorable secretary for foreign affairs for an explanation of the part of his letter which I have thus drawn under review, as a preliminary to any further proceedings in the proposed negotiation.

You will perform this in such a manner as to show that the explanation is asked in no querulous or hypercritical spirit. Secondly, you will perform it with reasonable promptness, so that the attainment of the important object of the negotiation may not be unnecessarily delayed; and, thirdly, you will assure the British government that while the United States at present see no reason to think that the stipulation proposed is necessary or expedient, yet, in view of the great interests of commerce and of civilization which are involved, they will refuse nothing which shall be really just or even nonessential and not injurious to themselves, while of course I suppose they are not expected in any way to compromise their own national integrity, safety, or honor.

I am, sir, respectfully, your obedient servant,

WILLIAM H. SEWARD.

CHARLES FRANCIS ADAMS, Esq., &c., &c., &c.

Mr. Seward to Mr. Adams.

No. 63.]

DEPARTMENT OF STATE,
Washington, August 17, 1861.

SIR: Alexander H. Schultz, a special messenger, will deliver to you this despatch, together with a bag containing papers addressed to Lord John Russell.

On the 5th instant I was advised by a telegram from Cincinnati that Robert Mure, of Charleston, was on his way to New York to embark at that port for England, and that he was a bearer of despatches from the usurping insurrectionary authorities of Richmond to Earl Russell. Other information bore that he was a bearer of despatches from the same authorities to their agents in London. Information from various sources agreed in the fact that he was travelling under a passport from the British consul at Charleston.

Upon this information I directed the police at New York to detain Mr. Mure and any papers which might be found in his possession until I should give further directions. He was so detained, and he is now in custody at Fort Lafayette, awaiting full disclosures. In his possession were found seventy letters, four of which were unsealed and sixty-six sealed. There was also found in his possession a sealed bag marked "Foreign Office, 3," with two labels, as follows : "On Her Brit. Maj. service. The Right Honorable the Lord John Russell, M. P., &c., &c., &c. Despatches in charge of Robert Mure, Esq.," signed Robert Bunch. "On Her Brit. Maj. service. The Right Honorable the Lord John Russell, M. P., H. B. M.'s Principal Secretary of State for Foreign Affairs, Foreign Office, London, R. Bunch." The bag bears two impressions of the seal of office of the British consul at Charleston, and seems to contain voluminous papers.

There were also found upon Mr. Mure's person, in an open envelope, what pretends to be a passport in the following words.—(See Annex A.)

Also a letter of introduction, which is as follows.—(See Annex B.)

There were also found several unsealed copies of a printed pamphlet entitled "A narrative of the Battles of Bull Run and Manassas Junction, July 18th and 21st. Accounts of the advance of both armies, the battles and rout of the enemy, compiled chiefly from the detailed reports of the Virginia and South Carolina press; Charleston, Steam Power Presses of Evans & Coggswell, No. 3 Broad, and 103 East Bay streets, 1861."

This pamphlet is manifestly an argument for the disunion of the United States. Several copies of it were found addressed to persons in England.

The marks and outward appearance of the bag indicate that its contents are exclusively legitimate communications from the British consul at Charleston to H. B. M.'s government. Nevertheless, I have what seem to be good reasons for supposing that they may be treasonable papers, designed and gotten up to aid parties engaged in arms for the overthrow of this government and the dissolution of the Union. These reasons are: 1st. That I can hardly conceive that there can be any occasion for such very voluminous communications of a legitimate nature being made by the consul at Charleston to his government at the present time. 2d. Consuls have no authority to issue passports, the granting of them being, as I understand, not a consular but a diplomatic function. Passports, however, have, in other times, been habitually granted by foreign consuls residing in the United States. But soon after the insurrection broke out in the Southern States a regulation was made by this department, which I have excellent means of knowing was communicated to the British consul at Charleston, to the effect that, until further orders, no diplomatic or consular passports would be recognized by this government, so far as to permit the bearer to pass through the lines of the national forces or out of the country unless it should be countersigned by the Secretary of State and the commanding general of the army of the United States. Mr. Mure had passed the lines of the army, and was in the act of leaving the United States in open violation of this regulation. Moreover, the bearer of the papers, Robert Mure, is a naturalized citizen of the United States, has resided here thirty years, and is a colonel in the insurgent military forces of South Carolina.

3d. If the papers contained in the bag are not illegal in their nature or purpose, it is not seen why their safe transmission was not secured, as it might have been by exposing them in some way to Lord Lyons, British minister residing at this capital, whose voucher for their propriety, as Mr. Bunch must well know, would exempt them from all scrutiny or suspicion. 4th. The consul's letter to the bearer of dispatches attaches an unusual importance to the papers in question, while it expresses great impatience for their immediate conveyance to their destination, and an undue anxiety lest they might, by some accident, come under the notice of this government. 5th. The bearer is proved to be disloyal to the United States by the pamphlet and the letters found in his possession.

I have examined many of the papers found upon the person of Mr. Mure, and I find them full of treasonable information, and clearly written for treasonable purposes. These, I think, will be deemed sufficient grounds for desiring the scrutiny of the papers and surveillance of the bearer on my part.

Comity towards. the British government, together with a perfect confidence in its justice and honor, as well as its friendship towards the United States, to say nothing of a sense of propriety, which I could not dismiss, have prevented me from entertaining, for a moment, the idea of breaking the seals which I have so much reason to believe were put upon the consular bag to save it from my inspection, while the bearer himself might remove them on his arrival in London, after which he might convey the papers, if treasonable, to the agents of the insurgents, now understood to be residing in several of the capitals in Europe.

I will not say that I have established the fact that the papers in question are treasonable in their nature, and are made with purposes hostile and dangerous to this country. But I confess I fear they are so, and I apprehend either that they are guilty despatches to the agents of disunion, or else that, if they are really addressed to the British government, they are papers prepared by traitors in the insurrectionary States, with a view to apply to the British government for some advantage and assistance or countenance from that government injurious to the United States and subversive of their sovereignty. Of course, I need hardly say that I disclaim any thought that Earl Russell has any knowledge of the papers or of their being sent, or that I have any belief or fear that the British government would, in any way, receive the papers if they are illegal in their character, or dangerous or injurious to the United States. It is important, however, to this government that whatever mischief, if any, may be lurking in the transaction, be counteracted and prevented.

I have, therefore, upon due consideration of the case, concluded to send the bag by a special messenger, who will deliver it into your care, and to instruct you to see that it is delivered accordingly to its address in exactly the condition in which you receive it.

You will also make known to the Earl Russell the causes and the circumstances of the arrest and detention of Mr. Mure and his papers, adding the assurance that this government deeply regrets that it has become necessary; and that it will be very desirous to excuse the brief interruption of the correspondence of the British consul, if it is indeed innocent, and will endeavor, in that case, to render any further satisfaction which may be justly required. On the other hand, you will, in such terms as you shall find most suitable and proper, intimate that if the papers in question shall prove to be treasonable against the United States, I expect that they will be delivered up to you for the use of this government, and that her British Majesty's consul at Charleston will, in that case, be promptly made to feel the severe displeasure of the government which employs him, since there can be no greater crime against society than a perversion by the agent of one government of the hospitality afforded to him by another, to designs against its safety, dignity, and honor.

I think it proper to say that I have apprised Lord Lyons of this transaction, and of the general character of this letter, while he is not in any way compromised by any assent given to my proceedings, or by any opinion expressed by him or asked from him.

I am, sir, your obedient servant,

WILLIAM H. SEWARD.

CHARLES F. ADAMS, Esq., &c., &c., &c.

Mr. Seward to Mr. Adams.

No. 64.]   DEPARTMENT OF STATE,
                                    Washington, August 17, 1861.

SIR : Among the letters found on the person of Robert Mure, mentioned in my despatch No. 63, of this date, there are many which more or less directly implicate Mr. Robert Bunch, the British consul at Charleston, as a conspirator against the government of the United States. The following is an extract from one of them:

"Mr. B., on oath of secrecy, communicated to me also that the *first step* to recognition was taken. He and Mr. Belligny together sent Mr. Trescot to Richmond yesterday, to ask Jeff. Davis, president, to ——— the treaty of ——— to ——— the neutral flag covering neutral goods to be respected. This is the first step of direct treating with our government, so prepare for active business by January 1."

You will submit this information to the British government, and request that Mr. Bunch may be removed from his office, saying that this government will grant an exequatur to any person who may be appointed to fill it, who will not pervert his functions to hostilities against the United States.

I am, sir, respectfully, your obedient servant,

WILLIAM H. SEWARD.

CHARLES F. ADAMS, Esq., &c., &c., &c.

Mr. Adams to Mr. Seward.

No. 32.]   LEGATION OF THE UNITED STATES,
                                     London, August 23, 1861.

SIR: I have the honor to transmit a copy of a note addressed to me by Lord Russell, transmitting to me a copy of a declaration which he proposes to make upon signing the convention, embodying the articles of the declaration of Paris, in conjunction with myself.

I have waited to communicate with Mr. Dayton until I now learn from him that Mr. Thouvenel proposes to him a similar movement on the part of France.

This proceeding is of so grave and novel a character as, in my opinion, to render further action unadvisable until I obtain further instructions; and I find Mr. Dayton is of the same opinion on his side. I propose to address a letter to his lordship stating my reasons for declining to proceed, as soon as possible, but I fear I shall not have time to get it ready and a copy made in season for the present mail. I shall therefore postpone any further elucidation of my views until the next opportunity. I do so the more readily that I am informed by Mr. Dayton that you have ceased to consider the matter as one of any urgent importance.

I have the honor to be, sir, your obedient servant,

CHARLES FRANCIS ADAMS.

Hon. WILLIAM H. SEWARD,
    Secretary of State, Washington.

FOREIGN OFFICE, *August* 19, 1861.

SIR: I have the honor to enclose a copy of a declaration which I propose to make upon signing the convention of which you gave me a draft embodying the articles of the declaration of Paris.

I propose to make the declaration in question in a written form, and to furnish you with a copy of it.

You will observe that it is intended to prevent any misconception as to the nature of the engagement to be taken by her Majesty.

If you have no objection to name a day in the course of this week for the signature of the convention, Mr. Dayton can on that day, and at the same time, sign with M. Thouvenel a convention identical with that which you propose to sign with me.

I have the honor to be, with the highest consideration, sir, your most obedient, humble servant,

RUSSELL.

C. F. ADAMS, Esq., *&c., &c., &c.*

Draft of Declaration.

In affixing his signature to the convention of this day between her Majesty the Queen of Great Britain and Ireland and the United States of America, the Earl Russell declares, by order of her Majesty, that her Majesty does not intend thereby to undertake any engagement which shall have any bearing, direct or indirect, on the internal differences now prevailing in the United States.

Mr. F. W. Seward to Mr. Adams.

No. 74.]

DEPARTMENT OF STATE,
Washington, August 27, 1861.

SIR: Your despatch of August 8, No. 25, has been received.

The account you have given us of the impression made by the reverse of our arms at Manassas does not surprise me. But there are to be very many fluctuations of opinion in Europe concerning our affairs before the Union will be in danger from any source.

The insurgents are exhausting themselves. We are invigorated even by disappointment. To-day the capital is beyond danger, and forces are accumulating and taking on the qualities which will render them invincible. The Union armies are preparing for movements which will, in a few weeks, remove the war from the present frontier. The blockade is effective, and is working out the best fruits.

We do not at present depart from that policy, but we are preparing for any emergency in our foreign relations.

The sentiment of disunion is losing its expansive force, and every day it grows weaker as a physical power.

I am, sir, respectfully, your obedient servant,

F. W. SEWARD, *Assistant Secretary.*

CHARLES FRANCIS ADAMS, Esq., &c., &c., &c.

Mr. Adams to Mr. Seward.

No. 34.]   LEGATION OF THE UNITED STATES,
                                              London, August 30, 1861

SIR: It is not without regret that I am compelled to announce the failure of the negotiation which I am led, by the tenor of your despatches, Nos. 55 and 58, to infer you considered almost sure to succeed. I have now the honor to transmit the copy of a note addressed by me to Lord Russell on the the 23d instant, assigning the reasons why I felt it my duty to take the responsibility of declining to fix a day for signing the convention agreed upon between us, burdened, as it was to be, with a contemporaneous exposition of one of its provisions in the form of an outside declaration made by his lordship on behalf of her Majesty the Queen. I have gone so fully into the matter in that note as to render further explanation unnecessary. At the same time I take the liberty to observe that, in case the President should be of opinion that too much stress has been laid by me upon the objectionable character of that paper, an opening has been left by me for the resumption of the negotiation at any moment under new instructions modifying my views. I transmitted to Mr. Dayton a copy for his information immediately after the original was sent. I have not received any later intelligence from him; but I do not doubt that he will forward to the department by this mail his representation of the state of the corresponding negotiation at Paris, so that the whole subject will be under your eye at the same moment. From the tenor of his last note to me, I was led to infer that M. Thouvenel contemplated a parallel proceeding in the conclusion of his negotiation, and that he regarded it there very much in the same light that I did here.

From a review of the whole course of these proceedings I am led to infer the existence of some influence in the cabinet here adverse to the success of this negotiation. At the time of my last conference with Lord Russell I had every reason, from his manner, to believe that he considered the offer of the project as perfectly satisfactory. The suggestion of a qualification did not make its appearance until after the consultation with his colleagues, when it showed itself first in the enigmatical sentence of his note to me of the 31st of July, of which, in my despatch No. 22 to the department, I confessed my inability to comprehend the meaning, and afterwards in the formal announcement contained in his note of the 19th of August. That the failure of the measure, by reason of it, could not have been altogether unexpected I infer from Mr. Dayton's report to me of M. Thouvenel's language to him, to the effect that his government would prefer to lose the negotiation rather than to omit making the exception.

Although the matter is not altogether germane to the preceding, I will not close this despatch without calling your attention to the copy of a letter of Lord John Russell to Mr. Edwardes, which I transmit as cut from a London newspaper, The Globe. It purports to have been taken from parliamentary papers just published, although I have not seen them, nor have I found it printed in any other newspaper. You will notice the date, the 14th of May, being the very day of my first visit to his lordship in company with Mr. Dallas, when he did not see us, as well as of the publication of the Queen's proclamation. I have reason to believe that the original form of that proclamation described the parties in America in much the same terms used by his Lordship, and that they were only qualified at a very late moment, and after earnest remonstrance. The tone of the letter corresponds very much with that used to me, a report of which was transmitted in my despatch No. 8.

I have the honor to be, sir, your obedient servant,

CHARLES FRANCIS ADAMS.

Hon. WILLIAM H. SEWARD,
    Secretary of State, Washington, D. C.

LEGATION OF THE UNITED STATES,
London, August 23, 1861.

The undersigned, envoy extraordinary and minister plenipotentiary of the United States, has the honor to acknowledge the reception of the note of the 19th instant, of Lord Russell, her Majesty's principal secretary of state for foreign affairs, covering the copy of a declaration which his lordship proposes to make upon signing the convention which has been agreed upon between her Majesty the Queen of Great Britain and Ireland, and the United States of America, embodying the articles of the declaration of Paris, and at the same time requesting him to name a day in the course of this week for the signature of the convention, in conjunction with a similar proceeding, to be arranged to take place at Paris, between Mr. Dayton and the minister of foreign affairs on the part of the French government.

The first step rendered necessary by this proposal was that the undersigned should communicate with Mr. Dayton in order to know whether a similar declaration was contemplated on the part of the Emperor of the French, and in case it was, whether Mr. Dayton was still prepared to proceed. Mr. Dayton's letter containing that information was received only yesterday, which fact, in conjunction with a brief absence of the undersigned, will account for the apparent delay in answering his lordship's note.

In order perfectly to understand the position of the undersigned, it will be necessary briefly to recapitulate the particulars of this negotiation. But a few weeks after the accession of the President of the United States to office, his attention was turned to the state in which the negotiation on the subject of the four articles of the declaration of Paris had been left by his predecessor; and his disposition manifested itself to remove so far as he could the obstacles which had been interposed in the way of completing it. To that end, among the duties with which the undersigned was charged immediately upon his arrival at his post, was an instruction at once to make overtures to her Majesty's government for a revival of the negotiation here. And, in case of the manifestation of a favorable disposition, he was further directed to offer a project of a convention, which he was properly empowered to sign, after satisfying himself that the incorporation of the amendment which had been proposed by Mr. Marcy for the government of the United States, at a former stage of the proceedings, was not attainable.

On the eighteenth of May last, being the day of the first interview had with his lordship, the subject was only opened by the undersigned as one on which he had power to negotiate, and the disposition of her Majesty's government to proceed here was tested. It was then that he received a distinct impression from his lordship that the matter had been already committed to the care of Lord Lyons at Washington, with authority to agree with the government of the United States on the basis of the adoption of three of the articles, and the omission of the fourth altogether. Considering this to be equivalent to declining a negotiation here, and at the same time relieving him from a duty which would be better performed by his own government, the undersigned cheerfully acquiesced in this suggestion, and accordingly wrote home signifying his intention not to renew the subject unless again specifically instructed so to do.

One month passed away, when the Secretary of State of the United States, after a conference with Lord Lyons, learning that his lordship did not confirm the representation of the powers with which the undersigned had understood him to be clothed, and, so far from it, that he did not feel authorized to enter into any convention at all at Washington, directed the undersigned to inform the government in London of this fact, and to propose once more to enter into convention, if agreeable, here.

Immediately upon the receipt of these instructions, the undersigned wrote a letter on the 11th of July, as his lordship may remember, reciting these facts and renewing the question whether a proposal of negotiation at this place would be acceptable to her Majesty's government. To this letter a favorable reply was received on the 13th, and an interview took place the same day, at which, after ascertaining that the amendment desired by his government would not be successful, the undersigned had the honor to present to his lordship the project in the same form in which it had been, nearly two months before, placed in his hands, and in which it has been since accepted, and to offer a copy of his powers to negotiate. His lordship, after examining the former, remarked that he would take it for consultation with his colleagues, and in the meantime that there was no necessity for a copy of the powers.

The next step in the negotiation was the receipt, by the undersigned, of a letter from his lordship, dated the 18th of July, calling his attention to the fact that the declaration of Paris contemplated a concurrence of various powers, and not an insulated engagement of two powers only, and requiring an assurance that the United States were ready to enter into a similar engagement with France and with other maritime powers, parties to the declaration, and not with Great Britain alone. But, inasmuch as this process itself might involve the loss of much time, that her Majesty's government would deem themselves authorized to advise the Queen to conclude a convention with the President of the United States so soon as they should have been informed that a similar convention has been agreed upon between the President and the Emperor of the French.

Upon receiving this reply the undersigned, not unwilling to do everything within his power to forward an object considered by him of the greatest value, immediately opened a correspondence with Mr. Dayton, the representative of the United States at Paris, to learn from him whether such an arrangement as that contemplated in his lordship's note could not be at once carried out by him. With some reluctance Mr. Dayton consented to promote it, but only upon the production of evidence satisfactory to his own mind that the amendment originally proposed by Mr. Marcy was not attainable. The undersigned then addressed himself to his lordship, and with entire success? The evidence was obtained, Mr. Dayton acted with success, and no further difficulties then seemed to be in the way of a speedy and simultaneous affirmation of concurrence in the principles of the declaration of Paris by the United States, in conjunction with the other powers.

The public law thus declared to be established, embraced four general propositions, to wit:

1. Privateering is abolished.
2. The neutral flag covers enemy's goods, except contraband of war.
3. Neutral goods safe under an enemy's flag, with the same exception.
4. Blockades, to be binding, must be effective.

The government of the United States, in proposing to join in the establishment of these principles, are believed by the undersigned to be acting with the single purpose of aiding to establish a permanent doctrine for all time. Convinced of the value of it in ameliorating the horrors of warfare all over the globe, they have, perhaps against their notions of their immediate interest, consented to waive temporary considerations of expediency for the attainment of a great ultimate good. They are at last prepared to sign and seal an engagement pure and simple, and by so doing to sacrifice the hope of attaining, at least for the present, an improvement of it to which they have always attached great value. But just at the moment when their concurrence with the views of the other maritime powers of the world would seem to be certain, they are met with a proposition from one, if not more, of the parties, to accompany the act with a proceeding somewhat novel and anomalous in this case, being the presentation of a written declaration, not making a part of the convention itself, but intended to follow the signature, to the effect that "her Majesty does not intend thereby to undertake any engagement which shall have any bearing, direct or *indirect*, on the internal differences now prevailing in the United States."

Obviously a consent to accept a particular exception, susceptible of so wide a construction to a joint instrument, made by one of the parties to it in its own favor at the time of signing, would justify the idea that some advantage is, or may be suspected to be, intended to be taken by the other. The natural effect of such an accompaniment would seem to be to imply that the goverment of the United States might be desirous, at this time, to take a part in the declaration, not from any high purpose or durable policy, but with the view of securing some small temporary object in the unhappy struggle which is going on at home. Such an inference would spoil all the value that might be attached to the act itself. The mere toleration of it would seem to be equivalent to a confession of their own weakness. Rather than that such a record should be made, it were a thousand times better that the declaration remain unsigned forever. If the parties to the instrument are not to sign it upon terms of perfect reciprocity, with all their duties and obligations under it perfectly equal, and without equivocation or reservation of any kind, on any side, then is it plain that the proper season for such an engagement has not yet arrived. It were much wiser to put it off until nations can understand each other better.

There is another reason why the undersigned cannot at this moment consent to proceed under the powers conferred on him to complete this negotiation when clogged with such a declaration, which is drawn from the peculiar construction of the government of his own country. By the terms of the Constitution, every treaty negotiated by the President of the United States must, before it is ratified, be submitted to the consideration of the Senate of the United States. The question immediately arises in this case, what is to be done with a declaration like that which his lordship proposes to make.

Is it a part of the treaty, or is it not? If it be, then is the undersigned exceeding his instructions in signing it, for the paper made no part of the project which he was directed to propose; and in case he should sign, the addition must be submitted to the Senate for its advice and consent, together with the paper itself. If it be not, what advantage can the party making the declaration expect from it in modifying the construction of the project, when the Senate have never had it before them for their approval? It either changes the treaty or it does not. If it does, then the question arises, why did not the undersigned procure it to be incorporated into it? On the other hand, if it do not, why did he connive at the appearance of a desire to do it without effecting the object?

The undersigned has ever been desirous of maintaining and perpetuating the most friendly relations between her Majesty's kingdom and the United States, and he continues to act in the same spirit when he deprecates the submission of any project clogged with a similar exception to the consideration of the Senate of the United States. He has reason to believe that already a strong disinclination exists in that body to the acceptance of the first of the four propositions embraced in the declaration itself, and that mainly because it is esteemed to be too much of a concession to the great maritime powers. Were he now to consent, without further instructions, to accept a qualification which would scarcely fail to be regarded by many unfavorably disposed persons as more or less directly an insult to the nation in its present distress, he should deem himself as incurring the hazard of bringing on difficulties which he professes an earnest wish to avoid.

For the reasons thus given the undersigned has reluctantly come to the conclusion to decline to fix a day for proceeding in the negotiation under its present aspect, at least until he shall have been able to submit the whole question once more to the judgment of the authorities under which he has the honor to act.

A copy of this letter will also be forwarded to Mr. Dayton for his information.

The undersigned prays Lord Russell to receive the assurances of the most distinguished consideration with which he is his obedient servant.

CHARLES FRANCIS ADAMS.

Right Hon. Earl Russell, &c., &c., &c.

Lord Russell to Mr. Edwards.

Foreign Office, *May* 14, 1861.

It is for the Spanish government to weigh in the balance of their judgment the advantages and inconveniences which may arise from the annexation of the territory of the Dominican state to the dominions of Spain; and any opinion which her Majesty's government may form on the subject can be founded on no other consideration than a regard for what they may look upon as the real and permanent interests of Spain.

Her Majesty's government would, no doubt, have felt a strong and decided dissatisfaction at the proposed annexation if it had been likely to lead to the introduction of slavery into a community which is free from the taint of that pernicious institution; but the formal and repeated declarations of Marshal O'Donnell, that under no circumstances will slavery be introduced into the Dominican territory, have removed the main cause which would have led her

Majesty's government to view the proposed annexation with dislike and repugnance.

Her Majesty's government certainly apprehended, when first this projected annexation was talked of, that it might, if carried into execution, involve Spain in unfriendly discussions, if not in conflict, either with France or with the United States, or with both. With regard to France, her Majesty's government have not learned that the French government has expressed any positive objection to the proposed arrangement, although she may not think it advantageous to Spain. It appears, also, from what has been stated to you, that there is no probability at present of any positive resistance to the measure, either by the northern or the southern confederation of North America. But the Spanish government should not too confidently rely on the permanent continuance of this indifference or acquiescence on the part of the North Americans; and it is not impossible that when the civil war which is now breaking out shall have been brought to an end, an event which may happen sooner than at present appears likely, both the north and the south might combine to make the occupation of the Dominican territory by Spain the cause of serious difference between the North American governments and that of Spain.

Her Majesty's government do not deny that Great Britain, as a power naturally inclined to peace, and systematically addicted to commerce, must always view a war between any two powers as an event not only at variance with her principles, but to a certain degree injurious to her interests. But with respect to Spain, the motives of the British government spring from far higher sources. Great Britain and Spain have for long periods of time, and in circumstances of high moment to each, been faithful and active allies; their alliance has been greatly useful and eminently honorable to both. It is a fundamental maxim of British policy to wish well to Spain, and earnestly to desire her welfare and prosperity; and therefore any combination of events which might at any time involve the possibility of Spain being engaged in a conflict which, from local circumstances and disadvantages, might be in the end seriously injurious to her rule over her ancient possessions, would be viewed by her Majesty's government with lively apprehension and sincere regret.

Mr. Seward to Mr. Adams.

[Extracts.]

No. 78.]   DEPARTMENT OF STATE,
                                    Washington, September 2, 1861.

SIR: Your despatch of the 16th of August, number 29, has been received.

*   *   *   *   *   *   *   *   *

Steadily for the period of four months our forces have been coming into the field at the rate of two thousand a day, and the same augmentation will go on nearly at the same rate until 500,000 men will be found in the service. Our supplies of arms are running low.

My despatch, No. 42, acknowledged by you in the paper before me, was written, as you will see by its date, July 21, during the progress of the battle at Bull Run, though sent a few days afterwards. From this fact you will see that our policy and our claims upon the government of Great Britain are not affected by the caprices of military fortune.

We have now reached a new and important stage in the war. The enemy is directly before us, invigorated and inspirited by a victory, which it is not the part of wisdom for us to undervalue. But that victory has brought with it the necessity for renewed and decisive action with proportionate results. The demoralization of our forces has passed away. I have already stated that they are increasing in numbers. You will learn through other channels that they are equally perfecting themselves in discipline. Commander Stringham and General Butler's success at Hatteras was not merely a brilliant affair. It brings nearly the whole coast of North Carolina under the surveillance of our blockade. *   *   *   *   *   *

I shall be entirely satisfied with the exercise of your own discretion as to the time and form you may choose for making the explanations to the British government on those subjects with which you are charged, and I regard the condition of things in that respect, as you have reported it to me, as, under the circumstances, quite satisfactory. No change of policy in regard to the blockade has been adopted since my former despatches.

I can well enough imagine that your position has been made a trying one by the exultations of enemies of our country and its institutions over the disaster of the 21st of July. But you will be able to comprehend what they cannot, that faction ripens fast, whence its necessities impel to action which exhausts its energies. Loyalty in any free country organizes less rapidly and gains strength from time and even from reverses. The previous success of this government is a sufficient guaranty of the safety of our cause, and is a fact too important to be misunderstood in the political circle in which you are moving.

I am, sir, respectfully, your obedient servant,

WILLIAM H. SEWARD.

CHARLES FRANCIS ADAMS, Esq., &c., &c., &c.

Mr. Seward to Mr. Adams.

No. 83.]

DEPARTMENT OF STATE,
Washington, September 7, 1861.

SIR: I have received your despatch of August 23, number 32. It is accompanied by a note which was addressed to you by Lord Russell on the 19th of the same month, and a paper containing the form of an official declaration which he proposes to make on the part of her Majesty on the occasion of affixing his signature to the projected convention between the United States and Great Britain for the accession of the former power to the articles of the declaration of the congress of Paris for the melioration of the rigor of international law in regard to neutrals in maritime war. The instrument thus submitted to us by Lord Russell is in the following words: "Draft of declaration.—In affixing his signature to the convention of this day, between her Majesty the Queen of Great Britain and Ireland and the United States of America, the Earl Russell declares, by order of her Majesty, that her Majesty does not intend thereby to undertake any engagement which shall have any bearing, direct or indirect, on the internal differences now prevailing in the United States."

Lord Russell, in his note to you, explains the object of the instrument by saying that it is intended to prevent any misconception as to the nature of the engagement to be taken by her Majesty.

You have judged very rightly in considering this proceeding, on the part of the British government, as one so grave and so novel in its character as to render further action on your part in regard to the projected convention inadmissible until you shall have special instructions from this department.

Long before the present communication can reach you, my instructions of August 17, No. 61, will have come to your hands. That paper directed you to ask Lord Russell to explain a passage in a note written to you, and then lying before me, in which he said: "I need scarcely add that on the part of Great Britain the engagement (to be contained in the projected convention) will be prospective, and will not invalidate anything already done;" which explanation I stated would be expected as a preliminary before you could proceed further in the transaction.

You have thus been already prepared for the information that your resolution to await special instructions in the present emergency is approved.

I feel myself at liberty, perhaps bound, to assume that Lord Russell's proposed declaration, which I have herein recited, will have been already regarded, as well by him as by yourself, as sufficiently answering the request for preliminary explanations which you were instructed to make.

I may, therefore, assume that the case is fully before me, and that the question whether this government will consent to enter into the projected treaty with Great Britain, subject to the condition of admitting the simultaneous declaration on her Majesty's part, proposed by Lord Russell, is ready to be decided.

I am instructed by the President to say that the proposed declaration is inadmissible.

It would be virtually a new and distinct article incorporated into the projected convention. To admit such a new article would, for the first time in the history of the United States, be to permit a foreign power to take cognizance of and adjust its relations upon assumed internal and purely domestic differences existing within our own country.

This broad consideration supersedes any necessity for considering in what manner or in what degree the projected convention, if completed either subject to the explanation proposed or not, would bear directly or indirectly on the internal differences which the British government assume to be prevailing in the United States.

I do not enlarge upon this branch of the subject. It is enough to say that the view thus adopted by the President seems to be in harmony equally with a prudent regard to the safety of the republic and a just sense of its honor and dignity.

The proposed declaration is inadmissible, among other reasons, because it is not mutual. It proposes a special rule by which her Majesty's obligations shall be meliorated in their bearing upon internal difficulties now prevailing in the United States, while the obligations to be assumed by the United States shall not be similarly meliorated or at all affected in their bearing on internal differences that may now be prevailing, or may hereafter arise and prevail, in Great Britain.

It is inadmissible, because it would be a substantial and even a radical departure from the declaration of the congress at Paris. That declaration makes no exception in favor of any of the parties to it in regard to the bearing of their obligations upon internal differences which may prevail in the territories or dominions of other parties.

The declaration of the congress of Paris is the joint act of forty-six great and enlightened powers, designing to alleviate the evils of maritime war, and promote the first interest of humanity, which is peace. The government of Great Britain will not, I am sure, expect us to accede to this noble act otherwise than upon the same equal footing upon which all the other parties to it are standing. We could not consent to accede to the declaration with a modification of its terms unless all the present parties to it should stipulate that the modification should be adopted as one of universal application. The British government cannot but know that there would be little prospect of an entire reformation of the declaration of Paris at the present time, and it has not even told us that it would accept the modification as a general one if it were proposed.

It results that the United States must accede to the declaration of the congress of Paris on the same terms with all the other parties to it, or that they do not accede to it at all.

You will present these considerations to Lord Russell, not as arguments why the British government ought to recede from the position it has assumed, but as the grounds upon which the United States decline to enter into the projected convention recognizing that exceptional position of her Majesty.

If, therefore, her Britannic Majesty's government shall adhere to the proposition thus disallowed, you will inform Lord Russell that the negotiation must for the present be suspended.

I forbear purposely from a review of the past correspondence, to ascertain the relative responsibilities of the parties for this failure of negotiations, from which I had hoped results would flow beneficial, not only to the two nations, but to the whole world—beneficial, not in the present age only, but in future ages.

It is my desire that we may withdraw from the subject carrying away no feelings of passion, prejudice, or jealousy, so that in some happier time it may be resumed, and the important objects of the proposed convention may be fully secured. I believe that that propitious time is even now not distant; and I will hope that when it comes Great Britain will not only willingly and unconditionally accept the adhesion of the United States to all the benignant articles of the declaration of the congress of Paris, but will even go further, and, relinquishing her present objections, consent, as the United States have. so constantly invited, that the private property, not contraband, of citizens and subjects of nations in collision shall be exempted from confiscation equally in warfare waged on the land and in warfare waged upon the seas, which are the common highways of all nations.

Regarding this negotiation as at an end, the question arises, what, then, are to be the views and policy of the United States in regard to the rights of neutrals in maritime war in the present case. My previous despatches leave no uncertainty upon this point. We regard Great Britain as a friend. Her Majesty's flag, according to our traditional principles, covers enemy's goods not contraband of war. Goods of her Majesty's subjects, not contraband of war, are exempt from confiscation though found under a neutral or disloyal flag. No depredations shall be committed by our naval forces or by those of any of our citizens, so far as we can prevent it, upon the vessels or property of British subjects. Our blockade, being effective, must be respected.

The unfortunate failure of our negotiations to amend the law of nations in regard to maritime war does not make us enemies, although, if they had been successful, we should have perhaps been more assured friends.

Civil war is a calamity from which certainly no people or nation that has ever existed has been always exempt. It is one which probably no nation ever will escape. Perhaps its most injurious trait is its tendency to subvert the good understanding and break up the relations existing between the distracted state and friendly nations, and to involve them, sooner or later, in war. It is the desire of the United States that the internal differences existing in this country may be confined within our own borders. I do not suffer myself for a moment to doubt that Great Britain has a desire that we may be successful in attaining that object, and that she looks with dread upon the possibility of being herself drawn into this unhappy internal controversy of our own. I do not think it can be regarded as disrespectful if you should remind Lord Russell that when, in 1838, a civil war broke out in

Canada, a part of the British dominions adjacent to the United States, the Congress of the United States passed and the President executed a law which effectually prevented any intervention against the government of Great Britain in those internal differences by American citizens, whatever might be their motives, real or pretended, whether of interest or sympathy. I send you a copy of that enactment. The British government will judge for itself whether it is suggestive of any measures on the part of Great Britain that might tend to preserve the peace of the two countries, and, through that way, the peace of all nations.

I am, sir, respectfully, your obedient servant,

WILLIAM H. SEWARD

CHARLES FRANCIS ADAMS, Esq., &c., &c., &c.

Mr. Adams to Mr. Seward.

[Extracts.]

No. 39.]   LEGATION OF THE UNITED STATES,
                                London, September 7, 1861.

SIR: I have the honor to acknowledge the reception of despatches from the department, numbered from 61 to 67, both inclusive.

Since the date of your No. 61, of the 17th of August, you will have learned ere this that the enigmatical extract from Lord Russell's note to me, of which you instructed me to ask an explanation, has taken a very distinct and unequivocal shape, superseding all necessity for further inquiry. I may take occasion to remark upon the similarity of some of the reasoning in your despatch with that which you will find already made use of in my letter to his lordship, of the 23d August, declining to conclude the negotiation. On the whole, it seems to me that it is perhaps as well to let it stay for the present in the situation in which her Majesty's ministers have placed it. But in this I remain to be directed at the pleasure of the President.

In this connexion I have the honor to transmit a copy of Lord Russell's note of the 28th of August, in reply to mine of the 23d of that month to him, already referred to in the preceding paragraph. I likewise send a copy of his instructions to Lord Lyons, which he seems to have furnished to me as an evidence of his good faith in the representation he made of them to me at the conference.

 * * * * * * * *

I have the honor to be, sir, your obedient servant,

CHARLES FRANCIS ADAMS.

HON. WILLIAM H. SEWARD,
 Secretary of State, Washington, D. C.

FOREIGN OFFICE, *August* 28, 1861.

The undersigned, her Majesty's principal secretary of state for foreign affairs, has had the honor to receive the note, of the 23d instant, of Mr. Adams, envoy extraordinary and minister plenipotentiary of the United States.

Mr. Adams has accounted satisfactorily for the delay in answering the note of the undersigned of the 19th instant. Her Majesty's government in all these transactions has acted in concert with the government of the

Emperor of the French, and the undersigned cannot be surprised that Mr. Adams should wish to communicate with Mr. Dayton, at Paris, before replying to his note.

The undersigned is quite prepared, following Mr. Adams, to recapitulate the particulars of this negotiation, and he is happy to think that in matters of fact there is no ground for any controversy between them. He need only supply omissions.

Mr. Adams, at his first interview with the undersigned, on the 18th of May last, mentioned the subject of the declaration of Paris as one on which he had power to negotiate, and the undersigned then told him that the matter had been already committed to the care of Lord Lyons, at Washington, with authority to agree with the government of the United States on the basis of the adoption of three of the articles and the omission of the first, being that relating to privateering. So far, the statement of Mr. Adams agrees substantially with that which is here made. But the representation of the undersigned was strictly accurate, and in faith of it he subjoins the despatch by which Lord Lyons was authorized to negotiate on the basis of the three latter articles of the declaration of Paris. Lord Lyons, however, was not empowered to sign a convention, because that form had not been adopted by the powers who originally signed the declaration, nor by any of the numerous states which afterwards gave their adherence to its articles.

At a later period, when Mr. Adams brought a copy of his full powers to the foreign office, the undersigned asked why the adherence of the United States should not be given in the same form as that of other powers, and he was told, in reply, that as the Constitution of the United States required the consent of the Senate to any agreement with foreign powers, that agreement must necessarily, or at least would most conveniently, be made in the shape of a convention.

The undersigned yielded to this argument, and proposed to the government of the Emperor of the French, with which her Majesty's government have been acting throughout in complete agreement, to concur likewise in this departure from the form in which the declaration of Paris had been adopted by the maritime powers of Europe.

But the British government could not sign the convention proposed by the United States as an act of Great Britain singly and alone, and they found to their surprise that in case of France and of some of the other European powers the addition of Mr. Marcy relating to private property at sea had been proposed by the ministers of the United States at the courts of those powers.

The undersigned concurs in the statement made by Mr. Adams respecting the transactions which followed. Her Majesty's government, like Mr. Adams, wished to establish a doctrine for all time, with a view to lessen the horrors of war all over the globe. The instructions sent to Lord Lyons prove the sincerity of their wish to give permanence and fixity of principles to this part of the law of nations.

The undersigned has now arrived at that part of the subject upon which the negotiation is interrupted.

The undersigned has notified Mr. Adams his intention to accompany his signature of the proposed convention with a declaration to the effect that her Majesty "does not intend thereby to undertake any engagement which shall have any bearing, direct or indirect, on the internal differences now prevailing in the United States."

The reasons for this course can be easily explained. On some recent occasions, as on the fulfilment of the treaty of 1846, respecting the boundary, and with respect to the treaty called by the name of the "Clayton-Bulwer treaty," serious differences have arisen with regard to the precise meaning of words, and the intention of those who framed them.

It was most desirable in framing a new agreement not to give rise to a fresh dispute.

But the different attitude of Great Britain and of the United States in regard to the internal dissensions now unhappily prevailing in the United States gave warning that such a dispute might arise out of the proposed convention.

Her Majesty's government, upon receiving intelligence that the President had declared by proclamation his intention to blockade the ports of nine of the States of the Union, and that Mr. Davis, speaking in the name of those nine States, had declared his intention to issue letters of marque and reprisals; and having also received certain information of the design of both sides to arm, had come to the conclusion that civil war existed in America, and her Majesty had thereupon proclaimed her neutrality in the approaching contest.

The government of the United States, on the other hand, spoke only of unlawful combinations, and designated those concerned in them as rebels and pirates. It would follow logically and consistently, from the attitude taken by her Majesty's government, that the so-called Confederate States, being acknowledged as a belligerent, might, by the law of nations, arm privateers, and that their privateers must be regarded as the armed vessels of a belligerent.

With equal logic and consistency it would follow, from the position taken by the United States, that the privateers of the southern States might be decreed to be pirates, and it might be further argued by the government of the United States that a European power signing a convention with the United States, declaring that privateering was and remains abolished, would be bound to treat the privateers of the so-called Confederate States as pirates.

Hence, instead of an agreement, charges of bad faith and violation of a convention might be brought in the United States against the power signing such a convention, and treating the privateers of the so-called Confederate States as those of a belligerent power.

The undersigned had at first intended to make verbally the declaration proposed. But he considered it would be more clear, more open, more fair to Mr. Adams to put the declaration in writing, and give notice of it to Mr. Adams before signing the convention.

The undersigned will not now reply to the reasons given by Mr. Adams for not signing the convention if accompanied by the proposed declaration. Her Majesty's government wish the question to be fairly weighed by the United States government. The undersigned, like Mr. Adams, wishes to maintain and perpetuate the most friendly relations between her Majesty's kingdom and the United States. It is in this spirit that her Majesty's government decline to bind themselves without a clear explanation on their part to a convention which, seemingly confined to an adoption of the declaration of Paris of 1856, might be construed as an engagement to interfere in the unhappy dissensions now prevailing in the United States—an interference which would be contrary to her Majesty's public declarations, and would be a reversal of the policy which her Majesty has deliberately sanctioned.

The undersigned requests Mr. Adams to accept the assurance of his highest consideration.

                                                            RUSSELL.

C. F. Adams, Esq., &c., &c., &c.

No. 136.]   FOREIGN OFFICE, *May* 18, 1861.

MY LORD: Her Majesty's government deeply lament the outbreak of hostilities in North America, and they would gladly lend their aid to the restoration of peace.

You are instructed, therefore, in case you should be asked to employ your good offices either singly or in conjunction with the representatives of other powers, to give your assistance in promoting the work of reconciliation. But as it is most probable, especially after a recent letter of Mr. Seward, that foreign advice is not likely to be accepted, you will refrain from offering it unasked. Such being the case, and supposing the contest not to be at once ended by signal success on one side or by the return of friendly feeling between the two contending parties, her Majesty's government have to consider what will be the position of Great Britain as a neutral between the two belligerents.

So far as the position of Great Britain in this respect toward the European powers is concerned, that position has been greatly modified by the declaration of Paris of April 16, 1856. That declaration was signed by the ministers of Austria, France, Great Britain, Prussia, Russia, Sardinia, and Turkey.

The motives for making that declaration, and for agreeing to the articles of maritime law which it proposes to introduce with a view to the establishment of a "uniform doctrine" and "fixed principles," are thus shortly enumerated in the declaration: •

"Considering that maritime law in time of war has long been the subject of deplorable disputes;

"That the uncertainty of the law and of the duties in such a matter gives rise to differences of opinion between neutrals and belligerents which ma occasion serious difficulties and even conflicts;

"That it is consequently advantageous to establish a uniform doctrine on so important a point;

"That the plenipotentiaries assembled in congress at Paris cannot better respond to the intentions by which their governments are animated than by seeking to introduce into international relations fixed principles in this respect—

"The above-mentioned plenipotentiaries, being duly authorized, resolved to concert among themselves as to the means of attaining this object, and having come to an agreement have adopted the following solemn declaration:"

1st. Privateering is and remains abolished.

2d. The neutral flag covers enemy's goods, with the exception of contraband of war.

3d. Neutral's goods, with the exception of contraband of war, are not liable to capture under enemy's flag.

4th. Blockades, in order to be binding, must be effective—that is to say, maintained by a force sufficient really to prevent access to the coast of the enemy.

The powers signing the declaration engaged to bring it to the knowledge of the states which had not taken part in the congress of Paris, and to invite those states to accede to it. They finally agreed that "the present declaration is not and shall not be binding, except between those powers who have acceded or shall accede to it."

The powers which acceded to the declaration are Baden, Bavaria, Belgium, Bremen, Brazil, Duchy of Brunswick, Chili, the Argentine Confederation, the Germanic Confederation, Denmark, the Two Sicilies, the Republic of the Equator, the Roman States, Greece, Guatemala, Hayti, Hamburg, Hanover, the Two Hesses, Lubeck, Mecklenburg Strelitz, Mecklenburg Schwerin, Nas-

.

sau, Oldenburg, Parma, Holland, Peru, Portugal, Saxony, Saxe Attenburg, Saxe Coburg Gotha, Saxe Meiningen, Saxe Weimer, Sweden, Switzerland, Tuscany, Wurtemburg, Anhalt Dessau, Modena, New Grenada, and Magnay.

Mr. Secretary Marcy, in acknowledging, on the 28th of July, 1856, the communication of the declaration of Paris made to the government of the United States by the Count de Sartiges, proposed to add to the first article thereof the following words : "and that the private property of the subjects or citizens of a belligerent on the high seas shall be exempted from seizure by public armed vessels of the other belligerents, except it be contraband ;" and Mr. Marcy expressed the willingness of the government of the United States to adopt the clause so amended, together with the other three principles contained in the declaration.

Mr. Marcy also stated that he was directed to communicate the approval of the President of the second, third, and fourth propositions, independently of the first, should the proposed amendment of the first article be unacceptable.

The United States minister in London, on the 24th of February, 1857, renewed the proposal in regard to the first article, and submitted a draft of convention, in which the article so amended would be embodied with the other three articles. But, before any decision was taken on this proposal, a change took place in the American government by the election of a new President of the United States, and Mr. Dallas announced, on the 25th of April, 1857, that he was directed to suspend negotiations on the subject ; up to the present time those negotiations have not been renewed.

The consequence is, that the United States remaining outside the provisions of the declaration of Paris, the uncertainty of the law and of international duties with regard to such matters may give rise to differences of opinion between neutrals and belligerents which may occasion serious difficulties and even conflicts.

It is with a view to remove beforehand such "difficulties," and to prevent such "conflicts," that I now address you.

For this purpose I proceed to remark on the four articles, beginning, not with the first, but with the last

In a letter to the Earl of Clarendon of the 24th of February, 1857, Mr. Dallas, the minister of the United States, while submitting the draft of a new convention, explains the views of the government of the United States on the four articles.

In reference to the last article, he says: "The fourth of those principles, respecting blockades, had, it is believed, long since become a fixed rule of the law of war."

There can be no difference of opinion, therefore, with regard to the fourth article.

With respect to the third article, the principle laid down in it has long been recognized as law, both in Great Britain and in the United States. Indeed this part of the law is stated by Chancellor Kent to be uniform in the two countries.

With respect to the second article, Mr. Dallas says, in the letter before quoted: "About two years prior to the meeting of congress at Paris, negotiations had been originated and were in train with the maritime nations for the adoption of the second and third propositions substantially as enumerated in the declaration."

The United States have therefore no objection in principle to the second proposition.

Indeed her Majesty's government have to remark that this principle is adopted in the treaties between the United States and Russia of the 22d of July, 1854, and was sanctioned by the United States in the earliest period of the history of their independence by their accession to the armed neutrality.

With Great Britain the case has been different. She formerly contended for the opposite principles as the established rule of the law of nations. But having, in 1856, upon full consideration, determined to depart from that rule, she means to adhere to the principle she then adopted. The United States, who have always desired this change, can, it may be presumed, have no difficulty in assenting to the principle set forth in the second article of the declaration of Paris.

There remains only to be considered the first article, namely, that relating to privateering, from which the government of the United States withhold their assent. Under these circumstances it is expedient to consider what is required on this subject by the general law of nations. Now, it must be borne in mind that privateers bearing the flag of one or other of the belligerents may be manned by lawless and abandoned men, who may commit, for the sake of plunder, the most destructive and sanguinary outrages.

There can be no question but that the commander and crew of the ship bearing a letter of marque must, by law of nations, carry on their hostilities according to the established laws of war. Her Majesty's government must, therefore, hold any government issuing such letters of marque responsible for, and liable to make good, any losses sustained by her Majesty's subjects in consequence of wrongful proceeding of vessels sailing under such letters of marque.

In this way the object of the declaration of Paris may, to a certain extent, be attained without the adoption of any new principle.

You will urge these views upon Mr. Seward.

The proposals of her Majesty's government are made with a view to limit and restrain that destruction of property and that interruption of trade which must, in a greater or less degree, be the inevitable consequence of the present hostilities. Her Majesty's government expect that these proposals will be received by the United States government in a friendly spirit. If such shall be the case, you will endeavor (in concert with M. Mercier) to come to an agreement on the subject binding France, Great Britain, and the United States.

If these proposals should, however, be rejected, her Majesty's government will consider what other steps should be taken with a view to protect from wrong and injury the trade and the property and persons of British subjects.

I am, &c., &c., &c.,

J. RUSSELL.

The Lord Lyons.

Mr. Adams to Mr. Seward.

No. 41.]   LEGATION OF THE UNITED STATES,
                                 London, September 9, 1861.

SIR: I have the honor to acknowledge the reception at the hands of your messenger, Captain Schultz, of a bag purporting to contain public despatches from Mr. Robert Bunch, the consul at Charleston, to Lord Russell, the head of the foreign office in London. In conformity with the instructions contained in your No. 63, dated the 17th of August, I immediately addressed a note to Lord Russell, explanatory of the reasons why such a bag was received through this channel, a copy of which is herewith transmitted. In it you will perceive that I have endeavored to adhere as closely as possible to the language of your communication to me. At the same time, in obedience to the directions contained in your No. 64, dated the 17th of August, I addressed another note to his lordship stating the grounds of dissatisfaction felt by the President with the conduct of Mr. Bunch, and requesting his removal. A copy of this note is likewise appended to the present despatch. These two notes, together with the bag in exactly the same condition in which I received it from Captain Schultz, I directed my assistant secretary, Mr. Benjamin Moran, to take with him to the foreign office, and there to deliver into the hands of his lordship if present, or, if absent from town, into those of one of her Majesty's under secretaries of state for foreign affairs. Accordingly, on the afternoon of Tuesday, the 4th instant, at about quarter past three o'clock, as Mr. Moran reports to me, he went to the foreign office, and finding Lord Russell to be absent from town, he delivered the bag and the notes into the hands of Mr. Layard, one of the under secretaries. Since that time I have had no reply from his lordship, although I received on Saturday last two notes from him on matters of minor consequence. I had hoped to send something by Captain Schultz, who returns in the Great Eastern, and I shall yet do so if it should come before the bag closes. I have consented to the departure of Captain Schultz, mainly because Mr. Dayton has expressed a great desire that he should take charge of his despatches as soon as possible.

I have the honor to be, sir, your obedient servant,

CHARLES FRANCIS ADAMS.

Hon. WILLIAM H. SEWARD,
    Secretary of State, Washington, D. C.

P. S.—I have just learned from Mr. Davy that the Bermuda put into Falmouth for coals. Her cargo in arms, ammunition, and clothing, is valued at £80,000 sterling. The importance of intercepting her cannot be overestimated.

Mr. Adams to Earl Russell.

LEGATION OF THE UNITED STATES,
    London, September 3, 1861.

MY LORD : I have the honor to inform your lordship that I have received by the hands of a special messenger of the government just arrived in the steamer Europa from the United States a sealed bag marked Foreign Office, 3, with two labels, as follows :

"On her Britannic Majesty's service. The right honorable the Lord John Russell, M. P., &c., &c., &c. Despatches in charge of Robert Mure, esq.
    "ROBERT BUNCH."

"On her Britannic Majesty's service. The right honorable the Lord John Russell, M. P., her Britannic Majesty's principal secretary of state for foreign affairs, foreign office, London.   ·
    "R. BUNCH."

Agreeably to instructions communicated by my government to me, to see that this bag is delivered accordingly to its address in exactly the condition in which I received it, I have the honor to transmit the same by the hands of my assistant secretary, Mr. Benjamin Moran, who is directed to deliver it into your own hands, if present, or, if absent, into those of one of the under secretaries of state for foreign affairs.

It now becomes my duty to explain the circumstances under which this bag has found its way from the possession of the person to whom it was originally intrusted into that of the authorities of the United States.

It appears that the Secretary of State of the United States, on the 15th of August last, received information deemed worthy of confidence that Mr. Robert Mure, the bearer of this bag, was at the same time acting as a bearer of despatches from the insurrectionary authorities of Richmond to your lordship. Other information came that he was a bearer of despatches from the same authorities to their agents in London. And still other information from various sources agreed in affirming that he was travelling under a passport issued by her Majesty's consul at Charleston. Upon this information, instructions were sent forthwith to the police of New York to detain Mr. Mure, and any papers which might be found in his possession. He was accordingly detained, and is now in custody at Fort Layfette, awaiting full disclosures. A large number of papers were found upon him, an examination of which was found fully to sustain some portions of the information which had been furnished, and to prove that Mr. Mure was acting as the bearer of a treasonable correspondence between persons acting in open arms against the government of the United States and their friends and emissaries in Great Britain. He had also with him several copies of a printed pamphlet purporting to be a narrative of the events of the 21st of July at Manassas Junction, addressed to persons in England, and evidently intended to further the purposes of the conspirators in South Carolina.

Robert Mure, the bearer of these papers, is represented to be a naturalized citizen of the United States, where he has resided for thirty years, and as actually holding a commission of colonel in the insurgent forces of South Carolina.

It turned out to be true that in the hands of this gentleman were found in an open envelope a paper purporting to be a passport, a copy of which I have the honor to append to this note as paper marked A ; and a letter of instructions, signed by Robert Bunch, her Majesty's consul for the United States, residing at Charleston, a copy of which is likewise appended, as paper marked B.

In the absence of all other evidence against Mr. Bunch to prove his departure from the line of his legitimate duty, it is quite enough to call the attention of your lordship to the fact that in issuing such a paper as this passport he has acted in direct contravention of a regulation issued by the proper department of the United States of which he had received notice, which forbids all recognition of any diplomatic or consular passport so far as to permit the bearer to pass through the lines of the national forces or out of the country unless it should be countersigned by the Secretary of State and the commanding general of the army of the United States. Mr. Mure attempted to do both with a paper bearing no such signatures.

There is, however, other and still more serious cause of complaint against Mr. Bunch, as disclosed by the papers of Mr. Mure, the exposition of which I am compelled to reserve for a separate communication. The present purpose is confined to an explanation of the reasons which have actuated the government of the United States in taking the extraordinary step which has had for one of its consequences the effect of diverting, be it but for a moment, a part of the official correspondence of her Majesty's government from the channel in which it was originally placed. I am directed to express the regret the government feels that such a measure had become imperative, and to assure your lordship of its earnest desire to make any suitable amends which may justly be required. If in the process there may have happened a slight interruption of the correspondence of the British consul, it is their desire that the pressing nature of the emergency may induce your lordship to excuse it.

It is needless to say that the bag passes into the hands of your lordship in precisely the same condition it came from those of Mr Mure. Comity towards the government of a friendly nation, together with a full confidence in its justice and honor, to say nothing of a sense of propriety, would deter the government which I have the honor to represent from entertaining the idea of breaking the seals which protect it even were there ten times more reason than there is to presume an intention under so sacred a sanction to perpetrate a wrong certainly on one and perhaps on both governments. Still less is it the intention of the American government to intimate the smallest suspicion of any privity whatever on the part of the authorities in Great Britain in aiding, assisting, or countenancing a supposed design injurious to the United States and subversive of their sovereignty. Much ground as there is for presuming that it never was the intention of those who prepared the package to forward it to its nominal address, but that it was rather the design, after bringing bad matter under this sacred sanction safely through the dangers of hostile scrutiny, to open the bag themselves and to disseminate the contents far and wide among the evil-disposed emissaries to be found scattered all over Europe; this consideration has never weighed a single moment to change their views of this trust when put in the balance with the strong reliance placed upon the good faith of her Majesty's constitutional advisers. Least of all has it been in the thought of any one that your lordship would consent in any way to receive the papers, if they are really illegal in their character or dangerous or injurious to the United States.

Should it, however, prove on inspection that any abuse has been attempted in America of the confidence to which her Majesty's government is in every way entitled, I am directed to express to your lordship the hope that any papers of a treasonable character against the United States may be delivered up to me for the use of my government, and that her Majesty's consul at Charleston, if shown to be privy to the transmission of them under such a form, may be made promptly to feel the severe displeasure of the government whose good faith he has sought to dishonor. For there can be no difference of opinion as to the nature of an offence which involves the perversion by the agent of one government of the hospitality afforded to him by another to conspire against its safety, dignity, and honor.

I pray your lordship to accept the assurances of the highest consideration with which I have the honor to be your lordship's most obedient servant,

CHARLES FRANCIS ADAMS.

The Right Honorable Earl Russell, &c., &c., &c.

Mr. Adams to Earl Russell.

LEGATION OF THE UNITED STATES,
London, *September* 3, 1861.

The undersigned, envoy extraordinary and minister plenipotentiary of the United States, deeply regrets the painful necessity that compels him to make a representation to the right honorable Lord Russell, her Majesty's principal secretary of state for foreign affairs, touching the conduct of Mr. Robert Bunch, her Majesty's consul for the port of Charleston, in the United States. It appears from the contents of one of the many letters found in the possession of Mr. Robert Mure, bearer of despatches from Mr. Bunch to the government of Great Britain, but detained as an agent of the enemies of the United States, that the following statement is made of the action of Mr. Bunch in Charleston.

"Mr. B., on oath of secrecy, communicated to me also that the *first step* to recognition was taken. He and Mr. Belligny together sent Mr. Trescot to Richmond yesterday to ask Jeff. Davis, President to —— the treaty of —— to —— the neutral flag covering neutral goods to be respected. This is the first step of direct treating with our government. So prepare for active business by 1st January."

The undersigned is instructed to submit this information to her Majesty's government with a request that, if it be found to be correct, Mr. Bunch may be at once removed from his office. The undersigned is further instructed to add that the President will cheerfully accord an exequatur to any person who may be appointed to succeed him, who will faithfully perform his functions without injury to the rights and the interests of the United States.

The undersigned avails himself of this occasion to renew to Lord Russell the assurances of his highest consideration.

CHARLES FRANCIS ADAMS.

The Right Honorable Earl Russell, &c., &c., &c.

Mr. Seward to Mr. Adams.

No. 84.] Department ot State,
Washington, September 10, 1861.

Sir: I send you an extract of a letter just received from Mr. Francis Bernard, in the island of Trinidad. It shows a clear case of connivance by the authorities of that island with the insurgents of the United States, in violation of the rights and dignity of this government, if the facts are truly presented. You will bring the subject to the notice of Lord Russell, and will, if the case shall not be satisfactorily explained, ask for such proceedings in the premises as shall make the authorities of the island sensible of the displeasure of the imperial government, and prevent such occurrences in the future.

For your satisfaction, I state that a new consul has been appointed at Trinidad, and that he is now on his way to that island.

I am, sir, your obedient servant,

WILLIAM H. SEWARD.

Charles Francis Adams, Esq., &c., &c., &c.

Mr. Bernard to Mr. Seward.

[Extract.]

Trinidad, *August* 7, 1861.

Sir: I beg to inform you that on the 30th ultimo a steam sloop-of-war (Semmes commander) carrying a secession flag, five guns, some of a large calibre, and a crew of from 120 to 150 men, sailed boldly in our harbor and reported herself to the authorities of this island as being on a cruise. She was last from Puerto Cabello; and since she succeeded in getting out of the Mississippi river she has already captured no less than eleven American vessels. I have ascertained the names of some of them, viz: the Joseph Maxwell, Abe Bradford, Minnie Miller, West Wind, of Westerly, with a cargo of sugar from Havana, and Golden Rocket, which was burnt by her off the coast of Cuba.

The Sumter landed eight of her prisoners here in a destitute condition; but a contribution has been raised here for their benefit, sufficient to supply their immediate wants, and I will take care that they are provided for till an opportunity offers to ship them to the States.

The Sumter remained here till the 5th instant, and was allowed to supply herself with coals and other necessary outfits. The British flag was hoisted on the government flag-staff for her arrival, and the officers of the British war vessel "Cadmus" appeared to be on amicable terms with those of the Sumter. The merchant who supplied the Sumter with coals did it with the consent and approval of our attorney general.

Being a loyal American, I consider it my duty to send you these informations, as there has been no consul of our nation in this island for many months.

     *   *   *   *   *   *

     *   *   *   *   *   *

I am, sir, your most obedient servant,

                                       FRANCIS BERNARD.

The Secretary of State *of the United States.*

Mr. Seward to Mr. Adams.

No. 85.]   Department of State,
                                       Washington, September 10, 1861.

Sir: I transmit a copy of an intercepted letter of the 30th of July last, from John P. Baldwin, of Richmond, Virginia, to Henry Adderley, at Nassau, New Providence, relative to the shipment of arms and powder from that place for the use of the insurgents in this country. The existing British statute for the prevention of armed expeditions against countries at peace with Great Britain is understood to be similar to our act of Congress of the 5th of April, 1818. Proceedings like that referred to in the letter of Baldwin, however, afford us special reason to expect legislation on the part of the British government of the character of our act of 1838, referred to in my instruction to you of the 7th instant, numbered 83. It may be, however, that the British executive government now has the power to prevent the exportation of contraband of war from British colonies near the United States for the use of the insurgents in the south. Should this be the fact, you will bring the subject to the attention of Lord Russell, and request that proper instructions in regard to it may be given to the colonial authorities.

I am, sir, your obedient servant,

                                       WILLIAM H. SEWARD.

Charles F. Adams, Esq.

Mr. Baldwin to Mr. Adderley.

                                 Richmond, *Virginia, July* 30, 1861.

My Dear Adderley: The secretary of the navy of the Confederate States of America has ordered from England, to be shipped to Nassau, a quantity of arms and powder. I have recommended them to be consigned to you, and

I have to ask of you, as a favor to me, to take good care of them. I will be with you soon, and will expect your aid in transhipping the same.

I must request you to regard this as a confidential communication, and will explain the reasons when we meet. You need not write me at all on the subject.

Hoping soon to see you, I remain your friend,

JNO. P. BALDWIN.

HENRY ADDERLEY, Esq.,
    Nassau, N. P., Bahamas.

Mr. Seward to Mr. Adams.

No. 86.]
DEPARTMENT OF STATE,
Washington, September 11, 1861.

SIR : Your despatch of August 23d has been received.

The inefficiency of the British laws to prevent violations of our rights is deeply to be regretted. We shall necessarily be obliged to exercise vigilance in detecting the unlawful character and objects of British vessels approaching our coasts, which will not be pleasant to the government whose flag they will be perverting to such unfriendly uses.

I am, sir, respectfully, your obedient servant,

WILLIAM H. SEWARD.

CHARLES FRANCIS ADAMS, Esq., &c., &c., &c.

Mr. Adams to Mr. Seward.

[Extract.]

No. 44.]
LEGATION OF THE UNITED STATES,
London, September 14, 1861.

SIR : I now have the honor to transmit copies of two notes received yesterday from Lord Russell, in answer to my notes of the 3d of September, transmitting to him the bag of Mr. Bunch. It appears from one of them that Mr. Bunch has been acting under secret instructions, which are only now acknowledged because they have come to light, and that his granting a safe conduct to an emissary of secession, charged with treasonable papers, is no objection to his neutral character in the eyes of his employers. With regard to the question presented in the other note, it is satisfactory to me, at least in so far as it devolves all responsibility for the further treatment of the question into more capable hands. I transmit also a copy of my reply.

*   *   *   *   *   *   *   *   *

Hon. WILLIAM H. SEWARD,
    Secretary of State, Washington, D. C.

FOREIGN OFFICE, *September* 9, 1861.

SIR : I received, with some surprise, from Lord Lyons an intimation that a sealed bag, directed by one of her Majesty's consuls to her Majesty's secretary of state, had been seized and detained by order of the Secretary of State of the United States.

It seems to have been suspected that her Majesty's consul had inserted in his official bag, and covered with his official seal, the correspondence of the enemies of the government of the United States now engaged in open hostilities against them.

Had her Majesty's consul so acted he would have, no doubt, been guilty of a grave breach of his duty both towards his own government and that of the United States; but I am happy to say there does not appear, on opening the bag at the foreign office, to be any ground for such a suspicion.

Her Majesty's government were advised that the suspension of the conveyance by post of letters from British subjects between the northern and the southern States, was a contravention of the treaty on this subject contracted by the two governments. Her Majesty's government have been unwilling to press this view on the United States; but this stoppage of the post has occasioned great inconvenience to individuals, and I enclose a copy of a note from Mr. Bunch to the under secretary of foreign affairs, showing the mode in which he has endeavored to palliate the evil by enclosing private letters in his consular bag.

I shall address any further communication I may have to make on this subject to Lord Lyons.

I have the honor to be, with the highest consideration, sir, your most obedient, humble servant,

RUSSELL.

CHARLES FRANCIS ADAMS, Esq., &c., &c., &c.

CHARLESTON, August 5, 1861.

Mr. Bunch presents his compliments to her Majesty's under secretary of state for foreign affairs, and takes leave to enclose to him herewith certain letters which are intended for the post.

They are principally letters of servants, governesses, &c., (British subjects,) which, owing to the discontinuance of the post, they are unable to send in any other way. Some also contain dividends, the property of British subjects, which they could scarcely receive without Mr. Bunch's intervention.

Mr. Bunch hopes that there is no irregularity in this proceeding. No expense of postage is incurred by the foreign office, as the bag in which the letters are contained goes by a private hand to Liverpool.

Her Majesty's UNDER SECRETARY OF STATE
For Foreign Affairs.

FOREIGN OFFICE, September 9, 1861.

The undersigned, her Majesty's principal secretary of state for foreign affairs, has received a communication from Mr. Adams, envoy extraordinary and minister plenipotentiary of the United States at this court, dated the 3d instant, giving some information regarding the conduct of Mr. Bunch, her Majesty's consul at Charleston, in the United States, and requesting, on the part of the government of the United States, that Mr. Bunch may at once be removed from his office.

The undersigned will, without hesitation, state to Mr. Adams that in pursuance of an agreement between the British and French governments, Mr. Bunch was instructed to communicate to the persons exercising authority in the so-called Confederate States, the desire of those governments, that the second, third, and fourth articles of the declaration of Paris should be observed by those States in the prosecution of the hostilities in which they were engaged. Mr. Adams will observe that the commerce of Great Britain and France is deeply interested in the maintenance of the articles providing that the flag covers the goods, and that the goods of a neutral taken on board a belligerent ship are not liable to condemnation.

Mr. Bunch, therefore, in what he has done in this matter, has acted in obedience to the instructions of his government, who accept the responsibility of his proceedings so far as they are known to the foreign department, and who cannot remove him from his office for having obeyed his instructions.

But when it is stated in a letter from some person not named, that the first step to the recognition of the southern States by Great Britain has been taken, the undersigned has to decline all responsibility for such statement.

Her Majesty's government have already recognized the belligerent character of the southern States, and they will continue to consider them as belligerents. But her Majesty's government have not recognized, and are not prepared to recognize the so-called Confederate States as a separate and independent State.

The undersigned requests Mr. Adams to accept the assurance of his highest consideration.

RUSSELL.

CHARLES FRANCIS ADAMS, Esq., &c., &c., &c.

LEGATION OF THE UNITED STATES,
London, September 13, 1861.

The undersigned, envoy extraordinary and minister plenipotentiary of the United States, has the honor to acknowledge the reception this day of two notes from the right honorable Earl Russel, her Majesty's principal secretary of state for foreign affairs, both dated the 9th of September, and both in reply to notes addressed to his lordship by the undersigned on the 3d instant, touching the case of Mr. Bunch, her Majesty's consul at Charleston, and the mode of transmission of his despatches. The undersigned has the honor to inform his lordship that copies of these notes will be transmitted by the next steamer for the consideration of the government of the United States.

The undersigned requests Earl Russell to accept the assurance of his highest consideration.

CHARLES FRANCIS ADAMS.

Right Honorable EARL RUSSELL, &c., &c., &c.

Mr. Seward to Mr. Adams.

No. 88.]   DEPARTMENT OF STATE,
                             Washington, September 14, 1861.

SIR: Your despatch of August 30 (No. 34) has just been received. Your note to Lord John Russell, which accompanies it, is approved. My despatch to you, (No. 83,) under the date of the 7th instant, will have reached you before this communication can arrive. You will have learned from that paper that your course, as now made known to me, was anticipated by the President, and that he had already directed that the negotiation for our adhesion to the declaration of the congress of Paris should be suspended.

It is due to the British government to say that the letter of Lord John Russell to Mr. Edwards, upon Dominican affairs, to which you refer, and a copy of which you enclose, was read to me by Lord Lyons, pursuant to instructions from Lord Russell.

I am, sir, respectfully, your obedient servant,

WILLIAM H. SEWARD.

CHARLES FRANCIS ADAMS, Esq., &c., &c., &c.

Mr. Seward to Mr. Adams.

No. 89.]   DEPARTMENT OF STATE,
                                        Washington, September 14, 1861.

SIR: Your despatch of August 30 (No. 35) has been received. While I regret with you that the administration of the laws of Great Britain is such as to render comparatively ineffectual your efforts to defeat there the designs of parties in that country injurious to the United States, I have great pleasure in saying that the information we receive from you concerning them is often very valuable, and enables us to put our own authorities here in a way of vigilant surveillance which promises good results.

I am, sir, respectfully, your obedient servant,

WILLIAM H. SEWARD.

CHARLES FRANCIS ADAMS, Esq., &c., &c., &c.

Mr. Seward to Mr. Adams.

[Confidential.]

No. 95.]   DEPARTMENT OF STATE,
                                        Washington, September 25, 1861.

SIR: Your despatch of September 7 (No. 39) has just been received. Your review of the correspondence between us and the British government since you entered upon your mission is quite satisfactory, and we have every reason to be content with the details as with the results.

The time which has elapsed since the insurgents made their first unnatural appeal to the sympathies and aid of foreign powers for the overthrow of our government has been sufficient to draw out all their strength and exhaust in some measure their passion. On the other hand, the strength of the Union manifests itself with constant augmentation. Every day brings two thousand men and some new ship-of-war into activity, and the insurrection, already, is finding itself obliged to provide for a long and merely defensive contest, desolating the States which should constitute the new confederacy, while the loyal States remain prosperous and happy.

I think that Great Britain will soon be able to see, what she has hitherto been unwilling to see, that, if she, like ourselves, seeks peace and prosperity on this continent, she can most effectually contribute to their restoration by manifesting her wishes for the success of this government in suppressing the insurrection as speedily as possible.

I am, sir, respectfully, your obedient servant,

WILLIAM H. SEWARD.

CHARLES FRANCIS ADAMS, Esq., &c., &c., &c.

Mr. Seward to Mr. Adams.

No. 97.]

DEPARTMENT OF STATE,
Washington, September 25, 1861.

SIR: Your despatch of September 6, No. 38, has been received.

Our naval force is rapidly increasing, and the command of it has recently been reorganized. We are preparing for some vigorous demonstrations on the coast, to begin in about ten days; and I trust, therefore, that we shall be able to defeat on this side the enterprises of the insurgents which we have been unable to prevent on the other.

I am, sir, respectfully, your obedient servant,

WILLIAM H. SEWARD.

CHARLES FRANCIS ADAMS, Esq., &c., &c., &c.

Mr. Adams to Mr. Seward.

[Extract.]

No. 50.]

LEGATION OF THE UNITED STATES,
London, September 28, 1861.

SIR: *   *   *   *   *   *   *   *

During my stay at Abergeldie I alluded to instructions received at the moment of my leaving London, in your despatch, No. 84, of the 10th of September, directing me to make a complaint of the authorities at Trinidad for their mode of reception of the insurgent privateer, the Sumter. I read to him the copy of the letter of Mr. Bernard, which was enclosed. But I contented myself with only mentioning the subject, as I said I supposed I should be obliged to present the case hereafter, in a more formal way, in writing.

His lordship expressed a wish that I should take that course. The matter had already come before the colonial office, and it had been referred to the law officers of the crown, to report what was the action proper to be taken in similar cases.

*   *   *   *   *   *   *   *

I have the honor to be, sir, your obedient servant,

CHARLES FRANCIS ADAMS.

Hon. WILLIAM H. SEWARD,
Secretary of State, Washington, D. C.

Mr. Adams to Mr. Seward.

No. 52.]   LEGATION OF THE UNITED STATES,
                                                    London, September 28, 1861.

SIR: I am much gratified to perceive, by the terms of your despatch, No. 83, dated the 7th of this month, a substantial ratification of the position taken by me in regard to Lord Russell's note of the 19th of August, and to the declaration which he proposed to append to the convention concerning neutral rights. I find in it, too, a general coincidence in the argument presented by me in my reply to his lordship on the 23d of August, a copy of which could not have reached the department down to the latest dates yet received. There are some views offered, however, in my note, which are not touched upon in that despatch. I am, therefore, not as yet fully certain whether, as a whole, it has met with the approbation of the President. For this reason I decided not to hold communication on the subject with Lord Russell, during the time of my late stay under his roof, but rather to wait until after the arrival of the next despatches from the department, which will probably bring a final review of the negotiation, as it appears, after an examination of all the papers that belong to it. I shall then be in a position to judge of the propriety of any further action which it may be advisable to pursue. His lordship informed me, on my taking leave of him, that he expected to return to London by the 14th of next month, after which I anticipate no delay, like the late one, in the transaction of important business.

I have the honor to be, sir, your obedient servant,
                                                    CHARLES FRANCIS ADAMS.
Hon. WILLIAM H. SEWARD,
    Secretary of State, Washington.

Mr. Adams to Mr. Seward.

[Extract.]

No. 53.]   LEGATION OF THE UNITED STATES,
                                                    London, October 4, 1861.

SIR: I have to acknowledge the reception of despatches from the department, numbered from 85 to 89, both inclusive.

The despatch, No. 85, dated the 10th of September, like its immediate predecessor, No. 84, of the same date, though received here a week earlier, relates to cases of violation of neutrality in the British islands in the West Indies. I have now the honor to forward copies of two notes addressed by me to Lord Russell, one of the 30th of September, and the other of the following day, touching these questions.

*   *   *   *   *   *

I have the honor to be, sir, your obedient servant,
                                                    CHARLES FRANCIS ADAMS.
Hon. WILLIAM H. SEWARD,
    Secretary of State, Washington, D. C.

Mr. Adams to Earl Russell.

LEGATION OF THE UNITED STATES,
London, *September* 30, 1861.

The undersigned, envoy extraordinary and minister plenipotentiary of the United States, regrets to be obliged to inform the right honorable Earl Russell, her Majesty's principal secretary of state for foreign affairs, that he has been instructed by the President of the United States to prefer a complaint against the authorities of the island of Trinidad for a violation of her Majesty's proclamation of neutrality, by giving aid and encouragement to the insurgents of the United States. It appears by an extract from a letter received at the Department of State from a gentleman believed to be worthy of credit, a resident of Trinidad, Mr. Francis Bernard, a copy of which is submitted herewith, that a steam vessel, known as an armed insurgent privateer, called the Sumter, was received on the 30th of July last at that port, and was permitted to remain for six days, during which time she was not only furnished with all necessary supplies for the continuance of her cruise, under the sanction of the attorney general, but that her Majesty's flag was actually hoisted on the government flag-staff in acknowledgment of her arrival.

The undersigned has been directed by his government to bring this extraordinary proceeding to the attention of Lord Russell, and, in case it shall not be satisfactorily explained, to ask for the adoption of such measures as shall insure, on the part of the authorities of the island, the prevention of all occurrences of the kind during the continuance of the difficulties in America.

The undersigned deems it proper to add, in explanation of the absence of any official representation from Trinidad to substantiate the present complaint, that there was no consul of the United States there at the time of the arrival of the vessel. The undersigned had the honor, a few days since, to apprise Lord Russell of the fact that this deficiency had been since supplied, by preferring an application for her Majesty's exequator for a new consul, who is already on his way to occupy his post.

The undersigned begs to renew to Earl Russell the assurances of his highest consideration.

CHARLES FRANCIS ADAMS.

The Right Hon. EARL RUSSELL, &c., &c., &c.

Mr. Adams to Earl Russell.

LEGATION OF THE UNITED STATES,
London, *October* 1, 1861.

MY LORD: It is with much regret that I find myself receiving, at every fresh arrival from the United States, instructions from my government to make representations to your lordship concerning alleged violations of her Majesty's proclamation of neutrality, committed by British subjects through the channel of the colonies situated near the United States. I have the honor now to submit to your lordship's consideration the copy of an intercepted letter from a person named John P. Baldwin, living at Richmond, in Virginia, in the service of the insurgents, addressed to Henry Adderley, esquire, of Nassau, New Providence. It appears by this letter that Nassau has been made, to some extent, an entrepot for the transmission of articles

Ex. Doc. 1——11

contraband of war from Great Britain to the ports held by the insurgents. It would be a great source of satisfaction to the government of the United States to learn that her Majesty's government felt itself clothed with the necessary power to prevent the exportation of such contraband from the colonies for the use of the insurgents, and that it would furnish the necessary instructions to the local authorities to attain that end.

I pray your lordship to accept the assurances of the highest consideration, with which I have the honor to be your lordship's most obedient servant,

CHARLES FRANCIS ADAMS.

The Right Hon. Earl Russell, &c., &c., &c.

Mr. Adams to Mr. Seward.

No. 58.]   Legation of the United States,
                                              London, October 11, 1861.

Sir: I have the honor to enclose a copy of Lord Russell's note to me of the 4th instant, in reply to my representation of the conduct of the authorities of the island of Trinidad, made under instructions from the department.

It will appear from this that the governor of Trinidad, by hoisting the British flag on the government flag-staff, probably desired to signify to the officers of the Sumter, on their arrival, the neutral character of the island, but that he in the meantime forgot that the act is susceptible of a very different construction in the popular mind.

*   *`   *   *   *   *

I have the honor to be, sir, your obedient servant,

CHARLES FRANCIS ADAMS.

Hon. William H. Seward,
     Secretary of State, Washington, D. C.

Earl Russell to Mr. Adams.

Foreign Office, *October* 4, 1861.

The undersigned, her Majesty's principal secretary of state for foreign affairs, has had the honor to receive a complaint from Mr. Adams, envoy extraordinary and minister plenipotentiary of the United States at this court, against the authorities of the island of Trinidad for a violation of her Majesty's proclamation of neutrality, by giving aid and encouragement to the insurgents of the United States.

It appears, from the accounts received at the colonial office and at the admiralty, that a vessel bearing a secession flag entered the port of Trinidad on the 30th of July last.

Captain Hillyar, of her Majesty's ship "Cadmus," having sent a boat to ascertain her nationality, the commanding officer showed a commission signed by Mr. Jefferson Davis, calling himself the President of the so-styled Confederate States.

The "Sumter," which was the vessel in question, was allowed to stay six days at Trinidad, and to supply herself with coals and provisions, and the attorney general of the island perceived no illegality in these proceedings.

The law officers of the crown have reported that the conduct of the governor was in conformity to her Majesty's proclamation.

No mention is made by the governor of his hoisting the British flag on the government flag-staff; and if he did so, it was probably in order to show the national character of the island, and not in acknowledgment of the arrival of the "Sumter."

There does not appear, therefore, any reason to believe that her Majesty's proclamation of neutrality has been violated by the governor of Trinidad, or by the commanding officer of her Majesty's ship "Cadmus."

The undersigned requests Mr. Adams to accept the assurance of his highest consideration.

RUSSELL.

CHARLES FRANCIS ADAMS, Esq., &c., &c., &c.

Mr. Seward to Mr. Adams.

No. 108.]
DEPARTMENT OF STATE,
Washington, October 22, 1861.

SIR : The receipt of your despatch of the 14th of September (No. 44) has been already acknowledged.

It was accompanied by Earl Russell's reply to the note which, in execution of my instructions, you addressed to him on the subject of the detention of a bearer of despatches sent by Robert Bunch, her Majesty's consul at Charleston, and the substitution by me of another person to convey his consular bag to Great Britain.

Earl Russell says, in his note, that if it had been true (as we apprehended) that Mr. Bunch had inserted into his official bag and covered with his official seal the correspondence of the enemies of this government in the United States, he would have been guilty of a grave breach of his duty towards his own government and that of the United States. Earl Russell says also, that on the opening of the bag at the foreign office (in London) no ground for that suspicion was revealed.

These declarations, made with unquestioned candor and freedom, are entirely satisfactory upon the main point involved in your note. It is therefore a pleasant duty for me to instruct you to reply to Earl Russell that this government regrets the interruption of the passage of the consular despatches, which has occurred in consequence of a mistaken suspicion that the agent who transmitted them was abusing the confidence of the two governments. I sincerely hope that no serious inconvenience resulted from the delay.

Earl Russell, after making the explanations which I have quoted, proceeds to remark that her Majesty's government was advised that the suspicion of the conveyance by post of letters from British subjects between the northern States and the southern States was in contravention of the treaty on this subject contracted between the two governments ; that her Majesty's government had been, nevertheless, unwilling to press this view on the United States ; but that this stoppage of the post has occasioned great inconvenience to individuals. His lordship then submits a copy of a note which Mr. Bunch had written to the under secretary of state, showing the mode in which he had endeavored to palliate the evil by enclosing private letters in his official bag. His lordship then dismisses the subject, saying that he shall address any further communication he may have to make thereon, to Lord Lyons.

Mr. Bunch, in his note, states that he encloses in the bag, to the under secretary's address, certain letters which are intended for the post, and that they are principally letters of servants, governesses, &c., British subjects, which, owing to the discontinuance of the post, they are unable to send in any other way ; also, that some of the letters contain dividends, the property of British subjects, which they could scarcely receive without Mr. Bunch's intervention. He adds that he hopes that there is no irregularity in this proceeding, since no expense of postage is incurred, because the bag in which the letters are contained goes by a private hand to Liverpool. I read this note under the light thrown upon it by the explanations of Earl Russell, which show that the whole correspondence contained in the bag was innocent.

In these circumstances, what remains open to special exception in Mr. Bunch's proceeding is, his substitution of his consular bag and official seal for the mail bag and mail locks of the United States, and of his own mail carrier for the mail carriers of the United States.

The proceeding of the consul in these respects, certainly is not defensible on any ground of treaty or international law ; nor does Earl Russell in any way imply that he deems it is so. The proceeding however was practically harmless, and it is not likely to be repeated.

I confess to the fact of the interruption of the post, and also that it works literally a non-fulfilment of a treaty stipulation. I deplore it for that reason, as well as for the public and private injuries that it occasions, not only abroad but at home. But the British government is well aware that the interruption has occurred, not through the deliberate or even voluntary consent of the government, but through the sudden violence of an insurrection which has not only obstructed the mails, but which even seeks to overthrow not only the treaty in question, but even the government of the United States and the Union itself, which constitutes them one treaty-making and treaty-observing nation. Suppression of the correspondence between parties in that nation with each other in this country and in foreign countries is a measure which is essential to the suppression of the insurrection itself, and to a complete restoration of the functions of the government throughout the Union. I feel sure that the magnanimity of the British government may be relied upon not to complain, at one and the same time, of the breach of our international postal treaty under such circumstances, and of our resort to a measure which is indispensable to complete our ability to fulfil it.

I am, sir, your obedient servant,

WILLIAM H. SEWARD,

CHARLES FRANCIS ADAMS, Esq., &c., &c., &c.

Mr. Seward to Mr. Adams.

No. 109.]   DEPARTMENT OF STATE,
                                          Washington, October 23, 1861.

SIR: I recur once more to your despatch of September 14, No. 44. On the 3d of that month you addressed a note to Earl Russell, in which you informed him, by my direction, that from the contents of the many letters found in the possession of Mr. Robert Mure, bearer of despatches to the government of Great Britain, but detained at New York as an agent of the enemies of the United States, the following statement is made of the action of Mr. Bunch in Charleston. "Mr. Bunch, on oath of secrecy, communicated to me also that the first step to recognition was taken; that he and Mr. Belligny together sent Mr. Trescot to Richmond yesterday to ask Jeff.

Davis, President, to —— the treaty of —— to —— the neutral flag covering neutral goods to be respected. This is the first step of direct treating with our government. So prepare for active business by first of January."

You submitted this information to her Majesty's government with a request on the part of the President of the United States that, if it should be found to be correct, Mr. Bunch might be at once removed from his office. And you further added, by my direction, that the President would cheerfully accord an exequatur to any person who might be appointed to succeed Mr. Bunch, who would faithfully perform his functions without injury to the rights and interests of the United States.

There is appended to your despatch now before me the written answer of the Earl Russell to your note thus recited.

His lordship answers that he will, without hesitation, state to Mr. Adams that, in pursuance of an agreement between the British and French governments, Mr. Bunch was instructed to communicate to the persons excercising authority in the so-called Confederate States the desire of those governments that the second, third, and fourth articles of the declaration of Paris should be observed by those States in the prosecution of the hostilities in which they were engaged. His lordship then asked you to observe that the commerce of Great Britain and France is deeply interested in the maintenance of the articles providing that the flag covers the goods, and that the goods of a neutral taken on board a belligerent ship are not liable to confiscation. Earl Russell thereupon proceeds to say that Mr. Bunch, in what he has done in this matter, has acted in obedience to the instructions of his government, who accept the responsibility of his proceedings, so far as they are known to the foreign department, and who cannot therefore remove him from his office for having obeyed their instructions. But his lordship adds that, when it is stated in a letter from some person not named that the first step to the recognition of the southern States by Great Britain has been taken, he, Earl Russell, begs to decline all responsibility for such statement; and he remarks on this branch of the subject that her Majesty's government have already recognized the belligerent character of the southern States, and they will continue to consider them as belligerents, but that her Majesty's government have not recognized, and are not prepared to recognize, the so-called Confederate States as a separate and independent State.

You are instructed to reply to this note of her Majesty's principal secretary of state for foreign affairs:

First. That her Majesty's government having avowed that Mr. Bunch acted under their instructions, so far as his conduct is known to the foreign department, and that government having avowed their responsibility for his proceedings in that extent, it is admitted that, so far as that portion of the subject is concerned, the matter is to be settled directly with her Majesty's government.

Secondly. That a law of the United States forbids any person not specially appointed or duly authorized or recognized by the President, whether citizen or denizen, privileged or unprivileged, from counselling, advising, aiding, or assisting in any political correspondence with the government of any foreign state whatever, with an intent to influence the measures of any foreign government, or of any officer or agent thereof, in relation to any disputes or controversies with the United States, or to defeat the measures of the government. The proceeding of Mr. Bunch was clearly and distinctly in violation of this positive law.

Thirdly. This government finds no sufficient justification or excuse for the proceeding of Mr. Bunch, thus shown to be in violation of the law of the United States, in the consideration that Great Britain was deeply interested in the maintenance of the articles which provide that the flag covers the goods, and that the goods of a neutral taken on board a belligerent ship are not liable to confiscation.

It is enough to say on this subject that, in our view, the proper agents of the British government, to make known that interest here, are the diplomatic, not the consular agents of her Majesty; and that the only authority in this country to which any diplomatic communication whatever can be made is the government of the United States itself.

Still less can the United States admit that communication by Mr. Bunch, while exercising consular privileges with which he was clothed by the consent of the United States, with insurgents in arms against the federal government, is justified by the declaration of the British ministry that they have already recognized the belligerent character of the insurgents, and that they will continue to consider them as belligerents. It is understood to be true that her Majesty's government have heretofore issued a royal proclamation which they interpret as declaring that they recognize the insurgents as a belligerent. But it is also true that this government has, with equal decision and with equal resolution, announced to the British government that any such declaration made by the British government would not be accepted as modifying, in the least degree, the rights or powers of this government, or the obligations due to them by Great Britain as a friendly nation. Still adhering to this position, the government of the United States will continue to pursue, as it has heretofore done, the counsels of prudence, and will not suffer itself to be disturbed by excitement. It must revoke the exequatur of the consul, who has not only been the bearer of communications between the insurgents and a foreign government, in violation of our laws, but has abused equally the confidence of the two governments by reporting, without the authority of his government, and in violation of their own policy as well as of our national rights, that the proceeding in which he was engaged was in the nature of a treaty with the insurgents, and the first step towards a recognition by Great Britain of their sovereignty. Moreover, the conduct of the person in question, even while this correspondence has been going on, as well as before it commenced, has been that, not of a friend to this government, or even of a neutral, but of a partisan of faction and disunion.

In reviewing this subject it would be unjust to her Majesty's minister residing here, as well as to her Majesty's government, to omit to say that that minister has, in all his proceedings, carefully respected the sovereignty and the rights of the United States, and that the arrangements which have been made by him, with the approval of this government, for communication between the British government and its consuls, through the national vessels of Great Britain entering blockaded ports without carrying passengers or private letters, seems to forbid any necessity for a recurrence of such proceedings as those which have brought about these explanations. You will inform the Earl Russell that the exequatur of Mr. Bunch has been withdrawn because his services as consul are not agreeable to this government, and that the consular privileges thus taken from him will be cheerfully allowed to any successor whom her Majesty may appoint, against whom no grave personal objections shall exist. It is a source of satisfaction to the President to reflect that the proceeding which I have been considering occurred some time ago, and that the part of it which was most calculated to offend, and to which exception is now especially taken, finds no support in the communication of Earl Russell.

I am, sir, your obedient servant,

WILLIAM H. SEWARD.

CHARLES FRANCIS ADAMS, Esq., &c., &c., &c.

Mr. Seward to Mr. Adams.

No. 112.]   DEPARTMENT OF STATE,
                                    Washington, October 29, 1861.

SIR: Your despatch of October 11, No. 58, has been received. It is accompanied by Lord Russell's reply to the note which you addressed to him by my direction, asking an explanation of the conduct of the colonial authorities in Trinidad on the occasion of the entrance of the piratical vessel the "Sumter" into that port.

Lord Russell admits that the "Sumter," (an armed American vessel,) bearing an insurgent flag, entered the port of Trinidad, and when boarded and required to show her nationality, her commanding officer showed no legal authority from this government, but a pretended commission from a citizen of the United States, notoriously engaged in arms against them. Notwithstanding these facts, it is not denied that the governor of the island hoisted the British flag on the government flag-staff, although it is stated by Lord Russell that, if he did so, it was probably done in order to show the national character of the island, and not in acknowledgment of the arrival of the "Sumter."

His lordship, however, admits that the "Sumter" was allowed to remain six days in Trinidad, and that during her stay she was allowed to supply herself with coals and provisions. The armament, the insurgent flag, and the spurious commission told the governor, as they sufficiently prove to her Majesty's government, that the "Sumter" is and can be nothing else than a piratical vessel. Her depredations on the commerce of this country form a part of the history of our times. The British government has, moreover, been directly informed by us that the "Sumter" is a piratical craft, and that the navigators and seamen on board of her are pirates, punishable by the laws of their own country with death. Lord Russell informs us that the law officers of the crown have nevertheless reported that the conduct of the colonial authorities of Trinidad is in conformity to her Majesty's proclamation. Her Majesty's government dismiss our complaint from their consideration.

In view of these facts, it becomes my duty to instruct you to inform the British government that the President deeply regrets that Lord Russell is altogether unable to give to our complaint a satisfactory solution.

When it is considered how important a part commerce plays among the interests of our country, it will be seen that the United States cannot consent that pirates engaged in destroying it shall receive shelter and supplies in the ports of friendly nations. It tends to the universal derangement of commerce when piracy is anywhere tolerated, and therefore its suppression is a common interest of all civilized countries. But if any one power fails to preserve this interest, and to act for the common welfare, then it is easy to see that each state must provide for its own security at whatever cost, and however it may disturb the general harmony of the commercial world.

This government will consider how its safety may be best secured; but it cannot forbear from expressing a hope that her Majesty's ministers, in view of the gravity of the question, may deem the subject worthy of a deliberate reconsideration.

I am, sir, your most obedient servant,

                                    WILLIAM H. SEWARD.

CHARLES FRANCIS ADAMS, Esq., &c., &c., &c.

Mr. Seward to Lord Lyons.

[Circular.]

DEPARTMENT OF STATE,
Washington, October 4, 1861.

My LORD: I regret to inform you that information has reached this department that foreign vessels-of-war, which have entered ports of States in insurrection against the government of the United States, under blockade,
have, in some instances, carried passengers, and in others private corres,
pondence. It is presumed that such proceedings could not have taken place
with the knowledge or approval of the governments of foreign countries.

With a view, however, to prevent any misunderstanding in future, it is
distinctly to be understood that no foreign vessel-of-war, which may enter
or depart from a blockaded port of the United States, will carry any person
as a passenger, or any correspondence other than that between the government of the country to which the vessel may belong and the diplomatic and
consular agents of such country at the ports adverted to.

I avail myself of this occasion to offer to your lordship a renewed assurance
of my high consideration.

WILLIAM H. SEWARD.
To the Right Honorable LORD LYONS, &c., &c., &c.

Lord Lyons to Mr. Seward.

BRITISH LEGATION,
Washington, D. C., October 12, 1861.

SIR : I have the honor to acknowledge the receipt of your note of the 4th
instant, relative to communications between ships-of-war and the ports in
the southern States, now under blockade.

You have apprised me in ·that note that information has reached the
Department of State that foreign vessels-of-war which have entered those
ports since they were blockaded, have in some instances carried passengers,
and in others private correspondence. You were so good as to assure me
verbally, yesterday, that no British ship-of-war was included among those
to which your note thus referred. Indeed, I have every reason to believe
that, with a single exception, no British ship-of-war has communicated with
any of the ports under blockade. The ship which I except is the "Steady;"
of my intention to request the commander of this ship to leave official despatches at Charleston, I had the honor to inform you on the 18th of last
month. The "Steady" accordingly sailed for Charleston a few days afterwards. She carried no letters except official despatches from me or other
authorities of foreign governments in the United States, and no passenger
excepting Mr. Fullaston, her Majesty's acting consul at Savannah, who was
landed at Charleston on his way back to his post.

As several of my colleagues have expressed to me their desire to send
official despatches to the consuls of their respective governments by any of
her Majesty's ships which may hereafter convey despatches for me to the
ports under blockade, I shall be much obliged if you will inform me whether
you see any objection to my forwarding to those ports, by her Majesty's

ships, despatches addressed by official authorities of foreign countries to other official authorities of their own countries.

I have the honor to be, with high consideration, sir, your most obedient, humble servant,

LYONS.

Lord Lyons to Mr. Seward.

WASHINGTON, *October* 14, 1861.

SIR: Her Majesty's government were much concerned to find that two British subjects, Mr. Patrick and Mr. Rahming, had been subjected to arbitrary arrest; and although they had learnt from a telegraphic despatch from me that Mr. Patrick had been released, they could not but regard the matter as one requiring their very serious consideration.

Her Majesty's government perceive that when British subjects as well as American citizens are arrested they are immediately transferred to a military prison, and that the military authorities refuse to pay obedience to a writ of habeas corpus.

Her Majesty's government conceive that this practice is directly opposed to the maxim of the Constitution of the United States "that no person shall be deprived of life, liberty, or property without due process of law."

Her Majesty's government are willing, however, to make every allowance for the hard necessities of a time of internal trouble; and they would not have been surprised if the ordinary securities of personal liberty had been temporarily suspended, nor would they have complained if British subjects falling under suspicion had suffered from the consequences of that suspension.

But it does not appear that Congress has sanctioned in this respect any departure from the due course of law; and it is in these circumstances that the law officers of the crown have advised her Majesty's government that the arbitrary arrests of British subjects are illegal.

So far as appears to her Majesty's government, the Secretary of State of the United States exercises, upon the reports of spies and informers, the power of depriving British subjects of their liberty, of retaining them in prison, or liberating them, by his own will and pleasure.

Her Majesty's government cannot but regard this despotic and arbitrary power as inconsistent with the Constitution of the United States, as at variance with the treaties of amity subsisting between the two nations, and as tending to prevent the resort of British subjects to the United States for the purposes of trade and industry.

Her Majesty's government have therefore felt bound to instruct me to remonstrate against such irregular proceedings, and to say that, in their opinion, the authority of Congress is necessary in order to justify the arbitrary arrest and imprisonment of British subjects.

I have the honor to be, sir, with the highest consideration, your most obedient, humble servant,

LYONS.

Hon. WILLIAM H. SEWARD, &c.

Mr. Seward to Lord Lyons.

DEPARTMENT OF STATE.
Washington, October 14, 1861.

MY LORD: I have the honor to acknowledge your lordship's note of the present date.

In that paper you inform me that the British government is much concerned to find that two British subjects, Mr. Patrick and Mr. Rahming, have been brought under arbitrary arrest, and that although her Majesty's ministers have been advised by you of the release of Mr. Patrick, yet they cannot but regard the matter as requiring the very serious consideration of this government.

You further inform me that her Majesty's government perceive that when British subjects, as well as American citizens, are arrested, they are transferred to a military prison, and that the military authorities refuse to pay obedience to a writ of habeas corpus.

You add that her Majesty's government conceive that this practice is directly opposed to the maxim of the Constitution of the United States that no person shall be deprived of life, liberty, or property, without due process of law. You then observe that her Majesty's government are nevertheless willing to make every allowance for the hard necessities of a time of internal trouble, and they would not have been surprised if the ordinary securities of personal liberty had been temporarily suspended, nor would they have complained if British subjects, falling under suspicion, had suffered from the consequences of that suspension. But that it does not appear that Congress has sanctioned, in this respect, any departure from the due course of law, and it is in these circumstances that the law officers of the crown have advised her Majesty's government that the arrests of British subjects are illegal.

You remark further, that, so far as appears to her Majesty's government, the Secretary of State for the United States examines upon the reports of spies, and assumes the power of depriving British subjects of their liberty or liberating them by his own will and pleasure; and you inform me that her Majesty's government cannot but regard this despotic and arbitrary power as inconsistent with the Constitution of the United States, as at variance with the treaties of amity subsisting between the two nations, and as tending to prevent the resort of British subjects to the United States for purposes of trade and industry. You conclude with informing me that upon these grounds her Majesty's government have felt bound to instruct you to remonstrate against such irregular proceedings, and to say that, in their opinion, the authority of Congress is necessary in order to justify the arbitrary arrest and imprisonment of British subjects.

The facts in regard to the two persons named in your note are as follows:

Communications from the regular police of the country to the Executive at Washington showed that disloyal persons in the State of Alabama were conducting treasonable correspondence with confederates, British subjects and American citizens, in Europe, aimed at the overthrow of the federal Union by armed forces actually in the field, and besieging the capital of the United States. A portion of this correspondence which was intercepted was addressed to the firm of Smith & Patrick, brokers, long established and doing business in the city of New York. It appeared that this firm had a branch at Mobile; that the partner, Smith, is a disloyal citizen of the United States, and that he was in Europe when the treasonable papers were sent from Mobile, addressed through the house of Smith & Patrick, in New York. On receiving this information William Patrick was arrested and committed into military custody at Fort Lafayette by an order of the Secretary of War of the United States, addressed to the police of the city of New York. These proceedings took place on the 28th of August last.

Representations were thereupon made to the Secretary of State by friends of Mr. Patrick to the effect that notwithstanding his associations he was personally loyal to this government, and that he was ignorant of the treasonable nature of the correspondence which was being carried on through the mercantile house of which he was a member. Directions were thereupon given by the Secretary of State to a proper agent to inquire into the correctness of the facts thus presented, and this inquiry resulted in the establishment of their truth. Mr. William Patrick was thereupon promptly released from custody by direction of the Secretary of State. This release occurred on the thirteenth day of September last.

On the second day of September the superintendent of police in the city of New York informed the Secretary of State, by telegraph, that he had under arrest J. C. Rahming, who had just arrived from Nassau, where he had attempted to induce the owners of the schooner "Arctic" to take cannon to Wilmington, in North Carolina, for the use of the rebels, and inquired what should he do with the prisoner. J. C. Rahming was thereupon committed into military custody at Fort Lafayette under a mandate from the Secretary of State. This commitment was made on the second day of September. On the 17th day of that month this prisoner, after due inquiry, was released from custody on his executing a bond in the penalty of two thousand five hundred dollars, with a condition that he should thereafter bear true allegiance to the United States, and do no act hostile or injurious to them while remaining under their protection.

I have to regret that, after so long an official intercourse between the governments of the United States and Great Britain, it should be necessary now to inform her Majesty's ministers that all executive proceedings, whether of the Secretary of War or of the Secretary of State, are, unless disavowed or revoked by the President, proceedings of the President of the United States.

Certainly it is not necessary to announce to the British government now that an insurrection, attended by civil and even social war, was existing in the United States when the proceedings which I have thus related took place. But it does seem necessary to state, for the information of that government, that Congress is, by the Constitution, invested with no executive power or responsibility whatever; and, on the contrary, that the President of the United States is, by the Constitution and laws, invested with the whole executive power of the government, and charged with the supreme direction of all municipal or ministerial civil agents, as well as of the whole land and naval forces of the Union; and that, invested with those ample powers, he is charged by the Constitution and laws with the absolute duty of suppressing insurrection as well as of preventing and repelling invasion; and that for these purposes he constitutionally exercises the right of suspending the writ of *habeas corpus* whenever and wheresoever and in whatsoever extent the public safety, endangered by treason or invasion in arms, in his judgment requires.

The proceedings of which the British government complain were taken upon information conveyed to the President by legal police authorities of the country, and they were not instituted until after he had suspended the great writ of freedom in just the extent that, in view of the perils of the State, he deemed necessary. For the exercise of that discretion he, as well as his advisers, among whom are the Secretary of War and the Secretary of State, is responsible by law before the highest judicial tribunal of the republic, and amenable also to the judgment of his countrymen and the enlightened opinion of the civilized world.

A candid admission contained in your letter relieves me of any necessity for showing that the two persons named therein were neither known nor supposed to be British subjects when the proceedings occurred, and that in every case subjects of her Majesty residing in the United States, and under their protection, are treated during the present troubles in the same manner and with no greater or less rigor than American citizens.

The military prison which was used for the temporary detention of the suspected parties is a fort constructed and garrisoned for the public defence. The military officer charged with their custody has declined to pay obedience to the writ of habeas corpus, but the refusal was made in obedience to an express direction of the President, in the exercise of his functions as commander-in-chief of all the land and naval forces of the United States. Although it is not very important, it certainly is not entirely irrelevant to add that, so far as I am informed, no writ of habeas corpus was attempted to be served, or was even sued out or applied for in behalf of either of the persons named ; although in a case not dissimilar the writ of habeas corpus was issued out in favor of another British subject, and was disobeyed by direction of the President.

The British government have candidly conceded, in the remonstrance before me, that even in this country, so remarkable for so long an enjoyment, by its people of the highest immunities of personal freedom, war, and especially civil war, cannot be conducted exclusively in the forms and with the dilatory remedies provided by municipal laws which are adequate to the preservation of public order in a time of peace. Treason always operates, if possible, by surprise, and prudence and humanity therefore equally require that violence concocted in secret shall be prevented if practicable by unusual and vigorous precaution. I am fully aware of the inconveniences which result from the practice of such precaution, embarrassing communities in social life, and affecting perhaps trade and intercourse with foreign nations. But the American people, after having tried in every way to avert civil war, have accepted it at last as a stern necessity. Their chief interest, while it lasts, is not the enjoyments of society, or the profits of trade, but the saving of the national life. That life saved, all the other blessings which attach to it will speedily return, with greater assurance of continuance than ever before. The safety of the whole people has become, in the present emergency, the supreme law, and so long as the danger shall exist, all classes of society equally, the denizen and the citizen, cheerfully acquiesce in the measures which that law prescribes.

This government does not question the learning of the legal advisers of the British crown or the justice of the deference which her Majesty's government pays to them. Nevertheless the British government will hardly expect that the President will accept their explanations of the Constitution of the United States, especially when the Constitution, thus expounded, would leave upon him the sole executive responsibility of suppressing the existing insurrection, while it would transfer to Congress the most material and indispensable power to be employed for that purpose. Moreover, these explanations find no real support in the letter, much less in the spirit, of the Constitution itself. He must be allowed, therefore, to prefer and be governed by the view of our organic national law, which, while it will enable him to execute his great trust with complete success, receives the sanction of the highest authorities of our own country, and is sustained by the general consent of the people, for whom alone that Constitution was established

I avail myself of this opportunity to offer to your lordship a renewed assurance of my very high consideration.

WILLIAM H. SEWARD.

The Right Hon. Lord Lyons, &c.

Mr. Seward to Lord Lyons.

DEPARTMENT OF STATE,
Washington, October 14, 1861.

MY LORD: I have had the honor to receive your note of the 12th instant, in answer to mine of the 4th, relative to the carriage of passengers and private letters in vessels of war of foreign powers to and from ports of the United States under blockade.

In reply, I have the honor to acquaint you that no complaint has been made to this department that any British vessel had indulged in this practice ; but insomuch as such a proceeding, if acquiesced in at all by this government, would defeat the objects of the blockade, it was deemed advisable to address a circular upon the subject to the representatives here of the principal maritime powers. No objection is entertained to the transmission, through the channel of vessels of war of friendly powers, of any *official* correspondence with the agents of those powers in blockaded ports.

I avail myself of this occasion to offer to your lordship a renewed assurance of my high consideration.

WILLIAM H. SEWARD.

The Right Hon. Lord LYONS, &c., &c., &c.

Mr. Seward to Lord Lyons.

CIRCULAR.

DEPARTMENT OF STATE,
Washington, October 16, 1861.

MY LORD: The judge of the court of the United States for the southern district of New York having recently decided, after elaborate argument of counsel, that the law of blockade does not permit a vessel in a blockaded port to take on board cargo after the commencement of the blockade, with a view to avoid any future misunderstanding upon this subject, you are informed that the law, as thus interpreted by the judge, will be expected to be strictly observed by all vessels in ports of insurgent States during their blockade by the naval forces of the United States.

I avail myself of this occasion to offer to your lordship a renewed assurance of my high consideration.

WILLIAM H. SEWARD.

The Right Hon. Lord LYONS, &c., &c., &c.

Lord Lyons to Mr. Seward.

WASHINGTON, *October* 17, 1861.

SIR: I beg to offer you my thanks for the note dated the 14th instant, which you have done me the honor to write to me in answer to that dated the 12th instant, which I addressed to you on the subject of transmitting official correspondence by her Majesty's ships of war to the blockaded ports.

It is with reluctance that I importune you further in this matter. But as I am very anxious to avoid all risk of misapprehending your wishes, I venture to ask you whether I am right in understanding that you have no objection to my sending to the blockaded ports, by her Majesty's ships of war, not only British official correspondence with British authorities, but also the official correspondence of other powers friendly to the United States, with the agents of the same powers in the southern States.

I have the honor to be, with high consideration, sir, your most obedient, humble servant,

LYONS.

The Hon. William H. Seward, &c., &c., &c.

Mr Seward to Lord Lyons.

DEPARTMENT OF STATE,
Washington, October 18, 1861.

MY LORD: I have the honor to acknowledge the receipt of your note of yesterday, and to state, in reply, that it was intended in my previous communication, to which it refers, to say that official correspondence of other powers with the agents of those powers in blockaded ports, as well as that of British authorities with their agents, might be sent by British vessels of war.

I am, &c.,

WILLIAM H. SEWARD.

The Right Hon. Lord Lyons, &c., &c., &c.

Lord Lyons to Mr. Seward.

WASHINGTON, *October 23,* 1861.

SIR: Having received information that a bag of despatches addressed by her Majesty's acting consul at Richmond, in Virginia, to her Majesty's consul at New York had been taken from a gentleman of the name of Crosse, at Baltimore, and sent to General Dix, I directed Mr. Bernal, her Majesty's consul at the latter place, to make inquiries of the general on the subject. You will perceive by the enclosed copy of a despatch from Mr. Bernal that the general referred him to you. I therefore do myself the honor to ask you to be so kind as to favor me with such information as it seems proper that I should receive with regard to the seizure of the despatches in question.

I have the honor to be, with high consideration, sir, your most obedient, humble servant,

LYONS.

Mr. Bernal to Lord Lyons.

BRITISH CONSULATE,
Baltimore, October 22, 1861.

MY LORD: In pursuance of the instructions in your lordship's despatch of the 19th (received this morning) having reference to the reported seizure of a bag of despatches, I proceeded to Fort McHenry, where I had an interview with General Dix. I asked him to be good enough to inform me if it was true that on or about the 16th instant a bag of despatches, addressed to her Majesty's consul in New York by her Majesty's acting consul at Richmond, was taken away from Mr. Thomas Crosse, a British subject, by the provost marshal in this city, and sent to him. General Dix replied very briefly that he must decline giving me any information, and referred me to Mr. Seward. In order that there should be no mistake, I repeated my question, and received the same answer.

I have, &c.,

F. BERNAL.

Mr. Seward to Lord Lyons.

DEPARTMENT OF STATE,
Washington, October 24, 1861.

MY LORD: I have the honor to acknowledge the receipt of your note of yesterday, requesting information in regard to a bag supposed to contain despatches from the acting British consul at Richmond, addressed to Mr. Archibald, the British consul at New York, which bag was taken from a man named Cross by the provost marshal of Baltimore.

In reply, I have the honor to inform you that having received information from General Dix that such a bag had been found concealed in the trunk of a man of that name—a spy of the insurgents, who escaped before he could be arrested—I directed the general to forward it hither. On its arrival, although it had a label attached to it, addressed to Mr. Archibald, and the words on her Britannic Majesty's service, there was nothing to identify it as having been forwarded by the British vice-consul at Richmond. This circumstance, in connexion with those under which the bag was brought through the military lines of the United States, naturally occasioned doubts as to its containing official correspondence. I consequently directed the bag to be opened, when it proved to contain not a single communication for Mr. Archibald, or for any other officer of the British government on this continent. It did contain a few apparently official letters to functionaries of the British government at London. These were promptly forwarded, as received, to Mr. Adams, with directions to cause them to be delivered to their address.

The other contents of the bag are, and will be, retained here. It is unnecessary to specify their character. I will only add that they are such as no consul, or acting consul, of a foreign government has a right to forward in any way from a place in rebellion against this government.

I avail myself of this occasion to offer to your lordship a renewed assurance of my very high consideration.

WILLIAM H. SEWARD.

To Lord Lyons.

Lord Lyons to Mr. Seward.

WASHINGTON, *October* 28, 1861.

SIR: Her Majesty's government have had under their consideration the note which I had the honor to address to you on the 22d ultimo, with the despatch from Mr. Consul Archibald which accompanied it.

Her Majesty's government have learned with much surprise, from those papers, the cruel treatment to which the nine British seamen who were imprisoned in Fort Lafayette were subjected by the United States authorities. Her Majesty's government are unable to comprehend the grounds on which persons, who were accused of no offence, were confined in irons and treated as criminals ; and although it has been satisfactory to them to learn, from the answer which you did me the honor to make to my representations on the subject, that orders were given for the release of these men, yet her Majesty's government cannot but consider that some amends are due to them for the sufferings to which they were thus causelessly exposed. Her Majesty's government have accordingly instructed me to bring the matter again to the notice of the government of the United States, and to express their hope that due compensation may be awarded to the sufferers.

I have the honor to be, with the highest consideration, sir, your most obedient, humble servant,

LYONS.

Mr. Seward to Mr. Adams.

No. 122.]   DEPARTMENT OF STATE,
                        Washington, November 11, 1861.

SIR: The case in regard to pirates engaged by the insurgents in this country practically stands thus: every naval power, and every commercial power except one, practically excludes them from their ports, except in distress, or for a visit of any kind longer than twenty-four hours, and from supplies, except of coals, for twenty-four hour's consumption.

Great Britain, as we are given to understand by the answer of Earl Russell, allows these pirates to visit her ports and stay at their own pleasure, receiving supplies without restriction.

We find it difficult to believe that the government of Great Britain has constituted this exception with full deliberation. I intimated in a preceding despatch, No. 112, a hope that the subject might be reconsidered before it should be necessary for us to consider what remedies we can adopt to prevent the evils which must result to our commerce from the policy thus indicated by Great Britain. I have consulted on the subject with Lord Lyons, and he may perhaps communicate with his government thereupon. Meantime, I am directed by the President to instruct you to recall the attention of her Majesty's government to the question, under the influences of a spirit of peace and friendship, and with a desire to preserve what remains of a commerce mutually important to both countries.

I am, sir, your obedient servant,

WILLIAM H. SEWARD.

CHARLES FRANCIS ADAMS, Esq., &c., &c., &c.

CASE OF THE PERTHSHIRE.

Lord Lyons to Mr. Seward.

BRITISH LEGATION,
Washington, D. C., October 11, 1861.

SIR : I have the honor to transmit to you a copy of a memorial addressed to Earl Russell, her Majesty's principal secretary of state for foreign affairs, by Mr. William Gray, owner of the British ship " Perthshire," which appears to have been interfered with by United States ships-of-war. I am directed by Lord Russell to ask the government of the United States for an explanation.

I have the honor to be, with high consideration, sir, your most obedient, humble servant,

LYONS.

Hon. W. H. SEWARD, &c., &c., &c.

Mr. Gray to Earl Russell.

HARTLEPOOL, *August* 28, 1861.

MY LORD : I take the liberty of directing your lordship's attention, in your official capacity as secretary of state for foreign affairs, to the following facts connected with the seizure and detention by a United States steamship of the ship " Perthshire," of the port of Hartlepool, whilst engaged in lawful commerce upon the high seas, and to request that your lordship will, through the British ambassador at Washington, bring the case before the government of the United States, and demand compensation for the loss I have sustained by the detention of my ship, and which loss I estimate at the sum of two hundred pounds sterling, besides rendering void all insurances effected upon the ship, her cargo and freight, (of the gross value of forty thousand pounds sterling,) by compelling the ship to deviate from her voyage.

The " Perthshire," a ship of 810 tons register, was chartered by a merchant in Liverpool, in March last, to proceed in ballast from Grimsby to Pensacola, and there load a cargo of timber for the United Kingdom ; the charterer, however, having the option, through his agent at Pensacola, of ordering the ship to Mobile to load cotton for Liverpool at a lump sum of £2,300.

The ship sailed from Grimsby in March last, and on the 13th of May was making for the harbor of Pensacola, when she was ordered to heave to by the commander of the United States steamship " Niagara." She was boarded by Lieutenant Brown, boarding officer, who informed Captain Oates, of the " Perthshire," that Pensacola was blockaded, and indorsed the vessel's register as follows :

"Boarded by the United States squadron May 13, 1861, and warned not to enter the harbor of Pensacola.

"GEORGE BROWN,
"Lieut. United States Navy, Boarding Officer."

Ex. Doc. 1——12

In reply to the inquiry of Captain Oates, the lieutenant informed him that Mobile was not blockaded. The ship then proceeded to Mobile, where she arrived on the 14th May. Mobile was not blockaded until May 26. At Mobile the "Perthshire" loaded a cargo of cotton for Liverpool, and proceeded to sea on May 31 ; outside the port she was again boarded by the boarding officer of the United States steamship "Niagara," who examined his [her] clearances, expressed himself satisfied with them, and said the ship might proceed on her voyage. She proceeded with light and variable winds until the 9th of June, when she was boarded by the boarding officer of the United States ship "Massachusetts," who, after communicating with his ship, sent a prize crew of 29 men and 2 officers on board the "Perthshire," who took possession of the ship and all the captain's papers, hauled down the British flag and hoisted the United States flag. They altered the course of the ship, and took her back towards Pensacola, off which place, on the 12th of June, after sailing about 200 miles back, they fell in with the United States squadron, the commander of which ordered the "Perthshire's" release, without, however, making any compensation for the detention to which she had been subjected, nor for the ship's stores, consisting of tea, coffee, and sugar, used by the prize crew whilst on board the "Perthshire."

On the ship being released, the captain's papers were returned to him, and his clearance indorsed as follows :

"Boarded June 9, 1861, by the United States steamship 'Massachusetts,' detained under note 159, page 339, Vattel's Law of Nations ; liberated by commanding officer of the Gulf squadron June 12, 1861."

This indorsement was without any signature.

A paper was given to the captain of the "Perthshire," on which was written, also without signature, as follows :

"Vattel's Law of Nations.   Sir Walter Scott's Opinion.   Note 159, page 339, article 3.   Things to be proved:
"1. The existence of a blockade.
"2. The knowledge of the party supposed to have offended.
"3. Some act of violation."

Such, my lord, is a plain, unvarnished statement of the facts connected with this extraordinary seizure and detention. The ship having reached her destination safely prevents a discussion as to liability in the event of loss after the deviation in the voyage, but which the Liverpool underwriters say they would have been exempted from had such taken place.

The ground upon which I base my claim for £200 is as follows: The ship had been nine days at sea when she was seized. She was taken back almost to the place from which she first started, and three days after that (or twelve days from leaving Mobile) she was as far from Liverpool as on the 31st of May, when she sailed from Mobile. Her freight was about £550 per month, and twelve days at that rate is about the sum I claim.

The case of the "Perthshire," my lord, has been commented upon by all the leading journals in Great Britain, and without exception they pronounce it a case in which our government ought to make a demand for damages. I venture to hope, therefore, that your lordship will take such steps with regard to this matter as will prevent a repetition of improper interference with British ships, and at the same time obtain for me the reasonable and fair compensation I claim.

I have, &c.

WILLIAM GRAY,
Owner of the ship "Perthshire."

The Right Hon. Earl RUSSELL, &c., &c., &c.

Mr. Seward to Mr. Welles.

DEPARTMENT OF STATE,
Washington, October 19, 1861.

SIR: I transmit herewith a copy of a note from the British minister of the 11th instant, and of its accompaniment, respecting an alleged interference with the British ship "Perthshire" by vessels of the United States blockading squadron.

I will thank you to furnish me with such information upon the subject as will enable me to reply to the note of Lord Lyons.

I have the honor to be, sir, your obedient servant,
WILLIAM H. SEWARD.

Hon. GIDEON WELLES,
Secretary of the Navy.

Mr. Seward to Lord Lyons.

DEPARTMENT OF STATE,
Washington, October 19, 1861.

MY LORD : I have the honor to acknowledge the receipt of your note of the 11th instant, accompanied by a copy of a memorial addressed to her Majesty's principal secretary of state for foreign affairs, by Mr. William Gray, owner of the British ship Perthshire, alleged to have been interfered with by United States ships-of-war.

A copy of those papers has been transmitted to the Secretary of the Navy with a view to a proper investigation of the matter. When the reply of that officer shall have been received, I shall lose no time in communicating to your lordship the result of the investigation.

Accept, my lord, the assurance of my high consideration.
WILLIAM H. SEWARD.

The Right Hon. Lord LYONS, &c., &c., &c.

Mr. Welles to Mr. Seward.

NAVY DEPARTMENT, *October* 24, 1861.

SIR : I have the honor to acknowledge the receipt of your letter of the 19th instant and enclosures, and to transmit herewith a copy of a report of Captain William W. McKean, commanding United States ship Niagara, and a copy of a report of Commander Melancton Smith, which contain such information as the department possesses in relation to the seizure of the British ship "Perthshire" by the United States steamer Massachusetts, and her subsequent release by order of Captain McKean.

I am, respectfully, your obedient servant,

GIDEON WELLES.

Hon. WILLIAM H. SEWARD,
Secretary of State.

Captain McKean to Commodore Mervine.

UNITED STATES STEAMER NIAGARA,
Off Southwest Pass of Mississippi, September 19, 1861.

SIR: Your communication of the 17th instant, with the accompanying document, was received on the 18th instant.

The English ship "Perthshire," Captain James Oates, left the harbor of Mobile on the 30th of June, 1861, and was boarded by Lieutenant Spicer, from this ship, and passed by my order, the fifteen days allowed by the proclamation of the President of the United States for neutral vessels to depart not having expired.

I am under the impression that no indorsement was made upon her register, as I did not consider it necessary.

I arrived off Fort Pickens in the Niagara early on the morning of the 12th of June, 1861. A large ship, which proved to be the "Perthshire," had just anchored.

Immediately after the Niagara had come to anchor, Commander M. Smith, commanding the United States steamer Massachusetts, came on board and reported having captured the Perthshire in latitude 27° 27' and longitude 85° 31'.

I stated to Commander Smith that the Perthshire had left Mobile within the time allowed by the President's proclamation ; that I considered the capture illegal, as, by order of the department, no neutral vessel not having on board contraband of war, was to be detained or captured unless attempting to leave or enter a blockaded port after the notification of blockade had been indorsed on her register. I therefore directed him to release the "Perthshire," and to replace such provisions and stores as might have been used by the prize crew.

She was accordingly released and immediately got under way, Commander Smith having reported to me that he had not only replaced such provisions as had been used, but had also supplied her with water.

I subsequently received from Captain Adams the report of Commander Smith, a copy of which is herewith submitted. It bears no date.

As I was in hourly expectation of your arrival from Key West, I had fully intended reporting the circumstances to you, but it escaped my memory.

I am, sir, your obedient servant,

WM. W. McKEAN, *Captain.*

Flag Officer WILLIAM MERVINE,
  Commanding Gulf Blockading Squadron,
    United States Steam Frigate "Colorado."

Commander Smith to commanding officer Gulf squadron.

U. S. STEAMER MASSACHUSETTS,
Off Pensacola, Florida.

SIR: I have to report that on the 9th instant, in latitude 27° 27', and longitude 85° 31', I boarded and seized as a prize the English ship "Perthshire," from Mobile, bound to Liverpool, with a cargo of 2,240 bales of cotton; said ship having been boarded by one of the blockading fleet off Pensacola, May 13th, and warned not to enter the harbor.

Two officers and twenty-nine men were placed on board the prize, and

Mr. Wm. R. Clark, acting master, was directed to proceed with all possible despatch and report to the senior commanding officer of the Gulf squadron for instructions.

In addition to the above, I boarded ship Janico from Mobile, ship Carl and bark Mary from New Orleans, all loaded with cotton, and with registers indorsed; also ship Bramley Moore, from New Orleans, register not indorsed, but allowed her to proceed upon her voyage, as the time granted vessels to clear, according to the notification of blockade, had not expired.

Very respectfully,

MELANCTON SMITH,
Commander.

The COMMANDING OFFICER
Gulf Squadron, Pensacola.

[Indorsement by Captain Adams.]

JUNE 10, 1861.

At the time the Perthshire was boarded from this ship and ordered off from Pensacola there was no blockade of Mobile or the Mississippi river.

H. A. ADAMS,
Captain U. S. Frigate " Sabine."

Mr. Seward to Lord Lyons.

DEPARTMENT OF STATE,
Washington, October 24, 1861.

MY LORD: Your letter of the 11th of October last, presenting the claim of Mr. William Gray, owner of the British ship "Perthshire," for damages incurred by the detention of that vessel by the blockading squadron of the United States, was referred by me to the Secretary of the Navy for information upon the subject.

I have now received the answer of the Secretary of the Navy thereupon, which fails to show me that the detention of the Perthshire by Commander Smith, commanding the United States steamer Massachusetts, was warranted by law or by the President's proclamation instituting the blockade, although I am satisfied that that officer acted under a misapprehension of his duties, and not from any improper motive. It will belong to Congress to appropriate the sum of two hundred pounds, claimed by Gray, which sum seems to me not an unreasonable one. The President will ask Congress for that appropriation as soon as they shall meet, and he will direct that such instructions shall be given to Commander Smith as will caution him against a repetition of the errors of which you have complained.

I avail myself of this opportunity to renew to your lordship the assurance of my high consideration.

WILLIAM H. SEWARD.

The Right Hon. Lord LYONS, &c., &c., &c.

AUSTRIA.

Mr. Seward to Mr. Burlingame.

[Extracts.]

No. 2.]
DEPARTMENT OF STATE,
Washington, April 13, 1861.

SIR: It seems to me that our mission to Austria has not been made as useful hitherto as it ought to have been. I think, indeed, that it has generally been undervalued, The causes for this are manifest. We are a commercial people, and of course cultivate acquaintance first and chiefly with other commercial nations. Situated on a long Atlantic coast, and confronting on the opposite shore the commercial countries from whence our population was first and principally derived, we have naturally fallen into relations with them of the most intimate kind. Austria is distant, and it has never been a maritime nation.

To go no further in the review of its history than 1815, the Austrian government has been that one of the great European powers which has maintained more studiously, firmly, and persistently than any other, the principles of unlimited monarchy, so opposite in their character to the principles upon which our own government has been established.

Again, Austria is not an unique country with a homogeneous people. It is a combination of kingdoms, duchies, provinces, and countries, added to each other by force, and subjected to an imperial head, but remaining at the same time diverse, distinct, and discordant. The empire is therefore largely destitute of that element of nationality which is essential to the establishment of free intercourse with remote foreign States. This absence of nationality is observable in the Austrian emigration to the United States. We meet everywhere here, in town and country, Italians, Hungarians, Poles, Magyars, Jews, and Germans, who have come to us from that empire, but no one has ever seen a confessed Austrain among us. So when a traveller visits Austria he passes through distinctly marked countries, whose people call themselves by many different names, but none of them indicative of their relation to the empire.

Our representatives at Vienna seem generally to have come, after a short residence there, to the conclusion that there was nothing for them to do and little for them to learn.   *   *   *   *   *

The President expects that you will be diligent in obtaining not only information about political events, but also commercial and even scientific facts, and in reporting them to this department. Austria is an interesting field for improvement of that kind. Although Lombardy, with other Italian provinces, has recently been lost, yet the empire still has a population little inferior in number to our own ; and though there are some nations whose people are more mercurial, there is no one in the whole world whose inhabitants are more industrious, frugal, cheerful, and comfortable ; none in which agriculture derives more wealth from hard soils and ungenial skies ; none where science, art, and taste mingle so perfectly with public and private economy. An undue portion of the country is mountainous. It has never-

theless a richness and variety of mineral and vegetable wealth unequalled
in any other part of Europe. Many of its productions could, if introduced
more freely, find a ready consumption here, while, on the other hand, we
could supply Austria with materials and provisions which are now at greater
cost received by her from other countries. Many of the Austrian productions
and fabrics which we do receive come to us through the hands of merchants
in other European States.

The insignificance of our commerce with Austria results in a large degree
from her policy of taxing exports as well as imports, and from monopolies,
by which she labors to create a national system of navigation. The subject
is one of great interest, and you can render an important service probably
to both countries by applying yourself to an examination of it with a view
to the negotiation of a more liberal treaty than the one now in force.

Just now a pressure upon this department, incidental to the beginning of
a new administration, renders it impossible for me to descend into the details
which must be considered in this connexion. It is, however, a purpose of
the President that the subject shall be thoroughly investigated, and you will
in due time be fully instructed. In the meanwhile you are authorized to
communicate his disposition in this respect to the government of his Imperial
Royal Majesty, and to ascertain, if possible, whether it would be willing to
enter into a revision of the commercial arrangements now existing between
the two nations.

The President is well aware that the government of Austria is naturally
pre-occupied with political questions of great moment. It must be confessed,
also, that painful events occurring among ourselves have a tendency to
withdraw our thoughts from commercial subjects. But it is not to be doubted,
in the first place, that political embarrassments would in both countries be
essentially relieved by any improvement of their commerce which could be
made; and, secondly, that the greater those embarrassments are the more
merit there will be in surmounting them so far as may be necessary to effect
that improvement. It certainly is not the intention of the President that
the progress in material and social improvement which this country has
been making through so many years shall be arrested or hindered unnecessarily by the peculiar political trials to which it seems likely to be subjected
during the term for which he has been called to conduct the administration
of its affairs.

There is a peculiar fitness in efforts at this time to enlarge our trade in
the Mediterranean, for it is never wise to neglect advantages which can be
secured with small expense, and near at home, while prosecuting at great
cost, as we are doing, great enterprises in remoter parts of the world. I
would not overlook Italy, Germany, and Hungary, while reaching forth for
the trade of China and Japan.

I shall allude to political affairs in Austria only so far as is necessary to
enable me to indicate the policy which the President will pursue in regard
to them. They present to us the aspect of an ancient and very influential
power, oppressed with fiscal embarrassments, the legacy of long and exhausting wars, putting forth at one and the same time efforts for material
improvement, and still mightier ones to protect its imperfectly combined
dominion from dismemberment and disintegration, seriously menaced from
without, aided by strong and intense popular passions within. With these
questions the government of the United States has and can have no concern.
In the intercourse of nations each must be assumed by every other to choose
and will what it maintains, tolerates, or allows Any other than a course
of neutrality would tend to keep human society continually embroiled in
wars, and render national independence everywhere practically impossible.

No institutions which can be established in a country through foreign intervention can give to it security or other advantages equal to those which are afforded by the system it establishes or permits for itself; while every nation must be regarded as a moral person, and so amenable to the public opinion of mankind, that opinion can carry its decrees into effect only by peaceful means and influences. These principles, hitherto practiced by the United States with great impartiality, furnish rules for the conduct of their representatives abroad, and especially for your own in the critical condition of political affairs in the country to which you are accredited.

This intimation is given so distinctly because an observance of it is peculiarly important in the present condition of our domestic affairs. We are just entering on a fearful trial, hitherto not only unknown, but even deemed impossible by all who have not been supposed to regard the career of our country, even under auspicious indications, with morbid distrust.

Ambitious and discontented partisans have raised the standard of insurrection and organized in form a revolutionary government. Their agents have gone abroad to seek, under the name of recognition, aid and assistance. In this case imprudence on our part in our intercourse with foreign nations might provoke injurious, possibly dangerous, retaliation.

The President does not by any means apprehend that the imperial royal government at Vienna will be inclined to listen to those overtures. The habitual forbearance of his Majesty, the friendship which happily has always existed between the two countries, and the prudence which the government of the former has so long practiced in regard to political affairs on this continent, forbid any such apprehension.

Should our confidence in this respect, however, prove to be erroneous, the remarks which I shall have occasion to make with a different view in this paper will furnish you with the grounds on which to stand while resisting and opposing any such application of the so-called Confederate States of America.

Vienna, as you are very well aware, is a political centre in continental Europe. You may expect to meet agents of disunion there seeking to mould public opinion for effect elsewhere.

I will not detain you with a history of that reckless movement, or with details of the President's policy in regard to it. Your experience as a prominent member of Congress has already furnished the former. The inaugural address of the President, with despatches to your predecessor, will be found in the archives of the legation, and will supply the latter.

Certainly I shall not need to anticipate and controvert any complaints of injustice, oppression, or wrong, which those agents may prefer against their country before foreign tribunals. Practically, the discontented party itself administered this government from the earliest day when sedition began its incubation until the insurgents had risen and organized their new provisional and revolutionary government. Never, in the history of the human race, has revolution been so altogether without cause, or met with forbearance, patience, and gentleness so long.

Nor shall I notice particularly the apprehensions of future injustice and oppression which, in the absence of real cause, are put forth as grounds for the insurrection. The revolutionists will find it very hard to make any European sovereign, or even any European subject, understand what better or further guarantee they could have of all their rights of person and property than those which are written in the Constitution of the United States, and which have never been by the government of the United States broken or violated either in letter or in spirit. They will find it quite as difficult to make either a European sovereign or subject understand how they can reasonably expect to improve their political security by organizing a new government under a constitution containing substantially the same provisions as the one they seek to overthrow.

There is reason to apprehend that the form of argument which the agents alluded to will chiefly employ will be an assumption that the independence and sovereignty of the new and irregular authority they represent is already *de facto* established.

If this were true, still you could reply that no public interest of other States, nor even any such interest of the new confederacy itself could suffer by a delay allowing sufficient time for the government of the United States, fully consulting the people, to acknowledge in the first instance the independence so claimed to have been established. The United States have a right to require such delay from all friendly powers, and a refusal of it would be an act offensive to their dignity and manifestly hostile. There is not the least ground to assume that the government of the United States would act otherwise than wisely, discreetly, and humanely, when it should come to act in such a case. Individual caprice finds no place in a government so entirely popular as ours, and partisan excitement sinks in great national emergencies here before the calm considerate judgment of the American people pronouncing upon considerations exclusively of their own security, freedom, and happiness. They would, indeed, regard the effectual dismemberment of the Union as fatal to the highest hopes which humanity has ever, with apparent reason, indulged. But they are not visionary nor impracticable, and they will not lack even the magnanimity to accept the fact of their ruin, and govern themselves in conformity with it, before other nations fraternally disposed need to intervene to reconcile them, or, if unfriendly, to profit by that last calamity.

At all events foreign governments may be expected to consult their own interests and welfare in regard to the subject in question, even though indifferent to the rights and interests of the United States. A premature declaration of recognition by any foreign State would be direct intervention, and the State which should lend it must be prepared to assume the relations of an ally of the projected confederacy and employ force to render the recognition effectual.

But, in point of fact, the assumption that the new confederacy has established its sovereignty and independence is altogether unfounded. It was projected, or favored, by the late administration during the four months that it remained in power after the election, which constituted practically an interregnum. The new administration, now only forty days old, has practiced forbearance and conciliation, relying hitherto, as it will hereafter rely, on the virtue and patriotism of the people to rescue the country and the Union from danger by peaceful and constitutional means, and content to maintain the authority and defend the positions which came into its hands on the fourth of March last, without employing coercion, so unnatural, and, as it has hitherto believed and still believes, so unnecessary for the national security, integrity, and welfare. The so-called confederacy has yet to secure its sovereignty either by war or by peace. If it shall, as now seems probable, have determined on war, it has only just thrown down the challenge. It must not assume that a nation so sound, so vigorous, and so strong as this, although it may forbear long, will not accept such a challenge when there is no alternative.

The government of the so-called Confederate States have still greater perils to incur if they are to establish their separation by the acts and processes proper for peace. They will have at some time to refer themselves and all their action to an intelligent people, who will then have had time to reflect and to inquire what all this revolution is for, and what good it can produce. They will have to satisfy that people and mankind that a republican government can be stable and permanent which is built on the principle that a minority, when defeated in the popular elections, may appeal to arms, and that a confederacy can be relied upon by creditors or nations that admits the right of each of its members to withdraw from it and cast off its obligations at pleasure.

I have treated the subject as if it were a question of war or of peace in the election of the insurrectionists. But, in truth, both the justice and the wisdom of the war must in the end be settled, as all questions which concern the American people must be determined, not by arms, but by suffrage. When, at last, the ballot is to be employed after the sword, then, in addition to the pregnant questions I have indicated, two further ones will arise requiring to be answered, namely, which party began the conflict, and which maintained in that conflict the cause of freedom and humanity.

The agents of the projected confederacy have hitherto affected to under-value the power which the Union can exercise for self-preservation, and they may attempt to mislead foreign States on this subject. It is true that the government was powerless to resist them so long as it was practically in their own hands and managed to favor their designs. Its executive department was panic-stricken, its legislature divided and distracted, its army demoralized and betrayed, its fortifications virtually surrendered, its navy dispersed, and its credit prostrated. Even the people themselves were bewildered by the sudden appearance of such unlooked-for and appalling dangers. All this demoralization is passing away as rapidly as it came on; and it will soon appear in this, as in all other cases, that the greatest vigor is found combined with the greatest power of elasticity. It will be deeply to be regretted if the energy of this great government is to have its first serious trial in a civil war, instead of one against a foreign foe. But if that trial cannot be averted, it will be seen that resources prudently left unembarrassed are more available than credit in foreign markets; that the loyalty of a brave and free people is more reliable than standing armies; that a good cause is worth more than allies, and self-defence is an attribute stronger than fortresses. Its assailants will have to defend themselves before an enlightened people, and even before other nations, at least so far as to show one State that the federal Union has actually oppressed or menaced, or one citizen who fared the worse for having lived under its authority.

The agents of the new confederacy it is supposed will offer more favorable conditions to foreign commerce than the United States have thought it wise to afford. Such offers may be met with a few direct propositions. The sagacity of the federal government is not likely to be found long at fault in giving such advantages to the insurrectionists. In the second place, how is a revolution to be carried on without taxes? Are the so-called seceding States abler than their sister States to endure direct taxation, or will faction reconcile men to burdens that patriotism finds intolerable? It will be well for the so-called confederacy if, instead of making good the promises in this respect made in its name, it do not find itself obliged to levy duties as large as those of the federal government on imports, and to add to its revenue system, what that government never has done, the ruinous feature of taxation upon exports. It is easily seen how little such a financial policy will commend the new government to the favor of European politicians and capitalists.

But I must draw these instructions to a close. You will on all occasions represent that the interests of Europe and of mankind demand peace, and especially peace on this continent. The Union is the only guarantee of peace. Intervention would be war, and disunion would be only endless war.

The Union is, moreover, the chief security for the stability of nations. When this experiment of self-government shall have failed for want of wisdom and virtue enough, either at home or abroad, to preserve it or permit it to exist, the people of other countries may well despair and lose the patience they have practiced so long under different systems in the expectation that the influence it was slowly exercising would ultimately bring them to the enjoyment of the rights of self-government. When that patience disappears, anarchy must come upon the earth.

I am, sir, your obedient servant,

WILLIAM H. SEWARD.

ANSON BURLINGAME, Esq., &c., &c., &c.

Mr. Jones to Mr. Seward.

[Extract.]

No. 20.]   LEGATION OF THE UNITED STATES,
                                                    Vienna, April 15, 1861.

SIR: I have the honor to acknowledge the receipt of your circular, dated the 9th of March, 1861.

I presented the copy of the inaugural address of the President to Count Rechberg on the 8th day of April, and at the same time verbally communicated, in accordance with the instructions contained in said despatch, the views and opinions of my government on the present disturbed condition of its domestic affairs, and the aspect in which it wished them to be regarded by the government of Austria.

He replied that Austria hoped to see us re-united. That she was not inclined to recognize *de facto* governments anywhere; her opinions had been made, however, and her minister and consuls in America instructed fully on the subject; that no application had yet been made to Austria for recognition as an independent sovereignty, by any portion of the confederacy of the United States, and he was of opinion that, as the views of Austria would soon be known on the subject, no such application would be made. Should it be otherwise, however, he would notify this legation and the subject could be resumed.

*   *   *   *   *   *   *   *   *

Very respectfully, your obedient servant,

J. GLANCY JONES.

HON. WILLIAM H. SEWARD,
        Secretary of State, Washington.

Mr. Jones to Mr. Seward.

No. 22.]   LEGATION OF THE UNITED STATES,
                                                    Vienna, July 20, 1861.

SIR: A few days since Count Rechberg, the imperial royal minister of foreign affairs, was interrogated in the house of deputies of the Austrian empire on the subject of the course pursued, or about to be pursued, by the imperial royal government in relation to American affairs in the present complication. The report of his remarks is as follows:

Count Rechberg rose to answer the question, "What measures has the government taken to protect its commercial relations with the United States of North America, under the warlike condition of things now existing there," put by Mr. Putzer and his associates. He said: "The minister of foreign affairs has, in connexion with the ministers of trade and the navy, caused information to be obtained through the imperial minister resident at Washington as to the measures which other governments have taken for the same reason. The answer received was, that England and France, as well as Holland, had strengthened their squadrons in the American waters, and had endeavored to bring the belligerent powers to the recognition of those principles, especially relating to the protection of private property, which were agreed upon at the congress of Paris in 1856. The imperial government has, for the present, abstained from sending ships-of-war, and has directed the minister resident to obtain from the belligerent powers the recognition of the following points established by the said congress:

"1. The neutral flag covers enemy's goods, with the exception of contraband of war.

"2. Neutral goods, with the exception of contraband of war, are not liable to capture under enemy's flag.

"3. Blockades, in order to be binding, must be effective; that is to say, maintained by a force sufficient really to prevent access to the coast of the enemy.

"The government hopes, on account of the friendly relations which have existed between it and the American States for years, to obtain the recognition of these three points on the part of the belligerents."

In an interview with Count Rechberg a day or two ago, he expressed to me a hope that the answer might be deemed satisfactory to my government, as it was his wish to make it so. I replied that, so far as I was advised, no exception could be taken to his language, but that I should transmit to my government both the question and answer, and if they had anything to say they would make it known to him through their minister here. He repeated his strong desire to see the integrity of the Union preserved in America, and said Austria was anxious to cultivate the most friendly relations with us, and would be the last to aid or abet any movement looking to the disruption of our confederacy, or weakening its power.

Very respectfully, your obedient servant,

J. GLANCY JONES.

Hon. WILLIAM H. SEWARD,
Secretary of State, Washington.

Mr. Hülsemann to Mr. Seward.

AUSTRIAN LEGATION,
Washington, August 7, 1861.

The undersigned, in pursuance of the understanding come to this morning, has the honor to transmit to the honorable Secretary of State a copy of the instructions received from Count Rechberg concerning the maritime rights of neutrals in time of war; and he takes this opportunity to renew his offer of high consideration to the honorable Secretary of State

HULSEMANN

Hon. WILLIAM H. SEWARD,
Secretary of State of the United States.

Baron Rechberg to Mr. Hülsemann.

[Translation.]

No. 6993.—H.]   VIENNA, *July* 1, 1861.

SIR: With deep regret we continue to follow events in the United States which, shaking the foundations of the Union, have effectively taken the character of an active warfare between powers; whence it has ensued that friendly nations, for the protection of their own commerce and navigation, are placed reluctantly in such position that they must reclaim their rights as neutrals.

You already know by my despatch of 14th June of last year what principles of international law bearing upon the questions of maritime rights in time of war we relied upon as between us and the government of the Union, whether under the provisions of old treaties, or under more recent arrangements; inasmuch as we have given our adhesion to the Paris declaration of maritime rights in 1856, as tending to improve the heretofore ill-advised mode of dealing with the political fluctuations that lie before us.

Albeit the government of the Union did not explicitly and at once accept, upon the first invitation, the declaration of the European powers, yet we still entertain an earnest expectation that such subsequent express assent may be given, as the abrogation of all hindrance to the security of private property on the seas was established on the broadest grounds.

By a proposal which, unfortunately, was not accepted on the other side, we, however, as you know, were always ready and willing to sustain the principle.

We await, however, in friendly expectation, at least, the express recognition of the second, third, and fourth principles of the Paris declaration on the part of the United States quite distinctly from that, because the government of the Union, on different occasions, has not only plainly expressed these principles in manner more or less forcible, but has upon its own motion set them forth and explicitly maintained them.

We therefore rest securely in the belief that we may soon receive a satisfactory communication upon this subject, and that under the high authority of the President, administering the relations of his government, the above mentioned three principles will be authentically asserted by the United States. But you also have it in express charge to invite the earnest attention of the Secretary of State to the matter, and to take the same steps as we see reason to adopt with the other European powers in what may be regarded as definitively settled.

You will, I hope, carry this important question through to a favorable close, and I present you the assurances of my cordial sympathies.

RECHBERG.

His Excellency the Chevalier HULSEMANN, &c., &c., &c., *Washington.*

Mr. Seward to Mr. Hülsemann.

DEPARTMENT OF STATE,
Washington, August 22, 1861.

The undersigned, the Secretary of State of the United States, has the honor to acknowledge the receipt of a communication from Mr. Hülsemann, minister resident of his imperial royal Majesty the Emperor of Austria, bearing date 7th August, instant. Mr. Hülsemann's letter is accompanied by an instruction sent to him by Count Rechberg, the Austrian minister for foreign affairs, calling for information on the subject of the views of this government concerning the rights of neutrals in maritime war. Count Rechberg expresses a hope that the government of the United States will give assurances that it adopts and will apply the 2d, 3d, and 4th principles of the declaration of Paris, viz:

2. The neutral flag covers enemy's goods, with the exception of contraband of war.

3. Neutral goods, with the exception of contraband of war, are not liable to capture under enemy's flag.

4. Blockades, in order to be binding, must be effective; that is to say, maintained by a force sufficient really to prevent access to the coast of the enemy.

The undersigned has great pleasure in assuring Mr. Hülsemann that this government does adopt, and that it will apply the principles thus recited and set forth, and that its liberal views in this respect have not only been long held, but they would have been formally communicated to the Austrian government several months ago but for the delay which has unavoidably occurred in the arrival of a newly appointed minister plenipotentiary at Vienna.

Of course the principles referred to are understood by the United States as not compromitting their right to close any of their own ports for the purpose of suppressing the existing insurrection in certain of the States, either directly or in the more lenient and equitable form of blockade which has already for some time been established.

Mr. Motley, who proceeds immediately to Vienna as envoy extraordinary and minister plenipotentiary of the United States, will be directly advised of this communication, while he will be charged with more ample instructions on the general subject involved.

The undersigned avails himself of this occasion to tender assurances of the good will of this government towards the government of Austria, and of his distinguished consideration for Mr. Hülsemann personally.

WILLIAM H. SEWARD.

The Chevalier Hulsemann, &c., &c., &c.

Mr. Seward to Mr. Jones.

No. 14.]
DEPARTMENT OF STATE,
Washington, August 12, 1861.

SIR: Your despatch of the 20th of July, No. 22, has just been received.

Owing to the change of Mr. Burlingame's destination, the instructions he conveyed have failed to reach your legation. A new appointment has just now been made in the person of Mr. Motley, who will, without much delay, proceed to relieve you of the mission which you have conducted so satisfactorily during the period of my connexion with this department.

Mr. Motley will have full powers to treat with the government of Austria on all the matters discussed by Count Rechberg in the speech to which, by his direction, you have called my attention, and I am sure that they will be disposed of to the entire satisfaction of Austria, as well as for the common advantage of both countries.

In the meantime, however, you are authorized to say to Count Rechberg that the United States adhere now, as heretofore, to the three principles enunciated by him in that speech, namely:

1. The neutral flag covers enemy's goods, with the exception of contraband of war.

2. Neutral goods, not contraband of war, are not liable to confiscation under enemy's flag.

3. Blockades, in order to be binding, must be effective.

Of course these principles are understood by us as not compromitting our right to close any of our own ports for the purpose of suppressing the existing insurrection, either directly or in the more lenient and equitable form of blockade which we have already some time since established.

You will not fail to assure the imperial royal government that the President had received with great satisfaction the assurances of the just purposes and good will of Austria towards the United States, communicated by Count Rechberg to yourself, and repeated by Mr. Hülsemann, the minister of Austria residing at this capital.

It shall be our purpose to cultivate the best understanding with all nations which respect our rights as Austria does.

I am, sir, respectfully, your obedient servant,

WILLIAM H. SEWARD.

J. Glancy Jones, Esq., &c., &c., &c.

Mr. Seward to Mr. Motley.

No. 2.]

Department of State,
Washington, August 27, 1861.

Sir: The despatch of your predecessor, Mr. Jones, No. 23, dated August 6, has been received and read with much interest. It relates, however, exclusively to the affairs of Austria, and does not seem to require any special remark from me at the present moment, when the attention of this department is so largely engrossed by the concerns of our own country at home as well as in foreign countries.

Should Mr. Jones be still remaining at Vienna when this communication arrives, you will express to him the entire satisfaction with which his conduct of the legation since it has fallen under the review of the present administration is regarded by the government of the United States.

I am, sir, respectfully, your obedient servant,

WILLIAM H. SEWARD.

J. Lothrop Motley, Esq., &c., &c., *Vienna.*

Mr. Seward to Mr. Motley.

No. 4.]

Department of State,
Washington, September 20, 1861.

Sir: The despatch, No. 24, of your predecessor, Mr. Jones, under date of August, has been received. I send you a copy of my latest instructions to Mr. Adams and Mr. Dayton on the subject of the proposed accession to the declaration of the congress at Paris. You will learn from these papers that the negotiations for that object with the governments of Great Britain and

France have been arrested, as well as the manner of suspension, and the reasons for it. You will already have discovered for yourself that this suspension of the negotiation with those two powers must operate, to a certain extent, upon the dispositions in the same respect of other European States, although it does not at all modify the views of this government. So far as such other European powers are concerned, all that remains to be said is, that acting in good faith we will cheerfully enter into convention with any State that may desire to receive our accession at this time, and that we shall not, at present, urge our proposition on those States which, for any reason of their own, may propose to await a more convenient season.

You will inform Count Rechberg that the friendly sentiments of this government towards Austria remain unchanged.

I am, sir, your obedient servant,

WILLIAM H. SEWARD.

J. LOTHROP MOTLEY, Esq., &c., &c., &c., *Vienna.*

Ex. Doc. 1——13

FRANCE.

Mr. Seward to Mr. Dayton.

No. 3.]

DEPARTMENT OF STATE,
Washington, April 22, 1861.

SIR: You enter a very important foreign mission at a moment when our domestic affairs have reached a crisis which awakens deep solicitude. Throughout a period of eighty years law and order have prevailed, and internal peace and tranquillity have been undisturbed. Five months ago sedition showed itself openly in several of the southern States, and it has acted ever since that time with boldness, skill, and energy. An insurrectionary government, embracing seven members of this Union, has been proclaimed under the name of the Confederate States of America. That pretended authority, by means chiefly of surprise, easily seen here to have been unavoidable, although liable to be misunderstood abroad, has possessed itself of a navy yard, several fortifications and arsenals, and considerable quantities of arms, ordnance, and military stores. On the 12th of April, instant, its forces commenced an attack upon, and ultimately carried, Fort Sumter, against the brave and heroic resistance of a diminutive garrison, which had been, through the neglect of the former administration, left in a condition to prevent supplies and re-enforcements.

Owing to the very peculiar construction of our system, the late administration, Congress, and every other department of the federal government, including the army and the navy, contained agents, abettors, and sympathizers in this insurrection. The federal authorities thus became inefficient, while large portions of the people were bewildered by the suddenness of the appearance of disunion, by apprehension that needless resistance might aggravate and precipitate the movement, and by political affinities with those engaged in it.

The project of dismembering the Union doubtless has some support in commercial and political ambition. But it is chiefly based upon a local, though widely extended partisan disappointment in the result of the recent election of President of the United States. It acquired strength for a time from its assumed character of legitimate opposition to a successful party, while, on the other hand, that party could not all at once accept the fact that an administrative political issue had given place to one which involved the very existence of the government and of the Union. These embarrassments are passing away so rapidly as to indicate that far the greater mass of the people remain loyal as heretofore. The President improved the temporary misfortune of the fall of Fort Sumter by calling on the militia of the States to re-enforce the federal army, and summoning Congress for its counsel and aid in the emergency. On the other hand, the insurrectionists have met those measures with an invitation to privateers from all lands to come forth and commit depredations on the commerce of the country.

To take care that the government of his Majesty the Emperor of France do not misunderstand our position, and through that misunderstanding do us some possible wrong, is the chief duty which you will have to perform at Paris.

It would have been gratifying to the President if the movements to which I have alluded had taken such a course as to leave this government free from the necessity in any event of conferring upon them in the presence of foreign powers. In this age of social development, however, isolation even in misfortune is impossible, and every attempt at revolution in one country becomes a subject of discussion in every other. The agitators in this case have, perhaps, not unnaturally carried their bad cause before foreign states by an appeal for recognition of the independence they have proclaimed, and which they are committed to establish by arms. Prudence requires that we oppose that appeal. The President believes that you will be able to do this in such a manner as will at once comport with the high consideration for his Imperial Majesty which this government habitually entertains, and a due sense of the dignity and honor of the American people.

The Emperor of France has given abundant proofs that he considers the people in every country the rightful source of all authority, and that its only legitimate objects are their safety, freedom, and welfare. He is versed in our Constitution, and, therefore, he will not need demonstration that the system which is established by the Constitution is founded strictly on those very principles. You will be at no loss to show also that it is perfectly adapted to the physical condition and the temper, spirit, and habits of the American people. In all its essential features it is the same system which was first built, and has since existed with ever renewed popular consent in this part of America. The people of this country have always enjoyed the personal rights guaranteed by the great statutes of British freedom, representation concurrent with taxation, jury trial, liberty of conscience, equality before the laws, and popular suffrage. The element of federation or union was early developed while the colonies were under the authority of, and during their revolutionary contest with, the British Crown, and was perfected afterwards by the establishment of the Constitution of the United States. Practically it has been voluntarily accepted by every State, Territory, and individual citizen of the United States. The working of the system has been completely successful, while not one square mile of domain that we at any time had occupied has ever been lost to us. We have extended our jurisdiction from the St. Mary's river to the Rio Grande, on the Gulf of Mexico, and in a wide belt from the Mississippi to the Pacific ocean. Our population has swollen from four millions to thirty-one millions. The number of our States has increased from thirteen to thirty-four. Our country has risen from insignificance to be the second in the world. Leaving out of view unimportant local instances of conflict, we have had only two foreign wars, and the aggregate duration of them was less than five years. Not one human life has hitherto been forfeited for disloyalty to the government, nor has martial law ever been established except temporarily in case of invasion. No other people have ever enjoyed so much immunity from the various forms of political casualties and calamities.

While there is not now, even in the midst of the gathering excitement of civil war, one American who declares his dissent from the principles of the Constitution, that great charter of federal authority has won the approbation of the civilized world. Many nations have taken it as a model, and almost every other one has in some degree conformed its institutions to the principles of this Constitution. The empire of France, and the new kingdom of Italy especially, are built on the same broad foundation with that of this federal republic, namely, universal suffrage.

Surely we cannot err in assuming that a system of government which arose out of the free consent of the people of this country, which has been often reconsidered and yet continually upheld in preference to every other throughout a period of two hundred years, which has commanded the acceptance or the approval of all other nations, and to the principles of which even those who attempt to overthrow it adhere in the very heat of insurrection, must be regarded as one which is not only well adapted to the condition and character of the American people, but is even indispensable and inseparable from their national existence.

Should it be answered that while all this has heretofore seemed true, yet that it is now disproved by the existing insurrection, you may truthfully reply that we must wait for that refutation until we see the end of the insurrection; that the insurrection proves in fact nothing else except that eighty years of peace is as much as human nature has the moderation to endure under circumstances the most conducive to moderation.

The attempted revolution is simply causeless. It is, indeed, equally without a reason and without an object. Confessedly there is neither reason nor object, unless it be one arising out of the subject of slavery. The practice of slavery has been so long a theme of angry political debate, while it has all the time been, as it yet is, a domestic concern, that I approach it with deep regret in a communication which relates to the action of a representative of this government abroad. I refrain from any observation whatever concerning the morality or the immorality, the economy or the waste, the social or the unsocial aspects of slavery, and confine myself, by direction of the President, strictly to the point that the attempt at revolution on account of it is, as I have already said, without reason and without object. Slavery of persons of African derivation existed practically within all the European colonies which, as States, now constitute the United States of America. The framers of our government accepted that fact, and with it the ideas concerning it which were then gaining ground throughout the civilized world. They expected and desired that it should ultimately cease, and with that view authorized Congress to prohibit the foreign slave trade after 1808. They did not expect that the practice of African slavery should be abruptly terminated to the prejudice of the peace and the economy of the country. They therefore placed the entire control of slavery, as it was then existing, beyond the control of the federal authorities, by leaving it to remain subject to the exclusive management and disposition of the several States themselves, and fortified it there with a provision for the return of fugitives from labor and service, and another securing an allowance of three-fifths of such persons in fixing the basis of direct taxation and representation. The legislators of that day took notice of the existence of a vast and nearly unoccupied region lying between the western borders of the Atlantic States and the Mississippi river. A few slaves were found in the southwest, and none in the northwest. They left the matter in the southwest to the discretion of the new States to be formed there, and prohibited the practice of slavery in the northwestern region forever.

Economical, moral, and political causes have subsequently modified the sentiments of that age differently in the two sections. Long ago slavery was prohibited by all the northern States, and, on the contrary, the increased production of cotton has resulted in fortifying the institution of slavery in the southern States. The accretions of domain, by purchase from Spain, France, and Mexico, brought regions in which slavery had either a very slight foothold, or none at all; and this new domain, as it should come under occupation, was to be constituted into new States, which must be either free States or slave States. The original States divided according to their own divers practices—the free States seeking so to direct federal legislation and action as to result in multiplying free States, and the slave States so to direct them as to multiply slave States. The interest became more intense because the several States have equal representation in the Senate of the United States.   This controversy soon disclosed itself in the popular elections, and more distinctly than ever before in the recent canvass, which resulted in the accession of the present administration.

It is now to be observed that, from the earliest agitation of the subject until that last election, the decisions of the people were practically favorable to the interest of the class which favored the extension of slavery, and yet their opponents always acquiesced.   Under these circumstances the executive administration, the national legislature, and the judiciary, were for practical purposes in the hands of that party, and the laws, with the administration and execution of them, conformed to their own policy.   The opposite class prevailed in the late election so far as to bring in the President and Vice-President, the citizens they had preferred, but no further— Congress and the judiciary remained under the same bias as before.   The new President could not assume his trust until the fourth of March, 1861, and even after that time, as before, the laws and the execution of them must remain unchanged.   He could not, without consent of his opponents in Congress, change either, nor appoint a minister or a ministerial officer, nor draw a dollar from the treasury even for his own defence or support.   It was under these circumstances that, on the very day when the election closed and its result became known, four months before the new administration was to come in, the disappointed party took their appeal from the ballot-box to arms, and inaugurated their revolution.

I need not further elaborate the proposition that the revolution is without a cause ; it has not even a pretext.

It is just as clear that it is without an object.   Moral and physical causes have determined inflexibly the character of each one of the Territories over which the dispute has arisen, and both parties after the election harmoniously agreed on all the federal laws required for their organization.   The Territories will remain in all respects the same, whether the revolution shall succeed or shall fail.   The condition of slavery in the several States will remain just the same whether it succeed or fail.   There is not even a pretext for the complaint that the disaffected States are to be conquered by the United States if the revolution fail ; for the rights of the States, and the condition of every human being in them, will remain subject to exactly the same laws and forms of administration, whether the revolution shall succeed or whether it shall fail.   In the one case, the States would be federally connected with the new confederacy ; in the other, they would, as now, be members of the United States ; but their constitutions and laws, customs, habits, and institutions in either case will remain the same.

It is hardly necessary to add to this incontestible statement the further fact that the new President, as well as the citizens through whose suffrages he has come into the administration, has always repudiated all designs whatever and wherever imputed to him and them of disturbing the system of slavery as it is existing under the Constitution and laws.   The case, however, would not be fully presented if I were to omit to say that any such effort on his part would be unconstitutional, and all his actions in that direction would be prevented by the judicial authority, even though they were assented to by Congress and the people.

This revolution, thus equally destitute of just cause and legitimate object, aims, nevertheless, at the dismemberment of the federal Union, and, if successful, must end in the overthrow of the government of the United States. If it be true, as the consent of mankind authorizes us to assume, that the establishment of this government was the most auspicious political event that has happened in the whole progress of history, its fall must be deemed not merely a national calamity, which a patriotic government ought to try to prevent, but a misfortune to the human race, which should secure for us at least the forbearance of all other nations.

It cannot be maintained that disunion would leave it still existing in its true character, and for its proper ends, although in two not very unequal and similar parts. Its integrity as a federal government, embracing all of the American independent, contiguous, and homogeneous States, protecting them all against foreign dangers and internal commotions ; securing to them all a common property, greatness, dignity, influence and happiness, is an indispensable feature of its constitution.

Dismemberment would be less effectually subversive of the character, objects, and purposes of the Union, if the two confederacies, which it is proposed shall succeed it, could severally be expected to exercise its great functions within their respective dominions. But this would be impossible. The several States are now held in union with each other by a confessed obligation of cohesion that only their common consent could dissolve, and that moral law, hitherto acknowledged by all, is substituted for the central military authority which, in other systems, secures the integrity as well as the peace and harmony of States. But if the revolution shall prevail and dismemberment ensue, the federal obligation in that case will be broken, its moral force spent, and in its place there must come up the principles which are the acknowledged elements of the revolution, namely, first, that in either confederacy each State is at liberty to secede at pleasure ; and secondly, the minority in each confederacy, and even in each State, may, whenever the will of the majority is ascertained, take an appeal from the ballot to the sword. It is manifest that the success of this revolution would therefore be not only a practical overthrow of the entire system of government, but the first stage by each confederacy in the road to anarchy, such as so widely prevails in Spanish America. The contest, then, involves nothing less than a failure of the hope to devise a stable system of government upon the principle of the consent of the people, and working through the peaceful expressions of their will without depending on military authority. If the President were addressing his countrymen at home on this occasion, instead of one of their representatives going abroad, he would direct me to set forth the consequences which obviously must follow the dissolution of the American Union. The loss of the ambition, which is a needful inspiration to a great people; the loss of the respect of mankind, and the veneration and respect of posterity; the loss of the enterprise and vigor which makes us a prosperous nation; and with the loss of sustained and constant culture, which makes us an intellectual people, the loss of safety, both at home and abroad, which directly involves the greatest calamity of all, the loss of liberty It is sufficient only to allude to these possible evils on this occasion to afford you the grounds for assuring the government of France that the President regards the revolution as one which in every event must and will be prevented, since it is manifest that the evils which would result from its success would be as incurable as they would be intolerable.

It is, indeed, an occasion of much regret that it has been found needful to employ force for this purpose. It is contrary to the genius and the habits of the people, as it is repugnant to the sentiments of the government of the country and of mankind. But the President believes that the country will accept that alternative with the less regret because sufficient time has been allowed to try every expedient of conciliatory prevention, and civil war is at last proved to be unavoidable. The responsibility of it must rest with those who have not only inaugurated it, but have done so without cause and without provocation. The world will see that it is an evil that comes upon us not from any necessity growing out of administration or out of our Constitution itself, but from a necessity growing out of our common nature.

It must not, however, be inferred that the reluctance of the government to employ force so long has demoralized the administration or can demoralize the American people. They are capable of a high, resolute, and vigorous defence of the Union, and they will maintain that defence with only the more firmness and fidelity, because they are animated by no hostile spirit, but, on the contrary, by a friendly and even fraternal one, being satisfied that its benefits will result equally to those who are engaged in overthrowing and those who are engaged in defending the Union.

I have thus, under the President's direction, placed before you a simple, unexaggerated, and dispassionate statement of the origin, nature, and purposes of the contest in which the United States are now involved. I have done so only for the purpose of deducing from it the arguments you will find it necessary to employ in opposing the application of the so-called Confederate States to the government of his Majesty the Emperor for a recognition of its independence and sovereignty.

The President neither expects nor desires any intervention, or even any favor, from the government of France, or any other, in this emergency. Whatever else he may consent to do, he will never invoke nor even admit foreign interference or influence in this or any other controversy in which the government of the United States may be engaged with any portion of the American people. It has been simply his aim to show that the present controversy furnishes no one ground on which a great and friendly power, like France, can justly lend aid or sympathy to the party engaged in insurrection, and therefore he instructs you to insist on the practice of neutrality by the government of the Emperor, as all our representatives are instructed to insist on the neutrality of the several powers to which they are accredited.

Not entertaining the least apprehension of the departure from that course by his Majesty's government, it is not without some reluctance that the President consents to the suggestion of some considerations affecting France herself, which you may urge in support of it. France is an agricultural and manufacturing country. Her industry depends very largely on a consumption of her productions and fabrics within the United States, and on the receipt, in exchange, of cotton, or other staples, or their equivalent in money, from the United States. The ability of the United States to thus consume and furnish depends on their ability to maintain and preserve peace. War here will in any case be less flagrant, and peace, when broken, will be restored all the more quickly and all the more perfectly if foreign nations shall have the sagacity, not to say the magnanimity, to practice the neutrality we demand.

Foreign intervention would oblige us to treat those who should yield it as allies of the insurrectionary party, and to carry on the war against them as enemies. The case would not be relieved, but, on the contrary, would only be aggravated, if several European states should combine in that intervention. The President and the people of the United States deem the Union, which would then be at stake, worth all the cost and all the sacrifices of a contest with the world in arms, if such a contest should prove inevitable.

However other European powers may mistake, his Majesty is the last one of those sovereigns to misapprehend the nature of this controversy. He knows that the revolution of 1775 in this country was a successful contest of the great American idea of free popular government against resisting prejudices and errors. He knows that the conflict awakened the sympathies of mankind, and that ultimately the triumph of that idea has been hailed by all European nations. He knows at what cost European nations resisted for a time the progress of that idea, and perhaps is not unwilling to confess how much France, especially, has profited by it. He will not fail to recognize the presence of that one great idea in the present conflict, nor will he mistake the side on which it will be found. It is, in short, the very principle of universal suffrage, with its claim to obedience to its decrees, on which the government of France is built, that is put in issue by the insurrection here, and is in this emergency to be vindicated, and, more effectually than ever, established by the government of the United States.

I forbear from treating of questions arising out of the revenue laws of the United States, which lately have been supposed to have some bearing on the subject. They have already passed away before the proclamation of the blockade of ports in the hands of the revolutionary party. Nor could considerations so merely mercenary and ephemeral in any case enter into the counsels of the Emperor of France.

You will, naturally enough, be asked what is the President's expectation concerning the progress of the contest and the prospect of its termination. It is, of course, impossible to speculate, with any confidence, upon the course of a revolution, and to fix times and seasons for the occurrence of political events affected by the excitement of popular passions ; but there are two things which may be assumed as certain : First. That the union of these States is an object of supreme and undying devotion on the part of the American people, and, therefore, it will be vindicated and maintained. Secondly. The American people, notwithstanding any temporary disturbance of their equanimity, are yet a sagacious and practical people, and less experience of evils than any other nation would require will bring them back to their customary and habitual exercise of reason and reflection, and, through that process, to the settlement of the controversy without further devastation and demoralization by needless continuance in a state of civil war.

The President recognizes, to a certain extent, the European idea of the balance of power. If the principle has any foundation at all, the independence and the stability af these United States just in their present form, properties, and character, are essential to the preservation of the balance between the nations of the earth as it now exists. It is not easy to see how France, Great Britain, Russia, or even reviving Spain, could hope to suppress wars of ambition which must inevitably break out if this continent of North America, now, after the exclusion of foreign interests for three-quarters of a century, is again to become a theatre for the ambition and cupidity of European nations.

It stands forth now to the glory of France that she contributed to the emancipation of this continent from the control of European states, an emancipation which has rendered only less benefit to those nations than to America itself. The present enlightened monarch of France is too ambitious, in the generous sense of the word, to signalize his reign by an attempt to reverse that great and magnanimous transaction. He is, moreover, too wise not to understand that the safety and advancement of the United States are guaranteed by the necessities, and, therefore, by the sympathies of mankind.

I am, sir, respectfully, your obedient servant,

WILLIAM H. SEWARD.

Hon. WILLIAM L. DAYTON, &c., &c., &c.

Mr. Faulkner to Mr. Black.

No. 111.] LEGATION OF THE UNITED STATES,
Paris, March 19, 1861.

SIR : I had the honor to-day to receive your despatch, No. 45, touching certain recent political movements in the United States. I had, of course, through the public journals, been made acquainted with the painful facts to which you refer ; but your communication brings them now, for the first time, officially to my notice.

I need hardly say to you that the events which have signalized the history of the United States for the last few months have occupied the attention of a very large share of the statesmen and people of Europe. In all my intercourse, public and private, from the Emperor to the peasant, embracing all grades of ministerial and diplomatic agents, it has been the engrossing, I might almost say the only topic of conversation. A revolution was as little anticipated in the United States as an earthquake in Paris.

That large communities should be casting off the protection of a government to which thousands on this continent were looking for the realization of all their dreams of happiness on earth ; that a system should be pronounced a failure which has produced, within a few years, the most extraordinary developments of national prosperity and power of which history has left any record ; that a flag should be trampled in the dust which has never been stained by oppression, and which is hailed as the emblem of civil and religious freedom in every corner of the globe, were problems well calculated to rouse the inquisitive and to puzzle the uninformed. The consequence was, that there has been, within the last four months, throughout Europe a more thorough and general discussion, by the press and by individuals, of American institutions than had occurred for the previous twenty years. In general the press of Europe is in able and skilful hands ; and if, in their late discussions, it has occasionally fallen into some egregious blunders, it shows how little familiar the best-informed were with the details of our system when those events arose which have attracted to our condition the gaze of Europe.

You inform me that it is not improbable that persons claiming to represent the States which have attempted to throw off their federal obligations will seek a recognition of their independence by the Emperor of the French ; that you would regard such an act, on the part of the French government, as calculated to encourage the revolutionary movements of the seceding States, and to increase the dangers of disaffection in those which shall remain loyal ; that it would be inconsistent with the friendship which the government of the United States has always heretofore experienced from the government of France ; that it would tend to disturb the friendly relations, diplomatic and commercial, now existing between those two powers, and prove adverse to the interests of France and the United States.

You have not in your despatch informed me what line of policy it is the purpose of the federal government to adopt towards the seceding States, a fact most material in determining my own action, as well as the views to be addressed to a foreign power on the points presented by your instructions. If I correctly construe the intentions of the government, it looks to a pacific solution of the difficulties which now disturb its relations with the seceding States. In other words, it does not propose to resort to the strong arm of military power to coerce those States into submission to the federal authority. If this be a correct view of its proposed action, and all who understand the genius of our institutions and the character of our people must hope that it shall be such, the only difficulty will be in making European governments appreciate the spirit of such wise and conciliatory policy, and comprehend the just application of the principles of international jurisprudence to a state of facts so novel and peculiar.

The fact which seems chiefly to have governed the conduct of nations in establishing diplomatic and commercial relations with States or provinces which have thrown off their allegiance to the general power—I mean, of course, apart from the fact of their ability to maintain international relations with the world—is the practical cessation of all attempts by arms to enforce obedience to the authority asserted. This rule is founded upon the idea that force, successfully exerted or resisted, is the only criterion by which the respective claims to sovereignty of the contending parties can be adjudged. And, unfortunately, the past history of the world exhibits no other influence which has been deemed fit and proper to be invoked to maintain authority or to suppress revolution. But it is obvious that this rule cannot be rigidly applied by foreign governments to our political system, nor to the course of policy which the federal government has thought expedient to pursue towards the seceding States, without exhibiting, on the part of such foreign government, a most unfriendly disregard of the rights and interests of the remaining twenty-eight States, and an eager desire to dismember the confederacy. Where the parties place the issue fairly upon the arbitrament of the sword, there the result of arms must naturally determine the action of foreign powers. But where force is *ab initio* repudiated as the means of terminating the contest; where the appeal is to the reason, judgment, and interests of the seceding States; where time is an essential element to moderate excited passion, to examine into alleged grievances, and to apply the remedies provided by our constitutional system; and especially when it is known that propositions for the adjustment of the points at issue are now being considered by some of the most influential States of the confederacy, a hasty recognition by any foreign power of the independence of the seceding States would exhibit, upon the part of such foreign government, proof as unequivocal of an unfriendly spirit towards the United States as if such recognition were made amidst the clash of arms, and with a view of exerting a moral influence over the result of the struggle. It would seem to me, therefore, that no principle of international law, nor any considerations of courtesy or commercial benefit could justify a foreign power in adding to the embarrassments of our present domestic position by recognizing at this time the independence of the confederated States. No appeal will be made to its sympathy by the allegation of grievous wrong and oppression in the presence of the fact that nine other States, with the same rights and interests involved, equally free, brave, and high spirited, have not deemed the evil sufficient to justify a remedy so extreme. Time has not yet made manifest to the world how far those movements have sprung from passion, or are the results of deliberate judgment; whether they have originated in fears which have since proved unfounded, or are the settled convictions of the popular mind. Nor has any adequate opportunity been afforded for the correction of the grievance complained of by the regular operation of our constitutional system. The foreign power which would, under such circumstances, recognize the independence of those States, and thus frustrate and embarrass the regular and pacific adjustment of our own internal difficulties, would subject itself to grave accusations of hostility to the Union, and give to the federal authority, as the agent and representative of the remaining States, just cause of dissatisfaction.

I have no hesitation in expressing it as my opinion, founded upon frequent general interviews with the Emperor, although in no instance touching this particular point, that France will act upon this delicate question when it shall be presented to her consideration in the spirit of a most friendly power; that she will be the last of the great states of Europe to give a hasty encouragement to the dismemberment of the Union, or to afford to the government of the United States, in the contingency to which you refer, any just cause of complaint. The unhappy divisions which have afflicted our country have attracted the Emperor's earnest attention since the first of January last, and he has never, but upon one occasion of our meeting since, failed to make them the subject of friendly inquiry, and often of comment. He looks upon the dismemberment of the American confederacy with no pleasurc, but as a calamity to be deplored by every enlightened friend of human progress. And he would act, not only in conflict with sentiments often expressed, but in opposition to the well understood feelings of the French people, if he should precipitately adopt any step whatever tending to give force and efficacy to those movements of separation, so long as a reasonable hope remains that the federal authority can or should be maintained over the seceding States.

The Emperor Napoleon has no selfish purpose to accomplish by the dismemberment of the American Union. As he has upon more than one occasion said to me: "There are no points of collision between France and the United States; their interests are harmonious, and they point to one policy, the closest friendship and the freest commercial intercourse." He knows full well that the greatness of our republic cannot endanger the stability of his throne, or cast a shadow over the glory of France. He would rather see us united and powerful than dissevered and weak. He is too enlightened to misapprehend the spirit of conciliation which now actuates the conduct of the federal authorities. He knows that appeals to the public judgment perform that function in our republic which is elsewhere only accomplished by brute force. And if armies have not been marshalled, as they would have been ere this in Europe, to give effect to the federal authority, he is aware that it is not because the general government disclaims authority over the seceding States, or is destitute of the means and resources of war, but from an enlightened conviction on its part that time and reflection will be more efficacious than arms in re-establishing the federal authority, and restoring that sentiment of loyalty to the Union which was once the pride of every American heart.

I have not, so far, heard that any commissioners have been sent by the seceding States to France. Should they, as you anticipate, arrive shortly, I think I am not mistaken in saying that they will find that the imperial government is not yet prepared to look favorably upon the object of this mission.

I have made this despatch longer, perhaps, than was necessary, for I have not had time to elaborate and digest my ideas very carefully, and submit them as suggestions to elicit more fully the views and instructions of the government.

I am, sir, very respectfully, your obedient servant,

CHAS. J. FAULKNER.

Hon. JEREMIAH S. BLACK,
        Secretary of State.

Mr. Faulkner to Mr. Seward.

[Extract.]

No. 119.]   LEGATION OF THE UNITED STATES,
                                    Paris, April 15, 1861.

SIR: I called to-day upon Mr. Thouvenel at the ministry of foreign affairs, and was promptly admitted to an interview. Agreeably to your request, I handed to him a copy of the inaugural address of President Lincoln, and added that I was instructed by you to say to him that it embraced the views of the President of the United States upon the difficulties which now disturbed the harmony of the American Union, and also an exposition of the general policy which it was the purpose of the government to pursue with a view to the preservation of domestic peace and the maintenance of the federal Union. Here Mr. Thouvenel asked if there was not some diversity of opinion in the cabinet of the President as to the proper mode of meeting the difficulties which now disturbed the relations of the States and general government. I replied, upon that point I had no information; under our system the cabinet was but an advising body; its opinions were entitled to weight, but did not necessarily compel the action of the President; the executive power was, by the Constitution, vested exclusively in the President.

I said that I was further instructed to assure him that the President of the United States entertains a full confidence in the speedy restoration of the harmony and unity of the government by a firm, yet just and liberal policy, co-operating with the deliberate and loyal action of the American people. Mr. Thouvenel expressed his pleasure at this assurance.

I further said that the President regretted that the events going on in the United States might be productive of some possible inconvenience to the people and subjects of France, but he was determined that those inconveniences shall be made as light and transient as possible, and, so far as it may rest with him, that all strangers who may suffer any injury from them shall be indemnified.

I said to him that the President thought it not improbable that an appeal would be made before long by the "confederated States" to foreign powers, and, among others, to the government of France, for the recognition of their independence; that no such appeal having yet been made, it was premature and out of place to discuss any of the points involved in that delicate and important inquiry; but the government of the United States desired the fact to be known that whenever any such application shall be made it will meet with opposition from the minister who shall then represent that government at this court.

I said to him that my mission at this court would very soon terminate, and that I should have no official connexion with the question which, it was anticipated, might arise upon the demand of the confederated States for the recognition of their independence ; that my place would soon be supplied by a distinguished citizen of the State of New Jersey, a gentleman who possessed the confidence of the President, who fully sympathized in his public views, and who would doubtless come fully instructed as to the then wishes and views of the government of the United States, and that the only request which I would now make, and which would close all I had to say in the interview, was that no proposition recognizing the permanent dismemberment of the American Union shall be considered by the French government until after the arrival and reception of the new minister accredited by the United States to this court.

Mr. Thouvenel, in reply, said that no application had yet been made to him by the confederated States, in any form, for the recognition of their independence; that the French government was not in the habit of acting hastily upon such questions, as might be seen by its tardiness in recognizing the new kingdom of Italy; that he believed the maintenance of the federal Union, in its integrity, was to be desired for the benefit of the people north and south, as well as for the interests of France, and the government of the United States might rest well assured that no hasty or precipitate action would be taken on that subject by the Emperor. But whilst he gave utterance of these views, he was equally bound to say that the practice and usage of the present century had fully established the right of *de facto* governments to recognition when a proper case was made out for the decision of foreign powers. Here the official interview ended.

The conversation was then further protracted by an inquiry from Mr. Thouvenel when the new tariff would go into operation, and whether it was to be regarded as the settled policy of the government. I told him that the first day of the present month had been prescribed as the period when the new duties would take effect; that I had not yet examined its provisions with such care as would justify me in pronouncing an opinion upon its merits; that it was condemned by the commercial classes of the country, and that I had no doubt, from the discontent manifested in several quarters, that the subject would engage the attention of Congress at its next meeting, and probably some important modifications would be made in it. The finances of the government were at this time temporarily embarrassed, and I had no doubt the provisions of the new tariff were adopted with a view, although probably a mistaken one, of sustaining the credit of the treasury as much as of reviving the protective policy. He then asked me my opinion as to the course of policy that would be adopted towards the seceding States, and whether I thought force would be employed to coerce them into submission to the federal authority. I told him that I could only give him my individual opinion, and that I thought force would not be employed; that ours was a government of public opinion, and although the Union unquestionably possessed all the ordinary powers necessary for its preservation, as had been shown in several partial insurrections which had occurred in our history, yet that the extreme powers of government could only be used in accordance with public opinion, and that I was satisfied that the sentiment of the people was opposed to the employment of force against the seceding States. So sincere was the deference felt in that country for the great principles of self-government, and so great the respect for the action of the people, when adopted under the imposing forms of State organization and State sovereignty, that I did not think the employment of force would be tolerated for a moment, and I thought the only solution of our difficulties would be found in such modifications of our constitutional compact as would invite the seceding States back into the Union on a peaceable acquiescence in the assertion of their claims to a separate sovereignty. *   *   *   *   *   *   *   *

I am, very respectfully, your obedient servant,

CHAS. J. FAULKNER

Hon. WILLIAM H. SEWARD,
    Secretary of State.

Mr. Seward to Mr. Dayton.

No. 7.]   DEPARTMENT OF STATE, '
                         Washington, May 4, 1861.

SIR: The despatches of your predecessor, Nos. 117, 119, and 120, have been received; the latter acknowledging the receipt of our letter of recall and announcing his intended return requires no special notice.

No. 117 bears the date of the 5th of April last. It contains only an exposition of Mr. Faulkner's views of the policy which this government ought to pursue in regard to the disturbed condition of affairs at home, but at the same time gives us no information concerning the state of our affairs in France.

The instructions heretofore transmitted to you will show you the President's views on the subject Mr. Faulkner has discussed, and these will be your guide notwithstanding any different opinions your predecessor may have expressed or left on record at Paris.

No. 119 bears date of the 15th of April last, and contains a report of an official conversation, and also of an unofficial one held between Mr. Faulkner and Mr. Thouvenel.

In the former conversation Mr. Thouvenel asked Mr. Faulkner whether there is not some diversity of opinion in the cabinet of the President as to the proper mode of meeting the difficulties which now disturb the relations of the States and the general government. Mr. Faulkner, in reply, said that he had no information on the subject.

The matter is of no great moment, yet it is desirable that there be no misapprehension of the true state of the government in the present emergency.

You may, therefore, recall that conversation to Mr. Thouvenel's memory, and then assure him explicitly that there is no difference of opinion whatever between the President and his constitutional advisers, or among those advisers themselves, concerning the policy that has been pursued, and which is now prosecuted by the administration in regard to the unhappy disturbances existing in the country. The path of executive duty has thus far been too plainly marked out by stern necessities to be mistaken, while the solemnity of the great emergency and the responsibilities it devolves have extinguished in the public councils every emotion but those of loyalty and patriotism. It is not in the hands of this administration that this government is to come to an end at all—much less for want of harmony in devotion to the country.

Mr. Thouvenel's declaration that the United States may rest well assured that no hasty or precipitate action will be taken on the subject of the apprehended application of the insurrectionists for a recognition of the independence of the so-called Confederate States is entirely satisfactory, although it was attended by a reservation of views concerning general principles applicable to cases that need not now be discussed.

In the unofficial conversation Mr. Faulkner says that he himself expressed the opinion that force would not be resorted to to coerce the so-called seceding States into submission to the federal authority, and that the only solution of the difficulty would be found in such modifications of the constitutional compact as would invite the seceding States back into the Union, or a peaceable acquiescence in the assertion of their claim to a separate sovereignty.

The time when these questions had any pertinency or plausibility have passed away. The United States waited patiently while their authority was defied in turbulent assemblies, and in seditious preparations, willing to hope that mediation, offered on all sides, would conciliate and induce the disaffected parties to return to a better mind.

But the case is now altogether changed. The insurgents have instituted revolution with open, flagrant, deadly war to compel the United States to acquiesce in the dismemberment of the Union. The United States have accepted this civil war as an inevitable necessity. The constitutional remedies for all the complaints of the insurgents are still open to them, and will remain so. But, on the other hand, the land and naval forces of the Union have been put into activity to restore the federal authority and to save the Union from danger.

You cannot be too decided or too explicit in making known to the French government that there is not now, nor has there been, nor will there be any the least idea existing in this government of suffering a dissolution of this Union to take place in any way whatever.

There will be here only one nation and one government, and there will be the same republic, and the same constitutional Union that have already survived a dozen national changes, and changes of government in almost every other country. These will stand hereafter, as they are now, objects of human wonder and human affection.

You have seen, on the eve of your departure, the elasticity of the national spirit, the vigor of the national government, and the lavish devotion of the national treasures to this great cause. Tell Mr. Thouvenel, then, with the highest consideration and good feeling, that the thought of a dissolution of this Union, peaceably or by force, has never entered into the mind of any candid statesman here, and it is high time that it be dismissed by statesmen in Europe.

I am, sir, respectfully, your obedient servant,

WILLIAM H. SEWARD.

Wm. L. Dayton, Esq., &c., &c., &c.

Mr. Dayton to Mr. Seward.

[Extracts.]

No. 5.]   Paris, *May* 22, 1861.

Sir: I have the pleasure to announce to you my arrival in this city on Saturday, May 11. On Monday, application was made through our legation for an audience with Mr. Thouvenel, minister of foreign affairs, which was granted for the 16th instant, on which day I was duly presented to him by Mr. Walsh, of the American legation.

Mr. Thouvenel, in the course of the conversation, took occasion to say that he deeply regretted the condition of things in the United States, and that in this expression of feeling he represented the views and feelings of the Emperor; that so deeply concerned was the Emperor that he had felt disposed to offer his good offices, but had been deterred from the fear that his offer might not be well received; but should occasion for this arise, he would always be ready and happy to be of use. He made special inquiry as to the policy of our government in regard to neutral rights, particularly in reference to neutral property found in southern ships. He went into considerable detail to show that historical precedents were in favor of treating southern vessels as those of a regular belligerent, and applying the same doctrine to them as had always been upheld by the United States. He dwelt particularly upon the fact that Great Britain, during our revolutionary war, had not considered our privateers as pirates. I understood him to say that, as respects an effective blockade, it would be fully recognized and respected; but he seemed much impressed with the importance of understanding clearly the intentions of our government in reference to these matters as respects the foreign world.

As respects a tender of the kind offices of the Emperor I could only thank him for the interest in our country which the suggestion manifested, but gave him no reason to suppose such offer at this time would be accepted. As to the doctrines which our government would apply in reference to the blockade of southern ports and neutral rights, I told him I had no specific instructions at present, and could only refer him to the proclamation of the President and the general principles of international law which might bear on the case. I further informed him that immediately after my reception by the Emperor I would apprise my government of the anxiety of the French government to learn the views of our government more definitively upon these questions. You will not fail to have observed that the action of France and England upon this question of belligerent rights has been upon a mutual understanding and agreement.

Throughout the conversation he seemed anxious to impress upon me the great interest which France took in our condition, and their desire for the perpetuation of the Union of the States. He referred to the fact that France had aided in its formation, and did not desire to witness its dissolution. The recognition of the southern confederates as possessing belligerent rights he did not consider at all as recognizing them as independent States.

After the conversation had closed, to save time I at once presented a copy of my letters of credence, and requested an audience of the Emperor, &c.

On the next day I was informed by a note from the minister that I would be received at the palace on the 19th instant, at which time I was presented in due form to the Emperor, in the presence of certain officers of the court.

A copy of my remarks to the Emperor will be found enclosed, (letter A.) In reply, the Emperor, after a courteous welcome, and one or two remarks of a character personally complimentary, said, in substance, that he felt great interest in the condition of things in our country; that he was very anxious our difficulties should be settled amicably; that he had been and yet was ready to offer his kind offices, if such offer would be mutually agreeable to the contending parties; that whatever tended to affect injuriously our interests was detrimental to the interests of France, and that he desired a perpetuation of the Union of the States, with some additional remarks of like tenor and character. His observations were in the same vein as those of the minister of foreign affairs, and I doubt not were the frank expressions of his views on this subject.

Immediately after the formal part of my presentation had closed, and my letters of credence been delivered, he entered for a short time into general conversation. Upon taking my leave of the Emperor I was conducted by the grand chamberlain to the apartments of the Empress, and there presented to her. She repeated to some extent the same views already presented by the Emperor. My reception at the palace was in every respect agreeable. On Monday, the 20th instant, I called again on Mr. Thouvenel, in company with Mr. Sanford, (our minister to Belgium,) for the purpose of obtaining, if possible, a little more distinct information as to what France meant by the terms "neutral rights" and "belligerent" rights; how far he considered such rights as extending to the capture and condemnation of prizes in the ports of France, &c. He said in reply, in substance, that they held that the flag covers the cargo; and that if a southern ship carrying neutral property was captured, the property would not be condemned, &c. He hoped our government would recognize principles for which it had always contended. I told him it would certainly do so, but the question here was, whether there was a flag; that our government insisted that the confederates, being merely in rebellion, had no flag, and I could not exactly understand how a foreign government which had not recognized them as an independent power could recognize them as having a flag. He said, furthermore, that the French government had given no warning to their citizens, &c., (as the English government had,) by proclamation, because it was unnecessary; that the statute law of France (of 1825, April 10, I think) declared that any French citizen taking service under a foreign power lost all claim to protection as a citizen; that if a subject of France should take service on board of a letter of marque licensed by the Confederate States, it would be, as I understood him, piratical on the part of such subject. He said, furthermore, that no letters of marque could be fitted out in their ports, or *even sheltered* there, unless they came in from necessity, (as stress of weather, &c.,) and then could remain, I think, but twenty-four hours; that consequently there could be no bringing of prizes into French ports, and while there a condemnation of them in the courts of the southern States. His conversation on this part of the case was very satisfactory, and he

Ex. Doc. 1——14

promised me a reference in writing to the French statutes bearing on the question. He added that the French government had addressed certain interrogatories to our government, and would await their answer. The disposition of this government to keep on friendly relations with us is, I think, manifest, and it will not, I judge, be diminished by the obvious fact that certain portions of the public men and the press of England are felicitating themselves on the condition of things in America. The policy of having a heavy commercial power in the west, as some counterpoise to the marine power of England, is too manifest to escape a mind so sagacious as that of the present Emperor of the French. I had taken the liberty before the reception of your last despatch, dated 4th instant, of assuring all persons, official and otherwise, with whom I came in contact, that the most effective measures were being taken by our government to crush out this causeless and wicked rebellion, and that I believed such efforts would be continued to the end; that the fears (which existed in some quarters) that the government would again temporize, and lose the advantage which the present determined enthusiasm of the people gave to it, were groundless. I find very strong feelings existing here in behalf of the Union among the American citizens from the northern States, and a determination to support the government with men and money.

*   *   *   *   *   *   *   *   *

I have had many applications since here by foreigners for service as officers in the army of the United States, and I understand from one of the former secretaries of the legation that many applications were made at the office of the legation before I came. There was one case only, as the secretary says, of an application at the office of the legation for service in the army of the south, and this was from an anonymous correspondent, the note seeking service being unsigned. To these applications I have said that our service was open to volunteers, but I had no authority to commit the government to appointments; that, in fact, we needed arms rather than men. * * *

No formal notice of the blockade of southern ports has been given to the government here, unless through the agency of the French minister at Washington. Indeed, I think I understood Mr. Thouvenel to say that they had received no such formal notice at all. I shall call the attention of Mr. Thouvenel to the original proclamation when I communicate to him (as I shall at once do) the additional proclamation (just received) of the blockade of the ports of Virginia and North Carolina.

*   *   *   *   *   *   *   *   *

I have opened, since here, (directed to my predecessor,) a copy of the President's proclamation as to the blockade of the ports of Virginia and North Carolina, dated 27th April, 1861. I received likewise despatch No. 4 last night, containing views of the government at Washington as to the abolition of privateering, and enclosing to me a commission to effect with the French government a treaty for that purpose, with the form of such treaty. This is of great importance, and will affect in a material degree the means of defence on the part of our country in time of war. I shall proceed in conformity, however, with these instructions to communicate with the minister of foreign affairs on the subject. But I cannot help feeling, in view of what the French law is, as heretofore stated, and the little danger to our commerce which can soon arise from any action of this government or of its subjects from privateers, that I had better attempt again to obtain a provision exempting from seizure *private* property afloat (unless contraband) the same as private property is now exempt on land. I should very much regret an opportunity lost to obtain such a treaty provision, if possible, before we give up that species of volunteer marine by which we are enabled in some degree to affect the commerce of other nations, having a heavier naval marine, while they are destroying our own. The Emperor is about to leave Paris for the country, and it is doubtful if great expedition can be had in this matter ; but, acting under the direct instructions of the government at home, I shall incur no unnecessary delay in carrying those instructions (if I can procure no better terms) into effect.

*　　*　　*　　*　　*　　*　　*　　*

I have received your despatch (No. 7) containing instructions as to matters to be communicated to Mr. Thouvenel in reference to the unity of the cabinet at Washington and the intentions of the government to prosecute the war with the utmost effect.

I will, at the earliest moment, so state to Mr. Thouvenel, though it will be to some extent a restatement of what has already been said. There has, I fear, been some misapprehension upon the minds of the authorities here upon this subject.

Since my arrival here my engagements, personal and official, have been constant ; so much so that it has not been in my power to communicate as promptly with your department as I would have desired.

*　　*　　*　　*　　*　　*　　*　　*

Your very obedient servant,

WM. L. DAYTON.

Hon. WILLIAM H. SEWARD,
Secretary of State.

A.

YOUR MAJESTY : I have the honor to present to your Imperial Majesty these, my letters of credence from the President of the United States of America, accrediting me as envoy extraordinary and minister plenipotentiary near to your Majesty.

By these letters it is made my especial duty, as it will certainly be my pleasure, with the assent of your Majesty, to cultivate and strengthen the friendship and good correspondence which has heretofore existed between France and the United States, and as far as possible to preserve and advance the interest and happiness of both nations. The people of the United States have not forgotten, nor can they ever forget, that France was their first ally, and throughout the whole period of their national existence has been (with a passing cloud only) their constant friend. An unbroken intercourse of good offices and kind feelings between two great nations for so long a period affords just cause of pride and congratulation to both. Each year has continued to enlarge those business interests which bind us together, and I am happy to know that at no period in our past history have those interests been more prosperous than under the wise, liberal, and enlightened policy of your Imperial Majesty. All our recollections of the past, all our interests of the present, and all our hopes for the future, prompt the United States to cultivate with sedulous care those friendly relations with the government of France which have existed so long and been productive to each nation of results so auspicious.

I have it specially in charge from the President of the United States to give assurance to your Imperial Majesty of his disposition to cultivate such friendly relations; to assure your Majesty personally of his high respect and appreciation ; to tender to you, to the Empress, your imperial consort, and to each of the members of the imperial family, his best wishes for their health, prosperity, and happiness. Permit me only to add that the mission near to your Imperial Majesty, with which I have been honored, is one most grateful to my feelings, and without neglecting the interests of my own government, I shall endeavor so to discharge its duties as to make my residence here entirely agreeable to your Majesty.

Mr. Dayton to Mr. Seward.

[Extracts.]

No. 6.] PARIS, *May* 27, 1861.

SIR: Immediately after closing my last despatch I wrote to Mr. Thouvenel a note apprising him that I was fully authorized to enter into a convention with the government of France in respect to privateering, the rights of neutrals, and the matter of blockade, and requesting him, if disposed to renew negotiations upon these subjects, to name a day for conference.

My note was not sent until the 25th instant. A copy is attached, marked letter A.

On the same day, to wit, the 25th of the present month, I sent to Mr. Thouvenel a copy of the President's proclamation of the blockade of the ports of Virginia and North Carolina, referring, at the same time, to the previous blockade of the other southern ports. A copy of my note is attached, marked letter C.

On the 24th instant I received from the minister of war a note as to certain fire-arms for the State of Virginia, applied for by my predecessor, Mr. Faulkner; a copy of which note, marked D, together with my answer thereto, marked E, is hereunto attached.

*   *   *   *   *

I recently received from the agent of our Havre line of steamers a request that I would (by application to the government for munitions of war) aid him to put the steamer Fulton in a condition of defence on her homeward voyage; which I did, so far as I could, by presenting his request to the government. A copy of his request, indorsed by me, is herewith attached, marked H. I presume the request was granted, as I have heard nothing since from the agent, and the steamer leaves her port to-day.

I have just received the despatches, by the last steamer, directed to Mr. Sanford, to whom I immediately delivered them; and likewise your circular to me upon the subject of passports, with which I shall carefully comply.

Mr. Thouvenel has promptly answered my note informing him I was authorized to enter into a convention as to privateering, &c., and has designated to-morrow, at 4 p. m., for a conference. In my next despatch I shall be able, doubtless, to give you some information as to the views of the French government on this subject. Mr. Marsh has been here, engaged in doing good service by matter communicated for use through the English press.

Mr. Burlingame is remaining here for a short time, acting under the advice of his brother diplomatists, owing to matter confidentially communicated from Vienna.

With much consideration, your obedient servant,

WM. L. DAYTON.

Hon. WM. H. SEWARD,
Secretary of State.

A.

PARIS, May 24, 1861.

SIR: I have the honor to inform your excellency that I am fully authorized by my government to enter into a convention with the government of France in reference to the subject of privateering, the rights of neutrals, and the matter of blockade.

If, therefore, the government of his Imperial Majesty remains disposed to renew negotiations upon these subjects, I shall be happy to have a conference with your excellency at such time as your excellency may indicate.

With great respect, I have the honor to be your obedient servant,

WM. L. DAYTON.

Mr. THOUVENEL, Minister of Foreign Affairs.

C.

PARIS, May 24, 1861.

SIR: I beg to enclose to your excellency a copy of a proclamation issued by the President of the United States on the 27th of April last, establishing a blockade of the ports of the States of Virginia and North Carolina.

A prior proclamation, dated 19th April last, established a blockade of the ports of the States of South Carolina, Georgia, Florida, Alabama, Louisiana, Mississippi, and Texas, of which your excellency has doubtless had notice.

With much respect, I have the honor to be your excellency's obedient servant,

WM. L. DAYTON.

Mr. THOUVENEL, Minister of Foreign Affairs.

D.

PARIS, May 24, 1861.

SIR: The 27th September, 1860, your predecessor having requested me to have the goodness to deliver to him, from the state arsenal, four fire-arms (4 armes à feu) and two other arms (armes blanches) for the State of Virginia, I authorized the said delivery, with the approbation of the Emperor; and the 22d of October, 1860, I informed Mr. Faulkner that the artillery board of Paris held these arms at the disposition of the Virginia commissioners.

Up to this moment there has not been a delivery, and the letters of the director colonel of artillery, as also my despatch of the 21st of March last to Mr. Faulkner, remain unanswered.

Interpreting this silence as a renunciation of the request of the State of Virginia, I have the honor to inform you that, unless you intimate a desire to the contrary in the course of a few days, I shall order the director of artillery at Paris to consider the authorization of the 22d of October, 1860, as null.

Accept, sir, the assurance of the most distinguished consideration with which I have the honor to be your very humble and very obedient servant,

RANDON,
Le Marechal de France, Ministre Secretaire d'etat de la Guerre.

E.

PARIS, *May* 26, 1861.

SIR: I have the honor to acknowledge your letter of the 24th instant, calling my attention to the fact that my predecessor, on the 27th of September last, requested you to have the goodness to deliver to him, from the government arsenal, four fire-arms (4 *armes à feu*) and two other arms (*armes blanches*) for the State of Virginia, and that you authorized the said delivery, with the approbation of the Emperor, on the 22d of October, 1860; and that you informed Mr. Faulkner that the artillery board of Paris held those arms at the disposition of the Virginia delegates; that up to the date of your note to me the letter from the colonel of the artillery staff and your own despatches of the 21st of March last, addressed to Mr. Faulkner, have remained unanswered, &c.

I beg to say to your excellency that I am altogether ignorant of the causes of delay on the part of my predecessor in answering the communications referred to, and asking for the delivery of the arms in question.

I pray you, sir, to accept for yourself, and convey to the Emperor, my grateful acknowledgments, in behalf of the United States, for the courtesy extended in the expression of a readiness to grant the request of my predecessor; while I deem it proper to say at once that the request for the arms referred to will not, under existing circumstances, be renewed by *me* in behalf of the State of Virginia.

I beg to assure you, sir, of the high consideration with which I have the honor to be your obedient servant,

WM. L. DAYTON.

Mons. le Marechal Comte RANDON,
    Minister de la Guerre.

H.

PARIS, *May* 23, 1861.

EXCELLENCY: The necessity which exists for arming our steamer, the Fulton, against any attack of the privateers of the southern confederacy obliges Captain Walton to provide himself with *two hundred rifles.* These guns, which we have purchased at Leige, (Belgium,) will be delivered to-day or to-morrow at Havre.

But we have no cartridges for these guns, and are obliged to buy them in France, and cannot obtain them without an authorization from the minister of war. We are thus obliged to appeal to you, to beg your powerful influence in obtaining the necessary munitions.

We desire that the French government furnish us, delivered on board the steamer Fulton, at Havre, *twenty thousand cartouches for hunting rifles*, of the calibre $17\frac{3}{10}$ for the muzzle of the guns. Either our house, at Paris, or that of Messrs. W. Selim & Co., at Havre, will pay the bills.

The steamer Fulton will quit Havre Tuesday morning, 28th instant, and it will be necessary that the munition should be delivered Monday.

We pray your excellency to accept, *in entram*, the expression of the profound gratitude and our distinguished consideration of your excellency's most obedient servants,

SHELBERT, KANE & CO.,
    8 *Place de la Bourse.*

His Excellency Mr. DAYTON,
    Minister of the United States of America, Paris.

Mr. Seward to Mr. Dayton.

No. 10.]   DEPARTMENT OF STATE,
                                                    Washington, May 30, 1861.

SIR: Mr. Sanford, who was requested by me to look to our interests in Paris in the interval which might elapse between the withdrawal of Mr. Faulkner and your own arrival, has transmitted to me (in his despatch No. 2) an account of a very interesting conversation which he has recently held with Mr. Thouvenel on our internal affairs.

In that conversation Mr. Thouvenel intimated that, in view of the great commercial interests which are involved in the domestic controversy which is now agitating the United States, the French government had felt itself constrained to take measures, in conjunction with the government of Great Britain, to meet a condition of things which imperiled those interests. That it had been decided that communications of a similar tenor should be addressed by both of those governments to the government of the United States, and that those communications would be forwarded in the current week. Mr. Thouvenel kindly foreshadowed the points of those communications.

As those papers may be expected to arrive by, perhaps, the next steamer, I shall reserve comments upon the propositions indicated until they shall thus be fully and directly brought to the attention of the President.

There are, however, some points in the conversation, or suggested by it, which I cannot properly suffer to pass unnoticed.

First. I desire that Mr. Thouvenel may be informed that this government cannot but regard any communications held by the French government, even though unofficial, with the agents of the insurrectionary movement in this country as exceptionable and injurious to the dignity and honor of the United States. They protest against this intercourse, however, not so much on that ground as on another. They desire to maintain the most cordial relations with the government of France, and would therefore, if possible, refrain from complaint. But it is manifest that even an unofficial reception of the emissaries of disunion has a certain though measured tendency to give them a prestige which would encourage their efforts to prosecute a civil war destructive to the prosperity of this country and aimed at the overthrow of the government itself. It is earnestly hoped that this protest may be sufficient to relieve this government from the necessity of any action on the unpleasant subject to which it relates.

Secondly. The United States cannot for a moment allow the French government to rest under the delusive belief that they will be content to have the confederate States recognized as a belligerent power by States with which this nation is in amity. No concert of action among foreign States so recognizing the insurgents can reconcile the United States to such a proceeding, whatever may be the consequences of resistance.

Thirdly. The President turns away from these points of apprehended difference of opinion between the two governments to notice other and more agreeable subjects.

The tone of Mr. Thouvenel's conversation is frank, generous, and cordial; and this government feels itself bound by new ties to France when her Emperor avows his desire for the perpetual union of the States. Especially does this government acknowledge that it is profoundly moved by the declaration of his Majesty, that he would be willing to act as mediator in the civil strife that unhappily convulses our country. These expressions of good will are just what have been expected from the Emperor of France. This government desires that his Majesty may be informed that it indulges not the least apprehension of a dissolution of the Union in this painful controversy. A favorable issue is deemed certain. What is wanted is that the war may be as short, and attended by as few calamities at home and as few injuries to friendly nations, as possible. No mediation could modify in the least degree the convictions of policy and duty under which this government is acting ; while foreign intervention, even in the friendly form of mediation, would produce new and injurious complications. We are free to confess that so cordial is our regard for the Emperor and our confidence in his wisdom and justice, that his mediation would be accepted if all intervention of that kind were not deemed altogether inadmissible. This government perceives, as it thinks, that the French government is indulging in an exaggerated estimate of the moral power and material forces of the insurrection. The government of the United States cheerfully excuses this error, because it knows how unintelligible the working of the American system and the real character of the American people are to European nations. This government knows, moreover, and painfully feels, that the commercial interests of European states are so deeply involved in the restoration of our domestic peace as to excite the highest anxiety and impatience on their part. But it desires the French government to reflect that our commercial interests involved in the issue are even greater than their own ; and that every motive that France can have for desiring peace operates still more powerfully on ourselves, besides a thousand motives peculiar to ourselves alone. The measures we have adopted, and are now vigorously pursuing, will terminate the unhappy contest at an early day, and be followed by benefits to ourselves and to all nations greater and better assured than those which have hitherto attended our national progress. Nothing is wanting to that success except that foreign nations shall leave us, as is our right, to manage our own affairs in our own way. They, as well as we, can only suffer by their intervention. No one, we are sure, can judge better than the Emperor of France how dangerous and deplorable would be the emergency that should intrude Europeans into the political contests of the American people.

I am, sir, respectfully, your obedient servant,

WILLIAM H. SEWARD.

William L. Dayton, Esq., &c., &c., &c.

Mr. Dayton to Mr. Seward.

[Extracts.]

Paris, *May* 30, 1861.

Sir: Since the date of my despatch No. 6 I have had an interview with Mr. Thouvenel.

I told him I was authorized to accept the propositions adopted at the congress of Paris in 1856, but with the desire expressed by the President that the provisions should be added exempting private property afloat, unless contraband, from seizure and confiscation. I did not say, nor did he ask, whether the four propositions would be accepted without amendment. He said nothing could be done except by conference with the other powers, but if I would submit the proposition in writing, which I shall at once do, he would.immediately address the other powers, and we would probably receive an answer in ten or twelve days.

I have been induced to suggest again the adoption of this amendment exempting private property afloat from seizure and confiscation: (1.) From the preference or wish of the President expressed in your letter of instruction. (2.) From the great importance, as it seemed to me, of securing the adoption of the principle, if possible, before the United States should give up the right of privateering. (3.) From the facts patent on the correspondence of this legation in 1856, whereby it appears that France and Russia were both favorably disposed at that time to the adoption of the principle of the amendment, (see Mr. Marcy's despatch to Mr. Mason, No. 94, dated October 4, 1856, and Mr. Mason's confidential letter to Mr. Dallas, of December 6, 1856,) and the obvious fact that it would be the interest of all the other powers (having little naval force) to concur in the amendment. (4.) From the fact that since the date of your despatch to me authorizing the acceptance of the four propositions adopted by the congress at Paris, Mr. Sanford, our minister to Belgium, on a visit to England, learned from Mr. Adams that the British government had given, as he understood, general instructions on the subject to Lord Lyons; and the impression made on the mind of Mr. Adams, as reported to me by Mr. Sanford, was that it was not improbable that England would now, to secure our concurrence in the other propositions, concur in the amendment. That in view of this information, Mr. Adams, who had like instructions with my own, had referred the matter back to be treated of and discussed at Washington. I could not, therefore, at once accept the four propositions, pure and simple, without running the hazard of conflicting with what might be done elsewhere.

I will probably receive an answer from Mr. Thouvenel (after he shall have communicated my proposition to the other powers) before even I shall receive my next despatch on this subject from Washington, which I shall await with some anxiety.

 * * * * * * * * *

The laws, however, in connexion with the practice of the tribunals of France are, I think, as follows:

1. That the captain who accepts a commission from a foreign government and takes command of a cruiser is guilty of a piratical act.

2. That all French subjects enlisting on board of such cruiser, without authority of the Emperor, lose their citizenship, and consequently forfeit their right to the protection of their government.

3. That the principle applied in the French tribunals is unlike that which has been applied in England (and I fear it will be found in the United States) as to harboring privateers; and while their prizes are in a neutral port having them condemned in courts of admiralty of the country licensing such privateer. The laws and practice of the French courts do not admit of this. But these matters, as Mr. Thouvenel now says, must be all left for determination to the tribunals of France.

I am happy to say that there is no disposition manifested here, so far as I have observed, to favor the rebellion in our southern States, or to recognize them as an independent power. All recognition of rights on their part is for commercial purposes only. But the government of France cannot, it says, look at this rebellion as a small matter. That, embracing as it does a large section and many States, they cannot apply to it the same reasoning as if it were an unimportant matter or confined to a small locality.

Mr. Thouvenel says he has had no application from southern commissioners for any purpose of recognition, and he does not know even that such persons are or have been in Paris.

 * * * * * * * * *

I send you a copy of "Gallignani's Messenger," containing a report of the

proceedings of a large and enthusiastic meeting of Americans yesterday at
the Hotel du Louvre.

With high consideration, your obedient servant,

WM. L. DAYTON.

Hon. WILLIAM H. SEWARD,
    Secretary of State.

Mr. Dayton to Mr. Seward.

[Extracts.]

No. 11.]   ·   PARIS, *June* —, 1861.

SIR: Your despatch (No. 10) was received by me on the 18th instant, and
its substance communicated to Mr. Thouvenel on the 19th. On that day I
had with him an interesting conversation. I communicated to him the very
kind language which you had used in behalf of the President in reference to
the Emperor and his willingness to mediate between the north and south,
should such mediation be desired. Nothing could have been better expressed
than the language of your own despatch ; and, without formally reading it
to him, I endeavored to repeat, substantially, its language. Mr. Thouvenel
seemed much gratified at its tone, and inasmuch as the Emperor had made
like remarks to me personally, I begged that your reply might be specially
communicated to him, which was readily promised. This, as you may infer,
was the most agreeable part of my duty, as connected with your despatch.

· A short editorial in reference to the recognition of the independence of
Italy, and in that connexion of the States of the south, which is herewith
enclosed, first appeared in the *Patrie,* (a newspaper published in this city,
and which has heretofore had a semi-official character.) It was republished
on Sunday last in the "Moniteur" without remark, thus giving it an official
significance which would not otherwise have been attached to it. It attracted
much attention here, and some anxiety. I resolved that, at the first opportunity, I would seek an explanation from the minister of foreign affairs.
After my communication of your kind remarks, before referred to, I availed
myself of the opportunity of calling his attention to this matter. He at
once said that his own attention had been arrested by it; that it was a
"silliness;" that Mr. Persigny (minister of the interior) was more dissatisfied with it even than he was; that the *Patrie* had ceased, ten days ago, to
be a semi-official paper; that he did not know how the paragraph had crept
into the *Moniteur,* but that Count Walewski (minister of state) had been
out of the city for ten days past, and that as a consequence matters had not
had the usual oversight. He read me a note from the count, in answer to
one he (Mr. Thouvenel) had written, inquiring if it would not be better to
insert something to show that the paragraph was printed in the *Moniteur*
by mistake, to which note the count replied that he thought it would be
giving an unnecessary importance to the matter, and in that view Mr.
Thouvenel, upon reflection, concurred. But he said he was vexed at the
insertion in the *Moniteur,* and at the commentaries likely to be made upon it.
He said, furthermore, (what he has so often said before,) that the French
government had no sympathy whatever with the seceding States of the
south; that it had no idea of recognizing them as an independent power;
that should they, in the course of time, obtain a status as an independent
power among nations, and show themselves able to maintain that posi-

tion, the French government might ultimately recognize them; but this would be after the expiration of a time ample to test their ability in this behalf. He said, incidentally, three or four years, though I do not suppose he intended anything by this, except to explain more fully his meaning.

He said, furthermore, he had received Mr. Rost, (one of the commissioners of the south,) who applied to him through a third party; that he had not applied to be received as a commissioner from the south; if he had so done he would not have received him. *   *   *   *   *   *
*   *   *   *   *   *   *   *   *   *
*   *   *   *   *   *   *   *   *   *

Mr. Thouvenel referred, in terms of satisfaction, to a private note which he had received from you, through this legation.

I have just received a note from Mr. Perry, our chargé d'affaires at Madrid, under date of the 16th instant, stating that on the next or following day a decree of that government would be made in reference to privateers and Spanish ports, of a like character, in the general, as that which has been made by the French government. This, in view of the locality of certain ports of Spain, will be an important benefit to us.

With a blockade of the ports of the south, and the ports of other nations closed against them, there will be little hope left for profitable marauding on the high seas.

I think I may say with some confidence that all the efforts of the agents of the confederates on this side of the channel have thus far been abortive. They have no encouragement to their hopes of recognition. They have met with no success in their attempts to negotiate a loan. I do not believe they have got any considerable supply of arms, and I think that we know substantially *what they have done* and are *attempting to do.* My only fear is of a possible, not probable, reverse to our arms in Virginia, and a rush, under the excitement of a first victory, upon the city of Washington. Should they get possession, by any possibility, of that point, the prestige it would give them (aside from any strategic advantage) might be productive of most unhappy results. God grant that no such future may hang over us.
*   *   *   *   *   *   *   *   *
*   *   *   *   *   *   *   *   *   *
*   *   *   *   *   *   *   *   *   *

With much respect, I have the honor to be your obedient servant,

WM. L. DAYTON.

Hon WILLIAM H. SEWARD,
    Secretary of State.

[Translation.]

The "Patrie" says:

It is asserted that negotiations will be opened to bring about the re-establishment of diplomatic relations between France and the court of Turin. If they take effect, the consequence will be the recognition of the Italian kingdom, composed of the provinces and states which have passed under the sceptre of his Majesty King Victor Emanuel, at the close of occurrences upon which France has not at this time occasion to express herself, but which have transpired through favor of the principle of non-intervention recognized in Europe.

The renewal of diplomatic relations with Turin would not imply on the part of France, on the subject of the policy of the Italian kingdom, any judgment upon the past, nor any solidarity for the future. It would make it appear that the government *de facto* of this new state is sufficiently established to render it possible to entertain with it those international relations which the interests of the two countries imperatively require.

France, in her new attitude, would not purpose to interfere at all with the internal or external affairs of the Italian kingdom, which must be sole judge of its administration, as it is of its future and its destinies. It will act towards it as at some future day the great European powers will act upon the American question, by recognizing the new republic of the southern States when that republic shall have established a government resting on foundations which will permit the formation of international relations with it conducive to general interests.

Mr. Dayton to Mr. Seward.

[Extracts.]

No. 9.] Paris, *June* 7, 1861.

Sir: I have the honor to acknowledge the receipt of a circular dated May 6, 1861, giving instructions in respect to granting passports.

* * * * * * * *

I understood him (M. Thouvenel) to say an answer could be got within ten or twelve days from the other powers. I was surprised at the briefness of the time stated, but supposed he meant to consult the representatives of those powers at this court; but his remark, as I am now informed, applied to a consultation with certain of the ministers of the French government only. The statement in the American newspapers, that the Department of State had authorized the acceptance of the Paris treaty of 1856 (if that is understood by Lord Lyons to be a distinct acceptance of the treaty, pure and simple) will, I fear, prevent all chance of other terms. The late annunciation of the course of the British government, shutting their ports against privateers, (which so much limits the belligerent rights of the so-called Confederate States,) you will consider, perhaps, renders the accession of our government to the treaty of Paris at this time of less importance than it otherwise would be. I think, from remarks in the New York press, (Herald and Times, and perhaps other prints which I have not seen,) that the force and efficacy of an accession by our government to the treaty of Paris is misunderstood. If I understand the view of these foreign governments, such accession by us would merely bind our hands as respects privateering; it would not at all enlarge our rights as against a belligerent power *not a party* to the treaty; nor would it bind these European governments to enforce the laws of piracy as against such belligerent power *not a party to the treaty.* If they admit the Confederate States as a belligerent power, and recognize them for even commercial purposes, (which, I take it, is what they mean to do,) our accession to the treaty of Paris will not change their action on this question. The status of these rebellious States as respects privateering will remain where it was; at least that is the view which I think is and will be taken of this question by England and France. But however this may be, I am happy to know that, in suggesting to the French government the amendment to that treaty, (securing private property afloat, unless contraband,) I have occasioned no unnecessary delay, inasmuch as Mr. Adams has referred the whole matter back to Washington, and as soon as you shall act there, or before, upon a notification to me, I can act here.

* * * * * * * * *

With high consideration, I have, &c.,

WM. L. DAYTON.

Hon. WM. H. SEWARD, *Secretary of State.*

Mr. Seward to Mr. Dayton.

No. 13.]

DEPARTMENT OF STATE,
Washington, June 8, 1861.

SIR : Your despatch of May 22d (No. 5) has been received. Your safe arrival at your post of duty in this crisis, when our relations to foreign countries, and especially to France, have assumed a degree of interest and importance never known before since the Constitution was established, is a source of sincere satisfaction.

The President approves the sentiments you expressed on your presentation to his Imperial Majesty. The manner in which he received you, and the friendly expressions made by himself, as well as those which were employed by Mr. Thouvenel, although not unexpected, have given us the liveliest satisfaction.

We appreciate highly the Emperor's assurance that he would mediate between the government and the insurgents, with a view to the maintenance and preservation of the Union, if such intervention were deemed desirable by us ; and that generous offer imposes a new obligation upon us toward France, which we acknowledge with sincere pleasure.

If mediation were at all admissible in this grave case, that of his Majesty would not be declined. But the present paramount duty of the government is to save the integrity of the American Union. Absolute, self-sustaining independence is the first and most indispensable element of national existence. This is a republican nation ; all its domestic affairs must be conducted and even adjusted in constitutional republican forms and upon constitutional republican principles. This is an American nation, and its internal affairs must not only be conducted with reference to its peculiar continental position, but by and through American agencies alone. These are simple elementary principles of administration, no one of which can be departed from with safety in any emergency whatever ; nor could it be departed from with the public consent, which rightfully regulates, through constitutionally constituted popular authorities, the entire business of the government.

I have set them forth in no invidious, uncharitable, or ungenerous spirit. I state them fairly and broadly, because I know the magnanimity of the Emperor of France, and I know that he can appreciate directness and candor in diplomacy. I know, moreover, that he is a friend of the United States, and desires that they may continue one great and independent nation forever. I know still further, that the principles I have thus stated will commend themselves to his own great wisdom. To invite or to accept mediation would be incompatible with these principles.

When all this has been said, you will then further say to Mr. Thouvenel, or to the Emperor, that if any mediation were at all admissible it would be his own that we should seek or accept.

You may say, at the same time, that this government has no apprehension whatever of its being unable to conduct our domestic affairs through this crisis to a safe conclusion ; that consummation is even not far distant, if foreign powers shall practice towards us the same forbearance from intervention which we have habitually practiced towards them in emergencies similar to our own; that intervention by them would only protract and aggravate the civil war in which we are unhappily engaged; that civil war is a scourge to which we are more sensitive than any other people, but that the preservation of national unity, which is national existence, reconciles us to every form of difficulty and to the longest possible endurance of the trial in which we are engaged.

Other subjects mentioned in your despatch will be the subject of a special communication after we shall have received the information from the French government which Mr. Thouvenel told Mr. Sanford that he should send with very little delay. It seems desirable to have the positions of the French government in regard to our affairs, as stated by itself, before we answer to inquiries bearing on the subjects to be discussed, which were referred to us through the conversation which took place at the time of your reception.

I am, sir, respectfully, your obedient servant,

WILLIAM H. SEWARD.

William L. Dayton, Esq., &c., &c. &c., Paris.

P. S.—I enclose a copy of a note of this date to Lord Lyons, which will dispel any uncertainty which the French government may entertain in regard to our recognition of a rule of international law which they may deem important.

Mr. Dayton to Mr. Seward.

[Extracts.]

No. 10.]   Paris, *June* 12, 1861.

Sir : Your despatch (No. 10) was duly received on the 9th instant, and, by the same steamer, certain enclosures which were delivered by me to Mr. Sanford as directed.

Your despatch (which is of great interest) was likewise handed by me to Mr. Sanford, to be read and copied if desired, with strict injunctions as to the necessary care to prevent all premature exposure of its contents. *   * You will observe in the first column of " Le Moniteur Universel " (a copy of which is herewith sent) that his Majesty the Emperor of the French, has published a formal declaration, setting out the principles by which this government will be controlled in respect to vessels of war or privateers of the United States and of those who *assume* to have formed ("prétendent former") a separate confederation. These principles are substantially the same as those set forth in my despatch No. 5, and, if they are thoroughly carried out by this government, I do not see that much danger can arise to our commerce from French subjects, or any facilities afforded by French ports. Indeed, if the insurrectionists of the south are recognized as belligerents, I do not see how we can justly ask or expect the French government to go further against the pretended confederacy than it has gone in this declaration. That part of the declaration which puts the vessels of the United States in the same category as the vessels of the Confederate States, may, I think, be justly complained of; but this grows almost necessarily out of the recognition of those States as belligerents. France has placed upon their rights as belligerents (as it seems to me) the utmost limitation that she could put upon them, consistently with the recognition of such rights at all. She has done this, moreover, without offensive promulgation of sympathy with the southern rebels either upon the part of the government or its statesmen, but with expressions of kindness and respect for us throughout.

I have not yet received from Mr. Thouvenel an answer to my written proposition to open negotiations for the accession of the United States to the treaty of Paris of 1856. A copy of that written proposition, marked A, is hereunto attached.

The European press, so far as I have observed, take it for granted that the accession of the United States to that treaty would not at all alter the relations of the several powers to the so-called southern confederacy. A treaty cannot of itself alter the law of nations, although it may restrict the rights of those States which become parties to it. The treaty of Paris certainly did not prevent the United States, while no party to it, from issuing letters of marque, nor would the accession of the United States to such treaty prevent the confederates of the south from doing the same thing if they are recognized by other nations as a belligerent power. The whole difficulty, every subsequent right which has been conceded to the confederates, grows out of that recognition.

It is doubtful, perhaps, whether the other powers will, under the circumstances, negotiate for the accession of the United States at this time to the treaty in question ; but should they do so, it will be with the understanding, I take it, that it imposes no new duties upon them growing out of our domestic controversy. I beg pardon, however, for these suggestions. They may, perhaps, be considered a little beyond the line of my official duties.

 * * * *. * *

With high consideration, I have the honor to be your obedient servant,

        WM. L. DAYTON.

Hon. WILLIAM H. SEWARD,
  Secretary of State, &c.

A.

          PARIS, *May* 31, 1861.

SIR: In conformity with the verbal promise I gave at our last conference, I now have the honor to propose to your excellency an accession, on the part of the United States of America, to "the declaration concerning maritime law," adopted by the plenipotentiaries of France, Great Britain, Austria, Prussia, Russia, Sardinia, and Turkey, at Paris, on the 16th of April, 1856, with the addition to the first clause, which declares "privateering is and remains abolished," of the following words: "And the private property of the subjects or citizens of a belligerent on the high seas shall be exempted from seizure by public armed vessels of the other belligerent, unless it be contraband."

Thus amended I will immediately sign a convention on the part of the United States, acceding to the declaration, which will, I doubt not, be promptly ratified and confirmed by my government.

With much respect, I have the honor to be your very obedient servant,

        WM. L. DAYTON.

His Excellency Monsieur THOUVENEL,
  Minister of Foreign Affairs.

Mr. Seward to Mr. Dayton.

No. 19.]   DEPARTMENT OF STATE,
Washington, June 17, 1861.

SIR: Every instruction which this government has given to its representatives abroad, since the recent change of administration took place, has expressed our profound anxiety lest the disloyal citizens who are engaged in an attempt to overthrow the Union should obtain aid and assistance from foreign nations, either in the form of a recognition of their pretended sovereignty, or in some other and more qualified or guarded manner. Every instruction has expressed our full belief that, without such aid or assistance, the insurrection would speedily come to an end, while any advantage that it could derive from such aid or assistance could serve no other purpose than to protract the existing struggle and aggravate the evils it is inflicting on our own country and on foreign and friendly nations. Every instruction bears evidence of an earnest solicitude to avoid even an appearance of menace or of want of comity towards foreign powers; but at the same time it has emphatically announced, as is now seen to have been necessary, our purpose not to allow any one of them to expect to remain in friendship with us if it should, with whatever motive, practically render such aid or assistance to the insurgents. We have intended not to leave it doubtful that a concession of sovereignty to the insurgents, though it should be indirect or unofficial, or though it should be qualified so as to concede only belligerent or other partial rights, would be regarded as inconsistent with the relations due to us by friendly nations. Nor has it been left at all uncertain that we shall, in every event, insist that these United States must be considered and dealt with now, as heretofore, by such nations as exclusively sovereign for all purposes whatsoever within the territories over which the Constitution has been extended. On the other hand we have not, at any time, been unmindful of the peculiar circumstances which might excite apprehensions on the part of commercial nations for the safety of their subjects and their property in the conflicts which might occur upon sea as well as on land between the forces of the United States and those of the insurgents.

The United States have never disclaimed the employment of letters of marque as a means of maritime war. The insurgents early announced their intention to commission privateers. We knew that friendly nations would be anxious for guarantees of safety from injury by that form of depredation upon the national commerce. We knew also that such nations would desire to be informed whether their flags should be regarded as protecting goods, not contraband of war, of disloyal citizens, found under them, and whether the goods, not contraband, of subjects of such nations would be safe from confiscation when found in vessels of disloyal citizens of the United States. This administration, free from some of the complications of those which had preceded it, promptly took up the negotiations relating to the declaration of the congress of Paris, just at the point where they had been suspended by President Buchanan. We found it just and humane in itself so far as it goes, and that it had only failed to be accepted by the United States because foreign nations had refused to accept an additional principle proposed by this government, yet more just and humane than any which it does contain, namely, that the property of private citizens, not contraband, should be exempted from confiscation in maritime war. While still willing and desirous to have that further principle incorporated in the law of nations, we nevertheless instructed you, and all our representatives in foreign countries, to waive it, if necessary, and to stipulate, subject to the concurrence of the Senate of the United States, our adhesion to the declaration of the congress of Paris as a whole and unmodified. This was done so early as the 25th day of April last, long before the date of the instructions which Mr. Mercier proposed to submit to us. We have ever since that time been waiting for the responses of foreign powers to this high and liberal demonstration on our part. We have, however, received no decisive answers on the subject from those powers.

It was under these circumstances that on the fifteenth day of June instant, the minister from France and the minister from Great Britain, having previously requested an interview, were received by me. Each of them announced that he was charged by his government to read a despatch to me and to give me a copy if I should desire it.

I answered that, owing to the peculiar circumstances of the times, I could not consent to an official reading or delivery of these papers without first knowing their characters and objects. They confidentially and with entire frankness put the despatches into my hands for an informal preliminary examination. Having thus become possessed of their characters, I replied to those ministers that I could not allow them to be officially communicated to this government. They will doubtless mention this answer to their respective states.

I give you now the reasons of this government for pursuing this course in regard to the despatch from France, that you may communicate them to the French government, if you shall find it necessary or expedient.

Some time ago we learned through our legation at St. Petersburg that an understanding had been effected between the governments of Great Britain and France that they should take one and the same course on the subject of the political disturbances in this country, including the possible recognition of the insurgents. At a later period this understanding was distinctly avowed by Mr. Thouvenel to Mr. Sanford, who had been informally introduced by me to the French minister for foreign affairs, and by Lord John Russell to Mr. Dallas, our late minister in London. The avowal in each case preceded the arrival of our newly appointed ministers in Europe, with their instructions for the discharge of their respective missions.

On receiving their avowals I immediately instructed yourself and Mr. Adams "that although we might have expected a different course on the part of these two great powers, yet, as the fact that an understanding existed between them did not certainly imply an unfriendly spirit, we should not complain of it, but that it must be understood by the French and British governments that we shall deal hereafter, as heretofore, in this case, as in all others, with each power separately, and that the agreement for concerted action between them would not at all influence the course we should pursue." The concert thus avowed has been carried out. The ministers came to me together; the instructions they proposed to me differ in form, but are counterparts in effect.

Adhering to our previous decision, which before this time has doubtless been made known to the government of France, we do not make this concert, under the circumstances, a reason for declining to hear the instruction with which Mr. Mercier is charged.

That paper does not expressly deny the sovereignty of the United States of America, but it does assume, inconsistently with that sovereignty, that the United States are not altogether and for all purposes one sovereign power, but that this nation consists of two parties, of which, this government is one. France proposes to take cognizance of both parties as belligerents, and for some purposes to hold communication with each. The instruction would advise us indeed that we must not be surprised if France shall address herself to a government which she says is to be installed at

Montgomery, for certain explanations. This intimation is conclusive in determining this government not to allow the instruction to be read to it.

The United States rightly jealous, as we think, of their sovereignty, cannot suffer themselves to debate any abridgement of that sovereignty with France or with any other nation. Much less can it consent that France shall announce to it a conclusion of her own against that sovereignty, which conclusion France has adopted without any previous conference with the United States on the subject. This government insists that the United States are one whole undivided nation, especially so far as foreign nations are concerned, and that France is, by the law of nations and by treaties, not a neutral power between two imaginary parties here, but a friend of the United States.

In the spirit of this understanding of the case, we are not only not wishing to seek or to give offence to France, but, on the contrary, we desire to preserve peace and friendship with that great power, as with all other nations. We do not feel at liberty to think, and do not think, that France intended any want of consideration towards the United States in directing that the instruction in question should be read to us. Outside of that paper we have abundant evidence of the good feeling and good wishes of the Emperor, and even his anxious solicitude for the same consummation which is the supreme object of our own desires and labors, namely, the preservation of the American Union in its full and absolute integrity.

Doubtless the proceeding has been the result of inadvertence. We feel ourselves at liberty to think that it would not have occurred if we had been so fortunate as to have been heard through you in the consultations of the French government. We think we can easily see how the inadvertence has occurred. France seems to have mistaken a mere casual and ephemeral insurrection here, such as is incidental in the experience of all nations, because all nations are merely human societies, such as have sometimes happened in the history of France herself, for a war which has flagrantly separated this nation into two co-existing political powers which are contending in arms against each other after the separation.

It is erroneous, so far as foreign nations are concerned, to suppose that any war exists in the United States. Certainly there cannot be two belligerent powers where there is no war. There is here, as there has always been, one political power, namely, the United States of America, competent to make war and peace, and conduct commerce and alliances with all foreign nations. There is none other, either in fact, or recognized by foreign nations. There is, indeed, an armed sedition seeking to overthrow the government, and the government is employing military and naval forces to repress it. But these facts do not constitute a war presenting two belligerent powers, and modifying the national character, rights, and responsibilities, or the characters, rights, and responsibilities of foreign nations. It is true that insurrection may ripen into revolution, and that revolution thus ripened may extinguish a previously existing State, or divide it into one or more independent States, and that if such States continue their strife after such division, then there exists a state of war affecting the characters, rights, and duties of all parties concerned. But this only happens when the revolution has run its successful course.

The French government says, in the instruction which has been tendered to us, that certain facts which it assumes confer upon the insurgents of this country, in the eyes of foreign powers, all the appearances of a government de facto, wherefore, whatever may be its regrets, the French government must consider the two contending parties as employing the forces at their disposal in conformity with the laws of war.

This statement assumes not only that the law of nations entitles any insurrectionary faction, when it establishes a *de facto* government, to be treated as a belligerent, but also that the fact of the attainment of this status is to be determined by the appearance of it in the eyes of foreign nations. If we should concede both of these positions, we should still insist that the existence of a *de facto* government, entitled to belligerent rights, is not established in the present case. We have already heard from most of the foreign nations. There are only two which seem so to construe appearances, and France is one of them. Are the judgments of these two to outweigh those of all other nations? Doubtless each nation may judge and act for itself, but it certainly cannot expect the United States to accept its decision upon a question vital to their national existence. The United States will not refine upon the question when and how new nations are born out of existing nations. They are well aware that the rights of the States involve their duties and their destinies, and they hold those rights to be absolute as against all foreign nations. These rights do not at all depend on the appearances which their condition may assume in the eyes of foreign nations, whether strangers, neutrals, friends, or even allies. The United States will maintain and defend their sovereignty throughout the bounds of the republic, and they deem all other nations bound to respect that sovereignty until, if ever, Providence shall consent that it shall be successfully overthrown. Any system of public law or national morality that conflicts with this would resolve society, first in this hemisphere and then in the other, into anarchy and chaos.

This government is sensible of the importance of the step it takes in declining to hear the communication the tender of which has drawn out these explanations. It believes, however, that it need not disturb the good relations which have so long and so happily subsisted between the United States and France.

The paper, as understood, while implying a disposition on the part of France to accord belligerent rights to the insurgents, does not name, specify, or even indicate one such belligerent right. On the other hand, the rights which it asserts that France expects, as a neutral, from the United States, as a belligerent, are even less than this government, on the 25th of April, instructed you to concede and guaranty to her by treaty, as a friend. On that day we offered to her our adhesion to the declaration of Paris, which contains four propositions, namely: 1st. That privateering shall be abolished. 2d. That a neutral flag covers enemy's goods not contraband of war. 3d. That goods of a neutral, not contraband, shall not be confiscated though found in an enemy's vessel. 4th. That blockades, in order to be lawful, must be maintained by competent force. We have always, when at war, conceded the three last of these rights to neutrals, *a fortiori*, we could not when at peace deny them to friendly nations. The first-named concession was proposed on the grounds already mentioned. We are still ready to guarantee these rights, by convention with France, whenever she shall authorize either you or her minister here to enter into convention. There is no reservation or difficulty about their application in the present case. We hold all the citizens of the United States, loyal or disloyal, alike included by the law of nations and treaties; and we hold ourselves bound by the same obligations to see, so far as may be in our power, that all our citizens, whether maintaining this government or engaged in overthrowing it, respect those rights in favor of France and of every other friendly nation. In any case, not only shall we allow no privateer or national vessel to violate the rights of friendly nations as I have thus described them, but we shall also employ all our naval force to prevent the insurgents from violating them just as much as we do to prevent them from violating the laws of our own country.

What, then, does France claim of us that we do not accord to her? Nothing. What do we refuse to France by declining to receive the communication sent to us through the hands of Mr. Mercier? Nothing but the privilege of telling us that we are at war, when we maintain we are at peace, and that she is a neutral, when we prefer to recognize her as a friend.

Of course, it is understood that on this occasion we reserve, as on all others, our right to suppress the insurrection by naval as well as by military power, and for that purpose to close such of our ports as have fallen or may fall into the hands of the insurgents, either directly or in the more lenient and equitable form of a blockade, which for the present we have adopted. It is thus seen that there is no practical subject of difference between the two governments. The United States will hope that France will not think it necessary to adhere to and practice upon the speculation concerning the condition of our internal affairs which she has proposed to communicate to us. But however this may be, the United States will not anticipate any occasion for a change of the relations which, with scarcely any interruption, have existed between the two nations for three-quarters of a century, and have been very instrumental in promoting, not merely the prosperity and greatness of each State, but the cause of civil and religious liberty and free institutions throughout the world.

This government understands equally the interest of friendly nations and its own in the present emergency. If they shall not interfere, the attempt at revolution here will cease without inflicting serious evils upon foreign nations. All that they can do by any interference, with a view to modify our action, will only serve to prolong the present unpleasant condition of things, and possibly to produce results that would be as universally calamitous as they would be irretrievable.

The case, as it now stands, is the simple, ordinary one that has happened at all times and in all countries. A discontented domestic faction seeks foreign intervention to overthrow the Constitution and the liberties of its own country. Such intervention, if yielded, is ultimately disastrous to the cause it is designed to aid. Every uncorrupted nation, in its deliberate moments, prefers its own integrity, even with unbearable evils, to division through the power or influence of any foreign State. This is so in France. It is not less so in this country. Down deep in the heart of the American people—deeper than the love of trade, or of freedom—deeper than the attachment to any local or sectional interest, or partizan pride or individual ambition—deeper than any other sentiment—is that one out of which the Constitution of this Union arose, namely, American independence—independence of all foreign control, alliance, or influence. Next above it lies the conviction that neither peace, nor safety, nor public liberty, nor prosperity, nor greatness, nor empire, can be attained here with the sacrifice of the unity of the people of North America. Those who, in a frenzy of passion, are building expectations on other principles do not know what they are doing. Whenever one part of this Union shall be found assuming bonds of dependence or of fraternity towards any foreign people, to the exclusion of the sympathies of their native land, then, even if not before, that spirit will be reawakened which brought the States of this republic into existence, and which will preserve them united until the common destiny which it opened to them shall be fully and completely realized.

I am, sir, respectfully, your obedient servant,

WILLIAM H. SEWARD.

William L. Dayton, Esq., &c., &c., &c.

Mr. Seward to Mr. Dayton.

[Extracts.]

No. 22.]
DEPARTMENT OF STATE,
Washington, June 22, 1861.

SIR:

*　　*　　*　　*　　*　　*　　*　　*　　*

Your answer to offers of service and of *materiel* of war seems to have been judicious. If the War Department should find need for the latter, it will commission proper agents. As for the former, the offers for military service, and by our own citizens, surpass equally our calls and our needs. Colonel Frémont's purchases are thankfully approved, and the drafts of yourself and Mr. Adams, mentioned by you, will be accepted. The President expresses great satisfaction with the promptness and decision manifested by you in the matter.

We wish to act singly and in good faith with the French government. We understand, and shall continue to understand, that France does not concede belligerent rights to the insurgents in contravention of our sovereignty. We shall insist that she does nothing adverse to our position, whatever may be *said* to the contrary.

She has proposed to tell us that she thinks the confederate States are entitled to belligerent rights. We have declined to hear that. We have not heard it. We shall continue to regard France as respecting our government, throughout the whole country, until she *practically acts in violation of her friendly obligations* to us, as we understand them. When she does *that*, it will be time enough to inquire whether, if we accede to the treaty of Paris, she could, after that, allow pirates upon our commerce shelter in her ports; and what our remedy then should be. We have no fear on this head.

We are dealing now as a nation at peace with France as a friend. We have told her that we shall not consent to her change of this relation.

She knows, distinctly, if she accepts our adhesion to the declaration of the congress of Paris, the ground on which it is given by us.

While saying this, however, we also confess that our solicitude on the subject is not so intense now, since the responsibility for the next step remains with France and not with us.

Still we wish you to act directly and frankly, being always ready to perform all we have offered.

This despatch is strictly confidential.

I am, sir, respectfully, your obedient servant,
WILLIAM H. SEWARD.

Mr. Dayton to Mr. Seward.

[Extracts.]

PARIS, *June 22, 1861.*

SIR: I have the honor to enclose to you a copy of the reply of Mr. Thouvenel to my proposition, on the part of the United States, to open negotiations for its accession to the treaty of Paris of 1856, according to the terms therein stated.

In our first conversation upon this subject, I understood from Mr. Thouvenel that on a written proposition from me for negotiation he would address the other powers (parties to the treaty) upon the subject. That a note from me would afford him a starting point for communicating with such powers. Upon further reflection, or upon conference with his associates in the government, he now writes that it will be necessary that I address myself jointly (if I understood him rightly) to all the powers associated in that treaty, before my proposition can be considered.

Our condition as respects privateering and the belligerent rights conceded to the south has been so changed by the action of Great Britain, France and Spain, subsequent to the first declaration of Lord John Russelll, (stating that such belligerent rights would be conceded,) that I know not what may be the views of the government of the United States at this time as respects an accession to the treaty of 1856, pure and simple. But as I have learned that nothing substantially has been done in that direction at other points, and I do not see that the interests of the country will be jeoparded by a little delay, I shall await further instructions upon this subject. My first despatch referring to this matter was dated 22d of May last, and I doubt not I shall now receive an answer at an early day. If the government of the United States shall, in view of the circumstances, direct me to make the proposition to the French government to accede to the Paris treaty, pure and simple, I will, acting under such express direction, lose no time in making the proposition.   *   *   *   *   *   *

With high consideration, I am yours, very truly,

WM. L. DAYTON.

Hon. WILLIAM H. SEWARD,
     Secretary of State.

Mr. Dayton to Mr. Seward.

[Extract.]

No. 14.]   PARIS, *June* 28, 1861.

SIR: Your despatches (Nos. 13 and 14) are duly received. The copy of your letter to Lord Lyons, recognizing the rights of neutrals to property taken in vessels of the insurgents, will be communicated on the first opportunity to Mr. Thouvenel. This will relieve any doubts the French government may have had heretofore on this subject.

*   *   *   The Emperor and most of the ministers being in the country, and the legislative chambers about to adjourn, there is little probability of anything of interest occurring here at an early day, unless something shall occur in America which shall give rise to it.

With much respect, I am yours, very truly,

WM. L. DAYTON

Hon. WM. H. SEWARD,
     Secretary of State.

Mr. Seward to Mr. Dayton.

[Extracts.]

No. 26.]   DEPARTMENT OF STATE,
                                              Washington, July 6, 1861.

SIR: Your despatch No. 11, dated on the —— day of June ultimo, has been received.

    *   *   *   *   *   *
    *   *   *   *   *   *
    *   *   *   *   *   *

The President is highly gratified by the disposition which Mr. Thouvenel has made of the application of the agents of the insurrectionists for recognition of their pretended revolution. What you have reported to us in this respect is happily confirmed in even more emphatic language by the communication which Mr. Mercier has made to us to-day under instructions from his government.

We are pleased that you called Mr. Thouvenel's attention to the mischievous paragraph in the *Moniteur,* because it has drawn out renewed and most satisfactory assurances of the friendly feelings and good wishes of the government of France. At the same time, it is but just to ourselves that you shall now inform Mr. Thouvenel that it is our settled habit never to overhear what the press, or the ministers, or even the monarch of a foreign country with which we are in amity, says concerning us, and never to ask any explanations so long as such observations are not directly communicated by the government itself to us, and it, at the same time, discharges all its customary functions without hostility or injury to us. Our reasons for this are that we know, first, there are state necessities which do not always permit, in any country, the practice of entire frankness concerning foreign questions; secondly, that unguarded and inconsiderate expressions, even by persons in high authority, ought not to disturb established and harmonious relations between friendly nations; and, thirdly, that we know that the maintenance of our rights and character depend, as they ought, chiefly on our own fidelity to ourselves, and very little on the favorable opinion of even the most candid and liberal nations. Friendship towards, and confidence in, the good will of France towards us are settled habits of mind on the part of the American people. If anything is hastily written or spoken on either side that would seem to indicate a different sentiment, it is wise to let it pass without sensibility, and certainly without querulous animadversion.

Mr. Burlingame will, before this time, have been advised of his appointment as minister to China. His delay at Paris is approved in consideration of the peculiar circumstances of the case.

I am, sir, respectfully, your obedient servant,
                                    WILLIAM H. SEWARD.
WILLIAM L. DAYTON, Esq., *&c., &c., &c.*

Mr. Seward to Mr. Dayton.

No. 27.]   DEPARTMENT OF STATE,
                                              Washington, July 6, 1861.

SIR: Your despatch No 12 (dated June 22) has been received. It relates to our proposition for accession to the declaration of Paris. This

affair has become very much complicated, by reason of the irregular
and extraordinary proceeding of the French government in proposing
to take notice of the domestic disturbance which has occurred in this
country. I do not know that even now I can clear the matter up
effectually without knowing what may be the result of the communication
which, in my despatch No. 19, I instructed you to make to the French government. I will try, nevertheless, to do so. The instructions contained in
my despatch No. 4, dated 24th of April last, required you to tender to the
French government, without delay, our adhesion to the declaration of the
congress of Paris, pure and simple.

The reason why we wished it done immediately was, that we supposed
the French government would naturally feel a deep anxiety about the safety
of their commerce, threatened distinctly with privateering by the insurgents,
while at the same time, as this government had heretofore persistently declined to relinquish the right of issuing letters of marque, it would be apprehended by France that we too should take up that form of maritime warfare
in the present domestic controversy. We apprehended that the danger of
such a case of depredation upon commerce equally by the government itself,
and by its enemies, would operate as a provocation to France and other
commercial nations to recognize the insurrectionary party in violation of our
national rights and sovereignty. On the contrary, we did not desire to
depredate on friendly commerce ourselves, and we thought it our duty to
prevent such depredations by the insurgents by executing our own laws,
which make privateering by disloyal citizens piracy, and punish its
pursuit as such. We thought it wise, just, and prudent to give, unasked,
guarantees to France and other friendly nations for the security of their
commerce from exposure to such depredations on either side, at the very
moment when we were delivering to them our protest against the recognition of the insurgents. The accession to the declaration of Paris would be
the form in which these guarantees could be given—that for obvious reasons
must be more unobjectionable to France and to other commercial nations
than any other. It was safe on our part, because we tendered it, of course,
as the act of this federal government, to be obligatory equally upon disloyal
as upon loyal citizens.

The instructions waived the Marcy amendment, (which proposed to exempt
private property from confiscation in maritime war,) and required you to propose our accession to the declaration of the congress of Paris, pure and simple.
These were the reasons for this course, namely: First. It was as well understood by this government then, as it is now by yourself, that an article of
that celebrated declaration prohibits every one of the parties to it from
negotiating upon the subject of neutral rights in maritime warfare with
any nation not a party to it, except for the adhesion of such outstanding
party to the declaration of the congress of Paris, pure and simple. An
attempt to obtain an acceptance of Mr. Marcy's amendment would require a
negotiation not merely with France alone, but with all the other original
parties of the congress of Paris, and every government that has since
acceded to the declaration. Nay, more: we must obtain their unanimous
consent to the amendment before being able to commit ourselves or to engage any other nation, however well disposed, to commit itself to us on the
propositions actually contained in the declaration. On the other hand, each
nation which is a party to the declaration of Paris is at liberty to stipulate
singly with us for acceptance of that declaration for the government of our
neutral relations. If, therefore, we should waive the Marcy proposition, or
leave it for ultimate consideration, we could establish a complete agreement
between ourselves and France on a subject which, if it should be left open,

might produce consequences very much to be deprecated. It is almost unnecessary to say that what we proposed to France was equally and simultaneously proposed to every other maritime power. In this way we expected to remove every cause that any foreign power could have for the recognition of the insurgents as a belligerent power.

The matter stood in this plain and intelligible way until certain declarations or expressions of the French government induced you to believe that they would recognize and treat the insurgents as a distinct national power for belligerent purposes. It was not altogether unreasonable that you, being at Paris, should suppose that this government would think itself obliged to acquiesce in such a course by the government of France. So assuming, you thought that we would not adhere to our proposition to accede to the declaration, pure and simple, since such a course would, as you thought, be effective to bind this government without binding the insurgents, and would leave France at liberty to hold us bound, and the insurgents free from the obligations created by our adhesion. Moreover, if we correctly understand your despatch on that subject, you supposed that you might propose our adhesion to the treaty of Paris, not pure and simple, but with the addition of the Marcy proposition in the first instance, and might afterwards, in case of its being declined in that form, withdraw the addition, and then propose our accession to the declaration of Paris, pure and simple.

While you were acting on these views on your side of the Atlantic, we on this side, not less confident in our strength than in our rights, as you are now aware, were acting on another view, which is altogether different, namely, that we shall not acquiesce in any declaration of the government of France that assumes that this government is not now, as it always has been, exclusive sovereign, for war as well as for peace, within the States and Territories of the federal Union, and over all citizens, the disloyal and loyal all alike. We treat in that character, which is our legal character, or we do not treat at all, and we in no way consent to compromise that character in the least degree; we do not even suffer this character to become the subject of discussion. Good faith and honor, as well as the same expediency which prompted the proffer of our accession to the declaration of Paris, pure and simple, in the first instance, now require us to adhere to that proposition and abide by it; and we do adhere to it, not, however, as a divided, but as an undivided nation. The proposition is tendered to France not as a neutral but as a friend, and the agreement is to be obligatory upon the United States and France and all their legal dependencies just alike.

The case was peculiar, and in the aspect in which it presented itself to you portentous. We were content that you might risk the experiment, so, however, that you should not bring any responsibility for delay upon this government. But you now see that by incorporating the Marcy amendment in your proposition, you have encountered the very difficulty which was at first foreseen by us. The following nations are parties to the declaration of Paris, namely : Baden, Bavaria, Belgium, Bremen, Brazils, Duchy of Brunswick, Chili, the Argentine Confederation, the Germanic Confederation, Denmark, the two Sicilies, the Republic of the Equator, the Roman States, Greece, Guatemala, Hayti, Hamburgh, Hanover, the two Hesses, Lubeck, Mecklenburgh Strelitz, Mecklenburgh Schwerin, Nassau, Oldenburgh, Parma, Holland, Peru, Portugal, Saxony, Saxe Altenburgh, Saxe Coburg Gotha, Saxe Meiningen, Saxe Weimar, Sweden, Switzerland, Tuscany, Wurtemburg, Anhault Dessau, Modena, New Granada, and Uruguay.

The great exigency in our affairs will have passed away—for preservation or destruction of the American Union—before we could bring all these nations to unanimity on the subject, as you have submitted it to Mr. Thouvenel. It is a time not for propagandism, but for energetic acting to arrest the worst of all national calamities. We therefore expect you now to renew the proposition in the form originally prescribed. But in doing this you will neither unnecessarily raise a question about the character in which this government acts, (being exclusive sovereign,) nor, on the other hand, in any way compromise that character in any degree. Whenever such a question occurs to hinder you, let it come up from the other party in the negotiation. It will be time then to stop and wait for such further instructions as the new exigency may require.

One word more. You will, in any case, avow our preference for the proposition with the Marcy amendment incorporated, and will assure the government of France that whenever there shall be any hope for the adoption of that beneficent feature by the necessary parties, as a principle of the law of nations, we shall be ready not only to agree to it, but even to propose it, and to lead in the necessary negotiations.

This paper is, in one view, a conversation merely between yourself and us. It is not to be made public. On the other hand, we confide in your discretion to make such explanations as will relieve yourself of embarrassments, and this government of any suspicion of inconsistency or indirection in its intercourse with the enlightened and friendly government of France.

I am, sir, respectfully, your obedient servant,

WILLIAM H. SEWARD.

WILLIAM L. DAYTON, Esq., &c., &c., &c.

Mr. Dayton to Mr. Seward.

[Extract.]

No. 15.]   PARIS, *July* 5, 1861.

SIR: *   *   *   *   *   *   *

Since writing the above I have received your despatches, Nos. 12, 19, and 20. I infer, from the contents of No. 19, that Mr. Mercier is aware of your original instructions to me on the subject of an accession to the treaty of Paris of 1856, and that you hold yourself open to negotiate with him there on that subject. As Mr. Adams has referred this question back to be treated of at Washington, and it is evident, I think, that Great Britain and France will act upon advisement at least with each other, it seems to me that it will be more convenient, in every respect, that you should take charge of the whole question at Washington, rather than have it dealt with by different persons, at the same time, each ignorant to a great extent of the action of the other. Besides, it is due to frankness to say that, if a convention is to be negotiated for an accession by the United States to the treaty of Paris, without amendment to the first clause, I would prefer it should be done at Washington rather than Paris. Still, I hold myself subject to the orders of the government in this as in other matters. I have already said I should await further instructions from your department on this subject.

With much respect, I have the honor to be, truly yours,

WILLIAM L DAYTON.

Hon. WILLIAM H. SEWARD,
    Secretary of State.

Mr. Dayton to Mr. Seward.

[Extracts.]

No. 21.]   PARIS, *July* 22, 1861.

SIR: Your despatches, Nos. 24 and 25, are duly received. Despatches 19, 22, and 24, treat in whole or in part of the same general matter.

I have read despatch No. 19 with great interest. It had not occurred to me that you might deny to France and Great Britain an official reading of their despatches which announced to our government their concession of belligerent rights to the south; or that, if you should do so, it would alter the relations of parties to the question. If it has that effect diplomatically, or relieves you from noticing their position, you were certainly right. Indeed, I cannot see how, upon the ground that you put the matter, France has just cause of offence. You say merely you want no notice of a *purpose* by her to do what you consider an unfriendly act; that you will wait until the act is done before you choose to notice it; that, in other words, you choose to consider her as a friend until she shows herself by acts, not words, to be the contrary.   *   *   *   *   *

The reasons assigned for your course you say I may communicate to the French government if I "shall find it necessary or expedient." I shall not fail to avail myself of this authority upon the earliest opportunity which shall be afforded for doing so. The just reasoning and friendly tone of your despatch will be invaluable for justification of your course and the prevention of difficulties. Unless, however, they refer to your action or make it a subject of complaint, it is, I suppose, not expedient for me to volunteer explanations. I was much surprised by one fact found in the despatch from the French government left with you for an informal reading, to wit: that you must not be surprised if France should address herself to a government which she says is to be installed at Montgomery for certain explanations. I could not have anticipated, from what had been said to me here, that such a course was in contemplation. Should they adopt it, the act would seem to me to approximate a recognition in this instance of the southern government more nearly than anything that has yet occurred. In that event, your future course will, no doubt, be guided by that wisdom which is so essential to carry us through the troubles of our present position.   *   *   *

With much respect, I have the honor to be your obedient servant,

WM. L. DAYTON.

Hon. WM. H. SEWARD,
        Secretary of State.

Mr. Seward to Mr. Dayton.

[Extract.]

No. 30.]   DEPARTMENT OF STATE,
                                                     Washington, July 26, 1861.

SIR: *   *   *   *   *   *   *   *

The President is not impatient about the negotiations concerning neutral rights. We trust that we have kept our own position right and clear.

You will probably find some anxiety on the part of the French government concerning a law which has passed Congress authorizing the President to close the ports held by the insurgents. I send you a copy of my instructions to Mr. Adams on that subject, which you will receive for your own government in that matter.

*   *   *   *   *   *   *   *

I am, &c.,

WILLIAM H. SEWARD.

WILLIAM L. DAYTON, Esq., &c., &c., &c.

Mr. Seward to Mr. Dayton.

[Extract.]

No. 31.]   DEPARTMENT OF STATE,
                                                        Washington, July 30, 1861.

SIR: *   *   *   *   *   *   *

You will receive the account of a deplorable reverse of our arms at Manassas. For a week or two that event will elate the friends of the insurgents in Europe as it confounded and bewildered the friends of the Union here for two or three days. The shock, however, has passed away, producing no other results than a resolution stronger and deeper than ever to maintain the Union, and a prompt and effective augmentation of the forces for that end exceeding what would otherwise have been possible. The heart of the country is sound. Its temper is now more favorable to the counsels of deliberation and wisdom.

I am, sir, respectfully, your obedient servant,

WILLIAM H. SEWARD.

WILLIAM L. DAYTON, Esq., &c., &c., &c.

Mr. Dayton to Mr. Seward.

No. 22.]   PARIS, *July* 30, 1861.

SIR: On the 21st of this month I received a note from Mr. Adams, a copy of which, marked A, is hereunto annexed, apprising me that, under renewed instructions from the government at Washington, he had proposed to the British government, on the 11th of this month, to negotiate on the basis of the project which had been transmitted to him soon after his arrival at London, touching the four points of the declaration of the convention at Paris in 1856, and inquiring whether I felt empowered and disposed to remove the obstacle of delay by entering at once into an arrangement for simultaneous action with the Emperor of the French. Accompanying his note was the copy of a communication from Lord John Russell, dated July 18, 1861, of which I send a copy, (though I doubt not Mr. Adams has anticipated me in doing so.) Feeling the great importance of this matter, and mindful of your request that we should confer together when we could, I immediately went over to London.

I found, by the date of your renewed instructions to Mr. Adams, that you did not intend the negotiation upon this question should be conducted at Washington, but that it should be done on this side; and further, that with a full knowledge of all the facts, the original purpose of acceding to the treaty of Paris of 1856 was adhered to. Under these circumstances, I felt it my duty to say to Mr. Adams that there need be no delay on my account.

To facilitate matters, while I was yet in London I made to him, in writing, a communication to that effect, of which I send you a copy, marked B.

You will observe that I ask Mr. Adams, in this communication, whether Great Britain has, at his instance, or otherwise, considered the Marcy amendment? This was done after conference with him, and after he had told me what would be his answer. He said that after I had made the proposition here it was considered at London, and Lord John Russell, upon his (Mr. Adams) suggesting this amendment to the treaty there, said at once that the principle was inadmissible; that the British government would not assent to it. This answer I thought it most desirable we should have on record, and therefore made a suggestion in my note which Mr. Adams said he would adopt. Great Britain, so far as I know, never has, before this, distinctly placed herself on record against the adoption of that humane and noble principle as a provision of maritime law.

I was much gratified that I had gone over to London. I felt a sense of relief in conferring with Mr. Adams upon questions of so much importance, and got knowledge of some facts of which I had no knowledge before. I was in England but two days, and then returned immediately to Paris. I missed, however, the mail by the steamer of last week, which I much regretted.

With much respect, your obedient servant,

WM. L. DAYTON.

His Excellency WM. H. SEWARD.

FOREIGN OFFICE, *July* 18, 1861.

SIR: Upon considering your proposition of Saturday last I have two remarks to make:

1. The course hitherto followed has been a simple notification of adherence to the declaration of Paris by those states which were not originally parties to it.

2. The declaration of Paris was one embracing various powers, with a view to general concurrence upon questions of maritime law, and not an insulated engagement between two powers only.

Her Majesty's government are willing to waive entirely any objection on the first of these heads, and to accept the form which the government of the United States prefers.

With regard to the second, her Majesty's government are of opinion that they should be assured that the United States are ready to enter into a similar engagement with France, and with other maritime powers, who are parties to the declaration of Paris, and do not propose to make singly and separately a convention with Great Britain only.

But as much time might be required for separate communications between the government of the United States and all the maritime powers who were parties to or have acceded to the declaration of Paris, her Majesty's government would deem themselves authorized to advise the Queen to conclude a convention on this subject with the President of the United States so soon as they shall have been informed that a similar convention has been agreed upon, and is ready for signature, between the President of the United States and the Emperor of the French, so that the two conventions might be signed simultaneously and on the same day.

I have the honor to be, with the highest consideration, sir, your most obedient, humble servant,

J. RUSSELL.

CHARLES FRANCIS ADAMS, Esq., &c., &c., &c.

B.

LONDON, *July* 25, 1861.

SIR: Yours of the 19th instant, enclosing a copy of Lord John Russell's of the 18th instant, was duly received by me at Paris. My powers to negotiate with France an accession by the United States to the treaty of Paris of 1856 are of the same general character as your own. Under those powers and the instructions received by me from Washington I did propose such accession to the government of France, but with an addition to the first clause of the following words: "And the private property of subjects or citizens of one of the belligerents shall not be seized, upon the high seas, by the vessels of war of the other belligerents, unless it may be contraband of war." To this proposition I received an answer from the French minister of foreign affairs, dated June 20, 1861, the substance of which was that the French government declined to consider the proposition (inasmuch as it differed from the provisions of the treaty of Paris) unless it was addressed to all the powers who were parties to that convention. In the meantime I saw it stated in the public press of Europe that the British, French, Spanish, and Belgian governments had made a declaration of their intentions as respects their conduct towards the United States government and the insurgents of the south, and I was not certain whether our government would desire, under the circumstances, that the proposition to accede to the treaty in question, without the amendment, should be made.

Your renewed instructions to proceed on the basis of that treaty are subsequent to and with a full knowledge by our government of the facts hereinbefore stated.

Under these circumstances, therefore, I feel authorized and required to proceed without further delay. Before, however, I shall communicate further with the French government, I wish to know whether Great Britain has, at your instance, or otherwise, considered the amendment of the treaty hereinbefore referred to. Before abandoning the hope of obtaining the incorporation, in our code of maritime law, of that great and humane principle, it seems to me desirable that we should have distinct assurance that the principle will not be admitted. I do not recollect that Great Britain has any time, heretofore, answered distinctly, if at all, upon that proposition, but seems rather to have avoided it. I think it desirable that that answer should be of record, (either in a note from or to you,) so that the responsibility may attach, through all time, where it properly belongs.

Immediately upon the receipt of your answer I will enclose a copy of your notes, in connexion with that from Lord John Russell to the French government, and, as soon as heard from, advise you of its reply.

Respectfully, your obedient servant,

WM. L. DAYTON.

His Excellency CHAS. F. ADAMS.

Mr. Dayton to Mr. Seward.

[Extract.]

No. 24.]   PARIS, *August* 2, 1861.

SIR: Your despatch No. 27 was not received by me until after my return from London.

By my note to Mr. Adams, written in London, and to be found in despatch No. 22, you will find your instructions were anticipated by my action; that immediately upon learning, from a reliable source, what were the views of the government in regard to an accession to the treaty of Paris, expressed with full knowledge of facts occurring since its original instructions to me, I at once took measures to comply with them, without attempting to balance the suggestions of my own mind against its known wishes. But I confess that in a matter of such grave importance as an accession by the United States to that treaty, I did want those wishes distinctly expressed with full knowledge of the facts. You will observe, by the copy of a communication to the minister of foreign affairs, (marked A,) and hereunto annexed, that I have already moved in the matter here.

* * * * * * * *

With much respect, I have the honor to be your obedient servant,

WM. L. DAYTON.

Hon. WILLIAM H. SEWARD,
    Secretary of State.

A.

PARIS, *August* 2, 1861.

SIR: I had the honor to inform your excellency some time since that I was authorized, upon the part of the United States, to treat with any person or persons authorized by the Emperor concerning the principles of maritime law which affect neutral and belligerent rights at sea, and other matters connected therewith, of interest to the two nations, and on the 31st of May last proposed to your excellency an accession by the United States to the treaty of Paris of 1856, with certain words of addition thereto.

Under date of 26th of June last I received a reply from your excellency stating that the protocols of the congress of Paris impose upon all the powers who signed the declaration of the 16th of April the obligation not to negotiate, separately, upon the application of maritime rights in time of war, any arrangement which differed from the declaration resolved upon in common, and that, as a consequence, it would be necessary that my offer include the other powers signing the declaration before it would be considered.

At the time the foregoing offer was made I had some reason to believe that it might be accepted by all the powers who negotiated that treaty, but subsequent information (the nature of which I have explained to you) has satisfied me that this was an error.

The government of the United States would have preferred the incorporation in the treaty of the amendment before referred to; and when there shall be any hope for the adoption of that beneficent feature by the necessary parties as a principle of the law of nations, the United States will not only be ready to agree to it, but even to propose it, and to lead in the necessary negotiations.

Under existing circumstances I am satisfied that I would not be justified in further delaying negotiations for an accession by the United States to the treaty of Paris of 1856, in the vain hope that the amendment in question, if proposed to all the powers, would, at present, be accepted. I have the honor, therefore, to apprise your excellency that I am prepared, on the part of the government of the United States, and hereby propose to your excellency, to enter into a convention with the Emperor of the French for accession by the United States to the "declaration concerning maritime law" adopted by the plenipotentiaries of France, Great Britain, Austria, Prussia, Russia, Sardinia, and Turkey, at Paris, on the 16th of April, 1856, and that I have special authority for this purpose from the President of the United States, dated 26th of April last, which I shall be happy to submit to your excellency. I beg likewise, in this connexion, to say to your excellency that a like proposition has been made by Mr. Adams to her Britannic Majesty, and herewith I deem it proper to enclose you a copy of the reply of Lord John Russell.

With much respect, I have the honor to be your very obedient servant,

WM. L. DAYTON.

MONSIEUR LE MINISTRE.

Mr. Seward to Mr. Dayton.

[Confidential]

No. 41.]   DEPARTMENT OF STATE,
Washington, August 17, 1861.

SIR: I send you a copy of a despatch, which is this day sent to Mr Adams, concerning the negotiations with Great Britain for the melioration of international law relating to the rights of neutrals in maritime war.

You will, of course, wait in your negotiations, at Paris, until the result of the explanations, which Mr. Adams is instructed to ask, shall have been received and duly considered. There is reason, however, to expect that the delay which thus becomes necessary will be moved for by Mr. Thouvenel himself when he shall have become advised of the new and singular position assumed by Lord John Russell.

I am, sir, respectfully, your obedient servant,

WILLIAM H. SEWARD.

WM. L. DAYTON, Esq., &c., &c., &c.

Mr. Seward to Mr. Dayton.

[Extract]

No. 42.]   DEPARTMENT OF STATE,
Washington, August 17, 1861.

SIR: *   *   *   *   *   *   *   *

You will learn from a distinct despatch, No. 41, which accompanies or which will soon follow this, that our negotiation in England has taken a new phase, which, of course, will soon present itself in discussion with the French government.

Treason was emboldened by its partial success at Manassas, but the Union now grows manifestly stronger every day. Let us see how Great Britain will explain.

I am, sir, respectfully, your obedient servant,

WILLIAM H. SEWARD.

WILLIAM L. DAYTON, Esq., &c., &c., &c.

Mr. Seward to Mr. Dayton.

No. 46.] DEPARTMENT OF STATE,
Washington, August 19, 1861.

SIR: Your despatch No. 22, under the date of July 30, has been received.

It relates to an interview, and is accompanied by a correspondence between yourself and Mr. Adams.

Your proceedings and your letter are deemed judicious, and are fully approved.

In communications which have preceded this I have already said all that the despatch now before me seems to require.

I am, sir, respectfully, your obedient servant,
WILLIAM H. SEWARD.

WILLIAM L. DAYTON, Esq., &c., &c., &c.

Mr. Dayton to Mr. Seward.

[Extracts.]

No. 29.] PARIS, *August* 19, 1861.

SIR: I have the honor to acknowledge the receipt of despatches Nos. 29, 30, and 31.

* * * * * * * * *
* * * * * * * * *

Your despatch No. 30 includes copies of despatches 42 and 46 to Mr. Adams. These are of great interest, as they affect the question of our blockade of the southern ports. I never think it wise to volunteer a subject out of which complaints may arise before they are brought to my notice by the party likely to complain; but should occasion arise, I shall avail myself fully of the views suggested by you as to the purpose and object of the late act of Congress authorizing the President to close the ports by proclamation. But I very much fear that difficulties will grow up between us and Great Britain and France upon this question. Unless the ports are hermetically sealed by blockade, not by proclamation—if these countries get short of cotton, and we are *not ourselves in possession of the interior*—excuses enough will be made for breaking the blockade. The tone of the public press here indicates this; the private conversation of public men indicate it.

* * * * * * * * *
* * * * * * * * *

With much respect, your obedient servant,
WILLIAM L. DAYTON.

WILLIAM H. SEWARD, Esq., &c., &c., &c.

Mr. Dayton to Mr. Seward.

No. 31.] PARIS, *August* 19, 1861.

SIR: On Thursday of last week I was informed by Lord Cowley that Mr. Adams and Lord John Russell had agreed upon the text of a convention in respect to maritime rights, &c. On the following day a copy of this convention was sent to me by Lord Cowley. I find it substantially, if not

Ex. Doc. 1——16

literally, the same as that which you enclosed to me, and directed me to execute. I am to see Mr. Thouvenel upon the subject by appointment to-morrow. Unless something shall occur, altering the existing condition of things, this convention will doubtless be executed at an early day. Your despatch No. 30 says, "the President is not impatient about the negotiations concerning neutral rights," but your prior despatches and the action of Mr. Adams have put any considerable delay out of my power. Besides, if the treaty is to be executed, whether it be done a few days or weeks earlier or later is, perhaps, not very important. I have felt much relieved in this negotiation by the specific character of my instructions.

With great respect, I have the honor to be your obedient servant,

WILLIAM L. DAYTON.

The Hon. WILLIAM H. SEWARD, &c., &c., &c.

Mr. Dayton to Mr. Seward.

No. 35.]   PARIS, *August* 22, 1861.

SIR: My anticipations expressed in despatch No. 10 are fully realized. Both Lord John Russell and Mr. Thouvenel refuse to negotiate for an accession by the United States to the treaty of Paris of 1856, except on the distinct understanding that it is to have no bearing, directly or indirectly, on the question of our southern or domestic difficulty, and to render the matter certain they each propose to make a written declaration simultaneous with the execution of the convention, of which I herewith send you a copy and a translation. I likewise send you a copy of Mr. Thouvenel's note to me with its translation.

I had an interview on Tuesday, the 20th instant, with Mr. Thouvenel by appointment in reference to the subject-matter of the convention, and then he gave me the first notice of the purpose of the French government to execute this outside declaration, predicated as it was, beyond all doubt, upon a note he had just received from Lord John Russell, dated only the day preceding. He said that both France and Great Britain had already announced that they would take no part in our domestic controversy, and they thought that a frank and open declaration in advance of the execution of this convention might save difficulty and misconception hereafter. He further said, in the way of specification, that the provisions of the treaty standing alone might bind England and France to pursue and punish the privateers of the south as pirates. That they were unwilling to do this, and had already so declared. He said that we could deal with these people as we chose, and they could only express their regrets on the score of humanity if we should deal with them as pirates, but they could not participate in such a course. He said, further, that although both England and France were anxious to have the adhesion of the United States to the declaration of Paris, that they would rather dispense with it altogether than be drawn into our domestic controversy. He insisted somewhat pointedly that I could take no just exception to this outside declaration, simultaneous with the execution of the convention, unless we intended they should be made parties to our controversy; and that the very fact of my hesitation was an additional reason why they should insist upon making such contemporaneous declaration. These are the general views expressed by him.

In answer, I assented at once to the propriety of such declaration being made in advance *if France and England did not mean to abide by the terms of the treaty.* I stated that I had no reason to suppose that the United States desired to embroil these countries in our domestic difficulties—that in point of fact our great desire had been that they should keep out of them; but they proposed now to make a declaration to accompany the execution of the convention which they admitted would vary its obligations. That my instructions were to negotiate that convention, and that I had no authority to do anything or listen to anything which would waive any rights or relieve from any obligation which might fairly arise from a just construction of its terms. He said they did not mean to alter its terms, that it was not like an addition of other provisions to the terms of the treaty itself. To this I replied, that for the purpose intended, it was precisely the same as if this declaration they proposed to make were to be incorporated into the treaty itself. That its effect was to relieve them (without complaint on our part) from compliance with one of the admitted obligations of the treaty. I then told him I would consult with Mr. Adams, and it was not improbable that we might feel ourselves under the necessity of referring again to our government, to which he answered that that must be a question for us to determine. In the course of our conversation I told him that any declaration or action which looked to or recognized a difference or distinction between the north and south was a matter upon which our government was, under the circumstances, peculiarly sensitive. That we treated with foreign governments for our whole country, north and south, and for all its citizens, whether true men or rebels, and when we could not so treat, we would cease to treat at all. He answered that they did not mean to contest our right to treat for the whole country, and that was not the purpose of the outside declaration they proposed to make; but having heretofore adopted a course of strict neutrality, the declaration in question was right and proper to prevent misconception and controversy in the future.

After my conference with Mr. Thouvenel closed, I immediately wrote to Mr. Adams, and suggested to him the propriety of either referring again to our government for instructions, or, if he thought that such reference would involve any unnecessary delay, then, at least, that at the time of executing the convention (if it were executed) we should in like manner make a counter declaration in writing, stating, in substance, that "we have no power to admit, and do not mean to admit, that this outside declaration by Great Britain and France is to relieve them, directly or indirectly, from any obligation or duty which would otherwise devolve upon them in virtue of said convention."

I have felt constrained to make these suggestions to Mr. Adams, for I am unwilling to act affirmatively in a matter of so much importance without being clearly within my instructions. I shall await his answer before I communicate further with the French government.

With much respect, your obedient servant,

WM. L. DAYTON.

His Excellency WILLIAM H. SEWARD,
        Secretary of State, &c., &c.

[Translation.]

PARIS, *August* 20, 1861.

SIR: I have the honor to communicate to you the text of the written declaration that I propose to myself to make, and of which I will take care to remit to you a copy, at the moment of the signing of the convention designed to render obligatory between France and the United States the principles upon maritime rights proclaimed by the congress of Paris. This declaration has for its object, as you will see, to prevent all misunderstanding upon the nature of the engagements which the government of the Emperor is disposed to contract.

If you were ready to sign the convention contemplated, we might be able to agree to make it the same day when Lord Russell should proceed from his side to the signing of a similar act with Mr. Adams.

Accept the assurances of the high consideration with which I have the honor to be, sir, your very humble and very obedient servant,

THOUVENEL.

Mr. DAYTON,
        Minister of the United States at Paris.

[Translation.]

Draft of declaration.

In affixing his signature to the convention concluded in date of this day between France and the United States, the undersigned declares, in execution of the orders of the Emperor, that the government of his Majesty does not intend to undertake, by the said convention, any engagement of a nature to implicate it, directly or indirectly, in the internal conflict now existing in the United States.

Mr. Dayton to Mr. Seward.

No. 37.]   PARIS, *August* 29, 1861.

SIR: Herewith I beg to enclose a copy of a communication made by me to Mr. Thouvenel, in answer to his formal notice of a purpose on the part of the French government to make an outside declaration of its intentions at the time of the execution of the treaty, copies of which were enclosed in despatch No. 35.

It is in part the same matter suggested to him by me in the conference in which he first notified me of his purpose. His written communication subsequent to that conference required a like formal reply. I am happy to learn from a communication received from Mr. Adams that he concurs with me in the propriety of stopping the negotiation where it is, and referring the matter to the government at home. I should have been most reluctant, under the circumstances, to execute this convention, had Mr. Adams insisted upon it, making only a counter declaration, such as was referred to in despatch No. 35; but I was very desirous, after what had passed, not to be considered an obstacle in the way of carrying out the wishes of the administration. I doubt now, however, if England and France would themselves have assented to proceed with the execution of the convention in the face of such declaration.

With much respect, I have the honor to be your obedient servant,
WM. L. DAYTON.

His Excellency WILLIAM H. SEWARD,
        Secretary of State, &c., &c.

Mr. Dayton to Mr. Thouvenel.

LEGATION OF THE UNITED STATES,
Paris, August 26, 1861.

MONSIEUR LE MINISTRE : I have the honor to acknowledge the receipt of your communication of the 20th instant, in which (carrying out the purpose expressed by you in our prior conversation of that day) you communicate to me the text of a written declaration which you propose to make simultaneous with the execution of the convention between the United States and France, in reference to the principles upon maritime rights proclaimed by the Congress of Paris in 1856. You further suggest in your note that if I were ready to sign the convention contemplated, we might be able to agree to do so the same day when Lord Russell should proceed, on his side, to the signing of a like convention with Mr. Adams.

The declaration which you propose to make in writing, simultaneous with the execution of the convention, has for its object, you say, "to prevent all misunderstanding as to the nature of the engagements which the government of the Emperor is disposed to contract," and this declaration is, that "in the execution of the orders of the Emperor the government of his Majesty does not intend to undertake, by said convention, any engagements of a nature to implicate it directly or indirectly in the internal conflict now existing in the United States."

My impressions, hastily thrown out when this proposition was verbally suggested, have been strengthened by subsequent reflection. I do not stop to inquire how such outside declaration as you propose may affect the rights or obligations of parties under the treaty. Indeed, it is so general that it may not be possible to anticipate its entire scope or operation. It gives us notice that the engagements of your government are not to be "*of a nature to implicate* it directly or *indirectly* in the internal conflict," &c. It may be that the conduct of the government of France, under this declaration, would practically extend no further than would be agreeable to the United States; yet I cannot act upon such assumption. My instructions are to negotiate a particular convention, the text of which has been examined and approved, as I understand, by your excellency. If the declaration which you propose to make does not alter the obligations or duties which would otherwise devolve upon France, in virtue of that convention, it is useless to make it. If it does alter such obligations or duties, then I am not authorized to execute the convention subject to such declaration. This, indeed, so far as my action at present is concerned, is the whole case. But the subject justifies, and perhaps requires some other remarks. You stated that you thought it more frank and loyal to make your declaration in advance, and in this I entirely concurred. If the treaty without such declaration would impose any duty upon France which she would be unwilling to perform, it was manifestly proper that she should declare her purpose in advance. It was proper, not only for the purpose of preventing misunderstanding as to the nature of her intended engagements, but for the other purposes of leaving to the United States the option of determining, with full knowledge, whether she would or would not enter into the treaty subject to such declaration. The declaration, it is true, is not strictly a part of the treaty, yet, for the purpose intended, its effect and operation would be the same as if it were incorporated into the treaty itself. It will prevent misunderstandings as to the nature of the engagements, or, in other words, it will prevent one party complaining of a non-performance of supposed engagements by the other under the treaty, just as effectively as if it were a condition added to the treaty itself. But for the interposition of this declaration I should have assented to the execution of the treaty at once; as it is, I have no power to do so.

From this it must not be inferred that there is now, or at any time has been, the slightest wish upon the part of the United States to involve France or any other foreign government in its domestic controversy. The wish, nay, stronger than this, the *right* to be let alone by other nations, has been claimed at all times, so far as I know, by our government and its representatives abroad. They have never failed to deprecate, in the most earnest manner, all interference in this question upon the part of foreign powers. Yet the declaration which it is now proposed to make would seem to imply that such interference might be claimed by us at the hands of those powers with whom such treaty might be made. I submit, with great respect, that there is nothing in the present position of the United States, or in the past history of this negotiation, which would justify such an inference. When the present administration at Washington came into power it almost immediately gave orders to its representatives abroad to open negotiations upon this general subject; not, it is to be assumed, for any small purpose or object growing out of what they then believed to be a mere temporary insurrection, but with a view to the settlement, so far as their assent could settle the same, of certain great principles of maritime law.

The second and third of those principles, enunciated in the declaration of Paris, has been already proposed and urged upon the attention of other nations by the United States.

The fourth of those principles, which requires that blockades to be respected shall be effective, had never been denied (at least by the United States) as a principle of international or maritime law. It was the first only of the points enunciated in that celebrated declaration about which hesitation existed.

The abandonment of the right, by belligerents, to issue letters of marque and reprisal, under proper restraints, was a serious matter to a country having the extended commerce and limited navy of the United States; yet such abandonment by all nations would, we well knew, tend much to lessen the afflictions incident to war; and so, too, the exemption of property of non-combatants at sea, (except contraband,) as it is on land, would, in a still greater degree, tend to the same end.

Hence the disposition manifested on the part of the United States, on every proper occasion, to connect in its negotiations the two; to make the concession of the one the equivalent, if possible, of the concession of the other. This was the condition of things when the present administration at Washington came into power. Not trammelled by certain considerations which had affected some of their predecessors, they immediately took up the negotiation where it had been left by a prior administration. Ascertaining definitely that the exemption of private property afloat (except contraband) would not be conceded by *all* the powers, they assented at once to the execution of a convention, adopting the four principles of the declaration of Paris as they are, without addition and without limitation.

Then, for the first time, we were informed that the government of his Majesty the Emperor (in connexion with that of her Britannic Majesty) would only execute such convention subject to a certain condition, which it declares for itself, and of the extent and operation of which it is itself to judge.

I cannot, of course, anticipate with certainty what view the government of the United States may take of this question, but I can scarcely suppose it will assent to the execution of a convention adopting the declaration of Paris, except upon terms of entire reciprocity, and subject to no other condition than those existing by and between the original parties; nor do I believe that it will, in its negotiations with foreign governments, at all assent to exceptions and reservations, verbal or written, predicated upon the existing state of things in that country. It will, I apprehend, exact no more and be content with no less than it would have been entitled to had the convention been executed in advance of its present internal controversy. If, therefore, the government of France shall consider that an unconditional execution of that convention will demand of it interference in our affairs, or will implicate it in any shape in the civil war now raging in our country, then it is obvious this is not a proper time for her or for us to enter into such agreements.

But these suggestions are made, of course, subject to correction from the government at Washington. To it I shall at once refer the communication of your excellency, together with a copy of the declaration which you have done me the honor to submit upon the part of the French government.

I avail myself of the opportunity to renew to your excellency assurances of the high consideration with which I have the honor to be, sir, your very humble and obedient servant,

WILLIAM L. DAYTON.

Monsieur THOUVENEL,
Ministre des Affaires Étrangères.

Mr. Seward to Mr. Dayton.

No. 53.] DEPARTMENT OF STATE,
Washington, September 5, 1861.

SIR: Your despatch of August 19, No. 31, has been received.

Before this shall reach you, my instruction, No. 41, will have come to your hands. In that paper you were informed that you would be expected to rest in your negotiation concerning maritime rights until after we should have received some explanations from Lord Russell on a point raised in the negotiation at London.

Those explanations have not yet been received here.

I am, sir, respectfully, your obedient servant,

WILLIAM H. SEWARD.

WILLIAM L. DAYTON, Esq., &c., &c., &c.

Mr. Dayton to Mr. Seward.

No. 44.] PARIS, *September* 7, 1861.

SIR: Your despatches, 41, 42, and 43, are duly received through Captain Schulz.

Your action, indicated in 41 and 42, has been anticipated by me. In a letter from Mr. Adams, dated London, August 1, 1861, he encloses me a copy of Lord John Russell's note of July 31, 1861, and in reference to the vague paragraph to which your despatches refer he says: "I do not quite comprehend the drift of the last paragraph, but I presume you will find it out in the progress of your negotiation." This I immediately answered by a letter, of which I herewith send you a copy.

Their subsequent offer to make a written outside declaration cotemporaneous with the execution of the treaty was a degree of frankness which I did

not anticipate, and for which I had not given them credit. I shall wait with
great pleasure, according to your instructions, "the result of the explanations
which Mr. Adams is instructed to ask," but I expect that both he and I have
already received all necessary explanations on that point. My conversations,
at least with Mr. Thouvenel, have covered the whole ground, as stated to
you in despatch No. 35. I add that I communicated immediately to Mr.
Adams the substance of that conversation with Mr. Thouvenel.

The exequatur of James Lesley, appointed consul of the United States to
Lyons, was applied for immediately on the receipt of his commission.

With much respect, I have the honor to be, your obedient servant,

                                              WILLIAM L. DAYTON.

His Excellency WILLIAM H. SEWARD,
              Secretary of State, &c.

                                              PARIS, *August* 5, 1861.

SIR : I acknowledge with pleasure the receipt of yours of the 1st instant,
enclosing a copy of your note to Lord John Russel and his reply. I feel
that we have done a good thing in getting the reply of the British government (declaring the amendment to the treaty of Paris inadmissible) in writing. At least, we can proceed now, under our instructions, with a consciousness that we have not only have not neglected this point, but that we have the
evidence of having pressed it affirmatively. You say you do not comprehend the drift of the last paragraph in Lord John's reply. I think I do, at
least, in part, and I shall not be surprised if the meaning, which he has purposely wrapped up in that general language, should in the end break off all
negotiation. He may not refer to this language again, but unless you ask
its meaning before the treaty is negotiated, it will be used by them afterwards as an excuse for not carrying it in effect as respects the insurrectionists of the south. The paragraph states, "the engagement of Great
Britain will be prospective, and will not invalidate anything already done."
The comment after the treaty, predicated upon this language, will be: "We
had declared before the treaty that the southern insurrectionists were a belligerent party, and entitled to belligerent rights, (among which is the right
to issue letters of marque,) and the treaty was to be prospective only, and
not to invalidate anything already done. That, in other words, it does not
bind your disloyal citizens, recognized by us as a belligerent party." I long
ago wrote Mr. Seward that these powers would, in my judgment, either
refuse to negotiate, or, if they did negotiate, it would be with the understanding that it secured us no rights not already conceded, and charged
them with no duties not heretofore acknowledged. It is advisable that we
raise no question in advance in reference to this matter, but it is necessary
that we know what they mean as we go along.

With much respect, I am yours truly,

                                              WM. L. DAYTON.

His Excellency CHAS. F. ADAMS,
              United States Minister.

Mr. Seward to Mr. Dayton.

No. 56.]   DEPARTMENT OF STATE,
                                               Washington, September 10, 1861.

SIR: Your despatch of August 22, No. 35, has been received. I learn from it that Mr. Thouvenel is unwilling to negotiate for an accession by the United States to the declaration of the congress of Paris concerning the rights of neutrals in maritime war, except "on a distinct understanding that it is to have no bearing, directly or indirectly, on the question of the domestic difficulty now existing in our country," and that to render the matter certain Mr. Thouvenel proposes to make a written declaration simultaneously with his execution of the projected convention for that accession.

You have sent me a copy of a note to this effect, addressed to you by Mr. Thouvenel, and have also represented to me an official conversation which he has held with you upon the same subject. The declaration which Mr. Thouvenel thus proposes to make is in these words:

"DRAFT OF DECLARATION.

"In affixing his signature to the convention concluded on date of this day between France and the United States, the undersigned declares, in execution of the orders of the Emperor, that the government of his Majesty does not intend to undertake by the said convention any engagements of a nature to implicate it, directly or indirectly, in the internal conflict now existing in the United States."

My despatch of the 17th day of August last, No. 41, which you must have received some time ago, will already have prepared you to expect my approval of the decision to wait for specific instructions in this new emergency at which you have arrived.

The obscurity of the text of the declaration which Mr. Thouvenel submits to us is sufficiently relieved by his verbal explanations. According to your report of the conversation, before referred to, he said that both France and Great Britain had already announced that they would take no part in our domestic controversy, and they thought that a frank and open declaration in advance of the execution of the projected convention might save difficulty and misconception hereafter. He further said, in the way of specification, that the provisions of the convention standing alone might bind England and France to pursue and punish the privateers of the south as pirates; that they are unwilling to do this and had so declared. He said, also, that we could deal with these people as we choose, and they (England and France) could only express their regrets on the score of humanity if we should deal with them as pirates, but that they could not participate in such a course. He added, that although both England and France are anxious to have the adhesion of the United States to the declaration of Paris, yet that they would rather dispense with it altogether than be drawn into our domestic controversy. He insisted somewhat pointedly that we could take no just exception to this outside declaration, to be made simultaneously with the execution of the convention, unless we intended that they (England and France) shall be made parties to our controversy, and that the very fact of your hesitation was an additional reason why they should insist upon making such contemporaneous declaration as they proposed.

These remarks of Mr. Thouvenel are certainly distinguished by entire frankness. It shall be my effort to reply to them with moderation and candor.

In 1856, France, Great Britain, Russia, Prussia, Sardinia and Turkey' being assembled in congress at Paris, with a view to modify the law of nations so as to meliorate the evils of maritime war, adopted and set forth a declaration, which is in the following words:

1st. Privateering is and remains abolished.

2d. The neutral flag covers enemy's goods, with the exception of contraband of war.

3d. Neutral goods, with the exception of contraband of war, are not liable to capture under enemy's flag.

4th. Blockades, in order to be binding, must be effective—that is to say, maintained by forces sufficient really to prevent access to the coast of the enemy.

The States which constituted the congress mutually agreed to submit the declaration to all other nations and invite them to accede to it. It was to be submitted as no special or narrow treaty between particular States for limited periods or special purposes of advantage, or under peculiar circumstances; but, on the contrary, its several articles were, by voluntary acceptance of maritime powers, to constitute a new chapter in the law of nations, and each one of the articles was to be universal and eternal in its application and obligation. France especially invited the United States to accede to these articles. An invitation was equally tendered to all other civilized nations, and the articles have been already adopted by forty-one of the powers thus invited. The United States hesitated, but only for the purpose of making an effort to induce the other parties to enlarge the beneficent scope of the declaration Having failed in that effort, they now, after a delay not unusual in such great international discussions, offer their adhesion to that declaration, pure and simple, in the form, words and manner in which it was originally adopted and accepted by all of the forty-six nations which have become parties to it. France declines to receive that adhesion unless she be allowed to make a special declaration, which would constitute an additional and qualifying article, limiting the obligations of France to the United States to a narrower range than the obligations which the United States must assume towards France and towards every other one of the forty-six sovereigns who are parties to it, and narrower than the mutual obligations of all those parties, including France herself.

If we should accede to that condition, it manifestly would not be the declaration of the congress of Paris to which we would be adhering, but a different and special and peculiar treaty between France and the United States only. Even as such a treaty it would be unequal. Assuming that Mr. Thouvenel's reasoning is correct, we should in that case be contracting an obligation, directly or indirectly, to implicate ourselves in any internal conflict that may now be existing or that may hereafter occur in France, while she would be distinctly excused by us from any similar duty towards the United States.

I know that France is a friend, and means to be just and equal towards the United States. I must assume, therefore, that she means not to make an exceptional arrangement with us, but to carry out the same arrangement in her interpretation of the obligations of the declaration of the congress of Paris in regard to other powers. Thus carried out, the declaration of Paris would be expounded so as to exclude all internal conflicts in States from the application of the articles of that celebrated declaration. Most of the wars of modern times—perhaps of all times—have been insurrectionary wars, or "internal conflicts." If the position now assumed by France should thus be taken by all the other parties to the declaration, then it would follow that the first article of that instrument, instead of being, in fact, an universal and effectual inhibition of the practice of privateering, would abrogate it only in wars between foreign nations, while it would enjoy universal toleration in civil and social wars. With great deference, I cannot but think that, thus modified, the declaration of the congress of Paris would lose much of the reverence which it has hitherto received from Christian nations. If it were proper for me to pursue the argument further, I might add that sedition, insurrection and treason would find in such a new reading of the declaration of Paris encouragement which would tend to render the most stable and even the most beneficent systems of government insecure. Nor do I know on what grounds it can be contended that practices more destructive to property and life ought to be tolerated in civil or fratricidal wars than are allowed in wars between independent nations.

I cannot, indeed, admit that the engagement which France is required to make without the qualifying declaration in question would, directly or indirectly, implicate her in our internal conflicts. But if such should be its effect, I must, in the first place, disclaim any desire for such an intervention on the part of the United States. The whole of this long correspondence has had for one of its objects the purpose of averting any such intervention. If, however, such an intervention would be the result of the unqualified execution of the convention by France, then the fault clearly must be inherent in the declaration of the congress of Paris itself, and it is not a result of anything that the United States have done or proposed.

Two motives induced them to tender their adhesion to that declaration—first, a sincere desire to co-operate with other progressive nations in the melioration of the rigors of maritime war; second, a desire to relieve France from any apprehension of danger to the lives or property of her people from violence to occur in the course of the civil conflict in which we are engaged, by giving her, unasked, all the guarantees in that respect which are contained in the declaration of the congress of Paris. The latter of these two motives is now put to rest, insomuch as France declines the guarantees we offer. Doubtlessly, she is satisfied that they are unnecessary. We have always practiced on the principles of the declaration. We did so long before they were adopted by the congress of Paris, so far as the rights of neutrals or friendly States are concerned. While our relations with France remain as they now are we shall continue the same practice none the less faithfully than if bound to do so by a solemn convention.

The other and higher motive will remain unsatisfied, and it will lose none of its force. We shall be ready to accede to the declaration of Paris with every power that will agree to adopt its principles for the government of its relations to us, and which shall be content to accept our adhesion on the same basis upon which all the other parties to it have acceded.

We know that France has a high and generous ambition. We shall wait for her to accept hereafter that co-operation on our part in a great reform which she now declines. We shall not doubt that when the present embarrassment which causes her to decline this co-operation shall have been removed, as it soon will be, she will then agree with us to go still further, and abolish the confiscation of property of non-belligerent citizens and subjects in maritime war.

You will inform Mr. Thouvenel that the proposed declaration on the part of the Emperor is deemed inadmissible by the President of the United States; and if it shall be still insisted upon, you will then inform him that you are instructed for the present to desist from further negotiation on the subject involved.

I am, sir, your obedient servant,

WILLIAM H. SEWARD.

Wm. L. Dayton, Esq., &c., &c., &c.

Mr. Dayton to Mr. Seward.

[Extract.]

PARIS, *September* 10, 1861.

SIR: *   *   *   *   *   *   *   *
I herewith enclose to you a copy and translation of a communication recently received by me from Mr. Thouvenel on the subject of the execution of the convention as to maritime rights. It contains nothing that I have not referred to before, but it is evident he wanted to put the specific grounds of exception to an unconditional exception of the treaty on record.

*   *   *   *   *   *   *   *   *

With much respect, your obedient servant,

WILLIAM L. DAYTON.

His Excellency WILLIAM H. SEWARD,
   Secretary of State, &c., &c., &c.

Mr. Thouvenel to Mr. Dayton.

[Translation]

PARIS, *September* 9, 1861.

SIR: I have received the letter which you did me the honor to write me, the 26th of the month of August, in order to explain to me the reasons which induced you to await further instructions from your government before proceeding to the signing of the convention relative to maritime rights.

In this state of affairs, I could but await the arrival of the instructions which you have requested, and, consequently, I do not wish to enter into the discussion of the motives which have prevented you from signing the contemplated convention, and which you were pleased to bring to my knowledge. I desire, however, to set forth clearly, by some further explanations, what is the train of thought followed by the government of the Emperor, in judging, like the government of her Britannic Majesty, that it is expedient to accompany the proposed treaty with a special declaration.

If the United States, before the actual crisis, had adhered to the declaration of the congress of Paris, as this adhesion would have bound the whole confederation from that moment, the cabinet of Washington might, at the present time, have availed itself of it to contest the right of the southern States to arm privateers. Now, if this supposition be correct, (fondée,) one could not be astonished that the government of Mr. President Lincoln, according to the principles which it has set forth in its manner of viewing the present conflict, should wish to consider the contemplated convention as much obligatory upon seceded States, in the present circumstances, as if it had preceded the hostilities. But if this opinion be quite explicable on the part of the cabinet of Washington in the situation in which events have placed it, it could not be thus with governments which have proposed to themselves to preserve the strictest neutrality in a struggle, the gravity of which it has no longer been possible for them to disregard. In accepting, then, a proposition presented (formulée) by the federal government, when the war had already unhappily broken out between the northern and southern States of the Union, it was natural that the government of the Emperor, having decided not to turn itself aside from the attitude of reserve which it had imposed upon itself, should consider beforehand what extension the cabinet of Washington might be induced, on account of its position, to give to an arrangement, by which it declared that the United States renounced privateering. The hostilities, in which the federal government is actually engaged, offering to it the opportunity of putting immediately into practice the abandonment of this mode of warfare; and its intention, officially announced, being to treat the privateers of the south as pirates, it was manifestly of importance to caution the cabinet of Washington against the conviction, where it might exist, that the contemplated treaty obliged us thus to consider the privateers of the south as pirates. I will not dwell upon the matter (n' insisterai pas) in order to show how much we would deviate from the neutrality we have declared ourselves desirous of observing towards the two factions of the Union, if, after having announced that they would constitute for us two ordinary belligerents, we should contest the primitive rights of a belligerent to one of them, because the other should consent voluntarily to the abandonment of it in a treaty concluded with us. There is no need to point out, further, how we would forcibly break through our neutrality as soon as we should be constrained, in virtue of the contemplated convention, to treat as pirates the privateers which the south will persist in arming. The cabinet of Washington might, then, I repeat, be led, by the particular point of view in which it is placed, to draw from the act which we are ready to conclude such consequences as we should now absolutely reject. It has seemed to us that it is equally important to the two governments to anticipate (prévénir à l'avance) all difference of interpretation as regards the application to the actual circumstances of the principles which were to become common to them both. Otherwise, it would have been to be feared, if the same explanations had had to be exchanged later, that there would have been attributed to them a character altogether different from that which they really possess. We would regret, too, sincerely that the least misunderstanding should be produced in our relations with the United States, not to be anxious, from this moment henceforth, to enlighten them upon a reserve, which, being officially stated to the cabinet of Washington before the signing of the convention, maintains strictly one line of neutrality, without taking away from the value of the agreement, which, in this case, we will be happy to establish with the United States.

Accept the assurances of the high consideration with which I have the honor to be, sir, your very humble and very obedient servant,

THOUVENEL.

Mr. DAYTON,
Minister of the United States at Paris.

Mr. Seward to Mr. Dayton.

No. 59.]   DEPARTMENT OF STATE,
                                                    Washington, September 23, 1861.

SIR: Your despatch of the 29th of August (No. 37) was duly received. The proceedings it relates had, however, been anticipated, and it only remains to be said in regard to them, that your conduct therein is fully approved

I am, sir, respectfully, your obedient servant,
                                                    WILLIAM H. SEWARD.

WILLIAM L. DAYTON, Esq., &c., &c., &c.

Mr. Seward to Mr. Dayton.

No. 66.]   DEPARTMENT OF STATE,
                                    Washington, October 10, 1861.

SIR: Some unaccounted for obstruction of the mails has caused a delay in the receipt of your despatch of the 7th of September (No. 44) until this time.

As I expected, you very properly anticipated my instructions on the subject of the conditional execution of the treaty proposed by Mr. Thouvenel, and your proceedings in that respect are entirely approved.

I am, sir, your obedient servant,

                                        WILLIAM H. SEWARD.
WILLIAM L. DAYTON, Esq., &c., &c., &c.

Mr. Dayton to Mr. Seward.

No. 59.]   PARIS, *October* 14, 1861.

SIR: After a careful examination of your despatch (No. 36) in reference to an accession by the United States to the declaration of the congress of Paris, I have thought it best to submit a copy of the same to Mr. Thouvenel, to be read.

As your despatch recapitulates the points made by Mr. Thouvenel in the conversation with me and reported by me to the government, it was perhaps due to him that he should see if he has been correctly reported. Upon one side, it was equally important that, in a matter of so much interest, the view taken by our government should not be misstated nor misunderstood. It seems to me now that the case stands, upon the whole correspondence, as well for the government of the United States as could be desired.

With much respect, your obedient servant,

                                        WM. L. DAYTON.
His Excellency WILLIAM H. SEWARD,
        Secretary of State, &c., &c.

Mr. Seward to Mr. Dayton.

No. 71.]   DEPARTMENT OF STATE,
                                    Washington, October 21, 1861.

SIR: Your despatch of September 30 (No. 54) has been duly received. Your vigilance in communicating to me Mr. Brown's comments on the subject of confiscation is approved. You will have learned, however, from the press, before this paper shall reach you, that the crises he apprehended were unreal.

I am, sir, your obedient servant,

                                        WILLIAM H. SEWARD.
WILLIAM L. DAYTON, Esq., &c., &c., &c.

Mr. Seward to Mr. Dayton.

No. 72.]   DEPARTMENT OF STATE,
                                    Washington, October 21, 1861.

SIR: Your despatch of September 30 (No. 55) has been received. I thank you for your diligence in transmitting the papers concerning our blockade, which it contains. The blockade is already very effective, quite as much so as any nation ever established. Proceedings are now on foot which will remove the premature objections of the French consul to which you allude.

I am your obedient servant,

WILLIAM H. SEWARD.

Wm. L. Dayton, Esq., &c., &c.

Mr. Dayton to Mr. Seward.

No. 69.]   Paris, *October* 22, 1861.

Sir: You will recollect that in despatch No. 59 I informed you that I had thought it proper, under all the circumstances, to submit a copy of your last despatch, No. 56, in reference to the projected treaty, &c., to Mr. Thouvenel, to be read and returned. Herewith I send you a translation of his note, acknowledging the reception of the copy of your despatch, and returning the same. He makes no comment on your despatch, and his note is of no importance except that you may have in your department the entire correspondence upon this important subject.

Respectfully, your obedient servant,

WM. L. DAYTON.

His Excellency William H. Seward,
        Secretary of State, &c., &c.

[Translation.]

Paris, *October* 18, 1861.

Sir: You have been pleased to transmit to me, the 14th of this month, a copy of a despatch in which Mr. the Secretary of State of the Union sets forth the motives which do not permit the cabinet at Washington to accept, in signing a convention of adhesion to the principles of maritime right proclaimed by the Congress of Paris, the declaration of which I had sent you the rough draft.

I have the honor to acknowledge the receipt of this communication, in returning to you, according to your desire, the despatch with which you have made me acquainted.

Accept the assurances of the high consideration with which I have the honor to be, sir, your very humble and very obedient servant,

THOUVENEL.

Mr. Seward to Mr. Dayton.

No. 80.]   Department of State,
                                        Washington, November 7, 1861.

Sir: I have the honor to acknowledge the receipt of your despatch of October 22, (No. 69,) which is accompanied by a note from Mr. Thouvenel on the subject of my despatch to you, No. 56.

I am, sir, your obedient servant,

WILLIAM H. SEWARD.

William L. Dayton, Esq., &c., &c., &c.

Mr. Dayton to Mr. Seward.

No. 75.]　　　　　　　　　　　　　　PARIS, *November* 7, 1861.

SIR: I acknowledge the receipt this morning of despatches Nos. 68, 69, 70, 71, and 72. Their contents relate principally to the reception of sundry despatches from me, with brief answers, for which I am much obliged. I asked any information that it might be proper to give as to the future course of events in the United States, (beyond what is found in the newspapers,) not from curiosity, merely, but because I am sometimes questioned here by parties in the government, and fear that I indicate an unwarrantable ignorance, for I am constrained to say that I know nothing beyond what is common to all the world; while the government and diplomats here take it for granted that I ought to know a great deal more.

Your despatch (No. 68) informs me of Mr. Adams's communication of an intended counter-proposition to be made by England and France to our government in respect to Mexican affairs. Of this I had heard before, and it made me less anxious as to the question here; for the fact that a counter-proposition was to be made and answered would, of necessity, as I thought, occupy time and give the United States a chance for reflection, and perhaps action. The prompt consummation of this matter in London has rather taken me by surprise. I fear that some misunderstanding of each other's meaning may have occurred upon the part of Mr. Adams and Earl Russell, or one of them. At all events a point has been reached at a much earlier day than an intimation of such intended proposition led me to anticipate.

I am, with respect, your obedient servant,

WILLIAM L. DAYTON.

His Excellency WILLIAM H. SEWARD, &c., &c., &c.

Mr. Seward to Mr. Dayton.

No. 84.]　　　　　　　　　　　　　　DEPARTMENT OF STATE,
　　　　　　　　　　　　　　　　　　Washington, November 23, 1861.

SIR: Your despatch of November 7 (No 75) has been received.

I have regretted quite as much as you have my inability at this moment to give advices to you and each other of our representatives abroad of the course of events occurring at home, and of the general drift of our correspondence with other nations; but this domestic commotion has ripened into a transaction so vast as to increase more than fourfold the labors of administration in every department. You can readily imagine how vast a machinery has been created in the War Department, in the Navy Deparment, and in the Treasury Department, respectively. The head of each is a man of busy occupations, high responsibilities, and perplexing cares. You would hardly suppose that a similar change has come over the modest little State Department of other and peaceful days; but the exactions upon it are infinite, and out of all that offers itself to be done, I can only select and do that which cannot be wisely or safely left undone.

Thus far we have no official notice from Europe of the proceedings there in regard to Mexico.

I am, sir, your obedient servant,

WILLIAM H. SEWARD.

WILLIAM L. DAYTON, Esq., &c., &c., &c.

SPAIN.

Mr. Seward to Mr. Schurz.

[Extract.]

No. 2.]
DEPARTMENT OF STATE,
Washington, April 27, 1861.

SIR: You receive the President's instructions for the discharge of your very important mission at a moment when a domestic crisis, long apprehended with deep solicitude, is actually reached. For the first time since the foundations of this federal republic were laid with such pious care and consummate wisdom, an insurrection has developed itself, and assumed the organization and attitude of a separate political power. This organization consists of several members of this Union, under the name of "The Confederate States of America." That irregular and usurping authority has instituted civil war. The President of the United States has adopted defensive and repressive measures, including the employment of federal forces by land and by sea, with the establishment of a maritime blockade. The revolutionists have opposed to these inevitable measures an army of invasion directed against this capital, and a force of privateers incited to prey upon the national commerce, and ultimately, no doubt, the commerce of the world. It seems the necessity of faction in every country that whenever it acquires sufficient boldness to inaugurate revolution, it then alike forgets the counsels of prudence and stifles the instincts of patriotism, and becomes a suitor to foreign courts for aid and assistance to subvert and destroy the most cherished and indispensable institutions of its own. So it has already happened in this case that the revolutionary power has, as it is understood, despatched agents to Europe to solicit from the States of that continent at least their acknowledgment of its asserted sovereignty and independence. To oppose this application and prevent its success will be your chief duty, and no more important one was ever devolved by the United States upon any representative whom they have sent abroad.

There would, indeed, be no danger of the success of the unpatriotic application if the governments addressed could be relied upon to understand their true interests, and fulfil the obligations of national justice and fraternity. But unhappily in the present condition of society nations are, to say the least, neither wiser nor more just or generous than individual men.

You will take care that you do not yourself misunderstand the spirit in which your duty is to be performed, nor suffer that spirit to be misapprehended by the government of her Catholic Majesty. The government of the United States, in the first place, indulges no profound apprehensions for its safety, even although the government to which you are accredited, and even many others of the European continent, should intervene in this unhappy civil war. The union of these States, with the maintenance of their republican institutions, is guaranteed by material, moral, and social necessities of this continent and mankind, that will, the President feels assured, overbear all aggression that shall be committed upon them, no matter how various its forms or how comprehensive its combinations. The trial involves only the questions how long shall the struggle be protracted, and

Ex. Doc. 1——17

what shall be the measure of the disasters and calamities it shall inflict. Secondly. The government neither expects nor asks, nor would it consent to receive, aid or favor from Spain or any other foreign state. It asks only that such states perform their treaty obligations, and leave this domestic controversy to the care and conduct of those to whom it exclusively belongs. Whenever this republic shall have come to need the protection or favor of any other nation, it will have become unable and unworthy to exist, however aided from abroad.

The President, in the absence of all information, is left to conjecture what are the influences upon which the so-called Confederate States rely to induce her Catholic Majesty's government to grant their disloyal application. The high consideration which he entertains for her Majesty enables him to assume that the appeal taken from this government to her royal favor, proceeds, in part at least, on the ground that the revolutionists affect to have suffered oppression and wrong at the hands of the government of the United States, which entitle them to the sympathy of the Queen of Spain, if not to redress through her intervention. Her Catholic Majesty's government has not been addicted to such intervention hitherto, and the wisdom of its forbearance is seen in the revival of the energies of that great and honored nation, which now seems renewing a felicitous career.

The President, however, will not rely merely on the forbearance of any foreign power, not even on that of the government of Spain.

That government well understands the Constitution of the United States, and has had opportunity to learn its practical operation It therefore knows that the several States which constitute the federal Union can respectively practice tyranny or oppression upon individual citizens, and may even hinder and embarrass the general government, while, on the other hand, that government, being armed with only a few though very important powers needful for preserving domestic peace, and defence against foreign nations, can neither oppress nor impoverish nor annoy any member of the Union or any private citizen.

In the present case there are some points which will not escape consideration, namely :

1st. The very interest which now resorts to insurrection, practically speaking, has directed the administration of the federal government from the hour when the first murmur of discontent was heard until now when it raises the flag of disunion.

2d. The federal government, now seventy years old, has never made a foreign war which that same interest, now so insurrectionary, did not urge or demand ; has never extended its dominion a square mile by discovery, conquest, or purchase except at the instance of the same party; has never exacted an irregular contribution, or levied an illegal or unequal tax, and only in war has imposed a direct tax. It has divided civil, military, and naval honors and trusts between all classes and sections, if not impartially, at least with preference of the same interest. It has constructed all the defences required for the section where that interest prevails, and for forty years has accommodated that interest with special legislation and beneficial arrangements with foreign powers. The administration of the government has been so just and so tolerant that no citizen of any one of the States claiming to be aggrieved has ever been deprived by it of his liberty, except on conviction of crime by his peers of the vicinage, nor of his property without due compensation, nor forfeited his life under its authority except as a volunteer in the battles of his country. I will not pursue the subject. It is enough to show that while this government will submit its action in domestic affairs to the judgment of no other nation, it does not fear to encounter the moral opinion of mankind.

Will the disunionists claim that they are the discoverers of a new and beneficent system of political government, which commends itself to the patronage of her Catholic Majesty? What are the salient principles of their system? First, government shall employ no standing military force in conducting administration of its domestic concerns, but shall always be constituted by popular suffrage, and be dependent upon it. But it shall, at the same time, be the right of the minority, when overruled in the elections, to resort to insurrection, not merely to reverse the popular decree, but even to overthrow the government itself, while, on the other hand, the government can never lawfully use force to coerce compliance with its laws.

2d. The several states, districts, intendencies, or provinces which constitute a nation, must be brought and held together not in any case by conquest or force, but by voluntary federation, which may be stipulated to be perpetual. But each constituent state, district, intendency, or province retains an inherent and absolute sovereignty, and its people may rightfully withdraw from the federal Union at pleasure, equally in war as in peace, leaving its common debts unpaid, its common treaties unfulfilled, its common defence frustrated. Moreover, the seceding party may seize all the federal treasures, defences, institutions, and property found within its own limits, and convert them to its own use, simply offering to come at its own future pleasure to an equitable account. It is not to be doubted that the kingdom of Spain could be dissolved by her Catholic Majesty's acceptance of this new system much more rapidly than by waiting the slow effect of foreign wars or domestic mal-administration. Castile, and Old Castile, Leon, Andalusia and Aragon, Cuba and the Philippine Islands, would be much more easily separated on this plan than New York and Louisiana, California and Massachusetts, Florida and Michigan.

Perhaps the so-called Confederate States will rest their appeal on some especial ground of sympathy with Spain and the states of Spanish America.

In such a case you will need only to say that the moderation which has thus far been practiced by the United States towards Spain, and the Spanish American states once her colonies, has been due chiefly to the fact that the several North American states of British derivation, exclusive of Canada, have been bound together in a federal Union, and the continuance of that Union is the only guarantee for the practice of the same moderation hereafter.

Will the so-called Confederate States promise liberal or reciprocal commerce with Spain or her provinces? What commerce can there be between states whose staples are substantially identical? Sugar cannot be exchanged for sugar, cotton for cotton, or rice for rice. The United States have always been willing, and undoubtedly they always will remain willing, to establish commerce with Spain and her provinces on terms as mutually reciprocal as the government of that country itself will allow.

These thoughts are presented to you by direction of the President, not as exhausting the subject, but only as suggestions to your own vigorous and comprehensive mind, and he confidently relies on your applying all its powers to the full discussion of the subject if it shall become necessary.

* * * * * * * *

I am, sir, your obedient servant,

WILLIAM H. SEWARD.

CARL SCHURZ, Esq., &c., &c., &c.

Mr. Preston to Mr. Seward.

[Extract.]

No. 41.]   LEGATION OF THE UNITED STATES,
                                                Aranjuez, April 22, 1861.

SIR: An interview has taken place between the minister of foreign affairs and myself in reference to the subject embraced in your circular.

In conformity with your instructions, I presented the inaugural address of the President as expressive of his policy towards the seceding States, and read to him your despatch, saying that the administration conceived that the unhappy differences existing in America owed their origin to popular passions and were of a transient character, and that the President was well assured of the speedy restoration of the harmony and unity of the government.

The minister replied with courtesy, expressing pain at the posture of affairs in the United States, but said that her Majesty's government was informed that extensive military and naval preparations were making in the north to enforce the federal supremacy in the south, and that the consequences were to be dreaded. I replied that I felt assured his information was erroneous.

No commissioners from the Confederated States have yet applied for the recognition of the Southern Confederacy, as I informed you in my former despatch. The minister has promised me that no negotiations for that purpose shall be conducted without my being fully informed. This is as satisfactory an arrangement as could be desired under existing circumstances.

*   *   *   *   *   *   *   *

I have the honor to remain your obedient servant,

                                                        W. PRESTON.

Hon. WILLIAM H. SEWARD,
        Secretary of State, &c., &c., Washington, D. C.

Mr. Preston to Mr. Seward.

[Extract]

No. 54.]   LEGATION OF THE UNITED STATES,
                                                Madrid, May 25, 1861.

SIR: *   *   *   *   *   *   *

The proclamations of the President declaring the blockade of the ports of Virginia, North Carolina, and other southern States, have been transmitted to the government of her Catholic Majesty for its official notification.

No commissioners have yet arrived in Spain to apply for the recognition of the southern States which have seceded from the Union, and none will probably come until the question has been determined by the cabinets of London or Paris.   *   *   *   *   *   *

I have the honor to remain your obedient servant,

                                                        W. PRESTON.

Hon. WILLIAM H. SEWARD,
        Secretary of State, &c., &c., Washington, D. C.

Mr. Perry to Mr. Seward.

[Extract.]

No. 4.]   LEGATION OF THE UNITED STATES,
                                               Madrid, June 13, 1861.

SIR: Your despatch of May 20, No. 1, has reached me, and varies the instructions of May 9.

Please find annexed copy of my note to Mr. Calderon, dated yesterday, which I placed in his hands accompanied by a copy of your despatch. I deemed it proper to provoke a repetition to myself of the assurance given to Mr. Preston, and fix it by a statement in writing.

On this subject, of the recognition by Spain of the pretended government of the Confederate States, I have had various interviews with influential personages, and with the sub-secretary and the first secretary of state. I have represented the position of the rebel party in a light which was evidently new to them.

Yesterday, in a long and very satisfactory interview with Mr. Calderon, I explained to him the connexion of Mr. Jefferson Davis and other leaders in the southern rebellion with the attempt made in 1854–'55 by the same parties to provoke a war with Spain for the conquest of Cuba. He was made to see that the former filibustering against Cuba had its origin, like the present rebellion at the south, in the political ambition of our slave owners. They then wished to re-enforce the slave power in the Union by the annexation of new slave States, but having failed in Cuba, in Nicaragua, in Kansas, and lastly in the recent presidential election, they had at length to turn their arms against the government of the United States, now passed out of their control.

Secession was filibustering struck in. I explained that, unhappily, a class at the south called by the slave owners "*mean whites*" were quite ready to follow their lead, and were a terrible instrument in their hands. Their own ignorance, their dependence upon the richer class, and their contact with the blacks had gradually reduced them, intellectually and morally, to a point of which, perhaps, there were few examples in the Anglo-Saxon race. They were as reckless of danger as they were of right, as ready to embark for the fever lakes of Central America as for the sugar fields of Cuba, or the wilds of Kansas, or a campaign against the government of their country.

This was good material for a rebel soldiery; and under the more intelligent lead of the slave owners this revolt was undoubtedly serious and would cost ·blood. But the result was not doubtful. The disparity of force and resources on the part of the government was too overbalancing to leave the rebels a chance of long prolonging the struggle.

Happily, between the ambitious class of slave owners and the so-called "mean whites," their instruments, there was a middle class in the south, more numerous than the two together, loyal to the Union and the Constitution. These loyal citizens were now held in a state of duress by the violence and intimidation employed by the slave owners and their instruments. His excellency would have noticed that from the beginning to this day the rebels had not obtained the sanction of a popular vote to any of their high acts. Nevertheless this was the only basis of political right known in America. We had no king, no church, no aristocracy, no other political guarantee or sanction in our nation than the will of the people fairly expressed. None of the so-called ordinances separating States from the Union had been ratified by the people of those States themselves; nor had the pretended new confederation of those States, nor the formation of a constitution and government for the so-called Confederate States, nor any other of the high acts pretended to have been accomplished in the name of the people of certain States, ever received their sanction or concurrence. The majority was against such proceedings in the southern States themselves. The whole was the work of a party which, by violence, was imposing its action upon those States.

Leaving out of view the question whether a State might or might not secede from the United States by its own will, really up to this time no such will had been manifested. The pretended acts of sovereignty exercised by those States in fact were not the acts of those States, but simply the acts of a party which shows itself a minority in those States.

They were hollow, they lacked the only sanction which could give them substance.

And the appearance of a confederate government set up by the faction operating in the south was an appearance only—convenient for their own purposes, but having no condition entitling it to the consideration of foreign States.

Without the sanction of the people it was a pretence and no reality. I mentioned the example of the court, or appearance of a court, set up by Don Carlos in the northern provinces of Spain not many years since, and asked Mr. Calderon whether that was a government either *de jure* or *de facto;* and yet Don Carlos and his rebel army and sympathizers held a large district for a considerable period subject to their duress.

Thus the appearance set up in our southern States was no government either *de jure* or *de facto.* It was at best a transitory form of violence, a phase of anarchy, a thing which could endure only whilst the violence might endure which had produced and still maintained it. But, aside from this violence, there was no political guarantee in Mr. Davis, nor in his followers, nor in the class from which they spring. Up to this time they had been unrestrained, and their demonstrations completely unchecked, by any show of force on the part of the government; but now it had been found necessary to display the power of the Union, and our forces were preparing by land and sea to quell this sedition and release the loyal people of the southern States from the duress of this rebel faction.

Much more was said, and questions asked and answered, which it is hardly necessary to repeat.

The result of this interview, I am happy to say, may be regarded by the President as decisive in regard to Spain. Much had been done previously, but it was brought to a termination yesterday.

The minister of state not only renewed to me the assurance given to Mr. Preston, but amplified it, stating absolutely that if any commissioners or other negotiators should appear in behalf of the so-called Confederate States, the government would not see them nor recognize them in any capacity; that Spain would have nothing to do with the rebel party in the United States in any sense.

I might write this to my government, and say besides that her Majesty's first secretary of state had promised me that within a few days, as soon as it could be declared, a decree would be issued by this government prohibiting all Spaniards from taking service on either side, and ordering all the subjects of Spain to maintain complete neutrality in the contest now begun in the United States; that she would prohibit the entrance of southern privateers into any of her ports, peninsular and colonial, and prohibit the furnishing of any supplies to the rebels, whether arms, provisions, coals, ships, or any other merchandise which might aid in their revolt against the government of the Union. Armed ships, with their prizes, would not be permitted to enter her ports. Spanish subjects would be forbidden to accept any letter of marque or other such document, or serve on board of any privateer; and no fitting out of vessels for the purpose of taking part in hostilities against the United States could be permitted, but impeded with vigor and severity.

I have again seen Mr. Calderon to-day, and he informed me that, in pursuance of these declarations, he had just come from a council of ministers, where he had been occupied with this business, and that the decree would appear in two or three days at most, and that he would also write to Señor Tassara, her Majesty's representative in Washington, to make you the same announcement on the part of his government.

* * * * * * * * *

With sentiments of the highest respect, sir, your obedient servant,

HORATIO J. PERRY.

Hon. Wm. II. Seward, *Secretary of State.*

Mr. Perry to Mr. Seward.

No. 7.]
LEGATION OF THE UNITED STATES,
Madrid, June 19, 1861.

Sir: I have the honor to enclose the royal decree, published by the official gazette this morning, with its translation, (explained in No. 6.)

The minister of state has to-day, whilst acknowledging that its provisions are in great part taken from the French decree, drawn my attention to the fact that he has avoided the use of the expression *belligerents* as far as possible, or any other which could be considered as prejudging the question of right in any manner.

He also drew my attention to the fact that, though the decree proclaims neutrality, it expressly prohibits any supplies to be furnished to privateers in the Spanish ports, whilst vessels-of-war may be provided and equipped with all they need; and this provision tells exclusively against the party issuing letters of marque.

The preamble also is less objectionable than some other documents which have seen the light in Europe.

With the highest respect, sir, your obedient servant,

HORATIO J. PERRY.

Hon. Wm. II. Seward, *Secretary of State.*

[Translation.]

MINISTRY OF STATE.—ROYAL DECREE.

Taking into consideration the relations which exist between Spain and the United States of America, and the desirability that the reciprocal sentiments of good intelligence should not be changed by reason of the grave events which have taken place in that republic, I have resolved to maintain the most strict neutrality in the contest begun between the federal States of the Union and the States confederated at the south; and in order to avoid the damage which might come to my subjects and to navigation, and to commerce, from the want of clear provisions to which to adjust their conduct in consonance with my council of ministers, I do decree the following:

ARTICLE 1. It is forbidden in all the ports of the monarchy to arm, provide, or equip any privateer vessel, whatever may be the flag she displays.

ART. 2. It is forbidden in like manner to the owners, masters, or captains of merchant vessels to accept letters of marque, or contribute in any way whatsoever to the armament or equipment of vessels-of-war or privateers.

ART. 3. It is forbidden to vessels-of-war or privateers with their prizes to enter or to remain for more than twenty-four hours in the ports of the monarchy, except in case of stress of weather. Whenever this last shall occur, the authorities will keep watch over the vessel and oblige her to get out to sea the soonest possible without permitting her to take in any stores except the purely necessary for the moment, but in no case arms nor supplies for war.

ART. 4. Articles proceeding from prizes shall not be sold in the ports of the monarchy.

ART. 5 The transportation under the Spanish flag of all articles of commerce is guaranteed, except when they are directed to blockaded ports. The transportation of effects of war is forbidden, as well as the carrying of papers or communications for belligerents. Transgressors shall be responsible for their acts, and shall have no right to the protection of my government.

ART. 6. It is forbidden to all Spaniards to enlist in the belligerent armies or take service on board of vessels-of-war or privateers.

ART. 7. My subjects will abstain from every act which, in violation of the laws of the kingdom, can be considered as contrary to neutrality.

ART. 8. Those who violate the foregoing provisions shall have no right to the protection of my governmer+, shall suffer the consequences of the measures which the belligerents ma y dictate, and shall be punished according to the laws of Spain.

Palace, on the seventeenth of June, one thousand eight hundred and sixty-one.

SIGNED WITH THE ROYAL HAND.

The minister of state,

SATURNINO CALDERON COLLANTES.

Mr. Seward to Mr. Schurz.

No. 6.]   DEPARTMENT OF STATE,
                                          Washington, June 22, 1861.

SIR: I send you an extract of a letter from Mr. Sanford, our minister at Belgium.

You will perceive, at once, how important it is that the Spanish government shall prevent the fitting out or departure of privateers from its friendly ports. We do not doubt your activity. You will need to see that our consuls in Spain are watchful and active.

I am, sir, your obedient servant,

WILLIAM H. SEWARD.

CARL SCHURZ, Esq., &c., &c., &c., *Madrid.*

No. 13.]   *Mr. Perry to Mr. Seward.*

LEGATION OF THE UNITED STATES,
Madrid, July 12, 1861.

SIR: I have been prevented, by my recent illness and the pressure of affairs, from communicating to you till this moment the import of various conversations which I had with Mr. Calderon Collantes, minister of state, previous to entering the protest of June 19, upon the subject of the commercial relations of the two countries and the West Indian colonies.

I confess this subject has been a favorite with me ever since I succeeded, in 1854, in inducing the Spanish government to consent to negotiate with me for the conclusion of a commercial treaty upon the liberal and advantageous basis of the eleven articles then drawn up and sent to the State Department, accompanied with this offer on the ———— September of that year.

On entering again upon the discharge of the duties of this legation, I took an early opportunity, therefore, to sound the dispositions of the present minister of state on this subject, as well as the feeling of other officers and personages influential in this government.

In no quarter has the idea of arranging the commercial intercourse of the two countries upon a more liberal basis been repelled. The minister of state told me, without hesitation, that he would enter with me upon the work of negotiating a treaty for this purpose readily, and with the idea that we should find no great difficulty in bringing it to a successful conclusion.

I mentioned, especially, the subject of the Cuban flour duties, and received the reply, now as in years before, that these would be yielded by Spain, and the Spanish colonial market thrown open to the introduction of our grains and provisions of all kinds.

Some compensation, or show of compensation, to the Castilian wheat-growers may be asked in the form of a reduction of our duties on the cheap wines of Castile; and whilst I see no great objection to such an arrangement, I am, at the same time, persuaded that practically it would amount to little in its effects either upon our revenue or upon the agricultural interests of Castile.

The motive of these conversations was to assure myself, for your information, what were the present wishes and dispositions of the Spanish government on this subject, prior to that coolness in our relations which must follow the presentation of the protest of June 19. I repeat, I have found these dispositions, now as heretofore, entirely favorable to the object mentioned, and I could have undertaken to carry a negotiation on this subject to a conclusion satisfactory to you, and highly advantageous to our people interested in the trade with the Spanish colonies.

As to the convention for the settlement of claims, which was signed by Mr. Preston, the minister of state expressed his regret that it had not received the ratification of the Senate, but had no doubt we should be able to arrange it so as to avoid the objections of that body. Other more pressing affairs induced me not to go much into the matter in the absence of your instructions.

But may I inquire what objection there would be on the part of the present administration, or of the Senate, to such a convention for this purpose, as I had the honor of offering to the acceptance of the administration of President Pierce, in September, 1854, a convention on the model of that concluded with Great Britain in February, 1853, free from especial clauses in reference to any particular claim, and embracing *all* claims by citizens or subjects of either country on the government of the other, without designation nor exception of any?

Should any change of circumstances lead you to recur to this subject, it will perhaps be useful to know that such an arrangement can be made.

With the highest respect, sir, your obedient servant,

HORATIO J. PERRY.

Hon. WILLIAM H. SEWARD,
    Secretary of State.

Mr. Schurz to Mr. Seward.

[Extracts.]

No. 2.]   LEGATION OF THE UNITED STATES,
                                     Madrid, July 15, 1861.

SIR:

*   *   *   *   *   *   *   *   *
*   *   *   *   *   *   *   *   *
*   *   *   *   *   *   *   *   *

Señor Calderon Collantes then asked me whether the declaration of neutrality on the part of Spain in regard to our domestic troubles was satisfactory to my government. I replied that the government of the United States asked for and expected from foreign powers nothing but to be left to dispose of our domestic controversy as it deemed best As to the declaration of neutrality on the part of Spain, I had received no expression of opinion from my government, and that I thought it would be considered satisfactory.

I then asked Señor Calderon Collantes whether any application had been made to her Majesty's government for the recognition of the so-called Confederate States. He replied that no such application had been made, and that to his knowledge none of the gentlemen said to have come to Europe for that purpose had touched the soil of Spain. He assured me, in addition, that if anything of the kind should occur he would immediately communicate the fact to this legation.

In relation to my presentation to the Queen, Señor Calderon Collantes said that it was uncertain whether her Majesty would be able to receive me previous to her departure for Santander, which was to take place on the 15th instant; but that he would bring the matter before a meeting of the cabinet, to be held the same evening, and advise me in due time of their decision. He requested me, at the same time, to communicate to him the draft of the speech which I intended to deliver at the reception.

In the course of the night Mr. Perry was advised that her Majesty would be pleased to receive me the next day, at 9.30 o'clock p. m.

*   *   *   *   *   *   *   *   *
*   *   *   *   *   *   *   *   *
*   *   *   *   *   *   *   *   *

At the appointed hour I was received by her Majesty. I have the pleasure to annex a copy of the speech I delivered in presenting my letter of credence, as well as her Majesty's answer.

Last night there was a general reception by the Queen and the King consort of the diplomatic corps, which I attended, accompanied by Mr. Perry. I may mention that on both occasions I was, contrary to the rules of court etiquette, admitted in a plain citizen's dress, the shortness of the time not having permitted me to prepare a proper court costume.

I cannot close this despatch without expressing my sincere gratification at the manner in which Mr. Perry had prepared for my reception here, and the many obliging attentions he has shown me since. Although my acquaintance with him is of but three days standing, yet I have no doubt our official and social intercourse will be of the most cordial nature.

I am, sir, your obedient servant, &c., &c.,

                                    C. SCHURZ.

Hon. WM. H. SEWARD,
     Secretary of State, Washington, D. C.

Copy of the speech of Mr. Schurz.

MADAM: In appearing before your Majesty as envoy extraordinary and minister plenipotentiary of the United States of America, I regard it as my most agreeable duty to communicate to your Majesty the friendly feelings which the President of the United States and the American nation entertain towards your Majesty and the people of Spain.

I beg leave to assure your Majesty that, for the purpose of maintaining amicable relations with the government of your Majesty, as far as may be consistent with the dignity and legitimate interests of the United States, the President could not have selected a more willing instrument than myself.

I have now the honor to place into your Majesty's hands the letter of credence confided to me by the President, and of presenting my best wishes for the health of your Majesty and the royal family, and for the prosperity of the Spanish nation.

Reply of the Queen to Mr. Schurz.

[Translation.]

MR. MINISTER: With true satisfaction I receive the letter which accredits you as envoy extraordinary and minister plenipotentiary of the United States of America in my court, and appreciate most highly the assurances which you give me of the sentiments of friendship which animate the President and those States towards my person and the Spanish people.

I take a lively interest in the prosperity of the nation which you come to represent, and cherish the hope that its relations with Spain will always be maintained in such a way as to satisfy the dignity and interests of both peoples.

I do not doubt that you will contribute with your enlightenment to this object, and that your comportment will make you worthy of the estimation of my government.

I am much gratified, Mr. Minister, with the wishes you express for my felicity, for that of my family, and for the prosperity of the Spanish nation.

Mr. Seward to Mr. Tassara.

DEPARTMENT OF STATE,
Washington, July 15, 1861.

The undersigned, Secretary of State, has the honor of addressing Mr. Tassara on the subject of certain vessels belonging to citizens of the United States now, or lately, detained at the port of Cienfuegos, in the Island of Cuba.

Information has been received at this department that a piratical armed steamer called Sumter, on the 6th July instant, entered that port with seven vessels belonging to citizens of the United States, which she had captured, with their officers, and also the officers and seamen of another such vessel which she had captured and burned on the high seas. The department is further informed that the Sumter was, on that occasion, manned by a full complement of seamen, marines, officers, and firemen; that she carried an armament of five or eight heavy guns, and that thus manned and armed the vessel was supplied with coal and water at Cienfuegos, and was allowed to depart on the same day to a destination unknown.

The undersigned is further informed that the captured vessels were detained in the port of Cienfuegos, and that their crews, together with that of the vessel which had been burned, were set at liberty.

It is the duty of the undersigned to bring this extraordinary transaction to the notice of the Spanish government. This government will cheerfully receive any explanations of it which the Spanish government may feel itself at liberty to give. But in the meantime, assuming the facts to be correctly presented as they are above stated, the undersigned is instructed by the President of the United States to inform the Spanish government that he deems the admittance of the said piratical vessel, the Sumter, into the port of Cienfuegos, with the captured vessels and crews before described, her supply there with coal and water, and her permitted departure, to have been in violation of the treaties existing between this government and Spain, as well as of the law of nations; and this government, in this view, will expect the immediate release and discharge of the captured vessels and their cargoes. Reserving the subject of indemnity for the injury inflicted upon the United States by the transaction, as recited, until time for explanation shall have been afforded, the undersigned is nevertheless instructed to ask at once that her Catholic Majesty's government will take effective measures to prevent the recurrence of transactions in the ports of Spain of the kind now in question, which are not more injurious to the commerce of the United States than toward that of Spain herself and of all other commercial nations.

The undersigned is induced to believe that those requests will not only meet prompt attention, but will even be answered in a manner satisfactory to the United States. This belief is founded on these facts: first, a correspondence which has taken place between the consul general of the United States and his excellency the governor general of the Island of Cuba relating to the subject has been submitted to this department, in which correspondence the governor general announces that he has been left without the aid of instructions in the matter, and that he shall abide the directions of his government, in the meantime taking your advice in the premises. Further, this government has been advised by a communication from Mr. Perry, lately acting as chargé d'affaires at Madrid, under date of the 13th of June last, that he was directed by the Spanish government to inform the government of the United States that Spain would prohibit the entrance of southern privateers into any of her ports, peninsular or colonial, and would also prohibit the furnishing of any supplies to the rebels, whether arms, provisions, coals, ships, or any other merchandise, and that armed vessels, with their prizes, would not be permitted to enter the ports of Spain. Moreover, the same mail which brought the information of this transaction, brought also a despatch from Mr. Perry, containing later assurances received from the government of Spain similar to those already recited, together with an official copy of a royal decree of the 15th June, giving legal effect to the promises thus so repeatedly made.

In specifying these particular grounds of confidence for an expectation of a satisfactory disposition of the subject of this communication, the undersigned is by no means to be regarded as excluding the more general assurances of amity and friendship which have been lately exchanged between the two governments, or their habits of good faith and reciprocal justice which have been confirmed by an almost unbroken experience of two-thirds of a century.

In order to elucidate the subject of this note, the undersigned causes to be annexed thereto a copy of some of the official communications to which allusion has been made, and especially the correspondence between his excellency the governor general of Cuba and the consul general of the United States in that island, and the recent communication from Mr. Perry, together with a copy of the royal decree to which reference has been made.

The undersigned avails himself of this occasion to offer to Mr. Tassara renewed assurances of his high consideration.

WILLIAM H. SEWARD.

Señor Don GABRIEL GARCIA Y TASSARA, &c., &c., &c.

Mr. Seward to Mr. Schurz.

No. 14.]   DEPARTMENT OF STATE,
                                                             Washington, July 20, 1861.

SIR: I send you copies of a correspondence which has taken place between this government and Mr. Tassara respecting the detention of several American vessels at Cienfuegos, which were carried into that port by the privateer Sumter, with copies of documents which illustrate the subject.

I regret very much that the captain general did not assume responsibility to deliver up the vessels, and that Mr. Tassara also declined it. It must be apparent that the entire commerce of Spain, as well as that of this country, is exposed to serious embarrassment if her Catholic Majesty's government, under whatever view of the subject, suffers privateers to find shelter, or supplies, or favor.

This government does not doubt that the Spanish government will promptly direct the release of the vessels, with their cargoes.

I am, sir, your obedient servant,

WILLIAM H. SEWARD.

CARL SCHURZ, Esq., &c., &c., &c., *Madrid.*

Mr. Schurz to Mr. Seward.

No. 5.]   LEGATION OF THE UNITED STATES,
                                                             Madrid, July 22, 1861.

SIR: I have the honor to enclose a copy of the royal order of the 16th of May last, addressed to the captain general of Cuba, and published in the Gazette of the Havana on the 16th June, just published in the official Gazette of Madrid.

It provides that, during the fourteen months after its publication at the Havana, all hard biscuit should be admitted free of duty in Cuba, no matter whence it come; and also the duties on Indian corn, and Indian meal and flour, potatoes, and beans, should be reduced one-half during the same period.

I suppose your attention will have been drawn to this order by the consul of the United States at Havana, and its provisions published for the benefit of our commerce.

It is another indication confirmatory of what has been said by Mr. Perry, in his despatch No. 13, and by myself, in my No. 3, of 18th instant, as to the apparent disposition of the Spanish government to listen favorably to any propositions for a change in the restrictive system of duties upon our commerce with their colonies.

With the highest respect, sir, your obedient servant,

C. SCHURZ.

Hon. WILLIAM H. SEWARD,
Secretary of State.

Mr. Schurz to Mr. Seward.

[Extract.]

No. 6.]   LEGATION OF THE UNITED STATES,
Madrid, August 5, 1861.

SIR: I have the honor to acknowledge the receipt of your despatches Nos. 10, 11, 12, and 13. The exequatur for Mr. Little has immediately been applied for.

In pursuance of the instruction contained in your despatch No. 11, I addressed a note to Señor Calderon Collantes, a copy of which is hereto annexed, (No. 1.) I would have solicited an interview with the secretary for the purpose of expressing to him the satisfaction with which the proclamation of the Queen was received by the President, had he not been absent from the capital. In my despatch No. 2 I informed you that on Monday, July 15, the second day after my reception, the Queen left Madrid for Santander, and that the secretary for foreign affairs accompanied her. Sandander not being one of the regular summer residences of the Queen, the diplomatic corps remained here, with the exception of a very few members who were specially invited to join the court, probably for the purpose of discussing Neapolitan affairs. It is for this reason that I have not seen Señor Calderon Collantes since the day of my reception by the Queen. Having no business on hand which called for immediate action, I deemed it prudent to follow the example of the rest of the diplomatic corps.

The court will leave Santander on the 13th instant, and then either spend a few days at Madrid, or go directly to La Granja, where the Queen will be joined by the whole diplomatic corps.

   *   *   *   *   *   *

I am, sir, with high esteem, your obedient servant, ·

C. SCHURZ.

Hon. WILLIAM H. SEWARD,
Secretary of State.

Mr. Schurz to Señor Calderon Collantes.

LEGATION OF THE UNITED STATES,
Madrid, July 31, 1861.

SIR: Yesterday I received a despatch from the Secretary of State of the United States, informing me that the President has read with the greatest satisfaction the proclamation of her Catholic Majesty concerning the unfortunate troubles that have arisen in the United States, and it affords me the sincerest pleasure to express to your excellency the high sense which the

President entertains of her Majesty's prompt decision and friendly action upon this occasion.

In connexion with the fulfilment of this most agreeable duty, I beg leave to call your excellency's attention to the following telegraphic report, contained in the London "Times" of July 27: .

"Advices have been received from Havana to the 10th instant. The privateer steamer Sumter had captured eight American ships laden with sugar on the south side of Cuba. One was burnt, and the other seven were taken by prize crews into Cienfuegos. One report states that the captain general of Cuba had released them. Another report asserts that he had detained them in order to refer the matter to Madrid."

In the latter case I trust her Majesty's government will not hesitate to cause the policy laid down in the royal proclamation to be loyally and promptly carried into effect.

I have the honor to remain, with sentiments of distinguished consideration, your excellency's obedient servant,

C. SCHURZ.

His Excellency Don SATURNINO CALDERON COLLANTES,
First Secretary of State, &c , &c.

Mr. Seward to Mr. Schurz.

No. 18.]
DEPARTMENT OF STATE,
Washington, August 8, 1861.

SIR: Your despatch of July 15 (No. 2) has been received.

Your conduct in regard to your presentation at court is approved.

Your speech was discreet in its points and felicitous in expression. The Queen's reply is entirely satisfactory.

I am, sir, your obedient servant,

WILLIAM H. SEWARD.

CARL SCHURZ, Esq., &c., &c., &c. *Madrid.*

Mr. Tassara to Mr. Seward.

[Translation.]

LEGATION OF SPAIN AT WASHINGTON,
Washington, August 9, 1861.

The undersigned, envoy extraordinary and minister plenipotentiary of her Catholic Majesty, has the honor to bring to the knowledge of the honorable Secretary of State of the United States that, according to an official communication of the 28th of July from the captain general of the Island of Cuba, the vessels belonging to citizens of the United States taken into the port of Cienfuegos by the steamer "Sumter" have been set at liberty, the examination of the case proving that they were captured in waters within the jurisdiction of the island, and under unlawful circumstances.

The undersigned avails of this occasion to reiterate to the Hon. William H. Seward the assurances of his highest consideration.

GABRIEL G. TASSARA.

Hon. WILLIAM H. SEWARD,
Secretary of State of the United States.

Mr. Seward to Mr. Schurz.

No. 21.]   DEPARTMENT OF STATE,
                                          Washington, August 15, 1861.

SIR: Mr. Perry's despatch, No. 13, dated July 12, was delayed, and only came to hand simultaneously with your own despatch (No. 3) of July 18, which relates in part to the same subject, namely, the negotiation of a treaty between the United States and Spain for the liquidation of claims, and for the melioration of the commercial arrangements between the two governments affecting trade with the Spanish West India colonies. My answer to your own (No. 3) includes all that it seems necessary to say concerning Mr. Perry's communication first mentioned, except one point. That point I shall now consider. Not only would this government cheerfully enter into a treaty raising a joint commission for the settling of pending claims between the two countries, or between their citizens and subjects, but it deems it essentially important and desirable that all such claims should be put into that very proper channel for settlement. But this government does not regard the so-called Amistad claim as having any valid obligation in law or conscience, and can in no case consent to negotiate upon it. While, therefore, we shall not be critical as to the form of words to be used in describing the claims to be submitted to the proposed joint commission, frankness requires that the exception of that supposed claim shall be expressed, or at least distinctly understood.

I am well aware that this instruction differs radically from admissions and acknowledgments heretofore made by several of the predecessors of the President. Each of them has considered the subject for himself, and pronounced upon it according to his own convictions. The new President, under the same obligation, instructs me to make known to you his disallowance of the claim in question. It were, indeed, to be desired that there should be consistency in the action of the government throughout successive administrations, especially where foreign nations are concerned, but justice and reason cannot be safely compromised by any government, even for the sake of preserving perfect consistency with itself through a series of years, and in its intercourse with foreign states.

I am, sir, your obedient servant,

                                          WILLIAM H. SEWARD.

CARL SCHURZ, Esq., &c., &c., &c., *Madrid.*

Mr. Seward to Mr. Schurz.

No. 23.]   DEPARTMENT OF STATE,
                                          Washington, August 20, 1861.

SIR: Your despatch of the 22d July, No. 5, has been received. The reduction of imposts on certain productions of the United States made by the Spanish government is a favorable step in the right direction, and, as such, will be very gratifying to the people of the United States. Due publicity to the regulation has been given.

I am, sir, respectfully, your obedient servant,

                                          WILLIAM H. SEWARD.

CARL SCHURZ, Esq., &c., &c , &c.

Mr. Seward to Mr. Schurz.

No. 26.]   DEPARTMENT OF STATE,
                                                    Washington, September 3, 1861.·

SIR: Your despatch No. 6, under the date of August 6, has been received. Your note written to Mr. Calderon Collantes on the subject of the reception of the piratical vessel Sumter with her prizes at Cienfuegos was eminently proper and is approved. You are already aware that the governor general of the Island of Cuba has released the prizes. I defer further remark concerning that transaction, if indeed any shall now be necessary, until the answer of the minister of foreign affairs to your note shall have been received.

Your attention to my request concerning certain matters in Paris is highly appreciated.

I am, sir, respectfully, your obedient servant,
                                                    WILLIAM H. SEWARD.
CARL SCHURZ, Esq., &c., &c., &c.

Mr. Seward to Mr. Schurz.

No. 28.]   DEPARTMENT OF STATE,
                                                    Washington, September 5, 1861.

SIR: Your despatch No. 7, dated August 6, has been received. I can very well understand that you were deeply distressed by the first reports of the battle at Bull Run. Those reports grossly exaggerated a disaster which was sufficiently afflicting in its real proportions. The exultation of persons and classes in foreign nations prejudiced against our country and its institutions is one of the penalties we pay for the civil discord into which we have fallen. But even a very limited experience of human nature will enable us to practice the necessary equanimity in such a crisis. Changes of habit and policy are necessary to national growth and progress. We have had little reason to expect that such changes in our case should always be effected without the occurrence of some disorder and violence. Let us be content that the country has virtue enough to pass the ordeal safely, and that when it is passed, our prosperity will be greater and more assured than ever.

I am, sir, your obedient servant,
                                                    WILLIAM H. SEWARD.
CARL SCHURZ, Esq.,
     &c., &c., &c., *Madrid.*

Mr. Seward to Mr. Schurz, with accompaniments.

No. 30.]   DEPARTMENT OF STATE,
                                                    Washington, September 18, 1861.

SIR: I write this despatch with a view that you shall ask permission of Mr. Calderon Collantes to read it to him, and if he shall be disposed to receive it you will deliver a copy of it to him.

Ex. Doc. 1——18

I think that the Spanish government can entertain no doubt that the United States earnestly and even anxiously desire to avert, if possible, any such alienation as might lead to a conflict between the two countries as an episode in the civil war which is unhappily prevailing at the present moment in the southern part of the republic. I am perfectly satisfied that the Spanish government is animated by the same desire. Upon this point I speak sincerely and upon full consideration. I am not equally confident, however, that the consuls of the United States in the Island of Cuba will always, in the absence of special instructions for unforeseen contingencies, exercise the discretion which the interests of our country require.

The government of the United States is not to be misunderstood as fearing to encounter the intervention of Spain in favor of the insurgents of this country, if her Catholic Majesty's sentiments and purposes have been misconstrued. We are aware, we think, of all the perils of our situation, and have not overlooked the not unnatural one of foreign alliances with our disloyal citizens.

The valuable commerce carried on between the United States and the Island of Cuba is often attended with incidents which require the exercise of great discretion and of mutual forbearance to prevent collisions between the consular authority of the United States, allowed by treaties and the law of nations, and the just sovereign authority of Spain.

I desire to state, in a spirit of perfect frankness, what deviation from the usages of revenue and commerce between sovereign states, as recognized by treaty and international law, this government tolerates in the transaction of American commerce in the ports of Cuba, and in all other foreign ports.

When an American merchant vessel arrives in a foreign port, having cleared from a port in the United States which, at the time of her departure, was in the possession of the insurgents, and for that reason she could not have obtained regular papers from officers acting under the authority of the United States, and conformable to the laws of Congress, this government does not insist that she shall be denationalized for that reason. But, on the other hand, it does expect that she shall, in the port where she arrives, be treated in all respects as an American vessel and subject to the consular authority of the United States, and that she shall not be treated as a vessel independent of the laws and consular authority of this nation.

The waiving of the irregularity of the papers in such cases is consented to *ex necessitate*, and for the present time only, and is not to be drawn into precedent. But when this government shall see fit to withdraw this concession, due notice will be given to foreign powers.

I send you copies of papers which have just been received from the vice-consul general of the United States residing in Havana, namely, despatches Nos. 56 and 60, dated the 6th and 10 instant, respectively, with their accompaniments.

These papers furnish some ground to apprehend that the Spanish authorities in Cuba, misinterpreting, as I am happy to think, the royal edict of the 17th of June, are practicing, or are about to practice, upon the principles of recognizing an insurgent flag upon American vessels, and denying the consular rights and privileges of the United States in reference to such insurgent vessels in Spanish ports.

I forbear from preferring any complaint concerning the cases mentioned in these papers, partly for the reason that the transactions mentioned therein are incompletely presented, and more for the reason that I am seeking the prevention of future difficulties by the government of Spain in an amicable spirit. I neither make nor ask explanations in these cases. But I desire that Mr. Calderon Collantes will examine the papers, and, after having satisfied himself of the true state of the case, will give such directions, if he shall find it necessary to do so, to the colonial authorities as will prevent any recognition whatever in the Spanish ports of the flag of the insurgents, or any disrespect to the flag of the United States, by the Spanish authorities, or any infraction of their consular authority in those ports.

I am, sir, your obedient servant,

WILLIAM H. SEWARD.

CARL SCHURZ, Esq., &c., &c., *Madrid.*

OCTOBER 4.

P. S.—The unavoidable delay which has taken place in the preparation of the accompaniments of this instruction has enabled me to add the transcript of another despatch from the vice-consul general of the United States at Havana, received at the department on the 1st instant, and dated on the 24th ultimo, (No. 63,) relating to the ship "Bamberg" and brig "Allen A. Chapman."

Mr. Savage to Mr. Seward.

No. 56.] CONSULATE GENERAL OF THE UNITED STATES OF AMERICA,
Havana, September 6, 1861.

SIR: Having learned, on the 30th ultimo, as I might say accidentally, that a vessel had come, several days before, into the port of Matanzas under the flag of the so-called Confederate States, and, notwithstanding the efforts of our consul there to prevent it, had been admitted by the authorities to entry, and to discharge her cargo, which course had been approved of by the superior authority of the island, I addressed the same day a letter to Mr. Martin, calling upon him for information on the subject. No reply having been received on the 2d instant to my letter, I wrote again, and yesterday morning his answer came to hand. A copy of it and the accompanying papers are herewith enclosed. This correspondence contains all the facts relating to that case.

On the same day that I wrote my first letter to Consul Martin I ascertained that the governor general had decided to admit into the ports of the island all vessels arriving under the flag of the insurgents, and to allow them to discharge and take cargo. On the next day I succeeded in obtaining a copy, and it is now accompanied with a translation thereof. This order was transmitted by the intendant general of the army and treasury to the collector general of the maritime revenue; has not been published nor communicated to me in any form; and, although its existence is known to many, the public journals, excepting the Weekly Report in a general way, have not even mentioned it.

In a matter of such import, and feeling the conviction that no suggestions of this office would cause the captain general to cancel that order, I have deemed it expedient not to enter into any correspondence or discussion with him without specific instructions from the department; more especially after reading what Mr. Wheaton advances upon the subject, in pages 32, 33, and 34, Elements of International Law. Moreover, as the Spanish government has always denied to consuls any diplomatic power, I felt apprehensive that my first communication on the subject would be unheeded, or acknowledged with the remarks that the question comes within the province of our respective governments, and to be settled at Washington or Madrid.

I have the honor to be, sir, with great respect, your obedient servant,

THOS. SAVAGE, Jr.,

U. S Vice-Consul General.

Hon. Wm. H. Seward,

Secretary of State of the United States, Washington.

His excellency the superior civil governor has, on date of 27th instant, resolved the following:

1st. All merchant vessels proceeding from and wearing the flag of the southern confederacy, employed in legitimate commerce, will be admitted in all the ports of entry of this island, if the documents they may present do not cause the slightest suspicion of piracy, fraud, or any other crime punishable according to the laws of all nations.

2d. Once in our ports, said vessels will be under the safeguard of the neutrality proclaimed by the government of her Majesty the Queen (whom God save) in the royal decree of the 17th of June, and in this understanding they cannot be molested by any foreign agent whilst engaged in their licit operations of entrance and discharge, loading and departure, in said ports.

3d. Therefore, all the civil, as well as naval and treasury, authorities in the ports of this island will consider such vessels, in relation to their admission and clearance, as vessels proceeding from a foreign nation which has no accredited consul in this territory.

Which, by order of the intendant general, I communicate to you for your intelligence and fulfilment of the part that concerns you.

Mr. Savage to Mr. Seward.

No. 60.]   Consulate General United States of America at Havana,

September 10, 1861.

Sir: I have the honor to lay before you copies of correspondence between this consulate and various authorities respecting the ship *Bamberg* and brig *Allen A. Chapman*. By reference to the communications that passed between the commercial court and myself, you will see that I objected to any interference on the part of that court against the action taken by this consulate in respect to the Bamberg. I have learned that on receipt of my letter the court cancelled the order it had issued granting permission for the survey and discharge of the ship, and has referred the matter to the governor general.

But on Sunday, the 1st instant, both the "Bamberg" and "A. A. Chapman," by preconcerted design, prompted by the governor general's order in relation to vessels arriving in open ports of the island under the flag of the so-called Confederate States, put up rebel flags at their fore and main mastheads. The A. A. Chapman had the rebel flag of the southern confederacy at the fore, and the flag adopted by Louisiana after she seceded from the Union at the main masthead, the American colors hanging from a rope at the stern. The Bamberg had the so-called Louisiana flag at the main masthead, the American at the peak. I consider the so-called flag of Louisiana to be an emblem of rebellion.

My correspondence with the captain general and captain of the port will show the course I have deemed proper to adopt, and I trust it will meet with your approbation.

I have no answer as yet from the governor general. He has probably referred the case for consultation before adopting a decision to communicate to this consulate.

I have the honor to be, sir, with profound respect, your obedient servant,

THOMAS SAVAGE, Jr.,
Vice-Consul General

Hon. WILLIAM H. SEWARD,
Secretary of State of the United States, Washington.

N. B.—I accompany also registers and crew-lists of the Bamberg and A. A. Chapman.

THOMAS SAVAGE.

CONSULATE GENERAL OF THE UNITED STATES OF AMERICA AT HAVANA,
September 1, 1861.

SIR: In the month of May last this consulate caused to be posted in the most conspicuous places frequented by American shipmasters the following notice:

" As the President of the United States has officially declared that certain States of the Union are in a condition of open rebellion against the government, and as in time of war *treason consists in giving aid and comfort to the enemy*, therefore I have to inform all masters of American vessels in the port of Havana that this consulate cannot give protection to any vessel claiming to be an American which hoists the rebel flag on any part thereof."

After some demurring on the part of three or four vessels that were at the time lying in this port, the practice of hoisting rebellious flags was discontinued, and the consulate entertained the hope that thereafter no case would occur requiring the enforcement of that notice. But in consequence of an order reported to have been issued recently by your excellency to the collectors of customs and authorities of the island, in respect to vessels that may arrive in her ports bearing the flag of the so-called Confederate States, that offensive practice has been revived to-day by the ship *Bamberg*, James E. Wilner master, and brigantine *Allen A. Chapman*, A. P. Laurent master. Both of these vessels are in this port under registers of the United States of America, and have been hitherto enjoying the protection of our government.

Under the present circumstances, and in obedience to the general instructions of my government, I deem it my duty to withhold from the two vessels above named the protection of the United States, consequently to forbid their using in future the flag of the United States of America. Their papers, evidencing their former American nationality, which are deposited in my office, will be forwarded by me to the government of the United States by the first conveyance.

Consequently, as no connexion can from this day forth exist between those vessels and this consulate, I hereby respectfully request of your excellency to make the above determination known to the masters thereof; and inasmuch as the crews of those vessels have become entitled to their discharge, and to be paid at the office of this consulate the wages and extra wages described by law, I have furthermore to request of your excellency that you will cause the said crews or such part thereof as may be yet attached to the vessels to be notified of this their right, and the payment of the wages that may accrue to each person to be enforced.

In calling on your excellency for this assistance, I trust that I am asking nothing incompatible with the strictest rules of propriety.

By a prompt attention to the subject-matter of this communication, and an early reply thereto, you will confer a favor on the undersigned, who has the honor to remain, with considerations of great respect and esteem, your excellency's obedient servant,

THOMAS SAVAGE,
In charge of the Consulate General.

His Excellency the GOVERNOR, CAPTAIN GENERAL OF CUBA, &c., &c., &c.

CONSULATE GENERAL OF THE UNITED STATES OF AMERICA AT HAVANA,
September 7, 1861.

SIR: Not having been as yet favored with an answer to the official letter I had the honor to address your excellency on the 1st instant, in relation to the ship Bamberg and brigantine Allen A. Chapman, I have now respectfully to advise that as to-morrow is Sunday, when all vessels in the harbor are bound, according to the port regulations, to hoist and keep up during the day their national colors, and those vessels will probably show their national colors at the peak, I shall be constrained, in this event, to call upon his excellency the brigadier captain of the port, and request him to cause the said flag to be hauled down. I beg leave to repeat that the said vessels, by the act of their commanders in hoisting rebellious flags at the fore and main mastheads, have forfeited their American nationality, and consequently cannot be permitted to wear the flag of the United States of America.

I avail myself of this occasion to renew to your excellency the assurances of respect and consideration with which I am your obedient servant,

THOS. SAVAGE,
In charge of Consulate General.

His Excellency the GOVERNOR, CAPTAIN GENERAL OF CUBA, &c., &c., &c.

CONSULATE GENERAL OF THE UNITED STATES OF AMERICA AT HAVANA,
September 8, 1861.

MY DEAR SIR, AND OF ALL MY CONSIDERATION: For the reasons set forth to his excellency the superior civil governor and captain general of this island in my communications of the 1st and 7th instant, I have deemed it proper to withhold from the ship *Bamberg* and brigantine *Allen A. Chapman* the protection of the United States flag, not recognizing them as American vessels any longer. As the said vessels have our flag hoisted, I find myself in the necessity of soliciting of your excellency to order that the same be immediately hauled down. And as I must transmit to my government by the steamer Columbia, which is to sail on the 10th, the papers of the said vessels, including the roll, I request of your excellency to place that of each of them at my disposal for the purpose. I will on my part furnish your office with authenticated copies, that it may possess the requisite evidence respecting the crews of both vessels.

I have much pleasure in repeating myself your very obedient servant,

THOS. SAVAGE,

In charge of the Consulate General.

His Excellency the Brigadier Captain *of this port.*

Note.—A notice came on the same day from the captain of the port's office, advising that he was absent, and no action could be taken but by himself.

(Translation.)

Molinos,
Captain General's country residence, September 8, 1861.

Sir: An accident, of those which are so apt to occur in public offices that have so much business as those of this government, has been the cause of the mislaying, without being able to find it, of your communication of the 1st instant relative to the ship "Bamberg" and brig "Allen A. Chapman." To avoid, therefore, greater delay in answering it, his excellency directs me to ask you to reproduce it, with the assurance that immediately you do it you will receive a reply thereto, and also to the other representation which you make in your second letter of the 7th.

With this motive, I have the honor of offering to you the assurance of consideration with which I am, very respectfully, your obedient servant,

ANSELMO DE VILLAESCUSA,

First Chief of Bureau, in the office of the
Secretary of the Superior Civil Government.

Thomas Savage, Esq.

Note.—The above, although appearing in the shape of a private letter, came under the seal of the superior government of Cuba.

[Translation.]

[SEAL.]   Captaincy of the Port of Havana.

I have received your polite communication of yesterday's date, in which you are pleased to state to me that for the reasons you have thought proper to lay before his excellency the superior civil governor, captain general of this island, in communications of the 1st and 7th instant, and that I am ignorant of, you have deemed it expedient to withhold from the ship *Bamberg* and brig *A. A. Chapman* the protection of the United States flag, not recognizing them as American vessels any longer.

The said vessels hoisted on yesterday the flag of the United States, because they appear at this office as such. And as it is ordained in the port regulations that all vessels therein hoist their respective flags, the Bamberg and A. A. Chapman put up the American, under which they entered the port, and appearing as American.

I felt great regret that I could not make them haul down their flag as you requested me on yesterday, owing to the lateness of the time in which I received your attentive letter, inasmuch as the masters of those vessels having asked of me on the preceding day (Saturday) to let them know what flag they had to put up on Sunday. I told them clearly that they had to hoist the American, being the only one they could put up, as being the same they had entered with, as evidenced in this office to the present time they are such vessels of the United States.

I have the honor of enclosing the crew lists of said vessels that you call for, hoping that you will please furnish certified copies thereof for record in this office. You will at the same time be pleased to inform me in what situation the said vessels remain after protection has been taken from them by the consulate of your worthy charge.

I have great satisfaction in offering to you the respects of the highest consideration.

God preserve you many years.

BLAS G. DE QUESADA.

HAVANA, *September* 9, 1861.

The CONSUL GENERAL *of the United States.*

CONSULATE GENERAL OF THE UNITED STATES OF AMERICA AT HAVANA,
September 10, 1861.

SIR: I had the honor to receive on yesterday your excellency's polite communication of the same date, in answer to mine of last Sunday, requesting you to cause the ship Bamberg and brig A. A. Chapman to haul down the American colors which they were flying.

The reason why those vessels have forfeited the protection of the United States under which they entered this port is, that their commanders on the previous Sunday hoisted rebellious flags at their fore and main mast heads, thereby showing their hostility to the government whose protection they had been enjoying and whose flag covered them.

In the first part of May last this consulate gave notice that it could not give protection to any vessel claiming to be American which hoisted the rebel flag, *or any part thereof.* This was made known to the government of the United States, who approved of it, directing the consulate not to recognize as vessels of the United States any that hoisted any other flag but that prescribed by law.

The masters of the "Bamberg" and "Allen A. Chapman" cannot allege ignorance; they deliberately disregarded the warning given them, and now must abide the consequences of their act; and having no longer the right to wear the American, they must remain without any flag to cover them, for I do not see that they are at liberty to use the colors of any other nation, being unprovided with the requisite papers.

By the United States registers, which the said vessels had been sailing under, the Bamberg is owned by—

Mr. Henry V. Baxter	10-32	
Mr. James C. Wilner, (master)	2-32	
Mr. Charles Sagory	10-32	Of New Orleans.
Mr E. M. Brown	4-32	
Mr. P. Pages	2-32	
Mr. Conrad Charles Maletta	2-32	Of New York.
Mr. William Tyson	2-32	

The Allen A. Chapman is wholly owned by Mr. Stanislas Plassan, of New Orleans.

I transmit herewith certified copies of the crew lists of both vessels for the purposes of your office; and regretting the trouble I have caused you with this annoying affair, I renew the assurances of respect and esteem with which I am your excellency's obedient servant,

THOS. SAVAGE,
In charge of the Consulate General.

His Excellency Brigadier Don BLAS G. DE QUESADA,
Captain of this Port, &c., &c., &c.

No. 63.] CONSULATE GENERAL OF THE UNITED STATES OF AMERICA AT HAVANA,
September 24, 1861.

SIR: The accompanying documents form the captain general's answer to my last communication in respect to the ship "Bamberg" and brig "Allen A. Chapman." I leave the matter now in the hands of the department, trusting that the course I adopted towards those vessels will be considered worthy of your approval.

The captain general advised me that the *Bamberg* is to discharge here. Such articles as armament and munitions of war will be deposited in the government stores, and the rest of the cargo will be entered for consumption. His excellency invited me to attend the inspection of her cargo, but I deemed it my duty to decline the invitation. The ship is now at the wharf. It is credited by many that she has since her arrival discharged arms, which have found their way to the southern ports. Though I have had a species of surveillance, nothing has been discovered; and yet I cannot but believe that arms, &c., have been taken out of her, not from under the hatches, but from places of concealment in the cabin and elsewhere, accessible without taking off the hatches. Such things were, of course, not manifested to this custom-house.

I wrote in my last despatch that Captain Laurent, of the A. A. Chapman, sailed for New Orleans in a French war steamer. I now confirm the report, and add that he took many letters from here. In all probability he will return in the same steamer, bringing powers of attorney for the sale of the "Bamberg" and the "Allen A. Chapman."

F. O. Sullivan finally did not go in command of the *Isilda*. A man named Emmerson, who belonged to the rebel steamer *Sumter*, and was prize mate on the Joseph Maxwell, went in her as master. Hicks, the midshipman of the Sumter, and two other gentlemen, formerly of the United States navy, went as passengers in the Isilda.

The United States schooner Nonpareil arrived here yesterday from Key West, to fetch despatches of the British commodore. No news from there.

I have the honor to be, very respectfully, your obedient servant,

THOS. SAVAGE,
Vice Consul General.

Hon. WILLIAM H. SEWARD,
Secretary of State of the United States, Washington.

[Translation]

GOVERNMENT, CAPTAIN GENERALCY, AND DELEGATED SUPERINTENDENCY
OF THE EXCHEQUER OF THE EVER-FAITHFUL ISLAND OF CUBA.

I transmit to you herewith, duly authenticated, a copy of the report made by his excellency the general commanding this naval station, in accordance with the opinion of the legal adviser of the same, upon the subject of the communication of the 13th instant, wherein you were pleased to answer mine of the 12th I fully concur in the opinions given by his excellency and pursuant thereto I address, under this same date, her Catholic Majesty's minister at Washington, in order that, by an understanding with the government, may be fixed, in a precise and definite manner, the course which, in cases analogous to those of the "Bamberg" and "Allan A. Chapman," should be pursued, respectively, by you and by the superior authority of Cuba. Thus barren debates will be avoided, and a course adopted consonant with the loyalty and harmony which this government always uses in the treatment of international affairs.

In the meanwhile I will state to you that, for the purpose of exhibiting practically my desire of acceding as far as possible to your requests, I have made known, confidentially, to the captains that they are not to hoist any more the flag of the United States; and they have pledged to the captain of the port their word of honor not to do it.

This communication should terminate here, inasmuch as I have stated I cannot accede in an official form to what is required by you, without anything else being thereby implied, but that I do not believe the moment has arrived for the aid of jurisdiction that you solicit. But I cannot allow to pass unnoticed two remarks made, respectively, in the communications of the 1st and 13th instants, without setting forth in regard to them my manner of appreciating them. The first is the relation you find between the cases of the "Bamberg" and the "Allan" and the circular, which you say was issued by my authority, to the collectors of customs respecting the toleration towards the flag of the seceded States. I will frankly confess to you that I find no connexion or link between the two subjects. In the first the object is not to injure the interests of our national trade, because you already understand Spain never could have bound herself to discontinue her commercial transactions with the south, whatever may be the state of its internal relations with the north. In the other the matter in question is that you require two vessels to be notified that they shall not use the flag under which they entered the port, which was hitherto, and still is officially, according to the papers they produced, that of their true nationality.

The second remark is that my declining to make the notification called for might be interpreted as a species of opposition to your consular authority. Upon this particular I will make only two observations. One is that you are well aware that in all questions hitherto occurring the government of this island has not spared any means of showing its deference to that of the United States, represented by you; examples of which might be adduced, which I omit, not to make this writing too long. The second is that such opposition could not in any way be supposed, when the subject in question solely is that you yourself wish to cut off vessels which till now have belonged to the United States, and have been by you, in conjunction with your government, denationalized, by the fact of taking their papers from them. I consider as sufficiently answered the observations you make upon the subject, without my entertaining, even remotely, the idea that the consulate could have doubted for a single moment of the good faith of this government, in the same manner that I have not doubted or will ever doubt of that which animates you, whose high qualities in all respects I take pleasure in acknowledging.

God preserve you many years.

F'co SERRANO.

HAVANA, *September* 20, 1861.

The CONSUL GENERAL *of the United States in this city*

[Translation.]

COMMANDANCY GENERAL OF THE HAVANA NAVAL STATION,
Havana, September 15, 1861.

MOST EXCELLENT SIR: The auditor of marine of this station, to whom I referred for his opinion upon your excellency's official letter of yesterday accompanying the new communication in which the consul general of the United States insists on his reclamation relating to the use of the American flag by the ship "Bamberg" and brig "Allan A. Chapman," says to me under this date as follows:

"MOST EXCELLENT SIR: I insist in considering that the aid of jurisdiction which, from the superior authority of the island, the consul of the United States again requires in respect to the ship 'Bamberg' and brig 'Allan' should be based or justified upon the opposition or resistance of the captains of those vessels to the orders and instructions given them directly by the consul himself in the circle of his consular functions. And this not from respect to the principle of neutrality, which has no application nor could be violated in the present case, but because his excellency the governor, captain general, is not the medium of communication between the consul of the United States and the masters of the vessels of his nation, nor has there been committed on board of the ship 'Bamberg' or the brig 'Allan A. Chapman' any act which was a disturbance of order or of the peace of the port, or which has violated the laws of the country—the only case that would justify the officious action of the local authorities against the captains and crews of those vessels. It is very true that every government has the exclusive right of prescribing the flags that their vessels are to use, and *which* they are not to use; but it is also true that the infraction of the laws of a country, while it does not affect others, is only to be proved in the country that made those laws. The ship 'Bamberg' and the brig 'Allan,' as the consul himself states, were received in this port as vessels of his nation duly authorized. Both have hoisted the flags of the United States at the stern, which is the principal place for the national flag; those which are said to be used at the same time at the fore and main mast heads have no official character or signification. If the use of them on any part of a vessel, or for whatever purpose, constitutes a crime in the eyes of the government of the United States, it should be tried before the courts of that nation. Had the consul limited himself to ask that through the captaincy of the port the captain should be ordered not to hoist those flags together with the one that denoted their nationality, he could have easily obtained this proof of deference to the American flag, and of consideration to his government. But in lieu thereof the consul has condemned those vessels to deprivation of their legitimate flag—a penalty which constitutes an indefinite embargo of the same in this port, and a simulated confiscation of the property—a penalty that does not affect the delinquent captains, but the owners and shippers, who may perhaps have no culpability in the proceedings of the former. So summary a proceeding against the property is not in conformity to our usages, and every species of confiscation is forbidden by our laws. For this reason the consul ought not to deem it strange that the superior authority of this island should hesitate to be officious in a foreign affair which is initiated with such grave proceedings on the part of him who has in this place the character of commercial agent to protect and support the interests of the citizens of the United States, and not the severe office of a judge. It is likewise well founded that if there is responsibility involved in the consul's action, it belongs solely to the government of his nation to demand it of him; but for the same reason his and his only should be the responsibility; and the consul should not unnecessarily demand the foreign assistance, as the authority rendering it might find itself involved therein. The apprehension of being disregarded by the captains is not a sufficient reason to justify that assistance, which, being extemporaneous, would have a character of officious and voluntary. As the consul has already referred the solution of this affair to Washington, transmitting the registers of the 'Bamberg' and the 'Allan,' he might await the resolution of his government, which may perhaps save all future difficulty; and to this end it might be expedient that his excellency the governor, captain general, should also, with a copy of all the communications and reports, bring the subject before his excellency the minister of her Catholic Majesty in Washington, in order that his excellency may be posted up for the event of any communication being addressed to him thereupon by that government, or may avail himself of the occasion, should it present itself, of avoiding other reclamations of the same nature from the consul, if he deems it expedient, or considers himself authorized therefor. Notwithstanding all that is stated, your excellency will be pleased to inform his excellency the governor, captain general, what you may deem most proper."

And in conformity with what is above set forth I have the honor of transcribing it to your excellency in answer, returning the two documents that your official letter refers to. God preserve your excellency many years.

Most excellent sir, in the absence of his excellency the commanding general, the 2d in command.

MANUEL SIVILA.

His Excellency THE GOVERNOR,
Captain General of this island.

Mr. Schurz to Mr. Seward.

[Extract.]

No. 27.]   LEGATION OF THE UNITED STATES,
Madrid, October 9, 1861.

SIR:

*   *   *   *   *   *   *   *   *

After having closed our conversation on the Mexican business, I called Mr. Calderon's attention to a report going through the American and European press that Spain was about to recognize the independence of the Southern Confederacy and to break up the blockade of our southern ports. I added that it was impossible for me to believe that Spain could entertain any such intentions, and inquired whether anything had occurred to give rise to such a rumor.

Mr. Calderon replied with the strongest protestations of good faith and friendship towards the United States. He assured me that nothing could be further from the intentions of her Majesty's government than to depart from the policy indicated in her Majesty's proclamation of neutrality. But, he added, there are things—and, interrupting himself, he asked me whether I had not, within the last two days, received despatches from my government. I answered in the negative. Then he went to his desk and took out a paper, which turned out to be a copy of your despatch (No. 30) addressed to me, bearing date September 18. This despatch, as he said, had been communicated by you to Mr. Tassara, and Mr. Tassara had sent it to him. He handed it to me, and you may well imagine that I was somewhat disagreeably surprised. Instead of my communicating this despatch to him, he communicated it to me, and I found myself obliged to confess that I had not the least official knowledge of a matter to which, according to the contents of the despatch, my government attached the highest importance. Mr. Calderon informed me that he had received the document the day before; that he had at once inquired whether any report had been sent in by the captain general of Cuba; and that, there being none, he was not prepared to give an answer to your despatch. I replied that I would not ask for an answer until I should have received the original of your instructions and the reports of our consular officers on the Island of Cuba; that as soon as I should be in possession of these documents, I would lay them before him, and then discuss the matter with him in all its bearings. He replied that this would be agreeable to him, but that it would be impossible for him to give a definite answer without having heard from the captain general of Cuba.

*　　　*　　　*　　　*　　　*　　　*　　　*　　　*　　　*

I am, sir, with the greatest respect, your obedient servant,

C. SCHURZ.

Hon. William H. Seward,
Secretary of State, Washington, D. C.

Mr. Schurz to Mr. Seward.

[Extract.]

No. 30.]　　　　　　　　　Legation of the United States,
Madrid, October 17, 1861.

Sir: After having waited for the arrival of your despatch No. 30 until yesterday, I deemed it necessary to make an effort to obtain an answer from Mr. Calderon as to the general merits of the case. I therefore called on Mr. Calderon yesterday, and have the honor to transmit a report of our conversation.

I noticed, in the course of that conversation, that Mr. Calderon, although he denied the receipt of official communications from the captain general of Cuba, seemed to be well informed of what had happened there, while I had no other knowledge of the facts referred to in your despatch than a general impression gathered from newspaper statements, which, in this case, had been distressingly indefinite and contradictory.

You will notice that, in my conversation with Mr. Calderon, I confined myself entirely to putting questions, partly because I was ignorant of what actually had happened, and partly because I consider it impolitic, under present circumstances, to join issue with foreign governments on things which may or may not happen. The latter is especially applicable to the case under consideration.

*   *   *   *   *   *   *   *   *

I am, sir, your obedient servant,

C. SCHURZ.

Hon. WILLIAM H. SEWARD,
    Secretary of State, Washington, D. C.

'Memorandum of a conversation between Mr. Calderon Collantes and Mr. Schurz
on October 16, 1861.

Mr. Schurz informed Mr. Calderon that the original of Mr. Seward's despatch [No. 30,] a copy of which had been forwarded by Mr. Tassara to him, (Mr. Calderon,) had not reached the American legation, and that he was therefore unable to lay before Mr. Calderon the reports of the consular officers of the United States alluded to in the despatch; but that he considered it important that a matter which was so apt to lead to disagreeable consequences should be promptly disposed of, and that he therefore requested Mr. Calderon to state the views of the Spanish government in a general manner, even if it was impossible, in the absence of special information, to judge of the exact merits of the cases which had occasioned Mr. Seward's despatch.

Mr. Calderon replied that he had received no official communication on this subject from the captain general of Cuba, but that he was prepared to make the following statement:

Spain had followed, in relation to vessels coming from the ports of the so-called Southern Confederacy, the same rules of action which she had adopted in the case of vessels clearing from the ports of the kingdom of the Two Sicilies after the assumption of royal authority in that kingdom by King Victor Emanuel. It was well known that Spain had not recognized the so-called kingdom of Italy, and that the consular agents of King Francis I were still exercising their functions in the Spanish ports. Nevertheless, Spain did not oblige the masters of vessels arriving in Spanish ports from the ports of the kingdom of Naples to submit to the authority of the consuls of Francis I, but permitted them to address themselves either to these or to the consular officers of King Victor Emanuel, as they saw fit. But this permission given to vessels coming from the Neapolitan ports to transact their business with the consuls of Victor Emanuel was by no means intended to imply a recognition of the Italian kingdom; for Spain recognized in the kingdom of the Two Sicilies no other authority as lawful and legitimate than that of King Francis I.

In like manner it was permitted to vessels coming from the ports now under the control of the so-called Confederate States, upon their arrival in Spanish ports, to address themselves to the consular authorities of the United States, if they saw fit to do so; but, as in the case of vessels coming from Neapolitan ports, Spain did not think proper to oblige them to do so. This practice, however, was by no means intended to imply, in any manner, a recognition of the so-called Confederate States as an independent nation.

But in the case of these vessels the action of Spain was still more justifiable than in the case of the Neapolitan vessels. The government of the United States was, with its naval forces, blockading the southern ports, and it was their business to see to it that no vessels should escape from the ports thus guarded. It could not be expected of Spain to supply the deficiencies of the maritime police of the United States, nor was it reasonable to expect that she should turn away from her ports vessels engaged in ordinary peaceful commerce, and which had not been able to obtain regular papers even if they had wanted to do so. Nor could Spain oblige such vessels by force to submit to the authority of the consular officers of the United States. Spain was acting solely with a view to the protection of her commercial interests, and nothing else.

Mr. Schurz replied that the only ground upon which such proceedings could legitimately be placed was that of necessity, and asked Mr. Calderon whether this was the ground taken by the government of Spain.

Mr. Calderon replied that it was. It was nothing but an *ex necessitate* proceeding, and that as soon as that necessity ceased the Spanish government would cease to follow that rule of action.

Mr. Schurz asked whether the Spanish government would admit into its ports vessels without papers regularly issued by the authorities of the United States as soon as the authority of the government of the United States should be re-established in the southern ports.

Mr. Calderon answered that they would not, because then the necessity would cease. But he would not admit the ground taken by Mr. Seward in his despatch, that the admission of vessels without regular papers under the actual state of things depended on a " concession " on the part of the government of the United States, which might be granted or withdrawn at pleasure. The Spanish government claimed a right to adhere to its rule of action as long as the necessity existed. But he protested most emphatically against the construction placed upon this rule as implying a recognition of the so-called Confederate States; the government of Spain did not think of taking such a step and of interrupting the friendly relations existing between the two countries, the preservation of which was undoubtedly considered important by the United States, and had always been sincerely desired by Spain.

Mr. Schurz replied that, as to these peaceful relations, the United States desired to preserve them with equal sincerity, not because they were afraid of a conflict, but because they loved peace. He added that if Spain in this case followed an established policy, founded on precedent, he did not wish to carry the discussion further at present, especially in the absence of all reliable information as to the recent occurrences in the ports of Cuba; but he wished to say that while the United States would set up no unreasonble pretensions, any act on the part of a foreign government which might be justly interpreted as a recognition of the independence of the States now in rebellion against the legitimate government of the North American republic would necessarily and inevitably lead to a rupture.

Mr. Calderon repeated that no such intention was entertained by the government of Spain, which entertained none but friendly feelings towards the United States. He informed Mr. Schurz that he was about to address a despatch on this subject to Mr. Tassara, which the latter would be instructed to read to Mr. Seward.

Mr. Schurz to Mr. Seward.

No. 33.] LEGATION OF THE UNITED STATES,
Madrid, October 20, 1861.

SIR: Last night I called upon Mr. Calderon, for the purpose of reading to him the memorandum of our conversation of the 16th instant. After having suggested some additions, which were forthwith incorporated into the report, he approved it as correct. He informed me that he had meanwhile received an official communication from the captain general of Cuba on the occurrences which had occasioned your despatch No. 30, and that he would read it to me at our next interview. He wanted to prove to me that the Spanish government had acted with entire fairness and loyalty in this transaction. I informed him that the London "Times," of October 16, contained the following telegraphic despatch:

"There are several vessels loading ammunition at Havana for the confederates."

And asked him whether he knew anything of this.

Mr. Calderon exclaimed at once, with great warmth: "That is impossible; it cannot be true. This would be a violation of the royal decree of the 17th of June, and will never be tolerated. General Serrano cannot have permitted this."

I replied that I was happy to hear him express his opinion so unequivocally and emphatically; for it would be impossible for the government of the United States to look on quietly while the Cuban ports were used as war depots for the rebels.

Mr. Calderon assured me repeatedly that this telegraphic despatch would most certainly turn out to be unfounded, and reiterated in very strong language the assurance of the loyal and friendly feelings of the Spanish government towards the United States, and of its firm determination to adhere faithfully to the principles laid down in the royal decree.

I am, sir, with high respect, your obedient servant,

C. SCHURZ.

Hon. WILLIAM H. SEWARD,
    Secretary of State, Washington, D. C.

Acting Secretary of State to Mr. Schurz.

[Extract.]

No. 46.]
                          DEPARTMENT OF STATE,
                          Washington, November 5, 1861.

SIR: Your despatch of September 2 (No. 13) was duly received.

  *   *   *   *   *   *   *

I am gratified to learn that the public opinion around you is less injurious than formerly. I trust that it is the beginning of a better understanding in Europe of the real character and determination of the American people.

I am, sir, your obedient servant,

F. W. SEWARD,
    Acting Secretary.

CARL SCHURZ, Esq., &c., &c., &c., *Madrid.*

Acting Secretary of State to Mr. Schurz.

No. 47.]
                          DEPARTMENT OF STATE,
                          Washington, November 5, 1861.

SIR: Your despatch of September 5 (No. 14) was duly received. It is very interesting, and I deeply regret that, owing to its having been accidentally mislaid, it failed to receive earlier attention.

Spain is engaged in her proceedings against Mexico. The United States are repressing an insurrection which, while it has attained formidable dimensions at home, reveals itself abroad in efforts to instigate foreign intervention. While it would be eminently desirable to make new friends, or at least to fortify existing friendships with foreign nations, the circumstances are so unpropitious as to make us content with averting new misunderstandings and consequent collisions.

You have correctly interpreted to Mr. Calderon Collantes the public sentiment of this country in regard to Spain. We not only seek no controversy with her, but are desirous to stand in the most friendly relations towards her. We are watchful, as we must be, of every fact or circumstance that seems to indicate a disposition on her part to favor or encourage the insurrection with which we are contending. We know our ability to maintain the integrity of the republic, and we intend to maintain it. We desire that when it shall have been completely re-established it shall be found that nothing has been done in the meantime by Spain, or by any foreign nation, to serve as causes for alienation. We are a peaceful state. Indeed, we think that the American Union is the guarantee of peace to the whole world. But like every other state we are jealous of our rights, and must maintain them.

Mr. Calderon Collantes could hardly have a better assurance of our desire for peace with Spain than the fact, which you might communicate to him, that even the unjust and ungenerous strictures of the Spanish press, which so naturally and so justly drew out your remonstrance, failed to excite the least sensibility on the part of this government.

This government neither has now, nor is likely to have, any schemes, or, indeed, any purpose, of conquest or aggrandizement. It seeks to extend its influence throughout this hemisphere and the world, not by the sword, but by commerce and by postal communication. It has practically guaranteed Cuba to Spain for many years heretofore, and it has no design against that possession or any other possession of Spain now; but it will not look with favor upon any policy that shall make that island the fulcrum of a lever for overthrowing either this Union or the institutions of human freedom and self-government which are identified with its existence.

We want a commercial treaty with Spain, and are willing to adopt a liberal principle of reciprocity to secure it; but we shall not urge such a measure now, when both parties are too deeply engaged to consider the matter with the intense attention necessary to a mutual understanding upon points so difficult.

We should be glad to effect a measure for the adjustment of mutual commercial claims, but we cannot admit that the Amistad claim has any foundation in justice or moral right. It is for Spain to refuse to treat with us upon this ground if she thinks it sufficient. We can only regret it, and wait for her to reconsider the subject.

I am, sir, your obedient servant,

F. W. SEWARD,
Acting Secretary.

CARL SCHURZ, Esq., &c., &c., &c.

Mr. Seward to Mr. Schurz.

No. 50.]   DEPARTMENT OF STATE,
                                        Washington, November 9, 1861.

SIR : Your despatch of October 20 (No. 33) has been received.

I trust that, with the good disposition manifested by Mr. Calderon Collantes on the occasion you have described, we shall be able to avert serious embarrassments of our affairs in the colonies of Spain.

I am, sir, your obedient servant,

                                        WILLIAM H. SEWARD.

CARL SCHURZ, Esq., &c., &c., &c.

Mr. Seward to Mr. Schurz.

No 52.]   DEPARTMENT OF STATE,
                                        Washington, November 11, 1861.

SIR : Your despatch of October 17 (No. 30) has been received. I am surprised at the miscarriage of my despatch No. 30. I have, however, directed a copy of it to be sent to you. Mr. Tassara has shown me certain explanations made to him by the captain general of Cuba, and I have in turn modified the opinion which I had formed concerning his action in relation to the matter complained of by the vice-consul general. I do not think it necessary to press the subject of my despatch No. 30 under these circumstances. With the gradual action of the government in restoring its authority at home, I look to see less disposition to treat it with disrespect abroad.

I am, sir, your obedient servant,

                                        WILLIAM H. SEWARD.

CARL SCHURZ, Esq., &c., &c., &c.

ROME.

Mr. Seward to Mr. King.

No. 2.]

DEPARTMENT OF STATE,
Washington, April 29, 1861.

SIR: I am to instruct you what to do, and of course what not to do, as resident minister of the United States at Rome. In order to understand the wishes and expectations of the President, please consider first the condition of Rome, and then the condition of the United States.

Rome, to a degree hardly comprehended in this country, is protected by the veneration of a large portion of mankind for his Holiness as the expounder of faith and the guardian of religion. Nevertheless, his government is surrounded by the elements of political revolution.

The United States are on the verge of civil war. It happens to them now, as it happened to ancient Rome, and has happened to many other republics, that they must make the trial whether liberty can be preserved while dominion is widely extended. What then shall we say or do in regard to Rome, or what ought Rome to say or do in regard to us?

Assure the government of his Holiness that the President and the people of the United States desire to cultivate with it the most cordial and friendly relations; that we will not violate the friendship already so happily existing by any intervention in the domestic affairs of the States of the Church. Assure his Holiness that it is the settled habit of this government to leave to all other countries the unquestioned regulation of their own internal concerns, being convinced that intrusion by a foreign nation anywhere tends only to embarrass rather than aid the best designs of the friends of freedom, religion and humanity, by impairing the unity of the state exclusively interested.

What ought Rome to do in regard to the United States? Just what I have thus said they will do in regard to Rome. We could not ask or consent to receive more, and the government of his Holiness will not propose to do less, for he is a friend to peace, to good order, and to the cause of human nature, which is now, as it always has been, our cause.

Let the government of Rome set this example and exercise its great influence in favor of a course of natural justice among nations, and the United States will still remain at peace with the whole world, and continue hereafter, as hitherto, to be the home of civil and religious liberty, and an asylum for the exiled and the oppressed.

I am, sir, your obedient servant,

WILLIAM H. SEWARD.

RUFUS KING, Esq., &c., &c., *Rome.*

Mr. Seward to Mr. Stockton.

No. 13.]

DEPARTMENT OF STATE,
Washington, April 30, 1861.

SIR: An instruction, numbered 2, and dated the 29th instant, has been addressed to your successor, Mr. King, of which, as it relates to a subject of present moment, I have deemed it expedient to send you a transcript, which you will find enclosed. It is thought desirable that the views therein expressed should be communicated to the Papal government without delay.

I am, sir, your obedient servant,

WILLIAM H. SEWARD.

JOHN P. STOCKTON, Esq., &c., &c., *Rome.*

Mr. Stockton to Mr. Seward.

WASHINGTON, *September* 14, 1861.

SIR: I have the honor to inform you that I left my post of duty on my return home on the 6th day of June last. But before doing so, according to the tenor of my despatch, (No. 48,) I communicated the contents of the instructions of the department to Mr. King (No. 2) to the government of his holiness

I translated all those points of the despatch which I thought necessary into Italian, and left it with his eminence as a memoranda. I informed his eminence, the secretary of state, that although the despatch was addressed to my successor, I should be most happy to take charge of a reply, as Mr. King had not yet arrived in Rome. His eminence said that he could not know the contents of instructions of the government of the United States to Mr. King except privately. Officially Mr. King should be received before any communication directed to him could be noticed. It was impossible for him to reply; a reply was not appropriate to the occasion.

I suggested that he could state to me privately his views, which I would communicate to the government, although my official position was ended.

His eminence consented to this, and then said, in substance, as follows: He said that the Catholics of the United States, as Catholics, as a church, would take no part in the matter; it would not be proper for them to do so. As citizens he had no doubt they would all feel a great concern at our internal dissensions. He added, you are aware that the government of his holiness concerns itself mainly in spiritual matters, but we are the supporters of law and order everywhere. He said he regarded the United States as a great and free country, and he hoped that I would be assured that the kind sentiments of our government to the Holy See were appreciated and reciprocated.

I do not pretend to give either the words or a verbal translation of the expressions of his eminence, but I am sure that I have fairly stated the substance of the conversation.

Perhaps it is not improper for me, in concluding my mission, to say that I parted from his holiness with a profound sense of the kindness and consideration I had always received from him, and with sentiments of the highest regard and esteem for his character.

I have the honor to remain, very truly yours,

JOHN P. STOCKTON,
Late United States Minister at Rome.

Hon. WILLIAM H. SEWARD,
Secretary of State.

RUSSIA.

Mr. Seward to Mr. Clay.

No. 3.]   DEPARTMENT OF STATE,
Washington, May 6, 1861.

SIR : Nations, like individuals, have three prominent wants; first, freedom; secondly, prosperity; thirdly, friends.

The United States early secured the two first objects by the exercise of courage and enterprise. But, although they have always practiced singular moderation, they nevertheless have been slow in winning friends.

Russia presents an exceptional case. That power was an early, and it has always been a constant friend. This relationship between two nations, so remote and so unlike, has excited much surprise, but the explanation is obvious.

Russia, like the United States, is an improving and expanding empire. Its track is eastward, while that of the United States is westward. The two nations, therefore, never come into rivalry or conflict. Each carries civilization to the new regions it enters, and each finds itself occasionally resisted by states jealous of its prosperity, or alarmed by its aggrandizement. Russia and the United States may remain good friends until, each having made a circuit of half the globe in opposite directions, they shall meet and greet each other in the region where civilization first began, and where, after so many ages, it has become now lethargic and helpless. It will be your pleasing duty to confirm and strengthen these traditional relations of amity and friendship.

Assure his Imperial Majesty that the President and the people of the United States have observed with admiration and sympathy the great and humane efforts he has so recently made for the material and moral improvement of his empire by the extension of telegraphs and railroads, and by removing the disabilities of slavery.

Make it your duty to inquire whether the sluggish course of commerce between the two nations cannot be quickened, and its volume increased. Russia is capable of receiving cotton and tobacco from us in much larger quantities than we now send. The former is not a staple of that country, and although it produces tobacco, yet not of so high a quality as that which we send abroad, and of which Russia consumes more than any other nation.

We can well receive from that country increased quantities of hemp and flax, tallow, and other productions in exchange.

Russia is liberal to our inventors, engineers, and machinists ; but vicious adventurers too often abuse this generous encouragement by fraudulent practices. See if you can devise a plan for correcting this evil. I suggest that it might be done by effecting free interchange of newspapers and scientific journals.

A Russian landing at New York can cross this western continent without once being required to exhibit a passport. Why will not Russia extend the same hospitality to us, and enable the American citizen, when he debarks at Revel, to cross the eastern continent in like manner unquestioned. The American abroad is not more than the Russian a propagandist, and while Russia pursues the general policy of the present reign it can have nothing to fear from American influences.

In another paper which accompanies this your attention is especially directed to the subject of amendments of the international code of maritime law in regard to neutrals, proposed in 1856 by the congress which was then sitting at Paris, of which body Russia was a member.

If nations were now, as in ancient times, morally independent and unsocial, the President would not have occasion to address our representatives in Europe on the painful events which are subjects of intense solicitude at home. But the world has, in a measured degree, become one commonwealth. Nations favor or discourage political changes in other nations, and exercise influences upon their success and fortunes, sometimes from interest, sometimes from sympathy, and sometimes from caprice.

Although this general fact is so well understood, yet the President indulges so uncompromising a sense of the national dignity and honor, that he, nevertheless, would not suffer a word on the subject to escape from the lips of one of our ministers abroad, if our discontented fellow-citizens who have raised the standard of insurrection had not sent out their agents to propitiate foreign powers and engage their co-operation in the desperate attempt they are making to overthrow the institutions and the liberties of the American people.

You will, of course, meet such agents in Russia. They have some advantages in Europe of which you should be warned.

What is now the insurrectionary party in the United States has been for near forty years, and until the fourth day of March last, the dominant party in the administration of this government. It has acquaintances and friendships in high places there, the growth of long intercourse in foreign courts, with the prestige of political authority. The late minister to Russia returned, however, to be the governor of South Carolina at the moment when that State was in the very act of inaugurating the present revolution.

When these agents shall present themselves at St. Petersburg, his Imperial Majesty, before granting them a hearing, will naturally address himself to you, and will ask you: What is the cause of this revolution? What is its object? Why does the government resist it? What is the present condition of the revolution, and what are its prospects? What are the probable consequences of its success, or of its failure? And, finally, what does the the President desire or expect from his Imperial Majesty in regard to it?

The President will not forget, nor will he allow you to forget, that he is the magistrate of the insurrectionary, as he is also of the loyal States, and in all his dealings concerning the plotters, aiders, and abettors of this great conspiracy he will constantly remember that the people in whose name they act, and whose power they abuse, are still citizens of the republic. He believes, however, that you may answer all the questions thus contemplated without compromising the impartiality of this government, or the dignity and honor of the federal Union.

As to the cause of the revolution, you will inform the Russian government that African slavery was found existing in nearly all the States, when, seventy years ago, they met, and by a written Constitution established that Union. It was expected that under the operation of moral, social, and political influences then existing the practice of slavery would soon cease. The foreign slave trade was adopted to favor that end, while the vacant common domain which lay between the Alleghany mountains and the Mississippi river was shut up against slavery by legislation then believed to be effective and eternal.

Cotton soon afterward became an object of great commercial demand; the soil and climate of those States of this Union which are situate near and upon the Gulf of Mexico were favorable to its growth, and African slave labor existed therein practically to the exclusion of the labor of free white men.

The raising of slaves of the African race to supply the wants of the cotton growing States became a prominent economical interest in the grain and tobacco growing States adjacent to the former class of States. The interest of slavery became at once the basis of the policy, and even of the polity of these two classes of States, and by political, social, and commercial connexions those interests secured a strong and even controlling influence throughout the whole Union, and even in all foreign commercial countries. This interest of slavery was jealous and apprehensive of danger from the growth of the democratic element of free white labor, which all the while has been constantly augmented by native increase and immigration from Europe.

The several States in the Union, whatever be their population, enjoy equal representation in the Senate. Congress may, and from manifest causes must, admit new States into the Union. The slave holding interest naturally desired to extend slavery and multiply slave States. The free States necessarily desired, as they constitutionally might, to prevent the extension of slavery in regions where it did not exist or had been abolished, and so to multiply free States.

The acquisitions of new domain by purchases from France, Spain, and Mexico, to be the seat of future States, opened a wide theatre for this contest, and the contest itself by degrees came to be a chief feature in the debates of Congress, and in the canvasses of the popular elections.

The interest of slavery was consolidated and compact in the slave States, and acquired great power by threatening that if overruled those States would secede and dissolve the Union, which the free States traditionally, as well as justly, regarded as fatal to the prosperity, safety, and happiness of the whole American people. Statesmen of all classes and all parties, on that ground, continually conceded, and Congress and the judiciary constantly compromised with the slave interest, in opposition to steadily advancing popular convictions of right, duty, and patriotism, until at last all legal barriers against the extension of slavery were, in one way or in another, thrown down. Transactions so unnatural roused the interest opposed to slavery to renewed effort in the popular election of the last year, and that election resulted in the choice of the present incumbent for the office of President of the United States, although without a majority of either house of Congress identified with this interest.

The party of slavery, which had thus, for the first time, been distinctly, though not completely, unsuccessful in a popular election, instantly, and four months before the constitutional period assigned for the inauguration of the new President, took an appeal from the verdict of the people, rendered through the ballot-box, to the sword, and organized a revolution with civil war.

Such was the cause of the revolution. Its object is to create a nation built upon the principle that African slavery is necessary, just, wise, and beneficent, and that it may and must be expanded over the central portion of the American continent and islands without check or resistance, at whatever cost and sacrifice to the welfare and happiness of the human race.

The government of the United States resists this revolution for reasons too many to be hastily set forth.

It is absolutely unnecessary. All existing interests of slavery are protected now, as heretofore, by our federal and State constitutions, sufficiently to prevent the destruction or molestation of the institution of slavery where it exists, by federal or foreign intervention, without the consent of the parties concerned. The policy of fortifying and extending slavery in regions where it has no existence is injurious, vicious, and eminently dangerous to our own country and to mankind.

Dismemberment of the Union, however effected and for whatever cause, would be destruction of the safety, happiness, and welfare of the whole American people, and would, by its influence, render the present establishment of any popular form of government impracticable in an age and in a region where no other than just such a form of government is known or could be tolerated.

The condition of the revolution is this, namely: In the United States the people always exercise a direct and potential influence upon the government. They were at first incredulous of the fact that a revolution so unnecessary, so unnatural, and so fatal, was seriously intended. They saw it move steadily on, but were beguiled by the appeals of mediators, who proposed at once to avert disunion and to prevent the calamity of civil war. The government was temporarily demoralized by the presence of the conspirators in controlling numbers in the administration, in Congress, in the army, in the navy, and in every department of the public service. But at last, when it became clearly revealed that nothing less than subversion of the federal republic would satisfy the insurgents, and that the forbearance and moderation of the government towards them were abused to the purpose of preparing a deadly and desolating war, the loyalty of the people suddenly awakened; the government, sustained by popular enthusiasm and energy, has put forth all the necessary power; the revolution has at once been checked, and it is no longer doubtful that it will be promptly and effectually suppressed.

It had its origin in disappointment; and it depends for continuance only on popular passions, the occasion for which has passed away, while such passions are not in harmony with the character, sentiments, and habits of the American people.

When it shall be seen, as it soon will be, that the effort to overthrow the government is hopeless, the misguided citizens who have joined themselves to the revolutionary standard will resume their accustomed habits of reason and reflection, and the Union, having surmounted a new and formidable danger, will be stronger than ever before.

What would be the consequences of the revolution if it could be successful? The answer is obvious. At first, division of this great and hitherto peaceful and happy country into two hostile and belligerent republics. Later, a resolution of each of those two republics into an indefinite number of petty, hostile, and belligerent States. Local jealousies, continually agitated, would, early or late, be aggravated by the horrors of a servile war, filling the whole country with desolation. The end would be military despotism, compelling peace where free government had proved an absolute and irretrievable failure.

The equilibrium of the nations, maintained by this republic, on the one side, against the European system on the other continent, would be lost, and the struggles of nations in that system for dominion in this hemisphere and on the high seas, which constitutes the chief portion of the world's history in the eighteenth century, would be renewed. The progress of freedom and civilization, now so happily inaugurated, would be arrested, and the hopes of humanity which this the present century has brought forth would be disappointed and indefinitely postponed.

What will be the consequences of the failure of the revolution? The continuance of the country in the happy career that it has pursued so auspiciously, to the repose of nations and to the improvement of the condition of mankind.

What does the President require or expect from the Emperor of Russia? That sovereign is expected to do just what this government does in regard to Russia and all other nations. It refrains from all intervention whatever in their political affairs; and it expects the same just and generous forbearance in return. It has too much self-respect to ask more, and too high a sense of its rights to accept anything less.

The high character of the government of Russia warrants these moderate and just expectations.

I am, sir, respectfully, your obedient servant,

WILLIAM H. SEWARD.

CASSIUS M. CLAY, Esq., &c., &c., &c.

Mr. Appleton to Mr. Black.

[Extract.]

No. 12.]   LEGATION OF THE UNITED STATES,
St. Petersburg, December 31, 1860, *(January* 12, 1861.)

SIR:

*   *   *   *   *   *   *   *   *

Here, as elsewhere in Europe, the late agitations in the United States, which have followed the election of the republican candidates for President and Vice-President, have been observed with the deepest interest. The President's message was published in full as soon as it was received, together with copious comments on it from the leading journals of England and France. A weekly letter on American affairs is also published in the St. Petersburg Journal, purporting to come from New York, but doubtless made up in London, while on the arrival of every steamer from the United States the same journal receives by telegraph its most important items of news. Yesterday, for example, we had news from New York to December 28. Although the intelligence thus far, in reference to the preservation of the Union, has been uniformly bad, I think the general belief here is still favorable to some amicable adjustment. European statesmen have seen so many violent agitations spring up and subside in our country, that they expect to see this one take the same course. They cannot understand, moreover, how a great government like ours, whose career has been eminently prosperous, can be suddenly destroyed without any apparent cause, by the very people who are themselves a part of it, and who are daily receiving its benefits. They have never seen an American citizen abroad who did not glory in the American name, and boast, with honest pride, of our popular institutions. They have never seen an American journal either where this same spirit was not manifested of satisfaction with the American Constitution, and of attachment to the American form of government. Under this government they have seen our country advance in population, and territory, and wealth, and honor, as no nation on earth was ever before permitted to do, and this progress, instead of exhausting its energies, has seemed to them to inspire it with new vigor for its future growth. They have regarded it, also, as one of the striking peculiarities of our republic, that while its national developments and national glory have been thus marvellously grand, they represent, at the same time, an amount of individual advancement and personal happiness which can be found nowhere else beneath the sun. They cannot persuade themselves that a government thus idolized apparently by its citizens, under which these great results have been already worked out, and under which still greater results may fairly be anticipated, is really about to be destroyed in the midst of its usefulness and by the hands of its own people. Still less can they comprehend the method of peaceable secession by which this destruction is sought to be accomplished. They have no idea of a government which exists only at the will of a small minority of its citizens, or of a revolution in which weakness is permitted to triumph over greatly superior strength. They have no sympathy with the idea of State secession any more than with the system of negro slavery, and they will be slow, therefore, to give back their old confidence in the United States, even if the present difficulties there should be happily surmounted, unless, indeed, they can understand at the same time that the right of secession, which is now so earnestly claimed, has been substantially abandoned throughout the country, and is not likely to be again insisted on in any practical form. If, however, the existing difficulties shall not be surmounted, and under the influence of this doctrine the Union shall be broken up, the result will be hailed undoubtedly by the cabinets of Europe as a conclusive proof of the instability of popular institutions; and the destruction of the American government will be a calamity, therefore, not only to those who enjoy its benefits at home, but to those oppressed people also in the Old World, whose hearts are now cheered by the knowledge of its existence, and whose eyes are turned daily towards it for support and consolation. Yet those governments on this side of the Atlantic, who have looked to our republic as the only maritime check in the world upon Great Britain, will not be quite satisfied to see this counterpoise disappear, and that haughty power restored to its old position of mistress of the seas.

The great events which are now in progress in the United States will continue to be regarded, therefore, with the deepest interest throughout Europe, until they shall have reached their end. In the meantime I cannot describe to you the painful anxiety with which those Americans who are abroad await now the arrival of every mail from home. Amidst the wars and convulsions of Europe we have been accustomed to look towards the great republic as the assured and constant abode of tranquillity and happiness, and we have rejoiced always in the conviction that, by our right of citizenship there, we possessed a title and an honor which, making each American himself the equal of a king, could receive no added dignity from any royal order or imperial decoration. We have all had the happy consciousness, moreover, that when our duties abroad should be closed we had a country to return to, where we should find safety for our lives and property, and numerous avenues wide open to prosperity and honor and happiness. To see all this crumbling away before our eyes—our country breaking into pieces—our citizenship changing from a glory to a shame—our hopes in the future clouded over with doubt—anarchy, possibly, taking the place of good government—civil war substituted, perhaps, for peace and harmony—and ruin threatened to every valuable interest which man can cherish. The bare possibility, I say, of such results as these, deeply painful as it must be to our fellow-citizens at home, who yet have the consolation of being able to struggle step by step against them, is even more painful to those of us who are abroad, and who hear of events only at fixed intervals, without the preparation of their gradual approach, and without any power whatever to prevent them. Let us hope even yet that the God of our fathers will not permit their children to be the instruments and the victims of so vast a calamity, but that oil may yet be poured upon the heaving waters, and the ship of state may yet outride the storm. I am one of those who have never believed that it could be possible to dissolve the American Union. I thought it was protected by too much plighted faith, by too many sacred associations in the past, by too much admitted usefulness in the present, and by too many thick coming glories in the future, ever to be seriously in danger of destruction. If in this, however, I have been mistaken, and the earth is really to be shadowed now by the great calamity, may God have mercy upon those misguided men by whose folly and wickedness it will have been accomplished.

*   *   *   *   *   *   *   *   *

I am, very respectfully, yours,

JOHN APPLETON.

Hon. J. S. BLACK,
   Secretary of State, Washington.

Mr. Appleton to Mr. Seward.

[Extract.]

No. 16.]   LEGATION OF THE UNITED STATES,
                             St. Petersburg, April 8–20, 1861.

SIR : The despatch of the department No. 10 and your circular of March 9th have been received, and I have had several interviews with Prince Gortchacow on the subject of them. Although no agent was here from the Confederate States, and none was immediately expected, I still thought it only prudent that your views in reference to these States should be known by the Russian government, in order that it might be prepared for the question of recognition whenever it should be presented. I, therefore, handed to Prince Gortchacow a copy of President Lincoln's inaugural address, and read to him, at the same time, such portions of the despatches I have mentioned as seemed to me most important, particularly calling his attention to those passages which declare the unquestioned legality of the existing government, the revolutionary nature of the movement which had been made against it, and the full confidence of the President that the harmony of the Union would be soon restored. In support of these views I added such suggestions of my own as I thought appropriate, and expressed the hope that our government might receive from Russia, at this crisis, a renewed manifestation of that friendly disposition which had always marked the intercourse between the United States and that empire. Prince Gortchacow replied that the question of recognizing the Confederate States was not now before the Emperor, and for the present he did not think it would be. I might assure you, he said, that his Majesty was not unmindful of the friendly relations which had so long subsisted between the two countries, and that he sincerely desired the harmony and prosperity of the Union. It was the only commercial counterpoise in the world, he added, to Great Britain, and Russia would do nothing, therefore, to diminish its just power and influence. It was only frank, however, to say, that while things continued as they were, the commerce between the Confederate States and Russia would not be interrupted. There was no blockade of southern ports, and any informality in the papers of ships which cleared there would be overlooked. This, he said, was the course determined on by England and France, and he understood it was pursued also by our own government. I told him I had no specific instructions on this point, and did not know what rule had been adopted concerning it by other nations. It seemed to me, however, that American ships ought to carry the American flag and be provided with American papers; and if this was not done or, still more, if the American character was repudiated, I hardly saw how they could be recognized as American ships. He said there were some difficulties certainly in the way, but it was better to overlook them, and to receive the ships for just what they were, vessels belonging to the

United States, but not provided, in consequence of existing troubles, with the usual evidence of nationality. I said, they might deny that they belonged to the United States.

He replied that this would not alter the fact. They came from ports in the United States, and the separation of the Confederate States was not yet recognized. The policy, he said, involved no recognition of nationality, but was only a concession in aid of commerce. I replied that my only interest was to prevent this recognition. We desired to be permitted to work out the pending questions in the Union in our own way, and, in our endeavors to restore its unity and harmony, we thought we had a right to rely upon the friendly aid and co-operation of other nations. He said no nation would witness the restoration with more satisfaction than Russia.

This is the substance of our conversations, and I need hardly trouble you with any comments. It is obvious that Russia does not expect to be called upon to decide the question of recognition until this decision has been made by England and France, and that she expects to find it then of easy solution. In the meantime she expresses the hope, which I am inclined to think she really entertains, that our difficulties may be amicably adjusted and the Union restored to its old harmony and power. In the commercial policy which she has adopted towards southern ports she has evidently followed the example of Great Britain and France. I ought to add that Prince Gortchacow read to me extracts from several letters of Mr. Stockl, the Russian minister at Washington, which indicated that the representatives of the three powers there were quite agreed upon this subject. Under these circumstances, after stating such objections to the policy as occurred to me, I contented myself with the assurance of Prince Gortchakow that it was not intended to involve any recognition of nationality.

I shall take care to inform you promptly of any attempts which may be made here "to embarrass or overthrow the republic," and you may rely also upon my best efforts to prevent and counteract them.

*   *   *   *   *   *   *   *

I am, very respectfully, yours,

JOHN APPLETON.

Hon. WILLIAM H. SEWARD,
 Secretary of State, Washington.

Mr. Appleton to Mr. Seward.

[Extract.]

LEGATION OF THE UNITED STATES,
St. Petersburg, May 11, (23,) 1861.

SIR: The circular of the department dated April 20, 1861, indorsing the President's proclamation on the subject of blockades and privateering, has been received. I have written to our consuls at the different ports of Russia, calling their special attention to the subject, and enjoining upon them the utmost vigilance to prevent the fitting out of privateers within their respective consulates. At Sebastopol, where we have no consul, I have written to Colonel Gowen, an American citizen, to the same effect, and have asked him to transmit to this legation any information which may come to his knowledge on this subject, concerning either ships or persons.

I have also received the circular of the department dated April 27, transmitting, for my information, a copy of the President's proclamation of that date directing a blockade of the ports of Virginia and North Carolina, in addition to that of the ports of the States mentioned in the proclamation of the 19th instant.

I have the honor to be, &c.,

JOHN APPLETON.

Hon. WM. H. SEWARD,
Secretary of State, Washington.

Mr. Seward to C. M. Clay.

No. 4.]
DEPARTMENT OF STATE,
Washington, May 21, 1861.

SIR: We have received Mr. Appleton's despatch of the 8th of April, (No. 16.) The manner in which Prince Gortchacow has expressed himself on the subject of the domestic disturbances in our country, and the anticipated application of the insurgents for a recognition of their assumed authority, is in harmony with the friendly spirit which Russia has always manifested towards the United States, and in the main is quite satisfactory. We might, indeed, have felt ourselves bound to except to the claim that while matters should remain as they were assumed to be when this conversation was held, irregularities in the observance of our revenue laws practiced by foreign nations would be expected to be overlooked by this government; but that question has passed by. We have put our land and naval forces in motion to suppress the insurrection, and have closed the ports which have been seized by the revolutionists by a blockade. You may, if occasion shall offer, assure the Russian government that we expect that the unhappy disturbance will not continue long, and that peace and harmony will return, and the Union be stronger and firmer than ever before.

Mr. Appleton's judicious and energetic conduct in this connexion is approved and appreciated by the President.

I am, sir, your obedient servant,

WILLIAM. H. SEWARD.

Mr. Appleton to Mr. Seward.

[Extract.]

No. 18.]
LEGATION OF THE UNITED STATES,
St. Petersburg, May 22, (*June* 3,) 1861.

SIR: I have the honor to enclose copies, which I have received unofficially, of two orders of the Russian government which have been recently issued for the guidance of its officers in respect to the flags and ships of the Confederate States. It will be seen that they conform to what was said to me on this subject by Prince Gortchacow in the conversation which I reported to the department in my No. 16. I ought to add that every American ship which has yet appeared at Cronstadt has shown the American flag and claimed the American character. In one case from a southern port the papers were not quite regular, but the irregularity was overlooked.

* * * * * *
* * * * * *

I am, very respectfully, your obedient servant,

JOHN APPLETON.

Hon. WILLIAM H. SEWARD,
Secretary of State, Washington.

To the commander-in-chief of the port of Cronstadt:

His imperial highness the general admiral, foreseeing the possibility of ships belonging to the southern States of the American Union, which have seceded from the United States of North America, arriving at our ports during the present navigation, has directed me to inform your excellency, for your guidance, that, according to the opinion of the minister of foreign affairs, the flag of men-of-war belonging to the seceded States must not be saluted.

That there may be no obstacle in the way of commerce, merchant vessels of the seceded States are to be treated according to the rules acted on by us with regard to Italian merchant vessels sailing under the Italian flag; *i. e.*, according to the treaties that are at present in force, (commercial treaty concluded between America and us December (6,) 10, 1832.) Should the crews of vessels belonging to the seceded States not wish to acknowledge the authority of the consuls appointed by the federal government of Washington, then, in case of dispute, they must abide by the decision of our local authorities, in the same manner as foreigners whose governments have no representatives in our empire.

General Major GREIG,
Director of the Chancellery of the Ministry of Marine.

Circular addressed to the custom-houses on the White, Baltic, Black, and Azoff seas.

By order of the minister of finance, the department of foreign trade prescribes: In case any merchant vessels arrive in our ports belonging to the southern States of the American Union, the same not acknowledging the authority of the government of the United States of America, the said vessels are to be treated and received as hitherto, according to the treaty of 1832, should even their ships' papers not be in order, which may occur in consequence of the present political condition of the United States of America.

General Lieutenant PASHKOFF,
Director of the Department of Foreign Trade.
SORNIN, *Chief of Section, &c.*

Mr. Clay to Mr. Seward.

[Extract.]

Legation of the United States,
St. Petersburg, Russia, June 7, 1861.

Sir: *   *   *   *   *   *   *   *   *

I find here your letters Nos. 1, 2, and 3. No. 1, giving me information which, if sooner received, would have avoided the necessity of my remarks in my last letter personal to myself, as I there find myself advised of my right to receive salary from the time of my leaving home to my arrival here I need only add that the documents referred to in No. 1 are also received, as well as your circular of the 6th May, (printed,) all of which shall receive my earliest attention.

I found the Emperor absent in the direction of Moscow; and being introduced by our minister, Mr. Appleton, to the assistant secretary of state, General Tolstoy, (the premier, Gortchacow, now being also absent,) I was advised by him to await the return of the Emperor; and I presumed it would not be agreeable to the Emperor for me to follow on, so I shall await his return to this city. I may add that the secretary gave me a very cordial meeting, speaking partly in English and partly in French; assured me of the continued feeling of friendship on the part of Russia for the Union, and *his hope that the Confederate States would not venture an embassy here.* In a word, I venture to say that the French and Russian Emperors are friendly to our Union.

* * * * * * * * *

I have the honor to be your obedient servant,

C. M. CLAY .

Hon. W. H. SEWARD,
 Secretary of State, &c.

Mr. Seward to Mr. Clay.

[Extract]

No. 8.]   DEPARTMENT OF STATE,
              Washington, July 8, 1861.

SIR: Your despatch No. 3, dated June 7, was duly received, and the intelligence of your safe arrival at your destination afforded us much satisfaction.

So also the President is highly gratified with the liberal and friendly sentiments concerning our domestic affairs, expressed to you by Prince Gortchacow.

I transmit for your confidential perusal a copy of my last despatch to Mr. Dayton, on the subject of our proposition to accede to the declaration of the congress of Paris. The views it presents will be the guide to your own action on that subject.

* * * * * * * * *

I am, sir, &c.

        WILLIAM H. SEWARD.

C. M. CLAY, Esq., &c., &c., &c.

Mr. Clay to Mr. Seward.

[Extracts.]

No. 4.]   ST. PETERSBURG, *Russia, June 21, 1861.*
 SIR :
 *   *   *   *   *   *   *
 *   *   *   *   *   *   *
 *   *   *   *   *   *   *

The Emperor returned from Moscow a few days ago, where, it is said, he was engaged in suppressing the insurrections of the serfs. By persuasion and arms, as the enemies of the liberation, the proprietors themselves, or their agents, were making them believe that they were at once freed from all claims of work, &c., and this was done, no doubt, to prejudice the great work of the Emperor. But it seems that everywhere the disaffection has been subdued, and very strong demonstrations of respect have been, here and at Moscow, by the peasants towards the Emperor, warmly exhibited.

On the 16th (28th) instant I called upon, by agreement, Prince Alexander Gortchacow III, minister of foreign affairs to his Majesty the Emperor. He received me in a cordial way, shaking hands, and causing me to be seated. He led the conversation by saying the Emperor having been advised of my arrival, had ordered him to express his continued friendship for the United States government; that he had heard with regret of our civil troubles, and hoped the Union a speedy triumph. I responded that no change of administration had changed the relations of the United States and Russia, whose natural position and traditionary friendship must ever keep them in the closest harmony, and that I was ordered by the President thus to express myself to his Imperial Majesty; that I was ordered also to explain at the proper time the causes of our difficulties at home; that at present I would only say that the rebel slaveholders made war upon us because, following in the wake of advancing civilization, we would not allow our government to be longer the propagandist of slavery. I stated how the slave States were divided, and my hope that the rebellion would be soon crushed out. To this he attentively listened, and responded that he hoped it would be most "*speedily* done."

Upon my giving him my office copy of the letter of credence, he said he would see the Emperor, and let me know at my hotel when I would be received by his Majesty. He also asked after Pickens, my family, and other things in a familiar way, when I was dismissed by again shaking hands. I have given the substance of the interview, and the words as near as may be, in order that you may for yourself draw your own conclusions. *

 * * * * * * *

 * * * * * * *

 * * * * * * *

According to the rule here, I day before yesterday called upon M. de Tchetestcheff, master of ceremonies. My visit was yesterday returned, and I now await further orders from the Emperor as to the presentation, of the which I will write you the particulars before sending you this. * *

 * * * * * * *

 * * * * * * *

Prince Gortchacow having returned my visit, gave me notice that the Emperor would receive me on Sunday, at twelve o'clock, the 2d (14th) July, at Peterhoff. So on to-day (14th July) I and my suite, Green Clay, William C. Goodloe, and T. Williams, private secretaries, set out at ten a. m. for Peterhoff by rail, the "geraut" of ceremonics meeting us at the station here, and three of the Emperor's carriages meeting us at the depot and taking us to the palace. We then witnessed a review of cavalry and infantry by the Emperor, and after it was over, at a little after one o'clock, we were sent for by the Emperor, and, as my secretary was told by the "master of ceremonics," who is the regular introducer, I was conducted into the presence by Prince Gortchacow, who, though the Emperor spoke (English?) American mostly, acted as interpreter as to the set speech, which was in Russian.

The Emperor received me standing, advancing and saying he was pleased to see me. I then went through, very briefly, the usual forms of such speeches, adding, that I ventured, by the orders of my government, to say further to him that the President of the United States and the American people looked with profound sympathy and admiration upon the great reforms which he was attempting in his empire, which, without considering the philanthropic view of the movement, by building up a middle class, he would add more to the physical power of his country than did Peter the Great by consolidation and extension; and that the success of his enterprise would, in the estimation of the western nations, place him even above that great ruler.

The Emperor seemed much gratified and really moved by this last remark, which he saw was from us a real appreciation of his great undertaking, and not an unmeaning compliment. He then said he would respond through the prince; and, turning to him, he spoke with very decided earnestness. In response to the first part of my address, he repeated the usual words. To the last he said, in conclusion, that "so much the more had he hopes of the perpetuity of the friendship between the two nations now, that in addition to all former ties we were bound together by a common sympathy in the common cause of emancipation." I give nearly the exact words. Among other things he expressed a very earnest wish that we would speedily recover the integrity of the Union. The more formal speech was done through the prince; the rest was spoken to me directly in English. He asked me what late advices I had; and when I told him how many of the border slave States were standing by the Union, he expressed great satisfaction. He wanted to know if I thought England would interfere. I told him we did not care what she did; that her interference would tend to unite us the more; that we fought the south with reluctance; we were much intermarried, and of a common history; but that the course of England had aroused our sensibilities towards her in no very pleasant manner. The Emperor seemed to like my seeming defiance of old "John Bull" very much. He wanted to know if I was a relative of Henry Clay, and what was my military rank. I told him I was only a distant relation of Clay, and that I wore the uniform of an American colonel, which rank I had filled in my own country. The Emperor then wished that our personal relations would advance the national friendship, as our former ministers had so succeeded; inquired after Mr. Appleton's health; regretted that he had not seen him before his departure; shook hands with me; when I accompanied him into the ante-chamber, and introduced to him my three attachés, to whom he made pleasant remarks, when, shaking hands once more, he dismissed us.

*　　*　　*　　*　　*　　*　　*　　*　　*　　*

I have already made this letter too long; but I cannot conclude without saying how much more and more I value the great and inestimable blessings of our government, and how I trust in God that no compromise will be made of the great idea for which we have so long fought, but that General Scott, following out the programme of Mr. Lincoln's inaugural, will *slowly* and *surely* subdue the rebellion, "stock, lock, and gun-barrel," "hook and line, bob and sinker," and that we may be all spared to see once more that glorious old banner restored. "Liberty and union, now and forever—one and inseparable."

I have the honor to be your most obedient servant,

C. M. CLAY.

Hon. W. H. SEWARD, *Secretary of State, &c., Washington, D. C.*

Mr. Seward to Mr. Clay.

No. 9.]

DEPARTMENT OF STATE,
Washington, July 9, 1861.

SIR: Mr. Appleton's despatch of May 22, (June 3,) No. 18, has been received.

It contains the orders in admiralty on the subject of the treatment of American vessels during the present condition of our internal affairs.

The subject seems to call for no special instruction to you, except to express to the Russian government the satisfaction which this government feels in regard to the conduct and friendly action of the Emperor.

Mr. Appleton is now with us, and we are deriving much profit from the information he gives. We learn your high appreciation of his conduct in his mission with pleasure.

I am, sir, respectfully, your obedient servant,

WILLIAM H. SEWARD.

CASSIUS M. CLAY, Esq., &c., &c., &c.

Mr. Clay to Mr. Seward.

[Extracts.]

No. 5.]

ST. PETERSBURG, *August* 3, 1861.

SIR:　　*　　　*　　　*　　　*　　　*　　　*　　　*

A few days since I laid before Prince Gortchacow the declaration of the seven powers at Paris, April 16, 1856, as you had prepared it. He expressed himself favorably inclined towards allowing us to become a party, saying that Russia had, in a friendly spirit, in 1856, asked that America and the parties not acceding should be exempt from its force; for he desired to see the United States flourish as a naval power;　　*　　　*　　　*
that he would take the scheme under consideration, and advise me of the Emperor's conclusion. I laid before him also an additional clause, embracing Secretary Marcy's proposition: "Private goods of citizens or subjects of neutrals, and of belligerents, at sea, not contraband of war, shall not be liable to capture." Of this also he spoke favorably, but said, as we could not enforce it without the accession of the great powers, it should be referred to them. I said that there must be a beginning, and that I hoped the Emperor would both accept it and urge it upon the maritime powers. Should this advance be made, (and why not?) it would, most of all, benefit the United States; whilst, in agreeing simply to the Paris declaration, we are most of all injured.

*　　　*　　　*　　　*　　　*　　　*

Your copy of despatch (No. 27) to Mr. Dayton you will see has just been exactly anticipated by me. I put the Paris declaration, "pure and simple," for immediate adoption, and reserved the Marcy addendum for future consideration. No doubt it will be ultimately adopted; for all the nations except France, England, and the United States, would no doubt be glad to have the commerce of the seas free from the perils of the war navies of these great powers.

*　　　*　　　*　　　*　　　*　　　*
*　　　*　　　*　　　*　　　*　　　*

I am, very truly, your obedient servant,

C. M. CLAY.

Hon. W. H. SEWARD.

Mr. Seward to Mr. Clay.

No. 12.]

DEPARTMENT OF STATE,
Washington, August 12, 1861.

SIR: Your despatch of 21st of June (No. 4) has been received. The account which it gives us of your reception by the Emperor of Russia, and of the just purposes and friendly wishes expressed by him in relation to the United States, is eminently satisfactory. I sincerely hope that the good understanding which now exists between the two governments may continue. I am sure you need no new instructions to enable you to say that we rejoice in the peaceful progress of the means which the Emperor has initiated for meliorating the condition of the people of Russia.

Your suggestions concerning certain modern improvements of rifled cannon have been commended to the consideration of the Secretary of War.

We wait with interest upon your negotiation on the subject of the rights of neutrals in maritime war, which your despatch leads us to suppose you will already have commenced before this communication shall have reached St. Petersburg.

I am, sir, respectfully, your obedient servant,

WILLIAM H. SEWARD.

CASSIUS M. CLAY, &c., &c., &c

Mr. Seward to Mr. Clay.

No. 13.]

DEPARTMENT OF STATE,
Washington, September 3, 1861.

SIR: Your despatch of the 3d of August (No. 5) has been received.

I have been quite well aware that our relations to Great Britain and France, in this crisis of our domestic difficulties, are attended by complications and dangers which altogether surpass any that we can have to encounter in our intercourse with Russia and other northern European powers. We hope and expect to be always in relations of amity and real friendship with those powers, and are very willing to negotiate with them, and especially with Russia, upon the basis of the declaration of the congress of Paris, either with or without the Marcy amendment, though greatly preferring that that amendment shall be incorporated into the treaty.

At the same time, it is well that you should know that thus far the propositions for similar treaties with Great Britain and France have not yet been acceded to by those governments. If the imperial government, for any reason, prefer to delay acting upon the subject until the decisive results of our negotiations with the two other powers named, we shall not expect you to be urgent upon the subject. We simply desire to act justly and candidly with all other nations, so as to give them all reasonable guarantees for the security of commerce during the continuance of our civil war. This done, we can cheerfully abide the coming of events, never doubting for a moment the complete restoration of the authority and high prestige of the federal Union.

Your remarks upon the subject of Mexico are very interesting, and they will have due weight in forming any determination which the rapid course of political events there shall require us to adopt.

I wish that it were compatible with my many cares at this critical moment to impart to each of our ministers abroad a full knowledge of the condition of our negotiations and discussions with all foreign powers. If I could do so, you would probably be satisfied that you are laboring under apprehensions of some imaginary foreign dangers. But such a proceeding is absolutely impossible, and I must be content to advise you, when necessary, of the President's wishes in regard to your own mission, and leave you, as to the rest, to await ultimate, and yet seasonable, developments.

I am, sir, respectfully, your obedient servant,

WILLIAM H. SEWARD.

Cassius M. Clay, Esq., &c., &c., &c.

Prince Gortchacow to Mr. De Stoeckl.

[Translation.]

St. Petersburg, *July* 10, 1861.

Sir: From the beginning of the conflict which divides the United States of America you have been desired to make known to the federal government the deep interest with which our august master was observing the development of a crisis which puts in question the prosperity and even the existence of the Union.

The Emperor profoundly regrets to see that the hope of a peaceful solution is not realized, and that American citizens, already in arms against each other, are ready to let loose upon their country the most formidable of the scourges of political society—a civil war.

For the more than eighty years that it has existed the American Union owes its independence, its towering rise, and its progress to the concord of its members, consecrated, under the auspices of its illustrious founder, by institutions which have been able to reconcile union with liberty. This union has been fruitful. It has exhibited to the world the spectacle of a prosperity without example in the annals of history.

It would be deplorable that, after so conclusive an experience, the United States should be hurried into a breach of the solemn compact which, up to this time, has made their power.

In spite of the diversity of their constitutions and of their interests, and perhaps, even, *because* of this diversity, Providence seems to urge them to draw closer the traditional bond which is the basis and the very condition of their political existence. In any event, the sacrifices which they might impose upon themselves to maintain it are beyond comparison with those which dissolution would bring after it. United, they perfect themselves; isolated, they are paralyzed.

The struggle which unhappily has just arisen can neither be indefinitely prolonged nor lead to the total destruction of one of the parties. Sooner or later it will be necessary to come to some settlement, whatsoever it may be, which may cause the divergent interests now actually in conflict to coexist. The American nation would then give a proof of high political wisdom in seeking in common such a settlement before a useless effusion of blood, a barren squandering of strength and of public riches, and acts of violence and reciprocal reprisals shall have come to deepen an abyss between the two parties to the confederation, to end definitively in their mutual exhaustion, and in the ruin, perhaps irreparable, of their commercial and political power.

Our august master cannot resign himself to admit such deplorable anticipations. His Imperial Majesty still places his confidence in that practical good sense of the citizens of the Union who appreciate so judiciously their true interests. His Majesty is happy to believe that the members of the federal government and the influential men of the two parties will seize all occasions and will unite all their efforts to calm the effervescence of the passions. There are no interests so divergent that it may not be possible to reconcile them by laboring to that end with zeal and perseverance in a spirit of justice and moderation.

If, within the limits of your friendly relations, your language and your councils may contribute to this result, you will respond, sir, to the intentions of his Majesty the Emperor in devoting to this the personal influence which you may have been able to acquire during your long residence at Washington, and the consideration which belongs to your character as the representative of a sovereign animated by the most friendly sentiments towards the American Union. This Union is not simply, in our eyes, an element essential to the universal *political* equilibrium. It constitutes, besides, a nation to which our august master and all Russia have pledged the most friendly interest; for the two countries, placed at the extremities of the two worlds, both in the ascending period of their development, appear called to a natural community of interests and of sympathies, of which they have already given mutual proofs to each other.

I do not wish here to approach any of the questions which divide the United States. We are not called upon to express ourselves in this contest. The preceding considerations have no other object than to attest the lively solicitude of the Emperor in presence of the dangers which menace the American Union, and the sincere wishes which his Majesty entertains for the maintenance of that great work, so laboriously raised, which appeared so rich in its future.

It is in this sense, sir, that I desire you to express yourself, as well to the members of the general government as to influential persons whom you may meet, giving them the assurance that in every event the American nation may count upon the most cordial sympathy on the part of our august master during the important crisis which it is passing through at present.

Receive, sir, the expression of my very distinguished consideration.

GORTCHACOW.

Mr. DE STOECKL, &c., &c., &c.

Mr. Seward to Mr. De Stoeckl.

DEPARTMENT OF STATE,
Washington, September 7, 1861.

The Secretary of State of the United States is authorized by the President to express to Mr. De Stoeckl, envoy extraordinary and minister plenipotentiary of his Majesty the Emperor of Russia, his profound sense of the liberal, friendly, and magnanimous sentiments of his Majesty on the subject of the internal differences which for a time have seemed to threaten the American Union, as they are communicated in the instruction from Prince Gortchacow, and by him read, by his Majesty's direction, to the President of the United States and Secretary of State. Mr. De Stoeckl will express to his government the satisfaction with which the President regards this new guarantee of a friendship between the two countries, which had its beginning with the national existence of the United States.

The Secretary of State offers to Mr. De Stoeckl renewed assurances of his high consideration.

WILLIAM H. SEWARD.

Mr. EDWARD DE STOECKL, &c., &c., &c.

DENMARK.

No. 2.]

DEPARTMENT OF STATE,
Washington, May 1, 1861.

SIR: The one subject in all our foreign relations which most anxiously engages the President's attention is the possible action of other nations in regard to the domestic controversy which is raging within our own borders.

Parties long ago found it their apparent interest to appeal to local interests and prejudices, and they have persevered in that policy so far and with such effect that masses large enough to control the action of the State authorities have at last come to prefer disorganization and disunion, rather than to acquiesce in the will of the majority expressed in conformity with the provisions of the organic law.

To a well-balanced mind it seems very strange that a citizen, ever without the excuse of intolerable oppression, passes the first stage of sedition, for it is at that very stage that the malcontent finds himself obliged to seek aid from aliens to defeat the equal laws and overthrow the beneficent institutions of his own country. Sedition in the United States is not merely unreasonable, it is altogether absurd. Human ingenuity has never yet devised, nor can it devise, a form of government in which the individual citizen can retain so large a portion of the natural rights of man, and at the same time receive so ample a protection against the dangers which so often threaten the safety and even the existence of nations. Nevertheless, an insurrection has broken out here; a pretended government has been constituted under the name of the Confederate States of America, and that government now has its agents abroad seeking to obtain a recognition of its sovereignty and independence.

It is hardly to be supposed that these agents will visit the capital of Denmark. They will seek the favor of powers supposed to be more capricious or more ambitious. Nevertheless political action even of the more commanding or more active States is influenced by a general opinion that is formed imperceptibly in all parts of the Eastern continent. Every representative of the United States in Europe has, therefore, a responsibility to see that no effort on his part is wanting to make that opinion just, so far as the true position of affairs in his own country is concerned.

It cannot be necessary to discuss at large the merits of the unhappy controversy. It is sufficient to speak of its nature and its probable result. The insurrection strikes at the heart of the nation. The country, so long accustomed to profound tranquillity and universal loyalty, was slow to believe that a parricidal purpose could be contemplated where it felt satisfied there was no just cause for serious discontent. Our government is at once a purely representative and simply federal one.

While the insurrection was gathering, the administration was practically paralyzed by the presence, in a very large proportion, of the plotters and abettors of the movement, in what, in Europe, would be called the ministry, in the legislative, in the army, in the navy, in the customs, in the post office, in the diplomatic and consular representations abroad.

Seventy years of almost unbroken peace had brought agriculture, mining, manufactures, and trade to the highest possible state of activity, and the people shrunk intuitively from a change of that peaceful activity, for not merely war, but needless and ruinous civil war, which even threatens to take on the revolting character of servile war.

The insurgents skilfully availed themselves of these doubts and fears, and by a course of affected moderation increased them. It seemed as if the nation would fall into ruins without even putting forth an effort to preserve its integrity. You could not, therefore, have been surprised at finding on your arrival in Europe that the same impression had obtained there, and that the Union of these States was assumed, in European circles, to be practically at an end. For a time loyal citizens occupied themselves with trying how, by compromise, to avert a civil war, rather than to accept as inevitable an event so unnatural and so fearful.

The crisis, however, came at last, a few days after your departure from the country. The insurgents, with the force gathered through immense preparations around a fortress in their own locality, opened a terrible fire upon it, to prevent the handful of men, which constituted the garrison, from receiving supplies when on the verge of famine, and continued the cannonade, though the barracks were in flames, and the brave men, thus imperilled, were obliged to abandon defence against assault to save themselves from destruction in another form. The defending force consented to a capitulation dishonorable only to their assailants.

This last and most violent pressure reached at once the very centre where the elastic force of the national spirit lay concealed. The government accepted the issue of civil war, and sent forth its appeal to the patriotism of the people. Never in any age or country was such an appeal responded to with so much promptness, enthusiasm, and resolution; and certainly never did any nation disclose and offer up at once such exhaustless resources for its self-preservation.

The revolution already is upon the recoil. Its failure is certain. All that remains is to see what shall be the measure of the disasters and calamities, affecting chiefly the insurgents themselves, which are to be endured before they consent to a restoration of peace, and to guarantee the inviolability of the Union.

Friendly nations may for a little time, perhaps, suffer some inconvenience from the blockade of the ports of the insurgent States, which this government has found it necessary to set on foot, as they will justly take alarm at the announcement that the revolutionary party have proclaimed their purpose to employ privateers to prey upon the commerce of the country. But the embarrassments attending the first measure will be mitigated by the strictness and efficiency with which it will be enforced, and it will not be maintained a day longer than is necessary. Our naval arm is already strong, and it will promptly be made stronger, so that the other evil will be, as we trust, effectually prevented.   *   *   *   *   *

I am, sir, your obedient servant,

WILLIAM H. SEWARD.

BRADFORD R. WOOD, Esq., &c., &c., &c.

Mr. Seward to Mr. Wood.

No. 3.]
DEPARTMENT OF STATE,
Washington, May 6, 1861.

SIR: Herewith I transmit a copy of a despatch of the 24th ultimo, which has been addressed to the several ministers of the United States accredited to the maritime powers whose plenipotentiaries composed the congress at Paris of the 16th of April, 1856, calling their attention to the importance of endeavoring to negotiate with those powers conventions upon the subject of the rights of belligerents and neutrals in time of war. The government of Denmark was not represented in the Paris congress; but the negotiation of a similar convention with that government is considered desirable, and you will therefore be governed by the instruction of which I enclose a transcript, and endeavor to effect that object. With this view I herewith send you a full power and a draft of the proposed convention.

I am, sir, your obedient servant,
WILLIAM H. SEWARD.

BRADFORD R. WOOD, Esq., &c., &c., &c., *Copenhagen.*

Mr. Wood to Mr. Seward.

No. 2.]
LEGATION OF THE UNITED STATES,
Copenhagen, July 11, 1861.

SIR: I have the honor to inform the department that, immediately on the return of Mr. Hall, the minister of foreign affairs, from Jutland, and by his request, I met him on the 10th instant. His reception was frank and cordial, and while he alluded to the opinions held by my predecessor as different from mine, he expressed himself decidedly in favor of the administration and against the so-called confederates. He also informed me that the King would not return to Copenhagen before the last of this month or the beginning of next.

I have the honor to remain your obedient servant,
BRADFORD R. WOOD.

Hon. WILLIAM H. SEWARD,
Secretary of State.

Mr. Wood to Mr. Seward.

No. 4.]
LEGATION OF THE UNITED STATES,
Copenhagen, July 19, 1861.

SIR: I have the honor to inform the department that, in an interview yesterday with the president of the council and minister of state, Mr. Hall, he readily acceded to the doctrine of the Paris convention in regard to privateering, though reluctant, in the present state of European affairs, to adopt the position of your predecessor, Mr. Marcy. He mentioned the fact that a

Danish man-of-war had been sent to the West Indies for the purpose of preventing privateering and preserving the neutrality of Denmark.

The King is still absent, in Jutland, and my reception as the representative of my government by the minister of state, without the formality of a presentation to the King, should be considered a compliment to that government.

I have the honor to remain your obedient servant,

BRADFORD R. WOOD.

Hon. WILLIAM H. SEWARD,
    Secretary of State.

Mr. Seward to Mr. Wood.

No. 6.]   DEPARTMENT OF STATE,
                                        Washington, August 1, 1861.

SIR: Your despatch of the 11th of July last has been received, and the President instructs me to say that the explanation of the views of the Danish government given to you by Mr. Hall, the minister for foreign affairs, is very satisfactory.

I am, sir, your obedient servant,

WILLIAM H. SEWARD.

BRADFORD R. WOOD, Esq., &c., &c., &c., *Copenhagen.*

Mr. Seward to Mr. Wood.

No. 8.]   DEPARTMENT OF STATE,
                                        Washington, August 22, 1861.

SIR: Your despatches to No. 5, of the 26th ultimo, have been received.

From your No. 4 I learn, with much satisfaction, that the Danish government adopts and practices the declaration of the congress of Paris, and I trust that nothing is likely to occur to produce any inconvenience affecting the commerce with Denmark, a power with which we have every desire to cultivate the most intimate relations.

Your admission by the minister to the duties of your mission under the circumstances of the absence of his Majesty is accepted by us as a proof of the friendly feelings of the government, deserving of especial acknowledgment.

The information given in your No. 5, on the subject of the purchase in Europe of clothing and arms for the United States, has been communicated to the Secretary of War.

I am, sir, your obedient servant,

WILLIAM H. SEWARD.

BRADFORD R. WOOD, Esq., &c., &c., &c., *Copenhagen.*

Mr. Seward to Mr. Wood.

No. 9.]

DEPARTMENT OF STATE,
Washington, September 5, 1861.

SIR: Your despatch of August 15 (No. 9) has been received.

The affair of the place of deposit for papers of Danish vessels, to which you direct my attention, has been already settled in a manner which will, I am sure, be entirely satisfactory to the government of Denmark.

I can well understand the depression you experienced on hearing of the reverse of our arms at Bull Run, and the unfavorable comments on our course which this misfortune elicits in Europe. There is, however, no occasion for apprehension of an unfavorable issue of the present civil contest.

Whatever speculations on the subject may be made at home or abroad, you may be assured that it is not in our day that treason is to prevail against the government in our country, based as it is on the rights of man and his capacity for self-government.

I am, sir, your obedient servant,

WILLIAM H. SEWARD.

BRADFORD R. WOOD, Esq., &c., &c., &c., *Copenhagen.*

ITALY.

Mr. Seward to Mr. Marsh.

[Extracts.]

No. 3.]

DEPARTMENT OF STATE,
Washington, May 9, 1861.

SIR: I know that you will be welcome at Turin. Count Cavour, a true exponent of the sentiments of a generous sovereign, will be rejoiced to receive from this country a minister who will not manifest repugnance to the aspirations of the Italian people for liberty and unity. The government of the United States practices non-intervention in all other countries and in the controversies between them. You are at liberty, however, and, indeed, are especially charged, to assure his Majesty that he is held in high consideration by the President and the people of the United States. You will further assure him that it is a source of sincere satisfaction to this government that Italy seems to be even more prosperous and happy now under his government, although enjoying only short respites from revolutionary struggles for independence, than it has been at many periods long gone by, when despotism shielded that classic region from turbulence and civil commotion.

You will learn from observation that government, even when its counsels are inspired by patriotism and humanity, has its trials and embarrassments as well in Italy as elsewhere. How to save the country from the ambitious designs of dangerous neighbors on either hand—how to reconcile the national passion for freedom with the profound national veneration for ecclesiastical authority—how to harmonize the lassitude of society in the Mediterranean provinces with the vigor that prevails along the Appenines, and how to conduct affairs with so much moderation as to win the confidence of the conservative interests, and yet not to lose the necessary support of the propagandists of freedom, are tasks witnessed there which will convince the American statesman that even in that country the establishment and maintenance of free government are attended with difficulties as formidable as those which sometimes produce political despondency in our own.

* * * * * * * * *
* * * * * * * * *

Since the inauguration of the President it has been my duty to prepare, under his directions, instructions to many of our ministers going abroad. The burden of them all has been, not the ordinary incidents of international hospitality and commerce, which reduce diplomacy to a monotonous routine, but the extraordinary and sometimes alarming condition of our own internal affairs, threatened with the complication, most of all to be deprecated, of intervention, in some form or other, by European nations.

This foreign danger arose chiefly out of the deplorable condition of affairs at home. The administration found the government disorganized by the presence of disunionists of high position and authority in all its departments. Some time was necessary to eliminate them before any decisive policy could be adopted. It was, moreover, necessary to forbear from demonstrations of federal authority that might be represented as aggressive, to allow the revolution to reveal its alarming proportions and boldly proclaim its desperate and destructive designs.

It was seen all the time that these needful delays were liable to be misunderstood abroad, and that the malcontents would endeavor to take advantage of them there. The government has, therefore, not been surprised, although it has been deeply grieved, to see the agents of the revolutionary party, perhaps even with the concurrence of some of our own demoralized ministers in Europe, insidiously seeking to obtain from some of its sovereigns a recognition of the projected treasonable confederacy.

It has been no easy task to study the sophisms, arts, and appliances which they might be expected to use in the highly commercial circles of Belgium, Paris, and London. It was nevertheless necessary to attempt it, for human nature is at least no more moral, just, or virtuous in courts than it is in private life. There is no such embarrassment, however, in the present case. It often happens that foreign observers, if candid, understand American questions quite as well as Americans themselves. Botta and De Tocqueville were of this class.

So Count Cavour cannot be at any loss to understand the present political condition of the United States.

The American revolution of 1776, with its benignant results, was due to the happy combination of three effective political ideas: First, that of emancipation from the distant European control of Great Britain; second, popular desire for an enlargement of the political rights of the individual members of the State upon the acknowledged theory of the natural rights of man; third, the want of union among the States to secure safety, tranquillity, aggrandizement, and fame.

The revolution attempted in 1861 is a spasmodic reaction against the revolution of 1776. It combines the three ideas which were put down, but not extinguished, in that great war, namely: First, European authority to regulate political affairs on this continent; second, the aggrandizement and extension of human slavery; third, disunion, dissolution, anarchy.

Any impartial thinker can see that an attempt at a revolution so unnatural and perverse as this could never have been embraced by any portion of the American people, except in a moment of frenzied partisan disappointment; that it has no one element of success at home, and that it is even more portentous to all other governments than to our own. It is painful to see faction stalking abroad in one's native land. But faction is incident to every state, because it is inherent in human nature. We prefer, if it must come, that it come in just its present form and character. It will perish by simply coming to confront the American people, for the first time brought to meet that enemy of national peace and safety in arms. The people are aroused, awakened, resolute, and determined. The danger is, therefore, already passed. We no longer fear—indeed, we hardly deprecate—the disaster of civil war brought upon us without fault. We now see that it may be regarded as a necessary trial to preserve the perfection of our Constitution, and to remove all remaining distrust of its durability and its adaptation to the universal wants of mankind.

I am, sir, your most obedient servant,

WILLIAM H. SEWARD.

George P. Marsh, Esq., &c., &c., Turin.

Mr. Seward to Mr. Marsh.

No. 5.]   DEPARTMENT OF STATE,
                                          Washington, June 21, 1861.

SIR: Your despatch No. 2, written at Paris May 29, has been received.

The government not only accepts your explanation of the delay you have made on your way to your post of duty, but also appreciates and thanks you for the faithful service you have rendered to the country in an important crisis by your labors to correct an erroneous public opinion in Europe through the use of the press in London.

We hear with sincere regret and sorrow of the death of Count Cavour, a statesman honored none the less by the people of this country because the theatre of his labors is remote from our own. If it shall seem proper to you, you may express these sentiments to his Majesty.

I am, sir, your obedient servant,

                                          WILLIAM H. SEWARD.

GEORGE P. MARSH, Esq., &c., &c., &c., *Turin.*

Mr. Dillon to Mr. Seward.

[Extracts.]

                                          UNITED STATES LEGATION,
                                          Turin, June 10, 1861.

SIR: Since my communication of the 16th of April last, to announce my arrival here the 12th of that month, from my late post, Rio de Janeiro, and of my having entered upon the discharge of my duties as *chargé d'affaires ad interim*, the event first in order of importance, though not of time, which it is my painful duty to communicate, is the sudden death, on the 6th instant, of his excellency the Count Camillo Benso de Cavour, late president of his Majesty's council and minister of foreign affairs. The count was taken ill on the evening of the 29th of May last at his residence, the hotel of his elder brother, the Marquis de Cavour, of what proved to be typhus fever. Injudicious and repeated bleedings at the commencement of the fever, though, I am told, at his own instance, hastened the sad event.

The count was never married.

Europe still echoes with eulogies to his memory. Among the most felicitous and important, as expressing at the same time a political programme, is a leading article in the *Constitutionnel* of Paris, semi-official, and supposed to emanate from the Emperor of the French. I extract a single sentence: "S'il y a aujourd' lui dans la péninsule un grand homme de moins il y a, grâce à Dieu, un grand peuple de plus. *Et ce peuple affranchi ne saurait desormais retomber dans la servitude.*" In common with my colleagues, of the diplomatic corps, I attended the funeral obsequies in the parish church of the Madonna degli Angeli the evening of the 7th instant, and the following morning the remains were transferred to the burial vault of the Cavour family, at Santena, some six miles distant from Turin, there to remain—thus contradicting the reports of the public prints that, in compliance with the King's wish, they were to be entombed in the royal basilica of the Superga.

> " Exegi monumentum ære perennius,
> Regalique situ pyramidum altius."
> ♀   ♀   ♀   ♀   ♀

Shortly after my arrival, in consequence of the warlike disturbances at home, the applications, written and verbal, by disbanded officers and men of the late Garibaldian army of Southern Italy, for enlistment into the United States army, became so numerous that I would call attention to a card, of which I annex a copy, published at my request by his Majesty's government in the official paper.

*　　　*　　　*　　　*　　　*　　　*

The President's proclamations of the 19th and 27th of April last, received at this legation, with the circular from the department, were by me duly communicated to his Majesty's government, and printed in extenso in the *Gazetta Officiale del Regno d'Italia* the 29th of May, 1861.

*　　　*　　　*　　　*　　　*　　　*

His Majesty has summoned the Baron Ricasoli, a very prominent conservative member of the chamber of deputies, from Florence, to form a new ministry, which, though not yet announced, will, it is thought, be soon completed, in continuation of the Cavour policy.

Mr. Marsh has arrived at Turin.

I am, sir, your obedient servant,

ROMAINE DILLON.

Hon. WILLIAM H. SEWARD,
　　Secretary of State, Washington.

CARD.

UNITED STATES LEGATION,
Turin, May 17, 1861.

In reply to numerous and continued applications to this legation, by letter and in person, of foreign volunteers for enlistment in the army of the United States of America, the undersigned takes this public means of declaring that he has no knowledge, official or non-official, of any instructions of his government authorizing any such enlistments out of the United States.

ROMAINE DILLON,
Chargé d'Affaires, &c.

Mr. Marsh to Mr. Seward.

[Extracts.]

No. 3.]　　　　　　　LEGATION OF THE UNITED STATES,
Turin, June 27, 1861.

SIR: The interruption of business in the foreign office of this government, occasioned by the illness and death of Count Cavour and a week's absence of the King, which immediately followed the formation of the new ministry, prevented me from obtaining an audience of his Majesty for the purpose of delivering my letters of credence until Sunday, the 23d day of this month.

On that day I was received by the King, and, in accordance with my instructions, conveyed to him assurances of the high consideration in which he is held by the President and people of the United States, and of their satisfaction in observing the apparent prosperity and happiness of Italy under his Majesty's government. I further expressed the personal gratification I had derived from being selected to represent the United States near the government of the Italian people—a people which I had long known, and which had always inspired me with deep interest—and especially from the honor of being the first diplomate accredited to the first King of Italy.

His Majesty received these remarks very graciously, using some terms personally complimentary to me, testified much respect for the President and for yourself, and expressed a strong interest in the welfare and prosperity of the United States, as well as much solicitude for an honorable termination of the present contest between the government and the seceding States.

The audience was strictly private, no person but his Majesty and myself being present, and the interview was therefore of a less formal character than is usual with royal receptions. It is, perhaps, proper to add that the communication was conducted in French, which is the usual language of oral intercourse between foreign ministers and the sovereign or the heads of departments at this court.

With Baron Ricasoli, the new head of the ministry and minister of foreign affairs, I have had several interviews, as well before as since my reception by the King, and I therefore am not aware that the public interests have sustained any detriment by the delay of my official reception. In all these interviews American politics have formed a leading topic of conversation, and, though Baron Ricasoli speaks with proper caution, the tenor of his remarks leaves no room for doubt that his personal sympathies, as well as those of his government, are entirely on the side of the President and the constituted authorities of the Union in their great struggle.

The first point which I brought to the notice of the minister of foreign affairs was the prevention of movements hostile to the United States in the territories of the King of Italy. I stated that I had been led to fear that some attempts were making at Genoa to fit out vessels or purchase arms for the service of the rebels, and begged that the attention of the local authorities at Genoa might be drawn to the subject. Baron Ricasoli replied that the government would not knowingly permit any such purchases to be made, and that he would request the minister of the interior to direct that the police of Genoa should be watchful to detect and prevent any negotiations for that purpose.

The suggestions I made to Baron Ricasoli on this subject were founded partly on a letter from Mr. H. S. Sanford and partly on vague rumors circulating here, which I have been unable to trace to any certain foundation, though I have made inquiry in all quarters known to me which seemed to be probable sources of information. In the course of the last week I employed an Italian gentleman, then about to proceed to Genoa, and whom I believe to be entirely trustworthy, to investigate the subject on the spot. He is still absent, and as he has not written to me since arrivng at Genoa I infer that he has made no discoveries.

I have communicated to Baron Ricasoli the substance of my instructions with regard to the proposed convention for the suppression of privateering and the exemption of private property from capture by national ships of war in certain cases. He replied that the Italian government had not yet become a party to the convention of 1856, and added that the pressure of business on his department would prevent his giving immediate attention to the subject ; but he expressed no objection to a negotiation on the basis proposed in your instructions of the 24th of April, 1861, or even on the broader ground of the total exemption of all private property not contraband of war from capture at sea by ships of war in all cases.

The Italian parliament is now in session, and will probably not adjourn before the 15th or 20th of July. The cabinet ministers are members, as in England, and regularly attend the sessions, which occupy a large part of the day. Many important topics are under discussion in parliament, and still more weighty questions of domestic and foreign policy are making large demands on the time and absorbing the thoughts of the administration. It is, therefore, not probable, as Baron Ricasoli intimated, that he will be able to consider the subject of the convention until the adjournment of the national legislature shall leave him more at leisure. In the meantime the negotiations with the English and French governments on the same subject will probably be brought to a close, and the final decision of the Italian government will be much influenced by that of England and France.

The death of Count Cavour, after an illness of a week's duration, and which, for the first few days, was not of a threatening character, was a great shock to the friends of constitutional liberty and progress, and an occasion of much ill-suppressed exultation among the advocates of temporal and spiritual despotism throughout Europe, and especially in Italy. To me, personally, it is a source of profound regret, both for less selfish reasons and because I had special grounds for expecting, more from his often expressed high regard for the President and yourself than from any other cause, agreeable private and official relations with this great statesman.

The successor of Count Cavour—and I may apply the same remark to most if not all of the members of the cabinet—is a man of a high order of talent, of great devotion to the interests of his country, of the same general doctrines of national policy as his predecessor, and of sincere attachment to the principles of civil and religious liberty. The remarkable unanimity with which the new cabinet is sustained by the parliament is a favorable omen, so far as respects the domestic success of the government; and there is some reason to think that the death of a prime minister, who was regarded with so much personal ill will by the reactionary party in Italy and elsewhere in Europe, may tend to diminish the asperity with which his policy has been hitherto opposed by that party.

*   *   *   *   *   *

I am, sir, respectfully yours,

GEO. P. MARSH.

Hon. WILLIAM H. SEWARD,
　　　Secretary of State.

Mr. Marsh to Mr. Seward.

[Extracts.]

No. 5.]   LEGATION OF THE UNITED STATES,
　　　　　　　　　　　　　　　　　　　　　　　　　　　　Turin, July 6, 1861.

SIR: Having heard a report that Mr. Patterson, consul of the United States at Genoa, expects a commission from the Southern Confederacy to act as consul of the rebel States at that port, I called on Baron Ricasoli yesterday morning, and protested against the recognition of Mr. Patterson, or of any other person, as a consular agent of the confederacy.

Baron Ricasoli assured me that, under present circumstances, at least, no such agent would be recognized at any Italian port, and he took occasion to repeat, in strong language, the expression of his own warm sympathy with the federal government of the United States, and his earnest hope that the present contest between the government and the seceding States would end in the re-establishment of the lawful authority of the Union, and be settled on terms which would secure the triumph of the principles of freedom, and the ultimate extinction of human slavery. He added that, in these expressions he was speaking the sentiments of his Majesty and of the entire government of which he was a member.

I then referred to apprehensions which had been expressed in America of the fitting out of privateers in remote Italian ports under the confederate flag. He replied that the government officers would endeavor to prevent such violations of the laws, but that it would be difficult to exercise a vigilant supervision over all the remote and unfrequented ports of the peninsula and islands, and he advised the appointment of American consuls at points favorable for observation along the coasts, as a good means of detecting and preventing such movements.

I had, on the same day, an audience of the Prince of Carignano, who expressed opinions and feelings similar to those of Baron Ricasoli with respect to our present national difficulties, and I may add that every member of the government, and almost every gentleman in public life, with whom I have conversed at Turin, coincides in these sentiments.

    *   *   *   *   *   *   *   *   *

    *   *   *   *   *   *   *   *   *

The favorable sentiments with which the present administration of the federal government is regarded by most continental statesmen, are founded (independently of the high personal regard felt for the President and his constitutional advisers) partly on the opinion that it is sustaining the cause of constitutional authority, of the entirety of nationalities and of established order against causeless rebellion, violent disruption of a commonwealth essentially a unit, and disorganizing and lawless misrule; but still more, I think, on the belief that the struggle in which it is now involved is virtually a contest between the propagandists of domestic slavery and the advocates of emancipation and universal freedom. If the civil war be protracted, I am convinced that our hold upon the sympathy and good will of the governments, and still more of the people of Europe, will depend upon the distinctness with which this issue is kept before them, and if it were now proposed by the federal government to purchase the submission of the south by any concession to their demands on this subject, or by assuming any attitude but that of, at least, moral hostility to slavery, I have no doubt that the dissolution of the Union would be both desired and promoted by a vast majority of those who now hope for its perpetuation.

    *   *   *   *   *   *   *   *   *

I am, sir, respectfully yours,

GEORGE P. MARSH.

Hon. WILLIAM H. SEWARD, *Secretary of State.*

Mr. Seward to Mr. Marsh.

No. 8.]
DEPARTMENT OF STATE,
Washington, July 23, 1861.

SIR: Your despatch of June 27, No. 3, has been received. The account it gives us of your reception and of the sentiments and feelings of the Italian government in regard to the United States is very satisfactory to the President. We are pleased with your prompt and vigilant attention to the matters affecting the public interest, especially the supposed project of fitting out hostile armaments at Genoa.

Renewing my best wishes for the prosperity of Italy under the new ministry so happily inaugurated, I am, sir, your obedient servant,

WILLIAM H. SEWARD.

GEORGE P. MARSH, Esq., &c., &c., &c., *Turin.*

Mr. Seward to Mr. Marsh.

[Extracts.]

No. 11.]   DEPARTMENT OF STATE,
                               Washington, July 30, 1861.

SIR: *   *   *   *   *   *   *   *   *
You will express to Baron Ricasoli the high appreciation which this government entertains of his decision in regard to our affairs.

    *   *   *   *   *   *   *   *

You will be pained by the intelligence of a reverse of our arms near Manassas Junction, and I fear it will, for a time, operate to excite apprehensions and encourage the enemies of the Union in Europe; but the blow has already spent its force here without producing any other effect than renewed resolution and confidence in the success of the government. The lesson that war cannot be waged successfully without wisdom as well as patriotism has been received at a severe cost; but, perhaps, it was necessary. It is certain that we are improving upon it.

I am, sir, your obedient servant,

                                 WILLIAM H. SEWARD.

GEORGE P. MARSH, Esq., &c., &c., *Turin.*

Mr. Marsh to Mr. Seward.

No. 14.]   LEGATION OF THE UNITED STATES,
                               Turin, September 2, 1861.

SIR: I have the honor to enclose herewith a copy of a note addressed by me to Baron Ricasoli on the 26th ultimo, in relation to the proposed convention for the accession of the United States to the declaration of the congress of Paris in 1856.

By my instructions, under date of April 24, 1861, I am directed as follows: "To ascertain whether it (the government of his Majesty the King of Italy) is disposed to enter into negotiations for the accession of the United States to the declaration of the Paris congress, with the conditions annexed by that body to the same; and if you shall find the government so disposed, you will then enter into a convention to that effect, substantially in the form of a project for that purpose herewith transmitted to you."

The project transmitted with the instructions makes no mention of the important conditions referred to in the instructions, and therefore, in drawing up the note, I thought it best not to notice the conditions specifically, but to make the proposal in general terms, leaving that point to be arranged, if suggested by the Italian government, as I shall be instructed hereafter.

I have the honor to be, sir, with high respect, your obedient servant,

                                 GEORGE P. MARSH.

Hon. WILLIAM H. SEWARD,
        Secretary of State.

Mr. Marsh to Baron Ricasoli.

LEGATION OF THE UNITED STATES OF AMERICA,
Turin, August 26, 1861.

The undersigned, envoy extraordinary and minister plenipotentiary of the United States of America, as he had the honor to state in one of his first interviews with his excellency the minister of foreign affairs, is instructed to propose the negotiation of a convention between the government of the United States and the government of his Majesty the King of Italy for defining the rights of belligerents and neutrals in maritime warfare, in accordance with the principles adopted by the congress of Paris in the year 1856.

Similar instructions have been given by the President to the American ministers at the courts of the other maritime powers, and negotiations to that effect are now in progress with all the governments represented at the congress of Paris.

It will be remembered by his excellency the minister of foreign affairs that in the year 1854 the President of the United States submitted to the several maritime nations two propositions, to which he solicited their assent as permanent principles of international law.

These were :

1. Free ships make free goods—that is to say, that the effects or goods belonging to subjects or citizens of a power or state at war are free from capture or confiscation when found on board of neutral vessels, with the exception of articles contraband of war.

2. That the property of neutrals on board an enemy's vessel is not subject to confiscation, unless the same be contraband of war.

These propositions were favorably entertained by most of the governments to which they were submitted, but no formal convention for their recognition was negotiated between them and the United States.

The congress of Paris, at which most of the European powers were represented, adopted, upon the 16th of April, 1856, an agreement embracing substantially these principles, with two additional propositions; all of which were embodied in a declaration composed of four articles, namely:

1. Privateering is and remains abolished.

2. The neutral flag covers enemy's goods, with the exception of contraband of war.

3. Neutral goods, with the exception of contraband of war, are not liable to capture under enemy's flag.

4. Blockades, in order to be binding, must be effective—that is to say, maintained by a force sufficient really to prevent access to the coast of the enemy.

The congress further agreed to invite the maritime states not represented in that body to accede to these propositions, and the assent of the government of the United States was asked to them accordingly.

The then President of the United States, Franklin Pierce, did not accede to the stipulations of the convention, but proposed an amendment to the first article which should exempt the private property of individuals, though belonging to belligerent states, from seizure or confiscation by national vessels in maritime war; and the ministers of the United States at Paris and London were instructed to inform the governments to which they were accredited that the United States would accede to the four points above recited, provided the first of them should be amended to the effect proposed by the President.

Neither of these governments is understood to have objected to this amendment, but the negotiations were not prosecuted to a conclusion.

The President of the United States adheres to the opinion expressed by his predecessor, that it would be eminently desirable for the good of all nations that the property and effects of private individuals, not contraband, should be exempt from seizure and confiscation by national vessels in maritime war. But the proposal to that effect not having been accepted by the nations represented in the congress of 1856, he now offers to accede to the invitation of the powers, and to accept the declaration promulgated by it, deferring to a future occasion the further prosecution of negotiations for the general adoption of the amendment above specified.

The undersigned is invested with full powers to conclude, on the part of the President, a convention between the government of the United States and that of his Majesty the King of Italy for the adoption of the declaration of the congress of Paris, and begs leave to invite the attention of his excellency the minister of foreign affairs to the proposal.

The undersigned avails himself of this occasion to renew to his excellency the minister of foreign affairs the assurance of his most distinguished consideration.

GEORGE P. MARSH.

His Excellency Baron RICASOLI,
President of the Council and Minister of Foreign Affairs.

Mr. Seward to Mr. Marsh.

No. 18.]

DEPARTMENT OF STATE,

Washington, September 20, 1861.

SIR: Your despatch of August 26th, No. 12, has been received.

I send you, in confidence, a copy of my latest instructions to Mr. Adams and Mr. Dayton, from which you will learn that the negotiations with Great Britain and France for an accession to the declaration of the congress at Paris have been suspended, and the causes of the suspension.

We are desirous to act in good faith, and to acquit ourselves of all responsibility for the failure of negotiations with enlightened powers for the advancement of the interests of peace and humanity; and yet we are at the same time resolved to maintain the independent position and the dignity of our government. We therefore hold ourselves ready to perfect a convention with the government of Italy for our accession; and at the same time you will not urge the proposition against any disinclination which that government may express or intimate.

We shall be the friend of Italy; and Italy, we are sure, cannot be otherwise than friendly to us, no matter what treaty relations exist or fail to be made.

I am, sir, your obedient servant,

WILLIAM H. SEWARD.

GEORGE P. MARSH, Esq., &c., &c., *Turin.*

Mr. Seward to Mr. Marsh.

No. 32.]

DEPARTMENT OF STATE,
Washington, November 22, 1861.

SIR: I have your despatch of October 29, (No. 29.)

The British and French governments, which stand at the head of the maritime powers, having declined our adhesion to the declaration of Paris without conditions which the United States cannot yield, there is no important object to be attained by pressing the same upon other powers. You will therefore let the matter rest in Italy for the present.

I think that when at no distant day it shall need to be renewed, the interest that shall move it forward will appear first on the other side of the Atlantic.

It is a matter of regret that we cannot consistently offer special inducements to military gentlemen in Italy who are unable to defray their own expenses in coming. to join our armies; but we are forbidden to do so by urgent considerations. First, we do not need to solicit foreign aid, and we naturally desire to avoid the appearance of doing so. Secondly, we wish to abstain from intrusion into the domestic concerns of foreign states, and, of course, from seeming to do so. Thirdly, our own countrymen are coming forward with just claims upon all positions requiring skill in the art of war, and we must avoid jealousies between native and foreign defenders of the Union. Already the forces in the field exceed half a million, and the officers charged with organizing them report to us that those recently recruited will swell the number to seven hundred thousand. If the insurrection should continue, it will be more difficult to keep them down to a million than to lift them up to that figure. Still, we do not yet revoke what we have thus far said, and we will receive from Europe those who may come.

A consul will be appointed for Ancona.

I am, sir, your obedient servant,

WILLIAM H. SEWARD.

GEORGE P. MARSH, Esq., &c., &c., *Turin.*

SWITZERLAND.

Mr. Seward to Mr. Fogg.

No. 2.]   DEPARTMENT OF STATE,
Washington, May 15, 1861.

SIR: I have delayed giving you the President's instructions so long because I was preoccupied. For the first time in our history the standard of civil war has been raised with the purpose of overthrowing the federal republic. It is a cardinal point with the seditions in modern revolutions to gain aid, or at least sympathy, in foreign countries. That sympathy is sought in the form of recognition of the simulated sovereignty set up by faction. An act of recognition carries moral weight, and material aid is expected soon to follow it. No state ought to lend its support to revolution in a foreign country except upon motives of justice and humanity. But in point of fact these motives seldom prevail, and nations generally act in such cases upon calculations of profit or ambition, or in the wantonness of mere caprice. It is well understood here that the revolutionary faction has its agents abroad, soliciting European powers to intervene in this unhappy civil war. It has therefore been my duty, under the President's authority, to instruct our representatives there how to meet them and counteract their designs. I could easily imagine that either Great Britain, France, Russia, Austria, Prussia, Belgium, Spain, or even Denmark, might suppose that it could acquire some advantage, or at least some satisfaction to itself, from a change that should abridge the dominion, the commerce, the prosperity, or influence of the United States. Each of them might be believed to have envious sentiments towards us, which would delight in an opportunity to do us harm. I have therefore first addressed myself to the consideration of our relations with those countries. It is otherwise with Italy and Switzerland. The former is yet hotly engaged in the struggle to secure freedom and unity, and the latter enviably distinguished by the rare enjoyment of both. Human nature must lose not only the faculty of reason which lifts it above the inferior beings, but also the benevolence which lifts it up to commune with superior orders of existence, when the security, welfare, and happiness of the United States shall have become even a matter of indifference to Italy or Switzerland. I salute Switzerland last among the European nations only because we esteem and confide in her most.

You will say this, or anything else that may occur to you that would more pleasantly or more effectually assure the government of Switzerland of the cordial good wishes cherished for it by the President and the people of the United States.

You will, of course, need to say nothing to the government on the subject of the domestic difficulties to which I have already adverted. You will, nevertheless, not be absolutely free from all responsibility on this head. You are in a region where men of inquiring mind and active habit seek a temporary respite from severe studies and exhausting labors. The world's affairs are discussed freely, and the sentiments and opinions which influence the conduct and affect the prospects of nations are very often formed in the mountains and dells of Switzerland. You will meet there, if no others, many of our own fellow-citizens, doubtlessly of both classes—the disloyal, sometimes, as well as those who are loyal to the Constitution and the Union. Improve the calmness and candor which the contemplation of nature inspires to dissuade the discontented American from his unnatural course and pernicious convictions, and to excite the loyal to return home as speedily as possible to speak, to vote, and, if need be, to enrol himself as a soldier or a sailor in the land or naval forces for the defence of his country, of freedom, and of mankind.

Seventy years of tranquillity and harmony, unparalleled in the experience of states, have made us misunderstand the stage in our national career at which we have arrived. We had to prove, by demonstration in war, that these institutions are adapted to defence against aggression, and even for aggrandizement of empire. The proof was given, and the world has nobly confessed the truth established.

We assumed that faction could not gain consistency and make head under institutions so free, so equal, so just, and so beneficent. This was a mistake less in regard to our institutions than in regard to human nature itself. But self-complacent, and consequently self-deceived, we have come all of a sudden to meet the emergency of civil war, and we find ourselves obliged to demonstrate that our government is adapted to resist and overcome domestic faction. It is a momentous but necessary trial. Perhaps it has not come too soon. . Certainly we have no apprehension of failure. Revolutions are seldom successful, even when they have just causes. Revolution without a good cause, amounting to absolute necessity, is never possible in a country where stable government is at all known by experience of its blessings. The present attempt at revolution is based on no alleged experience of oppression. It puts forth only apprehensions of danger of oppression, which the form of the Constitution and the experience of its actual working proves to be altogether impossible. It is a revolution originating only in disappointed personal ambition. Personal ambition is the least effective of all the political agencies that can be found in an extended federal republic. The revolution aims at the life of the country. It gathers the support of only that small, though very active, class of persons who are so thoughtless as to be insensible to the importance of having a country to protect and defend, with benefit to themselves and their posterity. Against it are arrayed the larger portion of our people with whom love of country is the first and strongest of all the social passions—that holy sentiment which in mature life is the strongest passion of our common humanity.

Tell the Swiss republic, then, that with God's blessing we will preserve this model of federal republican government by which they have reformed their institutions, and we invoke them to retain their own with no less fidelity. So Switzerland and the United States shall in after ages be honored as the founders of the only true and beneficent system of human government—a system that harmonizes needful authority with the preservation of the natural rights of man. Every free citizen of Switzerland who comes here, so long as he remains, is practically a citizen of the United States. He goes in and out everywhere unchallenged. Nevertheless, the American citizen in Switzerland is a stranger, and the reiterated demand for his passport at every angle in his course reminds him painfully that he is suspected. His least elevated motive for going there is trade and commerce ; but the objects of most of our citizens in visiting Alpine countries are health and study of the more sublime and attractive features of nature and a fervent admiration for the free people who dwell among them. In the United States there is not one man base enough to do or wish an injury to the enlightened government or to the people of Switzerland. Why, then, should not the government of that country make us conscious of its confidence by allowing us the enjoyment of national hospitality while we are sojourning in their beautiful country?

Please bring this subject to the consideration of the authorities, and if you find them well disposed you will be authorized to conclude a convention with them on the subject.

We very much want a good history of the Swiss Confederacy since its reformation, especially showing how faction developes itself there, and how the government works in preventing or suppressing designs subversive of the federal unity of the republic The President hopes that you will furnish it, as he knows your ability for such a task.

Please also send to the department a copy of the fullest and best history of the Swiss Confederation, (perhaps Muller's.) It is desirable, not only with a view to accurate information upon the points just adverted to, but also with reference to the legislation and its causes of the respective members of the confederation with regard to the Israelites, a subject in relation to which your predecessor has had much correspondence with that government.

I am, sir, your obedient servant,

WILLIAM H. SEWARD.

George G. Fogg, Esq.,
&c., &c., &c., Berne.

Mr. Fay to Mr. Seward.

[Extract.]

No. 421.]

United States Legation,
Berne, May 18, 1861.

Sir:

    *   *   *   *   *   *   *   *

Referring to my No. 417, I communicated, in addition to the English printed copy of the inaugural of the President, a carefully made German translation. I have some reason to suppose that the commissioners of the seceded States were, or would soon be, in Paris, and as Mr. Dudley Mann was informally my predecessor in Berne, and has personal friends in the governmental regions, and might profit by the occasion to slip over from London or Paris, I had another interview on the subject this morning with President Knüsel. A very severe illness had kept me some time from seeing him. As I have received not a word from the department with regard to my recall, I have not communicated officially with the government upon the subject, but the President commenced, and I am unwilling to repeat his friendly remarks. He alluded, however, to the affair of Neuchâtel, and said I must not think the government had forgotten the services I had rendered to Switzerland, and particularly on that occasion. He repeated several times; but I will not dwell further upon this point.

I asked if they had any news of the commissioners of the seceded States, and said I thought they might perhaps pay Berne a visit. I then addressed to him some earnest words upon a subject in which my whole heart is interested. I told him my public and private intelligence convinced me that the movement of the south would be suppressed ; that it was as insane as it was guilty; that the slowly rising spirit of the north, and the calm and efficient preparations made by the President, would, in due time,

bring it to a termination; that the United States had always loved Switzerland, but that I did not expect from him any sentimental engagements.
I wished, however, officially to express the opinion of my government, and,
privately, my own deep conviction, that the wise course of Switzerland
would be a flat refusal to receive, in any way, the commissioners of the
revolted States; that a different course would be painfully remembered,
while a prompt action in this direction would surely draw much closer the
bonds of friendship between the two republics. I called his attention to
the proclamation of the British government, in which the seceded States
are termed the "so-called Confederate States."

The President warmly acquiesced, and assured me that he completely
shared my opinion.

    *   *   *   *   *   *   *   *   *

I have the honor to be, sir, with the highest consideration, your obedient
servant,

THEO. S. FAY.

Hon. WILLIAM H. SEWARD,
    Secretary of State of the United States of America.

Mr. Fay to Mr. Seward.

[Extract]

No. 426.]   UNITED STATES LEGATION,
                                      Berne, June 3, 1861.

SIR:

    *   *   *   *   *   *   *   *   *

Mr. Fogg has not yet arrived, although the telegraph announces that he
is in London. Everything is ready for him here.

A despatch for him has been received but not opened. Your circulars of
April 27 and of May 6 have been received. The copies of the proclamation have been communicated to the federal council.

    *   *   *   *   *   *   *   *   *

I have the honor to be, sir, with the highest consideration, your obedient
servant,

THEO. S. FAY.

Hon. WILLIAM H. SEWARD,
    Secretary of State of the United States of America.

Mr. Fay to Mr. Seward.

[Extract.]

No. 428.]   UNITED STATES LEGATION,
                                      Berne, June 7, 1861.

SIR: *   *   *   *   *   *   *   *
I had an earnest conversation with Mr. Frei Herosée on the subject of the
possibility of the reception of any southern agent. He is an old friend of Mr.
Dudley Mann. He is also one of the oldest and most influential members of
the federal council and founders of the government, and has been several

times President. He confirmed warmly all that President Knüsel had said, and in plainer terms. Switzerland, he said, had always opposed rebellion and revolution everywhere. He alluded, I presume, to the days of 1848, during which this republic acted with equal liberality and wisdom. She has herself passed through the same ordeal as that through which God is now leading us, and she knows what it is for foreign powers to cast the weight of their open encouragement or secret intrigue into the wrong scale. Whatever importance may be attached to the course which Switzerland may pursue on this point, I am almost positive no agent would be received.

  *   *   *   *   *   *   *   *   *

I have the honor to be, sir, with the highest consideration, your obedient servant,

                    THEO. S. FAY.

Hon. WILLIAM H. SEWARD,
  Secretary of State of the United States of America.

Mr. Fay to Mr. Seward.

[Extract.]

No. 431.]   UNITED STATES LEGATION,
                 Berne, July 2, 1861.

SIR: It is with the permission of my successor, whom I learn to regard as a friend, that I address to you this my closing despatch.

I have placed him in possession of the legation office records, cipher, library, furniture, and all things pertaining to it. An inventory has been prepared, from the despatch books, of everything received; and he will doubtless inform you that he has verified it.

Yesterday, July 1, he accompanied me to the *Palais F.. ´ral*, where we were received in the state reception-room by the president and by the secretary of the federal chancery, Mr. Leutscher. I handed in my letter of recall, and read, in German, the remarks I had prepared. I then formally presented my successor, who gave his *lettre de créance*, and who requested me to read a German translation of his remarks, which I did. The president then replied to the latter. I have the honor to subjoin these documents in English.

Some conversation then ensued of a friendly character. On leaving, the president informed me he would make me a visit, and, taking me warmly by the hand, he said, (alluding to Neuchâtel,) "we shall never forget what you have done for us." We then drove to all the legations, and I presented the new minister to the *chefs de mission,* commencing with the French ambassador, the Marquis de Turgot. It gives me pleasure to say Mr. Fogg obviously made a favorable impression, and that it is a sincere satisfaction for me to see in my place a gentleman who I have no doubt will represent with dignity the new country, which God is disengaging from elements irreconcilable with its character as a Christian republic.

In my remarks to the president I thought it a proper occasion publicly to record my opinion, that I might throw into the scale the influence, however small, which I might possess from my long residence in Europe.

With regard to the French and English declarations of neutrality, the enclosed extract from the "New York Commercial Advertiser" emboldened me to express the hope that those governments, whatever might have been their original intention, would be careful as to the manner of applying the principle adopted.

* * * * * * * * * *

I have the honor to be, sir, with the highest consideration, your obedient servant,

THEO. S. FAY.

Hon. WILLIAM H. SEWARD,
  Secretary of State of the United States of America.

Mr. Fay's parting remarks to the president of the Swiss confederation.

Mr. PRESIDENT. I have the honor to hand to your excellency my letter of recall, and to present my estimable successor, against whom I have only one objection—that he will, I am afraid, perform the duties of his office better than I have done. I am instructed by the President of the United States on this occasion to repeat his sincere desire to continue to cultivate with you relations of the closest friendship.

I resigned my appointment as minister in Switzerland, not that I had any power or right to retain it contrary to the President's wish, but I thought it my duty, from certain considerations. This course was not induced by any discontent with Switzerland. On the contrary, I admire and love Switzerland. In my official transactions with the government, and with the different members of it, I have always found good sense and *loyauté*, and my private intercourse with the nation has caused it to rise always more in my esteem. I have been struck with the pure administration of justice, the universal love of country, the modest and yet effective character of the governments, and with the liberty of conscience asserted by superior authorities, even where embarrassed by local, contrary influences. Switzerland is peculiarly blessed by the Almighty, and she has it in her power, under Him, to be the happiest country in the world. Your free development in your present form is a necessity for Europe.

Neither has my resigna .on resulted from difference of opinion with the President of the United States. Our country is now occupied in a struggle with an institution as unmanageable as the hydra of Hercules. It is not my wish to misrepresent the proprietors of slaves. Many of them are sincere, Christian gentlemen. But the institution in its present form is irreconcilable with our national existence, with the religious sentiment of the majority, and with the Word of God. Nothing can be clearer than the right and duty of the American people to protect themselves from its uncontrolled development, and from being drawn downwards in their career of political and religious civilization. Man should not live by bread alone, nor by cotton alone.

The election of President Lincoln is the expression of this sentiment. The struggle in which he is engaged is one of light with darkness. Every Christian government in the world must be on his side, for he represents humanity, liberty, civilization, and religion. He represents also the principle of rational, popular government, and his course thus far has given reason to believe that he has been raised up by God to steer our nation through this tempest, by a union of moderation with energy, and of rapid decision with patient mercy and calm wisdom, if no encouragement from without be offered to the insurrection. No one who prefers good to evil would place an obstacle in his path.

The movement of certain southern States—not to say persons—represents not only rebellion against a Constitution and laws framed or freely accepted by themselves, but negro slavery and the African slave trade as one of its inevitable consequences. It represents also one of the greatest crimes recorded in history—a black, secret, long-matured, treacherous conspiracy, extending its ramifications into European countries, which, among other objects, aimed at the conquest of Cuba, Mexico, and Brazil, as the basis of a great, despotic, and African slave-trade empire, and which, by the mercy of God, must be shipwrecked against the steady firmness of the President, the honesty, the patriotism, and the religious sentiment of the American people. You will judge, Mr. President; also your government and your people; Europe and history will also judge how far any government, nation, or public press, can, consistently with its character, approve or in any way encourage such an enterprise, unless ignorant of its true nature. I have no doubt this insurrection, although it has reached such proportions, will be suppressed. We have the power, the right, and the will to suppress it. It is not a war between two powers entitled to equal international rights, any more than the rebellion in India was an international war. It is an insurrection, and nothing more, and one of the most unreasonable and unjust which the world has ever seen. The American Union, carried out according to its original intentions, offers to rapidly increasing millions material prosperity, political and religious liberty. It is a blessing for mankind; whereas the rise of a southern empire, built on such foundations, and aiming at such designs, could not but be a misfortune for itself and for all the world. It is one of the signs of our times that error not only boldly raises its head, but that it invites, with effrontery, the assistance of others, and sometimes receives encouragement from quarters where it would least be expected. I here in no way allude to the declarations of neutrality lately proclaimed by two great powers, but to opinions expressed by several journals. The declarations of neutrality have been prematurely considered unfriendly acts by a portion of my countrymen. They ought not to be so taken, unless applied in an unfriendly manner; and I have no fear that either of these enlightened and friendly governments would encourage the southern movement by receiving its representatives or suffering its marine prizes to be sold in their ports; and neither do I fear, Mr. President, that the government of Switzerland, which has always on such occasions proved itself wise and just, would ever throw its weight into the scale of insane revolution, and of negro slavery disengaged from all restraint, and of the African slave trade, by receiving any representative of that portion of our States.

In concluding, Mr. President, I have the honor to bid you farewell, and, in your person, to your estimable colleagues and to your free, well-conducted, and happy country. May it never forget whence this blessing comes, and what hand is indispensable for its continued preservation ! May your lakes and mountains—the admiration of the world—ever represent, as they do now, peace, prosperity, prudence in foreign policy, and, at home, Christian liberty !

Mr. Fogg's address to the President.

Mr. PRESIDENT : The just and lucid statement of the present condition and prospects of the United States made by my honored predecessor and friend leaves for myself little more than the agreeable duty of reaffirming what he has so well said.

There are crises in the lives of nations as well as of individuals. Swit-

zerland has had her crises. Times almost without number her brave moun-
taineers have been called to arms to put down sedition at home and repel
the invaders from abroad. Thanks to the God of liberty, they have always
triumphed, and the land of Tell is still the home of the free.

The United States has had her crises. In her infancy, when Washington
led her brave sons to maintain her right to be one of the nations of the
earth, then was her crisis. Her second great crisis is now, when a despotic
institution raises the standard of intestine war, and appeals to foreign governments for sympathy and aid to break down freedom and free institutions
in America. This crisis, like yours, shall be decided for liberty, and America, too, shall remain the land of the free. The cloud which is now charged
with destruction will soon be dispersed, and be followed by the sunshine of
a purer and broader realization of the rights of mankind.

I am instructed to assure your excellency of the cordial good wishes of
the President of the United States, and of his desire to cultivate and
strengthen those relations of amity and sympathy which have always subsisted and ought always to subsist between governments whose political
institutions are so nearly alike

In conclusion, let me say to your excellency and your associates that it
will be my highest ambition during my residence in your country to so discharge all my duties that, while jealously guarding the interests and rights
of American citizens, I may deserve the confidence and enjoy the personal
friendship of all the members of your government. Should I be as fortunate
in these respects as my predecessor has been, my highest hopes will be
gratified.

President Knuesel's reply.

The Swiss confederation has always taken a lively interest in everything
concerning the great sister republic beyond the Atlantic. How could it be
otherwise? The similarity of the democratic federative institutions, the
independence and liberty which both enjoy, and which they had to obtain
by force of arms, has necessarily led to a mutual approach, however great
the distance be which separates the old world from the new. In this may
be found, perhaps, a principal reason why for a long series of years numerous Swiss families emigrated to the United States, where they sought and
found a new home, and why the names of Swiss cantons and towns are now
to be found where for thousands of years uncultivated and unpopulated
forests and prairies existed. The intercourse between the two nations has
since steadily increased; the produce of one country finds its market in
the other, and numerous points of connexion develop themselves ever more
and more.

This harmony of political principles, sympathies, and interests has for its
consequence a steadily increasing approach of both nations, which has
already on different occasions shown itself by marks of mutual cordiality.
Names like that of William Tell, so dear to Switzerland, were given to sea
vessels by citizens of the United States. The federal council responded to
that salutation by hoisting the Swiss flag on the mainmast of those ships.
To the colossal monument which the United States erected in memory of
their liberator, the immortal Washington, Switzerland has contributed a
stone with an inscription. Many more similar marks of mutual esteem
might be enumerated; suffice it to add the remark that a treaty of friendship and commerce, concluded a few years ago, has but strengthened the
relations between the two countries.

Switzerland, from the sincere sympathy which she has for the welfare of
the Union, looks with anxiety upon the issue of the events which now shake

that country. Switzerland passed through a similar crisis fourteen years ago, which threatened to tear asunder the then loose connexion of the twenty-two cantons. But renewed rose the present confederation from that tempest ; strengthened internally and abroad, she now stands there, esteemed by the nations. May God grant that the connexion of the States of the United States of America may also emerge renewed and strengthened out of this crisis.

The president of the Swiss confederation presents his best thanks, through your excellency, to the President of the United States for his assurances of friendship and sympathy. He hopes that the new minister resident will thoroughly acquaint himself with our relations and laws. That would render the more possible for him a strict performance of his duties ; the protection of the rights and interests of American citizens, and the preservation of a good and ever friendly understanding with the Swiss government, which wishes to unite *loyauté* with their maintenance of authority. The President of the confederation may add that he thinks the retiring minister resident has learned to esteem Switzerland, her authorities and nation, and he may give to Mr. Fay the plain assurance that he has acquired the esteem and the love of the country and her magistrates. The President of the confederation doubts not a moment that the relations between the federal council and the present representative of America will always be of the most friendly character.

Mr. Fogg to Mr. Seward.

No. 1.]   UNITED STATES LEGATION,
                                          Berne, July 8, 1861.

SIR: Leaving New York for my post of duty on the steamer "Adriatic," the 14th day of May, I reached Berne *via* Galway, London, and Paris, June 27, having previously ascertained by correspondence with my predecessor that it would be agreeable to him for me to take possession of the office, legation property, &c., the 1st day of July.

Making it my first duty, after arriving, to call on Mr. Fay at his house, I was received with the utmost frankness and cordiality, and with the offer of every facility to render my entrance upon my new duties pleasant to myself and favorable to the non-interruption of that *entente cordiale*, now and for years past so happily existing between the American legation and the several members of the Swiss government.

Mr. Fay very kindly undertook to notify the president of the confederation of my arrival, and ask an audience to enable him to present his own *letter of recall*, and myself and my *letter of credence* on the Monday following. Having received promise of an audience on the day named, Mr. Fay called with his carriage, and we went together to the palace of the federal council. The sequel has been narrated and transmitted to the State Department by Mr. Fay in his despatch numbered 431, dated July 2, 1861.

Subsequently we called upon the other members of the Swiss government and upon the foreign ambassadors resident at Berne, to all of whom I was kindly introduced, and by all of whom as cordially received—not without uniform, and, I am sure I may add, sincere expressions of regret at the termination of Mr. Fay's official relations with the government and the diplomatic corps.

During our entire round of visits and presentations it was painfully pleasing to be constantly reminded of the profound interest with which the

Ex. Doc. 1——22

contest now going on in the United States, between liberty and union on the one hand, and despotism and secession on the other, is watched alike by the friends of republicanism and of absolutism. Here, however, the rebels have no friends—not even among the representatives of absolutism in Europe On all sides, the sanguine assurances I have felt at liberty to give of the certain triumph of our system and constitution of government over the conspirators for its overthrow, has seemed to give unalloyed satisfaction. That the future may justify these my assurances, will be my constant prayer, with that of millions in other lands.

I should not do justice to my own feelings did I omit to say that I have found Mr. Fay a true Christian gentleman, and an American whose heart has, by absence, lost none of its devotion to the liberties and good name of his native land. Thoroughly sympathizing with the principles and purposes of the present administration of the United States government, and possessing large experience and an enviable reputation in Europe, I trust it may not be deemed impertinent in me to express the hope that the State Department will not be a long time in finding some field where his familiarity with international and diplomatic affairs will be a necessity to the government.

With an ardent desire for the preservation of the free spirit of our government and the integrity of our national Union, I have the honor to subscribe myself, with the highest consideration, your obedient servant,

GEORGE G. FOGG.

Hon. WILLIAM H. SEWARD,
Secretary of State of the United States of America.

Mr. Seward to Mr. Fogg.

[Extract.]

No. 6.]   DEPARTMENT OF STATE,
                                      Washington, July 29, 1861.

SIR: Mr. Fay's despatch of July 2 (No. 431) has been duly received. The account he has given us of his retirement and your entrance upon the mission, as also the sentiments expressed by him and by yourself to the president of the republic, and the reply of that eminent magistrate, are exceedingly interesting. The President of the United States appreciates very highly the liberal and friendly feelings of the Swiss republic, and derives from them new motives to maintain relations so auspiciously established.
*   *   *   *   *   *   *   *   *

I am, sir, your obedient servant,

WILLIAM H. SEWARD.

GEORGE G. FOGG, Esq., &c., &c, *Berne.*

Mr. Seward to Mr. Fogg.

No. 8.]   DEPARTMENT OF STATE,
                                      Washington, August 6, 1861.

SIR: Your despatch No. 1, dated 8th July last, has been received. Your account of your interview with Mr. Fay, and of the circumstances of the audience granted you by the government of the republic of Switzerland, is interesting and entirely satisfactory.   The sentiments you expressed on that occasion are approved by the President of the United States, and the generous reply made to you by the president of the federal council of Switzerland, as narrated to us in the last despatch of Mr. Fay, has been received with deep emotion.   We feel assured that whatever may be the changes of existing relations between us and other countries, Switzerland and the United States will always remain friends.

I am, sir, your obedient servant,

WILLIAM H. SEWARD.

George G. Fogg, Esq., &c., &c., Berne.

Mr. Seward to Mr. Fogg.

No. 13.]   DEPARTMENT OF STATE,
                                          Washington, September 14, 1861.

SIR: Among the important instructions addressed to your predecessor are those concerning the restrictions of certain of the Swiss cantons against citizens of the United States professing Judaism—a subject which received at Mr. Fay's hands a large share of earnest attention, and upon which he addressed the department repeatedly and at much length.   It is very desirable that his efforts to procure the removal of the restrictions referred to—which, though not completely successful, have no doubt had much effect in smoothing the way to such a result—should be followed up by you.   You will, therefore, after having fully acquainted yourself with what Mr. Fay has done in the premises, and with the views of the department, as expressed to him in the despatches on file in the legation, take such steps as you may deem judicious and likely to advance the benevolent object in question.

It is not doubted that further proper appeals to the justice and liberality of the authorities of the several cantons whose laws discriminate against Israelitish citizens of the United States will result in a removal of the odious restrictions and a recognition of the just rights of those citizens.

I am, sir, your obedient servant,

WILLIAM H. SEWARD.

G. Fogg, Esq., &c., &c., Berne

NETHERLANDS.

Mr. Seward to Mr. Pike.

No. 4.]   DEPARTMENT OF STATE,
                                          Washington, May 16, 1861.

SIR: The government is preoccupied with the civil war which has been inaugurated with the reckless purpose of overthrowing the Constitution and the federal Union. It has little time to think of our foreign relations, and when it does think of them it is chiefly to consider how and in what way it can most effectually counteract the efforts of the revolutionists to procure European intervention in their favor.

The Netherlands lost even their independence for a time through the disastrous operations of the French revolution of 1789. They are slowly, but surely, recovering advantages and prestige which they enjoyed before that calamity occurred. Their policy is peace and friendship with all nations, and certainly they have always manifested the most liberal sentiments towards the United States. In view of these circumstances and dispositions the President does not apprehend any danger that the government of the Netherlands, or its very intelligent people, will lend aid, countenance, or sympathy to the misguided partisans who, in a frenzy of passion, are compassing the ruin of our country.

I have looked through the correspondence of this department with your legation, and I find that, although our commerce is known in every part of the world, and although the Netherlands have no insignificant possessions in each of its great continental divisions, yet that there is not even one case of controversy or dispute between the two nations.

What, then, will you do at the Hague? You can do much, and, first, in relation to Japan. The government of the Netherlands is probably an ally of Japan. I enclose the copy of a note of the 14th instant, addressed by this department to the respective diplomatic representatives of Christian powers here who have treaties with Japan. You will submit the suggestions contained therein to his Majesty's government, and if they should be frankly received, I shall be prepared to submit a project of a convention to carry them into effect.

I have especially called the attention of Baron de Limburg here to this matter, and invited him to consult with his government. Should he comply with this request, your own action will be merely in co-operation with him, and the needful negotiations may be had with him here if his government shall prefer.

The government of the Netherlands may perhaps have forgotten that New York, one of the largest and most prosperous of these States, was colonized by emigrants from that country, and that their descendants still cherish lively affection for the land of their ancestors. The flow of emigration from the Netherlands to this country was arrested by the revolutionary wars which occurred in both countries at the close of the last century; but it has resumed its course within the last twenty years, and the thrifty adventurers already constitute an important portion of the population in some of our new western States. The intercourse between persons of this class and their relations and friends is very intimate. All who come hither from the Netherlands, whether as settlers or transient passengers, are admitted and enjoy entire freedom of movement, and are never required to exhibit a passport under any circumstances. It is a fact very honorable to themselves, and to their native country, that not one of them has ever manifested a purpose or even a thought of hostility against this government. I am sure that the citizens of the United States who have occasion to visit the Netherlands are equally free from any sentiments of unkindness, or of hostility against the government or people of that country. Why, then, should not the government of the Netherlands relax the rigor of its police system so far as to dispense with the requirement that the citizen of the United States shall arm himself with a passport when visiting that country? The President desires that you submit these thoughts to the minister for foreign affairs in an earnest, but not importunate manner. If they should be favorably received, you will be authorized to enter into a convention to give them effect.

One of our first treaties was made with the Netherlands in the year 1782. Article XIX of that treaty was as follows:

"No subject of their high mightinesses, the states general of the United Netherlands, shall apply for or take any commission or letters of marque for arming any ship or ships to act as privateers against the said United States of America, or any of them, or the subjects and inhabitants of the said United States, or any of them, or against the property of the inhabitants of any of them, from any prince or State with which the United States of America may happen to be at war; nor shall any subject or inhabitant of the said United States of America, or any of them, apply for or take any commission or letters of marque for arming any ship or ships to act as privateers against the high and mighty lords, the states general of the United Netherlands, or against the subjects of their high mightinesses, or any of them, or against the property of any one of them, from any prince or State with which their high mightinesses may be at war. And if any person of either nation shall take such commission or letters of marque, he shall be punished as a pirate."

There have been several changes of the government of the Netherlands since that time, and it has thus become doubtful whether that treaty is now in force.

You will have perceived in the archives of the legation a letter which was addressed to you on the 10th instant, on the subject of the amendments to the law of nations in regard to the laws of maritime war applicable to neutrals, which was proposed by the congress at Paris in 1856. It is presumed that the government of the Netherlands will be well disposed to enter into a convention for the acceptance of these propositions, the material one being in effect the same as the treaty stipulations to which I have thus referred.

I am, sir, respectfully, your obedient servant,

WILLIAM H. SEWARD.

James S. Pike, Esq., &c., &c., &c.

Mr. Murphy to Mr. Seward.

[Extract.]

No. 52.]   LEGATION OF THE UNITED STATES,
                                              The Hague, April 2, 1861.

SIR: *   *   *   *   * ,   *   *   *   *

I have also to acknowledge the receipt of the despatch of your predecessor, No. 37, of the 28th of February last, in relation to the so-called "Confederate States of America." Upon receiving it I called upon the minister of foreign affairs and inquired whether any person or agent had presented himself to this government on behalf of those States; and, upon receiving an answer in the negative, I desired him, in case any person should do so, to inform me immediately, and before any action should be had to receive such representative, as I would in that case make a communication to him on the subject. He promised me that he would do so. I did not deem it necessary to be more explicit at the present time.

Since my former despatch there has been a resignation of all the members of the ministry, and a reconstruction of the cabinet. Some of the old members have been reinstated, but most of the members are new appointments. The ministry of foreign affairs has been devolved upon Baron T. P. P. de Zueglen de Nyevelt—not the late minister of the same name, though he occupied the same post a number of years since.

I have the honor to be, sir, yours respectfully,
                                                     HEN. C. MURPHY.

————————

Mr. Murphy to Mr. Seward.

No. 53.]   THE HAGUE, *April* 10, 1861.

SIR: I have the honor to acknowledge the receipt of your circular despatch of the 9th of March, in regard to the intervention of foreign powers in the domestic affairs of the United States at the present time. In compliance with the instructions contained therein, I immediately addressed the minister of foreign affairs of this government a communication, of which a copy is annexed to this despatch. The King is at present on his annual visit to Amsterdam, and will not probably return under ten days; and I presume nothing will be done in the ministry of an important character until he shall have returned. No person has yet appeared here on behalf of the seceding States; and if any one or more should come on their account, I apprehend nothing will be done by the Dutch government until the great powers shall have acted in regard to an acknowledgment of their independence or a treaty. You may rest assured that the present difficulties in the United States are regarded by this government with regret, and that it will do nothing to encourage the seceding States under existing circumstances. I speak, however, on this subject, as yet, of course without any official intimation, and merely from the tone and temper of the well-informed circles—as well those connected with the government as others. There is in the Dutch character a strong repugnance to political changes, except when a strong sense of wrong and injury exists. The government and people, as you well know, are conservative beyond any other nation. I will not fail, however, to inform you of everything which shall transpire here on this subject, and without delay.

I have the honor to be, sir, yours respectfully,
                                                     HENRY C. MURPHY.

Hon. WILLIAM H. SEWARD, &c., &c., &c.

Mr. Murphy to the Minister for Foreign Affairs.

THE HAGUE, *April* 8, 1861.

The undersigned, minister resident of the United States of America, has the honor to address his excellency Baron Van Zuylen Van Nijevelt, minister of foreign affairs of his Majesty the King of the Netherlands, on the subject of the present complication of the internal political affairs of the United States, and, for the better understanding of the views of his government in relation thereto, to invite the attention of his excellency to the accompanying address of the President on assuming the administration of the federal Union. His excellency will find therein a statement of the alleged grievances, of the revolutionary nature of the proceedings of a number of the States of the Union which have attempted to secede and have formed a provisional government of their own, and of the line of policy which the government of the Union will pursue for the purpose of preserving peace and for the maintenance of the Union.

The undersigned will further remark, in explanation of this statement of the President in regard to the character of the secession movement, that the government of the United States is not simply a confederation, but a union, which has been invested by the people of the different States, acting in their original sovereign capacity, with certain powers, which are exclusive and paramount throughout the republic, such as the making of war and peace, the regulation of commerce, whether between the States themselves or with foreign nations, the establishment of post offices and post roads, the defining and punishing piracies and felonies on the high seas, the maintenance of a navy, and the laying and collecting taxes and duties for the common defence and welfare, besides various others entirely of a domestic bearing, but all operating on all the States and the citizens thereof as one people. In other words, in all that concerns the foreign relations of the several States, as well as in many details of internal regulation, the United States are as much a consolidated government as the kingdom of the Netherlands, with its provincial divisions and assemblies—the only difference being, that in the United States all powers not granted to the federal government are reserved to the States and the people, and, consequently, original and more extensive powers are exercised by the legislatures of the several States. Any attempt, therefore, on the part of any State or number of States, or of any section of a State, to interfere with the exercise of the powers conferred on the general government by the Constitution is revolutionary; and any pretended or actual exercise of like powers by them is an usurpation.

The condition of affairs now existing in the United States is altogether of an anomalous character, arising from the principles upon which the government is founded. Those principles acknowledge the right of self-government in the people, and the exercise of perfect freedom of speech, of assemblage, and of the press. A majority of the electors, in the manner and under the forms prescribed by the Constitution, elect the President, and thus give administrative vitality to the government. In the canvass preceding the election, which takes place every four years, discussions of subjects of vital interest to the country are carried on in the press and on the stump with such effect that, although the voting body comprises over three millions of persons, probably not five per cent. of the whole number fail to vote on such occasions. Popular passion is aroused, every motive is appealed to by the rival parties, and, when a conclusion is reached, there is oftentimes a feeling of disappointment on the part of the minority. But this feeling has never heretofore interfered with their loyal submission to the will of the majority. In the recent canvass, the questions connected with the institution of slavery were almost exclusively agitated, principally in regard to its extension into the Territories, or, as it might be termed in this country, the lands of the generality. The decision of the people has been adverse to such extension, but altogether by the votes of the non-slaveholding States. Advantage has been taken of this circumstance by designing men to make the minority, or rather that portion of it residing in the slaveholding States, believe that their constitutional rights, in regard to that species of property known as slaves, were in danger of being destroyed by the majority. The fear of such a consequence is groundless; but, acting upon such apprehensions, the people of the seceding States have precipitated themselves into their present position.

No complaint has been made in any quarter of any improper act of the general government, or of any violation by it of its powers, or of the rights of slaveholders, as a ground for the existing discontent. The evils are anticipatory only, so far as the action of the general government is concerned. On the other hand it is true that, notwithstanding the apprehensions and fears which have been excited in the bosoms of a portion of the American people in regard to the policy of the government, and the steps which have been taken by them for the formation of an independent government, it is not to be doubted that the great majority of the people of those seceding States still cherish a love for the Union of their fathers, its memories, its prestige, and its blessings. Independent of this fact, the permanent dismemberment of the Union is fraught with so much evil to them, as well as to the country at large, as to justify the belief that a calm view of the consequences, combined with their patriotism, will cause them to retrace their steps. A separate government on their part entails the necessity not only of an entire new corps of officers of government, but also of a standing army where none now is necessary, of an independent navy, of a cordon of revenue officers along an extensive coast and frontier line; all attended with heavy expense and increased taxes. These consequences, and the severance of family ties and brotherhood existing between individuals residing in different States, are to come home to them when passion and delusion shall have passed away; and when they shall discover, as discover they will, that the general government entertains no designs against their peace or property, but on the other hand will, as it is bound to do, defend both.

The undersigned would also impress upon the government of his Majesty the fact that no one questions the election of the President according to the provisions of the Constitution. He is the choice of the country, and is fairly entitled to the exercise of all the powers conferred upon the executive head of the federal government by the Constitution. Every citizen within every State is bound to obedience to his lawful authority. It is the sworn duty of the President to administer faithfully the Constitution and laws of the United States, and the obligation of every citizen and individual is perfect to uphold and sustain him in its performance. But the President will seek by a just and liberal administration, and by a paternal regard for the rights and feelings of all sections of the country, to give occasion and opportunity for the deliberate and loyal action of the people. It is under these circumstances that the President entertains the fullest confidence in the restoration of the harmony and unity of the government at no very distant day.

The friendship and good will which his Majesty the King of the Netherlands has always manifested towards the United States, the President regards as an assurance that his Majesty's government will not yield to solicitations to intervene in any unfriendly way in the domestic affairs of the United States. It is evident that any encouragement to disaffection from abroad would thwart the efforts of the President for a reconciliation and defeat his just expectations in that regard. It is a question, moreover, which involves important interests to all nations with which the United States are in commercial relation, and to all constitutional governments. The form of government which the people of the United States have adopted is one which experience has proven is best adapted for the peace and protection of the States, for the welfare of the people, and for the development of the enterprise and resources of its vast territory. Nor has its influence, it is believed, been without its salutary effect upon the fatherlands, whence that population has originally sprung.

It has, however, been a government of example only as to other nations, and has steadily pursued the policy of not interfering with their internal affairs. Under it close commercial relations have sprung up, particularly with all the western powers of Europe, and with the kingdom of the Netherlands have never for a moment—now more than three-fourths of a century—been interrupted. If at present there happen some inconveniences to the trading interests of the subjects of his Majesty, it will be the endeavor of the President to render them as light and transient as possible; and should any injury be sustained therefrom by the subjects of his Majesty, the President is determined, the undersigned is instructed to say, that they shall, so far as it may rest with him, be amply indemnified. Should a state of civil war be precipitated, by any cause whatever, those inconveniences would be turned into evils of a wide-spread and disastrous character to other nations. Not only would the channels of commerce be closed, or, at least, seriously interrupted, and the agricultural and mining products of the United States, many of which have become necessary for other nations, be withheld; but the political systems of Europe and the cause of well regulated and constitutional government would suffer everywhere. A state of anarchy must ensue if the revolution be pursued. It is not to be expected that an empire of thirty-one millions of souls can be broken up, and the glories and blessings of its free government be thrown away at the behest of six millions, one-half of whom only are of the white race. The policy hitherto has been, on the part of the general government, and will continue to be, to avert such a calamity; and in asking the non-intervention of friendly nations, while it pursues a course of peace itself, it demands, it is confidently believed, what is most consistent with the cause of humanity and good government everywhere. And to no power is this caution addressed with more confidence than to his Majesty the King of the Netherlands.

The undersigned embraces this occasion to renew to his excellency Baron Van Zuylen Van Nijevelt the assurance of his high consideration.

HENRY C. MURPHY.

Mr. Murphy to Mr. Seward.

No. 55.]   THE HAGUE, *April* 30, 1861.

SIR: I have the honor to transmit to you hereunto annexed a copy of the reply of the minister of foreign affairs to my note addressed to him on the 8th instant, of which a copy was transmitted to you with my despatch, No. 53, of the 10th instant. After reciting very particularly the contents of that note, and expressing the regrets of his Majesty at the posture of our affairs and his hope that the difficulties will be surmounted, the minister concludes in these words:

"The undersigned, in acquitting himself of the orders of the King, has the honor to bring at the same time to the knowledge of Mr. Murphy that, already in the month of December last, the envoy of the King at Washington had recommended to the Dutch consuls in the United States to abstain from all intervention in the political affairs of the country within their jurisdiction, and that this requirement has been approved by the government of the Netherlands."

If the note required an answer at this time, it certainly should have received something more to the point than this paragraph. I apprehend, however, that this government will say nothing in regard to the recognition of the independence of the seceding States until the great powers of Europe have taken their ground, and that it will follow them if they be in accord.

I have also the honor to acknowledge the receipt of your despatch No. 39, with the gold medal for Captain Van Albuy, of the Dutch bark Hendrica. I have, in accordance with your direction, transmitted the medal to the minister of foreign affairs, with a request that it be presented to Captain Van Albuy in the name of the President.

I am, sir, yours respectfully,

HENRY C. MURPHY.

Hon. WILLIAM H. SEWARD, &c., &c., &c.

M. Zuylen de Nijevelt to Mr. Murphy.

[Translation.]

THE HAGUE, *April* 26, 1861.

The undersigned, minister for foreign affairs, has had the honor to receive the note which Mr. Murphy, minister resident of the United States of America, has pleased to address to him on the subject of the existing complications of political affairs in the United States; the said note being accompanied, for the better understanding of the views of his government, by the address delivered by his excellency the President on assuming the administration of the federal Union.

In calling, by his note, the attention of the undersigned to the exposition contained in the address of the wrongs alleged by some States of the Union, of their proceedings to attempt a separation, and the formation of a separated provisional government, as well as on the line of conduct which the federal government proposes to follow for the purpose of preserving peace and upholding the Union, Mr. Murphy further remarks, in explaining this part of the President's address, upon the character of the secessional movement, that the government of the United States is not merely a confederation but a Union, invested by the people of the different States with powers, exclusive and controlling throughout the republic—powers which, embracing the foreign relations and numerous details of domestic interest, operate over all the States and over their citizens collectively, so that, adds the note, any attempt of any State, of a number of States, or of any part of a State, to interrupt the exercise of the powers confided to the general government is revolutionary ; and any exercise, pretended or real on their part, of like powers, is usurpation.

After having enunciated these principles as the basis of the general government, and pointed out the mode established for the election of President, the minister resident enters into some details about the recent election of the actual President; the result is, that on former elections the will of the majority has been loyally submitted to, but that this example has not been followed by the minority in respect to Mr. Lincoln, whose election, furthermore, is in nowise contested in regard of its constitutional validity. This fact the said note attributes to apprehensions entertained in the slave States that a blow might be aimed at this portion of their property—apprehensions which nothing in the intentions of the general government justify, but which have prepared the way upon which those States have rushed.

Nevertheless and despite the fears excited among a noticeable portion of the American people, notwithstanding the attempt made to form an independent government, the government of the United States is persuaded, according to the note, that the great majority of the people in the separatist States will constantly preserve its regard for the Union of their fathers, their memory, their influence, and their greatness. But, independently of this fact, the mischiefs and disadvantages which a permanent dismemberment of the Union would draw, as well upon the separating States as upon the country generally, justifies the expectation that upon a calm review of the circumstances they will come back upon a better track.

The President, flattering himself that he will see the harmony and unity of the government soon established, and relying on the friendship and good understanding existing between the two countries, expresses through the channel of Mr. Murphy his confidence that his Majesty the King of the Netherlands will not lend himself to applications for interference in the domestic affairs of the United States, unless in an amicable and conciliatory sense, nor to any encouragement whatever of the disaffected, which would only counteract the efforts of the President to bring about a reconciliation.

Finally, Mr. Murphy wishes to give assurance that the President will strongly endeavor to lessen as much as possible the inconveniences which must result to commerce from the actual condition of things, and that he proposes to indemnify the injury which the subjects of his Majesty may suffer as far as may depend upon him.

The undersigned having placed the above-mentioned note before the King, his Majesty was particularly grieved by its contents. He has charged me to signify this to the minister resident, adding that if he deeply deplores the situation in which the United States are for the moment placed, nevertheless he has been happy to witness the confidence which the government expresses of being able to surmount existing difficulties; that he entertains the most sincere wishes for the success of the efforts which will be made for the purpose of saving and preserving not only the interests of the States of the Union, but also the interests of the political and commercial world in general.

The undersigned, in acquitting himself of these orders by these presents, has the honor at the same time to bring to Mr. Murphy's knowledge that, so long ago as the month of December, the King's envoy at Washington directed the consuls of the Netherlands in the United States to abstain from any interference whatever in political affairs in the districts of the consular offices, and that this prescription was approved afterwards by the government of the Netherlands.

The undersigned seizes this occasion to reiterate to Mr. Murphy the assurances of his high consideration.

DE ZUYLEN DE NIJEVELT.

Mr. Murphy to Mr. Seward.

No. 56.]   The Hague, *May* 27, 1861.

Sir: I have the honor to inform you that no communication has as yet been made to this government on behalf of the seceding States; nor, as far as I can learn, has any attempt been made by private persons to fit out vessels to attack our commerce. I have received a letter from an officer of the Dutch cavalry, tendering his services to the United States, but I have declined to forward the same to my government, assuring him that the people of the United States would dispose of the question themselves. On the other hand, it is not to be disguised that public sentiment here is much more favorable to the seceding States than it has been. The message of Mr. Davis, recently delivered to the congress of those States, has been extensively published here, in substance, not at full length, and has had much influence on the question from the specious ground of the Union being a mere confederation of independent States. Besides, Holland, or the Netherlands, has had a bitter lesson of experience under similar circumstances. The rebellion of Belgium, in 1830, was resisted with all the power of this government, which would probably have succeeded in crushing it if England and France had not interfered, and the immense public debt with which this country is oppressed was then mostly incurred, while Belgium was, notwithstanding, lost. Reasoning from this point of view, there are not a few who regard the present position of the United States an expensive and useless effort. I state these circumstances for your information.

The affairs of this country are in a prosperous condition. The great calamities by inundation both here at home and also in Java have shown that there is abundant resources to meet such misfortunes. They have called forth and received liberal contributions from private persons, without requiring any aid from the government. Political matters are quiet. The first chamber of the states general is now in session, and is engaged in considering the bills adopted by the other body, the most important of which are those relating to the budget and the reorganization of the judiciary.

I have the honor, sir, to be yours respectfully,

HEN. C. MURPHY.

Hon. William H. Seward,
Secretary of State, &c., &c., &c.

Mr. Pike to Mr. Seward.

[Extracts.]

No. 1.]   Legation of the United States,
                                         The Hague, June 8, 1861.

Sir: I hasten to inform you that his Majesty the King of Holland received me to-day in private audience, agreeably to the prescribed ceremonial, and that I delivered to him in person my credentials as minister resident of the United States at this court.

I arrived here on the first day of the present month and have waited till now for my audience. In my interview with his Majesty I took occasion to express the earnest desire of the President to maintain and cultivate those friendly relations that have so long and so happily subsisted between the United States and Holland, and especially with his Majesty's government.

I further observed that it would be my cherished aim, as it would be my most pleasing duty, in the discharge of my official duties, to foster and promote the good understanding now existing between the two countries. The King received me graciously, and promptly came forward to receive my credentials, and at once entered upon some friendly inquiries as to whether I had been in the country before or had been elsewhere in the diplomatic service. I replied that our American diplomatists generally were not educated after the European method, and that we labored under some disadvantage in consequence. His Majesty remarked that he had had the pleasure to meet Mr. Buchanan in Holland after he had served in Russia and in England. After some further brief conversation, in which the King expressed his pleasure at making my acquaintance, the audience terminated.

I found, on my arrival here, your despatch, No. 2, of the date of the 10th of May, covering a circular of the 6th of that month, in relation to agents of insurrectionary assemblages sent to Europe on errands hostile to the peace of the United States; also a copy of a despatch of the 24th of April, addressed to the several ministers of the United States accredited to the maritime powers whose plenipotentiaries composed the congress at Paris the 16th of April, 1856, calling their attention to the importance of endeavoring to negotiate with those powers conventions upon the subject of the rights of belligerents and neutrals in time of war; also the draft of a convention in reference to the subject therein discussed, with a full power and instructions to execute the same with the government of the Netherlands. I shall lose no time in communicating with the Dutch government upon the subject. Meantime I will observe that in an informal conversation with the minister of foreign affairs, since my arrival, I learned from him that Holland was the first power, not present at the convention referred to, to acquiesce in the propositions there laid down.

*   *   *   *   *   *   *

I cannot learn that any agent or agents of the seceding States have appeared in Holland for any purpose connected with their revolutionary or warlike plans, and from what I see and hear I conclude that no countenance would be given to them if they should.

The death of Count Cavour, the news of which reached here the morning of his decease, has created a profound sensation in diplomatic circles and is deeply deplored by the friends of Italy as an irreparable loss to that country.

I beg to add that I have found my predecessor, Mr. Murphy, unceasing in his endeavors to facilitate my labors here, and it gives me unfeigned pleasure to bear this testimony in his behalf, and to the highly honorable position which I believe him to hold among his colleagues.

I have the honor to be, with great respect, your obedient servant,

JAMES S. PIKE.

Hon. WILLIAM H. SEWARD,
    Secretary of State.

Mr. Pike to Mr. Seward.

[Extract.]

No. 2.]   LEGATION OF THE UNITED STATES,
                                           The Hague, June 12, 1861.

SIR : I have taken the earliest opportunity to have an interview with the minister of foreign affairs upon the condition of the internal concerns of the United States, and also upon the subject matter of your despatch No. 2, to which I referred in my last.

I assured him of the determined purpose of the United States government to put down the rebellion of the seceding States at all hazards, and stated its determination to adopt whatever measures are necessary to accomplish that object. I explained to him the character of the rebellion, and showed it to be merely a war in behalf of African slavery, and that if we had no slavery we should have no war and no rebellion. I further explained that the government possessed extraordinary means of ending the rebellion whenever it chose to employ them. The union of the States could be restored whenever the government saw fit to render the institutions of the several States homogeneous. For when they were once made free States there would be no wish to separate and no tendency to separation. But I observed that the government was desirous to adopt only moderate measures, and hoped that such measures would be sufficient to cause the leaders of the rebellion to succumb and to restore peace. But to accomplish the high object of maintaining the government and preserving the territory of the country from dismemberment, it was ready to make any sacrifice of mere material interests that necessity demanded. I showed that the government had abundant resources, and more men offering for the military service than it could employ.

The minister of foreign affairs, in reply to my inquiries, informed me that no agent or agents of the seceding States had appeared here, though he had heard they were in London. He said they would receive no countenance if they were to come. He observed that the Dutch government had considered the question of the proposed letters of marque to be issued by the seceding States, and were upon the point of issuing a proclamation and orders forbidding the use of their ports by privateers, a copy of which he said he would furnish me as soon as issued.

He expressed the opinion that the powers of Europe were unanimously in favor of the Paris declaration abolishing privateering, and said if the United States would concur in it, that privateers would have to be regarded as "sea-robbers." He believed there would be no opposition to negotiating treaties, based on the propositions of the Paris conference, with all the European powers which had agreed to them, of which Holland was one.

The minister seemed to be aware of the causeless character of the rebellion in the seceding States, and of the ability of the government to deal with it, concurring in the opinion that we had more men than were needed.

He informed me that his government had ordered four ships-of-war to be in readiness to sail for America to look after its commercial interests there, and that the first ship would be despatched on the 15th instant, and that the others would speedily follow. I subsequently learned from the minister of marine that the fleet would consist of two frigates and two brigs-of-war, and that after the flag-ship had communicated with the Dutch minister at Washington, the fleet would rendezvous at Curaçoa, and spend the winter in the West India seas.

I forebore to press the question of the immediate negotiation of a treaty in reference to privateering. Having satisfied myself of the favorable disposition of the government in respect to the question, and having learned its intention to issue the proclamation and orders referred to, and intimated with sufficient distinctness the ground the United States government was now disposed to occupy on that subject, I thought it prudent to await further developments of the question by our ministers at the courts of France and England, whose example Holland would be sure to wait for. I did not deem it advisable to ask the government here to take a lead to which I was aware it would be adverse. I shall be on the alert to seize the proper moment to recur to this subject.

*   *   *   *   *   *

I have the honor to be, with great respect, your most obedient servant,

JAMES S. PIKE.

Hon. WILLIAM H. SEWARD,
     Secretary of State, Washington.

Mr. Pike to Mr. Seward.

[Extracts.]

No. 3.]   LEGATION OF THE UNITED STATES,
                          The Hague, June 14, 1861.

SIR: I received yesterday your circular of the 20th of May, relating to the purchase of articles in Europe, contraband of war, for the use of persons in insurrection against the United States government.

*   *   *   *   *   *
*   *   *   *   *   *

The extraordinary unanimity and energy displayed by the government and loyal people of the United States in their measures to suppress the rebellion of the seceding States excites constant comment and high admiration in all quarters on this side of the Atlantic. The echoes of the first utterances of the British trading public, in favor of permitting the peaceable secession of the revolting States, have quite died away, and, instead, is now heard denunciation of the folly and madness of the secessionists, along with the expression of a general judgment that they will inevitably be forced to succumb. The growth of this sentiment, fostered by the character of the almost daily news from America, is strengthening the cause of the government on this side of the Atlantic and correspondingly weakening the cause of the secessionists. I think, therefore, that the whole weight of European opinion, which naturally desires a speedy end to the war, will soon be thrown in great force against the revolting States, and thus furnish important moral aid in putting an end to the struggle. I am satisfied, from what has come under my personal observation, that the high tone adopted by the United States government in regard to foreign interference in behalf of the secessionists has had a most salutary influence upon the action of European governments, great and small. Many of them have no objection to seeing the United States in difficulty; but they entertain a healthy apprehension that our government may find a speedy way out of it, and retain a lively recollection of those who would take advantage of its temporary embarrassments.

I have the honor to be, with high respect, your most obedient servant,

JAMES S. PIKE.

Hon. WM. H. SEWARD.
     Secretary of State.

Mr. Seward to Mr. Pike.

No. 6.]   DEPARTMENT OF STATE,
                                                       Washington, June 14, 1861.

SIR: Mr. Murphy's despatch of the 10th of April, (No. 53,) informing us that he had submitted our circular letter, with an appropriate communication of his own, to the Baron Zuylen, his Majesty's minister for foreign affairs, was duly received; and we have also received Mr. Murphy's despatch, No. 55, with which was transmitted a copy of the reply of the government of the Netherlands to the papers thus submitted to them.

Mr. Murphy executed the duty committed to him in a very proper manner, and you are instructed to express to his Majesty's government the President's high appreciation of the just and friendly sentiments which that government has manifested and expressed in regard to the domestic disturbance in our country, which, happily, now daily loses something of the formidable character which it at first assumed.

I am, sir, respectfully, your obedient servant,
                                                       WILLIAM H. SEWARD.
JAMES S. PIKE, Esq., &c., &c., &c.

Mr. Pike to Mr. Seward.

[Extract.]

No. 4.]   LEGATION OF THE UNITED STATES,
                                                       The Hague, June 16, 1861.

SIR: I have obtained from the minister of foreign affairs copies of the proclamations about to be issued by this government in relation to the letters of marque recently issued by the Montgomery revolutionists.

I have the honor to enclose the copies transmitted to me in the original Dutch. I see the instructions to ministers forbid the application of the contingent fund to pay translators, and I infer from this that the department prefers original documents. These papers warn the Dutch people against privateering, as an unlawful proceeding which may be deemed piracy, and they forbid the use of the ports of the Netherlands to privateers under any flag. They refer also to the fact of the adhesion of Holland to the declaration of the congress of Paris, in respect to maritime rights, made in 1856. It will likewise be observed that the Dutch government abstains from following the British example in excluding prizes brought in by ships-of-war.

*   *   *   *   *   *   *

I have the honor to be, with great respect, your most obedient servant,
                                                       JAMES S. PIKE.
Hon. WM. H. SEWARD.
     Secretary of State, Washington.

[Translation.]

In obedience to the King's orders the ministers for foreign affairs, of justice, and of the marine, present to the knowledge of all it may concern, that to guard against probable difficulties during the doubtful complications in the United States of North America, no privateers under any

Ex. Doc. 1——23

flag soever, or provided with any commission or letters of marque, or their prizes, shall be admitted into our havens or seaports, unless in case of marine disaster, and that requisite orders be issued that under any circumstances such privateers and their prizes be required to go again to sea as speedily as possible.

AT THE HAGUE.

The ministers above named.

[Translation.]

The minister for foreign affairs and the minister of justice, by the King's authority, warn, by these presents, all inhabitants of the kingdom, that during the existing disturbances in the United States of America they in nowise take part in privateering, because the Netherlands government has acceded to the declaration upon maritime rights set forth by the Paris conference of 1856, whereby, among other matters, privateering is abolished, and no recognition of commissions got for letters of marque permitted. Also that commissions and letters of marque, in conflict with the aforesaid prohibition, which may issue to inhabitants of the Netherlands, cannot have a lawful effect in behalf of the King's subjects, or of any abroad who are in subjection to the laws of the kingdom. Those who, under such circumstances, engage in or lend their aid in privateering to other people, will be considered as pirates, and prosecuted according to law in the Netherlands, and subjected to the punishment provided for the commission of such offences.

THE HAGUE.

The ministers above named.

[Translation.]

The minister for foreign affairs, apprised by a communication from the minister of marine, that the King has authorized the naval force in the West Indies to be seasonably strengthened by his Majesty's steam frigate Zealand, and the screw propellers Dyambi and Vesuvius, for the purpose of giving protection to the trade and navigation of the Netherlands during the contest which seems to be in existence in the United States of North America, wherever it may be desired, therefore esteems it to be his duty to direct the attention of ship-masters, consignees, and freighters, to the peril to which their insurance against loss will be exposed by any violation of the obligations imposed on neutral powers to respect actual blockades, and not to carry contraband of war, or despatches of belligerents.

In these cases they will be subject to all the resulting losses that may follow, without the benefit of any protection or intervention on the part of his Majesty's government. Of which take notice.

THE HAGUE, *June*, 1861.

The minister above named.

Mr. Seward to Mr. Pike.

No. 8]   DEPARTMENT OF STATE,
                                             Washington, July 1, 1861.

SIR: Your despatch of June 8 (No. 1) has been received. The President approves of your conduct and the sentiments you expressed on the occasion of your first audience by his Majesty. We are gratified by your confirmation of the high opinion we had formed of the fidelity and diligence of your predecessor.

I am, sir, respectfully, your obedient servant,
                                             WILLIAM H. SEWARD.
JAMES S. PIKE, Esq., &c., &c., &c.

Mr. Pike to Mr. Seward.

[Extracts.]

No. 7.]   UNITED STATES LEGATION,
                                             The Hague, July 4, 1861.

SIR: Referring to your last despatch, in which you say "the government has little time to think of its foreign relations, and when it does think of them, it is chiefly to consider how and in what way it can most effectually counteract the efforts of the revolutionists to procure European intervention in their favor," I beg to observe that within my circle of observation I find no occasion to change the opinion I have heretofore expressed in regard to the general good dispositions of the European governments towards that of the United States.

That there is any feeling of active sympathy, I should fear to allege. Every nation has its own peculiar, and to itself, important cares and difficulties, and each devotes the most of its time and attentions to these, caring comparatively little for those of others except so far as they affect their own. The domestic disturbances of a country three thousand miles away is thus regarded with a philosophic equanimity, and I think I may say with very great indifference except in respect to the commercial bearing of the events occurring there. But if little especial sympathy is felt for the United States government, still less is felt for the insurgents, whose revolt is seen to have caused the dire calamities now existing. So that we may still be allowed to claim a balance in our favor of the good wishes of European governments.

The revolutionary state of things in the United States has been, and is being very generally and thoroughly discussed in European journals, and all such discussion favors, of necessity, the cause of the government. This is especially true of the discussions in the German publications.   *

        *   *   *   *   *   *   *   *

In Germany, where discussion always partakes more of an absolute nature than anywhere else, from causes not necessary to delineate here, American affairs are more justly and comprehensively handled, and being more completely divested of their transitory features, results as I have stated.

On the whole, I think our government and the people it represents have not, thus far, any adequate cause to complain of the attitude of European governments, or the state of European opinion, toward them. The insurgents are nowhere in favor, and certainly have not received so much toleration and encouragement in Europe as was extended to them by a portion of

our own press and by the administration of Mr. Buchanan, previous to the breaking out of the war.   *   *   *   *   *
*   *   *   *   *   *   *   *
We all feel the deepest interest in the progress of events at home, and the utmost solicitude to do on this side of the Atlantic whatever is possible to further the ideas and purposes of our government. For my own part I am most anxious to go wherever, and to do whatever, I can to promote the designs and aid the labors of the administration in the great work devolved upon them.

I have the honor to be, with the highest respect, your obedient servant,

JAMES S. PIKE

Hon. WILLIAM H. SEWARD,
    Secretary of State, Washington.

Mr. Seward to Mr. Pike.

No. 9.]
           DEPARTMENT OF STATE,
           Washington, July 8, 1861.

SIR: Your despatch, No. 3, dated June 14th has been received, and the information which it brings is a cause of high satisfaction. Your proceedings in the various matters mentioned in that communication are approved.

I am, sir, respectfully your obedient servant,

WILLIAM H. SEWARD.

JAMES S. PIKE, Esq., &c., &c., &c.

Mr. Seward to Mr. Pike.

No. 11.]
           DEPARTMENT OF STATE,
           Washington, July 8, 1861.

SIR: Your despatch, No. 4, dated June 16 has been duly received.

You will, at the first convenient opportunity, make known to the minister of foreign affairs the satisfaction with which the United States has received intelligence of the prompt decision and friendly action of the government of the Netherlands on the subject of the disturbances occurring in our country.

You will receive herewith, confidentially, a copy of my last despatch to Mr. Dayton on the subject of the proffer of our adhesion to the declaration of the congress of Paris. It will serve, I think, to relieve your uncertainty, and to indicate the course you shall pursue. Only Great Britain and France have assumed to say to us that they regard our country as divided or broken, for any purpose, whether of war or of peace. And we have not thought proper to receive that communication from them. We treat as being the sovereign government over all the Union—the disloyal and the loyal, all alike—or we do not treat at all. This simple statement will, perhaps, be necessary to make the paper addressed to Mr. Dayton clearly intelligible to you.

These latter remarks you will consider as confidential.

I am, sir, respectfully, your obedient servant,

WILLIAM H. SEWARD.

JAMES S. PIKE, Esq., &c., &c., &c.

Mr. Pike to Mr. Seward.

[Extract.]

No. 8.]   UNITED STATES LEGATION,
                                              The Hague, July 12, 1861.

SIR: I have communicated to Baron de Zuylen, as directed, your high appreciation of the course of his government on our domestic affairs, as manifested and expressed in his reply to my predecessor's communication of the 8th of April last.

I have the honor to be, with great respect, your most obedient servant,
                                                          JAMES S. PIKE.
Hon. WILLIAM H. SEWARD,
     Secretary of State, Washington.

Mr. Seward to Mr. Pike.

No. 12.]   DEPARTMENT OF STATE,
                                              Washington, July 26, 1861.

SIR: Your very interesting despatch of June 22 (No. 6) has been received. The President is gratified with the just and proper sentiments expressed by the government of Holland concerning the United States.

Subsequently to the sending of my despatch to you concerning the affairs of the western powers in Japan, communications have been received from the Tycoon, and his ministers for foreign affairs, measurably supported by Mr. Harris, our excellent representatative there, urging a delay in opening the ports under the treaty in terms so strong that the President has concluded that I shall have a conference here with the representatives of the powers interested in the question. This conference will be held next week. You will be advised of whatever is considered.

We have met a reverse in arms. But though at first it seemed appalling, because it was as severe as it was unexpected, yet the result is even now seen to be only a signal for greater effort and more determined resolution.

I send you, confidentially, a copy of my most recent despatch to Mr. Adams.

I am, sir, respectfully, your obedient servant,
                                                          WILLIAM H. SEWARD.
JAMES S. PIKE, Esq., &c., &c., &c.

Mr. Seward to Mr. Pike.

No. 15.]   DEPARTMENT OF STATE,
                                              Washington, August 15, 1861.

SIR: We learn, in a manner which obliges us to give unwilling credit, that the Sumter, an armed steamer, well known through all the American seas to be a privateer fitted out for and actually engaged in depredations upon the commerce of the United States by some disloyal citizens, under the command of an officer named Semmes, on or about the 17th of July last, entered the port of Curaçoa and communicated directly with the local authorities of that island; that she was hospitably received there and was permitted to take a large quantity of coals, (said to be 120 tons,) and also to take on board a large supply of provisions; that the privateer's crew was allowed entire freedom in the place; that when one of the crew had deserted, an order was given by the authorities of the port for his arrest; that the attempt for that purpose having proved unsuccessful, the same authorities pledged themselves that the arrest should be afterwards effectually made, and that the deserter should be held in custody, to be surrendered to the pirate captain on his return homeward to the island.

You are instructed to bring this matter immediately to the notice of the government of the Netherlands. The subject of damages for so great a violation of the rights of the United States will be considered when we shall have properly verified the facts of the case. In the mean time you will ask the government of the Netherlands for any explanation of the transaction it may be able or see fit to give. You will further say that the United States, if the case thus stated shall prove to be correct, will expect, in view of the treaties existing between the two countries, and the principles of the law of nations, as well as upon the ground of assurances recently received from the goveror of the Netherlands, that it will disown the action of its authorities at Curaçoa, and will adopt efficient means to prevent a recurrence of such proceedings hereafter. If the case thus presented shall not be found entirely erroneous, or be very essentially modified, the United States will expect that the governor of the island of Curaçoa will be promptly made to feel the severe displeasure of the government of the Netherlands, a country with which we have lived on terms of unbroken friendship for three quarters of a century.

I am, sir, respectfully, your obedient servant,

WILLIAM H. SEWARD.

James S. Pike, Esq , &c., &c., &c.

Mr. Pike to Mr. Seward.

No. 13.]   United States Legation,
                The Hague, August 18, 1861.

Sir: I avail myself of the departure of my predecessor, Mr. Murphy, for America, who sails in the Arago from Havre on the 20th instant, to send you this communication.

The news from America to the 8th instant, which comes to-day by telegraph, is received with satisfaction. The continued successes in Missouri; the election of a majority of Union representatives to the Kentucky legislature, giving renewed assurance of the conservative position of that important State; the prevailing quiet in Maryland and Delaware; and the failure of the confederate commanders to take any advantage of their recent extraordinary good fortune, all tend to reproduce the general state of feeling that prevailed on this side of the Atlantic before the occurrence of the disaster at Bull Run.

But there has never been anything here to correspond to what appears to have been the momentary depression and alarm felt at home after the repulse of our troops. The event was never regarded here to be of great significance, as it was a flight without a pursuit, and a victory of which the victor was not aware.

The reverse seems now to be all summed up in the fact of a failure to advance on the part of the Union forces.

Still it is not to be disguised that the obstacles to be overcome in reducing the insurgents are regarded to be formidable when the large armed force they have been able to bring into the field is considered. There exists, however, a consideration which seems to check confidence in their ability to hold out, resting on the general belief of their destitution of resources to maintain a large body of troops in the field, and that the lapse of time will thus operate unfavorably on their levies.

Your despatch of the 26th of July (No. 12) is received. I am gratified to know that I am able to communicate anything which you deem of particular interest.

It affords me still greater satisfaction to have your assurance in the copy of your despatch to Mr. Adams, therewith enclosed, that "it is not likely anything will now be done here hastily or inconsiderately affecting our foreign relations."

I have the honor to be, with great respect, your most obedient servant,

JAMES S. PIKE

Hon. WILLIAM H. SEWARD,
   Secretary of State, Washington.

Mr. Pike to Mr. Seward.

[Extract.]

No. 14.] UNITED STATES LEGATION,
   The Hague, August 28, 1861.

SIR: The mails of to-day bring intelligence from America that the privateer steamer Sumter, bearing the so-called confederate flag, has been permitted by the authorities at Curaçoa to enter and replenish her exhausted stock of fuel and supplies with which to renew her career of depredation upon the commerce of the United States.

I have instantly called the attention of this government to these reports, and have assured the minister of foreign affairs that, if they shall be borne out by the facts of the case, in view of the recent prompt and friendly action of the Dutch government in relation to privateering, they will be regarded by the government and people of the United States with equal regret and surprise.

I think it will prove that the orders of the Dutch government to their colonial authorities to exclude privateers from their ports, which were issued about the middle of June, and of which I apprised you on the 16th of that month in my despatch No. 4, have by some means failed to reach Curaçoa. The ships which were sent out were expected to rendezvous at Curaçoa and winter in those seas. But they may be delaying their visit to avoid the heats of summer. I hope to be able to afford you more detailed information by the next mail, which want of time prevents me from obtaining now in season for this.

I thought of suggesting the publication in our newspapers of the Dutch proclamations, copies of which I forwarded to you with the despatch referred to, but I concluded the department did not need my suggestions on that head.

   *   *   *   *   *   *   *   *   *

I have the honor to be, with great respect, your most obedient servant.

JAMES S. PIKE.

Hon. WILLIAM H. SEWARD, &c., &c.

Mr. Pike to Mr. Seward.

No. 15.]   UNITED STATES LEGATION,
                                        The Hague, September 4, 1861.

SIR : Since writing to you on the 28th ultimo in regard to my action on
the strength of the public reports in respect to the steamer Sumter, I have
received your despatch, No. 15, under date of the 15th of August, and also
its duplicate.

I immediately addressed a communication to this government presenting
the substance of that despatch. I have since had two interviews with Baron
Van Zuylen, the minister of foreign affairs, on the questions involved and
likely to be involved in the case. Mr. Van Zuylen has informed me that his
government has received a brief communication from the governor of
Curaçoa stating that the vessel in question put into the port of Curaçoa in
distress, and was not a privateer.

In the course of our first interview Baron Van Zuylen dropped the remark
that it was probable the vessel was regarded as a ship-of-war of the so-
called Confederate States, but he subsequently seemed to desire to withdraw
the suggestion.

I felt it to be my duty to protest against the idea that aid and countenance
could be afforded by a friendly power to the Sumter, though she did assume
the character of a ship-of-war of the insurgents. I claimed that were she
afforded shelter and supplies on this ground by the authorities at Curaçoa,
and should the Dutch government approve the act, it would be, substantially,
a recognition of the southern confederacy, and that in my judgment such
an act would be regarded by the United States as an unfriendly, and even
hostile act, which might lead to the gravest consequences. I held that
nothing more need be asked by the so-styled Confederate States, as a practical measure of recognition, than that a ship like the Sumter, claiming to be
a national vessel of those States, should be permitted to enter the neighboring ports of foreign nations, and there obtain the necessary means to enable
her to depredate upon the commerce of the United States. That such a
course on the part of any power, aggravated by the fact that she was unable
to obtain such supplies at home, so far from being neutral conduct was
really to afford the most efficient aid to the men who were in rebellion
against their own government, and plundering and destroying the vessels
and property of their fellow citizens on the high seas. I protested against
such a doctrine as tending necessarily to the termination of all friendly
relations between our government and any government that would tolerate
such practices, whether that government were France or England, or Spain
or Holland. I remarked that it was not for me to judge of the purposes of
European powers in regard to the existing state of things in the United
States; but if there were to be exhibited a disposition anywhere to take
advantage of our present situation, I believed it would be found that such
a course could not be taken with impunity now, nor without leading to
alienation and bitterness in the future.

Baron Van Zuylen hereupon explained that the earnest desire of his
government was to maintain friendly relations with the United States, and
to do nothing to interrupt the existing harmony between the two countries.
That the point in question had not been considered by his government, and
that the whole case should receive careful attention so soon as the facts
relating to it could be ascertained. He has since sent me a note on the
subject, which I enclose.

The baron stated to me that the governor of Curaçoa had received the instructions of the Dutch government, and the baron was of the opinion that

the governor had paid too much attention to the letter, overlooking the spirit of the instructions, which remark I took to mean, that as the governor's instructions only ordered the exclusion of privateers and vessels *not* in distress, and that as the Sumter claimed to be a vessel of war, and to be *in* distress, the governor had sought to shield his action under this shallow and transparent device of the privateer, which could certainly deceive nobody who was not willing to be deceived.

I presume there is no danger of the Dutch government taking any position on this question *in haste*, as that is not their way. It is quite probable they will take time to send to Curçaoa for facts and particulars. Meantime the British government seem likely to have to act on the same question, as I see the Sumter has been at Trinidad, which will afford them a precedent, for which I am the more sorry, as I learned enough while I was in England to satisfy me that that government was likely to indulge in loose practices in regard to vessels sailing under the confederate flag.

But there is nothing in the circumstances or dispositions of this government, in my opinion, to induce them to exhibit unfriendliness to us or grant favors to the confederates, whatever there may be on the part of some of their slaveholding governors, of whom I infer him of Curaçoa to be one. I expect therefore to find the authorities here pursue a course void of offence towards the United States, however others may act. I shall make it my endeavor to induce the minister of foreign affairs to have sent out at once such instructions to the West Indies as will prevent the Sumter, or her confederates, from making use of the Dutch ports in future, whatever their pretensions.

Since penning the foregoing, and at the last moment before being compelled to close for the mail, I have had a third interview with Baron Van Zuylen. He states that the instructions sent out in June were framed purposely different from those of France, and excluded all reference to vessels of war, solely because that course was deemed more favorable to the United States government which had ships-of-war and no privateers. You will remember that I called attention to this peculiarity at the time.

In answer to my inquiry whether he would not immediately adapt his instructions to cover such cases as that of the Sumter, information of which I was desirous to transmit by the next steamer, he replied that the subject was now under consideration in the colonial department. He insisted, however, that the governor of Curaçoa declared the vessel was admitted on the ground of her being in distress, she having carried away one of her masts, and that before admitting her he convoked his council, who recommend the course he pursued.

I renewedly represented to Baron Van Zuylen the very grave character of this question and its vital importance to the commerce of the United States.

Since the government here must by this time fully understand that our government is very much in earnest on this subject, I entertain the hope that they will hurry their deliberations to a favorable conclusion.

Allusion having been made on my part to the possible influence of slaveholding sympathies in this case, I was pleased to be informed by Baron Van Zuylen that the question of slavery had been finally determined in Holland, and that emancipation is to take place in all the Dutch colonies within two years.

I have the honor to be, with great respect, your most obedient servant,
JAMES S. PIKE.

Hon. WILLIAM H. SEWARD,
Secretary of State, Washington.

Baron Van Zuylen to Mr. Pike.

[Translation.]

THE HAGUE, *September* 2, 1861.

SIR: I have the honor to acknowledge the receipt of your communications of the 28th of August and of 2d of September.

I hastened to communicate these notes to the minister of the colonies, and I hope to be enabled at an early day, and so soon as the reports of the Governor of Curaçoa respecting the affair of the steamer "Sumter" shall be known to me, to give you a reply upon this subject.

Be pleased, sir, to accept the renewed assurance of my high consideration.

DE ZUYLEN DE NIJEVELT.

Mr. PIKE,
    Minister Resident of the United States of America.

Mr. Seward to Mr. Pike.

No. 21.]   DEPARTMENT OF STATE,
         Washington, September 5, 1861.

SIR: Your despatch of August 18, (No. 13,) has been received, and the opinions it expresses seem to be just, while the information it gives is very satisfactory. Treason is apt to mature its energies before it strikes the first blow; on the other hand, loyalty is unapprehensive of danger and usually waits for conviction of the necessity for defence. The course of this domestic civil war illustrates this maxim. The fortunes of the insurrection hang on immediate success and despatch; efforts, therefore, are made to secure it. I feel sure, on the contrary, that the government has been continually gaining strength with every expenditure of vigor it has made. You will be gratified to learn that the paper issued by the government is at par in the market where gold and silver are recognized as the only lawful tender in the payment of debts.

While you will not hold out inducements of rewards or bounties for soldiers, you may say, whenever it shall seem expedient, that any foreigners arriving in this country will probably find no difficulty in finding military employment.

With a high appreciation of your discretion and vigilance, I am, sir, respectfully, your obedient servant,

WILLIAM H. SEWARD.

JAMES S. PIKE, Esq., &c., &c., &c.

Mr. Pike to Mr. Seward.

[Extract.]

No. 16.]   LEGATION OF THE UNITED STATES,
         The Hague, September 11, 1861.

SIR: Subsequently to the interviews I had with the minister of foreign affairs, of which I spoke in my last, and after the transmission to you of my despatch (No. 15) of the 4th instant, I addressed the following communication to Baron Van Zuylen:

"LEGATION OF THE UNITED STATES,
"*The Hague, September* 7, 1861.

"SIR: I do not understand this government to have yet distinctly conceded 'belligerent rights' to the self-styled Confederate States.

"In behalf of my government I beg to say that I trust Holland will not take this position now, and open the questions to flow therefrom. By doing so, this government may make an enemy of the United States, through the consequences growing out of that act. But Holland will not thereby make a friend of the rash and misguided men who lead the rebellion against the American government. For their object is to perpetuate and extend African slavery. With this object Holland can have no sympathy. Your government has just now determined to abolish that remnant of barbarism in your colonial possessions.

"The slaveholders' rebellion cannot be successful. The United States has determined it shall not be, and that it will preserve the union of the States at whatever cost.

"But even if we admit, for argument's sake, that some of the slaveholding States should be allowed hereafter to depart from the Union, still would the rebellion be unsuccessful in its objects, and hospitality shown to its progress be unavailing. The United States would be still resolute to defeat the purposes of the rebel slaveholder. They would do this by their own unaided efforts. They might readily co-operate with foreign powers to the same end. Such of those powers as hold possessions in America, wherein slavery has been abolished, would join in this object from motives of justice and humanity, as well as from considerations of policy and consistency. Those who have colonies where the practice still prevails would gladly concur in self-defence. England having abolished slavery, France having put it under her feet, the position of these two great maritime powers on this subject is fixed. The recent action of the French Emperor is conclusive as to the policy of that powerful monarchy. Spain, in her late trespass upon St. Domingo, has been constrained to formally stipulate that she will not reintroduce slavery in that island; Mexico and Central America will be only too eager to enter into stipulations that shall save them from any attempted spoliation, and preserve the condition of freedom from slavery for all their inhabitants now and hereafter. A common civilization throughout the world will look with favor on a common union to crush the offensive purposes of the rebellious slaveholder. His success, therefore, is out of the question. Unless the world is to go backward, and history reverse its lessons, this rebellion in its leading purpose is foredoomed. Even governments cannot save that against which humanity revolts. Surrounded by communities on the north, on the south, on the west, that have expelled slavery; the islands of the Caribbean sea nearly all emancipated from this pestilent system; the fabric of the rebellious slaveholder, which he is so madly ambitious to erect, were even its temporary establishment possible, would soon be washed away by the attrition of surrounding influence upon its crumbling foundations, and its remains left a ruin in the world.

"It is thus neither just nor politic, in any point of view, for the powers of Europe to do anything to encourage this abortive and criminal enterprise of the rebellious American slaveholder. For though they should do ever so much, the effort will be none the less abortive, through the operation of forces that governments cannot control.

"The recognition of 'belligerent rights' to the party in question by England and France was a precipitate and unnecessary act. It was surely time enough to do this when the alternative presented an embarrassing situation.

"The Dutch government has been wiser. In continuing to occupy the position of refusing all countenance to the authors of such a hateful rebellion, the Netherlands will do an act which will be viewed with the liveliest satisfaction by the United States, and, I may be permitted to add, one worthy the traditions of this ancient and renowned state, and will set an example well worthy the respect and consideration of other nations.

"The undersigned, &c., &c.

"Baron Van Zuylen, &c., &c."

On the 9th instant I had an interview with Baron Van Zuylen, again urging him in the most earnest manner to issue such instructions to the Dutch authorities in the West Indies as would peremptorily exclude from their ports every species of craft set afloat by the secessionists.

Baron Van Zuylen appears, and I have no doubt is, very desirous to do all he possibly can, under what he deems the requirements of public law, to carry out the wishes of the United States in this matter. He does not consider that his government has recognized belligerent rights, and desires not to be pressed on that point. I told him we had no desire to press him to do anything, except to issue such instructions to his colonial governors as will effectually exclude the piratical vessels of the secessionists from making use of the Dutch ports.

He asked then if we would consent to have our own ships-of-war excluded. I told him if that was necessary to relieve him from a dilemma, I did not know how far such an act might be tolerated for the sake of an advantage which we could procure in no other way. We might not find fault, if thereby we found our interests advanced. But, of course, I could not undertake to commit my government on the point. I remarked that exclusion would not operate to our disadvantage, inasmuch as we had command of the sea, while it would be fatal to the plunderers, as they had no retreat at home. He intimated that his government contemplated making the proposition to the United States. He also remarked that the course of our own government threw impediments in their way; for while we regarded the secessionists as rebels, we did not seem to treat them as such when taken prisoners, not even their privateers. I concluded the interview by renewedly urging every consideration I could adduce to induce him to issue the desired orders, and to lose no time in doing it.

He will soon make a written communication on the whole subject, which I will forward at the earliest moment after receiving it.

After my interview, I addressed Baron Van Zuylen the following note:

"United States Legation,
"The Hague, September 9, 1861.

"Sir: Referring to our conversation of to-day, I beg to suggest that what appears to you a practical difficulty may, it seems to me, be properly overcome by your government issuing orders to its colonial authorities to regard all armed vessels bearing the so-called confederate flag as privateers. They are so in fact, and they should not be allowed to shield themselves under any other pretext. Unless a vessel claiming to be a ship-of-war exhibit some prima facie evidence of being such, in her size, and in her other external symbols and aspects, which these piratical craft do not, the proper authorities may well claim the right to decline all investigation of the case, and assume her unlawful character.

"The undersigned, &c. &c.

"Baron Van Zuylen."

*   *   *   *   *   *   *   *   *

I have the honor to be, with great respect, your obedient servant,
                                        JAMES S. PIKE.

Hon. William H. Seward, Secretary of State.

Mr. Pike to Mr. Seward.

[Extract.]

No. 17.]   UNITED STATES LEGATION,
                                          The Hague, September 18, 1861.

SIR: The minister of foreign affairs has not yet furnished me with the promised communication on the Sumter case.

On the 12th instant I addressed him the following note:

"SIR: Referring to my recent communications to you on the case of the Sumter, I beg to say, in order to avoid all possibility of cavil or misapprehension, that, in speaking of or alluding to the marauding vessels of the persons in rebellion against the United States government as 'privateers,' I refer to them as such only in the sense of their own pretensions; the United States government, as you are well aware, regarding them solely as piratical craft, and the persons engaged thereon as pirates.

"I have the honor to be, &c., &c.

"Baron VAN ZUYLEN, &c., &c."

  *   *   *   *   *   *   *   *   *

I have the honor to be, with great respect, your most obedient servant,
                                              JAMES S. PIKE.
Hon. WILLIAM H. SEWARD,
    Secretary of State, Washington.

Mr. Seward to Mr. Pike.

No. 22.]   DEPARTMENT OF STATE,
                                          Washington, September 23, 1861.

SIR: Your despatch of August 28, No. 14, has been received. We await with some interest the explanations of the government of the Netherlands concerning the affair at Curaçoa, but at the same time with very great confidence that it will be conformable to the good and friendly relations existing between the two countries.

I am, sir, respectfully, your obedient servant,
                                              WILLIAM H. SEWARD.
JAMES S. PIKE, Esq , &c., &c., &c..

Mr. Pike to Mr. Seward.

[Extracts.]

No. 18.]   UNITED STATES LEGATION,
                                          The Hague, September 25, 1861.

SIR: I have the honor to enclose the communication from the Dutch government in reference to the Sumter case. Though dated the 17th, it did not make its appearance to me till the 20th.

You will perceive that the ground taken in regard to the harboring of the Sumter in the port of Curaçoa is, that it was the case of a vessel in distress.

This paper, however, goes beyond the case in hand, and argues the claim of the seceding States to be considered belligerents, and their rights as such, besides going over the whole ground of the rights of neutrals.

Baron Van Zuylen makes out to his own satisfaction that the secessionists hold that position, and that this carries with it the right of hospitality, in neutral ports, to their ships-of-war.

To my suggestion in my note of the 9th, that the Sumter was in no just sense a ship-of-war, but a privateer, or, as our government claims, a pirate, and that the want of the ordinary characteristics of a ship-of-war, besides the fact that she bore a strange flag of no recognized nationality, entitled us to ask of Holland, as a friendly nation, to *assume* her unlawful character. Mr. Van Zuylen opposes an argument to show that the Sumter was really a ship-of-war of the Confederate States, and that an impartial neutrality demanded that she be so treated. He finds his support of his position that this was the Sumter's real character in the declarations of her captain and in the allegation of *Harpers' Weekly.*

The minister of foreign affairs seems to admit the force of the argument I had previously urged, that it was inconsistent with all ideas of a just neutrality that these marauding vessels of the secessionists could be allowed to make free use of the neighboring ports of a power holding friendly relations with the United States, for hostile purposes, and this, too, while deprived of all shelter or resource at home. And, in reply to my earnest request that he would cause to be issued to the Dutch colonial authorities in the West Indies orders against such use of their ports, Baron Nan Zuylen de Nijevelt declares, under cover of his general principles, that orders shall be issued in the sense of forbidding the use of the Dutch ports as the base of operations against United States commerce, or, as he phrases it, by either of the belligerents.

In regard to this part of Mr. Van Zuylen's communication, I will here observe that much will depend upon the character of these instructions, and not less upon the spirit in which they are executed. It is in the power of the Dutch government, and of its colonial authorities, to so act, upon the basis of the rule laid down on this head, as to avoid further cause of complaint on the part of the United States, and to effectually prevent these sea robbers from making use of the Dutch ports as a means of pursuing their ravages; and I have so expressed myself to Baron Van Zuylen in the note of which I have the honor to annex a copy. I will add that I have confidence that such orders will be given.

*   *   *   *   *   *   *   *   *   *

The following is a copy of my note to Mr. Van Zuylen:

"UNITED STATES LEGATION,
The Hague, September 23, 1861.

"SIR: I have had the honor to receive your communication of the 17th instant, which will, in due time, receive that attention its importance merits.

"Meantime I desire to observe that, as must have been obvious to you, I have hitherto contented myself with advancing general considerations appealing to the friendly dispositions of Holland, rather than in invoking the application of the strict rules of public law to the case under review.

"The Dutch government exercises its undoubted right in overlooking such considerations, and in assuming the championship of a so-called neutrality, which insists upon treating a domestic disturbance as a war between equals.

"For those who so desire, as I am sure Holland does not, it is easy to be persuaded of an incipient nationality in an insurrection, and to see a ship-of-war in every pirate that insults mankind with her depredations or shocks it with her crimes.

"I have great satisfaction in learning from his communication that Baron Van Zuylen recognizes the force of the considerations I have had the honor to present to him touching the evident violation of a just neutrality which is involved in the free use of the ports of the Netherlands by the cruisers of persons engaged in piratical depredations upon the commerce and shipping of the United States, and also in learning that the government of his Majesty has determined that it will not permit its ports to be made the base of operations against that commerce, and that instructions in this sense will be addressed to the governors of the Netherlands colonial possessions.

"It is in the power of the Dutch government, acting upon the rule it has thus laid down, to issue such instructions to its colonial authorities as shall prevent further cause of complaint on the part of the United States, if those instructions shall be executed in good faith.

"The United States government will rely upon the action of Holland in this respect, and will still confidently look for such a course on the part of the Dutch government as will aid it in driving the instigators of rebellion and plunderers of property upon the high seas from the haunts they infest, and in bringing them to condign punishment.

"I have the honor, &c., &c.

"JAMES S. PIKE.

"Baron Van Zuylen, &c., &c."

To-day I have addressed Baron Van Zuylen the following note:

"UNITED STATES LEGATION,
"The Hague, September 25, 1861.

"SIR: I shall to-day forward your communication of the 17th instant to my government. I do it with reluctance, since its basis is found, as I have already remarked to you, in the assumption of the government of the Netherlands that the domestic disturbance in the United States is a war between equals.

"It cannot be supposed that the United States will consent to debate the question of an abridgment of their sovereignty with Holland or any other nation.

"The United States are one whole undivided nation, especially so far as foreign nations are concerned, and Holland is, by the law of nations and by treaties, not a neutral power between two imaginary parties there, but a friend of the United States. There is in the United States, as there has always been since the establishment of the government, one political power, namely, the United States of America, competent to make war and peace, and conduct alliances and commerce with foreign nations. There is none other, either in fact, or recognized by foreign nations. There is, indeed, an armed sedition seeking to overthrow the government, and the government is employing military and naval force to suppress it. But these facts do not constitute a war presenting two belligerent powers, and modifying the national character, rights, and responsibilities, or the character, rights, and responsibilities of foreign nations.

"That Holland should take a different view of the case will, I am sure, be a subject of very deep regret to the United States.

"The undersigned, &c., &c.

"JAMES S. PIKE.

"Baron Van Zuylen, &c., &c."

* * * * * * * * *

I have the honor to be, with great respect, your most obedient servant,

JAMES S. PIKE.

Hon. WM. H. SEWARD,
Secretary of State, Washington, D. C.

Baron Van Zuylen to Mr. Pike.

[Translation.]

THE HAGUE, *September* 17, 1861.

SIR: The department of the colonies has just communicated to me the information, transmitted by the governor of Curaçoa, concerning the affair of the ship "Sumter," and I hasten to bring to your notice the following observations, by way of sequence to the preliminary reply which I had the honor to address to you on the 2d of this month. According to the principles of the law of nations, all nations without exception may admit vessels of war belonging to a belligerent State to their ports, and accord to them all the favors which constitute an asylum. Conditions are imposed on said vessels during their stay in the port or roadstead. For example, they must keep perfect peace with all vessels that may be there ; they may not augment their crews, nor the number of their guns, nor be on the lookout in the ports or roadsteads for the purpose of watching after hostile vessels arriving or departing, &c. Besides, every state has the right to interdict foreign vessels of war from entrance to ports which are purely military. Thus it was that Sweden and Denmark, in 1854, at the time of the Crimean war, reserved the right to exclude vessels of war from such or such ports of their dominions.

The neutral power has also the right to act like France, who, by her declaration of neutrality in the war between the United States and the Confederate States, under date of 9th June last, (Moniteur of 11th June,) does not permit any vessel of war, or privateer, of one or the other of the belligerents, to enter and remain with their prizes in French ports longer than twenty-four hours, unless in case of refuge under stress.

In the proclamation of the month of June last, which was communicated to you with my despatch of the 13th, the government of the Netherlands has not excluded vessels of war from her ports.

As to privateers, the greatest number of the maritime nations allows them the privilege of asylum upon the same conditions nearly as to vessels of war.

According to a highly-esteemed author on the law of nations, (Hautefeuille, Droits et Devoirs des Nations Neutres, I, p. 139,) privateers may claim entrance into the ports of nations which have consented to accord asylum to them, not only in cases of pressing dangers, but even in cases in which they may deem it advantageous, or even only agreeable, and for obtaining rest or articles of secondary necessity, such as the refreshments they may have need of.

The terms of the proclamation of the Netherlands government, which admits privateers into Netherlands ports only in cases of distress, harmonize with this doctrine.

Moreover, according to the information received from the governor of Curaçoa, the "Sumter" was actually in distress, and that functionary could not, therefore, refuse to allow the said vessel to enter the port.

Strong in its amicable intentions, the King's government does not believe itself bound to confine itself to the defence of the conduct of one of its agents in the particular case under discussion. It is not ignorant that it can or may hereafter be a contested question in such cases as to the reality of the distress in which such vessel or other would be, and that thus the subject of the admission generally of the Confederate States vessels would rest untouched. I, therefore, sir, think it opportune to look into the question to determine whether the Sumter should have been admitted at Curaçoa outside of the condition of well-assured distress.

It is evident that the reply to be made is dependent on another question—that is to say, was this vessel a man-of-war or a privateer?

In the latter case, the Netherlands government could not, except in case of a putting in compelled by distress, (relâche forcée,) admit the Sumter into the ports of its territories.

It is not sufficient to dispose of the difficulty by the declaration that the Sumter is, as is stated in your despatches, "a vessel fitted out for, and actually engaged in, piratical expeditions," or "a privateer steamer." Such an assertion should be clearly proved, in accordance with the rule of law, "*affirmanti incumbit probatio.*"

After having poised, with all the attention which comports with the weightiness of the matter, the facts and circumstances which characterize the dissensions which now are laying desolate the United States, and of which no government more desires the prompt termination than does that of the Netherlands, I think I may express the conviction that the Sumter is not a privateer, but a man-of-war—grounding myself on the following considerations:

In the first place, the declaration of the commander of the vessel given in writing to the governor of Curaçoa, who had made known that he would not allow a privateer to come into the port, and had then demanded explanations as to the character of the vessel. This declaration purported "the Sumter is a ship-of-war duly commissioned by the government of the Confederate States."

The Netherlands governor had to be contented with the word of the commander couched in writing. Mr. Ortolan, (Diplomatie de la Mer, I, p. 217,) in speaking of the evidence of nationality of vessels of war, thus expresses himself:

"The flag and the pennant are visible indications, but we are not bound to give faith to them until they are sustained by a cannot shot."

The attestation of the commander may be exigible; but other proofs must be presumed; and, whether on the high seas or elsewhere, no foreign power has the right to obtain the exhibition of them.

Therefore the colonial council has unanimously concluded that the word of the commanding officer was sufficient.

In the second place, the vessel armed for war by *private persons* is called "privateer." The character of such vessel is settled precisely, and, like her English name, (privateer,) indicates sufficiently under this circumstance that she is a *private* armed vessel—name which Mr. Wheaton gives them.—(Elements of International Law, II, p. 19.)

Privateering is the maritime warfare which privateers are authorized to make, *for their own account*, against merchant vessels of the enemy by virtue of letters of marque which are issued to them by the State.

The Sumter is not a private vessel; is not the private property of unconnected individuals—of private ship-owners. She, therefore, cannot be a privateer; she can only be a ship-of-war or ship of the State armed for cruising. Thus the Sumter is designated, in the extract annexed from "Harpers' Weekly," under the name of "rebel ship-of-war."

Thirdly. It cannot be held, as you propose in your despatch of the 9th of this month, that all vessels carrying the confederate flag are, without distinction, to be considered as privateers, because the principles of the law of nations, as well as the examples of history, require that the rights of war be accorded to those States.

The government of the United States holds that it should consider the States of the south as rebels.

It does not pertain to the King's government to pronounce upon the subject of a question which is entirely within the domain of the internal regulation of the United States; neither has it to inquire whether, in virtue of the Constitution which rules that republic, the States of the south can separate from the central government, and whether they ought then, aye or no, to be reputed as rebels during the first period of the difficulties.

But I deem it my duty to observe to you, sir, that, according to the doctrines of the best publicists, such as Vattel, III, c. 18, § 292, and Mr. de Rayneval, Droit de la Nation et des Gens, I, p. 161, there is a notable difference between rebellion and civil war. "When," says Vattel, "a party is formed in the state, which no longer obeys its sovereign, and is strong enough to make head against him, or in a republic, when the nation divides into two opposing parties, and on one side and the other take up arms, then it is civil war." It is, therefore, the latter which now agitates the great American republic.

But, in this case, the rights of war must be accorded to the two parties.

Let me be allowed to cite here only two passages ; the one from Vattel, (II, c. 4, § 56,) which reads : "Whenever affairs reach to civil war the ties of political association are broken, or at least suspended, between the sovereign and his people. They may be considered as two distinct powers; and, since one and the other are independent of any foreign authority, no one has the right to judge between them. Each of them may be right. It follows, then, that the two parties may act as having equal right." The other passage is taken from the work of a former minister, himself belonging to the United States, Mr. Wheaton, who, in his Elements of International Law, c. I, p. 35, (Am. ed., part 1, p. 32,) thus expresses himself : "If the foreign state would observe absolute neutrality in the face of dissensions which disturb another state, it must accord to both belligerent parties all the rights which war accords to public enemies, such as the right of blockade, and the right of intercepting merchandise contraband of war."

As for historic evidence, it will suffice to call to mind from ancient times the struggle of the United Provinces with Spain, and from modern date the war between the Hispano-American colonies and the mother country since 1810, the war of independence of Greece from Turkey since 1821, &c.

It will doubtless be useless to recollect, on this occasion, that the principle to see only insurgents in the States of the south, having neither sovereignty nor rights of war, nor of peace, was put forward by England, at the breaking out of the war of independence of the Anglo-American colonies, in the vindicatory memoir published by the British court in 1778 in answer to the exposition of the motives for the conduct of France, which had lately signed, on the 6th day of February of that year, a treaty with the United States, in which they were regarded as an independent nation.

But the court of Versailles set out from other principles, which she developed in "Observations on the Vindicatory Memoir of the Court of London," saying, among other things: "It is sufficient to the justification of his Majesty that the colonies had established their independence not merely by a solemn declaration, but also in fact, and had maintained it against the efforts of the mother country."

Existing circumstances seem to present the same characteristics; and if it is desired to treat the States of the south as rebels, and accuse them of felony, there might here be cited as applicable to the actual conduct of the United States towards the confederates the following remark of the court of Versailles : "In advancing this proposition, (that the possession of independence, of which the French cabinet said the Americans were in the enjoyment in 1778, was a veritable felony,) the English minister had, without doubt, forgotten the course he had himself taken towards the Americans from the publication of the declaration of independence. It is remembered that the creatures of the court constantly called upon the rebellion vengeance and destruction. However, notwithstanding all their clamors, the English minister abstained, after the declaration of independence, from prosecuting the Americans as rebels ; he observed, and still observes towards them, the rules of war usual among independent nations. American prisoners have been exchanged through cartels," &c.

The rights of war cannot, then, in the opinion of the King's government, be refused to the Confederate States; but I hasten to add that the recognition of these rights does not import in favor of such States recognition of their sovereignty.

"Foreign nations," says Mr. Martens, (Précis du Droit des Gens, l. VIII, c. 3, § 264,) "cannot refuse to consider as lawful enemies those who are empowered by their actual government, whatever that may be. *This is not recognition of its legitimacy.*"

This last recognition can only spring from express and official declaration, which no one of the cabinets of Europe has thus far made.

Finally, and in the last place, I permit myself here to cite the example of the American privateer Paul Jones.

This vessel, considered as a pirate by England, had captured two of his Britannic Majesty's ships in October, 1779. She took them into the Texel, and remained there more than two months, notwithstanding the representations of Mr. York, ambassador of Great Britain at the Hague, who considered the asylum accorded to such privateer (pirate as he called it in his memoir to the states general of 21st March, 1780) as directly contrary to treaties, and even to the ordinances of the government of the republic.

Mr. York demanded that the English vessels should be released.

The states general refused the restitution of the prizes.

The United States, whose belligerent rights were not recognized by England, enjoyed at that period the same treatment in the ports of the republic of the United Provinces as the Netherlands authorities have now accorded to the Confederate States.

If the cabinet of the Hague cannot, therefore, by force of the preceding, class all the vessels of the Confederate States armed for war in the category of privateers, much less can it treat them as pirates, (as you call them in your despatch of the 12th of this month,) or consider the Sumter as engaged in a fillibustering expedition—"engaged in a piratical expedition against the commerce of the United States"—as it reads in your communication of the 2d of September.

Here again historic antecedents militate in favor of the opinion of the Netherlands government.

.Is there need, in fact, to remind you that at the outset of the war of American independence, in 1778, the English refused to recognize American privateers as lawful enemies, under the pretence that the letters of marque which they bore did not emanate from the sovereign, but from revolted subjects ?

But Great Britain soon had to desist from this pretension, and to accord international treatment to the colonists in arms against the mother country.

The frankness with which the King's government has expressed its convictions in relation to the course to be taken towards the States of the south will, without doubt, be estimated at its just value by the government of the United States.

It will perceive therein the well-settled intention to preserve in safety the rights of neutrality ; to lay down for itself and to follow a line of conduct equally distant from feebleness as from too great adventurousness, but suitable for maintaining intact the dignity of the state.

The government of the Netherlands desires to observe, on the occasion of existing affairs in America, a perfect and absolute neutrality, and to abstain therefore from the slightest act of partiality.

According to Hubner, (Saisie de Bâtiments Neutres,) "neutrality consists in absolute inaction relative to war, and in exact and perfect impartiality manifested by facts in regard to the belligerents, as far as this impartiality has relation to the war, and to the direct and immediate measures for its prosecution."

"Neutrality," says Azuni, (Droits Maritimes,) "is the continuation in a state of peace of a power which, when war is kindled between two or more nations, absolutely abstains from taking any part in the contest."

But if the proposition be admitted that all the vessels of the Confederate States armed for war should be considered *prima facie* as privateers, would there not be a flagrant inequality between the treatment and the favors accorded to vessels of war of the United States and the vessels of the Confederate States, which have not for the moment a navy properly so called?

This evidently would be giving proof of partiality incompatible with real duties of neutrality. The only question is to determine with exactitude the distinctive characteristics between a privateer and a ship-of-war, although this may be difficult of execution. Thus is ignored that which Count Reventlou, envoy of the King of Denmark at Madrid, drew attention to in 1782, that there exists among the maritime powers regulations or conventions between sovereigns, which oblige them to equip their vessels in a certain manner, that they may be held veritably armed for war.

You express also, in your despatch of September 2, the hope that the Netherlands government will do justice to your reclamation, grounding yourself on the tenor of treaties existing between the Netherlands and the United States, on the principles of the law of nations, and, finally, upon the assurances you have received from the King's government.

Amidst all the European powers there are few who have better defended the rights of neutrals, and have suffered more in this noble cause than Denmark; and one of her greatest statesmen of the close of the last century, Count Bernstorff, has been able to declare with justice, in his memoir of July 28, 1793, a document that will long continue to be celebrated: "A neutral power fulfils all its duties by never departing from the most strict impartiality, nor from the avowed meaning of its treaties."

I have endeavored, sir, to show, in what precedes, that the government of the Netherlands has fulfilled conscientiously its first duty, and will adhere faithfully thereto.

The cabinet of the Hague does not observe and will not observe less religiously the tenor of treaties.

The treaty of the 19th of January, 1839, and the additional convention of the 26th of August, 1852, only relate to commerce and navigation; the only treaties that can be invoked in the present case are those of the 8th of October, 1782.

I do not think it my duty to enter here upon a discussion of principles on the question of deciding whether these treaties can still be considered as actually in force, and I will not take advantage of the circumstance that the cabinet of Washington has implicitly recognized, by the very reclamation which is the object of your despatches, that the treaties of 1782 cannot any longer be invoked as the basis of international relations between the Netherlands and the United States.

I will only take the liberty of observing to you, sir, that the execution of the stipulations included in those diplomatic acts would be far, in the present circumstances, from being favorable to the government of the republic.

In fact, we should, in this case, admit to our ports privateers with their prizes, which could even be sold there by virtue of article 5 of the before-cited convention of 1782, on rescues.

It would, perhaps, be objected that the treaty of 1782, having been concluded with the United States of America, could not be invoked by a part of the Union which had seceded from the central government, and I do not dissent from the opinion that this thorny question of public law would give rise, should the case occur, to very serious difficulties.

But we cannot lose sight of the fact that the treaty spoken of was concluded, even before the recognition of the United States by England in 1783, with the oldest members of the republic, among others, to wit, with Virginia, North Carolina, South Carolina, and Georgia, and that those States actually figure among the secessionists.

In 1782 the republic of North America was only a simple confederation of states, remaining sovereign, united only for common defence, (Staatenbund) and it is only since the establishment of the Constitution, of the 17th of September, 1787, that the pact which binds together the United States received the character which is attributed to it by Mr. Wheaton, also, (Elements of International Law,) of a perfect union between all the members as one people under one government, federal and supreme, (Bundestaat,) "a commonwealth," according to Mr. Motley in his pamphlet "Causes of the Civil War in America," p. 71.

In view of this fundamental difference between the present character of the government of the United States and that of the party contracting the treaty of 1782, it would be difficult to refuse in equity the privilege of the secessionist States to avail themselves of it.

It will, therefore, not escape your penetration that it is preferable, as well for the Netherlands as for the cabinet of Washington, to leave the treaty above mentioned at rest, and that, in excluding privateers from its ports the government of the Netherlands has acted only in the interests of the government of the United States, to which it is bound by feelings of a friendship which dates even from the time of the existence of the republic of the united provinces, and which the King's government will make every effort to maintain and consolidate more and more.

According to the law of nations, the cases in which the neutrality of a power is more advantageous to one party than to the other do not affect or impair it; it suffices that the neutrality be perfect and strictly observed. The government of the Netherlands has not departed from it, therefore, in denying admission to the ports of his Majesty's territories to privateers, although at first glance this determination is unfavorable to the southern States.

The difficulties which have actually arisen, and which may be renewed hereafter, the desire to avoid as much as possible everything that could compromise the good understanding between the governments of the United States and the Netherlands, impose on the last the obligation to examine with scrupulous attention if the maintenance of the general principles which I have had the honor to develop might not in some particular cases impair the attitude of neutrality which the cabinet of the Hague desires to observe. If, for example, we had room to believe that the Sumter, or any other vessel of one of the two belligerent parties, sought to make of Curaçoa, or any other port in his Majesty's dominions, the base of operations against the commerce of the adverse party, the government of the Netherlands would be the first to perceive that such acts would be a real infraction, not merely of the neutrality we wish to observe, but also of the right of sovereignty over the territorial seas of the state; the duty of a neutral state being to take care that vessels of the belligerent parties commit no acts of hostility within the limits of its territory, and do not keep watch in the ports of its dominion to course from them after vessels of the adverse party.

Instructions on this point will be addressed to the governors of the Netherlands colonial possessions.

I flatter myself that the preceding explanations will suffice to convince the federal government of the unchangeable desire of that of the Netherlands to maintain a strict neutrality, and will cause the disappearance of the slightest trace of misunderstanding between the cabinets of the Hague and of Washington.

Accept, sir, the renewed assurance of my high consideration.

DE ZUYLEN DE NIJVELT.

Mr. PIKE, *Minister Resident of the United States of America.*

Mr. Seward to Mr. Pike.

No. 23.]   DEPARTMENT OF STATE,
                                        Washington, September 28, 1861.

SIR : By some accident our foreign mail missed the steamer. It is only just now that I have received your despatch of September 4, (No. 15.) The proceeding at Curaçoa in regard to the Sumter was so extraordinary, and so entirely contrary to what this government had expected from that of Holland, that I lose no time in instructing you to urge the consideration of the subject with as much earnestness as possible. I cannot believe that that government will hesitate to disavow the conduct of the authorities if they have been correctly reported to this department.

I am, sir, respectfully, your obedient servant,

WILLIAM H. SEWARD.

JAMES S. PIKE, Esq., &c., &c., &c.

Mr. Seward to Mr. Pike.

No. 24.]   DEPARTMENT OF STATE,
                                        Washington, October 4, 1861.

SIR : I am just now informed by a despatch from Henry Sawyer, esq., our consul at Paramaribo, that on the 19th day of August last the piratical steamer "Sumter" entered that port, and was allowed by the authorities there to approach the town and to purchase and receive coals, to stay during her pleasure, and to retire unmolested, all of which was done in opposition to the remonstrances of the consul.

You will lose no time in soliciting the attention of his Majesty's government to this violation of the rights of the United States. They will be well aware that it is the second instance of the same kind that has occurred in regard to the same vessel in Dutch colonies in the West Indies.

It is some relief of the sense of injury which we feel that we do not certainly know that the authorities who have permitted these wrongs had received instructions from their home government in regard to the rights of the United States in the present emergency. We therefore hope for satisfactory explanations. But, in any case, you will inform that government that the United States will expect them to visit those authorities with a censure so unreserved as will prevent the repetition of such injuries hereafter.

An early resolution of the subject is imperatively necessary, in order that this government may determine what is required for the protection of its national rights in the Dutch American forts.

I am, sir, respectfully, your obedient servant,

WILLIAM H. SEWARD.

JAMES S. PIKE, Esq., &c., &c., &c.

Mr. Pike to Mr. Seward.

No. 20.]   UNITED STATES LEGATION,
                              The Hague, October 9, 1861.

SIR : Since my last (under date of October 2) I have received a letter from the United States consul at Paramaribo, of which the following is a copy :

"UNITED STATES CONSULATE,
"*Port of Paramaribo, September 4,* 1861.

"SIR : I have the honor (but with chagrin) to inform you that the rebel steamer Sumter arrived at this port on the 19th of August, and left on the 31st, having been allowed to coal and refit. I used my best endeavors to prevent it without avail.

"I am, &c.,

"HENRY SAWYER."

Immediately on the receipt of it I addressed the following note to the minister of foreign affairs.

"THE HAGUE, *October* 8, 1861.

"SIR : I have just received a communication from the American consul at Paramaribo under date of the 4th of September last, which I lose no time in laying before your excellency.

"The consul states."

[See above.]

"The reappearance of the Sumter in a port of the Netherlands, after so brief an interval, seems to disclose a deliberate purpose on the part of the persons engaged in rebellion against the United States government to practice upon the presumed indifference, the expected favor, or the fancied weakness of the Dutch government.

"During a period of forty-six days, during which we have heard of this piratical vessel in the West Indies, it would appear that she had been twice entertained and supplied at Dutch ports, and spent eighteen days under their shelter.

"This can be no accidental circumstance.

"In the multitude of harbors with which the West India seas abound, the Sumter has had no occasion to confine her visits so entirely to the ports of one nation, especially one so scantily supplied with them as Holland. And the fact that she does so is, in my judgment, not fairly susceptible of any other interpretation than the one I have given.

"I feel convinced that the government of the Netherlands will see in this repeated visit of the Sumter (this time, it appears, without any pretext) a distinct violation of its neutrality according to its own views, as laid down in your excellency's communication to me of the 17th of September last, and a case which will call for the energetic assertion of its purpose expressed in the paper referred to, namely, not to allow its ports to be made the base of hostile operations against the United States. For that the Sumter is clearly making such use of the Dutch ports would seem to admit of no controversy.

"In view of the existing state of the correspondence between the United States and the Netherlands on the general subject to which this case belongs, and of the questions and relations involved therein, I shall be excused for the brevity of this communication upon a topic of so much importance and so provocative of comment.

"The undersigned avails himself," &c., &c.

I called to-day upon Baron Von Zuylen, but he was absent, and I shall not therefore be able to see him again before the close of the mail which takes this. And I do not know that an interview would in any way affect the existing state of things or give me any new information. This government's intentions are good; and it desires to avoid all difficulty with the United States, and with everybody else.

As I stated in my despatch of the 25th September, I have confidence that orders have been given that will impede the operations of these vessels in Dutch ports hereafter, and probably drive them elsewhere.

I have the honor to be, with great respect, your most obedient servant,

JAMES S. PIKE.

Hon. WILLIAM H. SEWARD,
 Secretary of State, Washington.

Mr. Seward to Mr. Pike.

No. 25.]
             DEPARTMENT OF STATE,
             Washington, October 10, 1861.

SIR: Your despatch of September 18 (No. 17) has been received.

The delay of the government of the Netherlands in disposing of the unpleasant questions which have arisen concerning the American pirates in the colonies of that country is a subject of deep concern; and you are instructed, if you find it necessary, to use such urgency as may be effectual to obtain the definitive decision of that government thereon so early that it may be considered by the President before the meeting of Congress in December next.

I am, sir, your obedient servant,

WILLIAM H. SEWARD.

JAMES S. PIKE, Esq., &c., &c., &c.

Mr. Pike to Mr. Seward.

[Extracts.]

No. 22.]
             UNITED STATES LEGATION,
             The Hague, October 12, 1861.

SIR: After reflection, upon the reappearance of the Sumter, and her prolonged stay in the port of Paramaribo, (this time apparently without pretext of any kind,) I have felt, in view of the position taken by the Dutch government in their communication to me of the 17th of September, that we were entitled to be specially informed of the precise interpretation which this government puts upon their general declaration in the communication referred to, namely, that it will not permit its ports to be made the base of hostile operations against the United States commerce.

I have accordingly made the direct inquiry of Baron Van Zuylen, without waiting to hear what you have to say in response to that communication. In reply to my inquiry, Baron Van Zuylen has informed me that, previous to his receiving information of the appearance of the Sumter at Paramaribo, orders were issued by the department of the colonies, instructing the colonial authorities not to permit the repetition of the visits of the Sumter, and other vessels of the so-called Confederate States; and if they did make their appearance in Dutch ports, to require them to leave within twenty-four hours, under penalty of being held to occupy a hostile attitude towards the government of the Netherlands. And further, that those authorities have also been instructed to forbid the furnishing of such vessels with more than twenty-four hours supply of fuel. These instructions, thus defined, are to the point. Whether they have been made general, and with that disregard of distinctions between the rights of mere belligerents and those of recognized nationalities, enjoying pacific relations and acting under treaties of amity and friendship, that mark the communication to which I have adverted, I did not deem it pertinent to inquire, nor do I consider the inquiry of any value as regards the practical bearings of this case.

In compliance with my request, Baron Van Zuylen has promised to furnish me with a copy of the order referred to, which, when received, I shall transmit to you without delay.

Although this order, as thus described to me by Mr. Van Zuylen, only sustains the expectations I have expressed to you on two former occasions as to what the action of this government would be, yet, considering the present attitude of the question, it is a matter of some surprise to me that a copy of it should not have been tendered without waiting to have it asked for.

*   *   *   *   *   *   *   *   *

Taking it to be as herein described, I do not see that the position of this government, so far as its action is concerned, is amenable to very grave censure, whatever may be said of its theoretic views, since the Dutch ports are now, substantially, shut to the vessels. The restriction in regard to supplying fuel, if adopted by other powers holding colonies in the West Indies, will put an end to rebel operations by steam in those seas.

I take some gratification in reflecting that my persistent appeals to the government to issue specific orders, on some ground, to their colonial authorities, looking to the exclusion of the piratical vessels of the seceding States from the Dutch ports, have not been wholly unavailing. That the government has argued against it, and declined acting on any suggestion I could make, is of small consequence, so long as they have found out a way of their own of doing the thing that was needed.

Baron Van Zuylen has renewedly expressed great regret that any questions should have arisen between the two governments.

I have the honor to be, with great respect, your most obedient servant,

JAMES S. PIKE.

Hon. WILLIAM H. SEWARD,
        Secretary of State.

Mr. Pike to Mr. Seward.

No. 23.]   UNITED STATES LEGATION,
                                                         The Hague, October 16, 1861.

SIR: I have the honor to enclose you the reply of the minister of foreign affairs to the communication I addressed to him on the 8th instant, in regard to the reappearance of the Sumter at Paramaribo. He states therein the character of the orders which have been sent to the colonial authorities, to which I referred in my last despatch, of October 12, (No. 22.)

The British minister here, Sir Andrew Buchanan, expressed incredulity and surprise when I informed him this government had issued the order in question. He declared the British government would not do it, and that the United States would not under similar circumstances. He said it was giving us an advantage, and was not therefore neutral conduct. He added that Russia asked Sweden to close her ports against both belligerents during the Crimean war, and England would not permit it, alleging that as Russia did not want to use them, and England did, it gave the former an advantage to which that power was not entitled. The British government held that Sweden, as a neutral, had no right to alter the natural situation unless it operated equally.

You see herein how thoroughly English officials (and it seems to me all others) are imbued with the idea that the rights of a mere belligerent are the same as the rights of a nation, in cases like the one under consideration.

I have received to-day a letter from our consul at Paramaribo, dated September 20, in which he says the United States steamer Powhatan arrived there on the 14th in search of the Sumter, and left for Brazil the same day; also that the Keystone State arrived on the 18th on the same errand, and left on the 19th for the West India islands.

Your despatch of the 28th of September, acknowledging receipt of mine of the 4th, has arrived. As you make no mention of mine of the 11th, it would seem another mail has missed. I wrote our despatch agent at London on the subject several days ago.

He replies that my despatch of the 4th of September went on the 7th, and that of the 11th on the 14th, which was in regular order.

I have the honor to be, with great respect, your most obedient servant,

JAMES S. PIKE.

Hon. WILLIAM H. SEWARD,
    Secretary of State, Washington.

Baron Van Zuylen to Mr. Pike.

[Translation.]

THE HAGUE, *October 15, 1861.*

SIR: By your despatch of the 8th of this month you have fixed my attention on the arrival of the "Sumter" at Paramaribo, and you complain that on this occasion the said vessel was admitted into ports of the Netherlands during eighteen days out of the forty-six in which the Sumter had shown herself in the West Indian seas.

You suppose that this is not a fortuitous case, and you demand that the government of the Netherlands, in accordance with the intentions mentioned at the close of my communication of the 17th September last, may not permit its ports to serve as stations or as base of hostile operations against the United States.

You have not deemed it your duty to enter for the moment on the discussion of the arguments contained in my above-mentioned communication, but you say that you wish to await preliminarily the reply of the cabinet at Washington.

I may, therefore, on my part, confine myself for the moment to referring, as to what regards the admission in general of the Sumter into the ports of the Netherlands and the character of this vessel, to the arguments contained in my communication of the 17th September, from which it follows, that if we do not choose to consider *prima facie* all the ships of the seceding States as privateers, and if, in the present case, the Sumter could not be, in the opinion of the government of the Netherlands, comprised among such, entrance to the ports of the Netherlands cannot be prohibited to that vessel without a departure from neutrality and from the express terms of the proclamation of the royal government.

It has already been observed that the latter, in forbidding access to the ports of the Netherlands to privateers, favors the United States much more, among others, than the declaration of the 10th of June by the French government, which, not permitting any vessel-of-war or privateer of the one or the other of the belligerents to sojourn *with prizes* in the ports of the empire for longer time than twenty-four hours, except in case of shelter through stress, (*relâche forcée*,) admits them without distinction when they do not bring prizes with them. But, without entering here into useless developments, I think I may observe to you, sir, that the royal government, whilst refusing to treat as pirates, or even to consider as privateers, all the vessels of the southern States, has striven, as much as the duties of strict neutrality permit, to keep the Sumter away from our ports. When this vessel arrived at Paramaribo, the commanders of two ships of the French imperial marine, which were there at the time, declared to the governor of Surinam that the Sumter was a regular vessel-of-war and not a privateer. The commander of the Sumter exhibited afterwards, to the same functionary, his commission as commandant in a regular navy.

Although there was no reason, under such circumstances, to refuse to the Sumter the enjoyment of the law of hospitality in all its extent, the governor, before referred to, strove to limit it as much as possible. Thus, although pit coal is not reputed contraband, if not at most, and within a recent time only, contraband by accident, it was not supplied to the Sumter except in the very restricted quantity of 125 tons, at the most sufficient for four days' progress.

However, the government of the Netherlands, wishing to give a fresh proof of its desire [to avoid] all that could give the slightest subject for complaint to the United States, has just sent instructions to the colonial authorities, enjoining them not to admit, except in case of shelter from stress, (*relâche forcée*,) the vessels-of-war and privateers of the two belligerent parties, unless for twice twenty-four hours, and not to permit them, when they are steamers, to provide themselves with a quantity of coal more than sufficient for a run of twenty-four hours.

It is needless to add that the cabinet of the Hague will not depart from the principles mentioned at the close of my reply of the 17th September, of which you demand the application ; it does know and will know how to act in conformity with the obligations of impartiality and of neutrality, without losing sight of the care for its own dignity.

Called by the confidence of the King to maintain that dignity, to defend the rights of the Crown, and to direct the relations of the state with foreign powers, I know not how to conceal from you, sir, that certain expressions in your communications above mentioned, of the 23d and 25th September last, have caused an unpleasant impression on the King's government, and do not appear to me to correspond with the manner in which I have striven to treat the question now under discussion, or with the desire which actuates the government of the Netherlands to seek for a solution perfectly in harmony with its sentiments of friendship towards the United States, and with the observance of treaties.

The feeling of distrust which seems to have dictated your last despatch of the 8th of this month, and which shows itself especially in some entirely erroneous appreciations of the conduct of the government of the Netherlands, gives to the last, strong in its good faith and in its friendly intentions, just cause for astonishment. So, then, the cabinet of which I have the honor to form part deems that it may dispense with undertaking a justification useless to all who examine impartially and without passion the events which have taken place.

The news which has reached me from the royal legations at London and at Washington, relative to the conduct of the British government in the affair of the Sumter, can only corroborate the views developed in my reply of 17th September last, and in the present communication.

It results from this, in effect, that not only has the British government treated the Sumter exactly as was done at Curaçoa, since that vessel sojourned six or seven days at the island of Trinidad, where she was received amicably and considered as a vessel-of-war, but that the crown lawyers of England, having been consulted on the matter, have unanimously declared that the conduct of the governor of that colony of England had been in all points in conformity with the Queen's proclamation of neutrality.

According to them the Sumter was not a privateer but a regular vessel-of-war, (duly commissioned,) belonging to a state possessing the rights of war, (belligerent rights.)

The Sumter, then, has been treated as a vessel-of-war of the United States would have been, and that vessel had the same right to obtain supplies at Trinidad as any vessel belonging to the navy of the northern States.

Accept, sir, the fresh assurance of my high consideration.

DE ZUYLEN DE NIJEVELT.

Mr. PIKE,
    Minister Resident of the United States of America.

Mr. Seward to Mr. Pike.

No. 26.]   DEPARTMENT OF STATE,
Washington, October 17, 1861.

SIR: Your despatch of the 25th of September, No. 18, has been received. It is accompanied by a note which was addressed to you by Baron Van Zuylen, on the 17th day of September last, on the subject of the admission of the pirate steamer Sumter into the port of Curaçoa.

I reproduce the account of that transaction, which was made by this government a subject of complaint to the government of the Netherlands. The steamer Sumter hove in sight of the port of Curaçoa on the evening of the 15th of July, and fired a gun for the pilot, who immediately took to sea. On his reaching the pirate vessel she hoisted what is called the confederate flag, and the same being unknown in that port, the pilot told the captain that he had to report to the governor before taking the vessel into port.

The pilot having made this report, the governor replied to the captain that, according to orders from the supreme government, he could not admit privateers into the port, nor their prizes, but in the case of distress, and therefore the steamer could not be admitted before her character was perfectly known.

In reply to this message the captain of the steamer remained outside of the port until the next morning, when he sent a despatch to the governor, by an officer, stating that his vessel being a duly commissioned man-of-war of the Confederate States, he desired to enter the port for a few days. The colonial court assembled the same evening, and, on the ground of the declaration and assurance of the privateer captain that the vessel is not a privateer, it was decided that she should enter the port, and she entered accordingly.

The consul of the United States thereupon informed the governor, by a note, that the steamer was, by the laws and express declaration of the United States, a pirate, and that on her way from New Orleans to Curaçoa she had taken and sent for sale to the Spanish island of Cuba several American merchant vessels, and on these grounds he asked upon what pretext and conditions the unlawful steamer had obtained admittance into Curaçoa.

The governor answered that, according to the orders received from the supreme government, neither privateers nor their prizes are to be allowed admittance to the ports or bays of this colony, save only in cases of distress. But that this prohibition does not extend to vessels-of-war, and that the Sumter being a man-of-war, according to the rules of nations, could not be repelled from that port.

The piratical vessel was then supplied, at Curaçoa, with 120 tons of coals, and departed at her own time and pleasure. On receiving this information you were instructed to call the attention of the government of the Netherlands to the proceeding of the governor of Curaçoa, and to ask that the proceedings, if correctly reported, might be disavowed, and that the governor might be made to feel the displeasure of his government.

You performed this duty in due season by addressing a proper note to Baron Van Zuylen. On the 2d of September he acknowledged your note, and promised you an early reply on the merits of the subject.

On the 17th of September he communicated this reply to you in the note which is now before me.

I encounter a difficulty in giving you instructions for your reply to that paper, because, first, since the correspondence was opened, a similar case of violation of our national rights has occurred in the hospitalities extended to the same piratical vessel in the Dutch port of Pernambuco, and has been made a subject of similar complaint, which, as yet, so far as I am advised, remains unanswered; and, secondly, the note of Baron Van Zuylen promises that special instructions shall be speedily given to the colonial authorities of the Netherlands in regard to conduct in cases similar to those which have induced the existing complaints. I cannot, of course, forsee how far those instructions, yet unknown to me, may modify the position assumed by the minister of foreign affairs in the paper under consideration.

Under these circumstances, I must be content with setting forth, for the information of the government of the Netherlands, just what the United States claim and expect in regard to the matter in debate.

They have asked for an explanation of the case, presented by the admission of the Sumter by the governor of Curaçoa, if one can be satisfactorily given; and if not, then for a disavowal of that officer's proceedings, attended by a justly deserved rebuke.

These demands have been made, not from irritation or any sensibility of national pride, but to make it sure that henceforth any piratical vessel fitted out by or under the agency of disloyal American citizens, and cruising in pursuit of merchant vessels of the United States, shall not be admitted into either the continental or the colonial ports of the Netherlands under any pretext whatever. If that assurance cannot be obtained in some way, we must provide for the protection of our rights in some other way. Thus, the subject is one of a purely practical character; it neither requires nor admits of debate or argument on the part of the United States. If what is thus desired shall be obtained by the United States in any way, they will be satisfied; if it fails to be obtained through the disinclination of the government of the Netherlands, its proceedings in this respect will be deemed unfriendly and injurious to the United States. The United States being thus disposed to treat the subject in a practical way, they are not tenacious about the manner or form in which the due respect to their rights is manifested by the government of the Netherlands, and still less about the considerations or arguments upon which that government regulates its own conduct in the matter. They regard the whole insurrection in this country as ephemeral; indeed, they believe that the attempt at piracy under the name of privateering, made by the insurgents, has already well nigh failed. While, therefore, they insist that shelter shall not be afforded to the pirates by nations in friendship with the United States, they, at the same time, are not unwilling to avoid grave debates concerning their rights that might survive the existing controversy. It remains only to say in this connexion that the course which the United States are pursuing in their complaints to the government of the Netherlands is not peculiar, but it is the same which has been and which will be pursued towards any other maritime power on the occurrence of similar grievances.

With these remarks, I proceed to notice Baron Van Zuylen's communication. You will reply to him that the United States unreservedly claim to determine for themselves absolutely the character of the Sumter, she being a vessel fitted out, owned, armed, sailed, and directed by American citizens who owe allegiance to the United States, and who neither have nor can, in their piratical purposes and pursuits, have or claim any political authority from any lawful source whatever.

The United States regard the vessel as piratical, and the persons by whom she is manned and navigated as pirates.

The United States, therefore, cannot admit that the Sumter is a ship-of-war or a privateer, and so entitled to any privileges whatever, in either of those characters, in the port of Curaçoa; nor can they debate any such subject with the government of the Netherlands. This will be all that you will need to say in reply to the whole of Baron Von Zuylen's note, except that portion of it which states, rather by way of argument than of assertion, that according to the information received from the governor of Curaçoa, (by the government of the Netherlands,) the Sumter was actually in distress, and that funtionary, therefore, could not refuse to allow the said vessel to enter the port.

If this position shall be actually assumed by the government of the Netherlands, two questions will arise: first, whether the fact that the Sumter was in distress was true, or a belief of the truth of that fact was the real ground upon which she was admitted by the colonial governor into the port of Curaçoa; secondly, how far a piratical vessel, roving over the seas in pursuit of peaceful commercial vessels of the United States, and fleeing before their naval pursuit, but falling into distress herself, is entitled to charity at the hands of a State, friendly to the nation upon whose commerce her depredations are directed.

It would hence be idle to occupy ourselves with a discussion of these questions until we know that the government of the Netherlands determines to stand upon the main position from which they are derived.

You will therefore ask the Baron Van Zuylen for an explicit statement on this subject.

I cannot but hope, however, that the government of the Netherlands will come to the conclusion that it is wisest and best, in view of the relations of the two countries, to give such directions to its agents as will render further prosecution of this discussion unnecessary, while it will prevent similar injuries in future to our national dignity and honor. Should it determine otherwise, and not be able to place the conduct of the governor general at Curaçoa in a better light than it has already done, it will become necessary to consider what means we can take to protect, in the ports of the Netherlands, national rights which cannot be surrendered or compromised.

I am, sir, your obedient servant,

WILLIAM H. SEWARD.

James S. Pike, Esq., &c., &c., &c.

Mr. Pike to Mr. Seward.

No. 24.]
United States Legation,
The Hague, October 23, 1861.

Sir: I had the honor to transmit to you, on the 16th instant, the last communication of this government in respect to the "Sumter" case, referring to the orders recently given to its colonial authorities, by which the stay of such vessels in Dutch ports is limited to 24 hours, and by which they are also forbidden to take on board more than 24 hours' supply of coal.

Considering these orders to be important, I have, in the following copy of my reply to the Dutch government, ventured to express a qualified satisfaction at their issue. I am in hopes you will adopt a similar view of the case, as I conceive this government to be well disposed towards the United States, and to consider that it has strained a point in our favor.

I doubt if England or France will do anything of the sort; but the course of Holland will, at least, furnish excellent grounds for some pertinent questions in case they decline.

I have informed Mr. Adams, and also Mr. Dayton and Mr. Schurz, of the final action of this government in this case. The copy of my note follows, (to Baron Van Zuylen.)

"United States Legation;
The Hague, October 22, 1861.

"Sir: In reply to your communication of the 15th instant, which I have had the honor to receive, I take pleasure in assuring your excellency that it has been far from my purpose to say anything at any time which should occasion painful impressions on the part of his Majesty's government, or to use language marked by impatience or irritation at the course of the government of the Netherlands. But while making this disclaimer, frankness compels me to add that I should not know in what more moderate terms to express my sentiments than those I have had the honor to employ in addressing his Majesty's government.

"I desire further to say, in respect to that part of your excellency's communication which refers to the recent orders given to the Dutch colonial authorities not to permit vessels engaged in pirating upon United States commerce to remain in their ports more than 24 hours, and, when steamers, not to be furnished with more than 24 hours' supply of fuel, that, while I receive the announcement with satisfaction, it is qualified by deep regrets at the position his Majesty's government has thought proper to take in placing the misguided persons in rebellion against the United States on a footing of equality, in a most important respect, with the government to which they owe obedience; for, though the orders in question deny shelter and aid to pirates, it is impossible to regard with complacency the fact that the exclusion operates equally against the vessels of the United States, denying to them that accustomed hospitality ever accorded by friendly nations.

"Abstaining, however, now as heretofore, from any discussion on this topic while awaiting the reply of my government to your communication of the 17th of September, I will only add that I feel assured the United States government will fully share these regrets, and I can only hope will not impeach my expressions of satisfaction at the orders which you inform me have been given in accordance with the rule of action laid down in that paper, notwithstanding the position falls so far short of that which the United States have confidently expected Holland would occupy on this question.

"I pray, &c., &c.

"Baron VAN ZUYLEN, &c., &c.

I have had the honor to receive your despatch of the 4th of October, (No. 24,) relative to the Sumter at Paramaribo, to which subject I have already given my attention.

I have the honor to be, with great respect, your most obedient servant,

JAMES S. PIKE.

Hon. WM. H. SEWARD,
    Secretary of State, Washington.

Mr. Seward to Mr. Pike.

No. 28.]   DEPARTMENT OF STATE,
                                    Washington, October 30, 1861.

SIR: Your despatch of October 9 (No. 20) has been received. We wait with much interest the result of your application to the government of the Netherlands for explanations of the hospitalities extended by its colonial authorities to privateers.

I am, sir, your obedient servant,

WILLIAM H. SEWARD.

JAMES S. PIKE, Esq., &c., &c., &c.

Mr. Seward to Mr. Pike.

No. 29.]   DEPARTMENT OF STATE,
                                      Washington, November 2, 1861.

SIR: Your despatch of October 12 (No. 22) has been received. I learn with much pleasure that you have assurances which, although informal, lead you to expect that a satisfactory course will be adopted by his Majesty's government in regard to the exclusion of privateers from the ports of the Netherlands. Awaiting with some solicitude more definite information,

I am, sir, your obedient servant,

WILLIAM H. SEWARD.

JAMES S. PIKE, Esq., &c., &c., &c.

Mr. Pike to Mr. Seward.

[Extract.]

No. 25.]

UNITED STATES LEGATION,
The Hague, November 6, 1861.

SIR: I duly received your despatch (No. 25) of the 10th of October, but have nothing by the last mail. I await your response to the communication of Mr. Van Zuylen of the 17th of September last.

I have the honor to enclose you the reply of the minister of foreign affairs to my note of the 22d of last month, a copy of which I forwarded to you in my last.

* * * · * * * * * *
* * * * * * * * *

I have the honor to be, with great respect, your most obedient servant,

JAMES S. PIKE.

Hon. WILLIAM H. SEWARD,
Secretary of State, Washington.

Mr. Van Zuylen to Mr. Pike.

[Translation.]

THE HAGUE, *October 29, 1861.*

SIR: I have had the honor to receive your letter of the 22d of this month, relative to the affair of the "Sumter," and it has been gratifying to me to learn from its tenor that you have received with satisfaction the information as to the measures adopted by the government of the Low Countries to prevent the return or the prolonged stay in its ports of vessels which, like the "Sumter," seemed to desire to use them as the base of their operations against the commerce of the adverse party.

You regret only that the government of the King should have adopted the same treatment towards the war vessels of the seceding States and those of the United States.

Without entering here into an extended discussion, rendered, moreover, almost superfluous by my two preceding communications, I shall merely permit myself, sir, in referring to their contents, to cause you to observe that, agreeably to the doctrine of the best publicists, neutrality imposes upon those nations which desire to enjoy its benefits a complete abstention from all that could establish a difference of treatment between the belligerent parties, and that this principle applies as well to the cases of civil war, or even of rebellion, as to that of an ordinary war.

Ex. Doc. 1——25

Your government having desired that measures should be taken to prevent a prolonged stay in our ports of the Sumter, or of other vessels-of-war of the seceding States, we have admitted the justice of this claim. But these measures could not reach exclusively one of the two parties; they were to be general, and the consequence of it is that the new instructions given to the governors of Curaçoa and of Surinam neither permit the vessels-of-war of the United States, except in the case of being compelled to put into a port, to sojourn in the ports of the Netherlands, in the West Indies, for a longer time than twice 24 hours, (and not for only 24 hours, as you seem to believe.)

Nevertheless, the privateers, with or without their prizes, are, as heretofore, excluded from the Netherland ports, and it is by an oversight, which I hasten to rectify, that the words "and the privateers" have been introduced into that part of my communication of the 15th of this month which calls your attention to the instructions transmitted to the colonial authorities.

Be pleased, sir, to accept the renewed assurance of my high consideration.

DE ZUYLEN DE NIJEVELT.

Mr. PIKE,
  Minister Resident of the United States of America.

Mr. Seward to Mr. Pike.

No. 31.]   DEPARTMENT OF STATE,
                                      Washington, November 11, 1861.

SIR: Your despatch No. 24, dated October 23, has been received.

I learn from it that the government of the Netherlands has made an order which will, it is hoped, practically prevent the recurrence of such countenance and favor to pirates in the ports of that state as we have heretofore complained of. You will express to Baron Zuylen our satisfaction with this proceeding, viewed in that light, but you will be no less explicit in saying that this government by no means assents to the qualifications affecting its claims as a sovereign power upon the Netherlands by which the proceeding is qualified.

Not only are we not seeking occasions for difference with any foreign powers, but we are, on the other hand, endeavoring to preserve amity and friendship with them all, in a crisis which tries the magnanimity of our country. Influenced by these feelings, I can only hope that no new injury or disrespect to our flag may occur in the ports of the Netherlands, to bring the action of their government again under review by us.

I am directed by the President to express his approval of the diligence and discretion you have practiced in this important transaction.

I am, sir, your obedient servant,

WILLIAM H. SEWARD.

JAMES S. PIKE, Esq., &c., &c., &c.

Mr. Seward to Mr. Pike.

No. 32.]   DEPARTMENT OF STATE,
                                      Washington, November 11, 1861.

SIR: Your despatch of October 16 (No. 23) has been received. It contains the reply of Mr. de Zuylen to the note you had addressed to him on the subject of the "Sumter" at Paramaribo.

In another paper I have already communicated the President's views of the disposition of that subject made by the government of the Netherlands, so that nothing remains to be said on the subject which you have had occasion to discuss in the despatch now before me.

I am, sir, your obedient servant,

WILLIAM H. SEWARD.

Mr. Seward to Mr. Pike.

No. 33.]
DEPARTMENT OF STATE,
Washington, November 23, 1861.

SIR: Your despatch of November 6 (No. 25) has just been received. I have already anticipated and disposed of the principal subject which it presents.

Felicitate the government of the Netherlands as we felicitate ourselves on the renewed auguries of good and cordial relations between friends too old to be alienated thoughtlessly, or from mere impatience.

I am, sir, your obedient servant,

WILLIAM H. SEWARD.

JAMES S. PIKE, Esq., &c., &c., &c.

TURKEY.

Mr. Brown to Mr. Seward.

[Extract.]

No. 2.] LEGATION OF THE UNITED STATES OF AMERICA,
Constantinople, May 29, 1861.

SIR:

*   *   *   *   *   *

I had the honor, on the 25th instant, to receive your circular of the 20th ultimo, with its enclosure, addressed to the late minister resident, respecting the fitting out of privateers in Turkey to act against the commerce of the United States, and shall give my faithful and vigilant attention to the orders which it contains. The minister resident, on his departure, gave me the "circulars" of the department, one of February 28, and the other of March 9, 1861, of which he had not either acknowledged the receipt, nor made any use in carrying out the injunctions of the President. These, also, call for my immediate attention, and shall be faithfully executed.

I would here take occasion to add that I am confident there is not now one citizen of the United States in this place animated with sentiments other than those of entire loyalty to the government of the United States, and of devotion to the cause of the Union. Not only from the members of all the foreign legations resident here, but also from all foreigners in this city, I receive expressions of the most friendly nature in favor of the American Union. The unhappy and misguided position assumed by some of its southern States is deeply deplored and strongly condemned by them, and all entertain the hope that a returning sense of patriotism, and a correct view of their own interests, will, before long, restore peace and happiness to our great and prosperous country. These are, also, the sentiments expressed by all of the functionaries of the Sultan's government; and I believe it will, at any time, be easy for the legation to invoke the most friendly conduct on the part of the Sublime Porte in behalf of the government of the United States of America.

I have the honor to be, sir, with great respect, your obedient servant,

JOHN P. BROWN.

Mr. Brown to Mr. Seward.

[Extract.]

LEGATION OF THE UNITED STATES,
Constantinople, June 11, 1861.

*   *   *   *   *   *

I do not believe that any agents of the "Confederate States" have, as yet, visited this place, and should any come here that the Porte would admit or recognize them. I receive from H. H. Aali Pacha, minister of foreign affairs, and H. H. Mehemed Kibrish Pacha, grand vizier, repeated assurances of the most friendly sentiments towards the government of the United States, and expressions of warm sympathy for the present unhappy state of popular excitement in the slave States of the Union.

I have the honor to be, sir, respectfully, your obedient servant,

JOHN P. BROWN.

Hon. WILLIAM H. SEWARD,
    Secretary of State.

Mr. Brown to Mr. Seward.

No. 4.]   LEGATION OF THE UNITED STATES OF AMERICA,
          Constantinople, June 12, 1861.

SIR: I have had the honor to receive your circular of the 6th of May, regarding the duties of the legation and consulates of the United States in Turkey, with reference to passports of American citizens and individuals found negotiating with this government for purposes hostile to the Union.

I have sent a copy of this circular to each consulate of the United States in this empire, and have the honor to enclose herewith copy of the reply of the present consul general for Constantinople, Mr. David P. Heap, in whose loyalty to the government of the United States and fidelity to the Union I have every confidence.

I have the honor to be, sir, with much respect, your obedient servant,

JOHN P. BROWN.

Hon. WILLIAM H. SEWARD,
    Secretary of State, United States of America.

Mr. Heap to Mr. Brown.

UNITED STATES CONSULATE GENERAL,
       Constantinople, June 12, 1861.

SIR: I have the honor to acknowledge the receipt of your communication of the 10th instant, enclosing a circular from the honorable Secretary of State, dated May 6, on the subject of the delivery of passports to citizens of the United States.

I will strictly conform to the instructions contained therein, and in no case will this consulate general grant its visa to the passport of any person of whose loyalty to the Union it has not the most complete and satisfactory evidence. This consulate general will exercise the utmost vigilance in counteracting the proceedings of any American citizen who, either personally or by agents, is found negotiating with the government or individuals for purposes hostile to the republic.

I remain sir, with high respect, your obedient servant,

D. P. HEAP,
    Consul General.

JOHN P. BROWN, Esq.,
    Chargé d'Affaires of the United States
       of America, Constantinople.

Mr. Brown to Mr. Seward.

[Extract.]

No. 10.]   LEGATION OF THE UNITED STATES OF AMERICA,
                                     Constantinople, July 17, 1861.

SIR: *   *   *   *   *   *   *

I have had several conversations with T. H. Mohammed Kibrisli Pacha, the grand vizier, or prime minister, and Aáli Pacha, minister of foreign affairs, on the subject of the troubles existing in the United States; and the latter recently requested me to offer you the strongest assurances on the part of the Ottoman government of its friendly sympathies, and its hopes that they may be soon settled in such a manner as will preserve the Union intact. H. H. warmly deprecated the principle of "secession," advocated by the southern States, as ruinous to all governments, and especially to the great American republic, the strength of which so much depends upon its unity. He expressed a warm interest in the future welfare and prosperity of the government of the United States, from which the sublime porte has received so many evidences of a sincere and disinterested friendship.

The Sultan is acting with much energy of character, and introducing many salutary and greatly needed financial reforms in the government. His activity and intelligence have already rendered him very popular among his subjects, and inspire them with great hopes for the future of the empire. There exists perfect harmony and co-operation among all his ministers and other public functionaries.

I have the honor to enclose a copy of the reply which I made to H. H. Aáli Pacha, in response to his circular on the subject of the accession of his Majesty, communicated to the department in my despatch No. 8; also copies of a letter from his highness, and my reply, on his recent appointment to the office of minister of foreign affairs, which he has latterly filled only *ad interim,* and hope they will meet with your approbation.

I have the honor to be, sir, with great respect, your obedient servant,
                                                    JOHN P. BROWN.
Hon. WILLIAM H. SEWARD,
    Secretary of State, United States of America.

LEGATION OF THE UNITED STATES OF AMERICA,
                                     Constantinople, June 26, 1861.

HIGHNESS: I have had the honor to receive the letter which your highness was pleased to address me yesterday for the purpose of informing me officially of the decease of his Imperial Majesty Sultan Abd ul Majid, and the accession to the throne of his brother and legitimate heir, his Imperial Majesty Sultan Abd ul Aziz Khan.

Deeply affected by the decease of a sovereign whose great goodness of heart and many generous impulses have engraved his memory in the minds of all, and which will distinguish the history of his reign, it is with much pleasure that I convey to the knowledge of the government of the United States of America the great qualities of his illustrious successor, his Imperial Majesty Sultan Abd ul Aziz Khan.

The President of the United States will receive with much interest the assurance which your highness has been pleased to convey to me of the in tention of his Imperial Majesty to continue to cultivate the friendly relations which have always so happily existed between the government of the United States and that of the Ottoman empire—relations to which he attaches a very high appreciation.

I avail myself, also, of the present occasion to renew to your highness assurances of my high respect and very distinguished consideration.

JOHN P. BROWN,
Chargé d'Affaires ad int.

[Translation.]

No. 5232 | 103.]   Sublime Porte, Bureau of Foreign Affairs,
July 15, 1861.

Sir : I have the honor to inform you that his excellency Fuad Pacha has been called to the presidency of the supreme council of justice, confided, until his return, to his excellency Kiamil Pacha, and that my august master has deigned to appoint me his minister of foreign affairs.

The kind assistance which you have been pleased to give me, during my provisional direction of this department, is an assurance that you will continue the same favor in my endeavors to strengthen still more the relations of friendship and harmony existing between our respective governments.

I take occasion to offer renewed assurances of my high respect and perfect consideration.

AALI.

Legation of the United States of America,
Constantinople, July 16, 1861.

Highness : I have had the honor to receive the letter you were so good as to write me, on the 15th instant, for the purpose of informing me that his excellency Fuad Pacha, having been appointed president of the supreme council of justice, with which his excellency Kiamil Pacha has been charged until his return, his Imperial Majesty the Sultan has been graciously pleased to nominate you his minister of foreign affairs.

I thank your highness for this communication and the kind expressions which it contains, and beg your highness to believe me most desirous of uniting with your highness in whatever may serve to strengthen the relations of friendship and harmony so happily existing between our respective governments, and which owe so much to the friendly sentiments entertained by your highness for the United States.

I hasten also to assure your highness of my perfect respect and most distinguished consideration.

JOHN P. BROWN.

Mr. Seward to Mr. Morris.

No. 3.]   Department of State,
Washington, August 28, 1861.

Sir: The despatch of Mr. Brown, secretary of legation, (No. 10,) dated July 17, has been received.

It is probable that, before receiving these instructions, you will have already assumed the responsibility of asking an audience of the new Sultan, and tendering him, on the part of the President, the proper congratulations. If this duty remains unperformed, you will take an early occasion for it, and will assure him that this government has learned, with sincere pleasure, of his accession to the throne under felicitous auspices, and of the favorable impression which his administration has made upon the minds of the people over whom he presides, as well as in foreign countries. Assure him that we shall suffer no occasion to pass by on which we can demonstrate the good will and friendship of the United States for the government of Turkey, and that we shall be happy if circumstances shall enable the two countries to modify their commercial arrangements so as to increase intercourse between them.

You will receive herewith new letters of credence addressed to his Imperial Majesty the present Sultan.

Mr. Brown's account of the favorable sentiments of his Majesty towards the United States is especially gratifying.

I am, sir, respectfully, your obedient servant,

WILLIAM H. SEWARD.

E. Joy Morris, Esq., &c., &c., &c., Constantinople.

SWEDEN

Mr. Angel to Mr. Seward.

[Extract.]

No. 76.]
LEGATION OF THE UNITED STATES,
Stockholm, May 22, 1861.

*   *   *   *   *   *   *   *   *

The Swedish law is very strict against the violation of the rights of neutrals, and I am assured that there is no apprehension that any of the ports of this kingdom or of Norway will be prostituted to the wicked purpose of fitting out privateers.

*   *   *   *   *   *   *   *   *

I have the honor to be, with much respect, your obedient servant,
B. F. ANGEL.

Mr. Angel to Mr. Seward.

[Extract.]

No. 77.]
LEGATION OF THE UNITED STATES,
Stockholm, May 30, 1861.

SIR:

*   *   *   *   *   *   *   *   *

Herewith I beg permission to enclose a copy of my note to Count Manderstrom, minister of foreign affairs, transmitting copies of the President's proclamations establishing a blockade of the ports in the seceding States, which I hope may meet your approbation.

I have the honor to be, with great respect, your obedient servant,
BENJ. F. ANGEL.

Hon. WM. H. SEWARD,
Secretary of State, &c., &c., &c.

LEGATION OF THE UNITED STATES,
Stockholm, May 22, 1861.

SIR: The President of the United States, in view of the disturbed and unhappy condition of public affairs in the southern portion of our confederacy, and in the exercise of what he regards as a legal right and constitutional duty, has ordered and established an effective blockade of the ports in the several States of South Carolina, Georgia, Alabama, Florida, Mississippi, Louisiana, Texas, Virginia, and North Carolina.

I have the honor herewith to transmit to your excellency copies of the President's proclamations upon this subject, for the information of his Majesty's government, and I avail myself of the occasion to offer to your excellency the renewed assurance of my high consideration.

BENJ. F. ANGEL.

His Excellency Count Manderstrom,
    Minister of Foreign Affairs, &c., &c., &c.

Mr. Angel to Mr. Seward.

[Extract.]

No. 79.]   Legation of the United States,
Stockholm, June 4, 1861.

Sir: In my conference with Count Manderstrom to-day I was informed that no application has been made to the Swedish government on behalf of the people of the so-called Confederate States for their recognition as an independent nation, and although passports are not now required, either in Sweden or Norway, I am quite sure no agents are here from the seceded States for any purpose whatever.   *   *   *   *   *

I have the honor to be, with great respect, your obedient servant,

B. F. ANGEL.

Hon. William H. Seward,
    Secretary of State, &c., &c., &c., Washington.

Mr. Angel to Mr. Seward.

[Extract.]

No. 83.]   Legation of the United States,
Stockholm, June 10, 1861.

   *   *   *   *   *   *   *   *   *

In the contest in which we are unfortunately engaged, it is of great importance to secure the good opinion of mankind, and I am gratified in being able to inform you that, so far as my reading and observations extend, the better informed European statesmen express the opinion that those charged with the administration of public affairs have acted with the greatest moderation and forbearance under circumstances which might perhaps have justified retaliatory measures, and in their defence of constitutional law and an organized government against treason and revolution they will have the sympathy and best wishes of all conservatives on this side the Atlantic.

   *   *   *   *   *   *   *   *   *

I am, sir, your obedient servant,

B. F. ANGEL.

[Extract.]

No. 1.]   Legation of the United States,
Stockholm, *June* 14, 1861.

Sir: *   *   *   *   *   *   *
Yesterday I called, by appointment, upon Count Manderstrom, minister of foreign affairs. Count M., in behalf of his government, welcomed me most cordially to Sweden as the representative of the United States of America. Count Manderstrom informed me of the absence of his Majesty in Norway, whose return was daily expected, and that an early day would be fixed for the audience to present my letter of credence. During the interview he referred to the condition of affairs in the United States, and expressed himself strongly in favor of our government.

From the limited opportunity I have had to judge, I have no hesitation in the declaration of the opinion that the sympathy of the entire north of Europe is almost unanimously in favor of the existing government of the United States. The emigration from this part of Europe having been to the northern or free States, they speak as if they would like to give active aid to their friends, relatives, and countrymen.

    *   *   *   *   *   *   *   *   *

I have the honor to be, with respect, your obedient servant,
J. S. HALDEMAN.

Hon. Wm. H. Seward,
Secretary of State, &c., &c., &c.

[Extract.]

No. 3.]   Legation of the United States,
Stockholm, *July* 4, 1861.

Sir: I have the honor, in reply to your circular of May 20, to inform you that I am almost confident no effort or attempt to purchase articles contraband of war, or to fit out vessels in any port of Sweden, under letters of marque, need be apprehended. The public voice of this nation, represented by a free press, is clearly and emphatically in favor of my government, and view secession as a causeless rebellion, which ought to be suppressed by the strong arm of military law. Should, contrary to my expectation, efforts be made by mercenary men to give in any manner assistance to the rebels, I have no doubt I shall receive information of the fact in time to call the attention of his Majesty's government to the subject.

Frequently application has been made to me by honorable discharged officers of the army of Sweden to know if their services would be accepted by my government, and on what conditions. I have replied that I have no instructions on that subject, and can make no promises or arrangements on the part of my government. The question is asked if their passage-money would be paid on their arrival in America and entering the service. Two of these officers are eminent military engineers. *   *   *   *   *

I have the honor to be, with great respect, your obedient servant,

J. S. HALDEMAN.

Hon. WILLIAM H. SEWARD,
    Secretary of State, &c., &c., &c.

Mr. Seward to Mr. Haldeman.

No. 2.]   DEPARTMENT OF STATE,
                                 Washington, July 8, 1861.

SIR: Your despatch of June 14 (No. 1) has just been received. Your safe arrival at your destination is a source of satisfaction, and the information you give concerning the tone and temper of public opinion in the north of Europe, with regard to the present embarrassment in our domestic affairs, is especially gratifying.

I am, respectfully, your obedient servant,

WILLIAM H. SEWARD.

JACOB S. HALDEMAN, Esq., *&c., &c., &c.*

Mr. Seward to Mr. Haldeman.

No. 3.]   DEPARTMENT OF STATE,
                                 Washington, July 25, 1861.

SIR: Your despatch of June 26 (No. 2) has been received. So much of it as relates to the preservation of the archives, and other matters of subordinate interest, will be noticed in a distinct paper.

The President is gratified by the account of the friendly reception you have received from his Majesty, and directs me to congratulate you upon the good auspices under which your mission is commenced. You will lose no good opportunity for assuring the government of Sweden that the United States entertain the highest consideration and cherish·the best wishes for his Majesty and the Swedish people.

I am, sir, respectfully, your obedient servant,

WILLIAM H. SEWARD.

JACOB S. HALDEMAN, Esq.,
    &c., &c., &c., Stockholm.

Mr. Haldeman to Mr. Seward.

[Extracts.]

No. 5.]

UNITED STATES LEGATION,
Stockholm, July 28, 1861.

SIR: Since I last wrote quite a change is visible in diplomatic circles in regard to American affairs. They now speak out openly that the government of the United States should act vigorously and efficiently; enforce the laws by the strong arm of military power; that the rebellion should be annihilated by force and not by compromise; that is a mistaken policy to suppose that delay and the holding out of the olive branch ever fitted rebels for grace, or brought them to a sense of their guilt.

* * * * * * * *

On the 29th of July the King joins his fleet in the Baltic, and will visit the coasts of Norway and Denmark; he will be absent some four or five weeks. Her Majesty at the same time visits her parents, the King and Queen of Holland. Count Edward Piper, who has been appointed minister to the United States, is one of the first noblemen in Sweden, with a thorough English education and manners, and whose appointment was intended as a compliment to the United States. Count Manderstrom informed me at our last conference that a large Swedish frigate would be sent to the American waters to protect Swedish interests against privateers if it should be necessary. From all quarters the firm and decided course of the administration is spoken of with respect and esteem; no one now seems to doubt of the speedy triumph of the government.

I remain, with great respect, your obedient servant,

J. S. HALDEMAN.

Hon. WILLIAM H. SEWARD,
Secretary of State, &c., &c., &c., Washington.

Mr. Seward to Mr. Haldeman.

No. 4.]

DEPARTMENT OF STATE,
Washington, July 30, 1861.

SIR: Your despatch of July 4, 1861, (No. 3,) has been received, and it is entirely satisfactory in regard to your own activity in your mission, and the favorable dispositions of the enlightened government to which you are accredited.

We notice with much pleasure the willingness of military gentlemen of talent and experience in Sweden, as in other nations, to enter the army of the United States. It is a proof of a sympathy with our great cause of inestimable value. We wish, indeed, that we were able to engage to accept all who should come. But this is impossible, for the reason that they are coming in unknown numbers from various European states, while at the same time a long repressed martial spirit has broken out among our own countrymen, which gives us more candidates than we have places for.

Gradually we have taken into the service several able and spirited military men from Prussia, Italy, France, and Hungary. I shall be happy to recommend any the government of Sweden may desire us to accept.

  *   *   *   *   *   *   *   *   *

  I am, sir, respectfully, your obedient servant,
            WILLIAM H. SEWARD.
JACOB S. HALDEMAN, Esq.,
   &c., &c., &c., Stockholm.

Mr. Seward to Mr. Haldeman.

No. 5.]   DEPARTMENT OF STATE,
            Washington, August 19, 1861.

 SIR: Your despatch (No. 4) of July 22 has been received.

 The announcement which you were requested to make, by his excellency Count Manderstrom, of the appointment of Count Piper as his Swedish and Norwegian Majesty's minister resident in the United States, has been received with much satisfaction. The filling of the mission in so acceptable a manner at this period is regarded by the President as an earnest of his Majesty's friendly feelings towards the government of the United States, and you are directed to assure Count Manderstrom that the new minister will receive at our hands a most cordial welcome, and that no opportunity will be neglected of strengthening the ties of amity between the government of his Majesty and that of the United States.

  I am, sir, respectfully, your obedient servant,
            WILLIAM H. SEWARD.
JACOB S. HALDEMAN, Esq.,
   &c., &c., &c., Stockholm.

Mr. Seward to Mr. Haldeman.

[Extract]

No. 6.]   DEPARTMENT OF STATE,
            Washington, August 19, 1861.

 SIR:
  * , *   *   *   *   *
  *   *   *   *   *   *

 The information which you give concerning the temper and feeling of the government and people of Sweden is very gratifying.

 This government will find a sincere pleasure in doing all that shall be in its power to favor the safety and freedom of the commerce of Sweden in the ports of the United States not closed by the blockade.

  I am, sir, respectfully, your obedient servant,
            WILLIAM H. SEWARD.
JACOB S. HALDEMAN, Esq.,
   &c., &c., &c., Stockholm.

Mr. Seward to Mr. Haldeman.

[Extract.]

No. 7.]　　　　　　　　　　　DEPARTMENT OF STATE,
　　　　　　　　　　　　　　　Washington, September 7, 1861.

SIR:
*　　*　　*　　*　　*　　*
*　　*　　*　　*　　*　　*
*　　*　　*　　*　　*　　*

Your communications concerning internal questions in Sweden are appreciated, and we hope that the succession to the throne may be settled in a manner satisfactory to the government, and conducive to the welfare of the enlightened people whom it so deeply concerns.

We have already forgotten the reverse of our arms at Bull Run, which affected you so deeply, and the prospect of the restoration of the authority of the Union is entirely satisfactory. Our volunteer army will, I have no doubt, vindicate its character and win back the confidence of the country and its friends.

I am, sir, your obedient servant,

JACOB S. HALDEMAN, Esq.,　　　　　　WILLIAM H. SEWARD.
　　&c., &c., &c., Stockholm.

Ex. Doc. 1——26

PORTUGAL.

Mr. Morgan to Mr. Seward.

[Extract.]

No. 66.]
UNITED STATES LEGATION,
Lisbon, April 6, 1861.

SIR: *   *   *   *   *   *   *   *   *

During the evening his Majesty inquired with interest as to the condition of affairs in the United States, but when I assured him, as I had before done on a similar occasion, that the Union would be preserved, his manner was more expressive of doubt than belief, though he replied that he hoped I was not mistaken, as it would be a great pity to see so fine a country ruined, and I regret to say that my colleagues, and European politicians generally, regard the disruption of the States as an established fact.

*   *   *   *   *   *   *   *

With high respect, I have the honor to be your obedient servant,

GEORGE W. MORGAN.

Hon. W. H. SEWARD, *Secretary of State.*

Mr. Morgan to Mr. Seward.

No. 67.]
UNITED STATES LEGATION,
Lisbon, May 29, 1861.

SIR: I have the honor to enclose a copy of my note to the government of H. M. F. Majesty on the subject of privateers.

I have notified our consular agents of the importance of vigilance.

Would it not be good policy to take into regular commission a considerable number of our clipper ships, till our navy can be placed on a basis commensurate with the crisis?

The telegraph announces that the President has notified the foreign powers that he will discontinue diplomatic relations with any nation that recognizes the so-called Confederate States.

I trust that it is true, for such a policy will produce good results, and is not less wise than it is dignified.

If we come out of this contest triumphant, and the Union be preserved, our nation will be more powerful and more glorious, more loved and more feared, than ever before in our history as a nation.

I have the honor to be, very respectfully, your obedient servant,

GEORGE W. MORGAN.

Hon. WM. H. SEWARD, *Secretary of State.*

UNITED STATES LEGATION,
Lisbon, May 27, 1861.

SIR: A combination of individuals in certain of the southern States of the United States have raised the standard of insurrection, and under the pretended authority of the self-styled Confederate States of America have threatened to grant pretended letters of marque for the purpose of committing assaults on the lives, vessels, and property of good citizens of the United States, lawfully engaged in commerce on the high seas, and in the waters of the United States. And in consequence thereof, on the 19th day of April, 1861, and the eighty-fifth year of the independence of the United States, the President, by formal proclamation, declared that if any person, under the pretended authority of the said so-called but unrecognized Confederate States, or under any other pretence, shall molest a vessel of the United States, or the persons or cargo on board of her, that such person will be held amenable to the laws of the United States for the punishment of piracy.

In the name, therefore, of the government of the United States, I have the honor to request that the government of H. M. F. Majesty may cause such measures to be taken as will effectually prevent any vessel from being prepared in any of his Majesty's ports for the aforesaid piratical purposes.

Under the conviction that reliable information as to said insurrection will be gratifying to his Majesty's government, I briefly submit the following statement:

1. The government of the so-called Confederate States has been neither recognized by any sovereign state, nor has it been acknowledged by the people it professes to represent. But, on the contrary, the combination of individuals who have usurped the title of a government refuse to submit their constitution to the ratification or rejection of the citizens of said States.

2. The insurrectionists are wanting in the great elements necessary to successful war. Their ports are strictly blockaded ; their supplies are cut off, by land and by sea, and within themselves they are destitute of the means of carrying on a prolonged struggle.

3. That while it may be difficult to predict the length of time which may be required to suppress the insurrection, yet in the future nothing can be more certain than are the vindication of the national flag, and the perfect restoration of order and prosperity under the Constitution of the United States.

It affords me great pleasure to renew to your excellency the assurance of my most distinguished consideration.

GEORGE W. MORGAN.

His Excellency M. ANTONIO JOSÉ D'AVILA,
  Secretary of State for Foreign Affairs, &c.

Mr. Harvey to Mr. Seward.

No. 6.]   LEGATION OF THE UNITED STATES,
Lisbon, July 25, 1861.

SIR: I have just had my first interview with Mr. d'Avila, the minister of
foreign affairs, since being presented to the King, and desire to report its
purpose and character. While no instructions have reached me in regard
to the desired action of this government concerning privateers, I considered
it proper, in view of the facilities offered by the ports of Portugal and her
colonies to prizes, to call the attention of the proper authorities to it at the
earliest opportunity when I was in an official position to do so with effect.

On the very day of my arrival here, and when I did not anticipate the
painful delays and difficulties which have since occurred, I told General
Morgan of my intention to ask for a proclamation excluding privateers, as
soon as I was presented. He addressed a note to the foreign office on the
2d instant, in which the general question was discussed at much length.
And although he afterwards called several times upon Mr. d'Avila, no
answer was obtained before his departure yesterday.

These were the circumstances under which I felt it necessary to go forward and to ask for some decisive action. I told Mr. d'Avila frankly that I
did not desire to signalize my advent here by any protracted correspondence,
and least of all by a controversy, and that the sentiments which I had expressed at my audience of presentation were those which really animated
me. I informed him that a condition of affairs existed in the United States
which required me to claim an early and positive expression of views by the
Portuguese government on this subject, and therefore he must excuse my
seeming urgency. He inquired if I adopted the note which General Morgan
had addressed to him. I answered that I accepted the principle, but was
willing to waive a correspondence, if the object could be accomplished by a
direct and candid interchange of opinions orally, when there would be less
difficulty in understanding each other, and a readier mode of reaching a conclusion promptly. He concurred in this suggestion, and said it reflected his
own sincere dispositions.

I then told him that a proclamation forbidding the ports of Portugal and
her colonies to privateers and their prizes, in explicit terms, would be satisfactory, and argued that, as Portugal had acquiesced in the treaty of Paris
of 1856, there ought to be no difficulty in making this declaration. In order
to strengthen the reason, I suggested that the proclamation might be made
broad and general, because I most desired the assertion of a practical principle which would cover the case completely. He seemed to assent to the
idea, and remarked that it was disembarrassed materially by the fact that the
government of the United States had discountenanced the issuing of letters
of marque. I told him that the government had not only done that, but that
it deprecated and denounced the system, which certain insurrectionary and
tumultuous assemblages of people had proclaimed with a professed authority.

In order that no misapprehension might occur, I notified Mr. d'Avila that
a proclamation or declaration which, in doubtful phrases or by implication,
recognized the existence of any pretended organization in the United States,
independent of the government which accredited me, and which alone has
power to make treaties and conduct diplomatic intercourse, would be regarded
as a most unfriendly act by the President.

After again urging upon him reasons for an early decision, he explained
that the cortes were now in session night and day, but expected to adjourn
soon, when he would lay the matter before the King's council, and obtain
their opinion, which he thought would conform to my request. I asked him

to name a convenient day when an answer might be expected. He declined fixing a time certain, but expressed the belief that by the middle of next week the council could be convened, and this subject should have precedence over all others.

In proposing a proclamation such as I have suggested, vessels-of-war and their prizes would be allowed entry to the ports of Portugal, which the English and French governments have expressly excluded, putting them on the same footing with privateers. As I have acted upon my own motion in this matter, I submit it to your approbation.

With high respect, your obedient servant,

JAMES E. HARVEY.

Hon. WILLIAM H. SEWARD,
    Secretary of State.

Mr. Harvey to Mr. Seward.

[Extract.]

No. 7.]   LEGATION OF THE UNITED STATES,
                                                 Lisbon, July 28, 1861.

SIR: Since my despatch (No. 6) of the 25th instant, information reached me   *   *   *   *   *   *   *   *   *   *   *   *   *
*   *   *   *   *   *   *   *   *   *   *   *   *
that plans were concerted by the parties who had recently applied for the privilege of fitting out a privateer, and others, to accept letters of marque from the so-called Confederate States, and to use some of the remote islands of Portugal as places of rendezvous for outfit and for the disposal of any prizes that might be taken.

In view of the facilities offered for these nefarious enterprises in the Azores, Madeira, Cape de Verd, and other islands, as well as in the small Indian possessions of that kingdom, I felt it proper to address the note, of which a copy is enclosed, to the minister of foreign affairs, yesterday, as a means of inducing him to take immediate and decisive action on the subject. These facts will serve to explain the seemingly urgent tone of my note, which I thought demanded by the necessity of the case.

I am, sir, very respectfully, your obedient servant,

JAMES E. HARVEY.

Hon. W. H. SEWARD,
    Secretary of State.

LEGATION OF THE UNITED STATES, *July* 27, 1861.

The undersigned presents his compliments to his excellency M. d'Avila, minister of foreign affairs of his most faithful Majesty, and begs leave to repeat in this form, for the convenience of a more precise understanding, the substance of the ideas which he had the honor to express in his interview with his excellency on the 25th instant.

Portugal has acceded fully to the anti-privateering doctrine established by the declaration of the congress of Paris of April, 1856, to which the assent of the United States has recently been given.

Opposed to the principle and practice of privateering, Portugal ought not to hesitate, as it appears to the undersigned, to declare by general proclamation, as a general principle and rule, that her ports are no longer open to privateers or their prizes.

This is the extent of the present request of the undersigned. He does not ask that Portugal shall make any particular application of the general rule to the peculiar and unhappy state of things now existing in the United States, nor that any unnecessary notice or cognizance should be taken of the disturbed condition of domestic affairs in the United States. Indeed, the government of the United States would not view with satisfaction any such superfluous and unnecessary expression of views or sentiments by any foreign power in regard to a state of things purely domestic, local, and temporary, to which a satisfactory termination will soon be placed by the ample power of the United States government. On the contrary, as the undersigned took occasion to assure his excellency M. d'Avila, at the personal interview referred to, any declaration which recognized the existence, even by implication, of a pretended organization in the United States, independent of the government, which alone has the power to make treaties, and to conduct diplomatic intercourse, and the authority of which cannot be questioned, would be considered as a most unfriendly act.

As little as the government of the United States would pretend to interfere in any analogous question that might possibly arise between the government of his most faithful Majesty and any of the provinces of his kingdom, can the United States be disposed to view with satisfaction any such expression as that suggested on the part of his or any foreign government. At the same time it is manifest that questions of the most embarrassing and even dangerous character are, at any moment, liable to occur, if unlawful and piratical privateers, with unlawful prizes, should make their appearance in the waters of Portugal or her colonies, and it is with a view to the amicable anticipation of such possible contingencies that the undersigned has requested, and now repeats the request, that the government of his most faithful Majesty should simply carry out, to its natural and necessary consequence and application, the principle of the declaration of Paris above referred to, as having been fully acceded to by the enlightened ·government of his most faithful Majesty.

The undersigned begs to add the expression of his hopes that in advance of the issue of the proclamation, which, under these circumstances, he believes and expects will be issued at the earliest convenient day by his most faithful Majesty, the undersigned may be favored with an opportunity of seeing the proposed terms of the same, in order that, by means of frank interchange of views, there may be the more perfect certainty of such a friendly and reciprocally satisfactory harmony of views between the two governments as shall correspond to the sentiments already fully expressed by the undersigned on behalf of the President of the United States, and most satisfactorily and cordially responded to by his most faithful Majesty.

In conclusion, the undersigned respectfully asks that this subject, in view of its importance and possible complications, may be brought to the early notice of his most faithful Majesty, so as to preclude the happening of events which might involve grave consequences, to which the interests and good will of both nations are alike opposed. He appreciates the reasons which have been assigned for the delay, since the subject was first presented by his immediate predecessor, in a note to his excellency M. d'Avila, dated on the 2d of July; but urgent considerations have recently arisen which require the undersigned to submit this request on behalf of the government of the United States.

The undersigned avails himself of this occasion to renew the assurances of his most distinguished consideration.

JAMES E. HARVEY.

Mr. Harvey to Mr. Seward.

No. 8.]   LEGATION OF THE UNITED STATES,
                                              Lisbon, July 30, 1861.

SIR: I received a note from Mr. d'Avila, the minister of foreign affairs, yesterday, requesting an interview with me at 4 o'clock. I called at the foreign office at the appointed hour, and he immediately presented the original draft, in Portuguese, of a proposed proclamation, of which I enclose a translated copy, marked No. 2. After hearing it read and reduced into English, I expressed my acceptance of its general scope and spirit, but expressly demurred to the declaration at the end of article 2, by which armed vessels are placed in the same category as privateers in regard to prizes. Although I knew it was of no practical importance to the United States under present circumstances, it was easy to foresee that in the event of war with England or France, and with their ability to blockade our ports, that prizes taken by American ships-of-war would be thus excluded from Portugal and her possessions. Hence my objection to that point. I told Mr. d'Avila that it went beyond the treaty of Paris, upon which the proclamation was professedly predicated, and that it did what I had sought to avoid by introducing indirectly our domestic question. He said his object was to exclude the prizes of vessels-of-war of the so-called Confederate States, in case they should create a navy, and thus to guard against any future complication. To this suggestion I answered that, as we were not dealing with suppositious or hypothetical cases, it was necessary to adhere to the practical question, and, as we had stated, on the basis of the declaration of Paris in regard to privateering and his own preamble set out with that statement, the introduction of any extraneous matter would be not only irrelevant, but likely to defeat the object which both sides alike professed to have in view. He did not respond to this suggestion, but agreed to let me take the rough draft, in order that I might submit whatever observations might occur to me as appropriate.

I prepared the accompanying note (marked No. 1) this morning, and sent it to Mr. d'Avila an hour ago.

There are two councils before which such questions are considered; first, the council of ministers or the cabinet; and second, the council of state, which is a larger body, and includes the cabinet and other distinguished persons. I understood Mr. d'Avila to say that the draft of the proclamation had been laid before the former, and approved by them, and that my proposed amendment must, therefore, be presented at another meeting. I have reason to believe that my note of Saturday precipitated this action, which, in a country where diplomacy is proverbially slow, exhibits unusual promptitude.

I am, sir, very respectfully, your obedient servant,
                                                   JAMES E. HARVEY.

Hon. W. H. SEWARD,
   Secretary of State, Washington City.

No. 1.

LEGATION OF THE UNITED STATES,
July 30, 1861.

The undersigned presents his most respectful compliments to his excellency M. d'Avila, and referring to the conversation he had the honor to have with his excellency yesterday, and repeating his thanks for his excellency's courtesy in showing him the draft of the proclamation contemplated by the government of his most faithful Majesty, as a proper consequence and application of the principles adopted by Portugal by her adhesion to the declaration of Paris of April, 1856, he begs leave to submit the following observations to his excellency's enlightened consideration:

The declaration of Paris abolished privateering. It would seem to follow as a necessary logical consequence to all powers acceding to the same, that under no circumstances (except those of force, *majeure*, and brief, indispensable hospitality, in view of the laws of humanity) ought their ports to be open to the admission of privateers or their prizes. So far, then, as regards privateers and their prizes, the undersigned sees nothing but what he must approve in the draft of the proclamation referred to.

But the declaration of Paris did not go further, and change the established maritime law of the world in regard to the legality of the capture of prizes by the regular men-of-war of the naval. forces whose fleets roam the ocean. Such prizes have always been deemed legitimate, and still remain so. It is no' application of the principles of the declaration of Paris to exclude such regular and lawful prizes, made by the regular vessels of one nation, from the ports of a friendly nation. In this respect the words, "*on por embarcacoes annadas,*" at the end of article 2, appear not only to go much beyond the principles of the declaration referred to, but even to be most unnecessarily introduced into a proclamation avowedly designed for the mere execution and practical application of the principles of that declaration. To introduce them at this moment in such a proclamation would be deemed by the government of the United States not only as a gratuitous deviation from the terms of the preamble to the same proclamation, but as a deviation prompted by a reason which would seem to involve an indirect, if not a direct, reference to the present rebellion of a small portion of the United States. It would be understood as placing on the same level the regular men-of-war of the United States and the privateers of the States now in rebellion, so far as regards the prizes made by them. It is only with reference to the principle involved, to the apparent inconsistency between the preamble and the sequence, and to the misconstruction to which it would be consequently liable, that the undersigned indulges the hope and expectation that the few words above cited may be omitted from the proposed proclamation, and takes occasion to say that in that form it will be perfectly acceptable to the government of the United States, and will add another to the many links of friendly relation and intercourse which already bind closely together the two countries.

It is only proper for the undersigned to notify his excellency M. d'Avila that information has been communicated to the government of the United States which authorizes the belief that some of the remote islands and colonies of this kingdom are proposed to be used by designing and reckless persons to engage in the nefarious enterprises referred to by the equipment of privateers, or the sale of prizes, if any should be taken. He knows perfectly well, in advance of any assurance, that such lawless undertakings would be sternly deprecated by the government of his most faithful Majesty; but his excellency cannot fail to discover in this fact an urgent reason why a proclamation of such sentiments, and in the unobjectionable form suggested, should be immediately made. It is with this view, and to provide against the contingency of future, and perhaps of impending, difficulty, that the undersigned has brought the subject thus promptly to the notice of his excellency, and with the most friendly spirit and purpose.

The undersigned begs leave to return the rough draft of the proclamation, and to repeat his assurances of respect and distinguished consideration.

JAMES E. HARVEY.

No. 2.

[Translation of proposed proclamation.]

It being convenient, under existing circumstances, to carry out the execution of the principles contained in the declaration of Paris of 16th April, 1856, made by the representatives of the signing parties to the treaty of peace of 30th March of the same year, to which my government hath adhered, I am pleased hereby, having heard the council of ministers, to decree the following :

ARTICLE 1.

It is prohibited to Portuguese subjects and foreigners to equip in the ports and waters of this kingdom, not only on the continent and adjacent islands, but also in the ultramarine provinces, vessels destined for privateering.

ARTICLE 2.

In the same points cited in the preceding article it is equally prohibited the entry of privateers and prizes made by them or by *armed vessels.*

§°. All cases of force, (*majeure,*) wherein, according to the rights of nations, hospitality becomes indispensable, are excepted from this clause without, however, allowing, under any form, that the sale of objects arising from prizes shall take place.

Let the ministers and secretaries of state of all the departments understand these presents, and cause the same to be executed.

PALACE OF NECESSIDADOS, *July* 29, 1861.

Mr. Seward to Mr. Harvey.

No. 2.]   DEPARTMENT OF STATE,
Washington, July 30, 1861.

SIR : Your despatches No. 1, of June 30, and No. 2, of July 7, have been received, and are under the consideration of the President.

Mr. Morgan's despatch No. 70, of the date of July 5, has been received. I am instructed by the President to say that Mr. Morgan's proceeding in addressing the Portuguese government on the subject of allowing the fitting out or harboring of privateers to prey upon the commerce of the United

States is approved, as well as the general tenor of his communication on that occasion.

The President cannot for a moment allow the belief that Portugal would be the only or even the first power to permit proceedings so injurious to the United States as a license or shelter granted to pirates engaged in preying on their commerce would be. Nevertheless, we shall look not without some solicitude for the result of the matter thus initiated by Mr. Morgan.

Please assure him, if he is yet remaining in Lisbon, of the entire satisfaction with which his conduct in the mission, so far as it has been reported to me, is regarded by the government.

I am, sir, your obedient servant,

WILLIAM H. SEWARD.

James E. Harvey, Esq., &c., &c., &c., *Lisbon.*

Mr. Seward to Mr. Harvey.

No. 5.]

Department of State,
Washington, August 17, 1861.

Sir: Your despatch No. 7, dated July 28, has been received. It is accompanied by a copy of a note which you on the 27th of July addressed to M. d'Avila, minister for foreign affairs in the government of Portugal, on the subject of privateering by or in the service of the insurgents of the United States. Your proceeding in this respect seems to have been eminently judicious, and the note itself, I think, very well and properly expressed.

It is hoped that you will before this time have received such a satisfactory reply as our good relations and treaties with the government of Portugal authorize us to expect.

I am, sir, respectfully, your obedient servant,

WILLIAM H. SEWARD.

James E. Harvey, Esq., &c., &c., &c, *Lisbon.*

Mr. Seward to Mr. Harvey.

No. 7.]

Department of State,
Washington, August 21, 1861.

Sir: Your despatch No. 4, under the date of July 20, has been received. Your address to his Majesty was appropriate, and even happy. His reply is very gratifying to this government.

We trust that you may find it easy to keep the relations between the two countries on a basis of mutual and cordial friendship.

I am, sir, respectfully, your obedient servant,

WILLIAM H. SEWARD.

James E. Harvey, Esq., &c., &c., &c., *Lisbon.*

Mr. Seward to Mr. Harvey.

No. 8.]

DEPARTMENT OF STATE,
Washington, August 24, 1861.

SIR: Your despatch No. 8, dated July 30, has been received, and I have the pleasure of informing you that the President entirely approves of your diligent and judicious action concerning the proposed proclamation of the government of Portugal. We look with much confidence for good results from it.

I am, sir, your obedient servant,

WILLIAM H. SEWARD.

JAMES E. HARVEY, Esq., &c., &c., &c., *Lisbon.*

Mr. Harvey to Mr. Seward.

No. 13.]

LEGATION OF THE UNITED STATES,
Lisbon, August 25, 1861.

SIR: I have the honor to enclose herewith the copy of a note from the foreign office, covering the copy of a proclamation in regard to privateers and their prizes, (Nos. 1 and 2,) in the form finally adopted by the council of state. This decree was published in the official paper (Diario de Lisboa) on the 23d instant, a copy of which has already been transmitted to the department.

By referring to my despatch No. 8, it will be seen that the preamble of the proclamation has been modified, so as to escape the logical inconsistencies which I then pointed out, in the hope of inducing the omission of certain phrases, which would have rendered it more acceptable. I have the best reason to know that the council of ministers, or cabinet, were not only well disposed to adopt my proposed amendment, but that they submitted the proclamation with the revision.

When this fact became known to me, I urged, with every influence and persuasion at my command, an immediate decision, so as to insure the promulgation before any interrupting cause or accident could intervene. But the King went away for a short time, and a council of state, to which the proposed action of the council of ministers on important questions is presented for examination, could not be convened. In the meantime intelligence from the United States of an eventful character affected opinion here, and gave increased weight to the objections which had been urged by the British minister and others against the form of proclamation which I had requested. A council of state was summoned upon the return of the King, and the result of their deliberations is to be found in the documents enclosed in this despatch.

While I should have been greatly gratified had my amendment been accepted, I have the satisfaction to know that it did not fail from any want of zeal, energy, or effort on my part, and that the proclamation as it now stands is mainly predicated upon your policy, in execution of the principle of the treaty of Paris, and is not open to the objections urged against those issued by England, France, or Spain.

I have the honor to be, sir, very respectfully,

JAMES E. HARVEY.

Hon. W. H. SEWARD,
Secretary of State.

Mr. d'Avila to Mr. Harvey.

[Translation.]

No. 1.] DEPARTMENT OF STATE FOR FOREIGN AFFAIRS,
August 22, 1861.

The councillor of state, Antonio José d'Avila, presents his most attentive compliments to Mr. James E. Harvey, and has the honor to remit him the enclosed copy of the decree of the 29th of July last, published according to the last form given thereto, after hearing the council of state.

[Translation.]

No. 2.] MINISTRY OF FOREIGN AFFAIRS.

It being proper, in view of the circumstances at present existing in regard to the United States of America, to carry into effect the principles established in the declaration of Paris of April 16, 1856, made by the representatives of the powers that signed the treaty of peace of the 30th of March of that year, to which declaration my government acceded, and likewise, for the same reason, to adopt other measures which I deem opportune, I have been pleased, after hearing the council of state, to decree as follows:

ARTICLE 1.

In all the ports and waters of this kingdom, as well on the continent and in the adjacent islands as in the ultramarine provinces, Portuguese subjects and foreigners are prohibited from fitting out vessels destined for privateering.

ARTICLE 2.

In the same ports and waters referred to in the preceding article is, in like manner, prohibited the entrance of privateers and of the prizes made by privateers, or by armed vessels.

§ The cases of overruling necessity, (*força maior*,) in which, according to the law of nations, hospitality is indispensable, are excepted from this regulation, without permission, however, being allowed, in any manner, for the sale of any objects proceeding from prizes.

The ministers and secretaries of state in all the departments will thus understand, and cause it to be executed.

PALACE OF NECESSIDADES, *July* 29, 1861.

KING.

MARQUEZ DE LOULÉ.
ALBERTO ANTONIO DE MORAES CARVALHO.
VISCONDE DE SÁ DA BANDEIRA.
CARLOS BENTO DA SILVA.
THIAGO AUGUSTO VELLOSO DE HORTA.
ANTONIO JOSÉ D'AVILA.

PERU.

No. 2.]

DEPARTMENT OF STATE,
Washington, November 12, 1861.

SIR: You are appointed a minister to represent the United States near the republic of Peru.

This appointment is an overture by this government, under the present administration, to renew the friendly relations with Peru, which had been suspended, on the motion of this government, when administered by the last President, James Buchanan.

The Peruvian government may naturally ask and be entitled to an explanation of this change of position on the part of the United States.

It is confessed to be unfortunate when any government has occasion to reverse its policy in any material respect, especially a policy of friendship or of hostility towards foreign nations. Inconstancy is always liable to be mistaken for inconsistency, and inconsistency is too often the result of caprice.

Moreover, when we come to explain such a change in any case, however necessary it may have been, we shall still find it necessary to explain in such a manner as shall not cause it to be understood that the reconsideration is due to personal or partisan considerations indulged by the government.

Keeping these points in view, you will be at liberty to say, in your communications with the representatives and statesmen of the country to which you are accredited, that the President of the United States entertains the opinions that the several states founded on the American continent have common interests arising out of their neighborhood to each other, their common attitudes towards states in the eastern hemisphere, and the similarity of their commercial, social, and political institutions; that owing to the inexperience of mankind in the conduct of republican representative institutions, and the incompleteness of assimilation in the population of these American states, there is always too much danger of faction at home, while faction at home inevitably tends to invite intrigues and intervention from abroad for the overthrow of the American powers with hopes of reconquest from Europe. For these reasons, the President of the United States, without at all reflecting upon the sentiments or the action of his predecessor, determined, on assuming the administration of the government, to resist rather than to yield to influences which might tend to introduce anarchy into any one of the American states, or produce alienation and war between them.

In reviewing the causes assigned by his predecessor for withdrawing our representative from Peru, he came to the conclusion that, although serious differences had arisen between the two countries, yet that there was no imperative necessity resulting from those differences for a declaration of war against Peru. Not being able to recommend to Congress the adoption of hostilities against Peru, it seemed to result that the differences between the two states might be accommodated by the two powers in case of renewed and pacific relations.

The questions in difference between the two countries will be a subject of special instruction in a distinct paper. I confine myself in this despatch to instructions for your conduct in presenting yourself at Lima.

You will assure the government of Peru that the United States are sincere and earnest in their friendship and affection for that republic; that they desire its prosperity and advancement, equally for the welfare of its own people and the best interests of civilization; and that consistently with that regard for own rights, which every nation must always cherish which is really independent, the United States will always be found to manifest the most cordial sympathies with the republic of Peru, and with other sister states on the American continent.

I am, sir, your obedient servant,

WILLIAM H. SEWARD.

CHRISTOPHER ROBINSON, Esq., &c., &c., &c.

GUATEMALA.

[Extract.]

No. 1.]
LEGATION OF THE UNITED STATES,
Guatemala, June 1, 1861.

SIR: *   *   *   *   *   *   *   *   *
His excellency the President of Guatemala and his ministers, as well as the other officers and gentlemen of the government and country, all express their great friendship for the government and people of the United States, and especially their fervent hope that the present administration might successfully suppress the disturbances in portions of the southern States, and maintain the Union in all its integrity.
*   *   *   *   *   *   *   *   *   *

I have the honor, &c.,

E. O. CROSBY.

Hon. W. H. SEWARD,
Secretary of State.

Ex. Doc. 1——27

NICARAGUA.

Mr. Seward to Mr. Dickinson.

No. 2.]
DEPARTMENT OF STATE,
Washington, June 5, 1861.

SIR: The Spanish American states are important characters in the interesting drama of advancing civilization. They occupy a virgin domain equal to about one-eighth of the habitable part of the globe. Its fountains of wealth are inexhaustible. Its position secures it nearly equal advantages of trade and intercourse with the listless nations of the east, and with the vigorous nations of the west. Its ports, as well as all its transit routes are essential features in the commerce of the world. With the advantages of youth and singular exemption from foreign oppression or aggression which the Spanish American states have enjoyed for near half a century, it might have been expected that they would within that period have become strong and influential nations. The fact, thus far, is otherwise. They are just strong enough to maintain independence without securing necessary fear or respect. With much versatility, respectable talent, high cultivation, and very generous aspirations, they are generally changeful and capricious. The very mention of a South American state suggests always the same inquiry: why a people so free, so virtuous, so educated, and so emulous, are not more secure, fortunate, and happy. Everybody wishes the Spanish American states well, and yet everybody loses patience with them for not being wiser, more constant, and more stable. Such, I imagine, is the temper in which every foreign state finds itself when it proposes to consider its relations to those republics, and especially the republics of Central America. I know, at least, that this has always been the temper of our best statesmen in regard to Nicaragua. Union, or, at least, practical alliance with Nicaragua has always been felt by them as a necessity for the United States, and yet no one ever deems it prudent to counsel the establishment of such intimate relations. Possessing one of the continental transits most interesting to the United States, Nicaragua is at once jealous of foreign intervention to render it available, and incompetent to open and maintain it herself. But Nicaragua, like the other Spanish American states, has far better excuses for its shortcomings than it generally has credit for. That state became precociously mature, and it adopted our model of government with little of that preliminary popular education and discipline which seem necessary to enable any people to administer, maintain, and preserve free republican institutions. The policy pursued by foreign nations towards Nicaragua has not been liberal or generous. Great Britain, in her wars with Spain, early secured a position in the state very detrimental to its independence, and used it to maintain the Indians in a condition of defiance against the creole population, while it did nothing, at least nothing effectually, to civilize the tribes whom it had taken under its protection. Unwilling to lend the aid necessary to the improvement of the country, Great Britain used its protectorate there to counteract domestic efforts and intervention from this government to make that improvement which was necessary for the interest of Nicaragua herself, and hardly less necessary for all the western nations. Our own government has been scarcely less capricious, at one time seeming to court the most intimate alliance, at another treating the new republic with neglect and indifference, and at another indirectly, if not directly, consenting to the conquest and desolation of the country by our own citizens for the purpose of re-establishing the institution of slavery, which it had wisely rejected. It may be doubtful whether Nicaragua has not until this day been a loser instead of a gainer by her propinquity to, and intercourse with, the United States.

Happily this condition of things has ceased at last. Great Britain has discovered that her Mosquito protectorate was as useless to herself as it was injurious to Nicaragua, and has abandoned it. The United States no longer think that they want slavery re-established in that state, nor do they desire anything at the hands of its government but that it may so conduct its affairs as to permit and favor the opening of an inter-oceanic navigation, which shall be profitable to Nicaragua and equally open to the United States and to all other maritime nations.

You go to Nicaragua in this fortunate conjuncture of circumstances. There is yet another comfort attending your mission. Claims of American citizens upon the government of Nicaragua have long been a source of diplomatic irritation. A convention which provides for the settlement of these claims has been already negotiated. It wants only the consent of the Senate of the United States to an amendment proposed by Nicaragu, which, it is believed, would not materially change the effect of the convention, and such consent may, therefore, be expected to be given at the approaching special session of Congress.

Your instructions, therefore, will be few and very simple. Assure the republic of Nicaragua that the President will deal with that government justly, fairly, and in the most friendly spirit; that he desires only its welfare and prosperity. Cultivate friendly dispositions there toward the United States. See that no partiality arises in behalf of any other foreign state to our prejudice, and favor, in every way you can, the improvement of the transit route, seeking only such facilities for our commerce as Nicaragua can afford profitably to herself, and yield, at the same time, to other commercial nations.

Let unpleasant memories of past differences be buried, and let Nicaragua be encouraged to rely on the sympathy and support of the United States if she shall at any time come to need them.

I am, sir, your obedient servant,

WILLIAM H. SEWARD.

A. B. DICKINSON, Esq., &c., &c., &c.

EGYPT.

No. 3.]   UNITED STATES CONSULATE GENERAL,
                                                Alexandria, Egypt, June 29, 1861.

SIR: I have the honor to inform you of my arrival at this port on the morning of the 26th instant. The interruption of travel between Washington and New York, consequent on the late riotous proceedings in Baltimore, and my illness in Europe, necessarily prevented an earlier appearance at my post.

Immediate notice of my arrival, coupled with a request for an early interview with the viceroy, was served on the minister of foreign affairs, who telegraphed accordingly to the Pacha, then sojourning at his palace in Benha, about one hundred and twenty miles distant. A reply arrived on the evening of the 28th instant, that his highness would visit Alexandria and give an official reception. The promptness of his response, and his obliging readiness in voluntarily foregoing the usage which has heretofore required diplomatic agents, when asking an immediate interview, to present themselves in whatever part of Egypt he may have happened to be, instead of his coming to meet them, are interpreted here as marks of special courtesy to the government of the United States.

At half-past eight, according to previous arrangement, the dragoman of the viceroy arrived at the United States consulate with the state carriage, in which, together with our vice-consul, Mr. Johnson, I was conveyed to the palace built by the late Mohammed Ali on the sea-shore. We were also accompanied by a cavalcade of guards and janizaries attached to the other consulates at Alexandria. As we entered the court-yard the troops were drawn up in a line, with quite a fine effect, on our right, and we were greeted with the vigorous music of a military band.

Passing up the steps of the palace, and between the numerous attendants and officers who stood in order on each side, I was welcomed by the minister of foreign affairs, and by him presented to the viceroy, who advanced towards the centre of the spacious hall of reception. I then addressed him as follows:

"YOUR HIGHNESS: I have the honor to present to your highness a letter of credence from the President of the United States, announcing that I have been duly appointed to be the consul general of the United States for Egypt and its dependencies.

"In thus accrediting me as a diplomatic agent, the President desires me to assure your highness of his cordial friendship, and of his satisfaction in the continuance of those amicable relations which have so long and so happily subsisted between the governments of your highness and of the United States.

"During my official residence it will be my pleasant duty, acting in harmony with these assurances of the President, to use all honorable means to protect the interests of my fellow-citizens, and at the same time to foster a good understanding between them and the subjects of your highness. May these purposes receive your highness's benevolent approval."

In accepting my credentials, his highness replied, in French, that he perfectly understood and was much pleased with what I had said; that he welcomed me to Egypt, and hoped that his relations with the United States woud be as agreeable hereafter as they had been in times past.

The viceroy then invited me to the divan, where we sat holding a few minutes of informal conversation, with the usual accompaniment of pipes and coffee. His highness was in his most affable humor. He hoped that Egypt would prove agreeable to me, though I might find it very different from the United States. Here in Egypt, he remarked, things go on very smoothly. I replied, in so far as things went smoothly, I trusted the United States would be able to imitate the government of his highness. The viceroy laughed, and then proceeding from gay to grave, mentioned the melancholy tidings he had heard the night before of the Sultan's death. I responded that I lamented the sad event, but was very glad, nevertheless, that the viceroy was in excellent health. His highness, whose domains are but nominally a dependency of the Sultan's, seemed to take pleasure in this compliment. To the suggestion that a voyage to the United States in one of the excellent steam yachts of his navy might be interesting to him, the viceroy answered that he could not leave his country for so long a time. This, I assured him, was the worst disability under which his highness labored. The viceroy made no explicit reference to the present domestic disturbances in the United States, but expressed his good wishes for the welfare and harmony of our government.

I was next invested with "the sabre of honor," and returned home, escorted in the state carriage as before. Immediately on my reception by the viceroy a salvo of cannon had been fired, and at the signal, the national flags of all the fifteen consulates in Alexandria were raised for the day in compliment to the occasion. A horse, handsomely caparisoned, awaited me as I left the palace, and was led to the consulate as the gift of the viceroy. The uniform usage in Egypt makes this present so essential a part of a first official reception by the viceroy, that the refusal of it would be deemed ungracious, and our government, in the case of all my predecessors, has permitted its acceptance. As the oriental custom on such occasions made it necessary for me to disburse a considerable sum of money in gratuities to the very numerous soldiers and servants of the viceroy, his gift may be regarded as in some degree reciprocated. The pecuniary value of the horse is by no means large.

On returning to the consulate I found the military band of the viceroy stationed in front, who continued their complimentary services during the whole day. The consuls general of other nations, and the viceroy's minister for foreign affairs, then called upon me, appearing in full uniform; and in the afternoon I returned their visits, paying my respects first to the minister. By the minister and by the consuls a deep and intelligent interest was manifested in the affairs of the United States, and warm wishes were expressed for the continuance of our Union. The vigor of our government, and the vastness, suddenness, and spontaneous character of the military movement of our people in the pending struggle for national integrity, seem to have filled them with surprise. Indeed, among all well-informed men here, as well as elsewhere abroad, the historic battle fields of Europe have paled in interest before the tremendous uprising of the great nation beyond the Atlantic. They almost forget the political complications nearer home in studying the military map of the United States. The book-shops of the principal transatlantic cities abound in maps, charts, and other publications illustrative of the American contest, and the United States will become to masses, hitherto ignorant of its geography, a ground more familiar than were India and the Crimea when the progress of armies made their localities significant to the whole world.

I have the honor to be, sir, your obedient servant,

WILLIAM S. THAYER.

Hon. WILLIAM H. SEWARD, *Secretary of State.*

Mr. Thayer to Mr. Seward.

[Extract]

No. 4.].

UNITED STATES CONSULATE GENERAL,
Alexandria, Egypt, July 20, 1861.

SIR: *   *   *   *   *   *   *   *

Mr. Haywood, secretary of the Manchester Cotton Supply Association, is expected here daily on a mission to Egypt and India, relative to the prospective deficiency of cotton produced by the pending conflict in the United States.

Mr. Haywood, while here, will endeavor to induce the Egyptian government to extend the cultivation of cotton. It is believed that the crop in Egypt could be increased tenfold if the government would tender its aid. Carelessness in allowing the small canals of irrigation to be obstructed is said to be a cause of the comparative meagreness of the average yield of this important staple.

This year, owing to the unusual height of the last overflow of the Nile, the crop promises to exceed considerably that which preceded it. In expectation of a scarcity in England, some of the commercial houses of Alexandria are sending agents into the interior to buy up the cotton in advance of harvest. But so well understood is the condition of the cotton growing region in the United States, even by the poorest fellahs, (peasants,) that it is difficult to persuade them to sell on terms which heretofore they would have been delighted to accept. The ruling price, at the last quotations, of Mako, which ranks next to Sea Island cotton, is 275 piastres ($13 75) per cantar (a quintal;) but some of the largest cotton growers insist on $17 00, and are holding back for that unheard of figure.

The following information is derived from intelligent men whose business connexions in Egpyt give authority to their statements in reference to this important question. I also communicate some tabular statistics which are appended to this despatch.

The cotton crop of Egypt commences to be gathered about the middle of September. There are two qualities, the Sea Island and the Mako.

The Sea Island cottons are divided into two kinds. The first is that of which the seed is new, and which is sown for the first time in Egypt. The second is that which has been sown for the second time. The Sea Island, after the second planting, are changed into fine Mako.

The Mako are divided into three kinds, which in commerce are called fine quality, medium quality, and inferior quality.

It is very difficult to give an exact statement of the number of quintals which Egypt annually produces. But, according to the official tables of exports, the total amount of crop is valued, on an average yearly, at from four hundred and sixty thousand to five hundred and fifty thousand, divided as follows:

Quintals.

Sea Island, 1st kind...............................	2, 000 to 2, 500
Sea Island, 2d kind...............................	1, 000 to 1, 500
Mako, fine..	100, 000 to 140, 000
Mako, medium	300, 000 to 380, 000
Mako, inferior	47, 000 to 56, 000

460, 000 to 550, 000

The prices during the six months ending June 30, 1861, have been—

Piastres per quintal.

Sea Island, 1st kind	450 to 500
Sea Island, 2d kind.......................................	320 to 390
Mako, fine..	250 to 360
Mako, medium...	230 to 270
Mako, inferior...	180 to 230

According to the statistics of exports, (they) have been as follows:

	1859.	1860	1861, 1st six months.
	Quintals.	*Quintals.*	*Quintals.*
For England.......................	325, 401	311, 253	264, 876
For Austria.......................	78, 372	41, 080	22, 020
For France........................	98, 672	78, 302	117, 656
For Italy.........................	200	160	20
For Spain.........................	....	620	....
For Antwerp.......................	....	....	156
Total	502, 643	431, 415	404, 728

The tabular results of the last six months indicate that England will absorb a far larger proportion of Egyptian cotton than heretofore.

As before remarked, a favorable expectation prevails respecting the new crop, because the waters of the Nile have now almost reached the level of the same period last year. But this expectation may fail, for the goodness of the crop depends, not solely on the overflow of the Nile, but also on the winds, which are more or less auspicious at the time of the efflorescence of the pods.

Thus far the disturbances in America, which have produced various fluctuations in the price of cotton, have not as yet caused an increase of more than two dollars (40 piastres) per quintal.

An informal application has been made to me in behalf of various Greek and Italian residents of Alexandria, who desire to enlist in the military service of the United States, if means shall be furnished to transport them thither. I replied that I should, while appreciating their benevolent wishes to our country, await instructions from my government before giving them any encouragement.

The 4th of July, in Alexandria, was observed in the usual manner. The flags of all the fifteen consulates were raised for the day. The minister of foreign affairs of the Egyptian government also paid me his annual visit in honor of the occasion, during which he expressed his wishes for the permanence of our Union, and his opinion of the hopelessness of the cause of its domestic enemies. He appeared quite astonished at the magnitude and efficiency of our military operations.

At a dinner, given by the vice-consul in honor of the day, which was attended by the consul general of the kingdom of Italy and other distinguished residents of the city, the occasion was enthusiastically commemorated.

*   *   *   *   *   *   *   *   *

Respectfully, your obedient servant,

WM. S. THAYER,
U. S. Consul General for Egypt.

Hon. W. H. SEWARD,
   Secretary of State, Washington, D. C. ·

Cotton exported from Egypt during the last five years, 1856–'57–'58–'59–'60.

1856.	1857.	1858.	1859.	1860.
Cantars, 539,885.	Cantars, 490,968.	Cantars, 519,537.	Cantars, 502,645.	Cantars, 501,324.
Or bags of 2 cantars each, 269,912.	Or bags of 2 cantars each, 245,484.	Or bags of 2 cantars each, 259,768.	Or bags of 2 cantars each, 251,322.	Or bags of 2 cantars each, 250,662.
Or pressed bales of 4 cantars each, 134,971.	Or pressed bales of 4 cantars each, 122,742.	Or pressed bales of 4 cantars each, 129,884.	Or pressed bales of 4 cantars each, 125,661.	Or pressed bales of 4 cantars each, 125,331.

This year's crop is not yet known, it being still growing, and will be gathered about the months of September to December, although it is estimated to be equal to that of the preceding years.

ALEXANDRIA, EGYPT, *July* 15, 1861.

Mr. Seward to Mr. Thayer.

No. 3.]
               DEPARTMENT OF STATE,
               Washington, August 13, 1861.

SIR: I have received and have read with much interest your despatch of the 29th of June, (No. 3,) announcing your arrival in Egypt, and giving an account of your reception by the viceroy. Your remarks on that occasion, as well as your conduct throughout the imposing ceremonial, are approved, and the friendly feeling towards the United States manifested by his highness in your interview with him, and subsequently by his minister of foreign affairs, and by the consuls general representing other nations in Egypt, is very gratifying.

I am, sir, your obedient servant,

WM. H. SEWARD.

WILLIAM S. THAYER, Esq.,
   Consul General of the United States, Alexandria, Egypt.

VENEZUELA.

Mr. Turpin to Mr. Seward.

[Extract.]

No. 45.]

LEGATION OF THE UNITED STATES,
Caracas, July 27, 1861.

SIR: *   *   *   *   *   *   *   *

The President has promised me to issue instructions to all *comandantes de puerto* of the republic prohibiting admission of all vessels under that [the confedate] flag into its ports, except in cases of distress. I could not obtain from him their complete denunciation as pirates.

*   *   *   *   *   *   *   *   *

I have the honor, &c.,

E. A. TURPIN.

Hon. WM. H. SEWARD, *Secretary of State.*

CHILI.

[Extract]

No. 136.]
LEGATION OF THE UNITED STATES,
Santiago de Chili, August 2, 1861.

SIR: I have the honor to enclose herewith, marked A, a copy of a note by me addressed to his excellency the secretary of foreign relations of Chili, dated July 31, 1861.

* * * * * * * * *

I have the honor to remain, very respectfully, your obedient servant,

JOHN BIGLER.

Hon. WILLIAM H. SEWARD,
Secretary of State of the United States.

A.

LEGATION OF THE UNITED STATES,
Santiago de Chili, July 31, 1861.

SIR: The undersigned, envoy extraordinary and minister plenipotentiary of the United States of America, has the honor to inform your excellency that, in consequence of the President of the so-called "Confederated States of America" having issued a proclamation announcing that he has been empowered and is prepared to issue letters of marque to all who are willing to enter the service of the said States as privateers, he, the undersigned, has been instructed by his government to be vigilant to the extent of his power to prevent vessels from being fitted out in the ports of Chili under the authority of the said "Confederated States." The government of the undersigned, denying the right of the States composing the so-called "Confederated States of America" to secede, as they have done, from the American Union, and maintaining that the people of the States which have so seceded still owe fealty to the Constitution and laws of the United States, has determined to enforce obedience thereto on the part of the whole people thereof, and has solemnly proclaimed and declared that any person who shall, "under the pretended authority of the Confederated States, or under any other pretence, molest a vessel of the United States, or the persons or cargo on board of her, such person will be held amenable to the laws of the United States for the prevention and punishment of piracy."

Information has recently been communicated to the undersigned of such a character and from such sources as to induce the belief on his part that there are now, or have very recently been, in Chili parties endeavoring to effect a purchase of munitions of war to be used in fitting out privateers for the service of the so-called "Confederated States of America."

Although the undersigned cannot vouch for the correctness of this information, he can assure your excellency that he regards the same of sufficient importance, in view of the before-mentioned instructions of his government, to require him to inform your excellency thereof, and to very respectfully suggest to your excellency's government to adopt such measures as it may deem advisable to secure vigilance on the part of the proper officials to prevent the fitting out of privateers in the ports of Chili with a view of committing assaults upon the lives and property of citizens of his country engaged in lawful commerce.

In conclusion, the undersigned begs to add that he has directed inquiries to be made at the different ports in Chili, and that he will promptly impart to your excellency's government any important facts relating to the object of this note which may hereafter come to his knowledge.

The undersigned avails himself of this occasion to renew to your excellency assurances of his sincere respect and high consideration.

JOHN BIGLER.

His Excel'y the SECRETARY OF FOREIGN RELATIONS
          Of the Republic of Chili.

Mr. Bigler to Mr. Seward.

[Extract.]

No. 138.]   LEGATION OF THE UNITED STATES,
                                    Santiago de Chili, August 17, 1861.

SIR: "In my despatch, No. 136, dated August 2, 1861, I had the honor to enclose a copy of a note by me addressed to his excellency the secretary of foreign relations of Chili, inviting his attention to the instructions given me by my government, and also to rumors which had reached me concerning efforts making in the city of Valparaiso to obtain munitions of war to be used, as was feared, in fitting out privateers, under the authority of the so-called 'Confederate States of America.'

"I now have the honor to enclose herewith, marked A, a copy and translation of his excellency's reply to my note above alluded to, and which, as it is exceedingly cordial, and in every respect highly satisfactory, it is hoped will be read with care and pleasure by you."

*   *   *   *   *   *   *

I have the honor to remain, very respectfully, your obedient servant,
                                                      JOHN BIGLER.

Hon. WILLIAM H. SEWARD,
    Secretary of State of the United States.

A.

Mr. Varas to Mr. Seward.

[Translation.]

L. S.]   SANTIAGO, *August* 7, 1861.

SIR : I have had the honor of reading the note dated the 31st ultimo, which your excellency was pleased to address me. In it your excellency informs me that you have received instructions from your government to endeavor to impede, as far as your powers will permit, that in the ports of Chili privateers be armed for the service of the States which have recently declined to recognize the authority of the government of the Union, and have constituted themselves under a *de facto* government, with the title of Confederated States of America—instructions given to your excellency in consequence of a recent proclamation of the President of these States, wherein he announces that he is empowered and prepared to issue letters of marque.

At the same time your excellency informs me that you have recently received information inducing you to believe that there are at present, or recently have been, in Chili, persons endeavoring to purchase munitions of war, in order to employ the same in arming privateers for the service of the said Confederated States of America; and in view of this information your excellency signifies to me a desire that my government adopt such measures as it may deem expedient, in order to prevent the fitting out of such privateers in the ports of the republic.

I must assure your excellency, in reply, that my government, complying with the duties which it owes to a friendly state, is disposed to prevent preparations of warlike character, or any other operations hostile to the United States, from being effected in any port whatever of the territory of the republic ; and that consequently the necessary orders will be given to the respective authorities to keep especial watch in this particular. However, as far as regards privateering expeditions which may prepare or arm themselves on the coasts of Chili, it might happen in many cases that the zeal and vigilance of the authorities might prove inefficacious to discover them ; so that it is to be desired that whatever news your excellency might obtain on the subject, you would have the kindness to transmit the same to me, in order that I might, in view thereof, issue the most opportune instructions to frustrate the carrying out of such expeditions.

In the mean time will your excellency be pleased to accept the assurances of my distinguished consideration, with which I remain your excellency's most obedient servant,

ANTONIO VARAS.

The ENVOY EXTRAORDINARY AND MINISTER PLENIPOTENTIARY
Of the United States of North America.

Mr. Bigler to Mr. Seward.

[Extract.]

No. 139.]   LEGATION OF THE UNITED STATES,
                                 Santiago de Chili, September 2, 1861.

"Herewith I have the honor to enclose, marked A, a copy of a communication by me addressed to his excellency the secretary of foreign relations of this republic, under date of August 21, 1861, in acknowledgment of a note from his excellency, dated August 7, 1861, upon the subject of the suppression of rumored privateering expeditions, which note formed enclosure A in my despatch No. 138."

 *   *   *   *   *   *

I have the honor to remain, very respectfully, your obedient servant,
                                                 JOHN BIGLER.

Mr. Bigler to Mr. Varas.

LEGATION OF THE UNITED STATES,
Santiago de Chili, August 21, 1861.

SIR: The undersigned, envoy extraordinary and minister plenipotentiary of the United States of America, has the honor to acknowledge the receipt of your excellency's note, dated August 7, 1861, in reply to his note of the 31st ultimo, wherein your excellency is pleased to give assurances that the necessary orders will be transmitted to the respective authorities to prevent the making of preparations of war, or any other operations hostile to the United States, within the territory of the republic, and requesting the undersigned to transmit to your excellency any information which he may obtain of contemplated privateering operations, in order to facilitate the frustration of the objects of such expeditions.

The undersigned, in acknowledging the receipt of these eminently satisfactory assurances, which he most cordially appreciates, as will also his government, desires to state that any information upon the subject, of a definite character, which he may receive, will be immediately communicated to your excellency's government.

The undersigned avails himself of this occasion to renew to your excellency the earnest assurances of his distinguished consideration and respect.

JOHN BIGLER.

His Excellency the SECRETARY OF FOREIGN RELATIONS
Of the Republic of Chili.

HAWAIIAN ISLANDS.

Mr. Dryer to Mr. Seward.

[Extract.]

No. 4.] LEGATION OF THE UNITED STATES AT THE HAWAIIAN ISLANDS,
Honolulu, September 5, 1861

    *   *   *   *   *   *

I have not been able yet to obtain from the Hawaiian government such a proclamation as I desired upon the subject of privateering, or the permission to enter the ports of this kingdom of any suspicious vessels.

The King and a portion of his counsellors are sojourning on the island of Hawaii during the summer months. Copies of the President's proclamation in relation to blockade of southern ports, together with the despatches from the Department of State accompanying them, have been furnished to the minister of foreign relations, since which I have had several interviews with that minister relative to the policy of this government towards privateering, and the occupancy of their ports by privateering vessels or prizes which might be captured by them.

    *   *   *   *   *   *

No. 1.] LEGATION OF THE UNITED STATES AT THE HAWAIIAN ISLANDS,
Honolulu, July 24, 1861.

SIR: I have the honor to enclose herewith copies of two despatches from the Hon. William H. Seward, Secretary of State of the United States, and of two proclamations (April 19 and April 27, 1861) issued by his excellency Abraham Lincoln, President of the United States, announcing the blockade of the ports of several of the southern States, and making known that all persons acting under the pretended authority of the aforesaid southern States, or under any pretence whatever, who shall molest vessels of the United States or their cargoes, shall be considered and dealt with as pirates.

You will observe, by a perusal of the copy of Mr. Seward's despatch to me of the 20th April, 1861, that I am instructed to be vigilant in preventing aggressions upon American commerce by vessels or persons acting under the pretended authority mentioned.

To this end I would respectfully call your attention to the fact that the American clipper ship Bald Eagle, bound from San Francisco to China, with a large amount of treasure on board, having been chased, on her passage to this group, by a suspicious vessel, and to officially inquire of you what course his Hawaiian Majesty's government intends to pursue with regard to vessels of this description found frequenting the King's waters, or touching for supplies or repairs at any of the ports in his Majesty's dominions.

I have the honor to be, with great respect, your obedient servant,
THOMAS J. DRYER.

His Excellency R. C. WYLLIE,
His Hawaiian Majesty's Minister of Foreign Affairs, &c., &c., &c.

Ex. Doc. 1——28

No. 1.]   DEPARTMENT OF FOREIGN AFFAIRS,
                                        City of Honolulu, July 27, 1861.

SIR: I have the honor to acknowledge the receipt of your despatch of the 24th instant, with its four enclosures, which you did me the great favor of delivering personally, along with verbal explanations, for which I beg to thank you in the name of the King's government.

By your despatch and its enclosures I am informed that the honorable Secretary of State, William H. Seward, apprehensive lest, "under the pretended authority of the so-called Confederate States of America," privateers might be fitted out in the ports of this kingdom for the purpose of aggression on the commerce of the United States, instructed you, on the 20th of April last, to be vigilant in preventing any such unlawful purpose; to make known to the proper authorities of this government the proclamations issued by the President; impart to them all facts upon the subject which might come to your knowledge; and to ascertain from the King's government, officially, what course they intended to pursue with regard to vessels of that description frequenting the King's waters, or touching for supplies or repairs at any of the ports in his Majesty's dominions; all which instructions you carried out very fully, and with great courtesy, in your precited despatch, and in the facts, no less important to the United States than to this kingdom, which you were pleased to impart to me verbally on the occasion of its delivery.

In reply, I have the honor to refer you to the proclamation of the late King of 16th May, 1854, asserting his neutral rights within the whole extent of his jurisdiction, declaring all captures and seizures made within that jurisdiction to be unlawful, and prohibiting his subjects from engaging, either directly or indirectly, in privateering, under the penalty of being treated and punished as pirates; to the resolution of his late Majesty, in privy council of 15th June, 1854, prohibiting the sale of prizes within his jurisdiction, and to the resolution of his late Majesty, in privy council of the 17th July of the same year, prohibiting all privateers, and prizes made by them, from entering the ports of this kingdom, unless in such circumstances of distress that their exclusion would involve a sacrifice of life, and then only under special permission of the King, after proof to his Majesty's satisfaction of such circumstances of distress; copies of all which you will find in your archives, for they were duly passed at the time to the Hon. David L. Gregg for his own and the information of his government.

I have the honor to enclose copy of the reply of the honorable judges of the supreme court, dated yesterday, in reply to my letters to them of the 5th, 10th, 13th, and 24th instant, from which you will see that, in their opinion, the said proclamation and resolutions are in accordance with the rights of the King, and with his Majesty's duties as a neutral sovereign to the United States ; and that under the same neither can privateers be fitted out in the ports of this kingdom, nor can its ports be used as a depot for the spoils or the prisoners made by privateers.

Therefore it only remains for me to make known to the King, who is at Kailua, your despatch and its enclosures, also the opinion of his Majesty's judges of the supreme court, and to suggest to his Majesty that he be pleased to issue a proclamation revalidating the aforesaid proclamation and resolutions, with an order that copies of such proclamation be published in the Polynesian, and served immediately by the pilots or harbor master upon any belligerent vessel that may appear in his Majesty's waters, until the conclusion of the civil war now unhappily devastating the United States.

You can assure the honorable Secretary of State of your government that the King, knowing well his obligations and responsibilities to the United States under the law of nations and the existing treaty, will neglect no means to fulfil them to the utmost extent of his power ; but destitute as you know him to be of either army, navy, or forts, that power is only *moral*, and if armed vessels should enter his waters, disregarding alike his neutral rights and the law of nations, captures might be made within his jurisdiction contrary to his proclamation, and in spite of all the efforts that he could make to prevent them.

Therefore I repeat what I had the honor to state to you verbally, that in a port where many millions of value in American whaleships, oil and bone, and in merchant vessels, are often to be found, and which might be captured or burnt by one strong privateer, in defiance of all the King's forces, it is of urgent necessity that Honolulu should not be left without the presence of a vessel-of-war of the United States of sufficient power to deter any such privateer from committing aggressions on the ships or property of the citizens of the United States within the King's jurisdiction. I was happy to understand from you that you had not neglected to make such a recommendation to your government.

In conclusion, let me assure you that in this and every other international matter it will afford me the utmost pleasure to confer and concert with you with all that frankness and confidence that, according to Martens and other publicists, ought to exist between a foreign representative and the minister of foreign affairs of the country to which he is accredited and sent ; but more especially be assured of the high respect and very distinguished consideration with which I have the honor to be, sir, your most obedient, humble servant,

R. C. WYLLIE.

Hon. Thomas J. Dryer, *Com'r of the United States to the Hawaiian Islands.*

Court-House,
Honolulu, July 26, 1861.

Sir: I have the honor to receive your communications of the 1st, 10th, 13th, and 25th instant, and their enclosures. The justices of the supreme court have examined the proclamation issued by her Britannic Majesty the Queen, and also the proclamation issued by the President of the United States, issued in consequence of hostilities having arisen between the government of the United States and certain States styling themselves the Confederate States of America, together with the communication of the Secretary of State, Mr. Seward, and the commissioner of the United States at this court accompanying them.

Mr. Seward is apprehensive that efforts may be made to fit out privateers in our ports for the purpose of aggression on American commerce. To permit it would unquestionably be a breach of neutrality and in derogation of our duty; neither can our ports be used as a depot for the spoils or the prisoners of privateers.

We have also examined the proclamation issued in 1854 by his Majesty the King, proclaiming neutrality in the war then pending between the great maritime powers of Europe, and the resolutions of the privy council which accompanied it, and we are of opinion that similar declarations at this time will be in accordance with our rights and duties as neutrals.

I beg to return to you the enclosures which accompanied your communications.

I have the honor to be, sir, your most obedient servants,

ELISHA H. ALLEN.
G. M. ROBERTSON

His Excellency R. C. Wyllie, *Minister of Foreign Affairs.*

Mr. Dryer to Mr. Seward.

No. 5.]   LEGATION OF THE UNITED STATES AT THE HAWAIIAN ISLANDS,
Honolulu, September 7, 1861.

SIR: Since my despatch of the 5th September was closed and mailed, Mr. Wyllie has sent to this legation another draft of a proclamation of the King in relation to privateering, &c., &c. This is an improvement on the former one sent to me, and which I returned.

I have only time to make a copy, which please find enclosed, and which I send for the information of the government at Washington.

I am, sir, with great respect, your obedient servant,

THOMAS J. DRYER.

Hon. WM. H. SEWARD,
Secretary of State, Washington.

Proclamation of Kamehameha IV, King of the Hawaiian Islands.

Be it known to all whom it may concern, that we, Kamehameha IV, King of the Hawaiian Islands, having been officially notified that hostilities are now unhappily pending between the government of the United States and certain States thereof, styling themselves "The Confederate States of America," hereby proclaim our neutrality between said contending parties.

That our neutrality is to be respected to the full extent of our jurisdiction, and that all captures and seizures made within the same are unlawful, and in violation of our rights as a sovereign.

And be it further known that we hereby strictly prohibit all our subjects, and all who reside or may be within our jurisdiction, from engaging, either directly or indirectly, in privateering against the shipping or commerce of either of the contending parties, or of rendering any aid to such enterprises whatever; and all persons so offending will be liable to the penalties imposed by the laws of nations, as well as by the laws of said States, and they will in nowise obtain any protection from us as against any penal consequences which they may incur.

Be it further known that no adjudication of prizes will be entertained within our jurisdiction, nor will the sale of goods or other property belonging to prizes be allowed.

Be it further known that the rights of asylum are not extended to the privateers or their prizes of either of the contending parties, excepting only in cases of distress or of compulsory delay by stress of weather or dangers of the sea, or in such cases as may be regulated by treaty stipulation.

Given at our marine residence of Kailua this 26th day of August, A. D. 1861, and the seventh of our reign.

KAMEHAMEHA.

By the King.

KAAHUMANU.

By the King and Kuhina Nui.

R. C. WYLLIE.

JAPAN.

Mr. Harris to Mr. Seward.

No. 28.]

Legation of the United States in Japan,
Yedo, July 9, 1861.

Sir: It is my unpleasant duty to inform you that a daring and murderous attack was made on the British legation in this city on the night of the 5th instant.

Mr. Alcock providentially escaped uninjured, but Mr. Oliphant, secretary of legation, and Mr. Morrison, consul for Nagasaki, were wounded. Four of the assailants were killed, and two wounded were made prisoners. Of the Japanese defenders of Mr. Alcock three were killed and fifteen wounded.

For full details of this bloody affair I beg to refer you to the following enclosures:

No. 1, Mr. Alcock to Mr. Harris, July 6.
No. 2, Mr. Harris to the ministers for foreign affairs, July 8.
No. 3, Mr. Harris to Mr. Alcock, July 8.
No. 4, Mr. Alcock to Mr. Harris, July 8.

The Japanese were evidently taken by surprise, but they soon recovered from it and fought with great bravery, and at last beat off the assailants.

This is the first instance in which a blow has been struck in defence of a foreigner in this country, and may be considered as proof of the desire of this government to give us protection.

I consider the present as a crisis in the foreign affairs of Japan, for if the government is too weak to punish the instigators, and agents of this nefarious affair, it may be believed that it will lead to some very decided action on the part of the English government, for the outrage was too great to be overlooked.

There is a party in this country who are opposed to the presence of any foreigners in Japan, and, in addition to this, there is a very strong dislike to the English in particular, which feeling seems to attach especially to Mr. Alcock. He was absent from this city for some three months, during which time the utmost quiet prevailed; yet within thirty-six hours after his return the attack in question was made on him.

I am happy to say that these prejudices do not extend to our citizens in this country, and I think that I am personally popular among all classes of the Japanese. Yet it must not be concealed from you that I am, in common with my colleagues, subject to the same unpopularity that attaches to the presence of all foreigners in Japan

I have requested the ministers for foreign affairs to give me an interview on the 11th instant, and I shall then endeavor to place before them, in a forcible manner, the great danger that will arise from any want of firm action on their part at this juncture.

I have the honor to be, very respectfully, your obedient servant,

TOWNSEND HARRIS,
Minister Resident.

Hon. William H. Seward,
Secretary of State, Washington.

Mr. Alcock to Mr. Harris.

HER MAJESTY'S LEGATION,
Yedo, July 6, 1861.

SIR : Last night between eleven and twelve o'clock the British legation was suddenly attacked, and an entrance effected at several points simultaneously by armed bands of Japanese, said to be Loonins, and by others, Prince of Mito's men. Two of the members of the establishment, Mr. Oliphant and Mr. Morrison, were met in a passage and both wounded ; the first, I am sorry to say, very severely, when a momentary diverson was effected by a shot from Mr. Morrison's revolver, which appears to have taken effect. A few minutes later the same or another division of the assassins sought to effect an entrance .to the apartments occupied by myself, by breaking through and hacking in pieces some glass doors opening into another suite, having mistaken their way. To this alone, under Providence, we probably owe our lives, for several minutes were thus lost to them ; at the end of which the Yaconins or Dainios guards appeared to have come to the spot, and the assailants were finally driven out of the house, after having penetrated into nearly every room except my own, leaving traces of their presence by slashing at all the beds and furniture. Marks of blood-were found in various directions, and a prolonged conflict took place outside, in the avenue and approaches to the legation, with the officers and men on service.

Such a deed of atrocity, perpetrated in the capital of a government to which foreign representatives are accredited by the western powers, needs no comment. I only feel it a duty to communicate to my colleagues the facts for their guidance and information, and to acquaint them that, as a temporary measure, I have ordered up her Majesty's ship "Ringdove," and caused a guard of men to be landed. What measures it may be expedient to adopt for future security of this and the other legations in Yedo, and the maintenance of those international rights and immunities so grievously attacked, becomes a serious consideration, and one the pressing importance of which cannot well be overlooked. But on this part of the subject I shall be glad to enter into further communication with you and the rest of my colleagues, should you feel disposed to favor me with your views.

I have the honor to be, sir, your most obedient humble servant,
RUTHERFORD ALCOCK,
Her Britannic Majesty's Envoy Extraordinary and Minister
Plenipotentiary in Japan.

TOWNSEND HARRIS, Esq.,
Resident Minister of the United States in Japan.

Mr. T. Harris to the Ministers for Foreign Affairs of Japan.

No. 70.]   LEGATION OF THE UNITED STATES IN JAPAN,
Yedo, July 8, 1861.

I am informed by Mr. Alcock, the British envoy, that an attempt was made on the night of the 5th instant to assassinate him and the persons attached to the British legation in this city. I am further informed that the house was broken into at the same moment of time in three different places ;

and that, during the contest, two persons in her Britannic Majesty's service were wounded.

This makes the seventh attack on foreigners within the period of two years; and in five of the attempts murder was committed. Up to this day not one person has been punished for these atrocious crimes. You have frequently assured me that you were making constant efforts to arrest these criminals, but that you were unable to discover them.

In the present case evidence is in your possession to enable you to arrest the persons concerned in the last atrocious attempt at murder, for you have made a prisoner of one of the men, and you have a pocket-book found on the ground which contains a list of the names of fourteen of the party; and these two sources of evidence will enable you to arrest and bring to condign punishment the whole of the gang. I feel it my duty to say to you that, in my opinion, your failure to arrest and punish the perpetrators of previous criminal acts has encouraged the present horrible attempt to take the life of Mr. Alcock.

I have given you too many evidences of my friendship for you to doubt my good will; and as your friend, who earnestly wishes to see Japan peaceful, prosperous, and happy, I now say to you, that if you do not promptly arrest and punish the authors of this last deed of blood, that the most lamentable consequences to your country will inevitably ensue; for if you do not punish these men, it will show that you do not wish to do so. I urge you earnestly to consider this friendly and serious warning.

I propose to have an interview with you in a few days, at which time I will enter more largely into details than I can do in a letter.

Stated with respect and courtesy.

TOWNSEND HARRIS,
Minister Resident of the United States in Japan.

Their Excellencies KUDSI YAMATO NOKAMI and ANDO FUSIMA NOKAMI,
Ministers for Foreign Affairs, &c., &c., &c., Yedo.

Mr Harris to Mr. Alcock.

No. 71.]

SIR: I have the honor to acknowledge the receipt of your letter of the 6th instant, giving me the particulars of an attack made the previous night, by a band of Japanese assassins, on her Britannic Majesty's legation, and informing me that Mr. Oliphant, secretary of her Britannic Majesty's legation, and Mr. Morrison, consul for Nagasaki, were wounded in the melee which ensued, and adding the gratifying intelligence that you had, providentially, escaped any bodily injury.

I cannot conceal from you the horror and indignation which the atrocious attempt on your life excites in my mind, exceeding, as it does, in the boldness of its design and in the extent of its intended slaughter, all previous essays of the kind.

In the nineteen months that followed the residence of the foreign representatives in this city, six distinct outrages were perpetrated on the persons of foreigners. Yet, up to this day, not one of the persons engaged in those criminal acts has been made to answer for his crime. The Japanese ministers have reiterated the assurance of their anxious desire to arrest and punish the offenders in question, but have declared their inability to identify them. In the present case no such plea can be set up, for two of your assailants are prisoners, and a pocket-book found on the ground near your legation contains a list of fourteen of the gang. With these two sources of information in their possession, there cannot be any difficulty in ascertaining the names of the whole band, and their consequent arrest and punishment.

Should this government fail in its duty in the present case, it will be almost conclusive that it is either unable or unwilling to give us that protection which the punishment of crime would secure by the repression of criminal designs, and it will then become a matter of serious consideration what line of conduct should be adopted to secure to us those rights which we have guaranteed to us by our solemn treaty stipulations.

I have addressed a letter to the Japanese ministers for foreign affairs in the sense of the foregoing, and I have pointedly shown them that any failure on their part at the present crisis will greatly endanger the peace of their country.

I propose to have an interview with the ministers in this behalf, when I intend to urge upon them the necessity that exists for their action in this matter.

In this connexion I beg to say that if you intend to have an interview with the ministers shortly, I will defer mine until after yours has taken place.

I renew to you my cordial congratulations on your truly providential escape from a daring and almost successful attempt on your life.

I have the honor to be, sir, your most obedient humble servant,

TOWNSEND HARRIS,
Minister resident of the United States in Japan.

RUTHERFORD ALCOCK, Esq., C. B.,
Her Britannic Majesty's Envoy Ext'y and Minister Plen'y in Yedo.

Mr. Alcock to Mr. Harris.

No. 37.]   HER MAJESTY'S LEGATION,
                                                        Yedo, July 8, 1861.

SIR: I have to thank you for the congratulations of escape from the assassins, conveyed in your letter of this date, and the expression of your views upon the present conjuncture, in which I am glad to say there is a general accordance with my own.

If there be any divergence, it is in the absence of all hope on my part that the Japanese government will behave otherwise on this than on every former occasion of the like nature. They have shown great supineness and indifference hitherto, and appear wholly unconscious of the gravity of the circumstances and the atrocious nature of the outrage offered to the flag.

I had proposed seeing the ministers to-morrow, but since the event of the 5th I have thought it better to wait an answer to a letter which I addressed them, urging them to give such full satisfaction as should relieve them of all charge of complicity or indifference.

I expect Admiral Hope here also in a few days, which may further induce me to postpone an interview. If you wish to see the ministers, therefore, I beg I may not be a cause of delay.

I have the honor to be, sir, your most obedient humble servant,

RUTHERFORD ALCOCK,
Her Britannic Majesty's Envoy Ext'y and Minister Plen'y in Japan.

TOWNSEND HARRIS, Esq., &c., &c., &c.,
United States Legation, Yedo.

Mr. Seward to Mr. Harris.

No. 23.]   DEPARTMENT OF STATE,
                                  Washington, October 21, 1861.

SIR: Your despatch of the 9th of July (No. 28) has been received.

The assaults committed upon the minister of Great Britain and the other members of that legation, in violation of express treaty, of the laws of nations, and of the principles of common humanity, have excited a deep concern on the part of the President.

Your prompt, earnest, and decided proceedings in aid of the just desire of her Britannic Majesty's minister to obtain adequate satisfaction for that outrage meet his emphatic approval. I have lost no time in assuring the British government directly of the willingness of the United States to co-operate with it in any judicious measure it may suggest to insure safety hereafter to diplomatic and consular representatives of the western powers in Japan, with due respect to the sovereignties in whose behalf their exposure to such grave perils is incurred.

I am, sir, your obedient servant,

                                  WILLIAM H. SEWARD.

TOWNSEND HARRIS, Esq., &c., &c., &c., *Yedo.*

Ex Doc. 1——29